A FOREST FLORA OF CHOTA NAGPUR INCLUDING GANGPUR AND THE SANTAL-PARGANAHS

A FOREST FLORA

OF CHOTA NAGPUR
INCLUDING
GANGPUR AND THE
SANTAL-PARGANAHS

A description of all the indigenous trees, shrubs and climbers, the principal economic herbs, and the most commonly cultivated trees and shrubs

(WITH INTRODUCTION AND GLOSSARY)

BY

H. H. HAINES, F.C.H., F.L.S., I.F.S. F.R. Met. Soc.

Conservator of Forests,
Late Imperial Forest Bolanist

GYAN

ISBN: 978-81-212-1398-1(HB)

First Published in 1910
Indian Reprint in 2017

Published by

Gyan Publishing House
5, Ansari Road
Daryaganj, New Delhi-110002
Phone: 9811692060
E-mail: books@gyanbooks.com

Cataloging in Publication Data—DK
Courtesy: D.K. Agencies (P) Ltd. <docinfo@dkagencies.com>

Haines, H. H., author.
A forest flora of Chota Nagpur including Gangpur and the Santal-Parganahs : a description of all the indigenous trees, shrubs and climbers, the principal economic herbs, and the most commonly cultivated trees and shrubs (with introduction and glossary) / by H.H. Haines.
pages cm
Reprint. Originally published: Dehra Dun : Bishen Singh Mahendra Pal Singh and Periodical Experts, Delhi, 1910.
ISBN 9788121213981 (HB)

1. Forest plants—India—Chota Na˜gpur. I. Title.

QK358.H35 2017 DDC 581.730954127 23

PREFACE.

The Flora is based mainly on notes and collections made during several years' residence in Chota Nagpur, as Divisional Forest and Working-Plans Officer, chiefly in Singbhum. These notes were very largely augmented during six weeks' leave (subsequently converted into special duty) devoted to a botanical walking tour in Manbhum, Ranchi, Hazaribagh and Palamau during the months of May and June 1905. A subsequent tour during the cold season of 1907-08 extended from the banks of the Sone through the districts of Palamau and Hazaribagh. and through the whole length of the Santal Parganahs.[1]

The last tour, and the actual writing of the Flora in its present form, were undertaken during the writer's short tenure of the office of Imperial Forest Botanist, and while on furlough in England.

It has been a source of regret that the notes and collections made during the comparatively lengthy stay in Singbhum were not compiled with any idea of subsequently writing a flora; had it been otherwise, not only would much of the later work have been saved, but the present attempt more satisfactory.

The book being intended for the use of those residents in Chota Nagpur[2] who may have no previous knowledge of systematic botany, as well as for forest officers and students, the writer has endeavoured to meet the requirements of all three classes. For the first, a glossary and an artificial key has been compiled, with which the approximate position of a plant in the Flora may be quickly located. The descriptions of the species usually starts with a fairly popular account of

[1] Spelt Sonthal Pargannahs on the map.

[2] Chota Nagpur in this, and in similar cases, where no confusion can arise, includes the Santal Parganahs.

the habit and other easily perceived characters, while fuller details, useful to the student, are added in smaller type. In some genera herbs have been described which have no known economic value. Such descriptions of the plants closely allied to a useful species often more effectively prevent its misidentification than a more particular account of the species itself, while they add to the botanical interest of the book. A few plants have been described in virtue of their beauty alone.

The economic uses are generally restricted to those to which the plants are put in Chota Nagpur. An exception has been made in the case of some trees, the value of which appears to have been overlooked on account of their rarity, and in order to claim their protection. A description of the timbers has also been omitted, as nothing could have been added by the writer to Gamble's account of them.

In regard to the limitation and multiplication of species the writer has adopted generally the views expressed by Sir D. Brandis on p. x of his introduction to "Forest Trees," but it is to be remembered that those views include the impossibility of a consensus of opinion in detail, and the limitation of particular species does not always coincide with that of "Indian Trees." Such differences of opinion are specially inevitable where the material on which conclusions have been based is different.[1] Where generic and specific names are given without explanation, or synonomy, they are believed to represent the plant or group of plants described under these names in the Flora of British India. Synonyms are given where the name employed differs from that for the same species in the Flora of British India, Brandis's Forest Trees, or Prain's Bengal Plants.

It is held that in attempting to completely describe the Forest Flora of any locality, the existence of those trees

---

[1] "It is moreover not to be forgotten that all taxonomic distinctions, which have not been confirmed by physiologic tests, are only provisional * * * * it is absolutely impossible to reach definite conclusions on purely morphologic evidence" De Vries, Origin of Species by Mutations, English Edition, p. 248.

should be referred to of which the material obtained may be insufficient to put their identification entirely beyond doubt. Specimens of twigs with buds and leaves can, by thorough examination of their stipules, venation,[1] and anatomy in comparison with known species, be usually quite correctly referred to their families, genera or even species. A very few of the species in this flora have had to be determined[2] solely from such material, but in such cases, either a (?) has been appended to the name, or the facts have been stated.

The books which have been most frequently consulted are "The Flora of British India" and Prain's "Bengal Plants." Much use has also been made of Wood's Plants of Chutia Nagpur (Records of the Botanical Survey of India) and of Campbell's Descriptive Catalogue (prepared for the Colonial and Indian Exhibition in 1886). A list of the principal works referred to will be found on p. vi. The writer's thanks are specially due to Mr. McIntire, Conservator of Forests, Bengal, without whose encouragement and help in the first instance the flora could not have been undertaken. Mr. Haslett, Bengal Forest Department, has rendered very great assistance in the collection of specimens, and in furnishing their Kharwari names, for most of which he is responsible. To him, Mr. Mee, and Mr. Modder the writer's thanks are also due for marking down and subsequently collecting several species which were not in flower or fruit at the time of observation. This aid was most valuable in the Santal Parganahs' tour which was undertaken at the worst time of year for obtaining complete specimens. Thanks are also due to Mr. Grieve, Mr. Kirkpatrick and Babu Sunder Singh for specimens. To Colonel Prain, C.I.E., formerly Director of the Botanical Survey of India, and to his successor, Major Gage, the writer is greatly indebted for their generous

---

[1] M. Laurent on p. 331 of the Progressus Rei Botanicæ, Vol. I, remarks that "Les botanistes ne considerent pas assez les feuilles dans leur derniere trame."

[2] Mr. N. E. Brown of Kew kindly determined for the writer an Aristolochia from the twigs and leaves alone. Subsequent comparison with other specimens showed the determination to be perfectly correct.

hospitality and assistance while he was working at the Calcutta herbarium. The writer regrets that more time was not available for a thorough examination of *all* the Chota Nagpur plants contained in that herbarium, and in the herbarium of the Revd. Dr. Campbell, who very kindly placed it at his disposal. Had such been practicable, some errors and omissions would no doubt have been avoided. Through the kindness of Mr. Gamble the whole of his excellent herbarium was examined on receipt of the first proof, and several additions to localities made. Advantage was also taken of his advice in other matters. It is with much gratitude that the writer recalls his visit to Dr. Campbell in Manbhum, who has collected in Chota Nagpur for over thirty years, and from whom practically all the Santali names given in this book have been obtained, either directly, or from his Descriptive Catalogue already referred to. Dr. Campbell also kindly corrected the spelling of these names in proof. The writer also wishes to acknowledge his indebtedness to Mr. Burkill for kindly checking the nomenclature of the Dioscoreaceæ, and lending specimens, to Dr. G. T. Walker, Meteorological Reporter to the Government of India, for assistance in obtaining some of the meteorological statistics; to the Director of the Geological Survey for naming rock specimens; to the Keeper and staff of the Royal Herbarium at Kew; to Dr. Ostenfeld and Dr. Paulsen of Copenhagen; and finally to the Hon. F. Slacke, C.S.I., C.I.E., formerly Commissioner of Chota Nagpur, for his sympathy and assistance in all matters concerned with forestry and botany during the writer's service in his division.

H. H. HAINES.

The 31st March 1908.

CONTENTS.

LIST OF WORKS CONSULTED

having a direct bearing on the botany of Chota Nagpur and the Santal Parganahs (excluding works on general botany).

Flora of British India, by Sir J. D. Hooker.

Indian Trees, by Sir D. Brandis.

Bengal Plants, by D. Prain.

Flora Indica, Vol. I, by J. D. Hooker and T. Thomson.

Flora Indica, by William Roxburgh.

Manual of Indian Timbers, by J. S. Gamble.

Descriptive Catalogue of the Economic Products of Chutia Nagpur, by Revd. A. Campbell, annotated by George Watt.

Dictionary of the Economic Products of India, by G. Watt.

Plants of Chutia Nagpur, including Jaspur and Sirguja, by J. J. Wood.

List of Trees and Shrubs found in Chota Nagpur, by J. S. Gamble and F. B. Manson (Appendix to Report on Forest Administration in the Chota Nagpur Division by Dr. W. Schlich, 1885).

Report on a visit to the forests of the Santal Parganahs made in November 1882 by J S. Gamble (published in the Forest Administration Report for British India for 1882-83).

On the Flora of Behar and the Mountain Parasnath, by Thomas Anderson (Journal of the Asiatic Society of Bengal, 1863. Vol. XXXII, p. 189).

Himalayan Journals, by Sir J. D. Hooker.

Noviciеæ Indicæ, by D. Prain (Papers published from time to time in the Journal of the Asiatic Society of Bengal).

Ferns of British India, by Col. R. H. Beddome.

A Review of the Ferns of Northern India, by C. B. Clarke.

Miscellaneous articles and descriptions of trees, published in the Journal of Botany, Journal of the Asiatic Society, Annals of the Botanical Gardens, Calcutta, Indian Forester, etc., are referred to in the place treating of the genus or species concerned.

LIST OF ABBREVIATIONS.

The abbreviated names of botanists are not here included. A fairly complete list of these may be found in several works, one of which, Watt's Dictionary of Economic Products, is available in all Collectors' and Forest Officers' libraries. The only other abbreviated name frequently used is *Camp.* for the Revd. D. Campbell.

alb.	albumen, endosperm.
alt.	alternate.
ant.	anterior.
anths.	anthers.
Beng.	Bengali.
C.N.	Chota Nagpur. Sometimes used to include the whole area embraced by the Flora.
cold.	coloured.
cor.	corolla.
c.s.	The cold season.
cult.	cultivated.
Dec.	Deciduous, or December, according to context, *e.g.*, Dec. Nov.-Dec implies that the plant in question drops its leaves, or is leafless from November to December.
diam.	diameter.
ell.	elliptic.
Ev.	evergreen.
exc.	except, or exceptions.
F., or Fem.	Female.
F.B.I.	Flora of British India.
Fl., fls.	Flowers; or, when followed by the names of months or seasons, the time of flowering.
Fr., frt.	Fruit; or, when followed by the names of months or seasons, the time of fruiting. If this period is a long one, only those months are mentioned in which the fruits are conspicuous, the last one or two months usually show those in which the seed ripens.
Ft.	Feet.
Gl.	Glume, in the family Gramineæ only.
H.	Hindi.
Him. Jour.	Hooker's Himalayan Journals.
h.s.	The hot season.
Hyp.	hypanthium.
Inflor.	Inflorescence.
K.	Kol *vide*, Intro. P.
L.	Leaves.
lanc.	lanceolate.
Lflts.	leaflets.
Mal P.	Mal Paharia.
m.s.	moderate or medium-sized.
M.	Mundari, or male.
M. fls.	Male flowers.
opp.	opposite.
oblanc.	oblanceolate.
Ped.	peduncle.
Ped. spkt.	pedicelled spikelet.
per.	perianth.
pet.	petals.
peti.	petiole.
prs.	pairs.
r.s.	rainy season.
S.	Santali.
Sec. n.	secondary nerves.
sep.	sepals.
S.P.	Santal Parganahs.
spkt.	spikelet (Gramineæ).
St.	stamens.
stmnds.	staminodes.
Syn.	Synonym
Var.	variety.
Vern.	Vernacular, where the particular language is not known.
	feet.
	inches.
∞	numerous.

ADDENDA AND CORRIGENDA.

[Obvious misprints are omitted.]

P. 51. Line 4 *for* Borgainvillea *read* Bougainvillea.

P. 52. *For* Gnetinee *read* Gnetineæ.

P. 63. In Gamboge Family, *for* Ovary 4 12-celled *read* Ovary 4-12-celled.

P. 67. Last line, *after* ovules 2 in each cell *read* or more in some Aurantieæ.

P. 76. In Ivy Family, *after* palmate *read* or digitate.

P. 80. In Urticales, *after* allied probably to Polygonaceæ *add* and Euphorbiales.

P. 82. In Myrsinaceæ, *add* Minute red glands usually present at the edges of the leaves and other places.

P. 83. In Olive Family, *the words* Ovary 2-celled *should be in italics.*

P. 86. See Bignoniaceæ, the star * is omitted from the foot-note.

P. 86. Acanthus Family, *after* exceptions see p. *read* 446.

P. 90. Dioscoreaceæ, the leaves are sometimes 3-5-foliolate.

P. 129. Alsophila. The indusium is absent in this genus. A tree-fern found in the hills of the Central Provinces with a very prickly and aspe.ous stipes and rachis is Cyathea spinulosa, *Wall.* Cyathea has an indusium which envelops the young sori and is more or less permanent below.

P. 143. Polyalthia cerasioides, L. sometimes glabrescent above.

P. 146. Saccopetalum tomentosum, Fls. greenish or dark purple. Frt. carpels purple-black.

P. 153. Litsæa sebifera, *Pers.* Cooke (Flora of Bombay) states that L. chinensis, *Lamk.* has long priority over Persoon's name.

P. 156. Crataeva religiosa, the flowers are variously coloured in cultivation.

P. 161. Casearia tomentosa, L. punctulate.

P. 164. Zehneria, Endl. The genus has been sunk in Melothria by Cogniaux, and the names of Z. umbellata and Z. Hookeriana become Melothria heterophylla *Cogn.* and M. perpusilla, *Cogn.* respectively.

P. 171. Bryonia laciniosa, Cooke gives Bryonopsis laciniosa, *Naud.* as the name of this plant.

P. 171. Mukia scabrella, this is called Melothria maderaspatana by Cogniaux.

P. 174. Cephalandra indica, *Naud.* should be Coccinia indica, *W. & A.* according to Cooke.

P. 176. Gulgul (Galgal) is also a Hindi name for Cochlospermum to which it properly belongs.

P. 191. Thespesia Lampas, *Dalz*, Syn. T. macrophylla, *Blume.* There are probably two species mixed up under these names. The common Singhbum species has globose woody 4-5-valved capsules which are only slightly dehiscent, the upper leaves are usually simple. The other, which is apparently the more common form in Western India has oblong or ovoid cuspidate, often 3-valved capsules, much more widely dehiscent and more resembling those of a Hibiscus, while the leaves are nearly always broad and 3-lobed.

P. 196. G. pilosa, the older stems are 3-4-angled.

P. 207. Eriolæna Hookeriana, line 13, *for* fid *read* fld.

P. 210. Tribe Phyllantheæ, line 5, add a comma after 'rarely few.'

P. 213. Euphorbia neriifolia, *L.* Cooke apparently considers that the correct name of this is E. ligularia, *Roxb.* and he calls E. Nivulia, *Ham.* 'E. neriifolia, *L.*' The matter appears to require further investigation. There is a much branched (from the root) species which is apparently undescribed and is found on quartzite and sandstone rocks in the Central Provinces not far from our area. It has broadly ovate leaves when young.

P. 219. G. velutinum, *after* capsule $\frac{1}{3}''$ *read* $\frac{1}{2}''$. *For* petiole $\frac{1}{4}''$ *read* Petiole $\frac{1}{8}$-$\frac{1}{4}''$. *For* Fls. April *read* Fls. April-May.

P. 222. Flueggea, *for* styles 3, *read* 2-3.

P. 227. A. Bunius, line 4, *for* fid *read* fld.

P. 239. B. Roxburghii. *For* Hingux *read* Hingan

P. 258. Buchanania latifolia. Cooke states that the name B. Lanzan, *Spreng.* has claim by priority.

P. 260. Sapindus trifoliatus, this is S. laurifolius, Vahl. according to Cooke.

P. 260. In Key, line 5, *for* H *read* Fl.

P. 270. Z. Jujuba, Var. It is probably a distinct species. The habit is very uniform. It is doubtless included in Z. rotundifolia, *Lamk.* in the Flora of the Gangetic Plain, between which and Jujuba it is intermediate.

P. 288. A. pennata. There are possibly two species under this name. One is arboreous in the Central Provinces. The shape of the pod is variable.

P. 291. A. odoratissima should have been placed next to Lebbek, to which it is more closely allied than to A. procera.

P. 297. B. Vahlii, line 13, *for* lama, K., *read* lamak'.

P. 338. D. scandens, line 3, *for* cold, *read* cold. (*i. e.,* coloured).

P. 354. Woodfordia floribunda, seeds minute linear. The seedlings are most minute with orbicular sessile cotyledons the size of a small pin's head. The first pairs of leaves are minute broadly ovate and glandular.

P. 356. Lawsonia alba, *Lamk.* Cooke gives L. inermis, *L.* as the name.

P. 369. Heptapleurum venulosum, Drupe spherical $\frac{1}{4}''$ diam., yellow, finally red with a compressed stone. Frt. June-July.

P. 369. Heteropanax, the so-called seeds are probably pyrenes.

P. 404. M. indica, first line, *for* A. R. amjani *read* *A. DC.* Ramjani.

P. 410. D. montana, *Roxb.* In the Central Provinces, not far from our area, is a third form, usually thorny, adult twigs and leaves beneath and or midrib above pubescent, sec. n. 6-10 prs., tertiaries not so numerous or reticulate, or so conspicuous when dry. L. dry green. Fl. and Fr. not seen.

P. 437. Dregea is included in Marsdenia by Mr. N. E. Brown and by Cooke. D. volubilis becomes M. volubilis, *Cooke*.

P. 452. Hygrophila spinosa, is a synonym for Asteracantha longifolia, *Nees* the name adopted by Cooke.

P. 465. Ipomæa, line 18, *for* ovary-2 or 4-celled *read* ovary 2- or 4-celled.

P. 468. I. Turpethum, L. attain 6" and more in luxuriant specimens.

P. 474. C. Macleodii, line 13, *for* on *read* or.

P. 482. P. barbata, line 4, *for* never quite entire *read* very rarely entire.

P. 482. P. nov. sp. I have since met this as a large tree in the Central Provinces, it appears to be undescribed.

Chota Nagpur. On the south the tract passes into the highlands of Orissa, and on the north it extends at one point to the banks of the Ganges. It belongs therefore to the Deccan Province of the Flora Indica, to Mr. Clarke's province of Coromandelia, and to Colonel Prain's province of Chota Nagpur.

TOPOGRAPHY.

The essential feature in the physical aspect of the country is the prevalence of plateaux and hills, often rising into mountains which rarely exceed 3,000 feet in elevation. A very small portion of the area can be said to lie in the plains. This is the narrow strip about 170 miles long in the east and north of the Santal Parganahs along the loop line of the East Indian Railway, which belongs both topographically and botanically to the Gangetic plain. On the other hand the plateaux are frequently very low and may not exceed 400 feet. This is the case in the open country near the Subarnekha in the east of Singbhum, and over much of eastern Manbhum. A subsidiary, but characteristic, feature of many of the plateaux are huge isolated rounded or conical bosses of rock rising abruptly from the general level and visible for many miles. Good examples may be seen near Chinpina (on the railway), near Jhalda, etc.

The edges of the higher plateaux, such as those of **Ranchi** and **Hazaribagh**, are usually broken into steep scarps which appear as ranges of hills seen from below, and sometimes *are* actually hills rising considerably above the general level of the plateaux. While the larger plateaux of Ranchi and Hazaribagh attain respectively an average elevation of 2,000 feet, and that of Palamau 1,200 feet, smaller ones or flat-topped mountains may rise as a third step to 3,000 feet or more. These are the so-called *páts.* They are best represented in **Sirguja** where the Main Pat [1] has an

[1] The Mainpat, or more correctly the Manipat, is 16 miles long and 12 miles broad. In summer it becomes a vast grazing ground for cattle from Mirzapur and Behar. *Vide* Imperial Gazetteer of India.

elevation of 3,850 feet. The tops of these pats "are open grassy plains with a few scattered bushes, they are now used as pasturage and were once good hunting grounds for Nilgai."[1]

The larger plateaux are usually under cultivation, and in the dry season offer but a monotonous expanse of dried up fields with scarcely any vegetation. From this cultivated country it is a relief to turn to their jungle-covered scarps, albeit most of the forest has now been reduced to a state of scrub. It is in the rugged mountainous tracts, especially of Singbhum, the former Tributary States, and Palamau, where the chief beauty and interest of Chota Nagpur now lies, and where the manifestations of the destructive hand of man are least apparent. These tracts being also those where there is most forest, coincide to some extent with the areas marked in green on the accompanying map. (The forest in the Native States is however not shown, *vide* note on p. 1.)

The districts of **Ranchi** and **Hazaribagh** are typically plateaux with forest on the scarps and on a few isolated hills, but the highest mountain of Chota Nagpur (Parasnath 4,479 feet) occurs on the eastern boundary of the latter district, as the culminating point of an east and west broken range of hills which lies partly in Manbhum, the eastern portion being known as the Tundi hills. Parasnath is classic ground for the botanist, as its flora was studied by Sir J. D. Hooker in the year 1848. There have recently been proposals of building on this beautiful mountain which, if carried out, would destroy most of its interesting vegetation.

The Parasnath range is divided from the higher Hazaribagh plateau and the broken hilly and jungle-clad country on its southern and eastern face by a tributary of the Damuda.

---

[1] Plants of Chutia Nagpur, by Lieutenant-Colonel J. J. Wood, p. 2. The writer has unfortunately never had an opportunity of examining these Pats.

TOPOGRAPHY.

The lower northern Hazaribagh plateau east of Chatra is flat, bare of forest and the streams mostly dry in December. Borassus palms are fairly abundant in northern Hazaribagh and lend a feature to the landscape absent from the greater part of Chota Nagpur. The upper Baraka basin is mostly an open barren plateau, sparsely cultivated and heavily grazed. The river is occasionally flanked by low hills. Towards Pachamba the scenery somewhat improves, and it is then flanked on the south by the Parasnath and Tundi ranges.

The Baraka joins the Damuda on the eastern boundary of Manbhum. The only reserved forests in Hazaribagh are at Koderma and Khurchuta. Koderma is situated on the scarps on the north of the lower plateau and also occupies hills at its base. This forest is continuous with that of the Ganwan zemindari forest and the other jungle of the scarps. The small forest of Khurchuta lies close to the Monghyr and Santal Parganahs boundary. In this direction the plateau character is more or less lost and the jungle-clad scarps have disappeared. The hilly scarps of northern Hazaribagh are, in fact, continued northwards into Monghyr, where they ultimately become the Karakpur hills.

There are still several private jungles in Hazaribagh chiefly belonging to the rajah of Ramgarh, and several patches of jungle attached to the villages called *Rakhauts.* The Damuda valley is much more diversified than that of the Baraka, and still contains considerable patches of jungle, though these are fast disappearing.

The Ranchi plateau, except in the western hills, is generally very flat and open, with occasional small hill ranges and barren rocks of granite or gneiss. Tea gardens, and occasional patches of Sal coppice are met with, but it is practically only on the scarps and in the river valleys that the forest still maintains itself. The Baragai mountain [1] on the northern ghats overlooking the Damuda is 3,445 feet high. Some of the

[1] Omitted from the map.

western mountains attain 3,600 feet and there is much forest about Biru and the watershed of the north and south Koel.

Manbhum is generally a low-level undulating plateau dipping to the east, but there are considerable hills in the south and west, the principal of which are the Dalma range, attaining 3,000 feet, and the hills of the Baghmundi plateau, attaining 2,220 feet (Gangabari Mountain). The last contains an area of Protected Forest situated in parganah Mahtah. The only other areas of Protected Forest in Manbhum are situated on the small hills of parganah Koelapal, to the east of the Dalma range, which last forms a natural boundary between Singbhum and Manbhum on the south.

The Dalma Range is interrupted where the Subhanarheka breaks through it, at the boundary of the two districts. Where this river crosses from Hazaribagh and Ranchi into Manbhum it forms a waterfall, known as the Hundru Gag, which is 320 ft. high Away from the mountains mentioned, however, Manbhum is flat or but slightly undulating, now and again dotted with the small isolated conical hills, or rocks, referred to above. The central portions are drained by the Kosai river, which flows ultimately into the Hughli. There are no reserved forests, and most of its zemindari forests and the recently protected blocks have long since been reduced to a condition of scrub. The desolation of the empty fields in the hot season, unrelieved by that touch of Nature which can even beautify the desert, resembles many parts of upper India.

Except for a considerable plateau in its eastern centre **Singbhum** is a mountainous country. On the north the Porahat plateau, adjoining the higher one of Ranchi, is much diversified by ranges of mountains and deep rocky glens; the homes of bears, leopards and tigers.

The high ridge in the north-west corner, on the borders of Ranchi, is sometimes known as the Layada Range, and reaches 2,900 ft. The Girga forest lies on some of its more rugged spurs. The valley of the North Karo, full of rocky pools, divides this from the main mass of Porahat, in which many mountains, such as the Bicha Buru, exceed 2,700 ft. The forest boundary is carried over the top of this mountain which lies on the western extension of the Dalma range. Parts of the Songra forest, with an elevation of 1,100 ft. to 2,000 ft., is characterized by large valleys which, towards the ghats, fall away in precipitous slopes and waterfalls. The ravines are filled with immense boulders, so that it is necessary to ascend them bare-footed. In the south of the Songra forest the Lokod Buru range attains 2,800 ft., and with the Seomari and Sunli ranges, protect some wide valleys on their northern slopes. These were jhumed many years ago, but still contain some magnificent old trees, remnants of the former forest. Such jhumed areas are very common in the Singbhum reserved forests near the sites of old villages long since deserted. They are occupied by a new type of forest, referred to in the flora as 'second growth' in which the species of the original forest only slowly reappear.[1] The pretty custom of the Kols which preserves near the village a *bongasarna*, or sacred grove, is the cause of the preservation of some of the ancient giants of the forest. Some of the hills and upper valleys in Porahat are too exposed to drought to contain good forest, and such names as the *jateserang* (signifying a carpet of rock) aptly describes their character.

Between Porahat on the north and the Kolhan Government estate on the south runs the Bengal-Nagpur railway in the valleys of the Sanjai (or Khorkai) and the Koil. These rivers run in opposite directions from a watershed through which the Goilkera tunnel is bored (elev. 1,100 ft.). The Sanjai flows east to the Subarnekha, the Koil, after receiving the North and South Karo and the Koina rivers, westwards to its confluence with the Sank in Gangpur, where the combined rivers flow south as the

[1] Jhumed areas in the Santal Parganahs are known as *Karao*. Gamble states that on old karaos bamboo frequently comes up in great abundance. and seedlings of Pterocarpus and Ougeinia are not uncommon.

Brahmini. The **Kolhan** Government Estate is generally very mountainous but there is a slightly undulating plateau in the east of it (and to the west of the estate of **Dalbhum** and **Seraikhela**), which is only about 750 ft. in elevation. On this Chaibassa is situated. The portion of the Kolhan west of the Karo R. known as "**Saranda**," the land of the seven hundred hills, is the most beautiful part of Singbhum and the richest in its flora and fauna. In consequence of the preservation of its forests the splendid streams of the South Karo, the Koina and others, contain an abundance of water all the year round and are well stocked with Mahseer and other fish. The mountain ranges strike generally N.-E. and S.-W. and usually rise to close on 3,000, ft.[1] sheltering deep valleys with perennial springs, where the comparative coolness and humidity has a marked effect on the flora (*vide* infra). The Saranda rivers, like those in Porahat, often have a gentle gradient for considerable distances and flow through broad valleys with fine forest. The whole aspect then suddenly changes, the valley closes in and rugged rocks, hung with bees' nests, overhang cascades and gigantic boulders 10-30 ft. in diameter. Wild elephants and considerable numbers of bison (Bos gaurus) still occur in these forests, which, however, have a somewhat less pleasant feature in their numerous man-eating tigers.

The district of **Palamau** is said to have an average elevation of 1,200 ft. On the south and south-east are the mountainous ghats of the Ranchi, Hazaribagh and Sarguja plateaux which throw out long spurs and hill-ranges far into Palamau, and on which are situated the Barasand and other reserved forests. Some of the highest mountains in the south, in continuation of the *pats* of western Lohardaga (Ranchi district) and Sarguja, attain 3,500 ft. Flowing north from the southern highlands is the Urunga river, afterwards known as the North Koil, which joins the Sone.

---

[1] The highest is 3,041 ft. situated on the Keonjhur frontier, while the lowest point of the Samta valley is only 750 ft.

The extreme west, occupied by the hills of Naga Untari and other zemindari estates, is fairly covered with a poor forest, from which all large timber has been removed, and is interspersed with villages. Similar jungle-clad hills also occur in the east of the district, where they join a confused mass lying in the west of Hazaribagh. From them tributaries of the Amanat river flow westwards. The high land in the extreme south-east of Palamau, in parganah Tori, is the watershed of the Amanat (which joins the Koil above Daltonganj) and the Damuda. It connects the Hazaribagh plateau with that of Ranchi. The forest on this watershed is not reserved. Below the ghats of the Palamau plateau in the North-West, is a small area near the Sone on a level with the Gaya plain.

The **Santal Parganahs** district is an oblong tract lying in a bend south and west of the Ganges. The south-west and western portion in continuation of the north-east of Hazaribagh is of low elevation, but generally undulating and with numerous detached hills and small hill ranges. The eastern half is chiefly occupied by the long north and south range of the Rajmehal Hills, which leave, however, a low alluvial highly-cultivated tract between them and the Ganges on the east The highest points of this range are only about 1,500 ft. and nowhere exceed 2,000 ft.; they are usually flat-topped. These hills must once have been covered with dense forest, but all the large timber was destroyed in the construction of the East Indian railway about 1857, and although a part was subsequently reserved under the Forest Act, control by the Forest Department has been again mostly withdrawn. Much of the area is jhumed or cultivated, and the greater portion of the remainder reduced to a state of scrub. The result of the denudation is that most of the streams become nearly dry early in the dry season, while they are violent torrents in the rains, only fordable with danger. The effects of excessive grazing and other destructive agencies is well seen about Barhait, where the Sal trees are found with a foot or more of their roots exposed, appearing to stand on stilts. It is interesting to compare the present condition of much of Chota Nagpur with the prophecies of Mr. Hewitt, formerly Commissioner of that province, in his Annual Administration Report for 1883-84, who foretold the results of the wholesale destruction of the forests.

GEOLOGY.

The land surface of Chota Nagpur is probably an extremely ancient one. Omitting deposits formed by recent süb-aërial denudation of the older rocks, including among these the laterites, there is no formation younger than the Gondwana system, which is believed to be contemporaneous with the Upper Lias and Trias, and these Gondwana beds were apparently all deposited in shallow water. The fossils of the Gondwana system are chiefly equisetales, ferns and cycadofilices, while conifers are very rare.[1] By far the greater part of the area is occupied by unfossiliferous metamorphic and submetamorphic rocks covered locally by shallow, or moderately deep, alluvial or sub-aërial deposits. The chief exception occurs in the Santal Parganahs, where enormous areas are covered with basalt and other trap rocks. Most of the rounded conical hills or bosses, alluded to on p. 2, consist of porphyritic granite,[2] sometimes called Dome Gneiss. The shelling off of the outer concentric layers of this rock, causing a continual exposure of fresh surfaces, renders it singularly bare of vegetation. On it species of Ficus, chiefly F. tomentosa and F. gibbosa, and more rarely the Banyan, are the commonest plants. The detritus at their base however will grow most species of trees, and among it natural sown Tamarind is not uncommon.

---

[1] "The plants of the Lower Gondwana include numerous Equisetales while those of the upper are chiefly Cycads and conifers. The species of ferns are distinct in the two divisions."—*Holland.*

[2] Much of the gneiss in Chota Nagpur, exhibits no trace of foliation and is lithologically granite. The Dome Gneiss is doubtfully granitic in origin.

The **Ranchi** and **Hazaribagh** districts are occupied especially by the metamorphic rocks. Granitoid Gneiss, mostly Hornblende gneiss, [1] is one of the commonest. It decomposes into a somewhat sandy unfertile soil much favoured by the wild Custard Apple. Much of the Tundi-Parasnath range is composed of it. It is also common about Markacho and over most of northern Hazaribagh and into Palamau. In **Palamau** it is found on the Kuru ghats, in the Betlah forest and numerous other places. The Koderma hill is composed of gneiss, but mica schists (submetamorphic) are here most abundant. Pegmatite is a handsome crystalline granite with large pink masses of dull felspar and translucent quartz. It is often met with (especially in Hazaribagh) and occurs apparently overlying (probably intruded into) the gneiss on the Sitagarh hill near Hazaribagh station between Banki and Barwadih, at Chorparan, and in Koderma among other places. Pegmatite is said to occur in Hazaribagh in *dykes in which* the workable mica is found.[2] Mica is extensively mined in Koderma and the vicinity. On ridges about Pachamba a form of quartz schist outcrops consisting of almost pure quartz with cavities lined with quartz crystals.

The *pats* on the western boundary of Ranchi and in Jashpur owe their flat-topped appearance to a horizontal layer of trap rock: [3] there is said to be but a small depth of soil on the top in which forest trees used to grow.[4]

---

[1] A pepper-and-salt looking rock, very crystalline on fracture but weathering black or deep grey-brown. Under the lens it appears to be composed of small blackish crystals of Hornblende and white crystals of quartz intimately associated.

[2] But the word pegmatite is used here in a somewhat different sense as a coarse mixture of quartz, felspar and mica. It often contains tourmaline, of which some fine specimens are found in the Koderma mines.

[3] *Vide* Gazetteer. This capping rock of the pats is however elsewhere referred to as laterite (Memoirs of the Geological Survey, Vol. VIII. The Daltonganj Coal-field, by W. H. Hughes). Probably the two rocks are associated as is so often the case.

[4] *Vide* p. 2.

In walking from **Hazaribagh** to **Ranchi** clays and carboniferous shales are met with at about the 21st mile which belong to the Damuda series of the Gondwana system. These rocks are more or less evident all down the Damuda valley, and contain the coal-fields of Ramgarh and Karanpur in Hazaribagh. The **Gondwana** system is also well developed in the Barakar valley, and tilted beds of sandstone north of Bagoda, as well as the micaceous shales composing some of the small hills north of the Barakar, possibly belong to it. The Gondwana system is important, as the Damuda series bears the coal measures of Raniganj (in Bardwan, but close to Chota Nagpur), Jheria (in the Damuda valley, Manbhum), Giridih (Barakar valley, Hazaribagh), Daltonganj (Palamau), and several less important fields. The formation is also interesting from the occurrence of similar coal-bearing Damuda beds in Sikkim and Bhotan, indicating a continuity of the land in that direction when sea occupied the greater part of the Indo-Gangetic plain and Himalayan area. In the subsequent elevation of the land we may assume the mountains of Chota Nagpur not only to have been on a far grander scale but to have borne much the same flora as their extension into Assam and adjacent areas. As these conditions are believed to have existed right up to tertiary times, the presence of so many eastern Himalayan and Malayan types in Chota Nagpur might thus be accounted for. Ball states that the outlying hills and prolongations of the Chota Nagpur plateau owe their character and origin to denudation modified only by the inclination of the beds, and not to local or special upheavals. "That the general level of **Manbhum** corresponded to the rest of Chota Nagpur in times previous to the scooping out of the Damuda and other valleys, and the deposition of the coal measures and associated rocks, is proved, not only by the scattered hills, a few of which approach in elevation that of the Chota Nagpur plateau, but by the fact that the Subarnareka and many of its smaller tributaries pass at right angles through gorges cut deep through hard ranges of trap, quartzite, and tough mica schists.[1] In the **Santal Parganans** the Rajmehal traps belong to the Gondwana system, and are often interbedded with coal and carboniferous shale. In the Bisrampur coalfield, in Sarguja, boulder beds of gneiss are characteristic of the lower Gondwanas. Of the less important areas of Gondwana rocks may be mentioned the Itkuri coalfield in northern Hazaribagh, one on the Balumath-Chatra road, and one called the Chope Coalfield well on the Hazaribagh plateau at nearly 2,000 ft. elevation! None of these is believed to be worked at the present day.

The low plateau of **Singbhum** is mostly metamorphic rock (gneiss) overlaid by a stiffish clay, and is much intersected by trap dykes. The series best represented in Singbhum however is the sub-metamorphic; in fact all the chief hill ranges are composed of these rocks. The sub-metamorphics are principally quartzites, ferruginous and mica schists, siliceous clay slates, shales and phyllite. Hæmatite and other iron schists are very widespread; whole ranges (*e.g.*, the Lokud Buru ridge in the Songra forest) are composed of them. The clay schists are usually interbedded with quartz laminæ. On weathering, the latter break up into numerous stones which often thickly strew the surface. The clays derived from these schists are usually very impermeable and are baked a stony hardness in the hot season; they support a poor forest growth often characterized by the presence of Gardenia gummifera both in Singbhum and in the protected forests of Manbhum. The soil derived from the iron-schists and quartzites is usually better or, at any rate, the forest growth is better, from the roots being better able to penetrate the numerous clefts and fissures which are characteristic of these rocks when superficial. In Kundrugutu, and some other places, magnesian schists (patra diri, *Kol*) are found, which are worked by the Kols into plates and ornaments. Deposits of laterite in Singbhum occur in Saranda in large amygdaloidal reddish masses especially about

---

[1] Ball, Memoirs of the Geological Survey of India, Vol. XVIII, Pt. 2.

Ratamatia. Trap dykes are very common, and occasional hills, *e.g.* the Kita Buru in the Saitba forest, are composed of serpentine. "This mountain is strongly magnetic and clothed chiefly with grass and Phœnix acaulis[1] (Kita, *K.*)"

Manbhum differs in some important respects from Singbhum, chief of which are firstly, the considerable areas of alluvial and sub-aërial deposits, among which the laterite is very conspicuous, and is the first rock met with in travelling westwards from Calcutta; secondly, the extensive remains of the Gondwana rocks especially in the valleys of the Damuda and Baraka; thirdly, the relatively poor development of the sub-metamorphics. Metamorphic and sub-metamorphic rocks are well represented, however, chiefly in the southern mountains. Here also, surrounded by the sub-metamorphics, is a large area of intrusive trap forming a long east and west band up to 3 miles in breadth, thinning out east of the Dalma mountain and extending into and across the valley of the Subarnarekha into Tamar (Ranchi district), and curving south to Bichia Buru in Singbhum. Manbhum shows the most perfect examples of the conical hills formed by the porphyritic or dome gnesis.[2]

In **Palamau** again the metamorphic and sub-metamorphic rocks compose most of the hill ranges, but in the west and south-west, in the neighbourhood of the Kanhar river the flat-topped hills are capped by massive sandstones and laterite.[3] In the north-western hills Biotite gneiss and a brownish amorphous-looking or slatey rock (with a quite black dull fracture, lydianstone?) are frequent.[4] In these hills again a crystalline limestone is abundant, *e.g.*, about Bonahatpur, where it is frequently hollowed out into cave

---

[1] Singbhum Working Plan, p. 2, and Appendix XIII, where the rocks in different compartments are enumerated.

[2] There is a good illustration of the Jhalda hill in Vol. XVIII of the Memoirs of the Geological Survey of India.

[3] But see note on p. 10.

[4] The "lydianstone" was found chiefly between Bonahatpur and Miral.

which form a refuge for bears. Limestone occurs in various forms throughout Chota Nagpur, and quarries of crystalline blue limestone are worked in Gangpur (where the rocks are similar to those of Singbhum) and to a less degree in Singbhum.

A considerable area of the central Palamau plateau, extending from near Loharsoe to Garhwa, across the junction of the Amanat, Jinjoi and Koel rivers (just north of Daltonganj) is occupied by Gondwana rocks (Talchir and Damuda series), chiefly sandstones, which are frequently calcareous, and some coal. Another area of these rocks also occurs near Latihar and in a few other places.

The predominant feature of the geology of the **Santal Parganahs** is the trap, which covers some three-fourths of the Rajmehal hills, and trap boulders are common in the valleys.

The trap rocks are usually very homogeneous, or amygdaloidal, brown or grey-black basalts, with a black or grey-black micro-crystalline fracture, which may be conchoidal, and usually breaks into sharp angular fragments. On the hills near Morjhora a variety (dolerite) is found with a grey fracture, with distinct blank or amber-coloured crystals under the lens. This weathers grey or red with a rough surface easily covered with crustaceous lichens. Laterite sometimes occurs on the top of the trap. Underlying the trap, and often including it, is a series of sandstones and grits, less often shales. These beds are usually met with in the valleys and outcropping on the slopes. Carbonaceous shales and coal beds, with occasional limestone and conglomerate also occur, and are often interbedded with the trap. The intertrappean sedimentary deposits often contain plant beds. Underlying the Gondwana system the metamorphic rocks are again met with, and they are sometimes exposed well inside the Rajmehal hills, *e.g.*, at Chandna. They are, however, chiefly noticeable on the western flanks and, outside the Rajmehals proper, the small hills are chiefly composed of them. "These rocks consist chiefly of gneiss alternating with micaceous and hornblendic schists."[1]

The soils in the Rajmehal hills are rarely of clay,[2] and thus contrast greatly with those of Singbhum. Cotton soil is very abundant in the valleys, perhaps due to the decomposition of the trap. It is also common in Hazaribagh, *e.g.*, from Chatra to Itkuri, in Palamau from Lesliegan] to Banki and at other places. The species of the cotton soil are largely Butea, Carissa, Zizyphus and Acacia arabica. Common trees on the basalt are Mohwa, Nyctanthes, Eriolæna, Terminalia tomentosa, Wendlandia exserta and Heteropanax, but none of these are peculiar to it.

CLIMATE.

The climate is characterized by a dry and comparatively cool season from the middle of October to the middle of February, a dry and very hot season from the middle of February to June, and a hot wet season from June or July to September. As might be anticipated from the great differences in elevation between the low plateaux on which, for instance, stands Chaibassa (760 ft.) or Naya Dumka, (489 ft.), and the high plateaux on which, for instance, Ranchi (2,128 ft.) stands, there are considerable local differences in the climate. The high plateaux are comparatively cool all the year round, and hygienically compare very favourably with most parts of Bengal. The climate of the jungle-clad hill tracts of Singbhum is, on the other hand, described in the Imperial Gazetteer as "so malarious that they cannot be visited with safety before the month of November." There are, again, considerable differences in the hot-weather temperatures between the open cultivated country and the high reserved forests, which is at once appreciable without the aid of instruments. Differences of

---

[1] Geology of the Rajmehal Hills, by V. Ball.

[2] Cp., however, Loc. cit., p. 68. "Again, on the eastern flank of the hills, there are many outlying deposits of laterite with which white and purplish clays are interbedded."

temperature between the open country and scrub jungles is, however, not thus perceptible. As, at present, we have no forest meteorological stations, such differences cannot be shown in figures.

The following table[1] shows the absolute maximum and minimum temperatures which have been recorded at Ranchi and Chaibassa, two of the stations for which records have been longest maintained, situated respectively on high and low-level plateaux :—

Absolute Maximum Temperatures.

	Jan.	Feb.	Mar.	Apl.	May.	June.	July.	Aug.	Sept.	Oct.	Nov.	Dec.	Highest mean Max. temperature of the year.	Highest mean daily Max. temperature of the year.
Ranchi	84·0	91·8	101·1	107·5	*110·3*	110·0	101·2	90·2	93·7	92·7	90·0	81·2	99·6	100·1
Chaibassa	90·5	100·5	108·1	114·1	*117·8*	113·9	103·7	95·1	97·4	96·9	94·7	88·2	105·1	106·6

Absolute Minimum Temperatures.

	Jan.	Feb.	Mar.	Apl.	May.	June.	July.	Aug.	Sept.	Oct.	Nov.	Dec.	Lowest mean Min. temperature of the year.	Lowest mean daily Min. temperature of the year.
Ranchi	37·9	40·9	46·2	56·4	58·9	65·4	68·4	68·4	64·9	52·3	46·4	40·9	50·6	49·5
Chaibassa	42·9	44·9	50·5	61·0	66·8	70·0	72·5	71·2	69·5	57·0	46·9	42·9	52·4	50·9

[1] The figures have been taken from Vol. XVII (1904) of the Meteorological Memoirs, combined with the records of the last four years.

The following table[1] shows the absolute maximum and minimum temperatures recorded during the last ten years (8 years in the case of Purulia) at five other stations. Bhagalpur, though no in Chota Nagpur, is mentioned as being the rarest recording station to the northern Santal Parganahs.

Absolute Maximum.

	Jan.	Feb.	Mar.	Apl.	May.	June.	July.	Aug.	Sept.	Oct.	Nov.	Dec.
Naya Dumka . .	86·9	91·5	103·5	112·0	111·4	*112·4*	97·5	95·5	96·0	95·4	91·5	83·2
Purulia . . .	90·8	93·5	105·7	113·2	113·8	*115·8*	100·6	96·6	96·6	98·5	92·5	87·1
Hazaribagh . .	86·2	88·2	99·5	107·1	*103·6*	106·1	102·2	91·2	91·2	92·2	87·1	80·5
Daltonganj . .	90·1	92·1	106·1	113·1	115·1	*115·6*	110·1	98·6	98·0	99·1	92·1	85·1
Bhagalpur . .	83·7	92·2	103·3	110·7	*112·8*	108·2	104·3	98·2	95·2	95·7	92·6	82·2

Absolute Minimum.

	Jan.	Feb.	Mar.	Apl.	May.	June.	July	Aug.	Sept.	Oct.	Nov.	Dec.
Naya Dumka . .	*41·9*	50·9	47·5	59·0	63·4	68·4	71·3	72·9	70·8	59·0	49·9	43·7
Purulia . . .	*44·4*	52·4	50·3	60·3	65·4	71·4	71·9	72·4	69·9	60·8	51·3	45·2
Hazaribagh . .	*39·3*	48·3	44·2	57·2	65·3	68·8	70·3	71·3	65·3	57·7	50·2	44·0
Daltonganj . .	*34·0*	46·0	42·0	53·5	64·5	68·0	71·5	73·0	63·0	51·0	44·2	36·2
Bhagalpur . .	*36·5*	49·6	46·7	57·2	64·6	68·1	73·3	75·6	70·1	58·7	47·4	42·7

[1] The figures have been extracted from the detailed statements of the ten years 1898-1907 kindly supplied by the Meteorological Reporter to the Government of India.

Temperatures of 105·5, 108·9, 109·8, 112·0, 113·1, 113·1, 110·1, respectively, were recorded from the 10th to the 16th June at the Meteorological station at Daltonganj during the writer's walking tour in 1905. On the other hand minimum temperatures of 32 F. have frequently been recorded on the grass, or the roof of a tent, in Singbhum during January. On the Khuria plateau hoar-frost is said to be usual in the winter, but below the *Pats* frost is rare.

The low temperature of the soil in December and January causes a very general cessation of growth and the fall of the leaf in many deciduous trees. The renewed activity of the root-system, as the soil becomes heated in the hot weather, is the cause of many trees putting out their new foliage at the hottest time of the year, and of many others bursting into flower. Others, of a different constitution, and in consequence of the excessive transpiration in the hot weather not being compensated for by the increased activity of the root-system, remain more or less dormant until the May storms, which are followed by a considerable increase in the relative humidity of the air (see below).

The following table shows the average means of maximum, minimum and diurnal range of temperatures and the average mean temperatures corrected to true diurnal means in Chaibassa and Ranchi respectively :—

Average Mean Temperatures.

	Jan.	Feb.	Mar.	Apl.	May.	June.	July.	Aug.	Sept.	Oct.	Nov.	Dec.	Year.
Ranchi—													
M. Max. .	74·4	78·2	87·6	97·1	*99·6*	91·1	84·0	83·3	84·4	83·0	77·8	73·7	84·5
M. Min. .	50·9	54·8	63·3	72·1	76·0	74·6	72·9	72·6	71·7	65·6	57·6	*50·6*	65·2
Means .	61·8	66·0	75·1	84·5	*86·6*	81·4	77·4	76·7	77·0	73·5	66·9	*61·3*	74·0
D. Range .	23·5	23·4	24·3	*25·0*	23·6	16·5	11·1	10·7	12·7	17·4	20·2	23·1	19·3

	Jan.	Feb.	Mar.	Apl.	May.	June.	July.	Aug.	Sept.	Oct.	Nov.	Dec.	Year.
Chaibassa—													
M. Max. .	81·1	85·2	94·8	103·6	*105·1*	96·2	89·6	88·6	89·9	88·7	83·5	79·7	90·5
M. Min. .	53·1	58·3	67·0	76·0	80·0	78·8	77·5	77·0	76·1	70·3	60·4	*52·4*	68·9
Means .	65·6	70·5	79·5	88·4	*90·8*	86·0	82·4	81·5	81·8	78·5	70·9	*64·7*	78·4
D. range .	28·0	26·9	*27·8*	27·6	25·1	17·4	12·1	11·6	13·8	18·4	23·1	27·3	21·6

The following mean maximum and mean minimum temperatures have been calculated from the detailed statements of the last ten years :—

Mean Maximum and Minimum Temperatures.

	Jan.	Feb.	Mar.	Apl.	May.	June.	July.	Aug.	Sept.	Oct.	Nov.	Dec.	Year.
M. Max.— Ranchi	72·9	76·1	87·2	95·6	98·4	94·3	84·8	83·9	84·2	83·9	78·4	73·6	84·4
Hazaribagh	72·4	75·5	86·9	96·6	99·1	95·4	86·1	84·7	84·8	83·5	78·7	73·2	84·9
Purulia .	77·3	80·5	91·7	101·4	101·6	98·4	90·4	89·2	89·0	89·1	83·6	77·8	89·2
Chaibassa . .	79·0	82·6	94·2	102·1	103·2	98·4	89·6	89·0	89·2	89·2	84·0	79·3	90·0
Daltonganj	76·1	79·5	92·2	102·3	106·8	102·7	91·9	89·7	88·2	90·1	83·6	77·5	90·3
Naya Dumka	74·5	78·9	90·9	99·4	98·7	94·5	89·1	88·9	88·6	88·0	82·1	76·2	87·6
Bhagalpur .	73·7	77·7	89·5	98·1	97·9	94·1	90·4	89·5	89·4	86·8	83·0	76·3	87·4
M. Min.— Ranchi .	51·4	54·9	63·6	71·6	75·1	76·7	73·7	73·4	72·1	66·5	57·8	52·0	65·7
Hazaribagh	50·9	54·3	63·3	72·2	75·8	77·6	74·6	74·0	72·5	67·0	57·8	51·2	66·0
Purulia .	54·2	57·6	66·1	74·3	77·2	79·2	77·1	76·7	75·7	70·2	60·8	53·7	68·9
Chaibassa .	54·0	58·3	67·0	74·9	77·2	79·9	77·6	77·3	75·9	70·3	59·4	53·7	68·8
Daltonganj	46·3	50·9	59·5	69·8	78·4	81·6	78·1	76·9	74·6	65·1	52·1	45·8	65·1
Naya Dumka	51·0	55·7	64·8	75·6	76·6	78·5	77·8	77·6	76·5	70·5	59·2	51·9	67·9
Bhagalpur .	51·2	54·6	63·2	71·7	76·1	78·9	79·2	79·1	77·7	71·5	59·3	51·2	67·8

From the above, it will be observed that the coolest months are December and January, that the temperature gradually rises until May, when it attains its mean maximum. The more overcast skies of June produce a lower mean temperature in that month, but the absolute maximum may occur in either May or June. From June the temperature decreases again till December or January, except that the decrease in cloud during September causes a temporary increase in temperature during that month. The damp tropical heat of the period from June to September produces a wealth of terrestrial orchids, Scitamineæ, Aroids and other tropical undergrowth, which dies back again to perennial rootstocks during the cool dry winter.

In the following table the stations are arranged in the order of the heaviest rainfall.

The figures are obtained from Volume XVII of the Meteorological Memoirs (1904), and are based on all available data to the end of 1903. They are not *exactly* comparable, inasmuch as some stations have a very much longer record than others. A comparison, however, of the figures with those recorded in the Meteorological Memoirs of 1886—1888 (Volume III, Part III) for the older stations, shows that there is no appreciable increase or diminution of the rainfall during the last twenty years.

Station.	No. of rainy days.	Inches of rain.	Station.	No. of rainy days.	Inches of rain.
Sirguja .	69·1	64·97	Ghatsila .	69·2	58·66
Palkot . .	67·7	64·73	Naya Dumka .	79·5	58·61
Monharpur .	65·5	64·67	Asanboni .	71·2	55·67
Jashpur .	82·9	64·58	Jhalda . .	66·0	55·20
Katikhund .	67·3	63·57	Gobindpur .	73·1	55·19
Gangpur .	69·9	60·95	Tamar . .	70·5	54·83
Pakaur . .	75·3	60·39	Ramgarh .	60·3	54·04
Sahibganj .	63·8	59·55	Chaibassa .	75·4	53·80
Goilkera .	72·4	59·47	Barabhum .	70·3	53·67

[1]In south Monghyr.

Station.	No. of rainy days.	Inches of rain.	Station.	No. of rainy days.	Inches of rain.
Rajmehal .	64·2	53·34	Giridih . .	75·3	50·82
Deoghar .	72·3	53·15	Sili . .	56·4	49·82
Purulia .	76·0	52·77	Raganathpur[2]	65·7	49·23
Chakardapur .	72·3	52·54	Bhagalpur .	60·8	49·35
Balumath .	62·1	52·42	Husainabad .	50·6	49·08
Sarath . .	70·0	52·14	Godda . .	66·4	48·68
Chatra . .	66·5	51·85	Barhi . .	62·0	48·04
Madhupur .	70·9	51·84	Monghyr .	60·0	47·19
Ranchi .	81·7	51·57	Garhwa . .	56·6	46·59
Hazaribagh .	75·8	51·49			
Sarwan[1] .	63·3	50·99	Daltonganj .	62·7	44·54

Local conditions often radically affect the rainfall at particular stations. Thus, Godda, situated in the lee of the Rajmehal Hills in respect to the moist winds from the Bay of Bengal, has a rainfall much below the average of the northern Santal Parganas. Ghatsila, situated in eastern Singbhum, in a belt where the same moist winds are first forced to rise on striking the eastern Singbhum mountains, has a heavier fall than Chaibassa situated to the west of them. Apart from such purely local variations, the heaviest rainfall is seen to be in two well-defined regions. The one embracing Jashpur, Sirguja, western Ranchi and western Singbhum and Gangpur, is a region of extensive high forest, as well as being nearest to the axis of minimum pressure towards which the two branches of the monsoon converge from the opposite coasts.[1] The other lies in the northern Santal Parganas, a region which is exposed to the moist breezes blowing up the Gangetic valley, and perhaps also to the deflected monsoon winds which sweep the base of the Himalayas.

[1] Cp. Blandford. Met. Memoirs, Vol. III, Part 3.
[2] Eastern Manbhum (not on map).

The driest region is seen to extend from western Palamau (Garhwa and Daltonganj) across northern Hazaribagh, to Giridih and southern Monghyr. It also embraces part of the high Ranchi and Hazaribagh plateaux, which on account of their elevation might be expected to have a larger rainfall. It is to be noted that these plateaux are singularly bare of forest. These differences in the distribution of the rainfall strikingly coincide with differences in the character of the vegetation noticed on p. 28 and which is there provisionally ascribed to differences in relative humidity.[1]

Figures on humidity are only available for very few stations. The following averages[2] are for the last ten years (Purulia, 8 years), but in view of the great divergence in some of the figures, the extremes have also been quoted.[3]

---

[1] The chapter on Climate was written after the completion of the rest of the Flora, as the figures were only received immediately before sending to the press.

[2] The averages are calculatod from the details kindly supplied by the Director General of Observatories.

[3] Figures in brackets are the extremes of *monthly means* of relative humidity, *not* extremes of relative humidity. Seeing that in some cases this mean is said to vary from 48 to ·86 for corresponding months in different years, and that hygrometrical instruments require a deal of attention which cannot perhaps be given by the observers at small meteorological stations, who are usually employees of other Departments, some of these figures may not be quite correct.

Mean Relative Humidity from 1898 to 1907.

	Jan.	Feb.	Mar.	Apl.	May.	June.
Ranchi . . .	67(58—80)	62(52—78)	45(28—57)	42(25—49)	51(39—60)	68(50—79)
Hazaribagh . .	63(56—79)	58(43—73)	44(31—58)	36(26—46)	48(36—55)	63(4—75)
Purulia	72(61—80)	67(46—85)	57(45—72)	50(39—64)	64(49—71)	75(59—84)
Chaibassa . .	82(77—90)	74(61—88)	66(48—86)	59(40—65)	65(59—75)	73(58—80)
Daltonganj . .	81(69—89)	74(56—89)	57(39—79)	42(31—66)	47(40—53)	61(43—75)
Naya Dumka . .	76(66—88)	67(51—85)	54(38—69)	52(38—72)	68(58—82)	80(76—89)
Bhagalpur . .	78(72—86)	68(54—75)	54(36—62)	55(38—72)	68(57—77)	80(72—85)

	July.	Aug.	Sept.	Oct.	Nov.	Dec.	Year.
Ranchi . . .	88(86—91)	89(88—92)	84(72—90)	69(53—80)	60(49—67)	62(51—73)	65(61—69)
Hazaribagh . .	83(78—87)	85(82—90)	81(73—88)	66(51—77)	56(42—64)	60(45—74)	62(59—65)
Purulia . . .	87(84—91)	88(84—96)	86(81—92)	77(72—84)	69(61—78)	68(60—77)	72(68—78)
Chaibassa . .	86(84—88)	86(74—88)	86(82—89)	81(72—87)	78(72—84)	80(69—84)	76(73—79)
Daltonganj . .	83(74—87)	86(82—91)	85(74—90)	81(70—89)	79(72—88)	73(74—92)	71(66—78)
Naya Dumka . .	88(86—91)	88(87—90)	86(83—90)	80(74—86)	75(67—83)	75(68—79)	74(71—77)
Bhagalpur . .	87(80—92)	87(84—89)	84(79—88)	77(70—81)	73(66—76)	73(64—81)	74(71—77)

Taking the averages, it is seen that the mean relative humidity in the hot dry season is, as would be expected, least in Palamau and Hazaribagh, greatest in Singbhum and the Santal Parganahs. In the cold season, however, the mean relative humidity becomes greatest in Palamau and Singbhum, least on the plateaux. The greatest drop in mean minimum temperature (*vide* p. 21) also takes place in Palamau, and indeed (though the table does not shew this), the mean relative humidity in the cold season frequently reaches 100 in the early mornings, and the copious dew has a most important effect in keeping the herbaceous vegetation green up to the end of January, and it is the season of flowering of many annuals and suffruticose perennials, esp. of Malvaceæ. The actual tension of aqueous vapour is much greater at Chaibassa than at Ranchi or Hazaribagh, but the statistics for other stations of equal elevation are wanting.

GENERAL CHARACTER OF THE FLORA.

The heavy rainfall confined to a few months of the year makes the climate essentially a forest one, and the province still contains a considerable percentage of forest-clad land, owing to the rocky nature of the surface preventing the spread of cultivation. This forest belongs to the monsoon type of the tropical zone, and is more or less leafless during the dry season, but the cool valleys, previously alluded to (p. 7), contain a flora which somewhat differs from the general type, and the tops of some of the highest hills, particularly Parasnath, possess species of a moister climate. Although essentially tropophilous, there is yet a marked tendency towards xerophilous structure, which is seen, *e.g.*, in the most characteristic tree of the area, the Sal. In the Sal tree the leaves[1] are very nearly persistent, and they thus

---

[1]The upper surface has a thick cuticle and large epidermal cells rather deeper than broad. Beneath this are 2-3 rows of thin-walled palisade cells. This tissue is interrupted at frequent intervals by large thick-walled sap tissue opposite the vascular bundles and, with the numerous bast fibres of these bundles and a similar tissue opposite to the bundle interrupting the spongey parenchyma, forms strong supporting strands which render the leaves very firm.

have to stand the hot dry winds of February and March, while the new ones appear in May, when the relative humidity of the air is very low. They are therefore markedly coriaceous, and possess a polished surface which reflects the sun's rays. On the hills the trees become low and gnarled with relatively massive stems and small leaves. The Sal, however, is neither long enough deciduous, nor sufficiently xerophilous, to grow on the driest aspects, and it is there supplanted by other trees, *e.g.*, Cleistanthus collinus, Anogeissus latifolia, Odina Wodier, Nyctanthes Arbor-tristis and other species which constitute much of the so-called "Mixed Forest" type. On the driest and most exposed rocks are found certain plants entirely xerophilous in structure. Such are fleshy Euphorbias with corky bark and fleshy leaves appearing only in the rains, and Sarcostemma with fleshy quill-like branches and pretty waxy flowers. Most of the trees, however, escape the dessicating influence of the long dry season by shedding their leaves, or even (some Phyllantheæ) their branches, and some, which are associated with the xerophilous plants above mentioned, have very thick twigs and remain without their leaves for an extraordinary time. Thus Sterculia urens is leafless from November to May or even to June, Odina Wodier and Cochlospermum Gossypium from November to May. A thin, papery, flaky bark, or a very white stem, is characteristic of species growing on sun-scorched hills, and these white leafless giants, flinging their bare arms to the furnace blasts of the western winds of May give a wild and weird look to many of the hill tops.

It is noteworthy that many of these trees which are leafless for prolonged periods have a chlorophyll layer under their white outer bark.

A very prominent rock-loving species is Gardenia latifolia. The minute seeds germinate in the crevices of bare rocks, the crevices becoming filled with the growing rootstock which also forms a cushion over the top. The tree has a clean white stem and large coriaceous leaves, covered with a resinous varnish while young.

Gardenia gummifera has polished coriaceous leaves, also varnished while young, and its buds are protected by a large drop of resin. It and Gardenia turgida, one form of which is covered with strong opposite and decussate spines, has also a white bark. Ficus infectoria (wild form), F. glabella, and F. tomentosa are all rock-loving species and often markedly xerophilous in structure. The leaves of F. tomentosa are covered with a dense felt of hairs. It may be seen growing freely on the old Palamau fort, the ruin of which it is helping to complete.

The most arid tract is in the extreme north-west o Palamau, which in addition to its being furthest from the moist winds of the Bay of Bengal, is exposed to a very dry wind which blows down the Sone valley. It is characterized by Capparis sepiaria, Hardwickia binata, and Balanites, plants common nowhere else in our area. South and east the country gradually becomes somewhat more humid. The most humid tracts are found in the deep valleys of the south-west of Singbhum, due apparently to the extensive clothing of vegetation, and again in the northern and north-eastern Santal Parganahs, due to the proximity of the Gangetic valley and the moist winds from the Bay.[1]

The increase in humidity is very marked in marching from Dumka northwards through the Santal Parganahs, and a number of plants re-appear which have only been elsewhere met with in the Saranda tract of Singbhum. Others are confined to the Santal Parganahs district, so far as Chota Nagpur is concerned, and belong rather to Bengal proper, Assam and the Sub-Himalayan region. The flora of the Rajmehal Hills must indeed, at one time, have been wonderfully rich, though now disappearing through the destruction of the forests. A number of plants, again, are found in the

[1] Cp. Climate, pp. 23 to 25.

eep Singbhum valleys but not in the Santal Parganahs or other parts of Chota Nagpur or Bengal, and these also belong, for the most part, to the Eastern Sub-Himalayan, Assam and Malay Flora.

Of plants peculiar to the Santal Parganahs (so far as our area is concerned) may be mentioned Glycosmis pentaphylla, Mallotus repandus, Bridelia tomentosa and B. stipularis, which are common in Bengal proper. Siphonodon celastrineus, Neuracanthus tetragonostachyus, Ochna squarrosa, Dalbergia tamarindifolia, Alphonsea ventricosa, Vitex glabrata and Ligustrum robustum, which are chiefly eastern species not found in Bengal proper, though occurring perhaps in Orissa.

The following are found both in the Singbhum forests and the Santal Parganahs, *viz.*, Mucuna imbricata, Sideroxylon tomentosum, Helinus, Cansjera Rheedii, Hyptianthera stricta, Lasia, Uvaria Hamiltonii, most of which are essentially Eastern Peninsular or Sub-Himalayan species.

The following are plants which are peculiar to the Singbhum (chiefly Saranda) forests of Chota Nagpur, *viz.*, Pygeum acuminatum, Lasianthus lancifolius, Ardisia depressa, Cyclostemon assamicus, Michelia Champaca, Litsæa nitida, Macaranga indica, Lysimachia peduncularis, Symplocos spicata, Trevesia palmata, Raphistemma pulchellum, Sauropus pubescens, Laportea crenulata, Homalium nepalense, Musa ornata, Licuala peltata, Caryota urens, and a sweet, wild form of the orange, nearly all of which, again, are species of Sikkim, Assam and the Malay Peninsula as well as all (except perhaps Raphistemma and Cyclostemon) belonging to Chinese genera.

Of the damp tropical flora Chota Nagpur possesses a few representatives besides those already mentioned as peculiar to special districts, such are Scindapsus and other Aroids, Piper longum, Heteropanax, numerous Ampelidaceæ, Garcinia Cowa, and many figs. One form of Beilschmiedia fagifolia occurs in Singbhum, and another in the Santal

Parganahs. Referring to the increased humidity of the top of Parasnath (in Hazaribagh), Sir J. D. Hooker says "Of plants eminently typical of a moister atmosphere I may mention the genera Bulbophyllum, Begonia, Aeginetia, Disporum, Roxburghia, Panax, Eugenia, Myrsine, ferns, mosses, and foliaceous lichens; which appeared in strange association with such dry-climate genera as Kalanchœ, Pterospermum, and the dwarf palm, Phœnix. Add to this list the Berberis asiatica, Clematis nutans, Thalictrum glyphocarpum, 27 grasses, Cardamine, etc., and the mountain top presents a mixture of the plants of a damp hot, a dry hot and of a temperate climate, in fairly balanced proportions." Of the strictly Peninsular Flora, Walsura piscidia from Koderma has hitherto only been known from south of the Godavery, and Nauclea purpurea from south of the Mahanadi.

The influence of the soil is, as usual, much less marked than that due to slight differences of climate. Soil is, however, chiefly accountable for the distribution of the Khair (Acacia Catechu) and Carissa. These occur over a very large area in Hazaribagh, Manbhum, and Palamau, chiefly on those rocks which yield a sandy soil such as the sandstones, quartzites, and horneblende gneiss. It is not always easy to say, however, how far the prevalence of these species is due to the soil alone. In parts of Palamau there is little doubt that human agency (including in this category fires, cattle-grazing, etc.) has favoured the Khair as against the Sal as, where the forests are protected, the Sal again tends to oust the Khair. Sal, probably, once reached the edge of the laterite plateau which extends into Midnapur. Its absence in many cases is almost certainly due to extermination, while its companion, the Mohwa (Bassia latifolia), has survived, according to the rule that timber trees are more liable to extermination than fruit trees. Its absence in many low-lying tracts is, on the other hand, due to edaphic factors, and it is also very frequently scarce or absent on some forms of trap and limestone. Gardenia gummifera is almost confined to clay schists.

Next to cultivation the first radical change due to man is to reduce the forest to a coppice or scrub condition in which the species are exposed to the effects of selective browsing. The species which survive longest are apparently those rich in tannic acid, or with a formidable armature of thorns. On some of the hills most subject to goat-grazing, as well as to annual fires, the coppice is nearly pure Cleistanthus collinus. In some cases, a coppice of Chloroxylon is very abundant although this is a comparatively rare tree in the forests. This also owes its preservation to the acrid nature of the leaves.

Although thorn woodland is, in the main, a formation due to climatic factors, there is ample evidence that its production or extension in Chota Nagpur is largely a result of selective cutting and grazing. Man in his cutting avoids thorny trees and bushes as animals avoid them. The quantity he removes for fencing purposes is comparatively trifling. In the mixed Sal and Khair forests of Palamau, the Sal is the more abundant in proportion to its distance from towns and villages. Carissa has found no footing at all in the comparatively dense forest areas of Singbhum; it thrives over the greater part of Hazaribagh, where the jungles are open formations, but more specially, as said above, on sandy soils.

A statement of the relative abundance and of the association of individuals of dominant genera and species frequently gives a better picture of a flora to a forester than can be obtained by mere numbers of species in dominant families. This is especially the case with small families containing gregarious species. The Sal is a case in point, which, though giving a peculiarly distinctive character to the Bengal-Deccan flora, does not appear at all in a list of dominant families. For the forester then, the province is well characterized by the almost general association in large numbers, on the one hand, of Sal, Anogeissus spp., Bassia latifolia, Gardenias, Butea spp., Schleichera, and the grasses

Ischaemum angustifolium (Sabai grass) and Andropogon contortus (Spear grass). On the other hand, by the scarcity of such common sub-Himalayan associates of the Sal as Dillenia pentagyna and indica, Careya arborea and herbacea, Stereospermum chelonoides, and Sterculia villosa; and by the complete absence in a wild state of all Cupuliferæ and Coniferæ, of Sissu and of Teak.

A second characteristic feature, or group of features, is the abundance of individuals of Rubiaceæ, notably of the genera Gardenia and Wendlandia (all the other Bengal species of Gardenia are confined to Chittagong), of Acanthaceæ, Bauhinia spp., Diospyros spp., Terminalia spp., Zizyphus spp., Cleistanthus collinus, Nyctanthes, Ægle Marmelos, and of the bamboo Dendrocalamus strictus.

Dillenia pentagyna, so common an associate of Sal in the Sub-Himalayas east of the 80th meridian, is in Chota Nagpur largely replaced by D. aurea, which appears to have been repeatedly confused with the former when in leaf, and with Cochlospermum when in flower. Dillenia aurea is a characteristic species and extends into the Karakpur Hills, which, as already remarked, might well have been included in this flora.

The Anonaceæ are fairly well represented, as also are the small families Menispermaceæ (5 spp.), Capparidaceæ (8 spp.), Polygalaceæ (6 spp.), Combretaceæ (10 spp.) and Lythraceæ (10 spp.). The families of Urticaceæ, Magnoliaceæ, Ranunculaceæ, Cruciferæ, Guttiferæ, Ternstrœmiaceæ, Rosaceæ, Umbelliferæ, and Lauraceæ are poorly represented both in species and individuals.

Following the method pursued to characterize the Botanical provinces in the sketch of the Flora of British India (prepared by Sir J. D. Hooker for the new edition of the Imperial Gazetteer), the approximate number of species in the dominant orders or families is given below :—

Gramineæ 150.

Leguminosæ 130 (Papilionaceæ 100, Cæsalpiniaceæ 20, Mimosaceæ 12).
Cyperaceæ 70.
Orchidaceæ 60.
Compositæ 60.
Euphorbiaceæ 50.
Acanthaceæ 45.
Rubiaceæ 45.
Scrophulariaceæ 40.
Filices 40.
Labiatæ 35.
Urticaceæ 35 (including Ulmaceæ and Moraceæ).
Cucurbitaceæ 30.
Scitamineæ 20 (including Zingiberaceæ, Marantaceæ and Musaceæ).
Verbenaceæ 20.
Commelinaceæ 17.
Araceæ 15.
Liliaceæ 11.

VERNACULAR NAMES, AND NOTE ON THE POPULATION.

Chota Nagpur is said to be a corruption of Chutia Nagpur from Chutia near Ranchi, the former seat of the old Munda Rajahs and with the Santal Parganahs, it contains the largest proportion of aboriginal races of any of the administrative divisions of Bengal. These races belong chiefly to the Kolarian and Dravidian stocks, though with regard to this distinction, Sir H. Risley[1] states that it rests solely upon linguistic peculiarities, and does not correspond to any differences of physiological type. Nevertheless it is usually possible for those who have lived among the aboriginal tribes to distinguish the two stocks, and it is more convenient to follow Hunter and Dalton and to treat them as distinct.

---

[1] *Vide* Sir H. H. Risley in Tribes and Castes of Bengal.

The word Kol is used in a variety of senses and requires definition. Broadly it includes both Mundas and Oraons and practically all the aboriginal tribes of Chota Nagpur. Col. Dalton,[1] however treats as Kolarian, or Kols, those races whose language is Munda or Kol, hence excluding the Oraons, Gonds, etc., but including the Santals, and of course including (though he does not specifically say so) those tribes obviously Kolarian who have now more or less lost the Kol language. Hunter again states that the scientific use of the word embraces the Kolarian tribes of Munda, Ho, Bhumij and Kharwar, and in another place he says that it is a generic word for the whole group of tribes included linguistically within the term Kolarian, but that it is often applied in a more restricted sense to embrace only the three principal tribes Munda Kols, Larka Kols or Hos, and Bhumij Kols. Inasmuch as the names of plants are usually the same or similar among these three tribes, the word Kol is used in the Flora in this last and restricted sense. In many cases Kol names will still be found in use among Kolarian tribes which have adopted Aryan languages,[2] but on the other hand the Mundari, Ho and Bhumij names may be distinct. The difference often only consists in the elision of the Mundari 'r' accompanied in the Ho with the peculiar partial reduplication of the final vowel,[3] equivalent to the c' or k' of the Santal. Thus a pot-herb is *ara* in Mundari or Bhumij *a : a* in Ho, *arak'* in Santal. Such trifling differences have sometimes been ignored in the Flora.

Owing to the spread of Aryan languages among the aboriginal races of Chota Nagpur, fostored by the primary schools and the law courts, the Kolarian and Dravidian languages are unfortunately disappearing. Unfortunately, because the

---

[1] Col. Edward Tuite Dalton, Ethnology of Bengal, a most interesting work, published in 1872 and long out of print.

[2] This is an instance of Sir H. Risley's contention that language is not a reliable guide to race.

[3] Usually written thus :, but diacritical signs have frequently been omitted in the Flora.

attributes of a people tend rapidly to change with their language, and few who have dwelled some time in the land of the Kols can desire the change. The non-Aryan languages are usually replaced by a jargon of Hindi, sometimes referred to locally as Gawnwari. In some cases, especially on the east of the tract, owing to association with Bengalis, a Bengali dialect has been adopted. For these reasons it has been necessary to include several Hindi and Bengali names. The latter, however, are not numerous, as Bengali names are chiefly confined to cultivated plants, and there are few really Bengali names for purely forest species. Most of those mentioned have been obtained from a comparison of the names quoted by Gamble and Watt. To how great an extent Aryan languages have replaced the non-Aryan may be gathered from the following table,[1] which also shows the total population and the number of persons per square mile in each district.

	Singbhum.	Manbhum.	Hazaribagh.	Ranchi.	Palamau.	Santal P.	Try. States.
Population	6,13,579	13,01,364	11,77,961	11,87,925	6,19,600	18,09,737	10,01,429
Pop. per sq. mile.	163	314	168	167	126	331	62
Percentage of aboriginal tribes.[2]	75	61	34	74	36	59	73
Percentage of persons speaking non-Aryan languages.	61-62	14-15	7-8	56-57	6-7	40	21-22

[1] Calculated from the figures given in the Census of India, 1901, by E. A. Gait, I.C.S.

[2] There is sometimes doubt as to which to consider aboriginal among the Hinduized tribes, and the figures can only be approximate. The writer has been guided as far as possible by Risley (Tribes and Castes of Bengal) and by Dalton (Ethnology of Bengal). Kurmis are not included in the Santal Parganas, but they are for the other districts. Koiris, Chamars, Goalas, Kumhars, Telis, etc., are all considered Aryan.

It might have been expected that the most isolated districts (*e.g.*, Ranchi), and those containing the largest proportion of forest (nearly 20 per cent. in Singbhum), would have been precisely those in which the aboriginal languages would die hardest but it is difficult to explain the progress of Aryan tongues among the Tributary States.

Singbhum.—The dominant tribe is the Ho, who form over 37 per cent. of the population, and next to them come the Santals. Among other Kolarian races the Bhumij are very numerous in the east along the Subarnarekha, and in Dalbhum, whence they extend into Manbhum, and in the north, in Porahat, the Mundas are predominant. The Dravidian element is not strong but there are over 6,000 Gonds and over 5,000 Oraons; the latter, however, chiefly confined to the towns. The Imperial Gazetteer (1887) states that the whole of Saranda (*vide* p. 7) contains but a few poor hamlets nestling in deep valleys, and belonging to one of the least reclaimed tribes of Kols. The reference is to the Hos, and may the process of so-called reclamation be a long one! The writer heartily endorses Col. Dalton's description of them; they have "a manner free from servility, but *never rude*; a love or at least the practice of truth; a feeling of self-respect, rendering them keenly sensitive under rebuke." They used to have, and indeed still maintain, a great reputation for bravery, and in 1820 a British force which entered the country with a view to bringing them under the subjection of the Rajah "had to fight every inch of its way out of the country again, leaving them unsubdued."[1] The Hos of the Singbhum jungles still carry their bows and battle-axes, and can use them with good effect. Although so essentially a forest tribe, it is to be noted that a considerable number of Saranda plants have really no Ho names. Unlike the Lepchas of the Eastern Himalayas, the Hos and other Chota Nagpur tribes only name the common plants and those of striking beauty or scent, and those of economic importance to them. Some

---

[1] Quoted from Hunter in the Imperial Gazetteer of 1887.

species have names given to them in one village but not in another, and generally speaking when plants have a large number of different and dissimilar names none of these are of much value, and the writer has usually rejected those names which have not been repeated in several villages. A large number of the more educated Kols and Santals are no more conversant with the correct names of their trees than is the ordinary Englishman with those of the trees of his native land, and they are the very ones to most readily supply names from their imagination. Descriptive and compound names, especially those formed with sandi (male), enga (female), huring (small), marang (large) and bir (forest, hence wild) as parts, are usually to be regarded with suspicion. The word *daru* (tree) is almost invariably added after the name of a tree by the Kols, but this has been omitted in the Flora.

The forest Kols are well versed in the edible properties of plants, but their medicine is usually very crude. Among them, as among other primitive tribes, the Law of Signatures is firmly believed in: a plant with milky juice is good for promoting the secretion of milk, the little plant Biophytum with sensitive leaves is valuable as a soporific. The Bhumij in the extreme east of Singbhum and in Manbhum speak a dialect of Bengali, but in other parts mostly Mundari. One of the wildest tribes in Singbhum are the Birhors (meaning "forest people"). They are a wandering, and now a very small, tribe whose encampments used to be occasionally met with in the north of Singbhum, and about Biru in Ranchi district, but they are also reported from Hazaribagh. They live by snaring monkeys and by collecting the fibre of the Bauhinia Vahlii. The monkey skins form the ends of the large deep-toned drum (dumung) of the Kols, the body of which is made of earth or of jack, while the smaller drum (dulki) is usually of Gmelina. The monkeys snared, which are the small brown Macacus, called *gari* in Birhor, and *gai*: in Ho; (the Hunaman, Semnopithecus, called Sara in Kol, I have never seen snared) also form their chief article of food, and the Birhor himself has acquired a very strong monkey odour. As far as could be ascertained from a slight acquaintance, the language of the Birhors is ordinary Mundari.

Manbhum.—The largest caste is the Hinduized Kurmis, and if these are really of Aryan blood, the proportion of aboriginal tribes in Manbhum is under 50 per cent. of the total population. In the north of Manbhum the Santals are very numerous, so that they form over 14 per cent. of the population of the whole district. Santal names are similar or distinct from the Munda and Ho, but in some cases they are now the same as the Hindi, and on this account it has sometimes been contended that the alleged Hindi names may be borrowed from the Santal. This, however, does not seem very probable when the other Kols still retain a distinct name for the plant in question, and seeing that so many Hindi words have been borrowed by the Santals. Most of the Santali names in the Flora have been obtained from the Rev. A. Campbell, who is most perfectly acquainted with the Santal language in addition to being a botanist.

Ranchi.—The Ranchi district is the great centre of the Kolarian Mundas and the Dravidian Oraons. Munda names of plants are very largely used and have already been referred to. The list is probably not quite complete as the writer has been unable to recognize a number of Mundari totems which are said to be names of trees.[1] Some of these, however, are certainly not trees native of the country now inhabited by the Mundas, and the names are usually considered Hindi; such for instance as Gua (Areca Nut), while others though native are under Hindi names, such as *aura* which is *miral* in Mundari, and *amba* which is translated as mango, though the wild mango is always known as *Uli*.

Oraon names are still a great desideratum[2] and of the few mentioned most have been gleaned from Mr. Gamble's works.

---

[1] See Risley's Tribes and Castes of Bengal.

[2] The writer, unfortunately, lost the notes of Oraon names collected for the trees of the Horhap forest.

Tradition says that the original home of the Oraons was in the Carnatic, whence they went up the Narbudda and settled in Behar on the banks of the Sone. Driven from Shahabad, the tribe split up into two divisions. One followed the Ganges and settled in the Rajmehal Hills, where their descendants are now known as Ma-le; while the others ascended the Sone into Palamau and turning eastwards along the Koel, took possession of the north-west portion of the Chota Nagpur plateau.[1] Some Oraon have a resemblance to the Kol names, possibly through long association, thus madgi in Oraon is the madkum of the Kols. Bara (Ficus bengalensis) and Bhelua (Semecarpus) are evidently the Hindi, but the former is also Bari in Munda so that the real origin of this word is doubtful. Other names such as Kirs Khochol = Pig's bones (quoted by Father Dehon) are among that class of descriptive names, which often appears to be applied by races to trees that they meet with in a new country, or when asked for the name of a tree which they do not know. It would be interesting were some residents among the Oraons to collect their names of the trees before they are finally lost. The Singbhum Oraons are usually singularly ignorant of them. The Oraons often tattoo themselves, and this is done with charcoal dust, mixed with Mohwa juice, and applied with the thorns of Flacourtia Ramontchi [2] (called Kandeh in Malto, perhaps the Khochol of the Oraons). Like other aboriginal tribes, they have a number of more picturesque and poetical customs, some of them in common with the Kols, such as the feast of *Sarhul*, or of the Flowering of the Sal Tree.

Hazaribagh.—In Hazaribagh the Hindus and semi-Hinduized tribes are predominant, and the names of the trees

---

[1] Rev. P. Dehon, S.J., in Memoirs of the Asiatic Society of Bengal, Vol. I, 9.

[2] B. B. Bainbridge in Memoirs of the Asiatic Society of Bengal, Vol. II, 4.

[3] Risley in Tribes and Castes of Bengal.

given are usually Hindi. In the Koderma forest (where, however, there is a very mixed population working in the mica mines) the names are often peculiar, and the word Koderma after a vernacular name has been used in place of specifying the language. Of the Hinduized aborigines in Hazaribagh the Bhuiyas are the most numerous of non-Hinduized tribes, the Santals

Palamau.—Palamau was originally included with Ranchi in the Lohardagga District, which had in 1881 53·4 per cent. of aboriginal races. It is now a separate district and the most numerous castes are the Bhuiyas, the Goalas and the Kharwars. There are, however, also a considerable number of Oraons. The Kharwars are aborigines whose original language is apparently entirely lost, but the mongrel Hindi dialect spoken in Palamau often contains names of trees dis tinct from the ordinary Hindi, and is referred to as Kharwar A few of the Kharwari names quoted were collected by the writer, but the bulk were collected by Mr. Haslett of the Forest Department.

Santal Parganahs.—The Santals form over 36 per cent. of the total population of the district. In the Ramgarh Hills, which are south of the Brahmini River but are often included collectively in the term Rajmehal Hills, dwell the Dravidian tribe known as the Mal Paharias who speak a dialect of Bengali. The few Mal Paharia names quoted have been obtained from Gamble's Manual of Indian Timbers. North of the Bansloi River, on the very summits of the Rajmehal Hills, dwell the Dravidian Saorias or Males (Mr. Bainbridge says that these are two distinct divisions), closely allied to the Oraons, and whose speech is known as Malto. Saoria names, as in the case of other Oraon names, are wanting, as the writer spent too short a time in the Saoria tract to render the collection of names of any value. Mr. Bainbridge says that "the disappearance of the forest on the north of the Saoria Hills and the shrewd councils of business men created the important industry in Sabai grass. To the native banker and middleman it has, in many cases, been profitable beyond the dreams of avarice; to the Saoria it has, in the majority of cases, brought a temporary affluence which is the portal to wretchedness—abject poverty is no misnomer among the Saorias of to-day."[1]

On this policy of permitting pushing races to indefinitely extend their cultivation at the expense of the forest tracts, Mr. Ball[2] says that the jungles may be regarded as the saving of the lower races from famine, and did they not afford nutritious food in abundance, the result of a famine like that of 1866-67 would probably be not merely decimation, but utter depopulation throughout extensive areas.

Tributary States.—The table above (p. 35) includes all the tributary states of Chota Nagpur as they stood at the time of the census of 1901. It has to be recollected, however, that politically most of these have since been excluded from Chota Nagpur. Their population varies much, and in Udaipur is only 43 persons to the square mile, in Sirguja there were 54 persons in 1891 and 58 in 1901, Gangpur had 76 and 95 respectively, while Kharswan has 252 persons to the square mile. The last as well as Seraikhela are practically in Singbhum, and include a very large percentage of Hos. In Gangpur the Oraons, Gonds and the Kolarian Kharias are the most numerous. Where *Gangpur* is shown after a plant name, this name is usually Kheria.[3] The Kharias are also frequent in Ranchi and Singbhum, and are said to frequent the Dalma range in Manbhum. The Kerwas are said[4] to be the sole inhabitants of the tableland forming the south barrier of Sirguja (or Sarguja) called the Main pat, but their plant names are not available and, taking the state

---

[1] Memoirs of the Asiatic Society of Bengal, Vol. II, 4.

[2] Journal of the Asiatic Society of Bengal, Vol. II, 1867.

[3] The caste name was not always specified in the field notes, hence the locality only is stated.

[4] Hunter, in Imperial Gazetteer.

as a whole, Gonds are the most numerous tribe, while in Jashpur the Oraons occupy this position.

THE MAP.

This has been compiled in the Forest Survey Office[1] chiefly from the topographical map of Bengal (Scale 16 miles to 1 inch) and the forest survey maps of the reserved and protected forests of Chota Nagpur. Reserved forests are shown in green, protected forests in deep red, and other forest tracts in light red. The distribution of the last has been taken from the excellent small map published with the Report on Forest Administration in the Chota Nagpur Division by Dr. W. Schlich (1885), and are only approximate. The Santal Parganahs were not included in that report, and the general light colouration of so much of the eastern portions of that district is an error. It should be remembered that many of the tributary estates now shown in the east of the Central Provinces were formerly in Chota Nagpur (see p. 1), and though they contain much forest this could not be depicted for want of precise information. The map is primarily intended to display the physical features of the area dealt with in the Flora, and to mark the position of the localities referred to. There are, however, some omissions owing to the impossibility of accurately fixing a number of these. Names printed thus LEDA are the names of Forest Blocks.

The following names mentioned in the Introduction are omitted from the Map :—

Baragori or Baragai Hill.—On the Ranchi-Hazaribagh border, south of Ramgarh, on the Damodar ghats.

Khuria plateau.—In northern Jashpur.

---

[1] By Mr. A. Descubes, Superintendent of Forest Map Records, under the supervision of Mr. T. A. Pope, Superintendent of Forest Surveys.

Main pát or Mani pat.—In southern Sarguja, extending to Udaipur.

CLASSIFICATION.

It is not possible to enter into much detail with regard to the reasons for the system of classification adopted. The two chief systems in use at the present day are those of Bentham and Hooker adopted in the Genera Plantarum, and the German system of Endlicher adopted more or less closely by Engler in die Naturlichen Pflanzenfamilien.[1] by Strasburger, Warming, and other European botanists. It is now generally recognized that the apetalous class as constituted in the first classification is unnatural as, of course, is the position assigned to the Gymnosperms in that classification.[2] On the other hand recent researches, especially in Fossil Botany, appear to show that the supposed phylogenetic arrangement (as far as a linear system can be phylogenetic) of the German system is probably still far from being a correct one. As there is for the moment no work yet complete [3] which embodies the most recent views on phylogeny, it has been rather difficult to decide on the correct line to adopt. Engler, believing that the apparent simplicity of the flowers of such families as the Willows and Peppers to be primitive, comparing them with those of the Coniferæ, which he believed to be somewhere near the main line of descent of the Angiosperms, commences the linear arrangement of the Dicotyledons with those orders (after having previously disposed of the Casuarinaceæ on the ground of its numerous embryo sacs [4]). But it is now more than ever doubtful whether the simplicity of the

---

[1] Die Naturlichen Pflanzenfamilien, Nachtrage, p. 341 *et seq.*

[2] *Vide* Genera Plantarum, Vol. III, Pt. I, p. vii, and Introduction to The Students' Flora of the British Islands, p. xi.

[3] Dr. Rendle's classification of Flowering Plants is not complete, or this might have been adopted in its entirety.

[4] A character which has since been shown not to possess the significance attached to it.

flowers in the above and similar cases is not a derived character, such flowers being due to suppression of parts present in more complex ancestors. It is also pointed out that these apparently simple flowers are usually combined into very complex inflorescences. In demonstration of the fact that some very primitive flowers were exceedingly complex, may be quoted Scott's very fascinating account[1] of the flowers of the extinct Bennettiteæ, which were probably much nearer the direct line of descent of the Angiosperms than the Coniferæ. "The centre is occupied by the gynæcium, seated on the convex receptacle, and consisting of numerous long-stalked ovules, imbedded among the interseminal scales. Surrounding this central body is the hypogynous whorl of stamens, fused below to form a tube, and expanding above into the pinnate sporophylls, bearing very numerous compound pollen-sacs or synangia, filled with pollen. The whole is surrounded by an envelope of spirally arranged bracts springing from the upper part of the peduncle. The general arrangement of parts is manifestly just the same as in a typical angiospermous flower, with a central pistil, hypogynous stamens, and a perianth. The resemblance is still further emphasised by the fact, long known, that the interseminal scales are confluent at their outer ends, to form a kind of pericarp or ovary-wall. When to these general features we add the practically exalbuminous character of the seed, with its highly organised, dicotyledonous embryo, the indications of affinity with the higher Flowering Plants become extremely significant. The comparison was drawn by Dr. Wieland in 1901, immediately on his discovery of the hermaphrodite flower.***The flower with its great stamens, 10 cm. long in some species, must have been a striking object when it opened. As, of course, we can know nothing of the colouration of the perianth and other parts, we cannot tell how brilliant its appearance may have been; the bright tints of

[1] Presidential Address to the Royal Micro. Society, published in the Journal Roy. Micro. Soc., April 1907, p. 139.

the carpels and ovules in some recent Cycads, such as species of Cycas and Encephalartos, suggests the probability that the attraction of colour were not wanting to the more elaborate flowers of the older Cycadophyta." The extraordinarily striking analogy which is presented between the Bennettitean flower and that of some of the Ranales leads to the conclusion that the earlier Angiosperms are not those with minute unisexual flowers, but some of those with large complex flowers and numerous sporophylls. To again quote from Dr. Scott :—[1] "The complexity of this earliest known type of a true flower indicates the probability, as Dr. Wieland points out, that the evolution of the Angiospermous flower was a process of reduction."

Again, in a most interesting paper[2] on the origin of Angiosperms by Messrs. Newell Arber and John Parkin, the Piperales, Amentiferæ, Araceæ and other orders with very simple flowers are regarded as derived from phyla with more complicated ones, while Nymphæaceæ, Magnoliaceæ, and other polycarpicæ among Dicotyledons, Alismaceæ, Butomaceæ, and Palmaceæ among Monocotyledons are taken as exhibiting many primitive features. But even if it be now a plausible theory that the Angiosperms sprung from seed-bearing plants, which had already large and well-developed flowers, and if it be conceded that on the whole the Ranales show most primitive characters, paleobotany still throws no direct light on the relative age of the several other Angiospermous groups. The appearance of the most widely separated groups is said to be sudden and simultaneous, and what are universally believed to be younger groups occur in the same beds with what are believed to be primitive. Even Gamopetalæ, and actually the Caprifoiaceæ (Viburnum) are, if leaf diagnosis can be relied upon, found as far back as the Cretaceous period.[3] No light is thrown, even, on the relative

---

[1] Journal, Roy. Micro. Soc., April 1907, p. 141.

[2] Journal of the Linnean Society, XXXVIII, p. 263.

[3] *Vide* Laurent in Les Progrès de la Paloébotanique angiospermique dans la dernière décade (Progressus Rei Botanicæ, Vol. I, pp. 360-361)

ages of Monocotyledons and Dicotyledons. Rendle in his Classification of Flowering Plants begins with the Cycads, Coniferæ, and Gnetaceæ, and follows with the Monocotyledons. The order of the two last groups adopted here is that of the Genera Plantarum, the Dicotyledonous phylum being considered on the whole as more ancient than that of the Monocotyledons,[1] which are probably a side branch of the main Angiospermic trunk. The arrangement adopted in this flora, then, is Ferns, Gymnosperms, Dicotyledons, Monocotyledons. The division of the Dicotyledons has been based on the German system in respect to the two great divisions of Choripetalæ and Sympetalæ, and in the distribution of the Apetalæ among the former; but for reasons indicated above the Choripetalæ start with the Ranales as in the Genera Plantarum. To those already acquainted with Bentham and Hooker's system, this arrangement will present little difficulty; most of them will already be familiar with the German system from their botanical studies, or from having used a German flora in the field. To those unfamiliar with systematic botany, it is believed that the abolition of the Apetalous class, as usually constituted, will be the removal of a stumbling block, and save such often-repeated queries as to the reason of Jatropha, etc., being included in the Apetalæ and not Casearia, etc., etc. They will, however, understand that in no linear arrangement is it possible to commence with the most primitive forms nor, while keeping obviously allied forms and groups together, to steadily proceed from the older and primitive to the younger and more highly evolved. Some groups may show, on the one hand, old and primitive types simultaneously with obviously allied but highly

[1] It will be recollected that the Monocotyledons show several points of resemblance with some of the Polycarpicæ or Ranales, and that Van Tieghem placed the Nymphæaceæ between the Monocotyledons and the Dicotyledons. Benettites had two cotyledons, and several Dicotyledons occasionally exhibit more than two, as is common among the Gymnosperms.

specialised or reduced forms. Sometimes a whole group of families may be allied to a single family in another group, yet it would be impossible in a linear arrangement to show this by the mere order of the families. As might be supposed, it is often the families at the *bases* of the several larger branches which show close affinities to the main trunk and hence to one another, but these could not be placed next to one another without at the same time severing the twigs from the branches.

These difficulties have been partly obviated by indicating supposed cross alliances of families or larger groups in brackets after the name of the younger or both groups, where one has had to be placed at a distance from its supposed relative.

DESCRIPTION OF CLASSES.

The vegetable kingdom may be divided into five main divisions, *viz.*, Mycetozoa, Thallophyta, Bryophyta, Pteridophyta (these two sometimes united as the Archegoniata), and Phanerogamia. Included in the large division of Thallophyta are the fungi, a group of importance to the forester, but not sufficient is known of the Chota Nagpur fungi to include them in this flora, which is limited to a few of the largest Pteridophyta, and to the Phanerogamia, or Flowering Plants.

Division—PTERIDOPHYTA.

Class—Filicinæ (Ferns).

Stems rarely much branched, roots arising from them in acropetal succession (or from the petioles). Leaves well developed and of large size in proportion to the stem, often very compound, rolled inwards (circinate) when young. Spores of one kind only (isosporous), which produce monœcious independent green prothallia, they (the spores) are formed in small roundish capsules (sporangia), which are produced in large numbers on the back or margin of leaves (fertile fronds, sporophylls) and are usually collected together in small groups (sori). Fertile fronds either altogether resemble the barren ones or are specially modified. The prothallia when fully developed produce archegonia and antheridia.

ORDER I. **Filicales.** (p. 54) ORDER II. **Marattiales.** (p. 56).

DIVISION—**PHANEROGAMIA.**

This division includes practically all the trees and shrubs of the present time. Spores of two kinds (heterosporous). Male spores (microspore, pollen-grain) borne on specially modified sporophylls (stamens) in sporangia (pollen-sacs). The female spore (macrospore, embryo-sac) never quits the macrosporangium (nucellus), which becomes invested by one or more envelopes (integuments) derived from the parent plant, and with them constitutes the ovule. The prothallium (if formed) develops entirely within the macrospore, and the fertilized oösphere forms an embryo inside the ovule, which after further changes consequent on fertilization becomes the seed. The microspore on germination gives rise to the pollen tube. Sub-divisions.—Gymnospermæ, Angiospermæ.

SUB-DIVISION I.—**Gymnospermæ.**

Trees or shrubs (including such well-known trees as the pines, yew, etc.), very rarely scandent. Fls. 1-sexual often cone-like. Female sporophyll (carpel) bearing the ovules on its margin or surface, *never infolded or cohering by the edges with other carpels to form a closed ovary* (*N.B.* the ovules may be concealed from view after fertilization by the overlapping of the carpels). Pollen grains borne by the wind direct to the exposed micropyle of the ovule. *Prothallium (endosperm, albumen) of the macrospore formed before fertilization and producing rudimentary archegonia* near the micropyle. Classes (I).—Cycadineæ (Cycads or Fern-palms) p. 56 ; (II).—Coniferæ (Pines, Cypress, etc.) p. 57 ; (III).—Gnetineæ (Shrubs, sometimes scandent) p. 57.

Sub-division II.—**Angiospermæ.**

Plants of very various habit (including all the wild trees and shrubs of Chota Nagpur except one). Fls. 1-2-sexual usually furnished with a perianth. Carpels infolded so that the edges unite, or several carpels in one whorl united to one another, in both cases *to form a one- or more-celled closed chamber* or *ovary*. Ovules enclosed in the ovary, so that the pollen grains are unable to directly come in contact with the ovule, and fertilization is effected by the pollen tubes growing through a *special conducting tissue of the carpel, which is often prolonged into a style bearing the stigma, or organ for the reception of the pollen grains*, (the styles of the several carpels may be free or connate, or absent ; if absent the stigma is sessile). Macrospore (embryo-sac) before fertilization contains nuclei *but no distinct prothallial tissue or archegonia.* An endosperm is formed after fertilization. Classes (I).—Dicotyledoneæ (contains most trees and shrubs) ; (II).—Monocotyledoneæ (contains the Palms, Bamboos, etc.) (p. 53).

Class I.—**Dicotyleledoneæ or Dicotyledons (p. 57).**

Plants of which the embryo has two seed-leaves or cotyledons. These often expand as the first green leaves of the plant, as in the mustard, bean, castor-oil, Grewia, Gmelina, etc., or they may remain in the seed and are then usually very thick and fleshy, *e.g.*, the Mohwa tree (Bassia). Rarely there are three cotyledons, *e.g.*, sometimes in Terminalia Arjuna.

The dicotyledons comprise the great majority of flowering plants, and practically all our forest trees. They usually have the venation of the leaf reticulate or much branched. Externally the arborescent forms are easily distinguished from the arboreous monocotyledons by the relatively copious branching of the stem. Anatomically the stem is generally well distinguished from the woody tissue uniting outside the pith into a solid cylinder enclosed by a distinct cylinder of bark. In between the two is a very thin tissue (the cambium) which continually adds more wood to the cylinder. The flowers when not reduced usually have their several parts (calyx, petals, etc.) in 2's, 4's or 5's, but 3's are common among the Ranales, and in a few other families.

Some leaves with palmate venation have the primary nerves more or less parallel and the secondary nerves more or less at right angles to these, *e.g.*, some Zizyphus, some Grewia, some Laurels, etc. The absence of a sheathing base to the petiole and the tertiary venation is however distinctive in these cases.

Sub-class I—**Choripetalæ** (Dialypetalæ or Polypetalæ) (p. 57).

Perianth leaves, when present, *free from one another* (not appearing as lobes of a tube), *or only those of the calyx united. Stamens free from the corolla* (see exceptions below) often many. Carpels rarely two, often one or more than two, free or united. Ovules *usually with 2 integuments and a large nucellus.*

The perianth in the Choripetalæ is very various. It may be of many spirally arranged leaves (cp. water-lily) *i.e.*, acyclic, or cyclic with 1, 2, or more whorls, one or more of which may be petaloid. In many cases the perianth is much reduced, *e.g.*, Urticaceæ, or obsolete, *e.g.*, Piper, Salix. White or brilliantly coloured bracts sometimes replace it functionally but usually surround an inflorescence not a flower, *e.g.*, Houttynia, Poinsettia. A gamophyllous perianth is not to be confused with a growth of a zone of the torus or receptacle around and above the ovary, termed a *hypanthium*, and on which may be placed sepals, petals and stamens (cp. a Rose, Pomegranate, or Woodfordia).

Exceptions :—

Petals sometimes united at their base or to the staminal tube in Malvaceæ, Meliaceæ, Ternstœmiaceæ, Polygala, and Leea. Corolla gamopetalous in the male flower only of some Papayaceæ, in both sexes in many

Cucurbitaceæ (the correct position of which is doubtful) and in many Mimosaceæ (where it is very small).

Where there is only one perianth whorl, this may be corolloid (petaloid) and gamophyllous, *e.g.*, Mirabilis, Borgainvillea, Loranthus, etc.

Carpels only two in Cruciferæ, Umbelliferæ, Moraceæ, Ulmaceæ, Polygalaceæ, and in certain genera or species of Ampelidaceæ, Euphorbiaceæ, Capparidaceæ, Burseraceæ, Amarantaceæ, Onagraceæ, Myrtaceæ, Lythraceæ, Tiliaceæ and a few others in which the carpels may be 2-3 in the same species.

Series A (includes Thalamifloræ, Discifloræ, some Apetalæ and a few others of the Genera Plantarum) (p. 57).

Perianth usually present 2- or more-seriate, of both calyx and corolla (heterochlamydeous) or acyclic with the sepals passing into petals. Sep., pet., and stamens all hypogynous. Orders I to VIII

Exceptions :—

Perianth haplochlamydeous, or homochlamydeous and sepaloid in Lauraceæ, many Euphorbiaceæ, some Menispermaceæ; homochlamydeous and petaloid in Moringa and a few others; wanting in a few Euphorbiaceæ

Petals are absent in some Ranunculaceæ, some Lauraceæ, some Sterculiaceæ, many Euphorbiaceæ, some Samydaceæ and Bixaceæ.

The flower is somewhat perigynous in some Capparidaceæ, Lauraceæ, Rhamnaceæ and other Celastrales, some Samydaceæ and Passifloraceæ. It is epigynous in some Rhamnaceæ and in Cucurbitaceæ.

Series B (includes most Calycifloræ and a few Apetalæ of the Genera Plantarum). Perianth present 2-seriate heterochlamydeous and perigynous or epigynous (*vide* also exceptions under A). Orders IX to XV. (p. 71).

Exceptions :—

Perianth homochlamydeous and sepaloid in Viscum, haplochlamydeous in Santalaceæ and perhaps in Loranthus.

Sepals very small or obsolete in some Umbellales, Olacales and Santalales (?)

Petals 0 in some Cæsalpiniaceæ, Combretaceæ, Lythraceæ, and perhaps in Loranthaceæ.

Fls. hypogynous in some Olacales, and nearly so in some Leguminosæ and Rosaceæ.

Series C (includes the remaining Monochlamydeæ and Achlamydeæ of the Genera Plantarum.

Perianth absent, or if present haplochlamydeous and sepaloid. Perianth leaves free or more or less connate, hypogynous or perigynous (*vide* also exceptions under A and B). Orders XVI to XXI. (p. 77.)

Exceptions :—

Fls. heterochlamydeous in some Caryophyllaceæ (see p. 77).

Perianth petaloid in some Portulacaceæ, Nyctaginaceæ, Polygonaceæ and Proteaceæ, coloured but dry in some Amarantaceæ.

SUB-CLASS 2.—**Sympetalæ** (or Gamopetalæ) (p. 82).

Perianth leaves always cyclic, and in two whorls, *viz.*, calyx and corolla. *Calyx persistent and often enlarged in fruit.* Sepals usually 5 or 4 *gamosepalous.* Corolla *gamopetalous* (see also some gamopetalous exceptions in Choripetalæ), the corolla-tube with an entire or 2-lipped or 4-5-lobed or -toothed limb. *Stamens usually adnate to the corolla*, and often appearing inserted on it (if the corolla tube is a petaloid zone of the torus, the stamens are actually inserted on it), usually 4 or 5 or by reduction 2. Carpels usually 2 median. Ovules with one thick integument and a very small nucellus.

Exceptions :—

The families at the bottom of this sub-class show many exceptions thus :—The petals are very slightly coherent in some Myrsinaceæ (or even free in Embelia spp.). Oleaceæ and Plumbaginaceæ.

Calyx annular or of 8-12 small teeth in Thunbergia.

Sep. and Petals more than 5 in some Ebenales, Jasminum (Oleales), Cordia and Symphorema.

Stamens free from the tube in Plumbago.

Stamens numerous and carpels several in many Ebenales. Carpels 4-8 in some Primulales.

Ovules with two integuments occur especially among Primulales and Ebenales.

A. Pentacyclicæ, or less specialized sympetalæ.

Floral whorls normally 5, *i.e.*, two whorls of stamens are

present, but Primulales has one whorl rudimentary or absent, or stamens are numerous; if only one whorl of St. present then ovary of 5 carpels and 1-celled. Flowers always regular. Corolla-tube often very short and stamens sometimes sub-hypogynous. Ovary superior (exc. some Styraceæ) of more than 2 carpels (rarely 2 in some Ebenales). Orders I and II. (p. 82).

B. Tetracyclicæ or Bicarpellatæ.

Floral whorls only 4 *i.e.*, stamens in one whorl only very often reduced to 4 or 2, never numerous. Carpels most usually 2 only, forming a 2-1-celled ovary. Fls. often irregular. Calyx as well as corolla often tubular.

Exceptions :—

Corolla-tube hardly any in some Oleales and some Boraginaceæ.

Ovary 2-many-locular in a few Rubiaceæ, 2-4-locular in a few Convolvulaceæ, often spuriously 4-locular in Boraginaceæ and Labiatæ, Datura and Pedaliaceæ.

1. Ovary superior Orders III to VII. (superæ, p. 83).
2. Ovary inferior Orders VIII and IX. (inferæ, p. 88).

Class II.—Monocotyledoneae or Monocotyledons.

Plants of which the embryo has only one cotyledon or seed-leaf, which may become free from the seed and forms the first green leaf, *e.g.*, Agave, or remains with its tip entirely or almost entirely enclosed in the seed from which it absorbs the albumen, *e.g.*, Dioscorea, Palms, the Grasses, etc. Sheathing bases to the leaves are very characteristic of Monocotyledons, even the cotyledon has a sheathing base which usually wraps round the young plumule. Sheathing bases are, however, found in some Dicotyledons, especially in the Ranales, Rosaceæ, Umbellales.

The monocotyledons are usually herbs, very sparsely branched. There are several exceptions: thus Asparagus is often copiously branched, and Smilax contains branched woody climbers. The root or perennial stem often develops into an underground tuber, or bulb or rhizome. The leaves usually have several more or less parallel primary nerves, and the secondary nerves, if any, are mostly at right angles to them ; in many

Musaceæ, however, there is a strong mid-rib with numerous parallel sec. nerves, while some Araceæ and Dioscoreaceæ and a few others have the venation copiously branched. Araceæ have usually sagittate or peltate leaves, while Dioscoreaceæ are climbers with underground tubers. In the few Monocotyledonous trees the stem is cylindrical and unbranched, *e.g.*, Toddy Palm; the woody bundles are scattered through the ground tissue of the stem which has no cambium, and therefore no secondary growth (some of the arborescent Liliaceæ and others are exceptions and have a secondary growth in thickness). The parts of the flower, when not reduced, are usually in threes. The inflorescence is very often enclosed, at least at the base, by a sheathing leaf base or spathe.

SUB-CLASS 1.

Flowers usually showy, regular or zygomorphic, if small or homochlamydeous then perianth petaloid or ovary inferior. Perianth always present 2-seriate. Ovary always syncarpous superior or inferior. Orders I to IV. (p. 89).

SUB-CLASS 2.

Fls. small. Perianth, if present, regular or somewhat oblique sepaloid or dry or fleshy, 2-seriate in the earlier orders, with the inner series somtimes differing in size from the outer, but not petaloid, reduced or absent in others. Fls. usually densely collected into spikes or very compound inflorescences. Stamens many-1. Ovary superior, sometimes apocarpous. Orders V and VI. (p. 92).

SYNOPSIS OF ORDERS AND FAMILIES.[1]

DIVISION—PTERIDOPHYTA.

CLASS—Filicineae (FERNS).

ORDER I—Filicales.

Stems rarely branched. *L. without stipules*, usually clothed at the base with chaffy scales. Sporangia either

---

[1] The diagnoses of Orders and families are, in general, limited to genera included in the Flora. The diagnosis is sometimes extended however, where such limitation would very poorly characterize the group concerned, and in order to embrace plants not included in the Flora, but found wild or cultivated in Chota Nagpur. Exceptions are similarly limited. Characters in italics are those which chiefly distinguish the group from allied groups.

aggregated into small groups (sori) situated on the veins at the back or margin of the frond; more rarely the sporangia are scattered over the whole of the lower surface. *Wall of the sporangia of one layer of cells and furnished with an annulus* (see glossary) which usually ruptures the wall by its straightening.[1]

1. The Tree-fern Family.

Stem erect, *often tall with a terminal crown of very large leaves.* Sori round on a more or less *convex hairy receptacle.* Sporangia sessile or stalked, obovoid, with *a complete nearly vertical* annulus. *Indusium O* **1. Cyatheaceæ (p. 129).**

2. The Common Fern Family.

Stem usually rhizomatous. Leaves in a terminal crown or scattered. Barren and fertile fronds sometimes dissimilar. Sori or sporangia naked, or covered by the recurved leaf margin, or by a variously shaped indusium. *Sporangia with a distinct pedicel,* and with *a vertical annulus, which is not quite complete on one side.* **2. Polypodiaceæ (p. 129).**

The Horned-fern Family.

A marsh fern with heteromorphous leaves. Fertile fronds with very narrow segments, their margins revolute. *Sporangia sub-sessile,* scattered dorsally on the nerves, *not united into sori. Annulus vertical nearly complete* of very numerous transversely elongated cells, *or* (*in the same species*) *more or less obsolete. Indusium O* **Parkeriaceæ.**

To this family belongs the very interesting fern Ceratopteris thalictroides, *Brogn.*, frequent in wet places.

3. The Forked-fern Family.

Ferns with a creeping rhizome and *scattered dichotomously-branching stem-like fronds with unlimited growth.*

---

[1] Microscopical characters are omitted as far as possible: the annulus can usually be seen with a good light and a pocket lens magnifying 10 diameters.

Sori terminal or on the back or fork of the veins, consisting *of few sessile or sub-sessile sporangia with a transverse or oblique annulus* and *vertical dehiscence. Indusium O.*

3. Gleicheniaceæ (p. 135).

4. The Climbing-fern Family. (Tribe Lygodieæ.)

Ferns with *unlimited apical growth to their leaf rachis,* which is solitary and *resembles a twining stem,* on which the primary pinnæ resemble leaves or branchlets. *Sporangia large borne dorsally on special spike-like lobes of the fertile pinnae; each on a vein with an involucre-like indusium.* Indusia imbricate. Annulus small apical.

4. Schizaeaceæ (p. 136).

ORDER II—**Marattiales.**

5. The Angiopteris Family.

Large ferns with a very short stout unbranched stem. *L. with a stipular sheath* at the base of the swollen petiole. *Pinnae articulate.* Sporangia sessile closely collected in two ranks into sori on the under-surface near the margin of the unmodified fertile frond. *Wall of sporangia of several cells thick opening by a fissure without an evident annulus.*

5. Marattiaceæ (p. 137).

DIVISION—PHANEROGAMIA.

SUB-DIVISION I.—**Gymnospermae.**

CLASS I.—**Cycadineae.**

1. The Cycad or Palm-fern Family.

Trunk short. L. large pinnate coriaceous. Male flowers in cones. Fem. sporophylls or carpels laxly imbricate on the main axis, carpels pinnatifid. **1. Cycadaceæ** (p. 137).

CLASS II.—Coniferae.

1. The Pine Family.

Trunk attaining large dimensions copiously branched. Leaves scale-like or acicular. Fem. flowers, as well as the males in cones. **1. Pinaceæ** (p. 138).

CLASS III.—Gnetinee.

1. The Gnetum Family.

A large climbing shrub with thickened nodes and unisexual minute flowers arranged in panicled annulate spikes. Fls. with a sheath resembling a rudimentary perianth Ovules erect. **1. Gnetaceæ** (p. 138).

SUB-DIVISION II.—Angiospermae. (p. 49).

CLASS I.—Dicotyledons. (p. 49).

SUB-CLASS I.—Choripetalae. (p. 50).

Series A (*vide* p. 51).

ORDER I.—Ranales or Polycarpicae.

Trees, shrubs, or herbs, often scandent, with simple alternate exstipulate sometimes dotted leaves. Fls. regular and 2-sexual, *acyclic or hemicyclic,* or if cyclic *then the whorls 3-merous. St. and carpels usually,* and perianth leaves sometimes, *numerous.* If stamens few then in 3-merous whorls. *Carpels free, sometimes stalked in fruit.*

Exceptions :—

L. opp. and compound in Clematis family, sub-opposite or opp. in a few Lauraceæ.

L. stipulate in Magnoliaceæ.

Fls. diœcious in Menispermaceæ, 1-sexual in a few Lauraceæ.

Fls. 2-4-merous in Cissampelos, sepals 6-10 in Stephania. Perianth sometimes 5-cleft in Lauraceæ.

Carpels reduced to 1 in some Menispermaceæ and Berberidaceæ.

Carpels 3 united into a 1-celled ovary in Lauraceæ. Carpels connate in Anona.

I. Anthers opening by slits. Carpels 3, several, or many.

1. Clematis Family.

Woody climbers *with opp. compound leaves.* Fls. showy. *Sepals petaloid* (4-8) valvate. Petals 0-12. Fruiting carpels capitate *with feathery styles.* **1. Ranunculaceæ**[1] (p. 139).

2. Magnolia Family.

Trees with the leaf-*buds* enclosed in *convolute* deciduous *stipules,* which leave an annular scar. *Flowers large solitary, sepals* passing gradually into *petals, in 3-merous whorls.* Torus elongate in fruit, *carpels spicate.*

2. Magnoliaceæ (p. 141).

3. Custard-apple Family.

Trees, shrubs or woody climbers. L. sometimes dotted. *Buds naked.* Fls. small or medium, often sub-solitary. Perianth of *three 3-merous whorls,* tepals often fleshy or coriaceous, one or more whorls petaloid or not. Fruiting *carpels* usually stalked and *umbelled.* Endosperm usually ruminate. **3. Anonaceæ** (p. 142).

4. The Moonseed Family.

Slender, rarely woody *climbers,* with *palmately-nerved* sometimes peltate *leaves.* Fls. *small or minute,* in a many-flowered inflorescence. *Perianth* sepaloid, *of several, usually 4, trimerous whorls.* Fruiting carpels 3-12, rarely 1, drupaceous with usually a *characteristic horse-shoe-shaped endocarp.* **4. Menispermaceæ** (p. 147).

Exceptions :—

M. of Cissampelos is 4-merous with connate petals.

II. Anthers 2-4-locular, loculi opening by valves. Carpels 1, or 3 united into a 1-celled ovary.

---

[1] Tribe Clematideæ only, which is poorly characteristic of the Family.

5. Barberry Family.

Shrubs often spiny. *Fls.* small or medium sized, *yellow*, in racemes. Perianth of four 3-merous whorls. Carpel 1 with a large sessile scutiform stigma. *Ovules several basal.*

5. **Berberidaceæ** (p. 149).

6. Laurel Family.

Trees or shrubs (Cassytha is a filiform parasite) with aromatic often dotted leaves. Fls. small *greenish or yellowish.* Perianth *perigynous* normally of two 3-merous whorls (sometimes apparently 5 cleft). Stamens in three or four 3-merous whorls (one usually reduced to staminodes). *Ovule* 1. Fruit baccate or drupaceous often surrounded or girt at the base by the enlarged hypanthium.

6. **Lauraceæ** (p. 150).

ORDER II.— Parietales.

Herbs, more rarely trees and shrubs, sometimes scandent L simple alternate. Fls. *regular*, 2-1-sexual, *cyclic*, with the whorls *often 2-merous or 4-merous.* Sepals and petals free. Stamens usually many (due to branching), or isostemonous or diplostemonous (3-5 in Cucurbitaceæ, tetradynamous in Cruciferæ), free. Disc present or not. *Ovary syncarpous*, sometimes on a gynophore, of 2-3 or several carpels, 1-*celled with parietal placentation.*

Exceptions :—

L compound in Moringaceæ, palmately divided in some Passifloraceæ and Cucurbitaceæ.

Fls. irregular in Moringaceæ, and homochlamydeous (sepals petaloid).

Petals are absent in some Bixaceæ and Samydaceæ.

Stamens sometimes connate in Cucurbitaceæ, sometimes united into a tube below in Samydaceæ.

Ovary apparently 2-celled in Cruciferæ by formation of a replum Ovary sometimes 2-4-celled by intrusion of the placentæ in Capparis, 2-8-celled in Flacourtia among Bixaceae, sometimes apparently 3-celled in Cucurbi taceæ.

N.B.—The Passiflorineæ are often placed as a separate order (Passiflorales) in the Calycifloræ (series B) and then include the Samydaceæ, but the latter come equally well under series A (Thalamifloræ). Passiflora again is not more perigynous than many Capparidaceæ, and Papayaceæ show wonderful variety in the insertion of corolla and stamens in a single species, varying from hypogynous to perigynous in the occasionally hermaphrodite flowers of the Papaya.

The affinities of the Moringaceæ and of the Cucurbitaceæ are very doubtful.

I. Families with polypetalous corolla and mostly superior ovary.

7. The Poppy Family.

Herbs *with milky juice, 4-petals, many stamens,* and a 1-celled ovary of 2-*many carpels* of which the margins may project inwards as plates. **7. Papaveraceæ** (p. 155).

8. The Cabbage Family.

Herbs with *4 petals and tetradynamous stamens.* Ovary of 2 carpels, divided vertically by a replum.

8. Cruciferæ (p. 155).

9. The Caper Family.

Trees, shrubs or herbs with *4 sepals, 4 petals and 4, or many stamens* (4-8 in some herbs). A large disc sometimes present. *Ovary* often *on a long gynophore.* Ovules numerous on 2-4 parietal placentæ. Fruit capsular or baccate. Seeds exalbuminous *with curved or spiral embryo.*

9. Capparidaceæ (p. 155).

10. The Arnatto Family.

Trees or shrubs with usually small (very large in Cochlospermum) *5-4-merous,* sometimes apetalous, *flowers* with *numerous stamens.* Disc often present. *Ovary sessile 1-8-celled.* Fr. capsular, baccate or drupaceous. Seed albuminous, often arillate, *embryo straight.* **10. Bixaceæ** (p. 157).

N.B.—The *disc* in Capparidaceæ is usually *adnate to a short hypanthium,* and bears the petals, in Bixaceæ usually *hypogynous* and *glandular.*

11. The Casearia Family.

Trees or shrubs with leaves *sometimes punctulate* and small deciduous stipules. *Fls. small 3-7-merous,* sometimes apetalous, stamens *isostemonous or diplostemonous. alternating with glands or staminodes,* and sometimes united at the base. Ovary 1-celled. *Fr. capsular, usually 3* (2-5-) *valved.* Seeds usually arillate. 11. **Samydaceæ** (p. 160).

12. The Tamarisk Family.

Small trees or shrubs *with scale-like leaves* and small white or pink flowers. *Sep. and pet. each 5.* St. iso- or diplo-stemonous on the margin of a crenulate disc. *Placentæ at the base of the ovary. Seeds comose.* (Perhaps allied to Salicaceæ.) 12. **Tamaricaceæ** (p. 162).

II. Families with either perigynous or epigynous flowers (*vide* also Capparidaceæ and Samydaceæ above) or gamopetalous corolla or both. *Sub-order Passiflorineæ.*

The Passion Flower Family.

Climbers with palmate leaves. Fls. perigynous 5-merous *with 3 bracteoles* and *furnished with a corona. Ovary on a gynophore.* Seed arillate. **Passifloraceæ.**

Passiflora fœtida, *L.* with greenish flowers has run wild in Singbhum in a few places. The Family is not further dealt with.

The Papaya Family.

Carica Papaya, *L.* a small cultivated tree (native of Mexico) *with milky juice and palmate leaves.* The flowers are *large and diœcious* (but sometimes bi-sexual) with a 5-merous corolla which is gamopetalous in the male. **Papayaceæ.**

13. The Gourd Family.

Herbs, rarely shrubs, *climbing by means of tendrils,* and usually with *palminerved or palmately-lobed leaves.* Fls. small to very large white or yellow 5-merous. *Sep. and petals superior* and hypanthium sometimes produced beyond the ovary. *St. 5 or apparently only 3*, often connate or with bent or conduplicate connate anthers. Ovary inferior with 3 (rarely 4-5) placentæ which may meet in the axis. (Müller in " Nat. Pflanzenfamilien " considers the placentation axile.) Fruit a berry, or a Pepo. 13. **Cucurbitaceæ** (p. 163).

III. Flowers irregular. Leaves compound.

14. The Horseradish Tree Family.

A small cultivated tree with *2-3-pinnate leaves* and 5-merous flowers with both perianth whorls petaloid. *Fruit an elongate 3-valved capsule.* 14. **Moringaceæ** (p. 174).

Order III.—Guttiferales (Allied to Orders I, II and VI).

Trees or shrubs with alternate simple and *usually entire penniveined leaves.* Fls. regular, 2-1-sexual, cyclic, *usually pentamerous* (sep. and pet. sometimes 4-7). Disc 0. *St. many, often more or less connate* (in bundles or a central mass) Ovary syncarpous *with 3-5, or several carpels, and as many cells as carpels. Ovules axile.* Fruit indehiscent or capsular, never coccous. Stellate hairs very rare.

Exceptions:—

Leaves of Garcinia are opposite. Dilleniaceæ has the carpels connate in the axis but with free styles, it is closely allied to Ranales.

Flowers of Ternstrœmiaceæ are sometimes acyclic as in Ranales.

Flowers of Guttiferæ often have sepals in decussate pairs as in many Parietales.

N.B.- The order is with difficulty separated from Parietales when considering genera outside Chota Nagpur, both parietal and axile placentation may occur in Hypericaceæ and other families, due to different degrees of the marginal infolding of the carpels.

15. The Dillenia Family.

Trees with large *strongly nerved leaves*, and *sheathing petioles* (as in many Ranales). *Flowers large.* Anthers opening by small slits or pores. *Carpels 5-20 cohering in the axis.* Fruit indehiscent, enclosed in the large fleshy accrescent calyx. 15. **Dilleniaceæ** (p. 175).

16. The Tea Family.

Trees or shrubs with usually evergreen exstipulate leaves and small or showy, sometimes diœcious flowers. *Outer stamens in bundles and connate with the bases of the petals* (and petals sometimes cohering). *Ovary 3-5 locular.* Styles free. Fruit capsular, often 1-locular by abortion of the other loculi. 16. **Ternstrœmiaceæ** (p. 177).

17. The Gamboge Family.

Trees with a *yellow milky juice*, evergreen rarely stipulate, *opposite* entire *leaves*, with the secondary venation often of very numerous fine parallel sec. n. at nearly right angles to the mid-rib. Fls. small or medium, often 1-sexual. Stamens often closely connate in bundles, or in a dense central mass. *Ovary 4 12-celled. Style connate or stigma peltate.* Fruit usually baccate.

17. **Guttiferaceæ** (p. 177).

18. The Sal Family.

Trees abounding in resin, with entire leaves and caducous stipules. Small or medium flowers panicled. Sepals 5 connate below. St. usually a multiple of 5. *Ovary 3-celled* with 2 ovules in each cell, *usually only 1 developing. Styles connate.* Stigma a point. Fruit a nut, enclosed in the calyx, of which 3 *or more sepals develop into linear wings.*

18. **Dipterocarpaceæ** (p. 178).

ORDER IV.—**Malvales.** (Allied to orders Parietales Guttiferales, and Geraniales.)

Trees or shrubs, more rarely herbs, with alternate *simple or palmately compound* usually stipulate leaves *with stellate hairs and palmate venation.* Fls. regular, or zygomorphous in some Sterculiaceæ, usually 5-merous. *Bracteoles often present* below the calyx as an epicalyx. Calyx gamosepalous valvate. Petals 5 sometimes adnate below to the staminal tube. *Stamens usually many, often mono- or poly-adelphous,* more rarely diplostemonous, or with one whorl suppressed or reduced to staminodes. Ovary of 2-many carpels with axile placentation, but *ovary often showing a tendency to become apocarpous in fruit* (each carpel then becoming a coccus, drupel, or follicle.)

Exceptions :—

Stellate hairs few or absent in some Corchorus, Bombax and very few Hibiscus. Petals 0 in Sterculia. Carpel only 1 in Waltheria.

19. The Hibiscus Family.

Trees, shrubs or herbs with regular flowers. *Calyx usually persistent* and *gamosepalous. Epicalyx usually present. St. many united into a tube,* or (Tribe Bombaceæ) more or less free and pentadelphous. *Anthers ultimately 1-celled,* cell often sinuous. Ovary of 5 (rarely 3) -many carpels, separating into cocci when ripe leaving a persistent columella, or fruit capsular. 19. **Malvaceæ** (p 179).

20. The Jute Family.

Trees, shrubs or undershrubs rarely herbs with regular flowers. *Calyx deciduous* with *free sepals. Epicalyx absent. St. many not united into a tube,* more rarely 10 or 5. *Anthers 2-locular.* 20. **Tiliaceæ** (p. 192).

21. The Sterculia or Udal Family.

Trees, shrubs and undershrubs with reg. or zygomorphous often polygamous flowers with *persistent calyx gamosopalous,* with or without epicalyx. *Stamens usually ten* (obdiplostemonous), with the alternate whorl often reduced to staminodes, sometimes numerous, rarely 5, *monadelphous or united into a tube below.* Anthers 2-locular (young 4-locular) and extrorse. Ovary usually 5-locular. Fruit usually capsular, but carpels follicular in Sterculia.

21. **Sterculiaceæ** (p. 203).

ORDER V.—Euphorbiales (probably allied to Malvales and Geraniales).

Habit very various. Juice often milky. Hairs sometimes stellate. L. simple, sometimes palmate or basal-nerved alternate, usually stipulate. *Fls. 1-sexual small or minute*, often trimerous, *sometimes much reduced* (even to a single pedicelled stamen or ovary in Euphorbia, in which case the flowers are always arranged in an involucrate inflorescence resembling single flowers, and this may be surrounded by brilliantly coloured bracts, as in the Poinsettia). Perianth usually *3-5-merous*, dichlamydeous, monochlamydeous or 0; inner whorl (petals) when present rarely conspicuous (*e.g.* Jatropha). Stamens *numerous*, or often only 3 or 5, frequently connate in a central column. Anthers usually 2-celled. *Ovary of 3 carpels and 3-locular*, or sometimes carpels several. *Ovules 1 or 2 in each cell, axile. Fruit often splitting into 2-valved cocci*, or pyrenes, or fruit capsular more rarely drupaceous with a 3-(1)-celled stone, or didymous. Embryo typically large and straight with flat foliaceous cotyledons (as in many Tiliaceæ) and copious endosperm.

22. The Croton and Castor-oil Family.

22. Euphorbiaceæ (p. 209).

Exceptions :—

L. 3-foliolate in Bischofia, opposite in Trewia.

Stamens 1-3, in Tragia, which has stinging hairs.

St. 2-5 in. spp. of Antidesma, 2-3 in Sapium, Anthers cells sometimes confluent in Phyllanthus and others, cells 3-4 in Macaranga. Fruit sub-baccate in Kirganelia, Flueggia, Bischofia and others, but even in these not truly so, as there is a thin endocarp which may be dehiscent, or the pericarp finally hardens.

ORDER VI.—Geraniales (allied to Guttiferales through Ochnaceæ.)

Trees, shrubs or herbs frequently with resin passages or secretory cells, with alt. or opp., simple or compound leaves *often gland-dotted and aromatic. Fls. regular*, 2-sexual. Sep. 3-5. Pet. usually 4-5 exceeding the sepals. *Stamens diplostemonous* (or obdiplostemonous), or second whorl of staminodes, free, or connate by the filaments into a tube. *Disc conspicuous* (exc. sub-order Gruinales), *sometimes tubular* hypogynous, *between the stamens and ovary. Ovary of 3-5*, rarely more (Ochnaceæ) or 2 *carpels, syncarpous* but *ovary frequently lobed*, and *carpels sometimes nearly free in fruit* (coccous). *Ovules 1-2 in each cell*, usually pendulous.

Exceptions :—

Fls. 3-6-merous in some Burseraceæ and Meliaceæ. Sep. and pet. often more than 5 in Ochnaceæ, some Citrus and other Rutaceæ, and stamens numerous in Ochnaceæ and some Rutaceæ. Stamens in the hermaphrodite flower of Ailanthus sometimes only 2-3. Ovules axile in Ochna. Ovules several in some Meliaceæ.

I. Sub-order Gruinales. St. obdiplostemonous. Annular disc 0, but disc glands sometimes present at the base of the petals.

23. The Flax Family.

Shrubs or herbs with alt. *simple entire* leaves, and pretty flowers with fugacious petals. Stamens 5 perfect connate at the base, alternating with staminodes. *Ovary* 3-5-celled *entire. Fruit capsular or drupaceous.*

23. Linaceæ (p. 235).

24. The Geranium Family (including Oxalidaceæ).

Herbs or undershrubs (or a tree : Averrhoa) with *pinnate palmate or palmately-nerved* usually stipulate leaves. St. 10 or 5 reduced to staminodes, free or connate at base. *Ovary* 3-5-celled, and as many *lobed. Fruit coccous, or a berry* (Averrhoa). 24. Geraniaceæ (p. 236).

II. Sub-order Rutales. St. diplostemonous. Annular disc well developed, sometimes tubular.

25. Ochna Family (closely allied to Dilleniaceæ).

Glabrous trees or undershrubs with alt. *simple* stipulate *leaves*. Fls. often showy yellow, sometimes umbelled.

Sepals persistent, and often deeply coloured in fruit. Petals 5-10. St. many. Anthers often opening by pores. Ovary deeply 3-10 lobed, the lobes becoming drupels in fruit.

25. **Ochnaceæ** (p. 237).

26. The Bitter Bark Family.

Trees or shrubs with alternate *pinnate leaves*. Fls. small. *Sepals* connate below, *deciduous*. *Pet. valvate*. St. 10, free. Ovary *deeply 2-5-lobed*. *Ovule 1 in each cell*. Fruit of as many samaras as fertile lobes of the ovary.

26. **Simarubaceæ** (p. 238).

27. The Desert Date Family.

Shrubs or herbs, *often spiny*. *L.* opp. or alternate, *pinnate* (with only one pair of leaflets in Balanites). Fls. white, yellow or greenish. Sep. deciduous, imbricate. *Pet. imbricate*. Disc annular or conical. St. 10, at the base of the disc. Ovary more or less sunk in the disc, of 5 *carpels* (sometimes more in Tribulus) lobed or, if entire, 5-angled in fruit. Fruit 5- or by abortion 1-celled, of spinous indehiscent cocci, or (Balanites) an oily 1-celled drupe. Seed exalbuminous. 27. **Zygophyllaceæ** (p. 239).

28. Myrrh Family.

Trees or shrubs often abounding in fragrant resins, with alt. *3-foliolate or pinnate leaves*. Fls. small. *Sep. 3-6* connate below, often minute, *Pet. 3-6* exceeding the sepals. St. 10 free. Ovary *usually 3- sometimes 2-5-celled*. *Ovules 2* in each cell. Fruit drupaceous, containing 2-5 (usually 3) pyrenes. 28. **Burseraceæ** (p. 239).

29. The Orange Family.

Trees or shrubs with simple or usually pinnate, alt. or opp. exstipulate leaves which are always *copiously gland-dotted*. Fls. small or medium, 4-5-merous. *St. free* usually diplostemonous (numerous in Ægle and Citrus) *Ovary 4-5-celled* (many-celled in Ægle and Citrus), sometimes lobed. Ovules 2 in each cell. Styles free or united

Fruit various, usually a copiously glandular berry. *Seeds never winged.* 29. **Rutaceæ** (p. 241).

30. The Toon Family.

Trees or shrubs with alt. exstipulate usually pinnate leaves, *not gland-dotted* (except Chloroxylon). Fls. small or usually medium. Sepals 3-6 usually connate. *Filaments connate into a tube* (except in tribe Cedreleæ). Ovary 2-5-celled. Ovules 2 (rarely 1), or 8-12. Styles always united into one. *Seeds often winged.* 30. **Meliaceæ** (p. 248).

ORDER VII.—**Sapindales** (closely allied to preceding through Anacardiaceæ and Malpighiaceæ.)

Trees or shrubs, rarely herbs, sometimes scandent. L. simple or compound, usually exstipulate. *Fls.* usually small, usually polygamous, *irregular* or corolla 0, or if calyx and corolla regular then stamens diclinous, or fewer than diplostemonous by reduction. *Disc* usually present, and *outside the stamens.* Ovary usually 3-celled with 1-2 ovules in each cell, axile or pendulous from the top or wall or from a basal funicle. Endosperm usually absent.

Exceptions :—

Fls. regular and diplostemonous in some Anacardiaceæ and the stamens inserted on or outside the disc ; reduction in such cases takes place in the gynæceum which usually consists of 1 carpel (Spondias is 2-5-carpellary and -celled) or if of more, the ovary is 1-celled or the other carpels early suppressed.

Disc 0 or inconspicuous in the M. fl. of Dodonaea, and st. outside the disc in the herm. fl. (but st. only 8).

Disc is obscure in Malpighiaceæ, *O in* Polygalaceæ, St. monadelphous in Polygala.

31. The Mango Family.

Trees or shrubs, often resinous, with simple or compound alt. leaves. Fls. polygamous small or very small, usually 4-5-merous. St. often less than 10 (only 1-5 in Mango) *inserted at the base of, rarely on the disc. Ovary 1-celled* rarely of 2-6 free carpels (Buchanania), or 2-5-celled

Spondias). *Ovule 1 in each cell,* often pendulous from a basal funicle. Fruit a drupe.

31. **Anacardiaceæ** (p. 255).

32. The Soap-nut Family.

Usually trees or shrubs (Cardiospermum is a slender climber) with alt. simple or compound leaves. Fls. inconspicuous. *St.* 4-10, *most usually 8* and declinate. Disc often oblique or unilateral. *Ovary 3- rarely 2-4-celled,* often lobed. Fruit a membranous capsule, or capsular, or indehiscent. 32. **Sapindaceæ** (p. 260).

Exceptions :—

Dodonæa in many respects approaches Anacardiaceæ.

33. The Meliosma Family.

Small trees with alt. simple or odd-pinnate leaves. Fls. with small bracteoles and sepals, *very unequal petals and 5 unequal stamens of which only 2 are fertile.* Fruit a small drupe. 33. **Sabiaceæ** (p. 262).

34. The Hiptage Family.

Climbing shrubs with opp. leaves. Petals 5-clawed, the 5th different. St. 10 declinate. *Ovary 3-lobed. Fruit of 1-3 winged samaras.* 34. **Malpighiaceæ** (p. 263).

35. The Polygala Family.

Herbs or undershrubs with alt. simple leaves and small irregular flowers with *two lateral sepals wing-like and often petaloid.* Corolla with 2 *lateral petals rudimentary* and the anterior developed as a keel. *St. 8 monadelphous,* adherent to the base of the keel. Ovary 2-locular.

35. **Polygalaceæ** (p. 264).

Order VIII.—Celastrales.

Trees or shrubs, often climbers, with simple (or compound in Ampelideceæ) alt. or opposite leaves, stipulate or not.

Fls. small greenish or white, *regular* 4-5-merous with *never more than 1 whorl of isomerous free stamens* (or monadelphous in some Ampelidaceæ). Perianth usually hypogynous, sometimes perigynous, or even epigynous (some Rhamnaceæ). *Disc well developed hypogynous or lining the hypanthium* and *usually bearing the stamens*, sometimes enclosing the ovary. Ovary usually 2-5-celled with 1-2 *erect or ascending ovules* in each cell. Style short or 0.

Exceptions:—

Petals 0 in a few Rhamnaceæ, and caducous or 0 in some Vitis. Ovary sometimes 6-celled in Leea, of numerous cells in the aberrant genus Siphonodon (Celastraceæ).

I. *Stamens alternate with the petals.*

36. The Spindle Tree Family.

Trees or shrubs, somtimes scandent. L. alt. or opp. Sep. 4-5 small usually connate. *Petals usually exceeding the sepals* sessile inserted below or at the margin of the large prominent disc. Filaments short alternate with the petals. Ovary sessile free or enclosed by the disc. 2-5-celled (or cells many in Siphonodon). *Ovules usually* 2. Seeds usually arillate. 36. **Celastraceæ** (p. 265).

II. *Stamens opposite to the petals.*

37. The Buckthorn or Jujube Family..

Trees or shrubs, sometimes scandent, leaves simple alt. *most frequently with 3-5 basal nerves.* Sep. and pet. usually 5 and perigynous or epigynous. Sep. valvate in bud and usually with a prominent mid-rib within. *Petals usually smaller than the sepals*, sometimes concealing the stamens which stand opp. to them. Disc thin and lining the hypanthium or filling it. Ovary free or united with the hypanthium, 3-2-(rarely 4) -celled with 1 basal *ovule in each cell.* Fr. 1-celled and 1-seeded (samaroid in Ventilago) or with a 2-4-celled endocarp, or 3-valved.

37. **Rhamnaceæ** (p. 268).

38. The Vine Family.

Herbs or shrubs with simple *digitate or pinnately compound leaves*, climbing by tendrils, or erect with jointed stems. Fls. small in umbels or panicles. Sep. and pet. usually 4-5. Pet. valvate, sometimes calyptrate, free or united at the base with the stamens. St. inserted at the base of the disc, free or connate into a tube. Ovary 2, rarely 3-6-celled, *with 2 collateral ovules in each cell.* Fruit-baccate.

38. Ampelidaceæ (p. 274).

Series B (*vide* p. 51.)

See also Parietales sub-order Passiflorineæ and Celastrales and other exceptions under A.

Order IX—Opuntiales (perhaps allied to Ranales and Parietales).

Stout fleshy usually prickly plants with the leaves reduced to scales with spines or setæ in their axils. *Flowers often very large,* usually solitary hemicyclic perigynous or epigynous. Hypanthium often produced beyond the ovary bearing the *many sepals and petals which pass into one another* and are often connate at the base. St. many. Ovary with many parietal placentæ.

39. The Cactus Family. **39. Cactaceæ** (p. 281).

Order X—Rosales (probably allied to Ranales).

Trees, shrubs or herbs with alternate simple or compound stipulate leaves (which, especially in the herbaceous genera, often have sheathing bases as in Ranales). Fls. rarely small, *regular, perigynous or epigynous* (or nearly hypogynous in some herbs) cyclic. *Calyx with 5-10 usually imbricate sepals, the odd sepal superior* (dorsal). Petals free, usually 5. *Stamens usually many*, usually incurved or circinate in bud. *Ovary apocarpous,* carpels 5-many free or if carpels adnate to the hypanthium then *styles free.* Carpel rarely only 1, and *then with only 1-2 ovules and fruit a drupe.* Ovules 1-several. Fruit of *achenes, drupels or drupaceous*, sometimes included in the fleshy hypanthium (as in the Rose) *or a pome* (Apple, pear).

40. **The Rose Family.** 40. **Rosaceæ** (p. 282).

ORDER XI.—**Leguminosæ.**

Trees, shrubs, or herbs often scandent, with alt. stipulate *compound or unifoliolate* rarely simple leaves. Fls. small or very showy, *usually zygomorphous* (always so in the gynæcium) perigynous, sometimes only slightly so, or even hypogynous. Calyx with 5-(4)-lobes, the *odd sepal or lobe inferior* (*ventral*). Sometimes calyx 2-lipped or sub-entire. Petals free, or ventral pair connate, or corolla gamopetalous (Mimosaceæ), if corolla regular then sepals and petals always valvate in bud. St. definite or many. *Ovary of 1 elongate* linear (short or even globose in a few small herbs, *e.g.*, Indigofera linifolia) *declinate carpel which bears usually several ovules in one or two series along the ventral suture. Fruit a legume* (pod).

41. **The Mimosa Family.**

Trees or shrubs, often scandent (rarely undershrubs) *with 2-pinnate leaves*, and small *regular 4-5-merous flowers*, conspicuous by being collected into dense heads or spikes. *Calyx and corolla valvate, usually gamopetalous.* St. free or monadelphous, *diplostemonous or many.*

41. **Mimosaceæ** (p. 284).

42. **The Cassia Family.**

Trees or shrubs, rarely herbs, *with pinnate or 2-pinnate leaves* (or apparently simple in Bauhinia) and small or showy flowers always *more or less zygomorphous. Corolla imbricate, dorsal petal interior in bud.* St. definite, diplostemonous, or fewer by reduction, free or united.

42. **Cæsalpiniaceæ** p. (294).

43. **The Pea Family.**

Trees, shrubs, or herbs with *simple, digitate or pinnate leaves* and small or showy *distinctly zygomorphous* (papilionaceaous) *flowers.* Corolla imbricate with *the dorsal petal (standard) exterior in bud,* the other petals in pairs, lowest pair (keel) often connate. Stamens 10 monadelphous, or diadelphous 9+1, or 5+5, rarely the 10th altogether absent, very rarely stamens all free (Sophora).

43. **Papilionaceæ** (p. 308).

ORDER XII—**Myrtales** (allied to Rosales).

Trees, shrubs or rarely herbs with opposite or whorled simple exstipulate and usually entire leaves. Fls. regular or (in some Lythraceæ and Onagraceæ) rarely zygomorphous, with *generally a well-developed hypanthium enclosing the ovary, and frequently produced beyond it into a green or coloured tube.* Petals not valvate in bud, sometimes very small. *Ovary inferior 2-7-celled adnate to the hypanthium* or rarely free in its tube, *always syncarpous* and *with connate styles.* Ovules axile. Seeds 1-very many. (The flowers are usually 4-5-merous in all the whorls with the stamens diplostemonous, sometimes however the stamens are numerous from branching and the ovary with 2-8 cells or carpels).

Exceptions :—

L. sometimes sub-opp. or alternate in Combretaceæ, Myrtaceæ (Careya and Barringtonia) and a few Onagraceæ. The submerged leaves in Trapa are pinnati-partite. Stipules present and interpetiolar in Rhizophoraceæ.

Perianth perigynous and ovary quite free in some Lythraceæ. Petals sometimes suppressed in Lythraceæ and Combretaceæ. St. haplostemonous in some Onagraceæ. Ovary only 1-celled in Combretaceæ, and 1-celled by absorption of the septa in some Ammannia.

Ovules pendulous from the top, or lateral near the top of the ovary in Combretaceæ, axile and parietal in the many-celled ovary of Punica.

44. The Myrtle Family.

Evergreen trees or shrubs with usually finely punctulate opposite leaves (exc. Careya and Barringtonia) which are *quite entire and usually coriaceous with an intramarginal nerve.* Fls. epigynous 4-5-merous *with numerous stamens* often in 4-5 bundles, and with *2-5 rarely more cells in the inferior ovary.* Fr. 1-many-seeded.

44. **Myrtaceæ** (p. 350)

The Pomegranate Family (included in Lythraceæ in the body of the flora) differs from Myrtaceæ in the leaf venation, in the ovary having the cells arranged in two whorls and in some of the ovules having axile placentation. The calyx has usually 6 (5-8) sepals as in Lythraceæ, but the ovary is quite adnate to the hypanthium. Fruit a berry with many cells and seeds.

Punicaceæ (p. 354).

45. The Henna Family.

Trees, shrubs or herbs with often 4-angled branches, leaves rarely gland-dotted. *Fls.* regular (zygomorphous in Woodfordia), *perigynous. Sepals 3-6,* often 6, valvate with sometimes intermediate smaller ones. Petals isomerous with the sepals (on the long petaloid hypanthium in Woodfordia) sometimes minute or 0. St. diplostemonous (2-8 in Ammannia) or very many, on the hypanthium which is long or very short. *Ovary free from the hypanthium 2-6 celled. Ovules very many.*

45. **Lythraceæ** (p. 354).

46. The Evening Primrose Family.

Herbs, sometimes aquatic. L. opp. or alternate. Fls. regular or slightly zygomorphous. *Seps. and petals 4* (4-6 in Jussiea). *St. 4 or 8. Ovary 2-4-celled adnate to the hypanthium* (only half inferior in Trapa). *Ovules many* (solitary in each cell in Trapa). Seeds many (1 in Trapa).

46. **Onagraceæ** (p. 356).

47. The Melastoma Family.

Shrubs or herbs with opposite leaves characterized by *sub-parallel primary nerves* and usually parallel cross sec. nerves. Fls. usually handsome, regular or slightly zygomorphous in the andrœcium. *Anthers opening by pores. Ovary united to the hypanthium by vertical walls.*

47. **Melastomaceæ** (p. 357).

48. The Mangrove Family.

Trees or shrubs with *opp. glabrous leaves and interpetiolar stipules.* Fls. small greenish 5-8-merous. *Petals and st. inserted on an outer disc lining the hypanthium* which is minutely bracteolate. *St. diplostemonous.* Inner disc lobed. *Ovary 3-5-celled,* septa soon disappearing so that the *fruit is 1-celled and -seeded.* Ovary cells 2-ovuled.

48. **Rhizophoraceæ** (p. 358).

49. The Myrabolan Family.

Trees or shrubs, sometimes scandent, with leaves sometimes sub.-opp. and alternate, occasionally ternate. *Fls.* usually small greenish (showy in the garden Quisqualis) *capitate, spicate or racemed, with the hypanthium enclosing and constricted above, or produced into a beak beyond, the ovary.* Sepals and petals 4-5, or pet. 0, rarely 6-7. St. diplostemonous. *Ovary 1-celled inferior. Ovules 2-7 pendulous from the apex.*

49. **Combretaceæ** (p. 359).

ORDER XIII.—Umbellales.

Trees, shrubs or herbs with alt simple or very compound leaves, the latter usually with a sheathing base. If simple then often with 3 or more primary nerves. Fls. *small regular polypetalous with valvate petals, frequently in umbels,* 4-5-merous with *isostemonous stamens* alternating with the petals (but see Alangium). Disc epigynous. *Ovary completely inferior of 2-5 carpels* and as many cells (or gynœcium polymerous in Araliaceæ) adherent to the hypanthium which is not or scarcely produced beyond the ovary. *Styles usually free. Ovule 1 in each cell pendulous.* Embryo in albumen.

Exceptions :—

Marginal flowers of umbels sometimes irregular.

Alangium is not at all typical of Cornaceæ and is perhaps allied to Olacales. The flower is 5-10-merous and with many stamens, the ovary is 1-celled and with 1 style.

50. The Carrot Family.

Herbs with usually *very compound leaves* and flowers in *simple or compound umbels. Sep. 5 small or abortive. Ovary cells always 2 only, and fruit a schizocarp.*

50. **Umbelliferæ** (p. 366).

51. The Ivy Family.

Trees or shrubs with pinnate, or *usually palmate leaves* and flowers small in crowded *umbels*, umbels often panicled. Sepals small or abortive. Ovary cells 5 or 2-many. *Fruit a drupe or berry.* 51. **Araliaceæ** (p. 368).

52. The Dogwood Family.

Small tree with simple entire leaves and medium-sized flowers in axillary fascicles. Sepals minute connate below. *Petals valvate 5-10 linear oblong. St. 2-3-times as many as the petals. Ovary 1-celled.* Fruit a *drupe crowned by the calyx tube.* 52. **Cornaceæ (Alangium)** (p. 369).

ORDER XIV.—**Olacales** (allied to Cornaceæ ?).

Shrubs or undershrubs often root parasites with alt. simple exstipulate leaves. Fls. regular. Calyx (*or calyculus* cp. Loranthaceæ) *minute or O, or a mere rim which may be accrescent in fruit. Tepals* 4-6 free or connate, *valvate. Stamens opp. to or near the edges of the tepals,* or 2-3-times as many, fertile or reduced to staminodes. Ovary free or enclosed in the accrescent calyx (or hypanthium), *1-celled, or 2-5-celled below. Ovules pendulous from the apex of the incomplete axis or 1 erect.* Style 1. *Fruit* drupaceous, sometimes enclosed in the hypanthium or calyx rim (see above), *1-seeded with the placenta sometimes embedded in the seed* (cp. some Cornaceæ). Embryo small in albumen.

53. **Olacaceæ** (p. 370).

ORDER XV.—**Santalales** (allied to Olacales.)

Parasitic shrubs or undershrubs (Santalum is a root parasite) with opp. rarely alternate simple exstipulate leaves, sometimes with 3-5 primary nerves, rarely leaves absent. Fls. small or medium green or coloured, regular or somewhat zygomorphous. *Calyx O,* or reduced to small teeth (*calyculus,* sometimes however the perianth is taken to be homologous with the calyx). *Tepals* 2-6 in one or two whorls, free or connate. St. perigynous or epigynous isostemonous and opp. the tepals, free or adnate to them. *Ovary 1-celled. Ovules 1-3, pendulous from a free central placenta, or placenta fused with the ovary walls.* Fruit drupaceous or baccate.

54. The Mistletoe Family.

Parasitic evergreen shrubs, leaves coriaceous or 0. Fls. racemed or fascicled, often with an entire or toothed calyculus. Perianth short, or long and tubular below, sometimes zygomorphous. *Ovary inferior. Ovule 1.*

54. Loranthaceæ (p. 373).

55. The Sandalwood Family.

A tree parasitic on roots (after the seedling stage) with opp. leaves and small haplochlamydeous 4-5-merous flowers in terminal 3-chotomous cymes. *Ovary at first free, ultimately half adnate to the hypanthium. Ovules 2-3 on a central placenta.* Fruit drupaceous.

55. Santalaceæ (p. 377).

Series C (*vide* p. 51.)

See also exceptions under A and B.

ORDER XVI.—**Chenopodiales or Curvembryeæ** (nearest ally Parietales ?).*

Herbs, rarely shrubs, with simple exstipulate entire leaves. *Fls. haplochlamydeous regular small and mostly greenish* (see exc.), usually in close spikes or clusters (solitary or cymose in many Caryophyllaceæ and Portulacaceæ), sometimes gamophyllous or perigynous. St. twice the number of the tepals or fewer, if isomerous then opp. the tepals, hypogynous or perigynous. *Ovary 1-celled of 2-5 carpels with basilar placentation, ovules usually solitary campylotropous. Embryo curved in a mealy perisperm.*

Exceptions :—

Caryophyllaceæ still retains numerous heterochlamydeous members and being least modified is placed at the base of this order, but there are few and very unimportant representatives in Chota Nagpur (*e.g.* Saponaria, Spergula and Polycarpæa). Some showy garden flowers, such as the Carnations belong to it. The calyx is frequently gamosepalous, st. often on a gonophore. Some members still have the ovary incompletely 3-5-celled and many ovules. The flower is sometimes perigynous and the nodes of the stem often swollen. The family is not further dealt with.

---

* *N.B.*—Orders XVI and XVII are sometimes placed after Parietales.

The two median bracteoles of Portulacaceæ are often regarded as sepals, if so the flower is hetero- or homo-chlamydeous.

Flowers are white, yellow, or brightly coloured in some Caryophyllaceæ Portulacaceæ and Nyctaginaceæ, sometimes coloured *but scarious* in Amarantaceæ, sometimes surrounded by brightly coloured bracts as in Bougainvillea.

Stamens and ovules sometimes numerous in Portulacaceæ. Ovules numerous in Deeringia among Amarantaceæ.

Sepals and stamens sometimes only 1-3 in Amarantus and Alternanthera (Amarantaceous herbs).

56. The Portulaca Family.

Herbs, often fleshy with inconspicuous (in garden species brilliantly coloured) flowers, and alt., opp. or sub-verticellate leaves with stipulary hairs. *Bracteoles or sepals 2. Tepals 4-6 perigynous.* St. 8-12. *Ovary with 3-8-fid style.* Seeds many. *Fruit a pyxidium.* 56. **Portulacaceæ** (p. 378).

The Bougainvillea Family.

Herbs or shrubs often with swollen nodes and opp. leaves. *Perianth single often brightly-coloured, e.g.,* Mirabilis or Marvel of Peru, which is semi-naturalized in parts, *gamophyllous,* more or less persistent in fruit. *Carpel 1. Ovule 1.*

Boerhaavia repens, *L.* A herb with minute pink capitate flowers is used as a sag. (Family not further dealt with).

Nyctaginaceæ.

57. The Amaranth Family.

Herbs or undershrubs (sub-scandent shrub in Deeringia) with alt. or opp. leaves and *rigid or scarious flowers in spikes or fascicles with scarious bracts and bracteoles.* Tepals 5-4 free or only slightly connate. *St. isomerous opp. the tepals connate into a short tube at the base,* sometimes alternating with staminodes, *hypogynous.* Fruit a utricle of 2-3 carpels with 1 seed (several-seeded berry in Deeringia). Rudimentary flowers, sometimes awn-like, are present in some genera.

57. **Amarantaceæ** (p. 378).

58. The Beet Family.

Herbs, sometimes climbing (Basella) and usually fleshy with alternate leaves. *Perianth sepaloid fleshy and enclosing the nut in fruit*, 5-fid. *St. 5 perigynous*, free. Stigmas 3. Embryo spiral. **58. Chenopodiaceæ** (p. 382).

ORDER XVII.—**Polygonales** (allied to Chenopodiales).

Herbs, rarely shrubs, sometimes scandent, *often with swollen nodes*. L. simple entire usually alternate, *with connate or ochreous membranous stipules*, which sheath the terminal bud. Flowers *spicate* or capitate, small regular mostly 3-5-merous and homo- or haplo-chlamydeous, or perianth 0. St. hypogynous or slightly perigynous, 5-8 or sometimes reduced to 2, opp. the tepals when isomerous. Ovary of 3 (-2) carpels, 1-celled with 1 erect basal orthotropous ovule.

59. The Buckwheat Family.

Herbs with *ochreous* stipules. L. convolute in bud, often dotted and acrid. Fls. small green, white, or pink. *Tepals 4-6*, rarely only 3, often connate. *St. 5-8*, rarely 9. *Ovary 2-5-carpellary*. Fruit a *2-3-cornered nut*. Embryo straight or curved, more or less excentric in the endosperm.

59. Polygonaceæ (p. 383).

60. The Pepper Family.

Herbs or shrubs with *palmi-nerved* dotted aromatic or acrid leaves, and *intrapetiolar stipules* which wrap round the terminal bud. Fls. much reduced, usually on a fleshy axis with peltate bracts, generally diœcious and *achlamydeous* St. 6-2. Carpels 3-1. *Fruit baccate.*

60. Piperaceæ (p. 383).

ORDER XVIII.—**Aristolochiales** (affinities unknown, both it and the Piperaceæ were at one time considered to belong to the Monocotyledons.)

61. The Snake-Root Family.

Climbers with *palmi-nerved* leaves and base of petiole dilated or decurrent. Flowers *2-sexual zygomorphic* haplostemonous with green or coloured *gamophyllous perianth* with inflated base and an entire limb. *St. 6* united into *a column with the style* of the inferior 6-celled ovary. Ovules many. Fruit capsular.

61. **Aristolochiaceæ** (p. 384).

ORDER **Proteales** is a large Australian and South African order to which the commonly cultivated Grevillea robusta, *A. Cunn.* belongs. This is a handsome tree with twice-pinnatifid leaves, and spicate 2-sexual 4-merous yellow flowers in unilateral spikes. Perianth petaloid tubular below. St. epiphyllous. Ovary 1-carpellary with 2 ovules and a very long style.

Proteaceæ (p. 385).

ORDER XIX.—**Urticales** (allied probably to Polygonaceæ).

Trees, shrubs or herbs, sometimes with milky juice, and with simple frequently *palmi-nerved* (esp. 3-nerved) *stipulate leaves.* Stipules sometimes intra-petiolar and leaves *often dotted* (due to cystoliths in the hypodermal cells). Inflorescence of cymes or clusters, rarely simple spikes, often developing into large pseudocarps. Fls. *small greenish unisexual* (exc. Ulmaceæ), regular, M. 4-5 (in Ulmaceæ 4-8) -merous with isomerous (fewer in some figs) *stamens opposite the perianth-lobes.* Fem. sometimes naked, usually with a 2-5-toothed or -partite perianth. Ovary *superior 1-celled* of 1-2 carpels. Style simple or 2-fid. Ovule 1 erect or pendulous.

Exceptions :—

Where the flowers are crowded inside a swollen fleshy axis (*e.g.* the figs) they are often much reduced, the perianth may be 2-6 fid. or 0, the stamens only 1-2. The leaves of Cannabis (the Hemp) are palmately divided and the seedling leaves of some Moraceæ are all but pinnate.

Fls. are polygamous or 2-sexual in Ulmaceæ.

62. The Nettle Family.

Shrubs or herbs without milky juice, sometimes with stinging hairs. L. alt. or opp. usually 3-nerved. Fls. in small heads or cymes, heads often spicate. M. usually 4-5-merous. F. with usually a 2-5-toothed or -partite perianth. *Ovary with only 1 style and stigma. Ovule erect orthotropous.* Fruit an achene, sometimes embraced by the more or less fleshy perianth. 62. **Urticaceæ** (p. 385).

63. The Elm Family.

Trees or shrubs *without milky juice,* alt. 3-nerved or penni-nerved leaves with caducous stipules and flowers in fascicles or cymes, *often polygamous. Perianth 4-9-partite,* polyphyllous or gamophyllous, with isomerou stamens. *Carpels 2. Ovule pendulous* anatropous or amphi tropous. Fruit a drupe or samara.

63. **Ulmaceæ** (p. 388).

64. The Mulberry and Fig Family.

Trees or shrubs, *often with milky juice,* alt. rarely opp. leaves, which may be lobed especially when young. Fls· densely aggregated in spikes, heads or outside or inside fleshy receptacles (Figs, Jack-fruits, etc.) *Carpels 2.* Ovule pendulous, more or less anatropous. Fruit of nuts, sometimes enclosed in the fleshy perianth (*e.g* Mulberry).

64. **Moraceæ** (p. 391).

ORDER XX.—**Salicales** (perhaps allied to Tamariscaceæ and Euphorbiaceæ).

Trees or shrubs with alt. simple stipulate leaves and *diœcious* flowers in *catkins. Perianth* reduced to *1 or 2 glands.* St. 2 or more. Ovary often stipitate, *2-3-carpellary, 1-celled with parietal placentation* and many anatropous ovules. Seeds with a pencil of hairs from the funicle.

65. The Willow Family.

65. **Salicaceæ** (p. 402).

ORDER **Casuarinales.**

The Beef Wood Family.

Trees with drooping branches, very slender sulcate branchlets *with whorls of 6-8 scale-like leaves* united into a sheath below. *Fls. monœcious* or sometimes diœcious. M. fl. in slender *catkin-like spikes* terminating the twigs. *F. capitate.* M. with 2 lateral bracteoles and 2 *median bract-like sepals,* connate below *Stamen 1.* F. with 2 lateral bracteoles which become woody and valvate in fruit. *Perianth* 0. Pistil of 2 median carpels, the posterior barren. Stigmas 2 filiform. Ovules 2 erect. Fruit a 1-seeded nut, the whole spike having in fruit a general superficial resemblance to a cone. Testa adnate to the wall. Embryo straight.

Casuarinaceæ

C. equisetifolia, *Forst.* is some times planted.

Sub-class II. Sympetalae (see p. 52).

A. Pentacyclicæ (see p. 52.)

Order I.—Primulales.

Herbs, shrubs or rarely small trees, usually glandular with alt. simple leaves and regular 1-2-sexual flowers. Stamens *opposite to the corolla lobes,* or sometimes a very rudimentary first whorl also present, adnate to the corolla or free. *Ovary 1-celled with free central placentation,* superior (half inferior in Mæsa).

66. The Plumbago Family.

Herbs or undershrubs. Fls. mod.-sized. Petals free or slightly coherent. St. free or adnate at base to the corolla. *Styles 5 free.* Ovules 1 basal anatropous.

66. **Plumbaginaceæ** (p. 403).

67. The Maesa Family.

Trees or shrubs. Fls. often 1-sexual, small or medium. Petals gamopetalous or free (some Embelia). St. adnate to the corolla. *Styles connate.* Ovules sunk in the swollen central placenta. Fruit baccate, 1-several-seeded.

67. **Myrsinaceæ** (p. 403).

Order II.—Ebenales.

Trees or shrubs with alt. or (Diospyros sp.) sub-opp. usually entire leaves. Fls. small or medium 1-2-sexual. Petals *often more than 5.* St. *diplostemonous or many* or one whorl reduced to staminodes. *Ovary 3-10 -(rarely 2) -celled.* Ovules 1-few in each cell.

68. The Mohwa Family.

Trees *with milky juice. Fls. 2-sexual* usually clustered. Calyx inferior with 4-8 imbricate sepals, sometimes (Mimusops) 2-seriate. Corolla tube short and broad. Petals as many or 2-4 times as many as the sepals. St. adnate to the corolla. Ovary 2-5- rarely 6-12-celled. *Style slender pointed.* Ovule 1 in each cell. 68. **Sapotaceæ** (p. 406).

69. The Ebony Family.

Trees *without milky juice. Fls. diœcious.* M. in 3-more-flowered cymes. F. solitary or several on abbreviated lateral branches. Calyx 4-5 rarely 3-lobed, often hardened in fruit. St. usually 16 (8-64), hypogynous or adnate to corolla. Ovary 4-10-celled. *Sub-sessile stigmas 1-4.* Ovule 1 in each cell. 69. **Ebenaceæ** (p. 408).

70. The Storax Family.

Small trees. *Fls. 2-sexual or polygamous. Calyx perigynous or epigynous,* sepals very small or almost obsolete. Petals spreading 5-10, almost free. *Stamens* numerous *perigynous or epigynous* adnate to the base of the corolla. *Ovary 2-5-celled, style slender.* Ovules 2 in each cell. Fruit drupaceous, 1-seeded. 70. **Styraceæ** (p. 412).

B. Tetracyclicæ (see p. 53).

1. Superæ. Ovary superior.

ORDER III.—**Oleales.**

71. The Olive and Jasmine Family.

Trees or shrubs without milky juice, with simple or pinnate penni-nerved exstipulate leaves. *Fls. regular* 2-sexual or polygamous, in terminal or axillary cymes or panicles. Calyx small 4 (5-9 in Jasminum) -lobed. Corolla 4 (5-9 in Jasminum) -lobed, petals sometimes nearly free, valvate or imbricate. *St.* 2, sometimes nearly free. Ovary 2 celled. Ovules 1-2 in the inner angle of each cell. 71. **Oleaceæ** (p. 414.).

ORDER IV.—**Gentianales.**

Trees, shrubs or herbs, often with milky juice, and with *opp. or ternate* simple entire exstipulate *often palmi-nerved* leaves. Fls *regular* 2-sexual usually cymose. Calyx and corolla 4-5-merous, corolla usually contorted in bud. *St. as many as the petals* and alt. with them, adnate to the corolla at least at the base, sometimes combined into a column with the pistil. *Carpels* 2 combined into a 2-or 1-celled ovary or distinct except in the styles. *Ovules many* parietal or covering a large axile placenta.

Exceptions :—

Stipules or stipular lines sometimes occur in Loganiaceæ, and L. sometimes toothed in Buddleia. Fls. irregular in a few Gentianaceæ and stamens fewer than the petals.

Corolla often imbricate or valvate in Loganiaceæ.

Ovules only 2-8 in each cell in a few Apocynaceæ.

72. The Strychnine Family.

Trees, shrubs or herbs with sometimes stipular lines. Juice not milky. Cymes usually dense. Calyx 4-5-toothed. *Ovary 2-celled.* Fr. dehiscent or indehiscent.

72. Loganiaceæ (p. 419).

73. The Gentian Family.

Herbs. Juice not milky. *Fls. 4-5-merous,* often showy in dichasial cymes. If irregular, fls. small and stamens reduced in number. *Ovary 1-celled* with parietal placentation, rarely placentæ meeting, and ovary 2-celled.

73. Gentianaceæ (p. 420).

74. The Oleander Family.

Trees, shrubs or herbs, often climbing, *abounding in milky juice,* with opp, or whorled leaves. Calyx 5-lobed. *Corolla 5-lobed, rotate or salver-shaped,* often with a corona. St. with their anthers rarely distant, usually conniving, and sometimes adhering by a point of the connective to the swollen base of the stigma. Ovary 2-celled, or *of two distinct carpels connate in the style.* Fruit baccate, drupaceous or of follicles. Seeds often with a coma of hairs. **74. Apocynaceæ (p. 423).**

75. The Asclepias or Mudar Family.

Climbing herbs, rarely erect shrubs, abounding in milky juice (with very few exceptions), rarely leafless (Sarcostemma) *differing from the apocarpous Apocynaceæ* essentially *in the pollen,* which forms one or two waxy, more rarely granular masses (pollinia) in each anther cell. Pollinia of the right hand cell of each anther united by a caudicle to a gland (corpuscle) to which is also attached the pollinia of the left-hand cell of the adjacent anther. Fruit always of 2 free or connate *follicles* and seeds winged or comose. Filaments usually connate in a column round the pistil.

75. **Asclepiadaceæ** (p. 430).

ORDER V.—Personales.

Shrubs or herbs, rarely trees, occasionally glandular and aromatic, with *alt. or opp.* exstipulate simple or compound leaves. Fls. *usually zygomorphic* (regular in most Solanaceæ, and sub-regular in the perianth in several genera of other families), but not contorted in bud. The posticous stamen nearly always rudimentary or altogether absent (perfect in Solanaceæ), sometimes only 2 stamens perfect. *Ovary 2-celled superior with many ovules.* Fruit capsular, or baccate.

Exceptions :—

Solanaceæ on account of the regular flowers is usually included in Polemoniales, but certain genera show zygomorphic flowers (not in Chota Nagpur), and the ovary is that of Personales.

Oroxylum (Bignoniaceæ) has 5 perfect stamens.

Ovary is 1-celled in Orobanchaceæ, Lentibulariaceæ (little marsh plants common in rice fields), Gesneraceæ (herbs of moist banks), and Martynia.

Ovary is 4-celled in Datura and by a false septum in some Pedaliaceæ.

Acanthaceæ has often only 2 or few ovules in each cell.

76. The Potato Family.

Shrubs or herbs with alternate simple, rarely deeply-lobed or (Tomato) pinnate leaves Fls. regular in cymes. Sep., pet., and stamens 5. *Ovary with 2 oblique carpels and 2 swollen axile placentas* covered with ovules. Fr. a berry or capsule. 76. **Solanaceæ** (p. 438).

The **Snapdragon Family** contains a very large number of herbs common in rice fields, etc., the leaves are opp. or alt. *fls. irregular* with *2 to 4 stamens.* Ovary as in Solanaceæ.

Scrophulariaceæ.

The **Broomrape Family** contains herbs parasitic on roots of other plants or saprophytes and are devoid of chlorophyll. *Orobanche indica* is common on tobacco and mustard and has purplish-blue flowers in spikes. *Æginetia indica* is found in damp forests in summer, and has curious rather large solitary rose-purple flowers on long scapes.

Orobanchaceæ.

77. The Bignonia Family.

Trees or shrubs (climbing in many garden species) with *opp.* pinnately compound,* (simple in Tecoma) leaves, and large or moderate-sized zygomorphic flowers. St. 4 or 5. *Fruit a linear capsule with winged seeds.*

77. **Bignoniaceæ** (p. 442).

78. The Sesamum Family.

Herbs with opp. or alt. simple or pinnatifid leaves, and drooping racemose flowers. *Ovary 1-2 or ultimately 4-celled.* St. 4 didynamous. Ovules 1-seriate in each cell. *Seeds not winged.*

78. **Pedaliaceæ** (p. 444).

79. The Acanthus Family.

Shrubs or herbs, rarely (Thunbergia) scandent, frequently with swollen nodes, simple usually entire often lineolate leaves, and *zygomorphic* capitate or spicate or panicled flowers usually 4-ranked and with *well-developed* subtending *bract* and two *bracteoles* (for few exceptions see p. 446-447.) *St. 2 or 4.* Ovary 2-celled. Ovules 2-several vertically 2-seriate in each cell. *Seeds* compressed *seated on retinacula.*

Exceptions :—

Thunbergia has two collateral ovules in each cell, and the retinacual are absent. Blepharis has sometimes only 1 ovule in each cell. Some herbs of the tribe Nelsonieæ have papillæ in place of hard retinacula.

79. **Acanthaceæ** (p. 445).

---

* L. often crowded and then not opposite.

ORDER VI.—Polemoniales.

80. The Convolvulus Family.

Climbers, rarely erect, often with milky juice. L. alt. mostly simple cordate and palmi-nerved, sometimes palmately compound (Pinnate in Ipomœa Quamoclit, O in Cuscuta) exstipulate. *Fls. regular* completely gamopetalous with frequently an entire or only slightly 5-lobed limb. Sep. sometimes free and unequal. *St. 5.* Disc usually prominent. *Carpels* 2 (rarely 3-5) combined into a 2-celled, rarely 1 (Hewittia) -3- or 4-celled ovary. *Style 1, stigmas 2* (styles 2 in Evolvulus). *Ovules 2 to each carpel.* Fr. capsular or baccate. **80. Convolvulaceæ** (p. 459).

ORDER VII.—Lamiales.

Trees, shrubs, or herbs very often with glands and aromatic, with alt., whorled or usually opposite simple exstipulate leaves. *Fls. zygomorphic* (or in most Boraginaceæ regular) usually cymose. Calyx gamosepalous often tubular. *St. 4 or 2* (5 in Boraginaceæ) with or without a rudimentary 5th. Ovary entire and *2-celled* or *deeply lobed* and *4-celled* by the formation of a septum. *Ovules 2 to each carpel, collateral.* Fruit 1-4-seeded, usually of *1-seeded pyrenes or nutlets.*

Exceptions :—

L. are digitate in Vitex.

Corolla is regular and 6-12-merous in Symphorema, regular 4-6-lobed in Cordiaceæ.

Styles 2 in Coldenia (a Boraginaceous herb), twice bipartite in Cordia, capitate in Rhabdia. One stigmatic lobe sometimes suppressed in various genera, as also occurs in Personales.

81. The Borage Family. Sub-family Cordiaceæ. (Allied to Polemoniales).

Trees or shrubs with *alt. leaves.* Fls. in *dichotomous scorpioid cymes* which are often corymbose (in few-fld. racemes in Rhabdia) regular. Calyx sometimes sub-entire. Corolla

4-6-lobed. Ovary not deeply divided. *Drupe with a 1-4-celled stone or 1-4 pyrenes.* 81. **Boraginaceæ** (p. 472).

NOTE.—While the fruit of Cordiaceæ resembles that of some Verbenaceæ, the typical Boraginaceæ are herbs characterised by the deeply lobed ovary, each lobe becoming a 1-seeded nutlet as in Labiatæ, the seeds, however, are epitropous and those in Labiatæ apotropous. Cordiaceæ is better kept as a distinct family as is done by Warming.

82. The Teak Family.

Trees, shrubs or herbs with opp. or whorled leaves. Corolla *sub-regular to 2-lipped. St. 4 or 2* (as many as the petals in Symphorema). Ovary 2-4-celled, entire or rarely 4-lobed *Style terminal.* Fruit a *drupe with a 1-4-celled stone or with 1-4 1-seeded* sometimes fleshy pyrenes.

82. **Verbenaceæ** (p. 476).

Exceptions :—

Rarely there is only 1 ovule in each carpel (Lantana and Stachytarpheta). Duranta has an 8-celled ovary.

83. The Labiate or Mint Family.

Herbs, rarely shrubs, abounding with *aromatic glands,* usually with a 4-angled stem, opp. or whorled often toothed leaves and dense axillary cymes or whorls of small flowers, or cymes or whorls spicate or panicled. Fls. from sub-regular to deeply lipped. Calyx sometimes 8-10-toothed (usually 5-toothed or 2-lipped). *St. 2 or 4.* Ovary *deeply 4-lobed* with a *gynobasic style. Ovule 1 in each lobe erect.* Fruit of *4 nutlets.* 83. **Labiatæ** (p. 489).

2. Inferæ. Ovary inferior (see p. 53).

ORDER VIII.—**Rubiales.** (Closely allied to Loganiaceæ, from which separated easily by the *inferior ovary.* Allied also to Cornaceæ among the Choripetalæ).

84. The Coffee and Gardenia Family.

Trees, shrubs or herbs with *opp. leaves* and *interpetiolar stipules.* Fls. small or medium, *regular,* 2-sexual. Sepals *4-5 usually small,* rarely obsolete. Corolla 4-5-lobed, valvate, imbricate or contorted in bud. Disc epigynous. St. isomerous with the petals and alt. with them on the tube or throat of the corolla. *Ovary 2-celled. Style 1.* Ovules 1 or many in each cell. Fruit various.

84. **Rubiaceæ** (p. 494).

Exceptions :—

L. whorled without stipules in Rubia.

Fls. 3-7-merous in Lasianthus (or ovary 7-9-merous).

Ovary 1-celled in Gardenia, 4-celled above in Anthocephalus, 4-celled in fruit in Morinda and some others, 5 (3-6)-celled in Vangueria and Hamiltonia.

Order IX.—**Asterales.**

85. The Daisy and Thistle Family.

Shrubs or herbs, rarely trees. L. alt. rarely opposite, very rarely stipulate. Fls. *small* sessile in a *dense head surrounded by an involucre of bracts*, the whole often appearing like a single flower. Fls. regular and tubular, or ligulate, sometimes filiform, 1-2-sexual. Calyx obsolete, or of scales or hairs (*pappus*). *Anthers connate. Ovary 1-celled.* Ovule 1 basal. Fruit dry indehiscent. 85. **Compositæ** (p. 511).

Class II.—**Monocotyledoneæ.**

Sub-class I.—(p. 54).

Order I.—**Liliifloræ.**

Shrubs or herbs, often with bulbous bases. Flowers regular with a *2-seriate 6-merous* usually homochlamydeous petaloid *perianth*, tepals free or connate, inferior or superior. *St. 6* in two whorls. Ovary 1 or 3-celled of 3 carpels with axile placentation. Ovules anatropous.

Exceptions :—

The flower is very slightly zygomorphic in a few species, *e.g.* the cultivated Aloe. The Dioscoreaceæ (and some Liliaceæ) are diœcious and the second staminal whorl is sometimes suppressed.

A. Ovary *superior.*

86. The Lily Family.

Herbs, or climbing rarely erect shrubs. L. simple with parallel or arcuate nerves sometimes reduced to scales (Asparagus). Fls. large and showy, or sometimes very small (Asparagus), perianth petaloid or sub-sepaloid (Smilax and Urginea spp.) 86. **Liliaceæ** (p. 517).

B. Ovary *Inferior.*

87. The Amaryllis Family.

Usually bulbous or tuberous based herbs (rarely shrubby *e.g.* Agave), with radical ensiform or lanceolate often plaited leaves and *flowers borne on naked scapes* (scape very short in Curculigo). Fls. with *superior* often gamophyllous petaloid *perianth, sometimes with a corona.* Ovary 3-celled.

87. **Amaryllidaceæ** (p. 522).

88. The Tacca Family.

Herbs with tuberous rootstock and *tripartite pinnatifid leaves.* Fls. unbelled greenish or purplish with filiform bracts. *Ovary 1-celled.* 88. **Taccaceæ** (p. 527).

89. The Yam Family.

Climbers with tuberous rootstock and *palmi-nerved simple or* 3-5-*foliolate* leaves. Fls. small *spicate diœcious.* Perianth in two 3-merous whorls. St. in 1 or 2-3-merous whorls. F. with a 3-cornered 3-locular ovary. *Fruit a 3-cornered capsule* with 2-winged seeds in each cell.

89. **Dioscoreaceæ** (p. 528).

Order II.—Commelinales.

Herbs, often tuberous. Fls. *usually zygomorphic* with heterochlamydeous perianth. Sepals 3 usually green. Petals free or connate below. St. in two whorls, 6 perfect or often only 2 or three perfect, the rest reduced to staminodes or obsolete, *filaments* usually *with long coloured hairs.* Ovary *superior* 3-celled, or 1 cell reduced or absent. *Ovules* few in each cell, *orthotropous.* 90. **Commelinaceæ** (p. 534).

90. The Spider-wort Family.

ORDER III.—Scitamineæ.

Usually tuberous-based herbs with erect simple leaves or leaves spreading from a short stem, rarely sub-arboreous as in the Plantain (Musa). Pseudo-stem often made up of convolute leaf sheaths. Flowers *zygomorphic* or *irregular,* sepals and petals often dissimilar. Calyx often spathaceous and *one or more of the stamens converted into staminodes* or suppressed. *Ovary* 1-3-celled, *inferior.*

91. The Plantain or Banana Family.

Pseudo-stem very stout, short or tall. L. very large with horizontal close sec. nerves. Fls. 1-sexual in the axils of large often coloured bracts. Calyx spathaceous. Corolla wrapped round the stamens and pistil. *Stamens* 5 perfect.

91. **Musaceæ** (p. 536).

92. The Ginger Family.

Stem leafy or leaves radical. Fls. in the axils of green or coloured bracts. Calyx spathaceous. Fls. zygomorphic. Cor-tube with 3 petals. *Outer whorl of stamens reduced* to 2 lateral staminodes or absent, inner whorl of *1 perfect dorsal stamen and two petaloid staminodes connate into a lip.*

92. **Zingiberaceæ** (p. 537).

93. The Arrowroot Family.

Stem usually developed, sometimes with only one large leaf. Fls. very irregular. Calyx with free or slightly cohering sepals. *Outer whorl of stamens reduced* to 1 or 2 staminodes, inner whorl of a *single stamen with only 1 anther-lobe perfect,* and adnate to the petaloid expansion of the other lobe, and of two hardened or petaloid *staminodes which do not form a lip.* 93. **Marantaceæ** (p. 544).

ORDER IV.—Gynandræ.

This includes the *Orchid Family.* Fl. *strongly zygomorphic,* usually with three petaloid sepals, two slightly modified petals and the third forming a lip. Only 1 (rarely two) stamen perfect, the *filament connate with the style into a stout column. Pollen grains* united into *masses* (pollinia), and anther often opercular. **Orchidaceæ.**

SUB-CLASS 2. (p. 54.)

ORDER V.—Spadicifloræ (The order is somewhat artificial, the families not being closely allied).

Trees, shrubs or herbs with simple or compound leaves, and the inflorescence always sheathed by a permanent or deciduous spathe. Fls. ebracteolate on a spike or spadix usually 1-sexual with either 3-merous 2-seriate perianth or flowers much reduced even down to a single stamen or naked ovary without bracts or bracteoles. Spikes often panicled and spathes sometimes petaloid.

94. The Palm Family.

Trees or shrubs, sometimes climbing (canes). *L. plaited in bud,* rarely simple and entire except in the seedling plant, usually palmate or pinnatisect. Fls. usually 1-sexual. Spikes often panicled. *Sepals and petals 3 each,* petals frequently differing in size from the sepals and often with different æstivation, but *more or less leathery* or *fleshy not* petaloid. *St. 3, 6 or many.* Ovary of 3 carpels free or 1-3-celled. Ovules 1-2 in each cell. 94. **Palmæ** (p. 545).

95. The Aroid Family.

Usually stout succulent or fleshy herbs, sometimes scandent. *L. palmi-nerved* and usually net-veined, simple or pedatipartite or pinnatifid, often sagittate. Fls. 1-2-sexual with a 4-6-phyllous perianth, or *perianth reduced to scales* or usually *obsolete*. Spadix fleshy, spathe green or coloured, often leathery. Ovary 1-3-celled. Ovules 1 or more.

95. **Araceæ** (p. 549).

96. The Screw Pine Family.

Trees or shrubs, often branched. Diœcious. *L. long narrow parallel-veined spinose-toothed 3-farious.* Fls. crowded on a spadix without bracts, bracteoles or perianth. *M. fl. with many stamens.* F. fl. *with a 1-celled ovary* the ovaries often confluent, and woody in fruit.

96. **Pandanacæ** (p. 555).

ORDER VI.—Glumifloræ.

Grass-like herbs or bamboos with narrow parallel-nerved leaves with a long sheathing base. Fls. 1-2-sexual with the *perianth reduced* to *hairs* or *minute scales* or *0*, situated in the axils of bracts *(glumes)* which are closely spirally or distichously imbricate in small spikes (*spikelets*). Bracteoles usually present. *St.* hypogynous *2-6*. Ovary 2-3-carpellary, 1-celled, with 1 erect anatropous ovule. Embryo minute at one end of a mealy albumen.

The Sedge Family.

Sedges number some 60-70 species in Chota Nagpur. The stems are solid often 3-cornered. L. 3-farious with *closed sheaths* and *ligule 0* or very inconspicuous. Spikelets usually with empty glumes below and often above, bracteoles 0. Perianth 0 or of 6 (2-6) scales or bristles. *Anthers basifixed.* Style branches slender *not feathery*. Fruit a *2-3-cornered nut* (in the Cariceæ enclosed in a utricle, which is said to be morphologically the bract of a secondary axis). The inflorescence is often corymbose, a very rare arrangement in grasses.

Cyperaceæ.

97. The Grass and Bamboo Family.

Stems terete, often hollow with solid often swollen nodes. L. *distichous* with *split sheaths* and usually with a conspicuous *ligule*. Spikelets composed of distichous imbricating bracts (glumes) of which the 2 lowest are usually empty, a bracteole (palea) is opposed to the glume on the very abbreviated floral pedicel, and often wraps round the flower and fruit (cp. Cariceæ above). Perianth 0 or of very minute swollen scales (lodicules). *Anthers versatile.* Styles 2, rarely 3 with *feathery stigmas.* Fruit *dry, usually terete.*

97. **Gramineæ** (p. 555).

ARTIFICIAL KEY.

Table I.

The following families have their minute flowers crowded in such a way that the number of stamens in each flower may be difficult to ascertain :—

A. Flowers without bracts or perianth (a few Araceæ have a very reduced perianth), but a sheath or spathe may enclose the whole inflorescence.

Stamens or anthers on a fleshy axis or spadix, the carpels or ovaries occupying a separate portion of the axis . Araceæ (p.549)

B. Perianth O. Stamens or ovaries crowded mixed with peltate bracts on a fleshy axis. Stamens always on separate axes from the ovaries . . . Piperaceæ (p. 383)

C Flowers crowded inside fleshy receptacles or figs . . . . . Moraceæ (p. 391)

D. Stamens included with a number of hairs, and often with a stalked ovary within an involucre of bracts. Plants with very milky juice . . . . Euphorbiaceæ. (p. 209)

E. Stamens on very delicate filaments in the axils of overlapping bracts. (Cyperaceæ are not dealt with. Grasses and bamboos belong to the family) . . Gramineæ (p. 555)

F. Flowers collected into dense heads or spikes, but where the distinct florets may be discerned and the stamens counted, are found in Compositæ, Rubiaceæ, Urticaceæ, and many other families, and will be found in Table II.

Table II.

This table includes all families, and may be used in all cases, where male or hermaphrodite flowers are available. In the case of plants bearing male and female flowers on separate individuals, and only the female flowers are available Table III may be used.

Stamen 1.

Dicotyledons. (For distinction between dicotyledons and monocotyledons see. p. 49)

Trees with slender branchlets and leaves reduced to scales.

Male flowers in slender spikes, female flowers in cones . . . . Casuarina (p.81)

Trees or shrubs with milky juice.

Fls. minute crowded inside (figs) or outside fleshy more or less globose receptacles . . . . . . Moraceæ (p.391)

Fls. crowded in involucres which resemble a perianth. Branches usually stout and fleshy. Juice milky	Euphorbia (p. 212)
Tree with evergreen foliage. Juice watery	Mangifera (p. 258)

Herbs.

Herbs with flowers as in Euphorbia (above) and milky juice . . .	Euphorbia (p. 212)
Herbs with opposite leaves, and irregular flowers with a distinct gamopetalous corolla. St. 1 perfect. Staminodes present	Canscora (p. 422)

Monocotyledons.

Herbs. Fls. crowded on a fleshy axis, sometimes sheathed by a spathe. Perianth O	Araceæ (p. 549)
Herbs. Fls. with an irregular, usually showy perianth. Stamen with a slender filament and 2 anther cells .	Zingiberaceæ (p. 537)
Stamen petaloid bearing one anther cell	Marantaceæ (p. 544)

Stamens 2.

Dicotyledons.

I. Fls. 1-sexual minute, without perianth or perianth green inconspicuous or simple.

A. Herbs.

a. L. alternate.

Flowers in dense spikes with peltate bracts. St. 2-4	Piperaceæ (p. 383)
Fls. in short slender racemes with 5-lobed perianth. St. 2-4.	Sebastiania

Fls. clustered in slender spikes with sepals 2-3 scarious	Amarantus. (p. 379)
b. L. opposite.	
St. 2-5 hypogynous, sepals unequal whitish	Alternanthera (p. 379)
St. 2-5 perigynous, sepals minute equal. Petals sometimes present .	Ammannia (p. 356)
B. Trees or shrubs.	
Fls. in slender spikes. St. 2-3 or 2-7	Euphorbiaceæ (Sapium and Antidesma) (p.209)
M. Fls. clustered. F. sub-solitary. St. 2-4	Putranjiva (p. 224)
Fls. in fig-like fleshy receptacles. Juice milky	Ficus. (p. 393)
II. Flowers with both calyx and corolla distinct.	
A. Petals free. St. 2-3 usually with staminodes. Trees with alternate leaves.	
L. simple.	Meliosma (p. 263)
L. pinnate with coarsely toothed leaflets	Ailanthus (p. 238)
B. Corolla gamopetalous. L. opposite.	
Trees or shrubs. Fls. regular. . .	Oleaceæ (p. 414)
Shrubs or Herbs. Fls. irregular.	
Ovary deeply 4-lobed. Calyx tubular .	Labiatæ (p.489)
Ovary not deeply lobed 2-celled	
Ovules 1-2 in each cell, not superposed .	Stachytarpheta (p.489)
Ovules 2-several in each cell superposed	Acanthaceæ (p. 445)

Monocotyledons.

Grasses. Petals O.	Gramineæ (p. 555)
Stamens 2 with staminodes present. Petals present	Comelinaceæ (p. 534)

Stamens or Anthers 3.

Dicotyledons.

I. Perianth 0, or small and inconspicuous, if white then not divisible into calyx and corolla.

1. Herbs.

Prostrate or scandent. Stamens among peltate bracts in spikes . .	Piperaceæ (p. 383)
Prostrate. L. opposite. Sepals dry or with scarious margins . . .	Alternanthera (p. 379)
Erect. L. alternate. Fls. in fascicles or spikes, as in Alternanthera .	Amarantus (p. 379)
2. Parasitic shrubs	Viscum (p.376)
3. Climbing woody shrubs, or a small undershrub. Fls. white with 3 fertile stamens and 5-6 2-fid staminodes .	Olax (p. 371)
4. Trees, shrubs, or herbs (scandent in Tragia) with small 1-sexual flowers in spikes or fascicles.	
Perianth 3-6-fid herbaceous. Stamens 3-6 often connate in the centre of the flower	Euphorbiaceæ (p. 209)

II. Perianth composed of both calyx and corolla, or if corolla absent (Saraca), then calyx highly coloured.

1. Trees or shrubs (Bauhinia Vahlii is a large climber).

L simple.

L. penni-veined. Fls. small white, with 2-3 perfect stamens .	Meliosma (p. 263)

L. palmi-nerved, usually deeply 2-lobed. Fls. irregular . . . . . Bauhinia (p. 295)

L. pinnate.

Fls. small regular in large panicles . Ailanthus (p. 238)

Fls. irregular in scarlet corymbs. Petals absent. St. 3-8 . . . . . Saraca (p. 303)

Fls. irregular in lax racemes. Petals 3 . Tamarindus (p. 303)

2. Herbs, rarely shrubs, climbing by means of tendrils. St. often conniving with curved anther cells. Petals white or yellow . . . . . Cucurbitaceæ (p. 164)

Monocotyledons.

I. Herbs.

Perianth 0.

Fls. concealed by overlapping bracts. Grasses . . . . . . Gramineæ (p. 555)

Flowers with conspicuous corolla. .

L. narrow often equitant. Ovary inferior . . . . . . Iridaceæ

L. not equitant. Ovary free. Staminodes present. . . . . Commelinaceæ (p. 534)

II. Climbers from a tuberous root. Fls. 1-sexual in slender spikes. . . Dioscoreaceæ (p. 528)

III. Trees or stout shrubs. Palms . Palmæ (p. 545)

Stamens or Anthers 4.

Vide also Cansjera and Zizyphus under st. 5.

Dicotyledons.

I. Perianth 0 or single or not distinctly differentiated into calyx and corolla. (Petals present or absent in Ammannia. Minute cupular corolla in Cissampelos).

ARTIFICIAL KEY.

1. Herbs or undershrubs.
   A. Stamens not connate in a column.
      a. Stamens hypogynous, or fls. 1-sexual.

Stout herb with stinging hairs and palmi-nerved leaves . . .	Girardinia (p. 386)
Stinging hairs absent.	
St. 4-5 free. Staminodes 0. L. with 3 primary nerves	Pouzolzia (p. 388)
St. 4-5 connate at the base with alternating staminodes	Aerua (p. 381)
b. Stamens 4-5 perigynous. Herbs of damp places often with petals . .	Ammannia (p. 356)
B. Anthers minute on the top of a minute column. Climbing under shrub with palmi-nerved leaves . . .	Cissampelos (p. 147)

2. Shrubs.

a. Parasitic.	Loranthaceæ (p. 373)
b. Scandent, or sub-scandent. Glabrous, without staminodes . .	Deeringia (p. 379)
Pubescent or woolly, with staminodes .	Ærua (p. 381)
c. Erect. Anthers reversed in bud.	
Fls. in 2-chotomous cymes. L. very large, sometimes stinging . .	Laportea (p. 386)
Fls. in spicate clusters. L. palmi-nerved	Bohmeria (p. 387)
Trees or in (Glochidion) shrubs.	
A. Leaves simple.	
1. Anthers connate in a sessile column	Glochidion (p. 217)
2. Anthers distinct	
a. Flowering while leafless, or with very young leaves.	
Fls. fascicled. Fruit a samara . .	Holoptelea (p. 389)

Fls. spicate. The Mulberry . . Morus (p. 392)

b. Flowering with the leaves.

Fls. capitate. (Female sub-solitary) . Streblus (p. 392)

Fls. in small axillary cymes . . Trema (p. 390)

Fls. in catkins. Perianth 0 or of glands. Filaments much exceeding the woolly bracts . . . . Salix (p. 402)

B. Leaves compound.

Leaves 2-3-pinnatifid. Fls. in yellow racemes . . . . . . Grevillea (p. 385)

Leaves pinnate. Fls. small greenish. St. 4-8 . . . . . . Schleichera (p. 261)

II. Perianth double, with both calyx and corolla. (The corolla of Vitis often falls off as a cap without expanding.)

A. Corolla polypetalous (or petals sometimes cohering to one another in Vitis, sometimes cohering at base only in Embelia) *vide* also St. 3-5 under St. 3 and St. 5.

1. Herbs or soft-wooded shrubs.

Aquatic, with floating deltoid leaves and white flowers . . . . . Trapa (p. 357)

Terrestrial. L. pinnate. Fls. yellow . Cassia (p. 299)

Climbers with tendrils. L. simple or digitate. St. 4-5 . . . Vitis (p. 275)

2. Trees or shrubs.

Small tree or shrub. Fls. small white racemed. St. 4-5 . . . Embelia (p. 404)

Tree with pinnate leaves. Fls. small white panicled. St. 4-6 . . . Cedrela (p. 249)

B. Corolla gamopetalous, or petals distinctly connate (sometimes only below in Boraginaceæ).

1. Fls. regular or sub-regular. Stamens not didynamous.

a. Ovary superior.

L. alternate. Style once or twice bifid	Boraginaceæ (p. 472)
L. opposite. Ovary deeply lobed. Shrubs or herbs, glandular . .	Labiatæ (p.489)
L. opposite. Ovary not lobed.	
Ovary imperfectly 2-celled. Ovules 2 in each cell	Callicarpa (p. 477)
Ovary 1- or 2-celled. Ovules many. Herbs	Gentianaceæ (p. 420)
Ovary 2-celled. Ovules many. Trees or shrubs	Loganiaceæ (p. 419)

b. Ovary inferior.

L. opposite with interpetiolar stipules or whorled	Rubiaceæ (p. 494)

2. Fls. distinctly 2-lipped, or if sub-regular then stamens didynamous.

a. L. simple or pinnatifid.

i. Ovary deeply 4-lobed with 1 ovule in each lobe. Shrubs or herbs . .	Labiatæ (p.489)
ii. Ovary not deeply 4-lobed (4-grooved in some Verbenaceæ).	
† Ovary with 4 ovules not superposed.	
Trees or shrubs, rarely herbs . .	Verbenaceæ (p. 476)
Weak climbing shrubs . . .	Thunbergia (p. 447)
†† Ovules 2 or more superposed on each placenta or in each cell of the ovary.	
Herbs with drooping tubular flowers. Upper leaves alternate . . .	Pedaliaceæ (p. 444)

Shrubs or herbs. Leaves all opposite. Seeds not winged . . . . . Acanthaceæ (p. 445)

Shrub with orange-scarlet flowers. Seeds winged . . . . . Tecoma (p. 444)

b. Leaves 1-3-pinnate. Seeds winged in long linear capsules . . . . . Bignoniaceæ (p. 442)

c. Leaves digitate . . . . . Vitex (p. 478)

Monocotyledons.

Stout climbers with aërial roots, or spinous marsh herbs. St. 4-6 . . Araceæ (p. 549)

Stamens or Anthers 5.

(Small alternating staminodes sometimes present. *Vide* also Ammannia st. 4-5 not repeated here, and Salix st. 4-10 without perianth).

Dicotyledons.

I. Perianth simple, or if 2-seriate not distinctly differentiated into calyx and corolla. (*Vide* also Umbelliferæ under II in which the sepals are often reduced or absent and some Rhamnaceæ in which the petals are exceedingly minute).

a. Leaves simple.

A. Fls. 2-sexual. Ovary superior (St. perigynous in Polygonaceæ).

Perianth sepaloid or petaloid. Herbs with ochreous stipules . . . . Polygonaceæ (p. 383)

Perianth fleshy. Climber with fleshy stems . . . . . . Basella (p. 382.)

Perianth petaloid. Fls. yellowish Climbing *or sub-erect shrubs.*

St. 4-5 alternating with staminodes . Cansjera (p.373)

St. 4-5. A sub-scandent shrub with stipular thorns . . . . Zizyphus (p.269)

B. Fls. 1-2-sexual. Ovary superior.

Herbs (or Deeringia, a rambling shrub) with dry or scarious or coloured and shining perianth. St. connate below. Stipules 0 . . . . . . Amarantaceæ (p. 378)

C. Fls. 1-sexual. Perianth sepaloid, or sub-membranous.

1. St. connate in a column in the centre of the flower, or if free, then alternating with disc glands, or anthers didymous, or anther cells divaricate on a broad connective . . . Euphorbiaceæ (p. 209)

2. St. free, usually spreading from the centre, one always opposite each tepal. Anthers more or less oblong, versatile or dorsi-fixed.

Trees. Anthers erect in bud . . Ulmaceæ (p. 388)

Shrubs or Herbs. Anthers reversed in bud . . . . Urticaceæ (p. 385)

D. Fls. 2-sexual. Perianth petaloid. Ovary inferior. Parasitic shrubs Loranthaceæ (p. 373)

β. Leaves 3-foliolate. Fls. small green panicled. Tree . . . Bischofia (p. 227)

γ. Leaves pinnate. Fls. in scarlet corymbs. St. 3-8 perfect. Tree . . Saraca (p. 303)

II. Perianth double, calyx and corolla both present (Sepals very minute in some Araliaceæ and Umbelliferæ. Petals very minute in some Rhamnaceæ).

A. Petals free (or somewhat connate in Leea) (see also Embelia under B. Myrsinaceæ.)	
1. Fls. 1-sexual. Petals small or minute	Euphorbiaceæ (p. 209)
2. Fls. all (or most of them in an inflorescence) 2-sexual.	
a. St. free (not united into a tube, or only connate at the base).	
† Leaves minute, scale-like . . .	Tamaricaceæ (p. 162)
†† Leaves simple, not scale-like.	
α. Herbs or under-shrubs, not climbing.	
Fls. Small yellow clustered. St. 5-10 free	Corchorus (p. 203)
Stamens connate at base, alternating with glands or staminodes	Linaceæ (p.235)
St. connate at base, without staminodes .	Sterculiaceæ (p. 203)
β. Trees or shrubs, sometimes scandent. Fls. regular or nearly so.	
Petals unequal. Ovary 2-3-celled. (Only 2 stamens usually fertile) . . .	Sabiaceæ (p.262)
Stamens opposite the petals. Ovary half-superior 1-celled	Homalium (p. 162)
Stamens alternate with the petals. Ovary superior 1-celled	Anacardiaceæ (p. 255)
Ovary 3-5-celled. St. alternate with the petals. St. perigynous . . .	Celastraceæ (p. 265)
Ovary 2-4-usually 3-celled. St. opposite to the petals. St. perigynous or epigynous	Rhamnaceæ (p. 268)

γ. Trees or immense climbers. L. palmi-nerved, usually deeply 2-lobed.

Fls. irregular. Fertile stamens 3-5, usually with staminodes . . . . Bauhinia (p. 37)

††† Leaves usually digitately compound, or deeply palmate or, if simple, palmi-nerved with tendrils.

Herbaceous or very soft-wooded climbers. Fls. usually very small . . . . Ampelidaceæ (p. 274)

Fls. large or medium-sized. Stamens on a gonophore . . . . Passiflora (p. 61)

†††† L. digitate. Large climbing shrub without tendrils . . . . . Heptapleurum (p. 369)

††††† L. pinnate or 2-3 pinnate.

a. Fls. in simple or compound umbels. Sepals sometimes obsolete. St. epigynous.

Trees or shrubs . . . . . . Araceæ (p. 549)

Herbs . . . . Umbelliferæ (p. 366)

β. Fls. racemed or panicled.

Fls. yellow. Leaves pinnate . . . . Cassia (p. 299)

Fls. small white regular panicled. L. pinnate . . . . Cedrela (p. 249)

Fls. white irregular. L. 2-3-pinnate. Staminodes 5 . . . . . . Moringa (p.174)

b. Stamens united into a tube.

A tree. L. pinnate with 3-7 leaflets . Aglaia (p. 255)

Herbs or shrubs. Leaves very large and simple, or 1-3-pinnate . . . . . Leea (p. 278)

B. Corolla gamopetalous.

1. Stamens free from one another (or slightly conniving in Solanaceæ).

a. Stamens alternate with the petals or corolla lobes.

i. Ovary superior.

† Leaves opposite. Juice not milky.

α. L. 2-3-pinnate. Small tree with a raceme of large irregular flowers .	Oroxylum (p. 413)
β. L. simple.	
Herbs. Ovary 1 or imperfectly 2-celled. Ovules many	Gentianaceæ (p. 420)
Trees or shrubs. Ovary 2-4-celled. Ovules many superposed (seeds 1-many) . .	Loganiaceæ (p. 419)
Trees. Ovary 2-4-celled. Ovules not more than 4	Verbenaceæ (Tectona, Callicarpa) (p. 476)
†† L. opposite. Trees or shrubs with milky juice	Apocynaceæ (p. 423)
††† Leaves alternate.	
α. Ovules 1-2 in each ovary cell, not superposed.	
Twiners, rarely erect, juice sometimes milky	Convolvulaceæ (p. 459)
Trees or shrubs, rarely herbs . . .	Boraginaceæ (p. 472)
β. Ovules numerous on two swollen placentas	Solanaceæ (p. 438)
ii. Ovary inferior.	
Trees, shrubs, or herbs with opposite simple leaves and interpetiolar stipules. Fls. sometimes aggregated in heads	Rubiaceæ (p. 494)

Climbers with palmi-nerved leaves and 1-sexual flowers	Cucurbitaceæ (p. 164)
b. Stamens opposite to the petals or corolla lobes.	
i. Juice not milky. Ovary 1-celled.	
Undershrub. Ovule 1. Styles 5 . .	Plumbaginaceæ (p. 403)
Trees or shrubs. Ovules more than 1. Style 1	Myrsinaceæ (p. 403)
ii. Juice milky. Ovary 2-8-celled. Trees or shrubs . . .	Sapotaceæ (Sideroxylon) (p. 406)
2. Stamens united into a column, or anthers connate, or conniving in a cone round the stigma and adherent to it.	
a. Leaves opposite, juice milky. Fls. not in dense heads surrounded by an involucre.	
Stamens in a column or, if free, pollen forming one or two masses.	
Climbers, rarely small trees or shrubs (leafless in Sarcostemma) . .	Asclepiadaceæ (p. 430)
Stamens not in a column. Pollen granular. Trees, shrubs or climbers .	Apocynaceæ (p. 423)
b. L. opposite or alt. Fls. in dense heads surrounded by an involucre of bracts (as in Daisy, Zinnia) .	Compositæ (p. 511)

Stamens or Anthers 6.

Note.—Many plants of which the stamens are normally 5, occasionally have 6 stamens. *Vide* also the following: Saraca St. 3-8. Schleichera St. 4-8. Salix St. 4-10. Symphorema St. 8-6.

Dicotyledons.—

I. Perianth simple, or of two or more whorls but not distinctly differentiated into calyx and corolla.

A. Perianth regular.

Herbs with ochreous stipules and fls. in spikes. St. 5-8. . . .	Polygonaceæ (p. 383)
Climbers with palmi-nerved leaves and small flowers with several floral whorls, of which inner may be petaloid	Menispermaceæ (p. 147)
Trees or shrubs.	
Stamens central or below the pistillode. Fls. 1-sexual . . .	Euphorbiaceæ (p. 209)
Stamens perigynous. Anthers opening by lids	Lauraceæ (p. 150)
B. Perianth irregular. Stamens united into a column with the style	Aristolochia (p. 384)

II. Flowers with distinct calyx, and corolla

A. Stamens free.

Herbs. Stamens 4 long and 2 short	Cruciferæ (p. 155)
Herbs. Stamens equal on a gynophore	Capparidaceæ (p. 155)
Shrub with yellow racemose flowers and spines. Anthers opening by lids	Berberis (p.149)

Tree. Stamens opposite the petals with alternating glands . . . Homalium (p. 162)

Tree with very large obovate leaves. St. 5-6 not opposite the petals . Semecarpus (p. 257)

B. Stamens united into a tube. Trees with pinnate leaves . . . Amoora (p.254)

Monocotyledons.

I. Perianth O, or brown, coriaceous or membranous. Inflorescence often enclosed in spathes.

Bamboos, and a few grasses . . Gramineæ (p. 555)

Stout climbers with aërial roots, or a stout prickly marsh herb, with flowers crowded on a spadix . . Araceæ (p. 549)

Tall trees with slender stems and large leaves, or if shrubs or shrubby climbers then leaves pinnate or pinnatifid . . . . . Palmæ (p. 545)

II. Perianth small regular of two 3-merous whorls, petaloid or sometimes sepaloid. Inflorescence never inclosed in spathes. Climbers, or young sub-erect.

Ovary superior. Leaves (cladodes) acicular . . . . Asparagus (p. 520)

Fls. 1-sexual. Ovary superior. Leaves broad. Fls. in umbels . . Smilax (p. 518)

Fls. 1-sexual. Ovary inferior. Leaves broad. Fls. in spikes . . . Dioscoreaceæ (p. 528)

III. Perianth moderate-sized, usually showy or coloured.

I. Ovary superior.

Fls. small blue cymose, often from imbricating bracts . . . . Commelinaceæ (p. 534)

Fls. solitary or racemose. Usually white or red . . . . Liliaceæ (p.517)

2. Ovary inferior.
Leaves simple . . . . Amaryllidaceæ (p. 522)

L. 3-partite and pinnatifid . . Taccaceæ (p. 527)

Stamens or Anthers 7-11 (usually variable).

Vide also stamens 8, St. 9, St. 10, and St. 12.

Dicotyledons.

I. Perianth simple or 0.

A. Trees or shrubs.

1. Leaves simple.

Fls. in the axils of bracts. Perianth of fleshy glands or scales . . . Salix (p. 402)

Fls. 2-sexual or polygamous. Tree flowering before the leaves. Stamens opposite the sepals. Fruit a samara . Holoptelea (p. 389)

Fls. 1-sexual. Stamens in centre of flower, or anther cells on a broad connective . . . . . . Euphorbiaceæ (p. 209)

Stamens alternating with glands or staminodes, united in a tube below . Casearia (p. 160)

2. Tree with pinnate leaves and scarlet corymbs . . . . . Saraca (p. 303)

B. Herbs.

Stipules ochreous. Green, white or pink flowers . . . . . Polygonaceæ (p. 383)

Dwarf fleshy. Stipules 0 or of hairs. Petals yellow . . . . Portulacaceæ (p. 378)

II. Calyx and corolla distinct (*vide* also Portulacaceæ above which have two deciduous sepal-like members).

Trees or shrubs.

A. L. simple. Fls. regular.

L. alternate. St. opposite the 5-7 petals	Homalium (p. 162)
L. opposite or fascicled. Ovary inferior	Rubiaceæ (p. 494)

(Petals and stamens occasionally 6-10 in Gardenia, Randia, Morinda, etc.)

B. L. pinnate. Fls. irregular. St. 3-9 perfect, often with staminodes .	Csalpiniaceæ (p. 294)

Stamens or Anthers 8.

Vide also St. 7-11. The following have normally 8 stamens.

Petals present in all except Schleichera and Dodonæa (Sapindaceæ).

I. Stamens free. Fls. regular. Petals free.

1. St. hypogynous. Leaves simple or pinnate (biternate in Cardiospermum).

Leaves simple or pinnate, copiously gland-dotted	Rutaceæ (p. 241)
Trees or shrubs (or Cardiospermum herbaceous) flowering with the leaves. St. 8-10	Sapindaceæ (p. 260)
Trees flowering before the leaves appear	Anacardiaceæ (Odina and Spondias). (p. 255)
Undershrubs or shrubs with clustered yellow flowers. St. 8-15 . . .	Triumfetta (p. 202)

2. Stamens perigynous. Leaves simple.

Ovary free. Petals 4-6 . . .	Lythraceæ (p. 354)

Ovary connected by vertical walls to the hypanthium. Petals 4. Herbs or shrubs with 3-5-nerved leaves .	Melastomaceæ (p. 357)
3. Stamens epigynous. L. simple.	
Herbs. Ovary 4-5-celled. . . .	Onagraceæ (p. 356)
Shrubs. Usually scandent or dwarf. Ovary 1-celled	Combretaceæ (p. 359)
II. Stamens united. Fls. irregular . .	Polygalaceæ (p. 264)
III. Stamens free, or somewhat monodelphous (in Mimosaceæ). Corolla gamopetalous.	
1. Leaves simple alternate.	
Fls. diœcious. Stamens 8-many .	Diospyros (p. 408)
Fls. 2-sexual. St. 8 with alternating staminodes	Mimusops (p. 407)
2. L. opposite. St. 6-8. Fls. in capitate cymes	Symphorema (p. 488)
3. L. 2-pinnate. Fls. very small in globose heads	Mimosa (p. 286)

Stamens 9.

Vide also St. 7-11, and stamens 8-10 (Sapindaceæ).

Dicotyledons.

Fls. regular. Anthers opening by lids. Staminodes usually present . .	Lauraceæ (p. 150)
Fls. irregular, papilionaceous . .	Papilionaceæ (p. 308)

Monocotyledons.

Trees or shrubs with pinnate leaves .	Palmæ (p. 545)

Stamens or Anthers 10.

Vide also stamens 7-11.

I. Perianth reduced to swollen glands.
Fls. in the axils of small bracts in catkin-like spikes . . . . . Salix (p. 402)

II. Perianth simple. Petals absent.

A. Stamens free, or only united into a tube at the base.

1. Leaves simple, not palmate, alternate. St. hypogynous or perigynous.
Stamens with alternating staminodes united at the base . . . Casearia (p.160)
Staminodes absent. A glabrous somewhat resinous shrub . . . Dodonæa(p.262)

2. Leaves simple opposite. Stamens epigynous . . . . . Combretaceæ (p. 359)

3. Leaves pinnate . . . . . Schleichera (p. 261)

B. Stamens in a column surmounted by a ring of sessile anthers.
Leaves palmi-nerved, palmate, or digitate. Fls. while leafless Sterculia (p. 204)

III. Calyx and corolla both present.

A. Flowers regular. Petals free or nearly so (except in some Mimosaceæ).

1. Leaves scale-like. Erectshrubs Tamaricaceæ (p. 162)

2. Leaves well-developed.

a. Stamens free. (*Vide* p. 116.)

i. Trees flowering while leafless, or occasionally (Boswellia) with the young leaves also.

a Fls. in very slender spikes, green. Lflts. entire . . . Odina (p. 256)

β Fls. in stout racemes, white. Lflts. opposite, coarsely toothed	Boswellia (p. 240)
γ Fls. in terminal panicles.	
Calyx campanulate, 5-fid., valvate. Ovary 4-5-celled. Lflts. crenate . . .	Garuga (p. 240)
Calyx small 5-toothed, imbricate. Ovary 4-5-celled. Lflts. entire . .	Spondias (p. 259)
Calyx deeply lobed. Ovary 3-celled, 3-lobed. Lflts gland dotted	Chloroxylon (p. 249)

ii. Flowering with the new leaves, or with fully developed leaves (exc. sometimes Limonia, a small thorny tree belonging to the Rutaceæ).

† Leaves simple.	
Tree. Carpels free, only one developing.	Buchanania (p. 258)
Undershrubs. Fls. small yellow. L. sometimes lobed . .	Tiliaceæ (p. 192)
†† Leaves simple or compound, copiously dotted with oil glands.	
Trees or shrubs. Ovary 4-6-celled, sometimes lobed . .	Rutaceæ (p. 241)
††† Leaves pinnate or 2-foliolate, not glandular.	
Tree. Lflts. mostly alternate, very coarsely toothed. Ovary deeply lobed	Ailanthus (p. 238)
Tree. Lflts. mostly opposite, entire or serrate. Ovary 3-5-celled entire	Bursera (p. 241)

Small tree or shrub. Thorny. L. pinnately 2-foliolate . Balanites (p. 239)
Herb with opposite pinnate leaves (Fam, Zygophyllaceæ). Tribulus
†††† Leaves 2-pinnate Small cultivated tree . . Leucæna (p. 285)

b. Stamens united at the base or throughout into a tube. (*vide* p. 114)

i. Leaves simple, not gland-dotted (external glands in Jatropha).

α. Ovary superior.

Leaves entire alternate with one primary nerve . . Erythroxylon (p. 236)
Leaves palmi-nerved, often deeply palmately lobed.
Fls. 1-sexual. Shrubs with thick branches . . Jatropha (p. 229)
Fls. 2-sexual . . . Sterculiaceæ (p. 203)

β. Ovary inferior. Leaves opposite.

Herbs . . . . Onagraceæ (p. 356)
Shrubs or undershrubs . . Combretaceæ (p. 359)

ii. Leaves pinnate, alternate.

Leaves gland-dotted. Stamens irregularly connate . Rutaceæ (p.241)
Stamens united at the base only. Styles 5. Cultivated tree . Averrhoa (p. 236)
Staminal tube long. Style 1 . Meliaceæ (p. 248)

iii. Leaves 2-pinnate. Corolla usually gamopetalous Mimosaceæ. (p. 284)

B. Flowers irregular (*vide* p. 114)

1. Leaves simple opposite . . . Hiptage. (p. 263)
2. Leaves alternate, simple 1-3-foliolate or pinnate. Fls. papilionaceous . . . . . . Papilionaceæ (p. 308)
3. Leaves alternate, 1-2-pinnate. Fls. not papilionaceous . . . Cæsalpiniaceæ (p. 294)

Stamens or Anthers 12-16.

See also Menispermaceæ with 6 stamens and 6 staminodes, and under stamens many.

Dicotyledons.

I. Herbs or undershrubs.

Sep. 0, Pet. 3. St. 9-12 (but only 3 usually perfect) . . . Olax (p. 371)

Sep. 2 deciduous. Pet. 4-5. St. 8-12 . Portulaca (p. 378)

Sep. 4. Pet. 4. St. 12-20 . . . Capparidaceæ (p. 155)

Sep. 4-5. Pet. 4-5. St. 8-15 . . . Tiliaceæ (p. 192)

II. Trees or shrubs.

A. Perianth simple or, if double, not differentiated into calyx and corolla.

1. Fls. 1-sexual or stamens hypogynous.

Anthers sessile in a ring on the top of a column . . . . . . Sterculia (p. 204)

Anthers not sessile.

Fls. axillary clustered . . . Cyclostemon (p. 225)

Fls. in long spikes or racemes . . Croton (p. 228)

Fls. in heads of close umbels surrounded by whorls of imbricating bracts. L. often aromatic . . (Lauraceæ) (p. 150)

2. Fls. 2-sexual or polygamous. St. perigynous or epigynous.

Fls. clustered or panicled Anthers opening by lids	Lauraceæ (p. 150)
Fls in dense heads, or in spikes. Anthers not opening by lids. Ovary quite inferior	Combretaceæ (p. 359)
Fls. scarlet in short axillary cymes. Petals 0 or 6 resembling the calyx lobes	Woodfordia (p. 354)

B. Perianth distinctly differentiated into calyx and corolla.

N.B.—*Vide* also Croton above which has greenish petals and Woodfordia which *usually* has petals.

1. Petals free, or only adnate at base to the staminal tube in Kydia.

Leaves opposite. Petals very small toothed. Ovary inferior . .	Carallia (p.359)
Leaves alternate. Petals white. Ovary superior	Kydia (p. 192)

2. Corolla gamopetalous.

Leaves alternate. Fls 1-sexual .	Ebenaceæ (p.408)
Leaves opposite. Corolla with 6-many entire lobes. Fls. 2-sexual . . .	Symphorema (p. 488)

Stamens or Anthers many.

Occasionally the number is only 15 or 16 *vide* also Lauraceæ above in which, from the fls. being collected in heads, the stamens may appear numerous.

Dicotyledons.

I. Perianth single. Petals absent.

A. Fls. 1-sexual.

1. Fls. green or yellow, not tubular.

Anther cells globose, terminal or adnate to a broad connective, rarely (Gelonium) anthers oblong and dorsifixed. L. alternate or in (Trewia) opposite. Sepals 3-6 imbricate or valvate . . Euphorbiaceæ (p. 209)

Anthers versatile. L. alternate. Sep. 4-5 imbricate . . . . . Bixaceæ (p. 157)

2. Calyx tubular green or coloured.

Anthers sessile on the top of a column. L. alt. palmate or palmi-nerved . Sterculia (p. 204)

B. Fls. 2-sexual Fls. with large white sepals. L. opposite, compound . . Clematis (p. 140)

II. Petals present, but flowers small green or yellowish, in racemes or spikes. L. simple. Chrozophora, Croton, Codiæum . . . . . . (Euphorbiaceæ) (p. 209)

III. Perianth pale or coloured of two or more 3-merous whorls, the inner one or more of which may be dissimilar and petaloid. Carpels free, except in Anona (Custard-apple.) .

Fls. large, solitary. Carpels on an elongate axis . . . . . . Michelia (p.141)

Fls. small or moderate-sized. Carpels in a head or umbel . . . . Anonaceæ (p. 142)

IV. Perianth distinctly separated into calyx and corolla.

A. Corolla polypetalous, or petals only united at the base (*vide* p. 122)

1. Stamens hypogynous, or on a hypogynous disc (*vide* p. 121).

a. Filaments completely united or only free at the apex.

Stamens united into a fleshy mass in the M. fl. or into 4 masses in the 2-sexual flower. Leaves opposite. Juice yellow . . . . Garcinia (p.177)

Fls. 2-sexual. Anthers 2-celled on a column or tube, usually in groups or alternating with staminodes. L. alternate, usually palmi-nerved . Sterculiaceæ (p. 203)

Fls. 2-sexual. Anthers 1-celled crowded on the tube above. Staminodes 0. Leaves as in Sterculiaceæ . . Malvaceæ (p. 179)

b. Filaments only united below, or quite free, or loosely connate in some Rutaceæ and Camellia.

i. Leaves simple or digitate alternate.

† L. palmi-nerved, palmate or digitate. Trees or shrubs.

Fls. small or medium, axillary, clustered or cymose. White or yellow . .. Tiliaceæ (p.192)

Fls. rather large, yellow, solitary or panicled on the new shoots, with 3-5 bracteoles and spathaceous calyx . Eriolæna (p. 207)

Fls. large in terminal panicles. White or rose. Leaves glandular beneath. Cultivated . . . . . . Bixa (p. 158)

Fls. in terminal corymbs. White, yellow or pink. Leaves 3-foliolate . . Cratæva. (p.156)

Fls. very large, scarlet, appearing before the leaves . . . . . . Bombax (p.192)

Fls. very large, yellow, appearing before the leaves. Carpels completely united. Style 1 (cp. Dillenia, below) . . Cochlospermum (p. 158)

†† L. penni-veined, simple. Trees.

Fls. very large or large, yellow and appearing before the leaves, or white and leaves evergreen. Carpels distinct above or with distinct styles. Styles 5, 10 or 20 (cp. Cochlospermum, above) . . . . Dillenia (p. 175)

The Sal Tree. Fls. white panicled. Style entire pointed . . . Shorea (p. 178)

††† L. penni-veined, simple. Shrubs or (Ochna squarrosa) a small tree.

Evergreen. Fls. white solitary. Styles 3-5 connate below. The Tea plant . Camellia (p.177)

Deciduous (O. pumila is a dwarf undershrub). Fls large yellow in corymbs. Ovary deeply lobed. Styles connate . Ochnaceæ (p. 237)

Thorny shrubs. Fls. white or pink. Style 0. Ovary on a gynophore . Capparis (p.156)

†††† Herbs with yellow juice and often pinnatifid or prickly leaves . . Papaveraceæ (p. 155)

ii. Leaves compound, or in some Rutaceæ 1-foliolate.

Leaves copiously pellucid punctate with oil glands . . . . . Rutaceæ (p.241)

Leaves not glandular. A climbing shrub with the terminal leaflet usually converted into a tendril . . . Naravelia (p. 140)

2. Stamens perigynous or, if epigynous carpels with separate styles . (*vide* p. 119)

Leaves alternate. Styles separate (N.B. Pygeum, as in the Plum, has only one carpel, and therefore only one style) . Rosaceæ (p.282)

Leaves opposite. Style 1. Sepals and petals usually 6 . . Lagerstroemia (p. 355)

3. Stamens epigynous. Styles connate into 1.

a. Fleshy prickly shrubs with large flowers . . . . . . Cactaceæ (p.281)

b. Trees, sometimes small. Leaves alternate.

Fls. medium-sized, white in axillary fascicles . . . . . Alangium (p.76)

Fls. very large, white or pink, in short spikes . . . . . . Careya (p. 353)

Fls. medium, in pendulous racemes . Barringtonia (p. 353)

c. Trees or shrubs. Leaves opposite.

Fls. scarlet . . . . . Punica (p. 356)

Fls. white. Leaves usually gland-dotted . Myrtaceæ (p. 350)

B. Corolla gamopetalous. (*Vide* p. 119)

1. Leaves simple alternate.

Fls. 1-sexual. Juice not milky Ebenaceæ (p. 408)

Fls. 2-sexual. Juice milky . . Sapotaceæ (p. 406)

2. Leaves 2-pinnate. Fls. very small in globose heads or in spikes . Mimosaceæ (p. 284)

Monocotyledons.

Small trees or shrubs with long narrow spinous-toothed leaves and small flowers crowded on a spadix with white spathes. Perianth 0. . . Pandanus (p. 555)

Palms with pinnate and pinnatifid leaves with flabelliform lflts. . . Caryota (p.547)

Table III.

This table may be used in the case of diœcious plants when the males are not available. Plants with 1-sexual flowers, but *monœcious* are included in Table II.

A. Ovary apocarpous with 3-12 free carpels each with a stigma.	
Climbing shrubs with palmi-nerved leaves	Menispermaceæ (p. 147)
B. Ovary syncarpous, or of one carpel only.	
I. Style 0 or 1. Stigma 1 (*vide* also Lauraceæ under III, in which stigmas sometimes scarcely lobed).	
a. Perianth 0.	
Ovaries with disciform stigma crowded on a spadix. Spathe present . .	Arisæma (p.553)
b. Perianth present simple green.	
Sepals 4, or perianth 2-3-toothed. Stigma slender papillose or penicillate. Ovule 1.	Urticaceæ (p. 385)
Sepals 3. Stigma subulate lateral. Ovary and capsule waxy. Ovule 1 . .	Macaranga (p. 232)
Sepals 4-5. Stigma capitate. Ovules few on parietal placentas . . .	Xylosma (p.159)
c. Perianth of calyx and corolla. Ovules few central	Embelia (p.404)
Stigma large 3-lobed vide *stigmas 3*. .	Cucurbitaceæ. (p. 164)
II. Styles, style arms or stigmas 2, sometimes bifid.	
a. Perianth 0, or reduced to a gland. Flowers in spikes or catkins.	
Trees with slender branches and leaves reduced to scales connate in sheaths. Fls. in ovoid heads, bracteate and bracteolate	Casuarina (p.81)
Trees or shrubs. Fls. in long spikes with small hairy bracts, each with a lunate	

fleshy disc. Stigmas 2 sub-sessile lobed, or 4. . . . . . . Salix (p. 402)

Climbing or prostrate herb with cordate leaves and ovaries crowded on fleshy spikes, mixed with peltate bracts . Piper (p. 384)

b. Perianth simple green; or, in Euphorbiaceæ, with green or very minute petals.

1. Ovary 1-celled. Ovule 1 pendulous.

Fls. in spikes. Styles 2, or 1-2-partite. Sepals 4 accrescent in fruit. The Mulberry . . . . . . Morus (p. 392)

Fls. in axillary cymes (often monœcious). Style with two linear arms. Sepals 4-5 . . . . Trema (p. 390)

Fls. peduncled solitary or few together axillary. Style with two long arms. Sepals 4 embracing the ovary . . Streblus (p.392)

2 Ovary 2-celled, or if ovary 1-celled ovules 2 (Antidesma) or several (Xylosma).

Ovary usually 1-celled. Fls. racemed. Stigmas lobed or bifid. . . . Antidesma (p. 225)

Ovary 1-or imperfectly 2-celled. Stigmas capitate. Fls. in short racemes. Sepals 3-5. Ovules on parietal placentas . . . . . . Xylosma (p.159)

Ovary 2-celled. Ovules 1-2 in each cell. Styles often twice-forked, stigmas often dilated and sessile, sometimes 2-lobed . . . . . . Euphorbiaceæ (p. 209)

c. Perianth double, with calyx and corolla. Corolla gamopetalous.

Styles or stigmas 2-4. Ovary cells 4-10, usually 6-8. Ovules 1 in each cell. Trees, sometimes flowering while leafless	Diospyros (p. 408)
III. Styles, style-arms or stigmas 3, sometimes bifid.	
a. Perianth O or small green, sometimes 2-seriate or with very small or green petals. Erect trees or shrubs (or Tragia, a climber).	
Ovary 3-celled or (Phyllanthus) several-celled. Stigmas 3 minute, or styles 3 often bifid, or stigmas simple or 2-lobed. Ovules 1-2 in each cell .	Euphorbiaceæ (p. 209)
Ovary 1-celled, 1-ovuled. L. often aromatic and fls. capitate . .	Lauraceæ (p. 150)
b. Perianth green or white, tepals usually 6 in two series.	
Monocotyledonous climbers, often prickly.	
Shrubby, not twining. Fls. umbelled. Ovary superior	Smilax (p. 518)
Herbaceous or shrubby. Twining. Fls. spicate. Ovary inferior . . .	Dioscorea (p. 528)
c. Calyx and corolla quite distinct. Fls. usually large.	
Dicotyledonous climbers with tendrils and inferior ovary	Cucurbitaceæ (p. 164)
d. Calyx and corolla distinct. Trees with gamopetalous corolla and superior ovary. (*Vide* also supra) . . .	Diospyros (p. 408)
IV. Styles or stigmas 4 or more.	

Vide also above Euphorbiaceæ under II and III. Several Euphorbiaceous genera, *e.g.*, Cyclostemon Bischofia, Trewia Mallotus have occasionally 4 styles or stigmas and a 4-celled ovary, but 2-3-celled ovaries may be found on the same individual. Cucurbitaceæ sometimes have a 4-lobed stigma.

a. Petals O.

Sepals 6, 2 seriate, or embracing the ovary as a tubular calyx. Disc glands O. Styles connate in a knob or column, stigmas very minute. Ovary 3-15-celled. Cells 2-ovuled . . .	Glochidion (p. 217)
Sepals 4-5. Disc-lobes 4-5. Styles 4-6, sometimes 4-11 capitellate small. Ovary 4-8-celled. Small, usually thorny, tree	Flacourtia (p. 159)
b. Petals 4-5, free imbricate, twice as long as the sepals. Stigma of 6-8 spreading papillose rays. Ovary several-celled, usually 6 . . .	Garcinia (p. 177)
c. Corolla gamopetalous. Styles 3-4 short, sometimes lobed or bifid. Ovary 4-10, usually 6-8-celled . . .	Diospyros (p. 408)

LIST OF THE ANGIOSPERMOUS FAMILIES.

LIST OF THE ANGIOSPERMOUS FAMILIES.

THE FLORA.

CLASS FILICINÆ.

[1]THE FERNS.

FAM. 1. CYATHEACEÆ (p. 55.)

1. Alsophila, Brown.

1. A. glabra, *Hook.*

A tree fern usually 10-20 ft. high. Petiole asperous. Rachis almost black-purple. Fronds 1-2-pinnate with pinnæ $1\frac{1}{2}$-$2\frac{1}{2}$ ft. long, pinnules 3-6″ by .5-9″ wide glabrous beneath pinnatifid $\frac{1}{4}$th to $\frac{1}{2}$ the way down. Veins simple or a few bifurcate (Beddome).

Chota Nagpur, *Prain.*

Prain (Bengal Plants) says "a tall tree-fern." I do not recollect any *wild* tree-fern in Chota Nagpur.

FAM. 2. POLYPODIACEÆ (p. 55.)

Stem never tall (unless scandent), usually underground, with the leaves scattered, or in a terminal crown. *Fronds* from simple to decompound. *Sori* usually dorsal, sometimes marginal. *Indusium* present or absent, or sori covered by the recurved leaf margin. *Sporangia* usually long-pedicelled with a vertical annulus, which is incomplete on one side near the pedicel, where it gives place to more transversely elongated but thinner-walled cells (stomium) across which the sporangium ruptures when ripe.

---

[1] Only the more striking ferns are described.

A. Sori roundish ' dorsal. Indusium roundish attached by its centre or a sinus, rarely evanescent, or present in some sori and absent in others.

Indusium kidney-shaped or evanescent. Veins not anastomosing, or only the tips joining those from the next costa . . . . 1. *Nephrodium.*

Indusium peltate. Veins copiously anastomosing 2. *Aspidium.*

B. Sori roundish close to the margin or marginal, not confluent. Indusium present.

Sori sub-apical on the lobes, indusium attached by base and sides . . . . 3. *Odontosoria.*

Sori within the margin, indusium attached by the base only . . . . 4. *Humata.*

C. Sori elongate dorsal, straight or curved. Indusium present.

Sori attached sideways to the fertile veins . . 5. *Asplenium.*

Sori short. Indusium often curved or hook-shaped over the vein . . . . 6. *Athyrium.*

Sori continuous along the rachis of the pinna . 7. *Blechnum.*

D. Sori linear, close to the margin or marginal.

1. Stipes not black and polished.

Sori on a marginal nerve, with a marginal indusium . . . . 8. *Pteris.*

2. Stipes black and polished.

Pinnæ not broadening apically. Sori at the thickened ends of the nerves, sometimes confluent. Leaf-margin recurved . . . . . 9. *Cheilanthes.*

Pinnæ or leaf segments fan-shaped apically) . . . . 10. *Adiantum.*

E. Sori without any indusium, usually sunk in the frond. Stipes articulate to the rhizome . 11. *Polypodium.*

1. Nephrodium, Schott.

Stout ferns with the fronds more or less coriaceous. Fronds 1-2-pinnate, the fertile similar to, or differing from, the barren. Venation quite free, or the veins of one tooth or segment uniting in an intermediate nerve with those of the adjacent segments. Indusium round-cordate, persistent (except in moulmeinense).

1. Veins quite free.
   - Fronds nearly or quite 2-pinnate. Fertile unlike the barren . . . . 1. *cochleatum.*
   - Fronds pinnate and pinnatisect, with narrow falcate segments . . . . . . 2. *falcilobum.*
2. One or more of the veins uniting with those of the next segment or costa.
   - Pinnæ pinnatilobed, lobes oblong . . . 3. *molle.*
   - Pinnæ toothed. *Indusium evanescent* . . 4. *moulmeinense.*

1. N. cochleatum, *Don.*

Barren fronds large, sub-2-pinnate, or pinnate and pinnatisect, old glabrous, reaching $3\frac{1}{2}$ ft. by 15″. Fertile smaller, thickly covered on the somewhat concave under-surface of the pinnules with the brown indusia of the large sori.

On shady banks and near streams, common in Sal forests etc. Singbhum; common on Parasnath (Hazaribagh); and on the Tundi Hills (Manbhum)[1]; Sant. Par.; Fr. *Nov.-Dec.*

Rhizome horizontal stout thickly covered with the old leaf-bases and with large light-brown shining scales at the apex. *Fronds* tufted. *Stipes* up to $1\frac{1}{4}$ft. in barren and 2 ft. in fertile fronds, base scaly and hairy. *Pinnæ* of barren frond 12-17 pairs sub-opp. lanceolate-acuminate, basal not parallel to the others; *pinnules* $\frac{3}{4}$-$1\frac{3}{4}$″ lobed or crenate and distinctly serrate; *sec. rachis* usually with a narrow wing. *Fertile frond* sometimes with long soft brown hairs on the firm round rachis; pinnules $\frac{1}{4}$-1″ serrate.

2. N. falcilobum, *Hook.* Syn. N. calcaratum, var. falciloba, *Bedd.*

A very elegant tufted fern with pinnate tufted fronds about 18″ long, with close linear lanceolate deeply pinnatifid pinnæ, and remarkable for the bract-like appendages on the stipes and also at the base of many of the lower pinnæ.

Along streams in the forest. Fr. *March-April.*

---

[1] *Campbell* under Lastrea Filix-mas.

Caudex erect often projecting considerably above the ground. *Stipes* short almost glabrous. *Pinnæ* about 4½" by ½". *Rachis* and sec. rachis with fine hairs. Lobes oblong-lanceolate or falcate with prominent costæ. *Sori* small, indusium reniform.

3. N. molle, *Desv.*

Fronds tufted oblong-lanceolate 1-3 ft. more or less, softly hairy all over, pinnate. Pinnae caudate cut about half-way down into rounded lobes. Lowest one or two veins of each costa uniting with an intermediate nerve opposite the sinus.

Common near streams. Fr. *Nov.-Dec.*

Stipes long, somewhat rough below. Lowest one or two pairs of *pinnæ* shorter and often deflexed. Costæ strong, veins rather obscure.

4. N. moulmeinense, *Bedd.* Syn. Polypodium multilineatum, *Wall.*

A large fern with the pinnate fronds 3-5½ ft. long arising separately from the underground rhizome. Pinnæ sharply serrate. Easily recognized by the strong parallel costæ, and the regular veins uniting obliquely with an intermediate zig-zag or nearly straight nerve joining their apices.

Damp shady places near rivers, Singbhum. Tundi hills. *Campbell.* Fr. *Nov.-Dec.*

Stipes not scaly. *Pinnæ* attain 12" by 1½", linear-lanceolate caudate, often with a large gland at the base. Pairs of veins 11-16 conjugate, and 5-8 in the serrature on the larger pinnæ, and with a marginal nerve. *Indusium* can only sometimes be found in nearly mature sori.

5. N. aridum, *Don.* Somewhat resembles the last. Fronds attain 5 ft., but the lower surface is hairy, and the pinnæ cut about ⅓rd of the way down, and indusium present.

6. N. truncatum, *Presl.* Has also fronds about 5 ft. Pinnæ cut about half way down and the lobes shallowly crenate. Indusium reniform. Chota Nagpur, *Wood.*

2. Aspidium, Swartz.

Fronds more membranous than in Nephrodium, simple to pinnate. Fertile and barren similar. Venation reticulate with generally free included veinlets in the areoles. Indusium peltate or somewhat reniform.

1. **A. cicutarium,** *Sw.*

A tufted fern with the fronds often $2\frac{1}{2}$-3 ft. by 1 ft. 8″ deltoid, pinnatifid, or pinnate below with the pinnæ deeply pinnatifid, rarely 2-pinnate. Sori at the ends of the free included veinlets. Indusium attached by the center, usually with a sinus.

Shady banks, common. Fr. *Nov.-Jany.*

Stipes deep chestnut brown flattened, with few oblong scales. *Pinnæ* pubescent above and on the nerves beneath, often much produced below pinnatifid with the lobes crenate.

3. Odontosoria, Présl. (*Stenoloma*, Fee.)

Sori quite terminal on the lobes of the frond, the indusium fused at the base and sides to the lobe, and with it forming a terminal cup containing the sporangia. L. several times pinnate with veins forked free. Stipes not articulate to the rhizome.

1. **O. chinensis,** *L.* Syn. Davallia chinensis, *Sw.*; Stenoloma chinensis, *Sw.*

A very beautiful fern with 3-pinnate fronds 2-$3\frac{1}{2}$ ft. long, the pinnules cut into linear-obcuneate forked lobes bearing the sori on their expanded tips.

Along streams in Saranda. Fr. *April.*

Rootstock tufted with shining-brown scales, *stipes* glabrous polished 8-18″; *pinnæ* $2\frac{1}{2}$-4″ distant alt. with the rachis flattened and grooved above. Apex of lobe minutely toothed. The *cups* often geminate.

To the closely allied genus Humata belong two ferns, *viz.*, **H. immersa,** *Wall.* and **H. pulchra.** *Don.* with widely creeping rhizomes and thin 3-pinnate fronds. The indusium is of similar shape to the last, but is not fused at the sides, and the sori are intra-marginal. The segments of the frond in H. immersa are roundly lobed with the lobes crenate above in H. pulchra, the lobes are narrow lanceolate.

5. Asplenium, L.

1. A. esculentum, *Presl.* Syn. Anisogonium esculentum.

A large fern with an erect stout candex and a terminal tuft of 2-pinnate fronds 3-5 ft. long. Veins from the costæ uniting in an intermediate nerve with those from the next costæ. Sori linear, one on each vein. Indusium opening towards the costa, rarely a sorus each side of the vein.

Marshy places, frequent. Fr. *Decr.-Jany.*

Stipes 1-2 ft. more or less 4-angled and grooved, pale with few scales. *Pinnæ* often 1 ft., alternate rather distant. *Pinnules* 1-4″ opp. or alt. linear-lanceolate acuminate sessile with a very truncate or slightly sagittate or auricled base, margin crenate-serrate. Lower surface puberulous. *Sori* $\frac{1}{16}$-$\frac{1}{12}$″ long.

Young fronds eaten.

Allied to this genus is **Athyrium**, to which belongs **A. Felix-femina**, *L.* a common European fern, frequent in damp forests in Chota Nagpur. Fronds lanceolate 2-3-pinnate and pinnatifid. The veins are quite free. The indusia are many of them curved.

7. Blechnum, L.

1. B. orientale, *L.*

A very large fern with simply pinnate fronds up to 4 or 5 ft. long on an erect candex. Pinnæ sessile entire linear-lanceolate caudate with very numerous fine close veins spreading from the mid-rib (rachis) of the pinna. Sporangia in a continuous line both sides of the rachis, with an indusium opening towards it.

Near streams, very common. Fr. *Nov.-Jany.*

8. Pteris, L.

Fronds tufted or not, on an erect or creeping candex 1-pinnate, or pinnate and pinnatifid. Sporangia continuous along the marginal nerve, excluding the tips of the lobes. Indusium marginal. Lowest pinnæ strongly produced on the lower side, with sometimes bipartite secondary depending pinnæ. Veins all free up to the margin, or the lowest uniting with those from the adjacent costæ.

1. **P. biaurita**, *L.* Syn. Campteria biaurita, *Bedd.*

A handsome fern with a rather stout erect caudex and fronds 3-4 ft. long including the stipes. Pinnæ all deeply pinnatifid, lanceolate caudate, lowest pair 2-fid with the basal segment reflexed.

Near watercourses.⁼ Fr. *April-May.*

Stipes 1¼-2¼ ft. naked and polished except at the base. *Pinnæ* 8-11 pairs sub-opp. 8-12″ long by 1½-2″. Lobes oblong entire, veins bifurcate, the lowest uniting with the adjacent ones from the next costa.

2. P. longifolia, *L.* has simply pinnate leaves with simple linear or linear-lanceolate pinnæ. 3. P. pellucida, *Presl.*, has pinnate leaves with the lowest pinnæ usually 2-fid. The veins are free in both.

⁼ To the genus **Cheilanthes**, or *Silver ferns*, belong two species, both common. **C. farinosa**, *Kaulf.* has the leaves quite white beneath. **C. tenuifolia**, *Sw.*, Nanha Dodhari, *S.* is less coriaceous and the leaves green beneath; it is used by the Santals when sickness or disease arises attributable to witchcraft or the Evil Eye.—*Campbell.*

Adiantum lunulatum, *Burn.* Dodhari, *S.* is a maiden-hair fern with simply pinnate leaves and fan-shaped leaflets 1-1½″ diam. on slender black petiolules ¼-¾″ long. A decoction of the root is given in throat affections, *Camp.* Very common.

A. caudatum, *L.* has wiry pinnate fronds often rooting at the tips.

FAM. 3. GLEICHENIACEÆ.

1. Gleichenia, Sm.

Ferns with a creeping rhizome, richly *dichotomously-branched* fronds not tufted on the rhizome, ultimate branching pinnate or pinnatifid. *Proliferous shoots* frequent from the froks. *Veins* free, forked from the base. *Sori* small dorsal, indusium 0. *Sporangia* sub-sessile 2-valved opening across the top. Annulus transverse, or (in the same individual) oblique and extending up each valve.[1]

1. G. linearis, *C. B. Clarke.*

A handsome fern, scandent and widely spreading by means of its often rooting proliferous shoots.

Saranda, near streams, and especially on white clay-schists in open forest, but not common. Fr. *Jany-Feby.*

Fronds coriaceous glaucous beneath with the pinnæ in divaricate pairs at the forks, the ultimate pairs of pinnæ sub-erect 6-9″ long. *Pinnæ* pinnatisect, lobes broadly linear often emarginate to the apex. *Innovations* densely covered with ferruginous hairs.

Fam. 4. SCHIZÆACEÆ.

1. Lygodium, Sw.

Fronds solitary on the rhizome with a *twining rachis* and unlimited growth. *Primary pinnæ* abbreviated ending in a bud-like tip, with one pair of divaricate secondary pinnæ. *Sporangia* in spikes, 2-seriate dorsal on special narrow fertile lobes of the pinnæ, one on each vein embraced, by a supporting indusium, the several indusia imbricate. *Annulus* very small, crown-like.

1. L. flexuosum, *Sw.*

A beautiful climbing fern. Primary pinnæ with the apex hardened and hairy. Sec. pinnae 1-2-pinnate or sympodially dichotomous, or sometimes (always in young plants?) palmate. Fertile pinnules sub-similar to the barren ones, but margins pectinate with the sporangial spikes or lobes.

Common in Sal forests. Fr. *Sept.-Dec.* The fronds are annual in Chota Nagpur, they spring up at the end of May.

[1] The annulus of Gleichenia is always described as equatorial, but it is sometimes very nearly vertical and may touch the short obpyramidal pedicel on the side.

Pinnules often crenate-toothed oblong, linear or lanceolate-oblong minutely serrulate ½-1″ wide with truncate or cordate base. Fertile lobes ⅛-¼″ long.

Fam. 5. MARATTIACEÆ.

1. Angiopteris, Hoffm.

Sporangia dorsal arranged in ellipsoid sori near the ends of the veins, *sessile*, opening by *a fissure* above *without* an annulus. About 7-12 sporangia in each sorus, somewhat laterally compressed by one another. *Indusium* O. Veins free, simple or forked.

1. A. evecta, *Hoffm.*

A magnificent fern with a very stout, short, erect caudex and 2-pinnate fronds 5-10 ft. long. Easily recognized by the stipular appendages at the base of the swollen articulate stipes, and by the swollen bases of the pinnæ.

In deep valleys along streams in Singbhum. Fr. *March-May.*

PHANEROGAMIA

GYMNOSPERMÆ (p. 48).

Class I. Cycadineæ. Fam. Cycadaceæ.

1. Cycas. L.

Woody plants intermediate in appearance between the Ferns and Palms, with an *erect* usually *short* trunk clothed with the hardened bases of the leaves and prophylls, and a crown of *pinnate coriaceous leaves.* Leaves of two kinds, large foliage leaves which appear in pseudo-whorls at intervals of a few months, alternating with similar whorls of scale leaves (prophylls). *Pinnæ* linear, 1-nerved circinnate towards the mid-rib in bud. *Fl.* diœcious. *M.* in large cones with crowded acyclic male sporophylls (stamens) bearing many sporangia (pollen sacs) on the under surface, which are sometimes collected into small sori. *F.* proliferous, the axis growing through the laxly imbricate leaf-like female sporophylls (carpels) which bear 2-several ovules on the margins below the dilated pinnatifid upper half.

1. **C. revoluta,** *Thunb.* Is grown in gardens in Chaibassa. The pinnæ have recurved margins. The male cones have a powerful and somewhat objectionable odour.

Class II. Coniferæ. Fam. Pinaceæ.

1. Pinus, L.

Richly monopodially branched trees with *simple acicular leaves*, one or more on abbreviated shoots in the axils of scale leaves. *M.* & *F.* sporophylls in *cones*, the latter woody in fruit. Ovules 2 at the base of each carpel, inverted.

1. **P. longifolia,** *Roxb.* The long-leaved Pine is grown at Ranchi. Each abbreviated shoot bears 3 leaves about 9″ long.

Class III. Gnetineæ. Fam. Gnetaceæ.

1. Gnetum, L.

Climbing shrubs with opposite broad penninerved leaves and thickened nodes. *Fls.* minute, monœcious or diœcious crowded in panicled spikes in the axils of annular bracts and mixed with dense cellular transparent hairs. *M.* perianth clavate in bud, the *apparently* single stamen breaking through it when ripe on a long filament, and opening by two terminal valves (two stamens). *Fem.* perianth double, inner with 3 filiform teeth, minute, obliquely ovoid ; outer with 3 minute obtuse teeth. *Ovule* 1 erect, with a single integument produced into a style-like tip. *Fruit* drupe-like, the seed enclosed in the fleshy accrescent perianth.

(*N. B.*—The nature of the so-called perianth is doubtful. The inner perianth may be an integument, or of the nature of an arillus as in Taxus, or again it may represent an open ovary.)

1. G. scandens, *Roxb.* Milgandi, *K.*

An immense, dichotomously branched, woody climber with elliptic or somewhat ovate entire leaves 3-8" by 2-4", and annulate spikes in trichotomous panicles, mostly from the old wood.

Kumbia and other valleys in Singbhum, but not common. Fl. *April-May.* Fr. *r. s.*

L. with 6-10 prs. *sec. n.* shortly acuminate. *Petiole* ½". *Fruit* ellipsoid silvery-scaly when young, 1½" long when ripe.

The flowers in this species are sometimes truly *monœcious*, and the female flowers which are in a whorl above the two series of males may be perfect or imperfect.

The flowers in bud are entirely enclosed in the peculiar annular bracts.

The fruit is eaten.

ANGIOSPERMÆ.

Class I. Dicotyledonæ.

Fam. 1. RANUNCULACEÆ.

(Tribe Clematideæ.)

Climbing shrubs with *opposite* compound exstipulate leaves. *Fls.* regular axillary or panicled. *Sepals* usually 4 petaloid, *petals* 0 or many. *St.* many hypogynous with adnate laterally dehiscing anthers. *Carpels* many free, each with 1 pendulous ovule, the styles becoming *feathery* in fruit. *Fr.* of achenes.

Petals O. Petiole or leaf rachis often twining 1. *Clematis.*

Petals 6-12, linear. Rachis ending in a tendril 2. *Naravelia.*

1. Clematis, L.

Sepals erect 1″ or more long. Filaments hairy . 1. *nutans.*
Sepals sub-patent 1″ by ⅓″ . . . . . . *var. patens.*
Sepals spreading under 1″ long. Filaments glabrous 2. *Gouriana.*

1. C. nutans, *Royle.* Bonga ghanti, *S.*

A shrub with pubescent angled branches and odd pinnate or 2-pinnate leaves with sharply, coarsely, doubly-serrate leaflets which are simple or lobed. Terminal leaflet about 2½″ by 1¾″. Fls. large cream coloured usually 5 on axillary leafy branches or panicles.

Singbhum, on hæmatite-schist rocks at 2,500 ft. Hazaribagh at Baragaon.—*Wood.* Common on Parasnath 3—4,000 ft. Kerhang (Lohardugga, 2,500 ft.), *Gamble.* Fl. *Nov.-Jany.*

Larger *leaflets* 5″ ovate with cordate base, smaller ovate-lanceolate. *Buds* oblong acute over 1″ long. *Sepals* 1½″ by ⅓″ with curled tips, silky pubescent.

Var. patens.

Buds ovoid under 1″. Sepals spreading 1″ by ⅓″, 5-7-nerved.

Top of Sundi Buru in Songra forest.

2. C. Gouriana, *Roxb.*

A shrub with adpressed-hairy grooved branches and 2-pinnate leaves and entire ovate acuminate leaflets. White flowers ½-¾″ diam. in pyramidal axillary and terminal panicles.

Very rare. Kundrugutu ravine (Singbhum). Parasnath. Fl. *Oct.-Nov.* Fr. *Dec.-Jany.*

Lflts. 1-3½″ ovate-lanceolate acuminate with cordate base, sometimes with a few distant teeth, nearly glabrous 3-5-nerved, articulate with some silky hairs at the joint. Sep. $\frac{5}{16}$″ ultimately revolute, ciliate.

It is said to abound in an acrid poisonous principle, *Watt.*

2. Naravelia, DC.

1. N. zeylanica, *DC.* Chagal-bate, *Beng.*

A climbing shrub with pubescent or tomentose branches, simply pinnate leaves with a single pair of leaflets, and the end of the rachis converted into a branched tendril. *Fls.* yellowish-green or whitish $\frac{1}{2}$-$\frac{3}{4}$" diam. in axillary and terminal panicles. Petals spreading equal to or shorter than the tomentose sepals.*

Along ravines and nalas in Singbhum, not common. Base of Parasnath, *And.* Fl. *Sept.* *Fr. Dec.*

Lflts. broadly or orbicular-ovate, sub-tomentose beneath, usually with a short cusp or acumination. *Panicles* 3-10". Hairy *styles* 2" in fruit.

Ropes are made from the stems.

Fam. 2. MAGNOLIACEÆ.

1. Michelia, L.

Trees with simple alt. entire leaves, with *convolute stipules* sheathing the bud and leaving a circular scar (resembling that of the figs) on falling off. *Fls.* axillary solitary usually showy, white or yellow. *Perianth-leaves* sub-similar free hypogynous in 3 or more 3-merous series. *Stamens* ∝. Fil. flat with adnate introrse anthers. *Carpels* many free spirally arranged on an elongate axis which is supported on a gynophore, coriaceous and dorsally dehiscent in fruit. Stigma decurrent. *Ovules* 2-12.

1. **M. Champaca,** *L.* Champa, Champaka, *H.* (the M. Champaca of Wood's list appears to be Artabotrys!).

A large tree 60-80 ft. high and 6 ft. girth with rusty-tomentose shoots, oblong-lanceolate or ovate-lanc. long-acuminate leaves attaining 12" by 4", and sweet-scented yellow fls. 2" diam. Fruiting spike of sub-sessile carpels, 3-4" long.

A rare and beautiful tree inhabiting deep valleys cooled by perennial springs, in the Tholokabad and Karampoda forests. Fl. *April-May*. Fr. *July*. Evergreen.

L. softly-tomentose beneath when young, adult rusty-hairy on the 15 prs. strong *sec. nerves* beneath, very reticulate between the sec. n. which are looped within the margin. *Petiole* $\frac{3}{4}$-1". *Peduncle* with 2 coriaceous silky caducous bracts which sheath the young flower-bud and leave an annular scar below it. *Ovules* 10-12, 2-seriate.

An excellent timber, especially suitable for planking, the tree should be carefully tended on working these forests.

Fam. 3. ANONACEÆ.

Trees, or climbing or erect shrubs usually with lanceolate scaleless buds and alt. exstipulate simple entire leaves. *Fls.* often greenish and pendulous, sometimes bright-coloured, perianth-leaves in 3 (rarely 2, in Anona) 3-merous whorls, outermost 'sepals' small. *St.* ∝ with adnate anthers, connective often produced or dilated. *Carpels* few or many, free (connate in Anona) on a rounded torus, usually stalked in fruit and resembling an umbel of distinct fruits, indehiscent, 1 or more seeded. The *ruminate,* often deeply lamellate, *endosperm* of the seeds is very characteristic of this family. Quite small leaves very frequently occur on the twigs below the ordinary-sized ones.

A. St. closely packed with overlapping connectives which conceal the anther-cells.
  1. Outermost perianth series small sepaloid, inner two series "petals" larger sub-similar.
    a. Petals flat without a concave base.
      Ovules many. Fl. (in our species) scarlet. Scandent shrubs . . . . . . 1. *Uvaria.*
      Ovules 1-2. Erect trees. . . . . . 2. *Polyalthia.*
    b. Petals with a concave base which conceal the stamens . . . . 3. *Artabotrys.*
  2. Innermost (3rd) series of perianth leaves very small or obsolete. . . . . . 4. *Anona.*

B. St. loosely imbricate, connectives *not* concealing the anther-cells.
  1. Outer two series of perianth leaves small sepaloid, innermost "petals" larger, petaloid.
      Base of petals not saccate. Ovules 1-2 . . 5. *Miliusa.*
      Base of petals saccate. Ovules 6-many. . . 6. *Saccopetalum.*
  2. Outermost perianth series small sepaloid, inner two series "petals" petaloid. Ovules 4-8 . . . . 7. *Alphonsea.*

1. Uvaria, L.

1. U. Hamiltoni, *H. f. & T.* Selauli, *K.*

A very large woody climber, often with circinate branchlets. Shoots rusty tomentose with ell. or oblong-obovate, finely acuminate strongly-nerved leaves stellately-tomentose beneath and deep scarlet flowers 2″ diam. Ripe carpels ½-1″ oblong tomentose many-seeded on stalks ¾-1″ long.

In damp shady valleys and stony ravines in Singhbhum and the S. P.

Fl. *May-July.* Fr. sometimes persistent till *Dec.* Evergreen.

L. from 3″ by 1¼″ to 12″ by 5¼″ on the same twig, base sub-cordate, sec. *n.* about 18 prs. *Fls.* 1-4 on abbreviated lateral branchlets usually below the leaves.

2. Polyalthia, Blume.

Usually straight growing trees with somewhat distichously-spreading leaves. Fls. often on small tubercles solitary or clustered axillary, extra-axillary, or below the leaves. Sep. 3. Pet. 2-seriate, flat. Carpels indefinite, succulent and 1-seeded in fruit. Ovules 1-2.

Cultivated. Branchlets glabrous. Fls. clustered with lanceolate petals. . . . . 1. *longifolia.*

Branchlets tomentose. Fls. 1-3 axillary with ovate or ovate-oblong petals . . . . 2. *cerasioides.*

Br. pubescent. Fls. 1-2 on small extra-axillary tubercles . . . . 3. *suberosa.*

1. P. longifolia, *Benth.* Deodar, debdar, Asoj, *Vern.*

A straight tree with narrowly-lanceolate glabrous long-acuminate undulate leaves and numerous fascicled green fls. with lanceolate acuminate petals ⅓-½″ long. Frequent in stations. Evergreen. Fls. and new leaves *March-April.*

2. P. cerasioides, *Benth. and Hook. f.* Sande Ome, *K.*; Panjon, *S.*; Kudumi, *H.*

A small tree 20-30 ft. with patent branches, distichous dark-green lanceolate or oblong-lanc. caudate-acuminate leaves 5" by $1\frac{5}{8}$" to $8\frac{1}{2}$" by 3" and usually solitary axillary greenish fls. $\frac{1}{2}$" diam. on bracteate curved pedicels in the axils of the new leaves and from the leaf scars. Fruit an umbel of many slender-stalked bright red globose-oblong fleshy carpels $\frac{1}{3}$" long.

Frequent in the valley forests of Singbhum, esp. of Saranda. Also in Manbhum, *Camp.* and along ravines in the S. P. Fl. *April-May.* Fr. *May-Aug.* Renews leaves *April.*

Mature *leaves* softly hairy on the nerves beneath, somewhat hirsute on midrib above. *Sec. n.* about 10 prs. oblique and arching forward within the margin. *Petiole* $\frac{1}{4}$". Fruiting *peduncles* woody 1-$1\frac{1}{2}$". *Stalks of carpels* $\frac{5}{8}$-$\frac{3}{4}$" somewhat pubescent. *Seed* brown ovoid $\frac{1}{2}$".

Fruit sweet, eaten.

3. **P. suberosa,** *Benth. and Hooker f.* Bara Chali, *Beng.*

Recorded by Gamble (Indian Timbers) from Singbhum with the vern. name of the last. I have met with no *wild* specimens in Ch. Nag. It is a small tree with very corky bark even on the twigs, which are pubescent and lenticellate. L. oblong to obl.-lanc. or oblanceolate-obtuse or shortly suddenly acute $1\frac{1}{2}$-6", base obtuse. Petiole very short. Petals reddish-brown. Fls. *April-May.* Fr. *June-July.* Sometimes cultivated.

Artabotrys odoratissimus, *R. Br.* Champa, *H.*

A large glabrous shrub with sarmentose branches, oblong or lanceolate leaves 2-8" long and solitary or paired green then yellow fls. on hooked or circinate ultimately woody peduncles. Ripe carpels large green or ultimately yellow. Fl. *April-June* and *r. s.*

This is probably the 'shrub' referred to in Wood's list under "Michelia Champaca." It is 'cultivated in gardens and has a heavy Jasmine odour.'

4. Anona, L.

An exotic genus of which species have become naturalized in India. Petals (2nd series of per. l.) triquetrous with concave base. Carpels sub-connate, ultimately confluent into an ovoid or globose syncarpous fruit. Carpels 1-ovuled.

1. **A. squamosa** *L.* Nenwa, Mandal, *K.*; Mandargom, *S.*; Saripha, *H.* The Custard apple.

A shrub or small tree with oblong or oblong-lanceo. leaves, the larger 4″ by $1\frac{1}{4}$″ to 6″ by 2″ acute, obtuse or sub-acuminate, nearly glabrous, pellucid-punctulate and slightly scented. Fls. drooping yellowish-green $\frac{3}{4}$-$1\frac{1}{4}$″ long; petals narrowly-oblong, 3rd series of *tepals* minute or 0. Fruit tubercled.

Completely wild now in the jungles of western Palamau, and on the scrub hills of Hazaribagh and Manbhum. Also run wild over the northern hills of the S. P. according to Gamble. Judging from the native names its introduction must be exceedingly ancient. Fl. *March-May*. Fr. *July-Sept.*

Cultivated largely and is one of the fruits that thrive in Ch. Nag. The root and leaves are used medicinally and are a valuable insecticide.

2. **A. reticulata,** *L.* Gom, *S.*; Bullock's Heart.

L. larger, 5-8″, acuminate glabrous. *Fls.* 2-3 together, innermost *tepals* narrow-oblong. *Fr.* larger, areolate, but not tubercled. Occasionally cultivated.

5. Miliusa, Leschn.

1. **M. velutina,** *H. f. and T.* Ome, *K.*; *S.*; Siarbhuka, *Kharw.*; Dom-sal, Kari, *H.*

A tree sometimes 4-5 ft. girth with large or very large broadly ell. or ovate leaves more or less permanently tomentose beneath and green flowers on very long drooping pedicels in few-fld. extra-axillary scorpioid cymes. Fruiting carpels $\frac{5}{8}$-$\frac{3}{4}$″ ellipsoid downy on short stalks, fruiting pedicels woody over $1\frac{1}{2}$″, often 3-5″.

In valleys throughout the area, rather common in some valley Sal forests.

Fl. *May* with the new leaves. Fr. *June*. Deciduous.

All young parts densely often villosely fulvous tomentose. *L.* $5\frac{1}{2}$″ by 4″ to 10″ by 6″ shortly acuminate, base rounded or cordate; *sec. n.* about 10-12 prs. strong nearly to margin. *Petiole* $\frac{1}{4}$″. *Cymes* 2-7-fld mostly on the new shoots. *Peduncle* 1″ or less. *Pedicels* 2-5″ villous

Sepals $\frac{1}{6}''$-$\frac{1}{5}''$. *Pet.* ovate with revolute margins, $\frac{1}{2}''$ or more, reflexed ultimately black. *Carpels* ∞ and villous, *ovules* 2.

The timber is used for yokes and axles and the fruit is eaten.

6. Saccopetalum. Benn.

(Sometimes united with Miliusa.)

1. S. tomentosum, *H. F. and T.* Ome, ombe, *K.*; *S.* Charra, *S.*; Kari, *Kharw.*; Ione, *Kheria* (*Gangpur*); Kirna, *H.*

A small or mod.-sized tree with softly pubescent or tomentose shoots, and solitary dark-purple flowers on slender pedicels nearly all lateral from the previous year's shoots. Leaves ovate-oblong obtuse or with short blunt acumen, aromatic.

Not very common in Singbhum and usually on the hills, very common in Palamau, found also in all the other districts. Fl. *May-June.* Fr. *June-July.* Deciduous, new leaves in *May* or *June.*

Attains 4-5 ft. girth, bu usually a small tree and frequently flowering as a bush like the last, which , some respects it much resembles, and has been confused with it. The bark and blaze are very similar, but the mature *leaves* rarely exceed 6″, usually $2\frac{1}{4}''$ by 2″ to 6″ by $3\frac{1}{4}''$ with obtuse rounded or sometimes cordate base, pubescent beneath, puberulous or quickly glabrescent between the nerves above; *sec. n.* 5-10 prs. omitting short intermediate ones, looped or branching some distance from the leaf margin. *Inflorescence* very distinct, short peduncles (very rarely on new shoot) with 1, very rarely 2, fls. on pedicels rarely exceeding $1\frac{1}{2}''$, usually much less (exceptional cases up to 3″ in fr.) *Petals* $\frac{1}{2}$-$\frac{5}{8}''$ erect saccate at base, ovate acute with recurved margins. Fr. much as in last.

Wood strong.

7. Alphonsea, H. f. & T.

1. A. ventricosa, *H. F. & T.*

A small (in C. N.) tree branched low down with appressed fulvous-hairy twigs, distichous oblong acuminate leaves 4″ by $1\frac{1}{2}''$ (at base of twig) to $9\frac{1}{2}''$ by $2\frac{3}{4}''$, beautifully polished above. Fls. clustered in brown-velvety sessile leaf-opposed bracteate cymes. Ripe carpels very large yellow tomentose.

Ravines near water in Rajmehal hills, from Narganj to Banjhi, rare. Fl. *Feby.* Fr. (in Br. Bhotan) ripens *Aug.* Evergreen. New shoots *Feby.-March.*

Buds tomentosely hairy. *L.* slightly hairy on the nerves beneath with obtuse or rounded base and 9-14 prs. very fine sec. n. visible both sides. *Petiole* thick $\frac{1}{4}''$ hairy. *Cymes* short and dense from the old wood mostly leaf opposed. *Pedicels* $\frac{1}{3}''$ with a minute ovate bract near the middle. *Calyx* $\frac{1}{6}''$ diam. with 3 broadly ovate brown tomentose lobes. *Petals* $\frac{3}{8}-\frac{7}{16}''$. Outer ovate valvate in bud, tomentose. Inner white ovate-lanceolate sub-erect acute with saccate base, brown pubescent. St. in 4 spirals, fil. very short broad, connective slightly produced, anth. cells extrose. *Carpels* 8 tomentose close elongate with about 15 ovules on the ventral suture. Stigma capitate.

If this is really the same as the tall tree of eastern Bengal, the fruiting carpels (which I have not seen in the S. P.) attain $2\frac{1}{2}''$ and resemble small tomentose yellow mangoes.

Fam. 4. MENISPERMACEÆ.

Climbing herbs or shrubs with alt. exstipulate *palminerved* simple leaves with lobed or usually quite entire margin. *Fls.* minute diœcious 3-5-merous in cymes or racemes. *St.* as many as petals, opp. to them, embraced by the petals, or anthers connate in a ring round the top of a column. *F. fl.*, carpels 1-6, when ripe drupaceous with usually a very characteristic *seed* and *endocarp*, the latter being generally a horse-shoe shaped, often thickened and tubercled tube containing the seed, curved round a solid depressed center.

M. fl. 4-merous. F. perianth leaves 2. Carpel 1 . . 1. *Cissampelos.*
M. sep. 6-10. pet. 3-5. F. sep. and pet, 3-5 Carpel 1 . 2. *Stephania.*
Sep. 6, petals 6, stamens 6.
  Pubescent. Carpels 3-6 . . . . . 3. *Cocculus.*
  Glabrous. Carpels 1-3 . . . . . 4. *Tinospora.*
  Glabrous. Carpels 9-12 . . . . . 5. *Tiliacora.*

1. Cissampelos, L.

1. C. Pareira, *L.* Pitu sing, Ranu-red, *K.*; Tejo mala, *S.*; Akanadi, *H.*, *Beng.*

A slender climber with usually peltate deltoid or broad-ovate leaves $1\frac{3}{4}''$ by $2''$ to $3\frac{1}{2}''$ by $3\frac{1}{2}''$ with 5-6 basal nerves. M.fl. in axillary corymbose often panicled cymes. F.fl. clustered in racemes in the axils of large leafy bracts.

Frequent throughout the area, esp. in open and rocky valleys. Shoots usually annual. Fl. *June-Oct.* Fr. *Nov.-Jany.*

L. obtuse, retuse or mucronate with straight or shallow-cordate base, somewhat glaucous and pubescent beneath or both sides. *Peti.* $1\text{-}3\frac{1}{4}''$. *M.fl.* minute whitish $\frac{1}{16}''$ diam. in densely hairy cymes in the axils of foliaceous bracts on slender shoots or 2-chotomously cymose on the capillary $\frac{3}{4}\text{-}1''$ long branches of axillary panicles. *Sep.* orbicular, *Corolla* cupular or peltate. *Anths.* sessile on a short column, *F. bracts* large reniform or orbicular. *Drupe* orange or scarlet, stone $\frac{3}{16}''$ long.

The plant has a long slender cylindric rhizome under $\frac{1}{2}''$ diam., often branched, this is used in the fermentation of rice beer [Ili], and in combination with Ruellia forms the "Ili-rann" of the Kols. The Santals give the root in diarrhœa and other complaints, *Camp.* Pelosine, a preparation of alkaloids derived from it, is an imperfect substitute for quinine; the Pareira root of the Pharmacopœia is an allied Brazilian plant.

Stephania hernandifolia, *Walp.* Akanadi, *Beng.*

Is a slender climber with somewhat peltate ovate or sub-deltoid leaves and capitate umbels. Anths. 6 on the column. Hedges and thickets, *Prain.* I have not seen it in C. N.

3. Cocculus, D.C.

1. C. villosus *D.C.*

A slender villosely tomentose climbing shrub with deltoid to ovate-oblong obtuse leaves attaining $3''$ by $2''$, smaller upwards and oblong on the flowering branches, and axillary short-peduncled small capitate cymes of minute greenish M.fls. $\frac{1}{10}''$ diam. F. peduncles 1-2-fld. Druplets dark-purple, compressed.

Very common over prickly bushes in the Sone valley, Palamau, and extending through Hazaribagh and the S. P., but scarcer. Manbhum, *Camp.* Fl. *Nov.-Feby.* Fr. *April.*

L. sometimes with large coarse teeth or triangular obtuse or acute lobes, old hairy beneath. *Peti.* $\frac{1}{12}$-$\frac{1}{2}$. *Petals* bifid. with 2 inflexed lateral auricles embracing the base of the stamens in the M., minute *staminodes* in the F. *Carpels* 3 glabrous.

Tinospora cordifolia, *Miers.* Gurach, *H.*; Gulencha, *Beng.*, is a climbing shrub with succulent corky stems, entire cordate leaves and yellow fls. in racemes longer than the leaves. It sends down numerous fleshy rootlets from the branches. Prain says "in hedges and thickets everywhere" but I have no record from C. N. nor can I find any either at Calcutta or Kew.

5. Tiliacora, Colebr.

1. T. racemosa, *Colebr.* Tiliakoru, *Beng.*

A large woody climber with striated bark and broadly ovate to ovate-lanceolate glabrous leaves $3\frac{1}{2}$-6″ long by $1\frac{1}{2}$-$3\frac{3}{4}$″. Fls. yellow in axillary racemes or panicles, females sub-solitary on the branches, males usually 3-7 together. Carpels about 10. Drupes reddish obovate laterally sub-compressed $\frac{1}{3}$″ long with a hard narrowly horse-shoe shaped putamen enclosing a bony plate.

Rajmehal Hills (Barhait) but not common. Fl. *May-June.* Fr. *r. s.*

L. shining, base rounded or sub-cordate, *sec. n.* raised beneath slender from near the base and decurrent on the mid-rib, finely reticulate between. *Petiole* articulate at the base $\frac{1}{2}$-1″ long. *Fem. racemes* 1-$2\frac{1}{2}$ long pubescent, *males* longer. *Fls.* 3-4-bracteolate with 3 imbricate and 3 valvate sepals and 6 small fleshy quadrate or cuneate petals. *Albumen* ruminate.

Fam. 5. BERBERIDACEÆ.

1. Berberis, L.

Shrubs with pinnate, or mostly dimorphic *leaves,* those on main branches converted into 3-5-partite spines bearing in their axils abbreviated branchlets with simple fascicled coriaceous leaves. *Fls.* yellow, solitary fascicled or racemed, with 2-3 appressed bracts. *Sep.* 3+3. *Pet* 3+3. *St.* 6 opp. the petals, anths. opening by 2 valves. *Carpel* 1 with a peltate stigma. *Ovules* few erect basal. Fr. a few-seeded berry.

1. B. asiatica, *Roxb.*

A very pretty shrub with the spines small 1-5-partite, and coriaceous entire or spinous toothed leaves 1-3″. Fls. $\frac{1}{4}$-$\frac{1}{3}$″ in short corymbose racemes. Berry purple-blue with a glaucous bloom $\frac{1}{3}$″.

Parasnath 4,000 ft. Fl., *Feby-April.* Fr. *May-June.* Evergreen.

Berries sometimes eaten. They are laxative.

Fam. 6. LAURACEÆ.

Trees (or, in Cassytha, a parasitic climber) with alt. rarely (*e.g.* Beilschmiedia) opp. or sub-opp. entire *leaves,* frequently clustered at the ends of the branchlets and with a characteristic aromatic smell, frequently gland dotted, ex-stipulate. *Fls.* usually small, greenish, regular, 1-2-sexual. *Sepals* and *petals* usually 3 each, sub-similar, usually connate into a 6-cleft perianth, or perianth lobes 5, occasionally rudimentary or 0. *St.* in 2-4 3-merous whorls, usually 3 whorls of stamens and one whorl of staminodes, more or less perigynous, inner fil. often 2-glandular at the base. Anths. opening by 2-4 deciduous lids. *Ovary* 3-carpellary 1-celled with one pendulous anatropous ovule. Stigma usually 3-lobed. *Fr.* a one seeded berry or drupe, often surrounded more or less by the swollen hypanthium. Albumen 0. Testa very thin.

The Laurels (though not well exemplified in C. N. species) have usually a very characteristic method of branching, only one or two of the axillary buds from the crowded leaves develops into a slender green shoot bare of leaves at the base.

Trees. Perfect *st.* 9-12, anthers 2-celled, innermost whorl extrorse.

L. alt. and opp., Perianth quite deciduous in fruit . . . . 1. *Beilschmiedia.*

Trees. Perfect st. 6-12, anthers 4-celled, all introrse.
L. usually sub-verticillate. Fl. bracts densely imbricate . . . . 2. *Actinodaphne.*
L. usually alt. scattered. Bracts forming a whorled involucre . . . . . . 3. *Litsæa.*
A leafless twining parasite . . . . . . 4. *Cassytha.*

1. Beilschmiedia, Nees.

L. penninerved, opp. or alt. Fls. usually panicled and 2-sexual. Perianth tube short. Filaments of innermost series of perfect st. 2-glandular at base with extrorse anthers, one whorl of ovoid or cordate staminodes. Fruit from globose to very narrowly oblong or obovoid unsupported by the perianth.

1. B. Roxburghiana, *Nees.* Syn, B. fagifolia, *Nees.*

B. fagifolia. *Nees,* is included in B. Roxburghiana by Brandis, working no doubt on a large series of specimens. The two following varieties however look so like distinct species that they are separately described.

Var. **fagifolia,** *Nees.* (sp.) Katea-Ratam, *K.*

A large tree attaining 6 ft. girth with rather smooth light bark, linear-oblong or oblong-lanceolate obtuse or slightly acuminate leaves 3″ by $\frac{5}{8}$″ to 6″ by 1$\frac{3}{4}$″. Fls. in short cymes $\frac{1}{2}$-$\frac{3}{4}$″ long from the leaf-scars. Fr. 1-1$\frac{1}{3}$″ long narrowly oblong-obovoid purple-black.

Along rivers on the Porahat plateau (e.g. Saikata R.), rare. Fl. *March* when nearly leafless. Fr. ripens *May*. Nearly evergreen.

L. tapering at the base, *sec. n.* 6-12 prs., intermediate very reticulate and fine, raised both sides. *Petiole* $\frac{1}{3}$-$\frac{3}{4}$″. *Per. lobes* $\frac{1}{3}$-$\frac{1}{6}$″ linear-oblong. *Perfect st.* in 3 or 4 series, usually 12, *staminodes* about 8 white fleshy sometimes, 2-seriate. *Testa* rather coriaceous.

It is said to be a good timber.

Var. **Dalzellii,** *Meissn.* (Sp.)

A small tree with green branches, alt. and sub-opposite shining ell.-oblong or narrow elliptic gland-dotted leaves 5″ by 1$\frac{3}{4}$″ to 9 by 3″, narrowed both ends, but scarcely acuminate.

Along streams in the S. P. Fl. and Fr. not seen.

Sec. n. distant about 7 prs., tertiaries obscure until the leaf is dried, when they stand out both sides as very fine reticulations as in the last, midrib strong. *Petiole* $\frac{3}{4}''$ puberulous above and buds shortly pubescent. It greatly resembles B. assamica, *Meissn.* in leaf and can only be distinguished in the absence of inflorescence by its short, pubescent buds, while the former has lanceolate glabrous ones.

2. Actinodaphne, Nees.

1. A. angustifolia, *Nees.*

A mod.-sized tree with large subverticillate elliptic-lanceolate to oblanceolate leaves glaucous beneath and shining above. Fls. $\frac{1}{6}''$ diam. diœcious in silky crowded shortly-peduncled umbels below the leaf-whorls. Fr. $\frac{1}{4}$-$\frac{1}{3}''$ diam. globose seated on the cup-shaped swollen perianth tube.

Valeys, esp. in the Saranda tract of Singbhum, not common.

Fl. *Aug.* Fr. *Nov.-Dec.* Evergreen.

Shoots tomentose. L. 5″-12″ by $1\frac{1}{4}$-$2\frac{1}{2}''$ acuminate with 4-10 prs. very oblique sec. n., the intermediate venation very obscure. *Petiole* $\frac{1}{3}$-$\frac{3}{4}''$.

3. Litsæa, Lamk.

L. nearly always scattered and alternate. Fls. several in an umbel surrounded by an involucre of 4-6 concave sepal-like bracts, umbels pedicelled, again umbelled, or racemed or fascicled, axillary or from leaf or bract scars. Perianth lobes usually 6 but sometimes very incomplete or absent, base or tube sometimes greatly enlarged in fruit. Filaments of the 3rd (and 4th, if present) whorl of stamens 2-glandular.

I. Perianth segments incomplete or rudimentary.
  Umbels clustered or corymbose, rarely racemose . 1. *sebifera.*

II. Perianth segments well-developed.
  Umbels clustered or corymbose. Per. base not much enlarged in fruit, tertiary nerves of L. strong parallel . . . . 2. *polyantha.*
  Umbels racemed. Fr. invested by the enlarged perianth . . . . 3. *nitida.*

1. L. sebifera, *Pers.* Chiur, *Kharw.* Medh, menda, *H.*

A small tree with tomentose shoots, narrowly to broadly elliptic rarely ovate leaves quickly glabrescent except sometimes on the nerves, slender petiole, umbels with pedicels $\frac{1}{4}$-$\frac{1}{3}''$ long usually corymbose on slender peduncles, sometimes few on short peduncles. Fruit black shining globose $\frac{1}{3}''$ diam. on the slightly enlarged perianth tube.

In valleys throughout the area but nowhere common, also on the cool aspects of hills. Fl. *June-July.* Fr. ripe *Oct.-Nov.* Evergreen. New shoots appear in May.

L. $3\frac{1}{2}''$ by $1\frac{3}{4}''$ to $8\frac{1}{2}''$ by $4''$ pale beneath usually acuminate, sometimes obtuse, base usually cuneate ; *sec. n.* 8-10 prs. rather strong with numerous very fine cross-nervules *Petioles* $\frac{3}{4}$-$2.''$ *Receptacle* and filaments densely softly hairy or villous. St. 12-15. This laurel is often scarcely aromatic and the glands very inconspicuous.

There are two forms or varieties :—

Var. *α L.* under $6''$ quickly glabrous beneath, peduncles of the corymbs $\frac{1}{4}$-$\frac{1}{3}''$ only with few umbels (sometimes only 1 or 2). Manbhum and Hazaribagh.

Var. *β.* glabraria, *J. D. H.* Leaves attaining $8\frac{1}{2}''$ more or less tomentose beneath until the fruit is ripe. *Peduncles* attain $1\frac{1}{2}''$ often with numerous umbels.

The usual form in Singbhum.

The wood is said to be durable and not attacked by insects but the tree in C. N. is usually too small to yield timber.

2. L. polyantha, *Juss.* Pojo, *S., K.* ; Kukur chita, *Beng.*; Baglal, *Mal Paharia.*

A small tree with brown-pubescent branchlets, strongly-nerved ell.-or oblanceo.-oblong obtuse or sub-acute leaves $4\frac{1}{2}''$ by $2''$ to $9''$ by $4''$ and tomentose stout-pedicelled umbels clustered along the branchlets and axillary. Fr. ellipsoid or ovoid $\frac{1}{4}$-$\frac{1}{3}''$ long, seated on the shallow saucer-shaped perianth base which is $\frac{1}{8}$-$\frac{1}{6}''$ diam.

In valleys chiefly along streams, throughout the area but nowhere common.

Fl. *April-May.* Fr. *July-Aug.* Evergreen. The leaves are renewed in *May.*

L. pubescent and glaucous beneath with 7-12 prs. strong sec. n. and raised parallel cross nervules. *Umbels* 2-several in a cluster sometimes or a very short common peduncle, 5-6-fld. *Special peduncle* in F. $\frac{1}{8}$—$\frac{1}{3}$ and fruiting pedicels $\frac{1}{4}$-$\frac{3}{4}$". *Sepals* usually 5 linear-oblong nearly free. *St.* 9-13, fil. hairy, reduced to 2-glandular staminodes in the F fl.

The powdered bark is applied to bruises of the body and to fractures in animals. The seeds yield an oil which is used medicinally, *Campbell.*

3. L. nitida, *Roxb.*

A straight small or mod.-sized glabrous tree branched low down with large shining oblong to oblanceolate leaves 12 by 3$\frac{1}{2}$", and long slender-pedicelled umbels in axillary racemes. Fr. $\frac{1}{2}$" red when ripe, invested by the enlarged fleshy perianth.

Deep valleys in the Saranda forests, Singbhum. Fl. *June.* Fr. *Sept.-Oct.* - Evergreen.

A very distinct and handsome tree. Branchlets 5-angled glossy as are the leaves. Nervation faint. Petiole stout $\frac{3}{4}$-1". M. racemes 1-4". F. $\frac{1}{2}$-2". Pedicels $\frac{3}{4}$".

Fls. about 4 in an umbel. *Peranth tube* and *filaments* tawny pubescent. *Tepals* unequal glabrous very glandular.

It is said to be a useful timber tree in Silhet.

4. Cassytha, L.

1. C. filiformis, *L.* Alag Jari, *S.*; Akasbel, *Beng* Amarbel, *H.*

A filiform leafless parasite attaching itself by means of haustoria to Sal, Carissa and other bushes, resembling Cuscuta but much greener. Fls. sessile $\frac{1}{12}$" white, with 3 broad, ovate imbricating bracts at base, in spikes $\frac{1}{2}$-1$\frac{1}{2}$" long.

Singbhum, Hazaribagh, Manbhum (along Barakha R.) and probably in other districts, locally abundant esp. near Chorparan in Hazaribagh chiefly on Carissa, Holarrhena, Zizyphus and Sal. Fl., Fr. most of the year, esp. *Sept.-Dec.*

Stems pubescent or glabrous. *Spikes* pubescent from the axils of scale-leaves. Outer *perianth lobes* small orbicular ciliate, inner oblong glabrous valvate. *St.* 3-seriate. First series petaloid with 2-cells adnate to linear face; second series smaller similar dilated below; third series hastate with 2 glands on the very short filament. *Staminodes* 3 fleshy. *Ovary* tapering to a minute capitellate stigma. Berry ¼″ enclosed by the inner perianth.

Fam. 7. PAPAVERACEÆ.

Herbs with milky juice. *Fl.* reg. *Sep.* 2 (or 3), *Pet.* 2+2 (or 3+3). *Ovary* 1-celled with 2-several parietal often lamellate placentæ. Stigmas radiating often connate.

Argemone mexicana, *L.* Sial Kanta, *Beng.* is a prickly thistle-like herb with yellow juice, sinuate pinnatifid green and white leaves and bright yellow flowers. Capsule opening at the top by small valves.

Naturalized and very common in waste ground. Fl. *Feby-June.*

Papaver somniferum, *L.* Aphim, *H.* The Opium Poppy. Fls. large usually white. Cultivated in Hazaribagh, but cultivation recently discontinued under the scheme for the reduction of Opium export.

Fam. 8. CRUCIFERÆ.

Herbs. *Fls.* racemed. *Sep.* 2+2. *Pet.* 4. St. 6, 4 inner longer in opp. pairs. *Ovary* 2-carpellary and usually 2-celled by a thin *placental membrane.* Ovules 2-seriate on parietal placentæ on the edges of the membrane.

Brassica Napus, *L.* var. dichotoma. Mani, *K.* and **B. campestris,** *L.* var. Sarson, *Prain.* Mustard.

Are largely cultivated, and form fields of a beautiful yellow in the cold weather.

The former is rather glaucous. *L.* radical and lower cauline lyrate pinnatifid 3″. *Sep.* erect or erecto-patent. *Corolla* pale-yellow under ½″ diam. *Pods* 1½″ excluding the ½″ seedless beak, erect on pedicels ¾″, glabrous.

The latter is a stouter plant with larger and hairy leaves and deeper yellow fls. (For vars. *vide* Prain in "Bengal Plants").

Fam. 9. CAPPARIDACEÆ.

Herbs, shrubs or trees, sometimes climbing by means of stipulary thorns, stipules sometimes 0. *L.* simple or digitate.

Fls. solitary umbelled or racemed, sometimes in extra-axillary vertical rows. *Sep.* 4. *Pet.* 4, hypogynous or on a large disc. *St.* 4-∞ sometimes on a gonophore. *Ovary* sessile, or more frequently on a *gonophore* or *gynophore* which may become long and woody in fruit, 1-celled with 2-4 parietal placentæ and numerous campylotropous ovules. *Style* short or 0, stigma depressed or capitate. *Fr.* capsular or baccate. Seeds exalbuminous, embryo incurved often spiral.

Trees or shrubs
- L. 3-foliolate. St. adnate to the base of the gynophore . . . . 1. *Cratæva.*
- L. simple. St. on torus at the base of the long gynophore . . . . 2. *Capparis.*

Herbs
- Gonophore 0 . . . . 3. *Cleome.*
- Gonophore conspicuous . . . . . . 4. *Gynandropsis.*

1. Cratæva, L.

1. C. religiosa, *Forst.* Barun, Varuna, *H.*, *Beng.*

A small tree very handsome in flower with 3-fol. leaves and greenish-yellow or white flowers in terminal corymbs 5-7″ diam.

Along streams in Singbhum, *e.g.* along Koina R. near Salai, very rare. Panchet in Manbhum, *Camp.* Fl. with the new foliage in *March* and *April.* Deciduous.

Twigs with white lenticels. *Lflts.* ovate-lanceolate or lanceolate, gradually acuminate, pale beneath, about $4\frac{1}{2}$″ by $1\frac{5}{8}$.″ *Petals* 1-$1\frac{1}{4}$″ with slender claws. *Gynophore* 2″ or more. *Fr.* a yellow berry 1″ diam.

Sometimes cultivated in gardens, *e.g.* the Mission compound in Chaibassa.

2. Capparis, L.

Trees or shrubs. *L.* simple often with stipulary thorns. Petals not clawed. *St.* at base of the long gynophore. Ovary 1-celled (in C. N. species.) Fruit baccate, but often hard. Seeds many, cotyledons spirally rolled.

1. C. horrida, *L.f.* Gaterna, *K.*; Buru asaria, *S.*; Bagnahim, *Kharw.*; Bagnai. *Beng.*

A shrub sarmentose or climbing by means of its recurved thorns densely brown tomentose on the innovations, with usually ovate leaves 2·3″ long and white fls. 1½-2″ diam. Fls. sub-solitary or in vertical lines above the leaf-axils, but as the leaves are often undeveloped at the time of flowering they may appear panicled. Berry ellipsoid 1½″ scarlet when ripe.

Chiefly along rocky nalas. Singbhum, Manbhum, Ranchi, Palamau (common). Fl. *March-April* with the new shoots. Fr. ripens *Sept.-Oct. Calyx* brown or purple *Filaments* and *petals* turning pink or purple with age. Gynophore often 2″ in fruit.

2. C. sepiaria, *L.* Kaliakara, *Beng.*

A large erect or straggling bush (a rather extensive wiry climber, *Prain*) with grey tomentose branches, sharp curved stipulary thorns, ell. oblong or obovate leaves ½-1¾″ long and small white flowers ¼″ diam. umbellate at the ends of the branchlets.

Palamau, chiefly in the dry scrubby zone near the Soane. Fl. *Nov.-Dec. L.* tomentose when young, old slightly pubescent, somewhat narrowed at the obtuse or retuse tip, base obtuse or rounded. *Petiole* ⅛″. *Pedicels* ½-½″ slender from the uppermost axils and in terminal umbels. *Fr.* black pisiform *F.B.I.*, only 1-seeded according to Roxburgh!

Three very common herbs of this family may be found flowering in the rains, they are all called "Chamani" by the Kols.

They are **Cleome monophylla,** *L.* with simple leaves; **Cleome viscosa,** *L.* with digitate leaves and yellow fls. with 12-20 st.; and **Gynandropsis pentaphylla,** *D.C.* with digitate leaves and pale purple fls. with 6 stamens.

Fam. 10. BIXACÆ.

Trees or shrubs with alt. simple or digitate leaves with minute or 0 stipules. *Fls.* reg. small and apetalous or large and showy, 1-2-sexual. *Sep.* 4-5 deciduous. *Pet.* 4-5 or

0 imbricate or contorted in bud. *St.* hypogynous, anths. with slits or pores. *Disc* hypogynous. *Ovary* of 2-several carpels 1-celled with parietal placentæ, which rarely form by intrusion an incompletely 2-8-celled ovary. Styles free or united. Ovules several or many. *Fr.* baccate or capsular, sometimes hairy, with fleshy albumen. Embryo with foliaceous cotyledons.

L. palmately-lobed. Fl. large yellow . . . . 1. *Cochlospermum.*
L. simple.
  Fls. 2″ diam. Fr. capsular covered with soft spines . . . . 2. *Bixa.*
  Fls. apetalous, small. Ovary 2-8-celled . 3. *Flacourtia.*
  Fls. apetalous small. Ovary 1-celled, or imperfectly 2-celled . . . . . . 4. *Xylosma.*

1. Cochlospermum, Kunth.

1. C. Gossypium, *DC.* Hupu, *K.*; Hopo, *S.*; Galgal, *H.*; Sisibaha *Vern.* (Wood).

A small straight very soft-wooded tree with palmately 3-5-lobed leaves 3-8″ diam. and bearing when leafless large handsome yellow flowers 4-5″ diam. which are succeeded by large pear-shaped pendulous fruits.

On dry hills throughout the area, rare in the S. P. Fl. *Jany.-March.* Fr. *March-June.* Deciduous *Nov.-May.*

L. tomentose beneath when young, shining above. *Petioles* 2-8.″ *Stipules* linear caducous. *Fls.* in few fld. terminal panicles. *Pet.* emarginate. *Capsules* 3-4″ by 2½″, 5-celled at the base, the coriaceous epicarp and papery endocarp dehisce on different lines. *Seeds* many large reniform densely cottony.

It yields a gum and a fibre. The wood is used for torches.

Bixa Orellana, *L.* Latkan, *H.*, *Beng.*

A small tree with cordate leaves and white and rose coloured flowers 1-2″ diam. Often cultivated in gardens. Fl., Fr. *r.s.*

3. Flacourtia, Commers.

1. **F. Ramontchi,** *L'Herit.* Merhle, *K.*; Merlec,' *S.*; Kanter, *S.*; Katai, *H.*, *Beng.*

A tree or shrub, usually thorny, with crenate-serrate often olive-green leaves and yellowish-green fls. $\frac{1}{4}''$ diam. either clustered or racemed or some also solitary in the axils of scales or leaves. Pedicels articulate below the middle. Sep. 4-6 pubescent or hirsute $\frac{1}{16}$-$\frac{1}{12}''$ in the M. very early disclosing the yellow stamens. Disc-lobes 4-6 rounded often lobulate. Styles usually 4-6 small capitellate. Ovules 2 superposed in each cell. Fruit a berry $\frac{1}{3}$-$\frac{1}{2}''$ diam. with as many pyrenes as seeds.

Very common throughout the area both in the valleys and on the hills, and in second growth forest. *Fl. Decr.-March.* Fr. ripens *April-May.* Deciduous just before flowering, but the new shoots appear with or, in some cases, a little later than the flowers.

The fruit is very palatable.

The following forms look very distinct:—

α (Var. sapida *F.B.I.*?, the racemes are pubescent.) Small tree or shrub, young twigs slender reddish pubescent. *L.* $2\frac{1}{4}''$ by $1\frac{1}{2}''$ oblong to obovate, glabrescent. *Sec. n.* 3-5 prs. *Petiole* $\frac{1}{3}''$, pubescent. Hills.

β. (Var. occidentalis *F.B.I.*) Similar but leaves often orbicular and permanently pubescent or tomentose beneath. Usually very thorny and shrubby. Hills.

γ. (Var. latifolia *F.B.I.*?). A tree. *L.* often 5 by $2\frac{3}{4}''$ ovate or ovate-lanceolate or narrow-ellip. acuminate, old glabrous except on mid-rib beneath. Mature twigs and petioles pubescent. *Sec. n.* 1-2 prs. from the base and 4-5 prs. above the base. Valleys. One specimen in Gangpur 4-5 ft. girth with leaves 3-6″ long and fr. $\frac{5}{8}''$ diam.

4. Xylosma, Fors.

1. **X. longifolium,** *Clos.* Dandal, Katai; Katari, *H.*

A small glabrous tree, often with long thorns when young, with lanceolate acuminate shallowly toothed leaves 3-6″ long and small greenish fls. in short axillary compound racemes. Ovary imperfectly 2-3-celled (or 1-celled according to works consulted).[1] A pretty tree in fruit with innumerable deep-red globose berries $\frac{1}{4}''$ diam. on pedicels $\frac{1}{6}$-$\frac{1}{4}''$ long, articulate near the base.

Ravines and along nalas, Singbhum (Tuia gara, Banskatta ravine, etc.); Kochang, *Gamble*. Fl. *Nov.-Dec.* Fr. ripens *April*. Evergreen. Renews leaves *Nov.*

L. narrowed both ends with 6-8 prs. oblique sec. n.; young somewhat gland-serrate. Petiole $\frac{1}{4}$-$\frac{1}{3}''$. M. *racemes* dense $\frac{1}{3}''$-1'' compound, fls. with 10 fleshy red disc glands and about 26 stamens. *Bracts* linear-oblong (ovate-acum. *FBI.*) *Stigmas* 2 small capitate (or stigma capitate *F.B.I.*) *Ovules* few parietal. *Berry* with coriaceous pericarp and about 6-angled seeds, seated on the persistent calyx and disc.

Fam 11. SAMYDACEÆ.

Trees or shrubs with alt. often distichous simple leaves with small deciduous stipules, and often minutely punctate beneath. *Flowers* small greenish-yellow or white in axillary fascicles, racemes or panicles. *Calyx-tube* hypogynous or perigynous with 3-7 lobes. *Petals* as many or 0 imbricate. *St.* definite or indefinite, sometimes with interposed staminodes, free or united. *Ovary* superior or half-superior 1-celled; style 1, capitate or 3-lobed, or styles 3-5. Ovules several, placentation parietal. Seeds few to many on the median lines of the 2-5 valves of a loculicidal often succulent *capsule*.

Fls. fascicled, petals 0 . . . . . 1. *Casearia.*
Fls. panicled, petals present . . . 2. *Homalium.*

1. Casearia, Jacq.

Trees or shrubs. *L.* distichous. Pedicels short, jointed. Calyx inferior, deeply 4-5-lobed; persistent. St. 6-10

---

[1] Flacourtia and Xylosma appear to me to be scarcely separable as distinct genera. The one style of Xylosma is sometimes so short that the stigmas appear distinct.

united into a tube with small petaloid staminodes or nearly free, hypogynous or sub-perigynous. Anthers introrse. Stigma capitate or 3-lobed. Capsule succulent, ellipsoid. Seeds many, with a fleshy usually scarlet aril and straight embryo.

L. oblong, more or less tomentose . . 1. *tomentosa.*
L. elliptic, glabrous . . . . . 2. *graveolens.*

1. **C. tomentosa,** *Roxb.* Rore, *K.*; Chorcho, *S.*; Churchu, *H.*; Beri, *Kharw.*; Maun, *Beng.*

A small tree, or flowering as a shrub, with pubescent or tomentose twigs, leaves oblong or the smaller ones somewhat ovate or elliptic, pubescent especially on the ribs beneath. Fls. axillary on the new shoots $\frac{1}{4}''$ diam. green. Capsules soft green axillary and from leafless axils oblong 6-angular.

Very common especially in waste ground in river valleys. Fl. *March-May.* Fr. *April-May.* Sub-deciduous *Feb.-March.* L. turn red before falling.

L. from 2″ at base of twigs to 7″ by 2″, obtuse entire or crenate. *Stipules* caducous, *petioles* $\frac{1}{3}$-$\frac{1}{2}''$. *Sepals* usually 5. *St.* 6-10 alternating with fleshy pubescent staminodes; tube short. *Fr.* $\frac{3}{4}$-$1\frac{1}{4}''$. *Seeds* with a scarlet aril. There are often 2-3 cymes together on peduncles $\frac{1}{3}''$ long.

The fruits pounded with mud are thrown into dammed up streams for killing fish. Campbell says that the pounded bark is applied externally in dropsy, fever and snakebite.

2. **C. graveolens,** *Dalz.* Syn. C. glomerata, *Roxb.* (according to Brandis) Reri, *K.*; Nuri, *S.*; Chilla, *H.* Benchu, *Koderma.*

A small tree with ell. or ell.-oblong or -ovate glabrous leaves. Fls. greenish in dense clusters from the leafless axils Frts. broadly ellipsoid $\frac{5}{8}$-$\frac{3}{4}''$ long obtuse yellow.

Common in the valleys. Fr. *May-June.* Fr. *May-July.* The tree is nearly or quite leafless at the time of flowering, the new leaves appear on the barren branches about the same time but not till later on the flowering branches. Old leaves turn copper-coloured in January.

Twigs glabrous. *L.* 4-8″ by 2-$3\frac{1}{2}''$ with often smaller ones at base of the twig, very shortly acuminate entire or crenate, usually rounded at the base. Petiole $\frac{1}{4}$-$\frac{1}{2}''$. *Sepals* 5, gland dotted. *St.* 6-8 alternating with linear oblong villous staminodes.

2. Homalium, Jacq.

1. H. nepalense, *Benth.*

A small tree 30-40 ft. with coarsely serrate prominently nerved leaves attaining $6\frac{1}{2}''$ by 3-4″ and axillary panicles of small white flowers $\frac{1}{5}$-$\frac{1}{4}''$ diam.

Singbhum, Birda Forest, rare. Fl. *May-June.*

Bark light coloured. Young twigs puberulous. L. ell. or ell.-ovate, dentate with a gland in each tooth, acuminate, nearly glabrous, narrowed into the $\frac{1}{2}$-1″ petiole. *Sec. nerves* very prominent 6-8 prs. *Panicles* 2-5″ dense pyramidal pubescent. *Pedicels* $\frac{1}{20}$-$\frac{1}{18}''$. *Fls.* densely hairy. *Calyx-tube* funnel shaped. *Sepals* 6-8 spreading linear. *Petals* as many linear-oblong valvate, perigynous. *St.* as many and inserted with and opposite to the petals alternating with fleshy glands. *Anther lobes* very short. *Ovary* half-inferior, hairy inside and out. *Styles* 3-5. *Ovules* about 6 parietal, anatropous.

Fam. 12. TAMARICACEÆ.

1. Tamarix, L. Tamarisk.

Shrubs or small trees with alt. scale-like often sheathing leaves and small regular white or pink flowers in spikes or panicled racemes. *Sep.* and *pet.* each 5 free persistent. *St.* 5 or 10 on the margin of a crenulate disc. *Ovary* free 1-celled with 3, rarely more, free styles dilated into the stigmas and as many parietal placentæ at the very base of the ovary. *Ovules* numerous and *seeds* erect comose, at the base of the 3-valved capsule.

1. T. ericoides, *Rottl.* Jao, *Beng., H.*

A handsome shrub with erect broom-like branches clothed with sheathing amplexicaul minute leaves and with 2-sexual pink fls. in terminal racemes 4-8″ long. St. 10. Capsule elongate beaked with 3 narrow-lanceolate valves.

In many of the river beds, *e.g.* Konor nadi, Hazaribagh; Urunga R. and Koel R., Palamau; Damuda valley, Manbhum; Sirguja, *Wood.* Fl., F. *Jany.-Aug.*

2. **T. dioica.** *Roxb.* Jao, *Beng.*

A glaucous shrub or small tree with elegant weeping branches, with sheathing leaves. The pink fls. are diœcious in dense panicled spikes 1-2″ long. M. with 5 stamens.

Santal Parganahs, banks of the Ganges. Fl. *Aug.*

Fam. 13. CUCURBITACEÆ.

Herbaceous, more rarely shrubby. climbing by means of tendrils.[1] *L.* alt. simple, lobed, or pedately divided. *Venation* palmate. *Fls.* 1-sexual monœcious or diœcious. *Calyx* and *corolla* superior springing from a common elongated zone of the torus (Hypanthium, Calyx-tube), which is often constricted above the ovary. *Corolla* either poly-or gamopetalous. *St.* inserted at various levels on the hypanthium, rarely 5, usually 3, two of which have 2-celled anthers and the third 1-celled. *Anthers* often connate, anther-cells straight or usually variously curved or twisted. *Ovary*[2] usually 1-celled, the three parietal placentæ often meeting in the ovarian cavity and only separated by mucilaginous lines, or ultimately 3-celled. *Ovules* anatropous, usually numerous. Style stout with 3-5 stigmas. *Fruit* a berry with an ultimately hard outer rind (when it is called a pepo) or entirely succulent, rarely dry. *Seeds* with a hard testa, exalbuminous, with straight embryo.

The following species all belong to the tribe Cucumerineæ in which the ovules are mostly horizontal, leaves not compound, female flowers usually solitary.

The ovarian cavity in Cucurbita and others becomes filled with a succulent tissue plentifully supplied with spiral vessels.

The affinities of Cucurbitaceæ are very doubtful. The family is sometimes placed near the Campanulaceæ.

---

[1] For the morphology of the tendril see Warming, "Systematischen. Botanik," Sec. German, Ed. P. 367.

[2] In all the genera examined by me, *viz.*, Trichosanthes, Luffa Momordica, Bryonia, Cucurbita and Cephelandra the ovary is always initially 1-celled. In some cases the apparent septum is an exceedingly small-celled tissue formed subsequently to the meeting of the placentæ, in Luffa the septa are the ingrown placentæ.

A. Petals free or connate only at base. Flowers white	
1. Fls. small.[1] Hypanthium tubular-campanulate. Petals minute	1. *Zehneria.*
2. Fls. large or m. s., Hypanthiun of M, long narrow-tubular	
Petals fimbriate	2. *Trichosanthes.*
Petals entire or toothed	3. *Gymnopetalum.*
3. Hypanthium funnel-shaped. Fls. 2-4" diam.	4. *Lagenaria.*
B. Petals connate at base or nearly half-way up. Fls. yellow. Hypanthium short.	
1. Fls. large (usually over 1½" diam.), not clustered (M. clustered in Luffa graveolens).	
Stamens inserted near the mouth of the hypanthium. Petals nearly free.	
M. fl. solitary and racemed in same axil .	5. *Luffa.*
Fls. all solitary	6. *Benincasa.*
2. Fls. mod.-sized, solitary on very slender peduncles.	
Corolla 5-partite. Tendrils simple . . .	7. *Momordica.*
3. Fls. small or m. s., clustered (except Citrullus).	
a. Anthers straight. Pedicels very short. Tendrils simple	8. *Mukia.*
b. Anthers curved or sigmoid.	
M. pedicels slender. Tendrils forked . .	9. *Bryonia.*
Fls. solitary. Tendrils 2-3-fid	10. *Citrullus.*
Anthers crested. Tendrils simple . . .	11. *Cucumis.*
C. Corolla gamopetalous half-way up or more.	
Fls. all solitary.	
Fls. very large, yellow. Tendrils 2-4-fid . .	12 *Cucurbita.*
Fls. m. s., white. Tendrils simple . . .	13. *Cephalandra.*

1. Zehneria, Endl.

Climbing herbs with a tuberous root. Leaves polymorphous abounding in cystoliths (showing superficially when dry as small pustules). Tendrils simple. Fls. small tubular-campanulate, monœcious or usually diœcious, in corymbose racemes or females solitary. Peduncles frequently with a long-stalked glandular bract at the base. Sepals minute.

[1] In the Fem. the part *above* the ovary only is referred to unless otherwise specified

Petals small triangular white. St. 3 free, inserted near the bottom of the short tubular-companulate hypanthium; anthers conniving, cells curved, sigmoid or transverse on a thickened papillose connective. Ovary 1-celled with 3 parietal placentæ.

(St. normally 3, 2 with 2-celled anthers and 1 with 1-celled anther. Fls. however have been found with 3 2-celled anthers, and again with 3 stamens bearing 2-celled anthers and a *fourth stamen* with a 1-celled anther.)

1. **Z. umbellata,** *Thw.* Chengor, *K.*; At, *S.*; Ban Kundri, *Beng.*

Climbing or usually procumbent. Tubers spindle-shaped 1″ diam. in chains and at the ends of fleshy roots. L. cordate or sagittate with petiole under $\frac{3}{4}$″. M. fls. $\frac{1}{4}$″ long articulate on slender pedicels in short dense usually corymbose racemes. F. solitary on $\frac{1}{2}$-$\frac{3}{4}$″ peduncles. Fruit ellipsoid $1\frac{1}{2}$″ scarlet with red pulp.

Singbhum, not common. Manbhum, common, *Campbell.* Baragaon Hill and Sarguja, *Wood.* Santal Parganahs. Fl. *May-July.* Fr. *June-Sept.*

Stem angled. *L.* minutely denticulate (end of nerves mucronate), glaucous beneath, base 5-7-nerved. *Petioles* shorter than the basal-lobes or auricles. There are two very distinct forms in Chota Nagpur.

(*a*) *L.* quite entire cordate or ovate with cordate base, attaining 6″ by $4\frac{1}{2}$″.
Rocky ravines in Singbhum. Gneissic hills of western Hazaribagh. Stems and foliage persistent, at least until after November.

(*b*) *L.* attaining 3″, sagittate or halbert-shaped, with the basal lobes sometimes again lobed. Center-lobe obtuse. Santal Parganahs, etc.

This, I believe, dies down in the cold season as I have never observed it then.

The tubers, leaves and fruit of both forms are eaten.

2. **Z. Hookeriana,** *Arn.*

L. cordate angular or 3-5-lobed half-way down but with the center-lobe acute and the petiole longer than the basal-lobes or auricles. *Fruit* globose $\frac{3}{8}$″ diam.

Jaspur, *Wood.* Wood states that the root is used in fever and diarrhœa.

2. Trichosanthes, L.

Climbers, sometimes very large. Tendrils 2-5-fid. Fls. white, males in long racemes (or raceme 1-fld. in dioica) with a solitary male or a *female* at the base of the raceme, or females separate. Calyx-tube above the ovary slender tubular dilated above. Corolla rotate, tube very short, petals narrow fimbriate. Filaments 3. Anthers connate (free in dioica) Fruit ellipsoid to elongate and globose, smooth. Seeds many, compressed, sometimes angular at margins.

Perennial, large. Raceme with large sheathing bracts . . . . 1. *palmata.*

Annual. Bracts minute. Anthers connate 2. *cucumerina.*

Annual. Anthers free. Raceme usually only 1-flowered . . . . . 3. *dioica.*

1. T. palmata, *Roxb.* Kaubutki *K.*; Makal, *H., Beng.*

A large climber with cordate denticulate often deeply lobed leaves 3 by 5″, white flowers $2\frac{1}{2}$-3″ diam. and bright scarlet globose or ellipsoid fruits 2-$2\frac{1}{2}$″ by 2″ on axillary short stout peduncles.

Singbhum, valleys, and on the Ranchi plateau. Palamau (the spinulose variety at Miral). Santal Parganahs (Junju gara). Fl. *Aug.* Fr. *Dec.-Jany.* Deciduous.

L. simple or lobed, lobes acute or acuminate, (in one variety sub-spinulose) smooth and bright green above and minutely pitted, (usually appearing scabrous with small round discs—cystoliths—when dry) pale beneath, base 3-5-nerved. *Petiole* 1-2″. *Calyx-tube* $1\frac{1}{2}$-$2\frac{1}{2}$″ long. Rind of *fruit* $\frac{1}{4}$″ thick, seeds embedded in dark green pulp, oblong flattened slightly narrowed at base, $\frac{3}{8}$-$\frac{1}{2}$″.

Fr. and root boiled with mustard oil used for headache.

2. T. cucumerina, *L.* Bir Kaita, *K.*; Ban potol, *Beng.*

A slender succulent climber with long-petioled deeply cordate 5-7-angular or lobed and dentate leaves 3-4″ diam. White fls. $\frac{3}{4}$-$1\frac{1}{3}$″ diam. with fimbriate petals and spindle-shaped sub-rostrate fruits 1-3″ long, green with white stripes, ultimately red.

Singbhum valleys. Fl. *Aug.-Sept.* Fr. *Sept.-Nov.*

L. smooth to touch above, almost velvety between nerves below, main nerves pubescent or somewhat scabrous beneath, basal sinus very broad, smell fœtid. *Tendrils* 3-fid. Monœcious. *Male racemes* 5-8″. Calyx-tube ¼-¾″.

Var. anguina, L. (sp.) Karta, K.; Chachinda, H. The snake gourd.

This is the cultivated form. *L.* 4-6″ or up to 11″ diam. sometimes very deeply lobed with narrow sinuses except the basal one which is very broad. *Fls.* 1½-2″. *Fr.* very long attaining 2 ft. and often twisted, green with white stripes when young. There are all gradations between this and the wild form.

3. **T. dioica,** *Roxb.* Potol, *Beng.*

Dioecious. *Male peduncles* usually only 1-fid. *Fruit* oblong or nearly spherical.

"In all the provinces," *Prain.* I have not seen it in Ch. Nagpur.

L. ovate to oblong, not palmate. *Sec. n.* excurrent as small teeth. *Petiole* ¼-½″ only. *Fls.* about ¾″ diam. white. *Hypanthium* very slender 2-3″ green striate with long white hairs. *Sepals* linear ½″.

3. Gymnopetalum, Arn.

G. cochinchinense, *Kurz.* Kaubutkila, *K.*

A pretty climber with bright green foliage, simple tendrils, and white flowers 2″ diam., M. solitary and racemed from same axil. Fem. solitary, or occasionally also panicled like the male. Corolla lobes oblong toothed. Fr. 2″ by 1¼″ bright orange-scarlet, ovoid-oblong, with 10 strong ribs when young.

Singbhum on Porahat plateau. Ranchi plateau. Fl. *Aug.-Oct.* Fr. *Sept.-Nov.*

Stems sparsely pubescent or hispid. *L.* lower deeply cordate orbicular 5-7-lobed and denticulate 2-4″, scabrous above hispidulous beneath, basal lobes rounded and sinus wide, others acute or acuminate. *Raceme* 5-9″, bracts foliaceous ½″, obovate cuneate, palmatisect. *Calyx-tube* curved pubescent 1″, sepals ¼″. *Anthers* connate. *Fem.* calyx-tube ½-⅝″ above pubescent ovary. *Seeds* 5/16″ by ⅛″ in a blackish-green pulp, somewhat compressed, brown.

4. Lagenaria, Seringe.

1. **L. vulgaris,** *Seringe.* Suku, *Ho.*; Kadu, *S.* Lao, *H.*, *Beng.* The bottle gourd.

A coarse glandular and softly hairy monœcious plant with 2-fid. tendrils, ovate or orbicular cordate dentate leaves 7-8″ diam. 2-glandular at base and large solitary white flowers 3-4″ diam. Ovary and young fruit hairy.

Largely cultivated. Fl. *July-Jany.*

Male peduncle 5-6″, *calyx-tube* $\frac{1}{2}$-$\frac{3}{4}$″ and *sepals* $\frac{3}{8}$″. *Petals* often 2″ by 1″ ovate with excurrent mid-rib. *Fem.* Ovary cylindric, villous, tube above very short. *Sepals* $\frac{1}{4}$″ linear.

Fruit (Tumba, *K.*) various, eaten when young, with a hard shell when ripe, used for bottles, etc.

5. Luffa, Cav.

Tendrils 4-5-fid. Fls. monœcious. Males in long racemes (pedicels clustered in L. graveolens) with a solitary male or a solitary female from the same node, or female in a different axil. Bracts often glandular. Male calyx-tube obconic or campanulate, sepals 5. Corolla rotate from the top of the tube or lining the calyx-tube to the base. Filaments 3-5 inserted at base of corolla tube, anthers free or in 3 groups, more or less exsert, cells sinuose or sigmoid on the margins of the often lamellate connective. Fem. calyx-tube scarcely produced above the ovary. Ovary narrow ultimately 3-celled. Fruit ultimately dry with a coriaceous epicarp and fibrous mesocarp, opening by a stopple.

The placentation in the genus becomes *axile* or nearly so from the ingrowing of the placentæ.

Fls. 2-3″ diam. Filaments 5 free inserted near mouth of tube . . . . . . 1. *ægyptiaca.*

Fls. $1\frac{1}{4}$-2″ diam. Fil. 3 inserted low in the tube . 2. *acutangula.*

Male pedicels clustered, ebracteate . . . . 3. *graveolens.*

1. L. ægyptiaca, *Mill.* Doro, *M.*; Pulu, *Ho.*; Ghiatorui, *H.*; Dhundul, *Beng.* Egyptian Loofah.

An extensive annual climber with orbicular-ovate 5-lobed leaves, attaining 13″ by 12″ scabrous both sides or slightly puberulous beneath. Fls. sulphur yellow often 3-4″ diam.

with a rotate corolla on racemes which attain 18″ long. Fr. 6-18″ clavate or cylindrical, not ridged.

Jungles in Singbhum, on old village sites apparently wild. This wild form has a fruit usually under 8″, quite smooth and cylindric. Cultivated throughout Ch. Nag. Wild plant Fl. *Aug.-Sept.* Fr. *Nov.-Dec.* The cultivated often also much later.

L. sinuate dentate or denticulate usually with well marked acuminate lobes. *Bracts* with 1 or more large disciform glands occupying the whole surface. *Calyx-tube* short campanulate, *sepals* longer $\frac{1}{3}$-$\frac{1}{4}$″ glandular. *Fem. fl.* solitary from same node as the male raceme, often abortive

2. **L. acutangula,** *Roxb.* Jui, *Ho.*; Paror Jhinga. *S.* Jhinga, Ara-torui, *H.*; Tita Dhundul, *Beng.*

L. orbicular, 5-9″ both ways, or broader than long usually faintly lobed or lobes obtuse, margin more or less repand and enuticulate; texture of last. Fls. $1\frac{1}{4}$-2″ diam., corolla inserted low down with the 3 filaments, anthers only shortly exserted. Male racemes 6-14″. Fruit with 10 sharp ridges.

Cultivated. Not found wild.

3. **L. graveolens,** *Roxb.*

L. 3″ diam., scabrous above, reniform-orbicular, 5-angled, punctulate, scabrous above. Male pedicels clustered axillary. Female peduncle short sometimes with 2-3 flowers each with a small ovate bract. Petals $\frac{1}{4}$″. Fruit 2′ by 1″, papillose, obscurely 10-striate.

Rajmehal Hills, *Roxb.*; Ch. Nagpur, *Prain.* Fls. *Sept.*

Stem grooved. *L.* ovate to kidney-shaped. *M.* and *F. fl.* from the same axils. *M.* on separate stalks, *F.* often sub-panicled, and peduncle bracteate. *Petals* under $\frac{1}{2}$″. *St.* 5 distinct. *Fr.* echinate.

6. Benincasa, Savi.

1. **B. cerifera,** *Savi.* Rakhsa *K.*; Kumra, *Beng.*, *H.*

Resembles a Cucurbita in its large solitary yellow flowers and foliaceous sepals, but the corolla is only very slightly gamopetalous, the stamens are inserted near mouth of the tube, the densely hairy ovary has 3 flexuose stigmas.

Occasionally cultivated. Fls. *Dec.-Jany.*

Hairy. *L.* cordate reniform-orbicular, toothed, sometimes also lobed *Tendrils* forked. *Fls.* solitary about 2″ diam., the corolla lobes exceeding the tube. *Fr.* hairy.

7. Momordica, L.

Tendrils simple. L. undivided or palmatisect. Fls. monoecious or dioecious, solitary peduncle often with a large bract. Calyx-tube campanulate. Corolla nearly polypetalous. Filam. 3. Anthers with horse-shoe shaped or conduplicate cells. Style long, stigmas 3. Fr. indehiscent or 3-valved, smooth, muricate or with soft spines.

L. deeply cut. Fruit tubercled . . . 1. *Charantia.*

L. not cut. Fruit densely softly spiny . . 2. *dioica.*

1. **M. Charantia,** *L.* Kirla, *K.*; Kanchan arac' (leaf), karla (fruit), *S.*; Karela, *H.*

A soft rather slender climber with softly hairy stems 7-palmatisect leaves, larger $4\frac{1}{2}''$, and solitary flowers $\frac{1}{2}$-$\frac{5}{8}''$ diam. on filiform peduncles with 1 orbicular foliaceous bract.

Apparently wild, hedges and roadsides in the cooler parts of Singbhum. Wild in Manbhum, *Campbell.* S. P., common in hedges. Fl. *Aug.-January.* Fr. *Aug.-Feby.*

L. segments lobed or sinuate and dentate. *Peduncles* often $3\frac{1}{2}''$ *Petals.* distinct to base, spreading. *Fruit* ovoid narrowed both ends 1-3″ with tubercled ribs, beaked, yellow when ripe.

Leaves as well as fruit are eaten.

2. **M. dioica,** *Roxb.* Ochen *K.*; Kaksa, *H.*

Slender nearly glabrous. L. cordate ovate acute denticulate mucronate 3-4″.

Fem. peduncles $1\frac{1}{2}$-2″ bracteate above the middle. Petals free to base, $\frac{3}{4}''$ pubescent.

Apparently wild in hedges. Fl. *Aug.-Sept.* Fr. *Sept.-Oct.* Fruit eaten.

8. Mukia, Arn.

1. **M. scabrella,** *Arn.* Kawa-tamar, *Vern.* (Wood) Bilari, *H.*

A very scabrous herb with simple tendrils 3-7-angular, lobed and toothed very rough deeply cordate leaves, larger about 4" by $3\frac{1}{2}$" with petiole 2", but floral much smaller and mostly sessile. Fls. small yellow, M. and F. clustered in the same axils, sub-sessile, $\frac{1}{8}$-$\frac{1}{6}$" diam. Anther cells straight.

Common, climbing over bushes in low jungle and open places. Fl. *Sept.-Oct* Fr. *Oct.-Nov.*

Very pretty in fruit with its clusters of scarlet berries $\frac{3}{8}$" diam.

The placentas and stigmatic lobes are sometimes only 2.

9. Bryonia, L.

1. **B. laciniosa,** *L.* Kahubotke, *S.*; Pachguria, *Kharw.* Mala, *Beng.*

A climbing fœtid herb with cordate deeply palmately 3-5-lobed or partite leaves and 2-fid tendrils. Male and fem. fls. small yellowish clustered in the same axils, pedicelled. Fil. 3, two double and one single anther free from one another, cells curved or sigmoid. Fr. $\frac{1}{2}$—$\frac{5}{8}$" diam. globose succulent green or red with white stripes.

Very common, scrub jungle and hedges. Fl. and Fr. *April-Oct.*

L. sometimes pedately lobed beyond the middle with narrow sinuses, 3-5" long and broad, nearly smooth, lobes toothed or denticulate. *Petiole* 1-$1\frac{1}{2}$". *M. pedicels* very slender $\frac{1}{2}$-1". *Fem.* short. *Petals* $\frac{3}{10}$" light yellow. *Seeds* in a blue-green pulp, pear-shaped with a corrugate vertical band.

Horses are fond of the fruit.

10. Citrullus, Schrader.

1. C. vulgaris, *Schrad.* Tarboj, *K.* Tarbuz, *H. Beng.* The Water-Melon.

Usually prostrate with rather slender stem pubescent or hairy or nearly glabrous and with somewhat scabrid petioles. *L.* 3-5-partite with the segments pinnatifid, sinuate and denticulate, about 6″ by 5″ with petiole 5″, dotted beneath, tendrils 2-3-fid. *Fl.* solitary, rarely geminate, on a peduncle 1½-2″, monoecious. *Hypanthium* short campanulate, *sepals* linear ¼″. *Corolla* 1″ diam. deeply-lobed, lobes strongly 3-5-nerved. *St.* 3 distinct with sigmoid anthers. *Peduncle* subtended at base (always?) by an obovoid entire 3-nerved foliaceous bract ¾″ long.

Frequently cultivated, and sometimes self-sown.

2. **C. Colocynthis,** *Schrad.* The Colocynth has very deeply pamately-divided leaves 2-3″ diam. very scabrous and hispid with tubercle-based hairs, and somewhat resembles Cucumis trigonus when wild. It is said to occur throughout India, but I have not met with it in Chota Nagpur.

11. Cucumis, L.

Hispid or scabrid herbs with simple tendrils. Fls. monoecious. Males fascicled and females solitary, in the axils, shortly peduncled. Hypanthium short. Filaments 3. Anther cells conduplicate or only flexuose. Connective *produced into a crest* above the anther. Ovary 3-septate or septa not meeting in the middle. Style short, stigmas 3, obtuse. Fruit fleshy.

1. **C. trigonus,** *Roxb.* Bing Dimbu, *K.* The wild melon.

Prostrate, with scabrous stems and petioles. Leaves small deeply palmately 3-5-lobed to about the middle or more, sometimes merely angular (see var.) Corolla, ½″ diam. lobed beyond the middle. Fruit smooth ellipsoid or globose 1¼″ diam., striped green and white.

Very common on banks and waste ground throughout the area. Fl., Fr. *Aug.-Oct.*

L. scabrous on both sides, lobes with broad tips, which are sometimes again lobed *Peti.* about ⅓-1½″. *M. fls.* sometimes solitary. Ped. ⅓″. *Calyx* and *cor.* and *ovary* hairy.

Var. *a.* L. sub-entire or lobed and fruit spherical. It only differs from a feral state of C. Melo in the leaves being under 2⅓" diam. and the absence of any soft hairs. Fl. r. s.

2. **C. Melo,** *L.* The Melon and 3. **C. sativus,** *L.* The Cucumber, are both cultivated and sometimes feral. C. Melo is distinguished from C. sativus by the smooth, not muricate fruit, and by the leaves having both soft hairs and harsh ones, while C. sativus has the hairs nearly uniform on the leaves which are not, or only slightly, scabrid, and the fruit is muricate. The ovary and young fruit is often densely hairy in both.

A variety of **Cucumis** with angular *leaves* 4½" diam., *fls.* ¾-1" diam., *frt.* sparsely muricate with scattered harsh *bulbous-based* hairs, and the leaves with many rather stiff hairs between the hispid nerves, may be an escape from cultivation of C. sativus, *L.* It is apparently wild in the Porahat jungles, between Nakti and Tebu. Fl., Fr. *Sept.-Oct.*

12. Cucurbita, L.

Coarse hispid or hairy herbs with 2-4-fid. tendrils. Fls. very large yellow solitary monœcious. Calyx-tube campanulate, sepals often leaf-like. Corolla gamopetalous. St. inserted low down, fil. 3 short, anthers connate in a column with conduplicate cells. Style short, Stigmas large fleshy, 3-5 often longitudinally lobed. Large epigynous cushion-shaped disc 5-lobed.

The ovary is filled with tissue and the ovules are on large swollen parietal placentæ which meet in the axis and are recurved.

The following diagnosis of the three commonly cultivated species is from Prain's "Bengal Plants."

1. **C. Pepo,** *D.C.* Karkaru, *K.* The Pumpkin.

Leaf-stalks beset beneath with rigid, pungent hairs; calyx lobes narrow-subulate; leaves deeply 5-lobed, with broad sinuses between the lobes.

2. **C. maxima,** *Duchesne.* The Gourd.

Leaf-stalks with hairs uniform, not rigid nor pungent. Calyx-lobes narrow-subulate; leaves not deeply lobed, sinuses narrow.

3. **C. moschata,** *Duchesne.* The Musk Melon.

Hairs of leaf-stalks as in 2. Calyx-lobes broad-spathulate, leafy; leaves very variously lobed.

13. Cephalandra, Schrad.

1. **C. indica**, *Naud.* Kundri, *K.*; Kanduri, Bhimb, *H.*; Tela-Kucha, *Beng*.

A climber with obtusely-angled, lobed, or palmately tripartite leaves with the basal lobes again 2-fid. or-lobed. Tendrils simple. Fls. diœcious white campanulate about 1″ long, hairy within, ribbed. Fr. oblong narrowed at each end or only apically, scarlet; green with usually 10 white streaks when unripe.

Common. Cultivated and in hedges. Fl., Fr. *July-August*.

Stems 5-angled somewhat scabrous, otherwise glabrous. *L.* attaining 4″ diam. and 3-4″ long punctate above, with raised points when dry, denticulate, glabrous, 1-6-glandular beneath near the petiole. *Petiole* about 1.″ *Calyx-tube* campanulate, lobes oblong acute spreading. *Corolla-lobes* $\frac{1}{3}$-$\frac{1}{2}$″ ovate. *St.* 3 with exsert anthers. *Style* with 3 large 2-lobed spreading stigmas.

The fruit is very commonly eaten as a vegetable.

Fam. 14. MORINGACEÆ.

1. Moringa, Lamk. Horse-radish Tree.

1. **M. pterygosperma**, *Gærtn.* Munga-ara (a :, *Ho*), *K. S.*; Munga, *H.*; Sojna, *Beng*.

A small tree with elegant tri-pinnate leaves and small leaflets, white irregular flowers in axillary panicles, and pendulous ribbed pods 9-18″ long.

Cultivated throughout Ch. Nagpur. Fl. *Jany-March*. Fr. *April-June*. Dec. *Dec.-Feby.*, or new leaves in *January*.

Fls. 2-sexual, 1″ diam. *Calyx* cupular with 5 linear-lanceolate reflexed sepals. *Pet.* 5, anterior largest. *St.* 5 perfect, opp. the petals, alternating with 5 staminodes, inserted on the disc which lines the calyx-tube. *Ovary* stipitate 1-celled. *Ovules* numerous on 3 parietal placentæ. *Capsule* 1-celled 3-valved, corky and with pits in the valves in which the 3-gonous winged seeds lie.

The leaves, flower and fruit are eaten as vegetables, and it is usually pollarded for the purpose of yielding the first and for fodder. It grows easily from cuttings. The pungent root is used as a vesicant and has the odour of Horse-radish, for which it is a substitute and is used medicinally.

Fam. Y5. DILLENIACEÆ.

1. Dillenia, L.

Trees with large simple exstipulate leaves with strong parallel *sec. nerves*, alt., often crowded at the tips of the branches. *Petiole* with a sheathing base. *Fls.* solitary or fascicled, white or yellow. *Sep.* 5 persistent, accrescent and fleshy in fruit which they envelope. *Petals* 5. *St.* ∞ anthers linear dehiscent by pores or small slits. *Carpels* 5-many, united in the axis with free spreading and recurved styles. *Ovules* many. *Fruit* globose, composed of the fleshy calyx enclosing the indehiscent carpels.

Fls. large white. Fr. (with calyx) 4″ diam. . . . 1. *indica.*
Fls. large yellow Fr. 2″ diam. . . . . . 2. *aurea.*
Fls. yellow mod.-sized 1″. Fr. ¾″ diam. . . . . 3. *pentagyna.*

1. D. indica, *L.* Korkotta, *K., S.*; Chalta, *Beng.*

A beautiful small tree with dense crown, deep-green leaves 8-10″ by 2-4″ and white solitary flowers 5-6″ diam.

Prefers muddy banks of streams, but in Singbhum is only found near villages and is probably always planted. S. P. (*Wood*) but I think doubtfully wild there also. Fl. *May-June.* Fr. *Dec.-Feby.* Evergreen.

L. lanceolate pubescent beneath with 30-40 prs. of close parallel sec. n. each running into a strong tooth. Petiole 1-2″. Carpels 20.

The large fleshy accrescent calyces which surround the fruit are eaten before they are quite ripe, usually after cooking.

2. D. aurea, *Sm.* Korkotta, Korkot, *K., S.*

A small crooked tree with obovate, broadly-oblong or elliptic leaves 12-20″ by 4½-7″ and a distinct petiole 1-3″ long

It bears large solitary beautiful yellow fls. terminating the leafless branches, and which much resemble those of Cochlospermum.[1]

Dry hills in Singbhum, very common in places on clay schists. Gangpur, Manbhum, Hazaribagh (Sitagarh hill, Koderma forest etc.) S. P. near Silingi, hills near Morjhora. Palamau, hills between Banki and Barwadih on trachyte, ghats near Chandwa on reddish grit. Fl. *April-May*. Fr. *May-June*. The leaves drop at end of *Jan.* and the new leaves appear at end of *May*.

I have cited localities rather fully from the curious fact that this tree has never before been recorded from Ch. Nag. It is, however, easily distinguished from D. pentagyna by both habit and habitat. The leaves are usually smaller, when young beautifully silky above, tomentose beneath between, and densely silky on, the close sec. n. (25-50 prs.); spinulose denticulate; adult pubescent or somewhat hairy beneath, margin sub-entire except for the excurrent nerves. *Peduncles* stout pubescent 1-3″ with 3-4 recurved bracts, lateral, but close to the terminal bud. Sep. ¾-1″. *Pet.* obovate-lanceo. 3″ by 2″. Styles 10 free ⅓″ spreading and recurved. Ovules many 2-seriate in each carpel.

The fruit is edible and is greedily eaten by wild elephants, which destroy the trees to obtain them.

3. D. pentagyna, *Roxb.* Rai, L.; Sahar S.

(Agor and Gulgul are vern. names acc. to Wood, but Korkot quoted in his list certainly belongs to the last. Agor is used in Monghyr.)

A mod.-sized tree with ell. or narrowly-elliptic leaves 12-36″ long decurrent below on a short petiole. Fls. very numerous in umbels along the leafless branches.

Confined to the valleys, not very common. Singbhum, Manbhum, Hazaribagh (2,000 ft. on Parasnath), Santal Parganahs. Fls. *March-April*. Fr. *May*. Deciduous end of *Feb.-May*.

L. much like the last but adult nearly or quite glabrous between the sec. n. beneath, margin distinctly repand crenate and together with the excurrent nerves forming teeth, the base is much more tapering and most often forms a wing on the petiole which hence rarely exceeds 1″ in length or is *absent*, base of leaf or of petiole broadly amplexicaul. Peduncles slender, 1-2″ ebracteate. *Carples* and *Styles* 5.

The wood gives an excellent charcoal. The fruit is eaten.

---

[1] I have found sheets of this placed under Cochlospermum in a herbarium.

Fam. 16. TERNSTRŒMIACEÆ.

This family contains the genus Camellia which includes the tea plant, and other handsome flowering shrubs. The tea, C. theifera, *Griff.* was formerly much cultivated on the Ranchi and Hazaribagh plateaux, but the climate of Chota Nagpur is far too dry for it, and the tea-planting industry has practically died out in competition with the large outturn of more suitable localities.

For botanical characters see Introduction.

Fam. 17. GUTTIFERACEÆ.

1. Garcinia, L.

Trees with a yellow milky juice, opp. rarely stipulate, simple entire leaves usually with numerous spreading close parallel sec. n. *Fls.* polygamous (or in G. Cowa usually diœcious), usually solitary or fascicled. *Sep.* 2+2, or 5. *Pet.* 4-5 imbricate. *St.* ∝ free or monodelphous, often in a central fleshy mass with 2- or 4-celled adnate or peltate anthers. *F. fl.* with staminodes. *Ovary* 2-12-celled with peltate stigma. *Ovules* 1 axile in each cell. *Fr.* a berry. *Seeds* arillate.

1. **G. Cowa,** *Roxb.* Soroa, *Ho.* *; Kowa, *Beng.*

An erect tree 30-40 ft. with many slender and drooping branches from quite close to the ground and dark shining broad-lanceolate leaves 3-5″ with slender rather obscure sec. n. meeting in an intramarginal one. Fls. yellowish rather fleshy usually 1-4 in the leaf axils. Fr. yellow about 2″ diam. grooved.

Along streams in the Saranda and Porahat forests, not common. Fl. ***April.*** **Fr.** ***May-June.*** **Evergreen.**

The fruit is edible.

*** But see footnote under Streblus as per p. 392.**

Fam. 18. DIPTEROCARPACEÆ.

1. Shorea, Roxb.

Trees, containing resin, with alt. entire simple leaves. *Stipules* caducous. *Fls.* in axillary and terminal panicles, bracts often caducous sometimes 0. *Calyx* 5-sepalous. *Petals* 5 contorted in bud. *St.* ∞ hypogynous, connective appendaged. *Ovary* 3-celled, cells 2-ovuled. *Style* subulate. *Fruit* a 1-seeded nut closely embraced by the bases of the greatly enlarged sepals. *Cotyledons* fleshy unequal, one embraced by the other, hypogeal in germination.

1. **S. robusta,** *Gaertn.* Sarjom, *K.*, *S.*; Sakua, *Kharw*; The Sal tree.

Throughout the area. In many of the deep valleys of Singbhum, Bonai and Gangpur it attains 12 ft. girth and 120 ft. high, the soil being a deep loam derived from the decomposition of gneissic rocks. On the hills of clay schist it is a stunted tree attaining 30-40 ft., and it occurs in a very stunted form on the top of Parasnath at 4,400 ft. elevation which is above the elevation it generally attains in the Himalayan region. Large trees are now very scarce in the other districts where the forests have been mostly ruined and the trees are mostly coppice shoots which frequently flower as mere bushes.

Gamble records a tree in a sacred grove in the S. P. (at Talpahari) 10½ ft. girth and 120 ft. high.

Fl. *March-April,* in some years the flowering extends into *May.* Fr. *June-July.* Nearly or quite leafless in *March.*

Stipules ¼-½" oblong, covering the young buds. The *panicles* arise direct from the old wood and on the new shoots, the *flowers* are unilateral on the branches. *Petals* with a twisted acumen free with overlapping bases. *Filaments* very swollen below.

Campbell says the best time for cutting is October, and that the timber is then much more durable. The logs should, of course, always be barked immediately after felling. The fuel and charcoal are excellent, and the latter is said by the Kols to be the best available for iron smelting. The seeds are eaten but are said not to be very wholesome. It was previously much tapped and destroyed for resin before the reservation of the forests. The resin (dunra, *K.*; sarjom lore, *S*) is used in medicine and for caulking. The leaf is the usual covering of the Kol cigarette (fikr). The seed should be sown as soon as ripe, but the earliest to fall are usually bad. The stalks of the cotyledons are very long, and if the primary shoot is injured or dies subsequent shoots arise from their axils. The first pair of foliage leaves are opposite.

Fam. 19. MALVACEÆ.

Trees, or more usually shrubs or herbs, mostly with stellate hairs and with very tough branches from the strength of the bast fibres. *L.* alt. stipulate with palmate venation, simple or digitate. *Fls.* regular usually showy, nearly always with *bracteoles* (not in Abutilon or Bombax) under the flower which often form an epicalyx. *Sep.* 5 valvate usually connate below. *Pet.* 5 imbricate and twisted, sometimes adnate below to the staminal tube. *St.* ∝ (only 15 in Kydia) more or less connate into a tube, from which free ends of the filaments may grow. *Anthers* variously shaped, ultimately 1-celled. *Ovary* 3-4- but usually 5-many-celled, capsular in fruit or breaking up into as many dehiscent or indehiscent cocci as carpels, which fall away from a persistent columella. *Ovules* 1-more axile curved. *Albumen* scanty or 0. *Cotyledons* usually crumpled or folded.

The family abounds in mucilage, and most of the species yield a fibre.

A. Shrubs or herbs, mostly undershrubs. Androecium tubular (filaments long in Abutilon sp.)	
I. Carpels numerous (only 5 in one species). Ovules 2 or more in each cell. Fls. usually orange . .	1. *Abutilon.*
II. Carpels 5 (rarely 4, sometimes 6-10 in Sida). Ovule 1 in each cell.	
Styles as many as carpels. Fls. yellow or straw coloured	2. *Sida.*
Styles 10. Fls. pink. Ovary cells opposite the petals	3. *Urena.*
Styles 10. Fls. pink. Ovary cells opposite the sepals	4. *Pavonia.*
III. Carpels 5. Ovules 3 or more in each cell. Fruit capsular.	
Stigmas spreading. Bracteoles 5 or more . . .	5. *Hibiscus.*
Stigmas coherent in a clavate mass. Brctls. 4-8 small	6. *Thespesia.*
Stigmas coherent in a clavate mass. Brctls. 3 large cordate	7. *Gossypium*

B. Large or small trees. Filaments all or some free above the base, usually pentadelphous.

L. simple or lobed. Bracteoles 4-5 . . . . 8. *Kydia.*

L. digitate. Bracteoles 0. Fls. very large . . . 9. *Bombax.*

1. Abutilon, Gaert.

Undershrubs more or less downy, with angled palmately-lobed or entire leaves and orange ebracteolate flowers usually 1" diam. or more, opening in the evening. Pedicels articulate. Pet. connate below and adnate to the st. tube which is divided at the apex into numerous filaments. Carpels exceeding 5 (exc. polyandrum), in fruit separating as 2-valved usually 2-3-seeded cocci from the persistent axis, apex of fruit depressed or truncate, awns or mucros, if present, on the shoulders.

Androecium only tubular at the base. Carpels 5 . . 1. *polyandrum.*

Staminal tube long. Carpels 15 or more.

Not hairy except the fruits, peduncles slender, cocci truncate usually shortly awned . . . . 2. *indicum.*

Hairy as well as pubescent, peduncles stout, cocci rounded muticous or mucronate . . . . 3. *graveolens.*

1. A. polyandrum, *Schlecht.*

A tomentose and hairy shrub with long-petioled orbicular or ovate cordate acuminate leaves and yellow flowers $1\frac{1}{2}$" diam. in loose panicles. Cocci awned.

Tundi forest, Manbhum. Parasnath, *Anders.*, *Campbell*! Kochang, *Gamble.* Not common. Biennial or lower portions perennial. Fl. *May* and *r. s.* Fr. *Oct.*

L. 4-5" repand-dentate densely shortly pubescent esp. beneath *Staminal-tube* forming a hispid cone over the ovary then dividing into about 40 long filaments. *Seeds* 3-4 in each carpel.

2. A. indicum, *G. Don.* Mirubaha, *S.*; Kakhi, *Khar.*; Kanghi, *H.*

An undershrub covered with a soft white close velvet with few or no long hairs intermixed. Fls. about 1" diam.

on very slender peduncles two to three times the length of the subtending petioles, and usually deflexed at the joint. Head of carpels truncate exceeding in diam. the fruiting calyx, usually with short awns on the shoulders, stellately hairy.

Waste ground and usually near villages in all the districts but rather local. Fl. *r. s.* and up to *December*. Fr. chiefly *Nov.-Jany.* Ripe seed, however, also collected in June, and it probably flowers at most times of the year.

L. usually dentate and acuminate (var. populifolium, *W.* and *A.*), sometimes lobed, 1½-3″. *Stipules* small deflexed. *Petiole* ¾ths as long as the blade. *Peduncles* solitary axillary 1½-2½″ sometimes appearing sub-panicled before the leaves develop.

3. **A. graveolens,** *W.* and *A.* Barkangbi, *H.*

Suffruticose 3-6 ft. high, the whole plant covered with a tomentum much as in A. indica, but also with glandular pubescence and long soft hairs on the branches, peduncles, etc. Fls. 1½″ diam. orange with a crimson centre, on solitary axillary peduncles together usually with another flowering branchlet. Head of carpels rounded, muticous or mucronate, densely pubescent. Fruiting calyx as broad as the fruit.

Similar localities to A. indicum. Singbhum, frequent. Manbhum, *Ball.* Palamau (common near Japla). Fl. *Aug.-Dec.* Fr. *Oct.-Jany.*

L. orbicular cordate, entire crenate or slightly toothed 3-6″ diam. *Petioles* 3-6.″ *Stipules* spreading or reflexed. *Peduncles* usually 1½-2″ stout. *Carpels* 2-3-seeded. *Seeds* with a yellow pubescence.

2. Sida, L.

Undershrubs or sub-herbaceous, with simple or lobed leaves, distinguished from Abutilon by habit (smaller size generally), smaller flowers (rarely 1″) generally a paler yellow with usually only 5 carpels and not more than 10. Fruiting head of carpels small not depressed at the top, and carpels awned near the apex, seed solitary. The sepals are connate below into a 5-angled or 10-nerved cup persistent long after the seeds have dropped.

I. Lower petioles long, ¾″ or more. L. ovate to orbicular with cordate base mostly 1″ or more long.
  Erect or trailing. Carpels 5 . . . . . 1. *veronicifolia.*
  Erect. Hairs glandular. Carpels 5 . . . . *var. glutinosa.*
  Erect. Tomentose. Carpels 10 . . . . 2. *cordifolia.*

II. Petioles under ¾″ longer than the stipules. L. variable mostly ¾″ (½-2″) hoary beneath. Carpels 5 3. *spinosa.*

III. Petioles ¼″ or less, shorter than the stipules. L. usually narrow, but if broad always with a cuneate base.
  L. pubescent beneath, often rhomboid or obovate. Peduncles ⅓-1″ long . . . . . . 4. *rhombifolia.*
  L. glabrous beneath, always narrow oblong or lanceolate. Peduncles ¼″ or less . . . 5. *acuta.*

1. S. veronicifolia, *Lamk.* Syn. S. humilis. *Willd* (*F.B.I.*) Bariar, *S., K.*; Junka, *Beng.*

Varies from a procumbent herb on open pasture land to an undershrub erect or trailing 1-3 ft. high, always hairy with sub-orbicular or ovate cordate obtusely serrate acuminate leaves attaining 3½″ by 2¾″ (only ½-1″ on some procumbent forms). Petiole and peduncles both slender ½-2″. Carpels mucronate or cuspidate, rarely awned.

In all situations and flowering and fruiting *throughout the year*, but especially at the *close of the rains.*

The trailing and erect forest form is usually covered with long spreading hairs as well as stellate hairs. *L.* 8-9-nerved at base. *Fls.* straw-coloured or yellow ⅓″ diam. 1-2 axillary and loosely arranged in racemes or panicles from the reduction of the leaves. *Peduncles* equal to or rather shorter than the petioles, jointed about half way.

Yields a good fibre. *L.* eaten as a sag, *Camp.*

Var. glutinosa, *Cav.* (sp.) Syn. S. mysorensis, *W.* and *A.* *F.B.I.*)

Erect and covered with glutinous hairs. *Carpels* awned.

2. S. cordifolia, *L.*

An erect undershrub 2-4 ft. tomentose all over and with thin hairs on the stem, with ovate or ovate-oblong cordate obtuse crenate leaves 1¼″ by 1″ to 3″ by 2½″ with petioles about

$\frac{1}{4}$th-$\frac{3}{4}$ths as long. Peduncles 1-2 axillary and sub-corymbose with the lower ones attaining 1″. Carpels 10-9 with 2 long retrorsely hispid awns.

Waste places throughout the area, esp. in scrub jungles in Palamau, elsewhere not common. Fls. *Aug.-Dec.* Fr. *Oct.-Jany.*

Easily recognized from the leaves being softly grey tomentose both sides, they are 7-9-nerved at the base. *Flowers* straw coloured $\frac{1}{2}$″ diam. *Carpels* with plaited sides and awns nearly as long as themselves.

3. S. spinosa, *L.*

An erect undershrub more or less stellately tomentose with linear-lanceolate ovate to obovate or sub-orbicular leaves $\frac{1}{2}$-2″ hoary beneath with obtuse apex and usually cuneate base, petioles $\frac{1}{2}$-$\frac{3}{4}$ths, as long as the leaves, often with 3 tubercles at the base. Fls. pale (white, *Roxb.*). Peduncles equal or exceeding the petiole jointed close to the flower. Carpels 5 beaked.

Chota Nagpur, *Prain.* On lands recently cultivated, *Roxb.*

4. S. rhombifolia, *L.* Ipirpijon, *K.*

An undershrub 1-4 ft. high with stellate hairs on the branches. L. narrowly or broadly rhomboid or obovate, always cuneate at the 3-nerved base,[1] pale or hoary and always more or less stellate pubescent or tomentose beneath. Peduncles slender jointed at or below the middle, the lower (at least) far exceeding the petioles. Carpels 5-9.

Very common and variable. In waste ground, forest glades, etc., throughout the area. Fl. Fr. *Aug.-Dec.* The following extreme forms occur :—

α. Stems slender, often procumbent. L. broadly-rhomboid, obovate or rounded, crenate or crenate-serrate, sometimes only $\frac{1}{2}$-1″ hoary beneath with stellate tomentum. Fruiting-calyx $\frac{1}{4}$″ or less. Peduncles under $\frac{1}{2}$″ often densely clustered. Tongue of seed broad. Beak not $\frac{1}{4}$th as long as the carpel, sometimes obsolete. In dry places.

β. Stems erect, thinly stellate. L. rhomboid to lanceolate attaining 3$\frac{1}{2}$″ by 1$\frac{1}{4}$″ acuminate or not, serrate except at the cuneate base. Glabrous above, pale and thinly stellate esp. on nerves beneath. Sec. n. 4-7 prs. Petiole $\frac{1}{4}$″. Stipules setaceous equal to or usually exceeding the petiole. Fls. solitary or few on short axillary branches or corymbose at the ends. Fruiting calyx $\frac{1}{4}$″ or more diam. Carpels usually 8-9 pubescent or hispid

---

[1] But apex of the wedge may be obtuse or sub-cordate.

with beaks or awns half as long as the carpel. Seeds black with a prominent tongue. In shady or damp localities.

Yields a good fibre.

5. **S. acuta,** *Burm.* Syn. S. carpinifolia *F.B.I.* Ipirpijon, *K.*; Ipirpichig, *M*; Bir miru baha, *S*.

An undershrub 2-3 ft. high with very tough sparsely stellate-hairy stems, lanceolate to obovate-lanc. serrate glabrous leaves $1\frac{1}{2}$-$3\frac{1}{2}''$ by $\frac{1}{2}$-$1''$ and pale-yellow flowers on jointed peduncles which are mostly shorter than the $\frac{1}{4}''$ petioles. Stipules hairy linear, or one linear and one setaceous in each pair, $\frac{1}{3}''$-$\frac{1}{2}''$ or more long.

Waste ground. Common. Fl. and Fr. *Aug.-Dec.*

Frequently variegated with yellow. *L.* gradually tapering at the tip, scarcely acuminate, base 3-nerved, sometimes rounded; *sec. n.* 5-8 prs. extending nearly to margin. *Ped.* jointed about the middle. Acuminate *calyx-lobes* ciliate. *Carpels* usually 5-6 reticulate, shortly 2-beaked.

Yields a good fibre.

3. Urena, L.

Undershrubs with stellate hairs, angled or deeply palmately-lobed leaves and pink solitary or clustered axillary fls., or clusters in more or less leafless terminal racemes. Bracteoles 5, adnate to the calyx and sometimes connate below into a cup. Petals 5 connate below and adnate below to the staminal tube. Anths. nearly sessile on the truncate or denticulate tube. Ovary 5-celled, cells 1-ovuled, stigmatic branches 10. Ripe carpels sub-indehiscent separating from the axis when ripe.

Carpels echinate. L. angled or somewhat lobed 1. *lobata.*
Carpels echinate. L. palmatifid . . . . 2. *sinuata.*
Carpels smooth. L. entire or slightly lobed . 3. *repanda.*

1. **U. lobata,** *L.* Bhidi janetet', *S.*

An undershrub 2-$4\frac{1}{2}$ ft. high with sub-orbicular angled or somewhat lobed leaves 2-4″ diam. often broader than long and with a gland on 1-3 of the nerves beneath. Pink flowers ¾″ diam. not racemose. Carpels glochidiate.

Very common in forest glades and waste land. Fl. and Fr. *Aug.-Dec.*

L. cordate or upper on flowering branches rhomboid and acute at base. Lobes 3-5 or more obscurely 7-9. Lower petioles long.

Yields a fibre.

2. U. sinuata, *L.* Mota bhidi janatet, *S.*

An undershrub closely resembling the last, but easily distinguished by its leaves being lobed beyond the middle into usually 5 oblong or lanceolate segments which are contracted at the base and often pinnatifid and serrated. Fls. 1″ diam.

Associated with the last and flowering at the same time and up to November.

Yields a fibre.

3. U. repanda, *Roxb.* Sikuar, *S.*

A shrub 2-4 ft. with stiff branches densely stellate-hairy, roundish repand or somewhat lobed denticulate leaves 2½-3½″ diam. and pink flowers axillary and racemose. Carpels smooth, easily dehiscent on slight pressure.

Frequent. Fl. *Sept.-Oct.* Fr. *Nov.-Dec.*

L. very reticulate beneath and mid-rib with a gland near the base. *Stipules* setaceous. *Bracteoles* united into a cup below, erect linear-subulate above ⅓-½.″ *Calyx* ⅓″, lobes linear-oblong connate ⅔ths the way up. *Cor.* ½-1″ diam. *St. tube* 1″ long.

Pavonia odorata, *Willd.* is an erect herbaceous glandular pubescent herb with slightly 3-5-lobed cordate-ovate leaves and long peduncled pink flowers about ¾″ diam. clustered at the ends of the branches. Bracteoles filiform 10-12. Carpels smooth. Chota Nagpur, *Prain.*

5. Hibiscus, Medik.

Trees, shrubs or herbs, usually suffruticose annuals or with a perennial root. L. more or less palmately lobed. Fls. axillary or becoming racemose by suppression of upper leaves. Bracteoles 5 or more, rarely fewer or absent, free or connate at the base. Sepals connate at base or combined into a 5-toothed or spathaceous calyx, valvate. Petals 5 adnate to st. tube at the base. St. tube truncate or 5-toothed at the top. Ovary 5-celled, ovules 3-more, style 5-fid. above. Capsule loculicidal with often a distinct endocarp.

I. Wild species (5 also cultivated).

A. Calyx spathaceous.

1. Fls. yellow with purple eye. Bracteoles many filiform.

Fls. mostly in terminal racemes. Capsule with dense spreading persistent hairs . 1. *cancellatus.*

Fls. mostly axillary. Capsule with appressed deciduous hairs . . . . . . 2. *Abelmoschus.*

2. Fls. yellow with purple eye. Bracteoles 4-5 lanceolate to ovate.

Branched from the base, slightly hispid below 3. *tetraphyllus.*

Stout erect unbranched, very bristly all over 4. *pungens.*

3. Fls. white or pink. Bracteoles very small caducous . . . . 5. *ficulneus.*

B. Sepals 5 nearly free or calyx 5-cleft.

1. Bracteoles not forked, linear, fls. white . 6. *micranthus.*

2. Bracteoles not forked. Fls. yellow with purple eye.

Pubescent and with pungent and glandular hairs. Capsule wingless . . . . 7. *panduræformis.*

Villous. Capsule 5-winged . . . 8. *vitifolius.*

3. Bracteoles forked. A prickly shrub . . 9. *furcatus.*

II. Cultivated species (*vide* also 5).

A. Herbaceous. Uses economical.

Calyx spathaceous. Fls. yellow. Fruit 5-10″ long . . . . 10. *esculentus.*

Calyx not spathaceous. Bracteoles not adnate to the calyx . . . . . . 11. *cannabinus.*

Calyx not spathaceous. Bracteoles and calyx accrescent red . . . . . . 12. *Sabdariffa.*

B. Large stout shrubs, grown for their showy flowers.

Bracteoles 6-7. L. ovate acuminate serrate above . . . . 13. *rosa sinensis.*

Bracteoles 6-7. L. cuneiform ovate 3-lobed dentate . . . . 14. *syriacus.*

Bracteoles 10. L. 5-angled cordate serrate downy . . . . 15. *mutabilis.*

1. H. cancellatus, *Roxb.* Usungid, *Ho.*; Jojo ara, Bir kaskom, *K.*, *S.* (names of little value).

A very hirsute or bristly herb with lower leaves sub-orbicular, upper often sagittate. Large yellow fls. with peduncles about 1″ in terminal racemes or few also axillary. Capsule subglobose to oblong 1-1¾″ very densely covered with yellowish spreading hairs, shortly beaked. Bracteoles filiform very *persistent* ¾-1¾″ with dense spreading stiff hairs.

In forests, esp. in the hills, throughout the area, frequent. Fl. *Aug.-Nov.* Fr. *Oct.-Jany.* It dies down after flowering.

Root fusiform. *Branches* often procumbent. *L.* very variable from round sub-entire deeply cordate coarsely crenate or dentate to acutely lobed (but not half way down) and (upper only) sagittate with very long linear-oblong entire auricles. Densely softly hairy or villous above and often with bristles on the nerves, beneath hairy and with stellate bristles. *Racemes* often dense flowered with filiform 2-several persistent bracts at the base of the short peduncles. *Capsules* hirsute inside and out. *Seeds* sub-reniform grey-brown ⅛″ glabrous with curved lines of dots. There are two forms :—α. Capsules ovoid 1-1¼″, bracteoles much exceeding the capsules. β. Capsules oblong 1¼-1¾″ often much longer than the bracteoles. Santara Forest division. This is very apt to be mistaken for the next species.

The root is eaten.

2. H. Abelmoschus, *L.* Mushk-dana, *H.*, *Beng.*

A hirsute or hispid herb with polymorphous leaves often resembling the last. Large yellow fls. with peduncles 2-3″ or more, usually solitary axillary, occasionally in few-fld. racemes. Capsule oblong 2-2¼″ beaked, with rather sparse adpressed stiff hairs, glabrescent. Bracteoles linear ½-1″ *deciduous*, not densely hairy.

A rare plant in Chota Nagpur. Hundrugagh (Ranchi), *Prain.* Fl. and Fr. same season as last.

The *leaves* are often 3-5-lobed half-way down or more, lobes serrate, sometimes very narrow. The leaves are less hairy than in *cancellatus,* hairs stiff and also a few stellate bristles beneath. *Peduncles* clavate above in fruit. *Seeds* reniform striate musky.

Var. **sagittifolius,** *Kew. Herb.* Nearly glabrous. *L.* sagittate. *Fl. and Fr.* small. The fruit is at once distinguished from that of H. cancellatus by absence of bristles.

Hazaribagh, *C.B. Clarke !*

3. **H. tetraphyllus,** *Roxb.*

A herb or undershrub branched from the base with a thick tap root. Branches with few short hispid or prickly hairs and deeply-lobed leaves with sparse stellate (3-forked) hispid hairs beneath and very few above. Fls. primrose-yellow $2\frac{1}{2}''$-$3''$ diam. Bracteoles 4-5, ovate, lanceolate or ovate-lanceolate. Capsule under 2″.

Ravines in the Santal P., on rocks. Fl. *Oct.-Nov.* Fr. *Dec.-Jany.* Perennial.[1]

About 3 ft. high only. *L.* radical attain 8″ diam., lobed more than half-way down, cauline usually about 3-4″ diam., deeply or shallowly-lobed; lobes usually 3 or 4 large and 2 smaller basal ones, ell. or oblong, acute or cuspidate, sometimes again lobed, coarsely toothed. *Petiole* as long or $\frac{3}{4}$ths as long as the leaf. *Stipules* linear $\frac{1}{2}$-$\frac{3}{4}''$. *Fls.* axillary and in short terminal racemes with the bract-like stipules. *Bracteoles* persistent $\frac{5}{8}$-$\frac{3}{4}''$. *Capsule* oblong $1\frac{1}{4}$-$1\frac{1}{2}''$ beaked covered with glandular and pungent hairs, 5-valved. *Seeds* black striate with rows of minute raised dots, striations with thin brown hairs.

4. **H. pungens,** *Roxb.*

A stout erect scarcely branched herb 6-12 ft. high, with bristly stem, palmately lobed or angled hairy leaves 5-12″ diam., and large yellow fls. 4-5″ diam. in terminal racemes. Bracteoles broad-lanceolate shorter than the large oblong $2\frac{1}{4}$-$2\frac{3}{4}''$ long hirsute capsule.

---

[1] Seeds of this sown by me in the Forest Park, Dehra, germinated *May-June* 1907 and flowered in the cold weather of the same year. Mr. Subramania Iyer kindly informs me that the plant is still vigorous April 1908, and looks as though it will flower again.

In cool ravines in Singbhum and the S. P. not common. Fl. *July-Oct.* Fr. *Nov.-Dec.*

Stems hollow often black or purple spotted. *Lower leaves* 5-7-lobed and coarsely toothed, *upper* 3-partite serrate hairy above, with scattered stellate hairs beneath. Lower *petioles* exceeding the blade. *Raceme* often 15″. *Bracteoles* connate at base. *Seeds* black striate with curved most minutely pubescent lines.

5. **H. ficulneus,** *L.* Naita, *Ho.*

A branched herb about 3 ft. with a thick taproot. Stems with small sharp tubercles or hispid hairs. L. palmately 3-5-lobed. Fls., 1-2″ diam, white with purple eye. Buds densely brown tomentose beaked with the 5 linear points of the spathaceous calyx. Bracteoles 4-6 caducous. Capsule $1\frac{1}{4}$-$1\frac{1}{2}$″ covered with glandular and pungent hairs. Seeds striate, the striæ with thin brown hairs.

S. P. as an escape from cultivation, also in fields. Cultivated in Singbhum and other districts. Fl. *Oct.-Nov.* Fr. *Dec.-Jany.*

L. somewhat hispidly hairy, not sparsely stellate, variable from lobed to 3-partite. Stipules caducous. Peduncles 1″ swollen above. Valves of capsule with long hairs on the margin (seen after dehiscence). Seeds somewhat as in the two last. Roxburgh, however, describes the bracteoles of H. strictus (the same plant) as small and subulate; Masters (in *F.B.I.*) as lanceolate. They are sometimes, at any rate, short and linear.

The plant yields an excellent fibre.

6. **H. micranthus,** *L.*

An erect weedy-looking undershrub with slender branches scabrid with stellate scattered bristles, and small ovate leaves $\frac{3}{4}$-1″. Fls. $\frac{1}{2}$″ diam. white or pink with reflexed corolla. Capsule globose.

Waste places, not common. Fl. *Feby.-June.*

L. crenate or toothed, simple or- 3-lobed. *Stipules* $\frac{1}{8}$-$\frac{1}{6}$″. *Peduncles* long slender articulate far exceeding the leaves, usually on short lateral branches.

7. **H. panduræformis,** *Burm.*

A very tall herb 10-12 ft. Stems pubescent and with pungent hairs. Lower leaves ovate and lobed, upper oblong-lanceolate, all coarsely irregularly toothed. Fls. solitary, axillary and sub-terminal 1-$1\frac{1}{4}$″ diam., yellow with purple eye on very short ($\frac{1}{4}$-$\frac{1}{3}$″) stout articulate peduncles. Ovary and capsule densely silky.

Waste ground, Palamau and Hazaribagh (near the boundary), rare. Fl. and Fr. *Nov.-Jan.*

L. hoary-tomentose both sides. *Peti.* 1-1½″, thickened above. *Stipules* and *bracts* filiform caducous. *Bracteoles* 8 united into cup at base, linear-spathulate appressed to and much shorter than the calyx which has oblong acute 3-nerved lobes. *Seeds* about 10 in each cell, brown, densely pubescent.

8. H. vitifolius, *L.*

Usually hoary-tomentose or villous not bristly, with simple or deeply 3-5-lobed long-stalked ovate leaves with acuminate lobes. *Petiole* as long as the blade. *Fls.* 2-2½″ diam. *Bracteoles* 8-12 linear persistent not spathulate. *Capsule* short sub-orbicular tomentose, but not with the long hairs of the last, beaked and *5-winged.*

Prain says common in all the provinces, but I have not seen it in our area nor are there specimens in the Cal. Herb. or Kew from Ch. Nagpur.

9. H. furcatus, *Roxb.*

An erect undershrub, stem covered with soft down and scattered recurved prickles, with entire or 3-5-lobed serrate leaves and yellow flowers 4″ diam. Bracteoles 10-12 linear and forked.

Pitorea, 2,000 ft. *Wood.*

10. H. esculentus, *L.* Mindijinga, *K.*; Ramjinga, *S.* Bindi *H.* Ochro. Lady's Fingers.

Erect hairy annual 4-6 ft. with cordate 3-5-lobed and toothed leaves and large yellow flowers. Peduncles and bracteoles about 1″.

Cultivated for its unripe fruits, which owing to their demulcent properties can be safely eaten in cases where other vegetables are interdicted.

11. H. cannabinus, *L.* Ji, Kotle, *K.*; Dare kudrum, *S.*

Tall unbranched 5-6 ft., rather prickly, with large leaves of which the lower are entire and cordate and the upper deeply palmate. Fls. large, over 2″ diam. white (yellow, *F.B.I.*) with purple eye.

Widely cultivated for its fibre in Singbhum. Also Manbhum, *Camp.* Santal Par., *Kurz.*; Chatra, *Wood.* Fl. *October.*

12. H. Sabdariffa, *L.* Arhaipila, *Ho.*; Arharjorjora, *M.* Arak Kudrum, *S.*; Patwa, *H.*: Rozelle, Red Sorrel

Erect glabrous with often purple stems, polymorphous usually simple leaves and yellow fls. 2½″ diam. The 8-10 linear bracteoles accrescent to the calyx which is red and fleshy (in one variety, however the calyx is green), and usually muricate or setose.

Cultivated everywhere. Fl. *r. s.* Fr. *Jany* The calyces are made into a jelly, and the leaves are eaten.

13. H. rosa-sinensis, *L.* Joba baha, *S.* is a well-known ornamental shrub usually with scarlet or crimson fls. Called Shoe flower from the fls. having been used to black shoes.

14. H. syriacus, *L.* Usually taller and more slender, the leaves sub-rhomboid and fls. usually lilac with purple eye.

15. H. mutabilis, *L.* A very large deciduous shrub, of which the handsome flowers open white and turn red by evening.

6. Thespesia, Corr.

1. T. Lampas, *Dalz.* Reke, *Ho.*; Bir katsom, or Kaskom *K.*, *S.*; Bon.-kapsi, *S.*; (both these names mean the wild or jungle cotton, a common epithet of these shrubs somewhat resembling cotton)

An erect shrub 3-5 ft. high with palmately 3-lobed leaves 4-5″ diam. and terminal solitary or 2-3 large yellow flowers 4-5″ diam. with crimson centre. It closely resembles Hibiscus, but the styles are not divided above but end in a club. Capsule woody sub-globose or ovoid, girt at base by the calyx-tube, not widely dehiscent.

Very common in the forests throughout the area. *Perennial* and deciduous or often dying down to the root, and shooting out again at the end of May. Fl. *Aug.-Oct.* Fr. *Oct.-Dec.*

Young parts covered with brown tomentum. *L.* sometimes simple softly pubescent beneath, hairy above, base cordate or rounded, mid-rib with a gland near the base beneath. *Peduncles* swollen above with 4-8 subulate or setaceous deciduous bracteoles.

Yields a strong fibre. The root and fruit given in gonorrhœa, *Camp.*

Gossypium herbaceum, *L.* Katsom, *K.*; Kaskom, *S.* Cotton is cultivated, but not on large scale, in Ch. Nag. The leaves, bracteoles and calyx are sprinkled with small black glands. Seeds covered with cotton wool. Fl. *Nov.-Jany.*

8. Kydia, Roxb.

1. **K. calycina,** *Roxb.* Bita-goinr, *K.*; Poska Olat', *S.*; Derki, Kharw; Pula, Baranga, *H.*

A moderate-sized tree, or (var.?) often flowering as a shrub, very handsome when bearing its pure white large panicles of flowers. L. sub-orbicular palmately 5-7-nerved stellate pubescent or tomentose and always with a gland on 1-3 of the nerves beneath. St. in a column with 5 spreading arms, each bearing 3 or 4 anthers. Bracteoles 4-6 spreading enlarged and persistent in fruit $\frac{1}{4}$-$\frac{1}{2}$".

Throughout the area in valleys and on hill slopes. Fl. *Sept.-Nov.* Fr. *Dec.-May.* Deciduous in *March.*

L. 4—6" diam. sinuate, angled, or somewhat lobed with strong parallel sec. nerves. *Petioles* 2-3". *Fls.* polygamous $\frac{3}{4}$" diam. *Petals* obcordate, very long clawed, densely pubescent (at least in the shrubby form), adnate to the staminal tube. Bracteoles oblong or oblong-spathulate, downy and glandular. *Ovary* 3-celled, cells 2-ovuled. *Styles* 3 hairy with peltate stigmas.

9. Bombax, L.

1. **B. malabaricum,** *D.C.* Edel, *K.*, *S.*; Simal, *H.* The Silk Cotton tree.

A large tree with prickly trunk and branches (when young), 5-7-digitate leaves, and large scarlet flowers which mostly appear when the tree is leafless. Capsule ovoid 5-7".

Generally distributed, chiefly in the valleys. Fls. *Jany.-March.* Fr. *March-May.* Leafless *Dec.-March* or even to *April.*

The tree is easily transplanted when 2-3 yrs. old, but it is largely eaten by elephants and cattle. The cotton which thickly lines the inside of the capsule is used for stuffing pillows. The wood is now largely used for tea-boxes in the Duars, but it requires careful storing or it develops a bad smell due to a fungus. Immersion in water improves its durability.

Fam. 20. TILIACEÆ.

Characters of the leaves, hairs, etc. of Malvaceæ, but leaves rarely deeply lobed. *Fls.* often small, *without* bracteoles under the flower. *Sep.* 3-5, usually free. *Pet.* as many, rarely 0, free, usually imbricate. *St.* (sometimes few in Triumfetta and Corchorus) *free* or sometimes 5-adelphous but *not* united into a tube, often on a *gonophore*; *anthers* 2-celled. *Ovary* 2-10-celled. *Ovules* anatropous. *Frt.* various, often *drupaceous* or deeply lobed. *Seeds* 1-many, exarillate, usually albuminous. Embryo straight or slightly curved.

A. Anthers globose or oblong, opening by slits.
- Trees or shrubs. Petals usually with a glandular base. Fruit drupaceous, smooth . . . . . 1. *Grewia.*
- Shrubs or herbs. Fls. in dense cymes. Pet. eglandular Frt. dry echinate . . . . . . 2. *Triumfetta.*
- Annuals. Peduncles 1-3-flowered. Frt. capsular . . 3. *Corchorus.*

B. Anthers linear, opening by pores. Frt. drupaceous. Trees . . . . 4. *Elæocarpus.*

1. Grewia, L.

Trees, shrubs or rarely undershrubs with stellate pubescence, simple 3-7-basal-nerved serrate or serrulate leaves and yellow, rarely white, flowers in axillary (not panicled in C. N. species) sessile or stalked umbels. Petals shorter than the sepals, the base usually occupied by a large gland with a pubescent rim.* St. numerous on a short gonophore (but see Note). Ovary 2-4-celled. Style 1 with 2-4 spreading stigmas or multifid peltate stigma. Ovules 2-several in each cell. Fruit often lobed of 1-4 pyrenes enclosed in a succulent or ultimately fibrous mesocarp. Pyrenes 1-2-seeded. Seed albuminous with large flat thinly-fleshy cotyledons.

The number of species is greater according to some authors than those here retained, esp. in the *asiatica* series. The *extreme* forms of these variable groups can no doubt be easily distinguished, but the way in which others have been repeatedly changed about from one cover to another in herbaria by those who maintain their distinctness as species shews how many intermediate and connecting forms exist. Whether the

---

*NOTE.—The glandular area at the base of the petals may be absent, as was noted by Sir D. Brandis, who founded the species *leptopetala* on this character. The absence of the gland is, I find, always correlated with the reduction of the gonophore and I hold the character to be variable in certain species.

extreme forms of such groups in the present state of evolution of the series should receive specific rank is of course a matter of opinion, in the absence of data as to their constancy.

A. Fls. white, or sepals first white then turning colour inside. *Shrubs* (*exc.* 4) Top of gonophore (or top of pedicel in 2) ciliate or hirsute.

I. Stigma capitate of radiating long papillæ. Pet. under ¼" half, or not half, as long as sepals. Gonophore and sometimes pedicel pilose above.

Peduncles very short. L. ovate-oblong or ovate-lanceolate . . . . . . 1. *hirsuta.*

Peduncles slender. L. lanceolate or linear-lanceolate . . . . *Var. helicterifolia.*

II. Stigma with 4 linear arms. Petals over half as long as sepals . . . . . 2. *pilosa.*

III. Stigma peltate, more or less lobed. Fls. with sepals over ½". Petals rarely half as long.

L. large sub-orbicular. Frt. large globose. A shrub . . . . 3. *sclerophylla.*

L. lanceolate. Frt. didymous or 4-lobed. Usually a tree . . . . 4. *lævigata.*

B. Fls. bright yellow. Stigmas peltate entire, lobed, or somewhat fimbriate on margins when old, sometimes 2-fid (in 8). Gonophore, when present, pubescent or tomentose above (rarely almost hirsute). Ovary villous.

I. Tree. Fruits mostly didymous, small. Petioles over ⅓" (exc. on very small leaves) slender (or thickened at top). L. glabrescent, very oblique or auricled at base. Stipules mostly falcate with auricled base.

Peduncles usually shorter than petiole and usually numerous . . . . . . 5. *tiliæfolia.*

II. Fruits globose. Petioles stout uniform or clavate, short (rarely over ½" in very large leaves). L. never auricled at base, often oblique.

Stiples subulate, linear or with setaceous tip (rarely some with subauricled base when young).

(*a*) Peduncles long (up to 1¼"); slender and usually erect. Fl. buds ellipsoid or oblong, over ¼" or if smaller then leaves about as broad as long, old green beneath (in C. N.), not (or very shortly) acuminate.

Tree, cultivated (always?). L. subrotund. Petiole $\frac{1}{3}$-$\frac{1}{2}$" . . . . 6. *asiatica*.

Undershrub. L. oblong, orbicular or obovate. Petiole under $\frac{1}{3}$" . . . . . 7. *sapida*.

(*b*) Peduncles unequal, rarely 1" long, usually divaricate. Leaves ovate to oblong, never as broad as long, sometimes persistently white or tomentose beneath, 5-7-nerved. Fl. buds globose or oblong, under $\frac{1}{4}$".

Very tomentose. Buds globose. Fls. large. L. ovate, usually white beneath . . . 8. *elastica*.

Less tomentose. Buds oblong. Fls. smaller with peduncles not longer than pedicels. L. oblong, finally green beneath . . . *var. vestita*.

(*c*) Peduncles very slender. L. narrow, lanceolate, rarely narrowly oblong or lanceolate-ovate, permanently white beneath but never coarsely tomentose, often only 3-nerved. Usually a shrub . . . . 9. *Rothii*.

1. **G. hirsuta,** *Vahl* (Em. polygama, *F.B.I.*, polygama *Roxb.* ?[1] pilosa, *Roxb.*?) Seta beli, *K.*; Seta kata, Seta andir *S.*; Kukur bicha, *H.*; Gursukri, *Kharw.*

A shrub $1\frac{1}{2}$-3 ft. high, usually with many stems from the root, tomentose or stellately villous all over, with linear-oblong to ovate-lanceolate or broadly oblong serrulate very shortly petioled usually acuminate leaves stellate-tomentose beneath and also closely stellate above when young. Fls. polygamous or 1-sexual, buds ovoid under $\frac{1}{4}$". Fr. pilose with long deciduous hairs, fleshy with a crustaceous rind.

Throughout the area, chiefly in open forest, common. Fls. *July-Sept.* Fr. *Nov.-Jany.*

Very variable. The following forms occur :—

G. *hirsuta proper.* (G. hirsuta *Roxb.* and perhaps G. pilosa, *Roxb.*)

---

[1] G. polygama, *Roxb.* is not the narrow-leaved shrub described under that name in the *F.B.I.* and by Duthie and others. Roxburgh's original figure shews broadly-lanceolate leaves and very short peduncles as in hirsuta *proper*.

L. lanceolate to ovate-lanceolate, hoary and densely clothed with stellate and pilose-stellate hairs beneath, hairs deciduous above leaving a simple base. *Peduncles* few, or clustered, equal to petiole. *Pedicels* as long. *Fls.* opening white, turning light-yellow and finally brown. *Sep.* $\frac{1}{4}$ to nearly $\frac{1}{3}$" *Pet.* $\frac{1}{10}$"-nearly $\frac{1}{7}$" oblong entire, blade not much longer than the gland. *M. gonophore* cylindric but slightly expanded into a sinuous rim above, top densely pilose, stamens 45 or more much longer than the hairs. *Herm. fl.* gonophore not margined, hairs rather longer than the stamens. *Ovary* hirsute. In fruit the hairs at the top of the gonophore spread beneath it.

Form α. *L.* oblong, suddenly acute or acuminate, sometimes wider upwards and 3-lobed, green or scarcely hoary beneath, base often oblique. Singbhum and Palamau.

Form β. *L.* much larger, often 5" by 2", more membranous, green beneath. Palamau and Hazaribagh.

Var. **helicterifolia**, *Wall.* Syn. G. angustifolia, *Wall.*, G. polygama *F.B.I.* non *Roxb.*

As in G. hirsuta proper but stems slender, *leaves* very narrow, almost white but not tomentose between the raised nerves beneath, 2½-4" long, under $\frac{3}{4}$" broad. *Peduncles* 1-4 slender, attaining 1⅛". M. st. about 30 only. *St.* in the herm. fl. slightly exceeding the hairs.

Common in scrub jungle in the west of Palamau.

Form γ. *L.* linear-oblong, under ⅜" broad, often 3½" long with peduncles longer than petioles, but otherwise as in hirsuta *proper* is intermediate. Mr. Witt has sent a similar specimen from Nimar, C. P.

The fruit of all varieties is pleasant eating, and is given in diarrhœa and dysentery.

A decoction of the leaves is also said to be used, *Watt Dic.*

2. G. pilosa, *Lamk.*[1] Syn. G. carpinifolia, *Roxb.* non *Juss.* Gursukri, *Kharw.*; Gursikri (Sirguja, *Wood*).

A large straggling shrub with branchlets, leaves and inflorescence hirsute with stellate hairs, not villous. L. oblong or sometimes slightly broader upwards, suddenly narrowed to the tip, or more rarely acuminate. Fl.-buds oblong mostly constricted in the middle $\frac{1}{3}$-$\frac{1}{2}$" long before opening. Stigmas 4 linear spreading. Style stellate. Frt. closely covered with very *short* stellate hairs.

---

[1] Lamarck's description seems at first excellent, except that the fruit described is that of hirsuta. The plant is certainly Wight and Arnott's G. pilosa, *Lamk.* Mr. Drummond has, however, pointed out that Lamarck's pilosa is not this plant at all but G. orientalis, *L.*, and he considers that the one here described is G. commutata, *D.C*

Hazaribagh, at Pachamba, *Camp.*; Parasnath, *Anderson*; Sirguja, *Wood*; Ranchi (at Kuru ghat), *Wood.* Very rare. Fls. *July-Oct.* Fr. *Dec-Jany.*

Easily distinguished in flower, similar to some states of *hirsuta* in leaf it may however be distinguished by the stiff not softly villous hairs on the branches and fruit which break off with age leaving a *stellate* base, also by the remarkable short medianly constricted terminally dilated cup-shaped gonophore which is recognizable in fruit and after this has fallen. Mr. Witt in forwarding excellent specimens from the Central Provinces points out that the bare straggling habit, and especially the *square* stems below make it very easily recognizable in the field.

L. 2″ by 1″ to 4″ by $1\frac{1}{2}$″ with rounded or sub-cordate base, often doubly serrulate. Sec. n. 4-5 prs. *Petiole* $\frac{1}{8}$″. *Peduncles* few $\frac{1}{4}$″. *Sep.* $\frac{1}{2}$-$\frac{2}{3}$″. *Petals* more than half as long bifid. *Anthers* with a few long hairs. *Ovary* hirsute.

3. **G. sclerophylla,** *Roxb.* Syn. G. scabrophylla, *Roxb.* Gaphni, *K.*; Tarse Kotap, *S.*

A coarse bushy shrub about 4 ft. high with large roundish or broadly elliptic leaves. Fls. large white 1-$1\frac{1}{2}$″ diam. Frt. globose $\frac{3}{4}$-1″ diam. with 4 rugose pyrenes.

Singbhum, on wooded slopes; Manbhum, *Camp.* and *Watt* (under G. villosa). Fl. *May-Aug.* Fr. *June-Nov.* the dried fruit may be often found up to *Feby.* of the following year along the branches below the leaves.

Branchlets stellately tomentose, young densely shaggily tomentose. *L.* 4-6″ by 3-5″ often slightly lobed, serrate or denticulate, scabrid above and stellate pubescent beneath, base rounded with 3 strong and 2 weaker nerves, cross nervules prominent. *Petiole* $\frac{1}{2}$-1″ (in C. N.) *Stipules* linear caducous. *Peduncles* and pedicels about $\frac{1}{4}$″ or shorter. *Pet.* obovate white about $\frac{1}{3}$rd as long as sepals, sometimes notched. (In Campbell's No. 8712 the sepals are unusually short, only $\frac{1}{3}$″.)

The fruit is eaten.

The distinction of the fruits of Grewia into fleshy and those with crustaceous rind is not tenable in the field. The rind of this species only becomes crustaceous or coriaceous when old or dry, the rind of hirsuta, described as fleshy in the *F.B.I.* is crustaceous when fresh.

4. **G. lævigata,** *Vahl.* Gara Bursu, *K.*; Marang jowar, *S.*

A small tree with shortly pubescent slender branchlets, narrow leaves green both sides usually 3-6″ by $1\frac{1}{4}$-2″, and white flowers 1-$1\frac{1}{2}$″ diam., succeeded by simple didymous or 4-lobed green fruits, drupels $\frac{1}{4}$-$\frac{3}{8}$″ diam.

Singbhum, Manbhum, Ranchi, Hazaribagh (Panchet), and S. P. Especially frequents the vicinity of streams at 1,000-2,000 ft. elev. Fl. *June-Oct.* Fr. *Dec.-Feby.* Evergreen.

L. narrow elliptic or oblong-lanceolate acuminate serrulate attaining in favourable localities 9″ by 3″, slightly stellate beneath, base acute 3-nerved. Sec. n. 3-5 prs. oblique, cross nervules distinct. *Petiole* $\frac{1}{4}$-$\frac{1}{3}$″. *Peduncles* $\frac{3}{4}$-1″. *Pedicels* $\frac{1}{2}$-$\frac{3}{4}$″. *Buds* $\frac{1}{2}$″ long or more. *Sepals* 3-nerved, $\frac{1}{2}$-$\frac{5}{8}$″ long. *Petals* less than $\frac{1}{4}$th as long orbicular or quadrate glandular with very small blade.

5. **G. tiliæfolia,** *Vahl.* Syn. G. asiatica, var. tiliæfolia, *Brandis.* Jang Olat', *S.*; Dhaman, Ahsing, *K.*; Dhaman, *Kharw.*, *H.*

A tree with very broadly ovate to obovate obtuse or shortly cuspidate usually crenate (more serrate with age) glabrescent leaves with the *cordate* base usually auricled on one side, *slender* petioles usually thickened at the top, mostly *falcate* stipules and peduncles usually much shorter than the petioles. Gonophore 0 or long or short.

Fruits mostly *didymous.*

Fl. *April-June.* Fr. *Oct.* Very common.

α tiliæfolia *proper.* *L.* large 5-7-nerved mostly auricled on one side, 6″ or more long at the time of flowering, crenate. *Petiole* $\frac{1}{2}$-1″, only very young tomentose. *Stipules* falcate semi cordate at base. *Peduncles* $\frac{1}{4}$-$\frac{1}{3}$″ usually numerous and much shorter than the petioles. *Buds* shortly ellipsoid to oblong somewhat tomentose, ribbed. *Sepals* under $\frac{1}{4}$″.

(Vahl's type shews the leaves fully developed while the plant is still in flower, 6-7″ long, nearly glabrous, with 5 primary nerves and very distinct cross nervules. *Petiole* $\frac{1}{2}$-$\frac{3}{4}$″. *Peduncles* few below but *fl.-buds* crowded above. *Buds* 2-4 mm. long ellipsoid tomentose ridged, buds however, vary much in shape according to age. *Fls.* small, but too crumpled for measurement.)

Common throughout the area.

β. *L.* only half-developed at the time of flowering, oblong to oblong-ovate with often sub-regular base but very falcate and sub-cordate stipules. *Peduncles* very numerous. *Fls.* larger. *Sep.* over $\frac{1}{4}$″. *Buds* oblong.

Singbhum. Palamau.

γ. *L.* not over $3\frac{1}{2}$″ at the time of flowering. *Stipules* only falcate while young. *Buds* globose and tomentose (sometimes ellipsoid just before expanding). *Fls.* larger. *Sepals* over $\frac{1}{4}$″ oblong.

Palamau. (also Central Provinces).

δ. *L.* very membranous, oblong to ovate with sub-regular or oblique base, half developed only at the time of flowering. *Stipules* linear or only slightly falcate. *Peduncles* few very slender and often as long as petiole, about $\frac{1}{8}$″. *Buds* oblong. Linear *bracteoles* sub-persistent (they are usually very caducous).

Santal Parganahs.

The wood is the most highly prized of all the species in Chota Nagpur for banghy poles, etc. The branches are lopped for fodder.

6. **G. asiatica,** *L.*? Olat', *S.*; Pat-dhaman. *Kharw.* Phalsa, *H.*

A tree with tomentose shoots, very broadly ovate or sub-orbicular obtuse or shortly cuspidate leaves with regular or usually oblique very rarely cordate base, sharply (often doubly) serrate leaves, tomentose when young. Petioles short $\frac{1}{8}$-$\frac{1}{2}$″ uniform or clavate, usually stout. Peduncles several long slender, about twice length of petiole. Gonophore long. Fruit globose.

Cultivated in Chota Nagpur for its fruit, Hazaribagh, etc. *Fl.* *May* *Fr.* *June.*

The C. N. plant is certainly G. asiatica of Roxburgh, but somewhat differs from the Linnean type. This was collected at Surat by Braad, and was almost certainly a cultivated specimen. It has tomentose shoots, sub-orbicular cuspidate sharply doubly serrate *leaves* about 3″ long (still young), *white* beneath, with 5-7 primary nerves. *Petiole* about $\frac{3}{8}$″ rather slender and clavate. *Stipules* sharply subulate about as long. *Peduncles* up to 1″ long. *Buds* very broadly oblong. According to a note by Braad (kindly translated by Dr. Daydon-Jackson) the berries are red and sour (this corresponds to an unripe condition).

The C. N. plant has *leaves* about 4″, sometimes slightly lobed, more or less permanently pubescent beneath but *green*, *petioles* stout, *buds* up to $\frac{1}{4}$″, and much larger flowers. *Peduncles* up to 1″. *Petals* usually 2-fid. *Drupe* purple when ripe $\frac{1}{3}$-$\frac{1}{2}$″ diam.

7. **G. sapida,** *Roxb.* Syn. G. Campbellii *Watt* (in Descriptive Catalogue). Barsa pakor. *S*

An undershrub with more or less perennial shoots (if not burnt) from a woody rootstock, with broadly oblong to sub-orbicular or obovate rounded or obtuse serrate leaves often with cuneate 5-nerved base, very short petioles $\frac{1}{10}$-$\frac{1}{4}$″, lanceolate or subulate stipules, and very long peduncles $\frac{1}{2}$-$1\frac{1}{4}''$. Buds large clavate, $\frac{1}{4}''$ or more before opening. Drupes globose, sometimes somewhat lobed with 1-3 1-seeded nuts.

Singbhum, Manbhum, Hazaribagh and Palamau on the hills and fire-lines, or in scrub jungle annually burnt. Fl. *April-June.*

Like *asiatica* and *elastica* this species shows a series of forms from glabrescent (in C. N.) to white or white-tomentose (in the U. P.), or brown-tomentose (in the Sikkim Terai). The C. N. form (var. Campbellii) has shoots with few stellate hairs. *L.* attaining 4'' sometimes sub-lobate, very rarely acute, with scattered stellate hairs, nearly glabrous except on the nerves when old. *Peduncles* hispid, usually 3-fid., *pedicels* $\frac{1}{4}$-$\frac{1}{2}''$. *Sepals* about $\frac{1}{3}''$. *Pet.* $\frac{1}{8}''$ usually 2-fid. *Drupes* $\frac{1}{4}''$.
The fruit is eaten.

8. **G. elastica,** *Royle* (em. G. cinnamomea, *Gamble* G. vestita, *Wall.*) Syn. *G. asiatica* pro parte *Brandis.* Gonyer *K.*; Nanha Olat', *S.*

Tree with tomentose shoots, ovate oblong or elliptic acuminate serrate or serrulate 5-7-nerved leaves tomentose when young and often persistently white or tomentose beneath when old, with oblique base but not cordate. Petioles short (usually under $\frac{1}{2}''$ in large leaves) stout uniform or only slightly thickened upwards. Stipules linear to setaceous, more rarely subulate. Peduncles few to many usually stout tomentose and divaricate, but sometimes slender in var. γ. Bracteoles narrowly linear or setaceous, more persistent than in *asiatica.* Buds sub-globose to oblong. Gonophore present or absent. Fruit globose under $\frac{1}{4}''$ diam.

Throughout Chota Nagpur. Fl. *April-May.* Fr. *Oct.-Jany.* Campbell and Watt say that *vestita* (the tree referred to is *elastica* proper) is very plentiful on the summit of Parasnath at 4,500 ft.; but as far as Parasnath is concerned, it nowhere occurs below 3,500 ft., its place at the lower elevations being taken by G. asiatica (G. tiliæfolia?). On the Tundi Hills both species grow side by side at an elevation of 1,500 ft.

The typical G. elastica, *Royle,* is a very tomentose form with ovate leaves, found chiefly in the north-west Himalayas. Leaves on some shoots will attain 11 inches. Typical G. vestita, *Wall.* is a green form with oblong leaves, short peduncles and smaller flowers, found chiefly in Nepal and the Eastern Himalayas. The following forms occur in C. N.

α. elastica proper. *Branches* often drooping. *Shoots* shaggily tomentose when young with tomentum white or (var. cinnamomea) tawny or rufous. *Twigs* reddish when old. *L.* 3-5″ obliquely broadly ovate acuminate or acute, persistently white beneath when old, serrulate. (Royle's type is lobed). *Stipules* broadly linear or subulate. *Petioles* about $\frac{1}{3}$″. *Peduncles* $\frac{1}{3}$-$\frac{3}{4}$″. *Bracts* linear or subulate. *Buds* large globose ver-tomentose. *Sepals* persistently tomentose without about $\frac{3}{8}$-$\frac{5}{8}$″. *I* oblong $\frac{1}{8}$-$\frac{6}{32}$″. *Stigma* capitate with much lobed or fimbriate margin or deeply 2-fid. with lamellate branches. Fruit $\frac{1}{4}$″.

Singbhum, frequent in the forests: Manbhum, Tundi hills and Hazaribagh, especially on Parasnath.

Well described by Campbell and Watt as a "small, much branched tree crowded with ovate oblique acute or acuminate leaves, densely rufescent, hoary beneath, above deep dark green. Foliage thick dark coloured. Fruit less than $\frac{1}{4}$″, 2-seeded."

β. Less tomentose. *L.* becoming quite green beneath, but permanently stellately puberulous, attaining $6\frac{1}{2}$″ by $3\frac{1}{2}$″. Singbhum.

γ. **vestita** (*Bengal Plants*, not typical). Less densely tomentose or villous than in *α*. *L* oblong or narrowly ovate 3-6″, scarcely or very finely tomentose, ultimately green or hoary beneath, finely acuminate. *Stipules* as long as petiole linear to setaceous, but sometimes with sub-auricled base. *Peduncles* slender $\frac{1}{3}$-$\frac{3}{4}$″. *Pedicels* shorter than peduncles. *Buds* oblong or clavate before opening. *Bracts* setaceous. *Sep.* $\frac{5}{16}$-$\frac{3}{8}$″ *Pet.* linear or linear-oblong $\frac{1}{8}$-$\frac{3}{16}$″.

Singbhum, frequent. (Some specimens, *e.g.*, Singbhum No. 152 with leaves hoary beneath are placed in G. excelsa in the Cal. Herb.)

δ **vestita,** *Wall*, is more densely brown-villous on twigs and peduncles. *Peduncles* very short and *pedicels* equalling or exceeding them. Oblong-acuminate *leaves* stellately villous beneath. *Sep.* $\frac{7}{32}$-$\frac{9}{32}$″. *Pet.* $\frac{3}{32}$″ linear-oblanceolate. Not seen in C. N.

The wood is much valued, but not quite as much as is that of *tiliæfolia*.

9. **G. Rothii,** *D.C.* Syn. G. excelsa, *F.B.I.* non *Vahl*, G. salvifolia, *Roxb.* non *Heyne*.

Bursu, *K.*; Cheli, K (f. *Watt*); Bichra (Sirguja, f. *Wood*).

A pretty shrub or, rarely a small tree with hoary branchlets, oblong or ovate-lanceolate or lanceolate, rarely oblong or lanceolate-ovate, acuminate serrulate or crenulate 3-5-nerved leaves always beautifully white beneath, short petioles rarely over $\frac{1}{4}$″. Stipules broadly linear to linear-subulate (never setaceous as in elastica) equalling or exceeding the petiole. Peduncles 1-6, very slender, $\frac{1}{2}$-1″, with usually 3 very slender pedicels clavate beneath the flower and linear bracts $\frac{1}{8}$″ long.

Gonophore distinct, finely tomentose above. Ovary long-villous. Stigma not deeply lobed. Fruit about $\frac{1}{4}''$, sub-persistently hoary, rarely lobed, ultimately purple.

Singbhum forests, common; Palamau; Santal Parganahs; Sirguja and Jaspur, *Wood*; not reported by Campbell from Manbhum! Fl. *April-Sept.* Fr. *June-Oct.* Evergreen.

a. Rothii *proper.* A *shrub* with the bright-yellow flowers often borne in great profusion. *Twigs* purple when old. *L.* lanceolate to ovate-lanceolate, never lobed, 2-3″ but attaining 4-5″ by $1\frac{1}{3}''$, acuminate rarely acute. *Peduncles* $\frac{1}{3}$-$\frac{3}{4}''$, *pedicels* $\frac{1}{4}$-$\frac{1}{2}''$. *Sepals* $\frac{1}{3}''$ linear or linear-oblong. *Pet.* about $\frac{1}{8}''$ entire oblong, blade $1\frac{1}{2}$-2 times the claw.

Distribution as above.

β. A *tree. L.* often lobed, ovate-lanceolate to broadly oblong with broad base mostly 5-nerved, attaining $4\frac{1}{2}$ by 2″, serrulate or sometimes even coarsely serrate, in one specimen blunt. *Peduncles* sometimes 6, and 3-4-fid. Santal Parganas.

G. Rothii, is one of the woods used by the Kols in producing fire from dry sticks.

2. Triumfetta, L.

Herbs, undershrubs or shrubs with simple or lobed serrate leaves, and small yellow flowers in dense cymes or fascicles. Fascicles axillary or running into terminal spikes from the reduction of the upper leaves. Sepals and petals 5. Stamens 8-15, on a fleshy lobed glandular torus. Ovary 2-5-celled. Cells 2-ovuled. Style filiform. Stigma 5-toothed. Fruit bristly or with hooked spines, indehiscent or capsular. Seeds 1-2 in each cell.

1. T. pilosa, *Roth.*

A shrub 3-6 feet high with stellately hairy stems and simple ovate lanceolate subcordate leaves, softly stellately hairy both sides. Conspicuous in fruit from the heads of hooked spines.

Shady moist woods in Singbhum. Fls. *Sept.-Nov.* Fr. *Nov.-Jany.* The flowers close in afternoon.

Stellate hairs on stem with red bulbous bases. *L.* attain 6″ by $2\frac{1}{4}''$ pale and densely hairy beneath. *Petiole* $\frac{1}{2}''$-2″ *Stipules* $\frac{1}{4}''$. *Sepals* $\frac{5}{16}''$-$\frac{3}{8}''$ linear stellate-hairy apiculate. *Petals* linear-oblong or oblanceolate $\frac{1}{4}''$ spreading. *Stamens* 10. Fruit $\frac{3}{4}''$-1″ diam. including the $\frac{1}{4}''$-$\frac{1}{3}''$ long spines 4-celled 8-seeded. Spines hairy all round (glabrous one side, *F.B.I.*)

2. T. rhomboidea, *Jacq.* Chikti, *H.*

A herb, or undershrub 3-4 feet with more or less pubescent branches and 3-lobed 5-7-nerved leaves, stellately hairy especially on the ribs beneath. Fruits pubescent $\frac{1}{4}''$ diam. including the minutely-hooked spines.

Throughout the area, attaining its largest size in damp shady places.

Fl. and Fr., *Oct.-Jany.*

Stems usually more pubescent on one side. *L.*, lower with round base attaining $5\frac{1}{2}''$ by $5''$, 3-lobed and coarsely toothed with a petiole up to $4''$ long. *Upper leaves* gradually smaller and uppermost lanceolate. *Fls.* fascicled axillary and running into terminal spikes. *Sep.* linear $\frac{1}{4}''$ apiculate. *Pet.* oblong or spathulate, somewhat shorter.

Yields a soft glossy fibre. Mucilaginous.

The following species of **Corchorus,** viz., **acutangulus**, *Lamk.* with narrow winged capsules and 3-fid beak; **fascicularis**, *Lamk.* with narrow leaves and beaked capsules; **olitorius**, *L.* and **capsularis**, *L.* are found outside the forests. The last two give the fibre known as Jute. **C. capsularis**, Kaskomrau, *S.* with globose capsules is found sometimes apparently wild. the others are all probably truly wild. They flower in the rains. **C. olitorius**, Vern. Hatempa, *Ho.* Bir Narcha, *S.* is eaten as a vegetable. It has broad ovate serrate leaves some, or all of them with a slender tail each side of the base, and a linear long-beaked capsule with transverse partitions between the seeds.

Elæocarpus serratus, *L.* A tree with evergreen foliage and axillary racemes of white flowers with laciniate petals is sometimes grown in gardens.

Fam. 21. STERCULIACEÆ.

Characters of leaves, hairs, etc., of Malvaceæ but *fls.* often zygomorphic, 1-2-sexual or polygamous. *Petals* sometimes absent. St. sometimes definite and *anther-cells* always 2. parallel or divergent. *Ovary* sessile or stipitate, of 2-5 carpels loosely united and follicular in fruit, or connate into as many cells, rarely carpel 1 (Waltheria). *Ovules* anatropous. *Frt.* capsular or follicular. *Cotyledons* leafy. *Alb.* present or 0.

A. Petals 0. St. column bearing a head or ring of anthers. Carpels in fruit distinct follicular. L. simple or digitate . . . . . . 1. *Sterculia.*

B. Petals present. Carpels not follicular in fruit. (but see Helicteres)

I. Fil. completely connate into a tube, or free above. Ovary on a long gynophore

Anthers and staminodes subsessile on the dilated tube . . . . 2. *Helicteres.*

Free part of filaments and staminodes long and filiform . . . . 3. *Pterospermum.*

II. Stamens with the filaments only connate below. Ovary sessile . . . .

Stamens very many. Shrubs . . . . 4. *Eriolaena.*

Stamens 15 fertile, staminodes 5. Herb . . 5. *Pentapetes.*

Stamens 5. Staminodes 5. Petals appendaged 6. *Buettneria.*

Stamens 5. Petals spathulate. Ovary 5-celled 7. *Melochia.*

Stamens 5. Petals oblong-spathulate. Ovary 1-celled . . . . 8. *Waltheria.*

1. Sterculia, L.

Trees, characters as above. Fls. polygamous. The 5 follicles stellately spreading in fruit, sometimes dehiscing long before the seed or seeds are ripe, so that these ripen fully exposed.

1. L. angled or palmately lobed.

L. shallowly 5-lobed tomentose beneath. Lobes entire. Fls. very small greenish-brown. Inflorescence densely glandular . . . . 1. *urens.*

L deeply 5-7-lobed tomentose beneath lobes again 3-lobed rarely entire. Fls. $\frac{1}{2}''$ diam. yellowish with pink centre . . . . 2. *villosa.*

L. 3-lobed or in young plants deeply 5-7-lobed glabrescent. Fls. scarlet . . . . 3. *colorata.*

2. L. digitate. Fls. dull orange . . . . 4. *foetida.*

1. S. urens, *Roxb.* Teley, *K.*, *S.*, Telhec', *S.*; Kaunjii, *Kharw.*, Gulu, *H.*

A large or mod.-sized tree with thin papery bark which appears white in the distance and gaunt spreading branches marked with large scars. Panicles 4-7″ densely viscidly pubescent. Fls. $\frac{1}{6}''$ diam. Follicles pungent with bristles.

A conspicuous feature of the dry rocky hills of Ch. Nag. and less so in the S. P. Fls. *Dec.-Feby.* Fr. *April.* It drops its leaves in *Nov.* or *Dec.* and often remains leafless until the May storms.

L. 9-16" both ways not deeply lobed (never half-way down) but usually broadly 5-cuspidate, base deeply cordate rounded. Petiole 6-12". *Fls.* reddish-brown tomentose outside, green inside the oblong acute lobes which are bearded within at the base, and crimson inside the tube.

It yields a gum "used by the Santals in throat affections". *Camp.* The seeds are eaten. The bark yields a fibre.

2. S. villosa, *Roxb.* Sisi, *K.*, Ganjher, *S.*, Walkom, Pironja, *M.*? ; Sisir, *Oraon* ; Udal, *Kharw.*, *H.* ; Baringa, *Gond.*

A large tree with pale but not papery bark. Branches with large scars. Panicles pendulous 9-12" rusty pubescent. Fls. ½" diam. membranous. Ripe follicles tomentose, scarlet inside.

Essentially a tree of the valleys. Singbhum, frequent, but not common. Parasnath, in Hazaribagh. Palamau. S. P. Probably in other districts. Fl. *Jany.-March.* Fr. *May-June.* Leafless *Dec.-May.*

L. appressed villosely-tomentose beneath 9-16" both ways, usually cut to the middle, lobes caudate or again 3-partite ; base deeply cordate. *Petiole* as long as leaf. *Seeds* several brown with a black shining aril, ⅓-½.

A very strong fibre is obtained from the bast which accounts for the scarcity of the tree in some places. The wood is now used for tea boxes in the Duars, it is a very bad fuel. The tree coppices freely ; the seeds germinate soon after falling in June.

3. S. colorata, *Roxb.* Sisi, *K.* ; Udal, *S.* ; Sisir. *Oraon.*

A large or mod.-sized tree very beautiful in flower when the numerous panicles resemble masses of scarlet coral. In fruit it is easily distinguished by the very membranous green or rosy follicles which open widely, bearing one seed on one or both of the margins.

Valleys in Singbhum ; Manbhum, *Manson, Campbell* ; Tamar, *Wood* ; Parasnath. Neterhat 2,500 ft. (Palamau) *Gamble!* S. P. (Mahuagarhi *Gamble.*)

Fls. *March-April.* Fr. *April-May.* Leafless *Jany.-May.*

Bark grey. *L* 6-12", with only scattered stellate hairs beneath. In young plants very deeply 7-lobed or partite (Campbell's No 8792 is almost certainly this), in old trees usually with only 3 caudate lobes and deeply cordate base. *Fls.* ¾" clavate, orange-scarlet stellately tomentose with pedicels and rachis of panicle of the same colour.

Yields a strong fibre.

4. S. fœtida, *L.*

Has been introduced into Purulia. It was also reported by Anderson from Parasnath!

Fl. 1¼″ diam. red and yellow or dull purple in narrow panicles 6-12″ long, and with a most offensive smell, *Brandis*. Fl. *April-May*.

2. Helicteres, L.

1. H. Isora, *L.* Poto-porla, sinkari, *K.*; also called Goinr from a confusion with Grewia; Petcamra, *S.*; Aitem, *Kharw*; Maraphal, *H.*

A shrub or small tree with oblique usually cordate broadly oblong or rounded pubescent 5-7-palmi-nerved leaves, scarlet lateral zygomorphic flowers 1½″ long, and a woody fruit of 5 spirally rolled carpels on a very elongated gynophore, tardily follicular when ripe, and dehiscent along their inner edge.

Very common and often gregarious both in the valleys and especially on northern aspects in the hills. Fls. *April-Dec.* Fr. *Oct.-Jany.*, but the open carpels may be found up to June. Deciduous in *March* and renews leaves in *April*.

Shoots softly villous. *L.* rarely symmetrical, bifarious 3-6″ often scabrous above, densely stellate pubescent beneath, often somewhat lobed, serrate. *Petiole* ⅛-½″. *Peduncles* axillary or extra axillary 2-4 together short. *Calyx* ⅓-¼″ oblique, stellate. *Petals* reflexed. *Staminal tube* embracing the gynophore cupular above and 5-toothed.

The root, bark and fruit are given for colic, *Camp.*

3. Pterospermum, Schreb.

1. P. acerifolium, *Willd.* Muchu kundi, *K.*; Machkunda, *S.*

A large handsome tree with large palmately-nerved cordate leaves white tomentose beneath and large white flowers. Capsule oblong woody 5-valved with winged seeds.

Doubtfully indigenous. Messrs. Campbell and Watt believe it to be so in the Tundi forest. It is commonly planted near villages throughout the area. The name Muchokunda is Sanscrit and is the Hindi and Bengalee name for P. suberifolium, *Lam.*

Fls. *March-July*. The capsules open at the time of flowering in the following year. Evergreen.

Rusty tomentose. *L.* 6-15″, lobed entire or coarsely toothed. *Fls.*, regular or sub-regular. *Sepals* 4-5″. *Petals* $3\frac{1}{2}$-$4\frac{1}{2}$″ linear-oblanceolate. *St.* 15, shorter than the staminodes, with filiform filaments and linear anthers. *Staminodes* 5, $3\frac{1}{2}$-$3\frac{3}{4}$″ long (including tube), pubescent, filiform slightly clavate. *Capsule* rough.

4. Eriolæna, D.C.

Trees or shrubs with palmately-nerved leaves and regular yellow flowers axillary or panicled, bracteolate. Calyx spathaceous, 5-toothed or partite. St. tube short with many anthers, cells parallel. Staminodes 0. Ovary sessile 5-10-celled. Style with as many spreading stigmas. Ovules many. Capsule woody loculicidal. Seeds winged above. The woody peduncles are often sharply flexed in fruit.

Bracteoles pinnatisect large . . . . . 1. *Hookeriana*.
Bracteoles entire or lobed very small and caducous. 2. *quinquelocularis*.

1. **E. Hookeriana**, *W. & A.* Bundun, Uidbulung, Hakehomo, *K.*; Guaguli, *S.*; Ponra, *Oraon*.

A shrub or small tree with the new shoots densely, stellately scaly, leaves white tomentose beneath 3-6″. Yellow flowers $1\frac{1}{2}$-2″ diam., 1-few on axillary or extra-axillary long peduncles. Capsule tubercled, ovoid.

Common on the hills in Singbhum, Manbhum, Hazaribagh and Palamau. Also found in the Santal Parganahs; Sirguja, *Wood*.

Fls. *April-June*. Fr. *Nov.-Jany*. New leaves at time of flowering

L. broadly cordate coarsely toothed shortly acuminate, base 7-9 nerved. *Peduncles* from the axils of deciduous bracts or of the young leaves, rarely terminal, far exceeding the petioles at the time of flowering, 2-4″, either simple and 1-fid. or branched and few-fid. often with 1-2 or a whorl of pectinate bracts about the middle. *Bracteoles* 3 laciniate $\frac{1}{3}$-$\frac{1}{2}$″. *Calyx* ovoid crowned by the free tips of the valvate sepals in bud, tomentose.

The wood is strong and used for axe (hake) handles. The bark is said to yield a good fibre.

2. **E. quinquelocularis**, *Wight*. Bhawat, *Vern.* (Wood).

Much resembling the last but the flowers in large terminal panicles exceeding the leaves and the bracteoles as above. The capsule also is smoother and more oblong.

Parasnath, *Prain*; Jaspur, *Wood*.
Poultices of the root cures wounds, *Wood*.

Pentapetes phoenicea, *L.* Bare baha, *S.*, is a branched herb 2-5 ft. high, glabrous, or with a few scattered hairs, easily recognized by its long lanceolate sharply toothed leaves 3-5" long with only 1 primary nerve. Fls. large, red nodding on short 2-flowered peduncles. *Capsule* subglobose, bristly.

In wet fields, not common. The root is used medicinally, *Camp*.

6. Buettneria, L.

Trees, shrubs, or herbs, sometimes climbing, with simple entire or toothed leaves. Fls. purplish small or minute cymose, cymes often umbellate and panicled. Petals with a hooded base and variously shaped horns or appendages. Staminal tube short with 5 fertile anthers and 5 staminodes. Ovary 5-celled, cells 2-ovuled. Capsule globose more or less echinate, septifragally 5-valved.

1. B. aspera, *Colebr.*

A large woody climber (or tree ?) with large cordate sub-orbicular or oblong leaves with 6 basal nerves, and the minute flowers in axillary hoary cymose panicles.

Rajmehal Hills, *Prain*. Fl. *May-June*.

L. glabrescent shortly acuminate with 4-6 prs. sec. n. above the basal. *Sep.* triangular valvate, lurid purple-green. *Pet.* linear blackish with yellow pilose horns on the back, *Clarke*. *Capsule* 1¼" diam. 5-celled with long curved spines.

This plant is described as a tree in the *F.B.I.* and in Bengal Plants. All the herbarium sheets (I have seen none from Chota Nagpur), which bear remarks as to its habit describe it as *scandent*.

2. B. herbacea, *Roxb.* - Idel sanga, *K.*; Deku sindur, *S.*

A branched herb with a perennial woody rootstock, distant ovate-lanceolate acuminate toothed leaves 1-2½" long and axillary cymes of small purplish flowers, remarkable for the long slender tips and 2-fid appendages of the petals. Capsule softly spiny, $\frac{1}{4}''$ diam.

Rocky ground in the forests, and also sometimes in the open. Fl. *Aug.-Oct.*

The rootstock is ground and rubbed on swellings of the legs by the Kols. It is also used in combination with Bael fruit, hesel gum, and Banyan root in cholera and diarrhœa. 'It is given in the female complaint known in Santali as pordhol,' *Camp*

Melochia corchorifolia, *L.* Thuiak'. *S.* An undershrub with oblong-ovate serrate plaited leaves 1-3″ long with rounded or cordate base. *Fls.* small white or pink collected in dense heads. *Calyx tube* $\frac{1}{8}''$ surrounded by 4-5 bracteoles $\frac{1}{4}$-$\frac{1}{3}''$ long. *Capsule* depressed globose. pubescent, 5-grooved.

Common in waste places, bunds of rice-fields, etc. Fl. and Fr. r.s.

The leaves are eaten as a vegetable and the stem yields a fibre.

Waltheria indica, *L.* A perennial hoary-tomentose undershrub 2-4 ft., partially dying down in some situations and shooting out again in *May* and *June*. *Leaves* velvety-ovate or ovate oblong sub-plicate toothed with 5-nerved base, larger $2\frac{3}{8}''$ by $1\frac{1}{8}''$, rarely 3″ long. *Fls.* yellow or pink in axillary sessile or stalked dense capitate cymes with small lanceolate bracts and also running out into leafless spikes. Petals $\frac{1}{6}$-$\frac{1}{4}$ narrow oblong, with a long claw. *St. tube* with 5 oblong anthers without staminodes. *Capsule* $\frac{1}{12}''$ ovoid villous 2-valved with 1 black seed.

Especially on rocks in open dry jungles, also common in waste land. Fl. r.s.

Fam. 22. EUPHORBIACEÆ.

Trees, shrubs, or herbs, sometimes with milky juice. *Leaves* alternate (exc. Trewia) simple (exc. Bischofia), usually stipulate. *Fls.* small or minute, 1-sexual, monœcious or diœcious. In Euphorbia reduced to single pedicelled stamens and naked ovaries surrounded by an involucre. *Perianth* 0, single or double, usually sepaloid. *St.* 1-6 or numerous; often central in the flower, with or without a pistillode. *Anthers* 2-celled, usually small on a broad connective. *Ovary* superior of 3 carpels and 3-celled, more rarely of 2 or many carpels and cells (only 1-celled in Antidesma spp.), often 3-lobed. *Styles* or *stigmas* as many as the carpels, sometimes 2-fid. *Ovules* 1-2 in each cell, pendulous from the inner angle. *Fruit* usually capsular of three or more 2-

valved cocci, or a drupe with a 1-more-celled putamen. *Seed* sometimes arillate or with a caruncle. *Embryo* straight with flat foliaceous cotyledons in a fleshy albumen, very rarely exalbuminous with fleshy cotyledons.

I. Cells of ovary 2-ovuled.

A. Male fls. reduced to single pedicelled stamens, surrounded by a calyx-like involucre, which sometimes also includes a solitary pedicelled ovary.

Trees, shrubs, or herbs, often fleshy, with milky juice . . . . 1. *Euphorbia.*

B. Fls. not reduced to single stamens and pistils.

1. Tribe Phyllantheæ. Perianth 1-2-seriate. Petals sometimes present. St. 3-6 (sep. and anths. 4-12 in Glochidion spp.) free or connate. Ovary 2-many-celled. Fls. fascicled, rarely few in the axils. Stigmas not dilated. The leaves are often small and distichous, the twigs bearing them simulating pinnate leaves, the resemblance to such being very striking when, as is often the case, the whole twig is deciduous.

(*a*) Petals present, very small. Sepals valvate. Stamens united into a column below.

Ovary 2-celled. Fruit a drupe . . . . 2. *Bridelia.*

Ovary 3-celled. Fruit dry, ultimately dehiscent . 3. *Cleistanthus.*

(*b*) Petals absent. Sepals imbricate.

(i) Calyx 4-6-lobed or partite, campanulate or spreading. St. 3 or more.

Disc 0. Styles united in a column round a depressed center. Frt. multilocular capsular . . . . 4. *Glochidion.*

Disc of small glands. Stigmas sessile or sub-sessile. Frt. baccate . . . . 5. *Kirganelia.*

Disc of distinct scales (exc. P. Emblica). Styles slender. Pistillode 0 . . . . 6. *Phyllanthus.*

Perianth sub-petaloid. Styles slender recurved connate at base. Pistillode large . . . 7. *Flueggea.*

(ii) Calyx of male swollen, sometimes thickened round a minute mouth, St. 3.

Male calyx turbinate or hemispheric . . . 8. *Breynia.*

Male calyx rotate or disciform . . . . . . 9. *Sauropus.*

(iii) Calyx 3-6-lobed or partite, not swollen. St. 2 or more, free. Ovary 1-4-celled. Stigmas dilated or if minute, then flowers racemed. Disc 0 or annular, sometimes lobed but never of distinct glands. Frt. a 1-2-celled drupe. Fls. in axillary clusters spikes or racemes (M. axillary clustered and F. sub-solitary in 10).

St. 2-3. Ovary 2-3-celled. Stigmas dilated . . 10. *Putranjiva.*

St. 4 or more. Ovary 2-4-celled. Stigmas dilated. Fls. clustered . . . . 11. *Cyclostemon.*

St. 2-5. Ovary 1-2-celled. Styles and stigmas minute. Fls. spicate . . . . 12. *Antidesma.*

2. Leaves trifoliolate. Fls. panicled. Frt. baccate . . . . 13. *Bischofia.*

II. Cells of ovary 1-ovuled

A. Calyx valvate or imbricate in bud. Petals present in male or both sexes.

1. Fls. in spikes or racemes. Stamens indefinite.

Trees or shrubs. Racemes axillary and terminal. Petals villous . . . . 14. *Croton.*

Glabrous cultivated shrubs with ornamental leaves. Racemes axillary . . . . *Codiæum.*

Tomentose undershrubs. Racemes axillary. St. 5-15 15. *Chrozophora*

2. Fls. in terminal 2-3-chotomous cymes. St. 8-many . . . . . . 16. *Jatropha.*

B. Calyx valvate in bud. Petals 0. Styles long, often 2-multi-fid.

1. L. opposite. M. fl. racemose. F. solitary or few. Large tree . . . . . 17. *Trewia.*

2. L. alternate. Fls. spiked, racemed, or panicled. Stamens many.

(*a*) Filaments not connate in bundles. L. 3-5-palmi-nerved.

Anther-cells 2 erect slender. F. fls. with large bracts 18. *Acalypha.*

Anther-cells 2 globose. Trees or shrubs . . . 19. *Mallotus.*

Anther-cells 3-4 (rarely 2), or anther 4-valved. Trees 20. *Macaranga.*

Anther-cells 2 adnate on the sub-reniform anthers. Undershrubs . . . . 21. *Baliospermum.*

(*b*) Filaments connate in bundles. Anther-cells sub-globose divergent.

L. narrow. Fls. spicate. Shrub . . . . . 22. *Homonoia.*
L. very broad palmi-nerved. Fls. panicled. Castor-oil plant . . . . 23. *Ricinus.*
3. L. alt. pellucid punctate. Fls. in axillary contracted cymes or clusters, or sub-racemose. Stamens numerous . . 24. *Gelonium.*
4. L. alt. St. 1-3. Herb usually scandent, with stinging hairs . . . . . 25. *Tragia.*
C. Calyx of male open in bud. St. 2-3. An introduced tree . . . . 26. *Sapium.*

Manihot utilissima, *Pohl.* Taresan, *S.* The Cassava. A soft-wooded shrub with tuberous roots and Simal-like digitate leaves is occasionally cultivated.

1. Euphorbia, L.

Trees or shrubs, often with swollen fleshy thorny branches, or herbs, always with milky juice. M. fl., a naked pedicelled stamen. F. fl. a pedicelled 3-celled ovary with 3 styles. The males are clustered in a calyx-like 4-5-lobed turbinate or disciform or campanulate involucre, the lobes of which have swollen glands at the sinuses which sometimes develop a petaloid limb. One F. fl. is usually included in each involucre, the first of the cyme being generally male, and subsequent ones 2-sexual. Capsule of three 2-valved cocci separating from a columella when ripe.

Of the several small herbaceous species, the commonest is **E. pilulifera,** *L.* Pusi-toa, *K.*, *S.*, (Cat's milk), an erect (or, in one variety, prostrate) herb 6″-2 ft. high, with opp. shortly petioled very oblique serrulated leaves $\frac{3}{4}$-$1\frac{1}{2}$″ long. Involucres in axillary and terminal dense-flowered sessile or peduncled cymose heads. The root is given to allay vomiting, *Camp.*

1. Fleshy small trees or shrubs armed with stipulary thorns.
   Branchlets prominently sinuately 3-5-winged Stipular thorns in the sinuses. . . . . 1. *antiquorum.*
   Branchlets somewhat 5-angled from the sub-confluent prominences. Stipular thorns on the prominences (tubercles) . . . . . 2. *neriifolia.*
   Branchlets terete, tubercles flat, not confluent 3. *Nivulia.*
2. Fleshy small tree or shrub, without thorns . 4. *Tirucalli.*
3. Cultivated shrub, not fleshy, bearing brilliant red leaf-like bracts . . . . 5. *pulcherrima.*

1. **E. antiquorum,** *L.* Etkec', *S.*

A shrub or small tree up to 20 ft., usually leafless, or leaves few and deciduous, obovate-oblong with rounded tip. Involucres 3-nate, forming short-peduncled cymes in the sinuses. Styles 2-cleft.

Occasional in village hedges. Given as a cure for cough, *Camp.*

2. **E. neriifolia,** *L.* Etke, *K.*; Etkec', *S.* Syn. E. ligularia, *Roxb.*

A shrub or small tree 6-15 ft. with sharp stipular thorns on sub-confluent tubercles, arranged in vertical or spiral lines. L. usually present, narrowly obovate or obovate-oblong, usually acute. Involucres 3-nate in small short-peduncled cymes $1\frac{1}{2}$-2″ long above the leaf-scars. Style 3-lobed.

Apparently wild in western Palamau, among rocks. Frequent in villages.

Fl. *Feby.-March.* Deciduous *March-June.*

This is perhaps the E. ligulata which is referred to as being common along the Soane, in the Himalayan Journals.

The *cymes* begin as single male receptacles, bearing two ovate-lanceolate bracts at the base of the short stout pedicel. In the axils of these arise two turbinate receptacles bearing female flowers, and again subtended by a pair of bracts as long as the involucre, which are 3-lobed, mid-lobe being somewhat fimbriate.

3. **E. Nivulia,** *Ham.* Etke, *K.*; Etkec', S.; Sij, *Beng.*

A tree 15-30 ft. high with thick rugose corky bark below when old, and spreading often whorled branches. Branchlets terete armed (or some unarmed). Prominences absent or represented by flat corky areas. L. obovate or oblanceolate to spathulate-obovate, 4″ by $2\frac{1}{4}$″ to 9″ by $5\frac{1}{2}$″ with rounded or slightly retuse tip. Style columnar, 3-lobed.

Frequent on barren rocks in Singbhum, Palamau and the Rajmehal Hills (on trap). It is sometimes also grown in villages, and is the true Etke of the Kols, who take the milky juice as a violent purgative in cases of fever.

Fls. *Feby.-April.* Fr. *April.* Leafless usually *Feby.-June.*

• *Branches* often jointed. *Stipulary thorns* $\frac{1}{8}$-$\frac{1}{4}$." *L.* pale beneath, nerves only visible by transmitted light. *Involucres* yellow usually 3-nate in cymes from above the leafscars, and near the ends of the branches. *Old cymes* about twice forked $1\frac{1}{2}$" long with yellow involucres. Young with a central sessile disciform male and two lateral funnel-shaped female, or central neuter with linear-spathulate staminodes. *Anthers* purple with yellow pollen. *Bracteoles* between the stamens numerous fimbriate, as also in the last, between the fls. and inflorescence of which and of E. Nivulia good distinguishing characters are still wanting. *Capsule* $\frac{1}{2}$" broad, on a pedicel $\frac{3}{8}$".

4. E. Tirucalli, *L.* Siju, *Beng.*

A small tree 12-20 ft. high. Prain says quite naturalized in the western parts of Bengal. I have rarely seen it in C. N. It is a native of Africa. The branchlets are slender quill-like.

5. **E. pulcherrima,** *Willd.* The Poinsettia, a well-known garden plant, with brilliant scarlet leafy bracts surrounding the cymes of involucres. Fl. *Nov.-Feby.*

2. Bridelia, Willd.

Trees or shrubs, sometimes scandent, with entire usually strongly nerved leaves and small monœcious or diœcious flowers in axillary clusters, or the clusters in terminal spikes. Calyx 5-lobed valvate persistent. Petals 5 shorter than the sepals, inserted outside the prominent annular slightly perigynous disc. St. 5 on a gonophore with the pistillode. Ovary 2-celled. Styles free or partially connate, or stigmas sessile. Fruit a drupe with a 2-celled stone, ultimately splitting into two 1-seeded 2-valved (always ?) pyrenes.

1. Erect trees with very strong parallel sec. nerves and straight cross nervules.

Nerves 15-20 prs. Clusters axillary and in long spikes. Fr. globose . . . . 1. *retusa.*

Nerves 8-16 prs. L. broadly obovate. Clusters all axillary. Fr. ellipsoid or oblong . . . . . 2. *montana.*

Clusters axillary and in short spikes. L. elliptic acuminate. Fr. ellipsoid . . . . . . 3. *pubescens.*

Large scandent shrub. Venation as in 1 . . 4. *stipularis.*

3. Small tree or a shrub. Leaves only 1·3″, rarely 6″, sec. n. not very strong . . . . . . 5. *tomentosa*.

1. B. retusa, *Spreng.* Karaka, *M.*; Kaka, *Ho.*; Karke anum, Kadrupala, *S.*; Kaj, kaji, *Kharw.*

A small tree usually with long conical thorns on the trunk when young, stiff ell.-oblong strongly nerved leaves, glabrous or pubescent, grey or glaucous beneath, and diœcious or monœcious fls. in axillary and spicate clusters.

Common in all the districts. Fl. *Aug.-Oct.* Fr. *Nov.-Jany.* Evergreen.

L. shining above, sometimes somewhat obovate, always acute with rounded base, 4″ by 2″ to 10″ by 4½″, usually somewhat pubescent beneath. *Petiole* swollen ¼-½″. *M. fls.* pedicelled. *Petals* of M. obovate coarsely toothed, of Fem. entire. *Calyx* ¼″ diam. in frt. *Fr.* ¼″-⅓″ diam. greenish-yellow or flesh-coloured, globose. *Pyrenes* ridged.

The *drupes* are quoted as purplish-black by Brandis and in the *F.B.I.* This is so when over-ripe and when dried. They are usually eaten by birds before this stage, and are a favourite food of Hornbills, parrots and green pigeons.

The leaves are largely used for buffalo fodder.

1. B. montana, *Willd.* Vern. as in the last.

A small, often straggling tree, without thorns, with glabrous brown pustulate twigs and leaves sometimes rather resembling those of *retusa*, but mostly obovate with a rounded tip, smaller and of a much brighter green. Fls. never spicate, and even the quite young fruit ovoid or ellipsoid.

Common in rocky ravines in the Santal P. On Parasnath in Hazaribagh. Fl. *Oct.-Dec.* Fr. *Feby.*

There appears to be some confusion in the *F.B.I.* between *B. retusa* and this species, the fruit of which is described (in the *F.B.I.*) as globose, and the leaves as shining above, whereas when the trees are seen growing in the same locality, one of the most obvious distinctions is the dull and lighter green colour of the leaf surface of *montana* compared with that of *retusa*.

L. obovate or broadly elliptic, shorter in proportion than *B. retusa* and rounded or retuse at the tip, narrowed but not acute at the base, glabrous or puberulous beneath. Size about 4″ by 2½″ to 6″ by 3½″, though occasionally some abnormally very large leaves occur as in other species of the genus. *Petiole* ¼″. *Fls.* sessile or sub-sessile, monœcious. *M.* with lanceolate or oblong-lanc. sepals, and obovate coarsely toothed petals. *F. sepals* triangular-lanceolate, *pet.* oblong entire.

3. B. pubescens, *Kurz.*

A small tree with pubescent or tomentose twigs, narrowly elliptic *acuminate* leaves, pilose or pubescent on the nerves beneath, and white flowers in axillary or spicate clusters. Drupe ellipsoid or oblong ½″ by ¼″.

Along streams in the northern valleys of Saranda, generally above 2,000 ft.

Fl. *April.* Fr. ripens the following cold weather, but like other Bridelias, if not eaten it dries on the tree, and may remain till the following April.

L. 4½″ by 1¾″ to 10″ by 4″, some of the lower leaves on a twig sometimes broadly elliptic, base rounded or acute. The leaves are much more membranous than in the two last, venation similar but the tertiary nerves much weaker, pubescent or pilose. *Fls.* sometimes ¼″ diam. when fully expanded, tomentose *Sep.* deltoid acuminate. *Pet.* obovate or obcordate. *Disc* prominent, filling the tube.

4. B. stipularis, *Blume.* Babu janga, *S.*

A large woody climber with pendent branches, broadly ell.-oblong strongly nerved leaves and numerous axillary or spiked or panicled clusters of green monœcious flowers, succeeded by oblong drupes ½″ long.

Santal P. from Chandna northwards, along the banks of nalas and in ravines. Fl. *May-Oct.* Fr. *Dec.-Feb.*

Branches pubescent. *L.* 4½″ by 3½″, much reduced on the flowering branches, sometimes obovate, obtuse or rounded at the tip, and with rounded or sub-cordate base, hairy beneath. *Sec. n* 7-12 prs. strong and tertiaries strong and parallel. *Calyx* ⅜″ diam. in fruit. *Pet.* obovate. *Drupe* reddish until over-ripe.

5. B. tomentosa, *Blume.*

A shrub or a very small tree with usually small, lanceolate to elliptic leaves, pale glaucous beneath with the venation of the other species but very much finer. Clusters of flowers always axillary (in C. N.). Drupes blue-black ¼″ diam. globose.

Singbhum valleys, very rare. Ranchi, *Wood.* Valleys to the north of Burio in the S. P. Fl. *Sept.* Fr. *Nov.* but the dry fruits will remain till end of *Jany.*

Twigs rusty tomentose, *L.* usually 1″ by ⅓″ to 3″ by 1″, but variable and few sometimes attain 6″ by 2¼″ membranous, acute or obtuse rarely sub-acuminate, not shining, softly pubescent beneath or quite glabrous with age, base acute or obtuse. *Sec. n.* 6-12 prs. *Petiole* $\frac{1}{10}$-$\frac{1}{8}$" rarely $\frac{1}{4}$" pubescent. *M. fl.* shortly pedicelled. *Pet.* broader than long, crenate. *Fem. calyx* $\frac{1}{10}$—$\frac{1}{8}$" diam. in fr. *Sep.* triangular. *Pet.* sub-orbicular entire.

If the drupes are not eaten, the pericarp dries and splits into 6 valves, each of the pyrenes split into 2 valves. Seed black somewhat cordate.

3. Cleistanthus, Hoof, k.

1. C. collinus, *Benth.* Syn. Lebidieropsis orbicularis, *Muell.* Parasu, *M.*; Pasu, *Ho.*; Kargali, *S.*; Kargeli, *Kharw*; Kirla, *H.*

A small tree with dark-coloured bark, distichous orbicular obovate or elliptic leaves 1-4" by $\frac{3}{4}$-3" glaucous beneath. Small green flowers $\frac{1}{4}$-$\frac{1}{3}$" diam. appearing with the new leaves, the males clustered, the F. often solitary sessile. Capsules chestnut coloured woody when ripe $\frac{3}{4}$" diam., ultimately breaking up into three 2-valved cocci.

Very common on dry hills in Singbhum, and less common in other districts. A large form occurs also along nalas. S. P. only south of the Brahmini R. *Gamble.*

Fl. *April-May,* occasionally flowers may also be found in *Sept.* Fr. ripens *March-April* of the next year, and burst with slight reports on hot evenings. Leafless *March-April.*

Twigs slender. *L.* entire with rounded or retuse tip and rounded base, nerves fine reticulate glabrous, or faintly pubescent beneath when young. *Petiole* $\frac{1}{8}$-$\frac{1}{4}$". *Stipules* deciduous, hairy. *Clusters* 2-6-fid. Buds conical 5-angled. *Fls.* softly pubescent, petals minute fleshy, sometimes 0. *Calyx-lobes* often $\frac{1}{4}$" in F. and often twisted. *Capsule* somewhat 3-gonous.

All parts of the tree are very astringent, and the roots and fruit are poisonous. They are also used to poison fish. Campbell says that the bark is applied in cutaneous diseases. The tree coppices freely, and as it is not eaten by goats, it sometimes forms the only vegetation on rocky hill sides. The wood is durable.

4. Glochidion, Forst.

Evergreen trees or shrubs with distichous shortly petioled entire leaves and small greenish or yellow flowers in axillary monœcious or diœcious clusters, the males frequently on much more slender pedicels than the females. Sepals 6, spreading in 2 series, rarely 5, or 7-12; in the young female fl. calyx often campanulate toothed. St. 3-6, rarely 8-12, connate in a central column over the minute pistillode, or pistillode 0. Ovary 3-15-celled, styles connate in a short column lobed or toothed at the tip, or styles obsolete. Fruit globose or frequently depressed and intruded at base and apex, of 3 or more 2-valved coriaceous or crustaceous cocci, which separate from a central axis.

Anths. 4-12. Sep. 6-12. Ovary 10-15-celled. . . 1. *multiloculare*.
Anths. 4-6 (rarely 3). Sep. 6-7. Ovary 6-8-celled . 2. *lanceolarium*.
Anths. 3. Sep. 6. Ovary 4-7-celled . . . . . 3. *velutinum*.

1. G. multiloculare, *Muell.* Nanha baria, Nandhum, *S.*

(So named from the resemblance of the fruit to the pad which the bania pedlars wear on their back under the basket they carry, *Camp.*).

A small gregarious bush pubescent tomentose all over or sometimes glabrous with angular twigs, oblong or ell.-oblong leaves 3-5″, with 3-5 prs. of very oblique nerves and numerous fine cross nervules. Pedicels short stout. Capsules $\frac{3}{4}$″ diam., three-times as broad as long, intruded at the base and apex.

Manbhum and S. P. (along Barakar R.). Fl. *April-Oct.* Fr. *May* (and probably at other seasons).

L. acute or obtuse, and with acute base, shining and very minutely puberulous above, glaucous beneath. *Petiole* $\frac{1}{10}$-$\frac{1}{8}$″ stout. *Stipules* shorter acuminate $\frac{1}{10}$-$\frac{1}{8}$″. *Stylar-column* short and broad. *Seeds* with red aril.

The description is taken mainly from Duars and Champaran specimens.

2. G. lanceolarium, *Muell.* Barhia Kandhum, *S.*

A small glabrous tree, or often a shrub with green rather flexuous and angular twigs, coriaceous glabrous dark green shining leaves and small axillary flowers, the females green 1-3 or many together sessile, the males yellowish $\frac{1}{8}$″-$\frac{1}{4}$″ ($\frac{1}{3}$″ *F.B.I.*!) diam. numerous on slender pedicels. Capsule orbicular depressed $\frac{2}{3}$-$\frac{3}{4}$″ diam. and $\frac{1}{2}$-$\frac{5}{8}$″ long.

Common throughout Ch. Nag. and S. P., especially near streams. Fl. *March-May*. Fr. *Sept.-Jany.* New shoots in *March*.

L. $4\frac{1}{2}$" by 2" to $6\frac{1}{2}$" by $2\frac{1}{2}$" rarely 7 by $3\frac{1}{2}$", lower on the twigs much smaller, oblong to elliptic acuminate with 5-7 prs. slender *sec. n.* *Petiole* $\frac{1}{4}$", *Stipules* $\frac{1}{8}$" acuminate sometimes hardened. *M. fls.* on pedicels $\frac{1}{8}$-$\frac{3}{4}$" long. *F. fls.* $\frac{1}{8}$" long campanulate. *Ovary* and prominent *stylar-column* pubescent stalked.

"Bark given medicinally when the stomach revolts against food," *Camp.* The seeds give an oil used for burning.

Var. *L.* narrowly lanceolate acuminate with very unequal acute base closely resembles G. Gamblei, *Hook f.*, but petioles somewhat pubescent. Silingi, S. P.

3. G. velutinum, *Wight.*[1]

A small tree with nearly all parts pubescent or tomentose, L. elliptic to oblong or oblong-lanceolate 3-$6\frac{1}{2}$" by 1-$2\frac{1}{2}$" shortly cuspidate or acuminate. Fls. axillary solitary and fascicled, M. and F. usually in same cluster, M. yellow, F. green. Capsule $\frac{1}{3}$" diam. pubescent.

Valleys, rare. Singbhum. Fls. on the new shoots in *April.* Fr. *Aug.* till the following April. Evergreen.

New shoots densely tomentose. *L.* persistently pubescent on the nerves beneath, with 4-7 pairs strong sec. n. and cross nervules. Base narrowed into the petiole. *Petiole* $\frac{1}{4}$". *Stipules* persistent subulate shorter than petiole. *M. fl.* about $\frac{1}{8}$" diam. on pedicels $\frac{1}{2}$", *sepals* 6 nearly free. *F. fl.* on shorter stouter pedicels. *Styles* in a sub-globose or sub-terete-column larger than the ovary, unaltered in fruit. *Capsule* depressed.

5. Kirganelia, Baill.

This genus which is sunk in Phyllanthus in the *F.B.I.* seems better kept distinct, it has 4-7 stamens, free or connate below, with or without a pistillode. Anthers with longitudinal dehiscence. Ovary 5-12-celled with as many minute sessile or sub-sessile stigmas surrounding a hollow umbo of the ovary more resembling Glochidion than Phyllanthus. Ovules and seeds 2 superposed in each cell. Fruit with a fleshy epicarp and soft 5-12-celled endocarp.

---

[1] Gamble's specimens from Tatkora and Sonua are placed under G. Heyneanum, *Wight.* The specimens are not in flower. Heyneanum is less pubescent and has a cylindric style twice the length of the sepals, while that of velutinum is short columnar and 4-8-toothed. The capsules have pedicels $\frac{1}{8}$" to nearly $\frac{1}{4}$", while those of velutinum are sub-sessile.

1. **K. reticulata**, *Baill.* Syn. P. reticulatus, *Poir.* Panjoli, *H.*, *Beng.*

A climbing shrub with slender glabrous or pubescent branches, oblong leaves about $1\frac{3}{4}''$ by $\frac{3}{4}''$, minute fls. and small black berries $\frac{3}{16}$-$\frac{1}{4}''$ diam.

Chiefly along ravines and nalas in Hazaribagh (Damuda valley), Ranchi, and Gangpur. Fl. *Feby.-May.* Fr. *April-June* (perhaps all the year). Dec. *Jany.-Feb.*

Branchlets sometimes deciduous at their base. The subtending bract and its two stipules often become converted into three recurved thorns by means of which it climbs. *L.* sometimes attain 3″, obtuse both ends, pale beneath, glabrous with 6-8 prs. of slender sec. n. *Fls.* usually 1 male and 1 female in each axil, frequently racemed from the reduction of the leaves, racemes sometimes fascicled. *M. fl.* $\frac{1}{20}$-$\frac{1}{16}''$ long, green or purplish, campanulate, 3 outer sepals smaller than the inner, disc of 5 fleshy glands.

6. Phyllanthus, L.

Trees, shrubs or herbs with entire leaves often pinnately arranged and small or minute monœcious flowers in axillary clusters, male and female pedicels often of unequal length. Sepals 4-6 imbricate in 2 series. Disc usually of scales or glands (or sometimes 0 in M. of P. Emblica). St. 3-5 free or connate in the center of the flower, anths. 2-celled or didymous. Pistillode 0. Ovary 3-celled. Styles elongate, free or connate. Fruit of 3 2-valved cocci with sometimes a coriaceous or fleshy epicarp, or drupaceous.

A tree, leaves pinnately arranged on the twigs. Frt. a drupe . . . . 1. *Emblica.*

An erect shrub, leaves pinnately arranged Fr. nearly dry . . . . 2. *Lawii.*

Undershrubs or herbs St. 3. Styles 3. Fr. capsular.

a. Anths. erect, slits vertical. Fr. echinate. 3. *urinaria.*

b. Anths. didymous or reniform, cells subglobose.

L. narrowly oblong to elliptic. Anths. sessile on a short column. 4. *Niruri* (*pendulus*).

Stipules lanceolate. Fil. short, more or less free. L. elliptic. 5. *debilis* (*rotundifolius*).

Stipules semisagittate. Fil. free. L. narrow linear or linear oblong. 6. *simplex.*

1. **P. Emblica,** *L.* Miral, *K.*; Miral, *S.*; Aura, Aonla, *H.*; Amla, *Beng.* The Emblic Myrabolan.

A small or m. s. tree with distichous close-set small linear-oblong leaves $\frac{1}{3}$—$\frac{3}{4}$" long. Fls. minute yellowish densely fascicled in the axils of the new leaves. Fruit globose succulent $\frac{3}{4}$" diam. with a 6-ridged putamen.

Common in the valley forests.

Fl. *May.* Fr. *Oct.-April.* Dec. *March-April.*

A well-known tree, the branchlets of which closely resemble pinnate leaves and are often deciduous. *Sep.* 6. *Disc* of male of 6 minute glands or 0, of *fem.* cupular. *St.* 3 monadelphous.

The putamen is very tardily dehiscent.

Fruits astringent, but sialagogue, and hence often taken by natives when thirsty. Largely used in Hindu medicine, the properties are said to resemble those of the chebulic myrabolan. It is eaten as a cure for cough in Ch. Nag., and the juice of the fresh fruit is used for inflammation of the eyes. Campbell says that boiled till it becomes of an oily consistency, it is used for *Khasra*, a skin disease.

The fruits boiled with sugar make an excellent preserve.

2. **P. Lawii,** *Grah.* Tirsibirsi, *M.* (possibly fictitious); Jhawar Khandera, *S.*

A shrub with numerous erect rigid stems 3-4$\frac{1}{2}$ ft. high, close spreading slender branchlets with distichous crowded sub-sessile small leaves $\frac{1}{4}$" by $\frac{1}{12}$", and solitary or few minute pinkish flowers.

Usually gregarious along the banks of rocky rivers with a constant water supply. Throughout the area, but very local.

Fl. *Jany.-March.* Fr. *Jany.*

Branches terete glabrous. *L.* linear-oblong obtuse glaucous, base subcordate, sec. n. 3-4 prs. faint. *Stipules* linear subulate 3-4 times as long as the minute petiole. *Pedicels.* $\frac{1}{16}$-$\frac{1}{8}$". *Fls.* $\frac{1}{12}$" diam. *Disc* of m. of glands, of fem. a crenulate ring. Filaments connate to above the middle. *Styles* lamellate 2-partite. *Frt.* $\frac{1}{8}$-$\frac{1}{6}$" diam. 3-lobed.

3. **P. urinaria,** *L.* is a slender sometimes decumbent plant with spreading or ascending branches like pinnate leaves, leaves close often imbricate, numerous minute subsessile flowers and capsules which are echinate or pustulate. Fl., Fr. *July-Jany.*

4. **P. Niruri,** *L.* somewhat similar, is an erect herb or undershrub 1-2$\frac{1}{2}$ ft., branches 4-6" long and close glabrous linear, oblong or elliptic

leaves $\frac{1}{8}$-$\frac{1}{3}$". Fls. shortly pedicelled 1-2 axillary, or on very abbreviated axillary shoots crowded with setaceous imbricating bracts. Capsule $\frac{1}{8}$" diam. smooth.

P. pendulus, *Roxb.* appears to be a form of this with the 'bracteate peduncles.' It is common in Chota Nagpur.

5. **P. debilis**, *Ham.* An erect herb or undershrub 1-4 ft. with often a woody rootstock and numerous erect stems, glabrous leaves $\frac{1}{3}$-$\frac{3}{4}$" elliptic or obovate. Fls. pedicelled, often on abbreviated bracteate axillary shoots.

I am inclined to think that much of the material in the P. debilis cover at the Cal. Herb. is P. rotundifolius, and that P. rotundifolius is more common in Ch. Nag. than P. debilis, the latter has nearly free stamens and a more slender male pedicel, whereas the common Ch. Nag. plant has filaments combined half to three-fourths of the way up or more.

7. Flueggea, Wild.

1. **F. microcarpa**, *Blume.* Sikat, *Kharw.*; Remre Horte *S.*

A glabrous straggling shrub, often large, with thin elliptic or more often orbicular or obovate leaves 1-3" long rarely attaining 4$\frac{1}{2}$" by 2" glaucous beneath, axillary fascicled minute flowers on capillary $\frac{1}{6}$-$\frac{1}{2}$" long pedicels, and pretty white berries $\frac{1}{3}$" diam., or fruits rarely dry and $\frac{1}{6}$-$\frac{1}{8}$" diam. only.

Valley forests in Singbhum, frequent. Also in Manbhum (Tundi hills, etc.); Ranchi (Baragaon) *Wood*; Hazaribagh (Bagodhar); S. P. (hills east of Dharampur, etc.) Palamau (Bhirla Hat). Fl. *May-Aug.* Fr. *July-Sept.* Evergreen, new leaves in *May.*

Rarely thorny. *Branchlets* angled or compressed. *L.* with usually rounded tip rarely acute, base cuneate, *sec. n.* slender, or (in a S. P. variety) raised and prominent, 5-8 prs. with fine cross nervules. *Petiole* $\frac{1}{8}$-$\frac{1}{4}$" slender. Sep. 5 broad thin. *St.* 5. *Disc* of 5 glands in M., annular in F. *Pistillode* large 3-angled and with 3 recurved tips. *Ovary* 3-celled with 3 recurved bifid styles.

8, Breynia, Forst.

Shrubs or small trees with small entire usually bifarious leaves and very small axillary monœcious flowers. M. fleshy turbinate or campanulate truncate with 6 minute inflexed calyx lobes. St. 3 united into a short column at the bottom of the tube, anths. linear 2-celled adnate to the column. F. perianth 6-lobed, sometimes spreading. Ovary 3-celled with a fleshy often depressed top, stigmas 3 minute sessile in the cavity, or style exserted with 3 2-fid arms. Frt. drupaceous with 3 pyrenes, each splitting into 2 indehiscent cocci.

Stigmas capitellate in depression on top of the ovary . 1. *rhamnoides.*
Style stout with 3 short 2-fid arms . . . . . 2. *patens.*

1. B. rhamnoides, *Muell.* Kadrupala, Karki, *S.*

A pretty shrub, when well grown, up to 10-ft. high, with close-set distichous small glabrous leaves about 1″ by $\frac{5}{8}$″ and minute green or pinkish flowers succeeded by red globose berries nearly $\frac{1}{4}$″ diam. with a depressed umbo.

Valleys in Manbhum *e.g.* Topchanchee. Along streams in S. P., frequent in the northerly half. Fl., Fr. *Jany.-June* (perhaps all the year). Evergreen.

Somewhat resembles Kirganelia reticulata. *L.* $\frac{3}{4}$″ to $2\frac{1}{4}$″ oblong or ovate-oblong or sub-orbicular with rounded apex and usually oblique rounded obtuse or sub-cordate base. *Sec. n.* 4-7 prs. slender. *Petiole* $\frac{1}{12}$-$\frac{1}{8}$″ longer than the setaceous stipules. *Fls.* in axillary few fld. clusters, *M.* and *F.* often on separate twigs. M. green or pink turbinate $\frac{1}{12}$-$\frac{1}{10}$″ with 6 small inflexed teeth, *pedicel* $\frac{1}{10}$″, *F.* calyx campanulate 6-lobed, rapidly developing, and in fruit spreading and irregularly split $\frac{3}{16}$″ diam.

2. B. patens, *Benth.*

A graceful little shrub with small distichous glabrous leaves and axillary small flowers on slender pedicels, the males being yellow and drooping, with campanulate calyx; the females green with broader funnel-shaped calyces.

Tundi Hills, Manbhum, *Campbell.* Chota Nagpur, *Prain.* Fl. *April-May.*

2-4 ft. high. *L.* $\frac{1}{2}$-1″ with 3-5 prs. of sec. n. *Fem. fl.* $\frac{1}{10}$-$\frac{1}{8}$″ diam. larger and shorter-pedicelled than in male, *calyx* greatly enlarged in fruit and often exceeding it. *Fr.* $\frac{1}{2}$″ diam.

9. Sauropus, Blume.

Small shrubs or undershrubs with distichous entire leaves and minute axillary solitary or clustered monœcious flowers. M. calyx disciform or turbinate with a very small mouth 6-lobed and with thickenings which meet round the 3-gonous staminal column. Anths. sessile on the angles of the column. F. calyx 6-cleft accrescent in fruit. Ovary 3-celled with rounded or concave top and 3 sessile spreading styles with 3 curved arms. Fruit as in Breynia but surrounded by the calyx.

1. S. quadrangularis, *Muell.*

A dwarf glabrous shrub with angled branchlets and very shortly petioled ell. or broadly ovate or obovate obtuse or subacute leaves about $\frac{1}{2}''$ by $\frac{1}{3}''$. Fls. shortlv pedicelled, M. $\frac{1}{16}''$ diam., F. $\frac{1}{6}''$.

Manbhum, *Cal. Herb.*; Karakpur Hills (near Monghyr).

L. with 4-5 prs. sec. n., margin minutely hispid. *Petiole* $\frac{1}{12}$-$\frac{1}{10}''$ *Sep.* of M. linguiform obtuse, of F. rounded. *Fr.* $\frac{1}{5}''$ diam. depressed globose, narrower than the enlarged calyx.

2. S. pubescens, *Hook, f.*

An undershrub with compressed 2-ridged branches, and leaves on both surfaces pubescent or finely tomentose, glabrescent above. L. $\frac{1}{2}$-$1\frac{1}{4}''$ by $\frac{3}{8}$-$\frac{3}{4}''$ broadly ovate o elliptic with 3 prs. sec. nerves. Fls. $\frac{1}{12}$-$\frac{1}{10}''$ solitary red Pedicels $\frac{1}{8}''$ very slender.

Along dry nalas in the Singbhum forests. Fl. *May-July* Deciduous in *February*.

Stems 3-4″ high with pubescent sometimes sub-alate branchlets. *L.* acute or sub-obtuse with rounded base, pubescent beneath and margins recurved. *Petiole* $\frac{1}{10}''$ Stipules and bracts minute, very persistent.

Fls. not noted in the C. N. plant.

10. Putranjiva, Wall.

1. P. Roxburghii, *Wall* Pitonj, *S.*; Putranjiva, jiaputa, *Beng.*

A handsome mod.-sized tree with drooping branches. bifarious broadly lanceolate leaves 1-3½″ inclined forwards, often with a wavy or somewhat serrate margin. M. fl. in numerous minute yellow axillary heads or contracted racemes. F. fl. green solitary on current year's shoots or in few-fid. racemes on the previous year's. Drupe ellipsoid hoary ⅝″ crowned with the style bases.

Manbhum *Campbell* ; S. P. but where I have seen it, probably planted. Mahuagari hill, *Gamble* ! Sometimes planted on railway platforms. Evergreen. Fl. *March-April* ; Fr. *Jany.-Feby.*

Twigs and petioles tomentose. *L.* slightly pubescent both sides with obtuse or rounded base, very finely nerved. *Sepals* 5. *St.* usually 3, *fil.* more or less connate. *Seed* with copious albumen and flat somewhat bent cotyledons. Fruiting pedicels ½-¾″. The stones of the fruit are strung into rosaries.

11. Cyclostemon, Bl.

1. C. assamicus, *Hook. f.* Ban Bokul, *Beng.*

A small much-branched tree with exstipulate deep-green glabrous shining elliptic-lanceolate, ell.-oblong to ovate-lanceolate leaves 3-6½″ by 1½-3″ and greenish globose diœcious fls., M. clustered ¼″ diam. St. many. F. solitary. Fruits scarlet ovoid-oblong somewhat didymous ½-¾″ long.

Ravines in the Tholokabad forest, Singbhum. Fl. *Nov.-Dec.* Fr. ripens *April* Evergreen.

Young *twigs* and petioles somewhat rusty pubescent. *L.* rarely attaining 8″ by 3″ entire acute or acuminate with rounded or acute usually oblique base. Sec. n. 7-10 prs. fine and nervules reticulate. *Petiole* ¼-⅓″. *Perianth* with 2 outer orbicular lobes and 2-3 inner imbricate larger ones, shortly appressed hairy. *Disc* annular thin hirsute on margin. *Fil.* and connective pubescent. *Ovary* densely silky, stigmas 2 large subsessile half-orbicular, fleshy. *Fr.* velvety pubescent on the remains of the perianth, usually 2-celled and 2-seeded with red coriaceous epicarp, pulpy endocarp and seed with hard coriaceous testa, flat cotyledons and copious albumen.

12. Antidesma, L.

Small trees or shrubs with alt. entire stipulate leaves, and small or minute diœcious fls. in slender spikes or racemes produced on the new shoots. Calyx 3-5-lobed or partite. St. 2-5, rarely 6-7 inserted on or around the disc, anther-cells globose often on a broad connective. Ovary 1- rarely more-celled, stigmas 2-4, 2-fid. Ovules 2 pendulous. Frt. a small more or less compressed drupe. Seed with broad flat cotyledons.

St. 2 (rarely 3). Fls. pedicelled. Calyx 4-lobed . 1. *diandrum.*
St. 3-4.
Calyx 3-4-fid. Fls. shortly pedicelled . . . . 2. *acuminatum.*
Calyx of M. shortly 4-lobed, of F. entire. M. fl. sessile . . . . 3. *Bunius.*
St. 5 (4-7). Spikes wooly. Fls. sessile. Calyx 5-7-partite . . . . 4 *Ghaessmbilla.*

1. A. diandrum, *Roth.* Mata-ara. Mata-sura, *K.*; Matha arak', *S.*; Amti, *Kharw.*; Mutta, *Beng.* Amtua sag. *Mal Pahari.*

A shrub with obovate-lanceolate or somewhat rhomboidly elliptical leaves usually glabrous rarely 5″ long, minute green flowers in mostly simple spikes; M. 1-2″ long, F. often 3″ in fruit. Fr. sub-globose $\frac{1}{8}''$-$\frac{3}{16}''$ diam. with a slightly compressed and rugose keeled seed.

Common, chiefly in the valleys, throughout the area. Fl. *May-June.* Fr. *Nov.-Jany.* Leaves turn red from *Jany.-March* and then fall.

Shoots usually pubescent, and a form occurs in Singbhum with the leaves permanently sub-tomentose beneath. *L.* acute or acuminate with cuneate base, and 4-5 prs. slender sec. n., usually $1\frac{1}{2}$-$3\frac{1}{2}''$ by $\frac{3}{4}$-$1\frac{1}{4}''$ *Disc* lobed glabrous or pilose.

The young leaves make an excellent spinach. The fruits are eaten.

2. A. acuminatum, *Wall.*

A small tree with oblong to elliptic usually caudate-acuminate nearly glabrous leaves about 6″ by 2″, minute fls. in *panicled* pilose spikes 2-5″ long. Fr. ell. $\frac{1}{8}''$ long crowned by the style.

Along streams in the Saranda forests. Evergreen; new leaves and fls. in *May.*

Branchlets pilose or tomentose. *L.* very dark green, sometimes 12″ long or only 3-4″ at time of flowering with generally rounded base and 7-12 prs. of inarching sec. n. which are pubescent beneath.

Fls. unequally pedicelled. M. sep. 3-4 glabrous outside. *Disc* fleshy glabrous 3-4-angular. St. 3-4, long. Pistillode distinct.

3. A. Bunius, *Spreng.*

A small tree, sometimes 30 ft. somewhat resembling the last and distinguished by the characters given above. *L.* oblong-oblanceolate glabrous and shining both sides. *Racemes* rather lax fid., 3-4″ long simple or branched. *Fr.* ell. $\frac{1}{6}$-$\frac{1}{4}$.

Parasnath. Fl. *April-May.* Fr. *August.* New shoots sometimes in August.

4. A. Ghæsembilla, *Gaert.* Mata-sura, *K.*; Bhabiranj, *Kharw.*; Umtoa, (Hazaribagh) *Wood*, appears to be same word as Amtua (*vide* A. diandrum).

A shrub with broadly elliptic or orbicular grey- or hoary-tomentose leaves 2—4½ by 1½ —2½″. Fls. in densely tomentose panicled spikes. Frt. red to black oblong ¼″.

A plant of much drier localities than the other species; found chiefly on hill sides in Singbhum, Manbhum (also along Barakar R.), Hazaribagh, Palamau and S. P. Fl. *May-June.* Fr. *September-October.*

L. rounded both ends. Sec. n. strong beneath 3-6 prs. *Spikes* ¾″ to 2¼″ in fruit. *Disc* 5-partite pubescent. *F. fl.* pedicelled. *Ovary* glabrous, pubescent or tomentose, exserted from the wooly perianth.

13. Bischofia, Bl.

1. B. javanica, *Bl.* Hajam, *M.*; Pader, *S.*

A mod.-sized tree easily recognized by its long-petioled 3-foliolate leaves, crenate or serrate leaflets and 1-sexual green or greenish-yellow fls. Berry ⅓″ diam. brown or black.

Ravines in Singbhum and the S. P.; Parasnath. Evergreen. Fl. *March-April.* Fr. *Oct.-Dec.* New shoots *March-April.*

Lflts. 3-6″ oblong to obovate or ell., always with a sudden acumination, glabrous, rather strongly nerved and sometimes with glands in the nerve axils. *Petioles* 2½-6″ and terminal petiolules ¾-1½″. Panicles from the scale axils of the new shoots. *Fls.* usually diœcious. *Sep.* 5, hooded over the young stamens, caducous in the F. *St.* 5, inserted under the peltate pistillode. *Ovary* 3-4-celled with linear recurved styles.

An excellent wood for planking.

14. Croton, L.

Trees or shrubs usually with scurfy, stellate or scaly hairs and leaves 2-glandular at the base. Fls. green monœcious or diœcious, solitary or clustered on the rachis of axillary and terminal bracteate racemes. Calyx 4-6-partite. Petals and disc glands as many as the sepals. St. on a hairy receptacle indefinite. Ovary 3-(rarely 2-4) celled with as many 2-4-cleft styles. Capsule of 3, 2-valved cocci.

Old leaves glabrous, inflor. lepidote, St. 10-12 1. *oblongifolius.*
L. and inflor. glabrous or nearly so. St. 15-25 2. *Tiglium.*
L. and inflor. scurfily stellately hairy. St. 18-30 3. *caudatus.*

1. C. oblongifolius, *Roxb.* Kuti, Kuti-konyer, *K.;* Gote, Kote, *S.;* Poter, *Oraon?* Bhainswan, *Kharw.;* Putol, *Mal Paharia;* Maisonda (Koderma); Putri, *Beng.*

A small tree with rather large coriaceous more or less toothed or repand oblong or elliptic-oblong penni-nerved leaves and long racemes of diœcious (or monœcious) fls. which appear when the tree is more or less leafless.

Very common throughout the area, esp. in open and scrub jungles. Fl. *Jany.-Feby.* Fr. *April.* More or less deciduous at the time. *L.* turn red before falling.

L. 6-12″ with long or short petiole, lepidote when young, acute. *Racemes* numerous from the uppermost axils and terminal with numerous linear or sub-foliaceous oblanceolate bracts at their base, rachis nearly glabrous 5-12″ long with minute subulate bracts. *M. fl.* rather large on pedicels $\frac{1}{4}$-$\frac{5}{16}$″ long lepidote. *Calyx* $\frac{1}{8}$″ long, sep. villous ciliate. *Pet.* villous free $\frac{1}{8}$″ between the disc-lobes. *F.* racemes and pedicels shorter. Some of the *Pet.* often aborted. *Ovary* lepidote with 3 long branched styles. *Capsule* $\frac{1}{3}$″ diam.

The plant is usually described as monoecious, I have often found it diœcious.

The bark and root are given as a purgative and also as an alterative in dysentery, *Campbell.*

2. C. Tiglium, *L.* Jaiphal, *H.*

A small tree with ell. or ovate leaves 3-nerved at the base and with stellate hairs beneath when young.

Chota Nagpur, *Wood's list*. The tree is indigenous in the Eastern Himalaya and the Malay Archipelago. Fl. *June*. Fr. *Aug.-Sept.* (in Bhotan). The seeds yield the well-known Croton Oil.

3. C. caudatus, *Geisel.*

A sub-scandent shrub with stellately-pubescent leaves with 3-5-nerved base and long slender racemes 4-10″.

Chota Nagpur, *Wood's list*. Loc. ? It is common in the damper parts of Bengal and fls. *March*.

N.B.—The shrubs with brightly variegated foliage commonly known as Crotons belong to the genus **Codiæum**. The styles are entire.

15. Chrozophora, Neck.

1. C. plicata, *A. Juss.* Pango nari, *S.* ?

A coarse herb or undershrub, often prostrate, stellate tomentose all over with sinuate more or less rugose or plaited leaves and fls. in axillary short bracteate racemes.

A common weed of waste land, described by Campbell as a common and abundant *scandent bush* in the Tundi hills ! Fl., Fr. *August—April*.

L. variable in size 1-4″ hoary, ovate. *F. fl.* pedicelled usually few or solitary at the base, and the *male fls.* pale yellow crowded in the upper part of the raceme.

16. Jatropha, L.

Usually shrubs, frequently glandular, with palmately nerved, entire or palmately-lobed leaves at the ends of the branches. Fls. monœcious in terminal corymbose cymes, usually petaliferous and calyx frequently petaloid, petals 5 often more or less connate. St. 8 or more, the inner or all connate. Fr. capsular.

Pet. red free or connate at base. Glandular . 1. *gossypifolia*.
Pet. yellow. Eglandular . . . . . 2. *Curcas*.

1. J. gossypifolia, *L.* Bhernda, verenda, *K.*; *S.*, and *H.*; Lal-bherenda, *Beng.*

A shrub 3-6 ft. with palmately 3-5-lobed leaves, easily recognized by the stipitate yellow viscid glands which cover the leaf margins, peticles and stipules, and the small red flowers in glandular corymbose cymes. St. 10-12.

A native of Brazil (*F.B.I.*) very common in waste ground and by road-sides. Deciduous in *C. S.* Fl., Fr. *r. s.*

A glandular Jatropha *occurring in rocky ravines* in the Santal P., seen by me in Jany. *without leaves or flowers* was possibly a completely naturalized form of this, or else **J. glandulifera**, *Roxb.* which can be distinguished by its greenish-yellow fls. with only 8 stamens.

2. **J. Curcas,** *L.* Kulajara, *K.;* Totkabindi, *M.;* Bhernda, *S., H.* The Physic-nut.

A shrub or small tree 10-20 ft. with glabrous (exc. when quite young) 3-5-angled or -lobed leaves 4-6″ diam. and small yellow flowers with a campanulate 5-lobed corolla in terminal cymose panicles.

Very commonly planted in village hedges. Dec. in the cold season when it is frequently covered with the capsules. Fl. *May-October.*

The oil of the seeds is a violent purgative and emetic.

J. multifida, *L.* with multifid leaves, and other species are very ornamental garden shrubs with scarlet flowers.

17. Trewia, L.

1. **T. nudiflora,** *L.* Gara Loa, *K.;* Gada Lopong, *S.;* Pitali, *Beng.*

A large tree, superficially much resembling Gmelina arborea (some vernacular names *e.g.* Khamara, Gamhar applied to this belong to Gmelina), with opp. long-petioled broadly-ovate cordate entire 3-5-basal-nerved leaves, and diœcious fls. M. in long drooping catkin-like racemes 3-8″ with slender pedicels. F. solitary or 2-3 on long stout peduncles. Frt. globose hard drupaceous 2-5-celled, 1-1½″ diam.

Chiefly in river-beds, Saranda and Gangpur. Also in S. P. (Bokhraband, etc.) Fl. *Jany.-March.* Fr. *May.* Leafless *Dec. or Jany.-Feby.*

Young shoots mealy with stellate hairs. *L.* 4-6″ sometimes tomentose or pubescent green *not* glaucous beneath, base rounded or cordate. *M. fl.*

1-3 in a bract, pedicels jointed on a small bracteolate peduncle. *Sep.* 3 orbicular, reflexed in fl. *St.* ∝. Ovary closely invested by the urceolate 5-toothed calyx, often 5-celled with as many large fimbriate stigmas as cells.

N.B.—The first few seedling leaves are *alternate*.

18. Acalypha, L.

A large genus containing several shrubs with copper-coloured, or otherwise ornamental, leaves common in gardens.

1. A. indica, *L.*

A stiff erect herb or undershrub 18″-2½′ with spreading long-petioled rhomboid-ovate serrate leaves and very numerous axillary spikes with foliaceous bracts bearing green F. fl., the top of the spike ebracteate with minute M. fl.

Hazaribagh, near Chorparan, etc. Fl. *Dec.-Jany.*

19. Mallotus, Lour.

Erect trees or sarmentose or scandent large shrubs generally covered esp. on the leaves beneath with small peltate glands or stellate hairs. L. 3-7-nerved at the base and with strong cross nervules, sometimes peltate. Fls. diœcious, rarely monœcicus in spikes or racemes, the males clustered on the rachis. St. ∝ free, with two small globose or very short anther cells adnate to the frequently broad connective. Ovary and capsule 2-3- (rarely 4-) celled. Styles entire.

Small tree. L. peltate 7-9-nerved . . . . 1. *Roxburghianus.*
Small tree. L. not peltate, base 3-nerved . . . . 2. *philippinensis.*
Large sarmentose or scandent shrub . . . . . . 3. *repandus.*

1. M. Roxburghianus, *Muell.* Barui, *S.*; Dopsinga, *Mal.*

A small tree softly pubescent with simple and stellate hairs all over, with long petioled orbicular or broad-ovate peltate sinuate-toothed leaves 4-7″ diam. and terminal racemes as long as the leaves.

Santal P., in ravines, rare. Fl. *May*. Fr. *Sept*.

L. stellately-hairy and with yellow glands both sides, densely so beneath, above *also* simply pubescent (or, *vide* Prain. *only* simply pubescent) *Petioles* 1½-4″. *Stipules* linear ½″. *M. sep.* 2-5, *Capsule* densely echinate and glandular.

2. **M. philippinensis**, *Muell.* Gara Sinduri, *K.*; Rora, *S.*; Rori, *Kharw.*; Kamala, *H.*; Daosindra, *Mal.*

A tree 20-30 ft. branched low, with ovate or rhomboid acute or acuminate leaves covered beneath when young with a greenish-yellow glandular pubescence (as are the shoots) and permanently with small red glands. M. fl. clustered in racemes 6-10″ long, F. racemes 2-3″ long. Capsule densely covered with red glands.

Common throughout the area, in valleys. Fl. *Oct.-Nov.* Fr. *Feby.-March.*

L. attain 9″ by 5″. Sec. n. 3-4 prs. above basal. *Petiole* 2-3½″. *Calyx* 4-fid. in both sexes.

The red glands from the capsule yield the *Kamela* dye.

3. **M. repandus**, *Muell.*

Sub-scandent with tomentose branches, ovate or cordate acute leaves 2½″ by 2″ to 3″ by 2½″, softly stellate-pubescent and closely covered with glands beneath.

Dalbhum, *Gamble!* S. P., foot of Rajmehal hills in the Gangetic valley. Fl. *Jany.-Feby.*

L. with 2-3 prs. of sec. n. above the 3-nerved base, nervules often ending in minute teeth. *Petiole* 1″. *M. fl.* yellow, calyx 3-5-fid. *F.* green, sep. linear caducous. *Ovary* 2-lobed. *Stigmas* plumose sessile.

20. Macaranga, Thouars.

A genus with most of the characters of Mallotus, and somewhat artificially separated therefrom by the anthers, which are usually said to be 3-4-locellate. The anthers are variable, in some species they are very distinct, opening by 4 valves like the 4-valvate sepals of a flower; usually they have 3-4 2-valved terminal cells, but in M. indica there are sometimes only 2 cells and the anther may exactly resemble those of Mallotus except in the smaller connective.

Ovary only 1-2-celled in the C. N. species.

1. M. indica, *Wight.* Boura, *Beng.*

A soft-wooded tree with green or glaucous branches exuding a large quantity of very gummy sap when cut, long-petioled large peltate leaves and fls. in axillary panicles 2-4½" long with glandular bracts.

Ravines in the Saranda forest, elev. 2,000 ft., very rare. Fl. *Oct.* Fr. *April.* Evergreen.

L. sometimes attain 12" by 10" orbicular-ovate glaucous and hairy beneath and covered with small glands. *Sec. n.* 4-8 prs. above the numerous basal nerves. *Stipules* lanceolate or ovate acuminate ⅜". Frequently a large gland on 1 or 2 of the principal nerves. In the inflorescence the bracts may be reduced to these glands or be more or less foliaceous. *Rachis* of M. panicles zig-zag. *Fls.* minute, *St.* 3-8. *F. fl.* with a glandular and pubescent ovary. *Capsule* usually globose and 1-celled waxy, rarely didymous and 2-celled.

[This tree was named M. Roxburghii, *Wight,* in the Calcutta Herb. The latter tree however differs in its densely rusty tomentose inflorescence and bracts, and in the large lateral *peltate* stigma. The stigma of M. indica is also basal or lateral, but is *subulate.* The C. N. tree *differs* from *typical* M. indica in its greater hairiness.]

21. Baliospermum, Bl.

1. B. axillare, *Bl.*

A shrub with numerous erect herbaceous shoots from the root, with variously lobed, sinuate or serrate ell., oblong or (upper) lanceolate leaves attaining 6-10", and greenish fls. in fascicles either axillary, or from the axils of bracts on proliferous shoots or in contracted leafless panicles. Capsule ⅓" 3-lobed pubescent. Seeds with a brown caruncle.

Valleys, esp. in shady places. Singbhum; Palamau (Betlah); Santal P.

Fl. *Dec.-March* and more or less all the year round. Sub-deciduous in *March.*

Twigs pubescent. *L.* with 3-5 nerves at or near the base which is often 2-glandular. Fls. monœcious in the *type*. *Disc* of 5-6 fleshy glands in M., annular in F. *Anth. cells* vertical on the very broad connective.

Var. dioica. L. with very strong parallel tertiary nerves. Fls. *diœcious*, with the males fascicled in narrow panicles and the females 1-3 axillary. Common.

22. Homonoia, Lour.

1. H. riparia, *Lour.* Gara-huri, gara-hui, *K.*; Sunukui, Gurjor, *S.*

A large shrub with numerous erect branches from near the root marked with prominent leaf scars. L. willow-like lanceolate or linear-oblong $3\frac{1}{2}''$ by $\frac{3}{4}''$ to $10''$ by $1''$. Fls. in long axillary spikes.

Rocky river-beds, throughout the area but somewhat local. Fl. *March-April* with the young shoots. Fr. *May-Sept.* Usually described as evergreen, but it is often completely deciduous in cold weather.

L. pubescent and nerves raised reticulate beneath, the areolæ closely lepidote: glabrescent above and shining. *Petiole* $\frac{1}{4}$-$\frac{1}{2}''$. *Stipules* linear $\frac{1}{4}''$ deciduous. *F. spikes* 2-4" long, *M.* longer. *M. sepals* 3, *F.* 5-8. *Capsules* $\frac{1}{8}$-$\frac{1}{4}''$ diam. tomentose seated on the spreading calyx. *Seeds* bright crimson.

Ricinus communis, *L.* Jara Bindi, *K.* is the well-known Castor-oil plant. The fls. are in panicled racemes, the lower female, often with brightly-coloured styles, the upper M. with copiously branched stamens. Capsules echinate.

24. Gelonium, Roxb.

1. G. multiflorum, *Roxb.*

A small glabrous tree with oblong or oblong-lanceolate obtuse leaves $2\frac{1}{2}$-$6''$ long narrowed into a petiole $\frac{1}{4}$-$\frac{1}{3}''$, diœcious yellow odorous fls. in peduncled contracted cymes or clusters. Fr. fleshy globose $\frac{1}{2}$-$\frac{3}{4}''$ diam.

Parasnath, *Campbell* ! Fl. *April.*

Nodes with stipular lines, *stipules* sheathing caducous. *L.* pellucid dotted, entire or serrate. *M. fl.* $\frac{1}{3}$-$\frac{1}{2}''$ diam. *St.* 40-60. *Fil.* free *Disc* 0. *F. disc* cupular, *ovary* 2-4-celled. "Fruit tardily dehiscent, the valves separating from a persistent axis, seeds arillate," *Brandis.*

25. Tragia, L.

1. T. involucrata, *L.* Jipenda, *Ho.*; Sengel sing, *S.*; Barhanta, *H.*; Bichati, *Beng.*

A perennial undershrub, woody below, with erect or scandent hairy branches, some of the hairs with pungent points, nettle-like serrate leaves, and minute green fls. in bracteate leaf-opposed or terminal spikes, or on short axillary branches.

Singbhum, not rare; S. P., common; Hazaribagh. Probably in the other districts. Usually in open waste ground, scrub jungle or among rocks. Fl., Fr. *Dec.-Feby.*

L. 2-4½" by 1-2", young tomentose beneath, base 3-5-nerved rounded. *Spikes* ⅓-½" long usually with a solitary female below and several minute yellowish-green m. above. *M. Sep.* 3 broadly ovate, *F. Sep.* 6 linear persistent, villous with pectinate lobes. *Capsule* septifragal of 3 2-valved cocci. *Seeds* globose strophiolate.

26. Sapium, P. Br.

1. S. sebiferum, *Roxb.* Chinese Tallow Tree.

A tree superficially resembling Sissu, the *leaves* being broadly rhomboid acuminate or of much the same shape as Sissu *leaflets.* Fls. monœcious greenish, M. clustered in simple terminal spiciform racemes 2-4" long, usually fem. at the base. Capsule 3-valved.

Native of China. Frequently planted, esp. in Daltonganj. Fl. *Aug.-Sept.* The open capsules may remain on the tree till *Nov.*, Deciduous *Nov.-March.*

Fam. 23. LINACEÆ.

Herbs or shrubs with alt. simple leaves and regular 2-sexual flowers with 5 sepals and petals and 10 stamens, or the alternate stamens reduced to staminodes. *Filaments* united at base into a hypogynous or slightly perigynous ring, *anthers* versatile, 2-celled. *Disc* 0 or of 2-3 or 5 glands usually adnate to the staminal ring. *Ovary* entire, 3-5-celled. *Styles*

3-5 free, or somewhat connate. *Ovules* 1-2. axile, pendulous, anatropous. *Fruit* a septicidal capsule usually splitting into 3-8 1-2-seeded cocci or (in Erythroxylon) a drupe. *Embryo* nearly as long as seed, cotyledons broad.

Shrub or undershrub. Fls. showy yellow . . . . . 1. *Reinwardtia.*
Cultivated shrub, Fr. a drupe. Fls. white . . . . 2. *Erythroxylon.*
Cultivated herbs. Fls. blue . . . . 3. *Linum.*

1. Reinwardtia, Dumort.

1. R. trigyna, *Planch.* Lungora, *Vern.* (Wood).

A very pretty small shrub 2-4 ft. high with green herbaceous branches, ovate-oblong to elliptic-lanceolate entire or crenate-serrate leaves and bright chrome-yellow flowers 1-1½″ diam. on numerous small axillary branchlets, rarely solitary or in terminal cymes.

Usually on damp shady banks near nalas, throughout the area.

Fl. *Oct.-Feby.*

Glabrous. *Branches* erect or prostrate and rooting. *L.* up to 3-4″ rarely sometimes with minute teeth, mucronate, narrowed into the slender ½-1″ petiole. *Sepals* erect. *Petals* obovate. *Styles* 3, or 4-5 (R. tetragyna, *Planch.*)

Erythroxylon Coca, *Lamk.* has been grown on the Ranchi plateau for the drug Cocaine derived from its leaves, without, it is believed, much success. It is a native of the Andes and Peru where the leaves are used as a masticatory.

Linum usitatissimum. *L* Vern. Unchi, *K.*; Tisi, *H.* The Linseed, is a common cold weather crop, and sometimes cultivated in gardens for its pretty blue flowers.

Fam. 24. GERANIACEÆ.

Tribe. Oxalideæ.

Averrhoa Carambola, *L* Vern. Karmaranga, H is a tree with drooping branches alt. imparipinnate leaves and small regular flowers variegated with white and purple which are borne in panicles, sometimes from the old wood. Fr. 3″ long oblong 5-angled, fleshy. Occasionally cultivated on the Ranchi plateau. The fruits are eaten.

Fam. 25. OCHNACEÆ.

Ochna, L.

Trees, shrubs or undershrubs with glabrous alt. simple serrate stipulate leaves. *Fls.* large yellow, in racemes or umbels. *Sep.* 5-7, persistent. *Pet.* 5-10, imbricate. *Disc* thick. *St.* ∞ inserted on the disc, filaments persistent, with deciduous anthers. *Ovary* deeply 5-10-lobed, lobes 1-ovuled, entirely separated on the enlarged torus in fruit, ovule axile. *Styles* connate. *Fruit* of distinct drupels. Seed erect, albuminous.

1. O. pumila, *Ham.* Champa Baha, *S.*

A pretty undershrub with a long stout rootstock from which it sends up annually shoots 8-18″ high bearing umbels of showy bright yellow flowers $1\frac{1}{2}$″ diam. Conspicuous in fruit from the spreading deep red sepals.

In open, especially grassy places. Singbhum, not common; Manbhum *Camp.*; Hazaribagh; Ranchi; Palamau.

Fl. *Feby.-June.* Fr. *March-July.*

L. broadly oblanceolate, 3-6″ by 1-2″, narrowed into the short petiole finely sub-spinulosely serrate. *Fls.* on pedicels 1-2″ long, peduncle axillary 1-3″. Petals $\frac{1}{2}$-$\frac{3}{4}$″. *Anthers* opening by pores. *Stigmas* as many as ovary lobes. *Drupels* usually 4-6, greenish.

Campbell states that the root is used by the Santals as an antidote to snakebite and medicinally for certain menstrual complaints, consumption and asthma.

2. O. squarrosa, *Roxb.* Champa baha, *S.*

A small glabrous tree or shrub with ell., ell-lanceolate-or oblanc. acute or somewhat acuminate leaves 3″ by 1″ to 7″ by $2\frac{1}{2}$″ with very numerous fine oblique sec. n. Handsome bright-yellow fragrant fls. $1\frac{1}{2}$″ diam. in short lateral sub-corymbose rarely panicled racemes from the leaf scars. Sepals $\frac{3}{4}$″ erect after flowering but again spreading and deep purple in fruit.

Rajmehal hills, in ravines and on rocky slopes, from Barhait northwards.

Fl. *May*. Fr. r.'s. Sub-deciduous *Feby.-March*.

Buds perulate. *L.* often clustered, finely spinulose-serrate but points deciduous and then crenulate or serrulate, base acute. *Petiole* $\frac{1}{6}$-$\frac{1}{4}$." *Pedicels* 1-1½" articulate.

Fam. 26. SIMARUBACEÆ.

Ailanthus, Desf.

Large trees with bitter bark, large, alt., exstipulate pinnate leaves which continue to grow for a considerable time at the apex and are approximated at the ends of the branchlets. *Fls.* small polygamous, in axillary panicles. *Calyx* 5-6-lobed, lobes imbricate. *Petals* 5-6 spreading, induplicate valvate. *Disc* 10-lobed. *St.* in male fl. 10, in herm. fl. sometimes only 2-3. *Carpels* 5-6 nearly free entirely free in fruit, 1-ovuled, 1 or more developing into a large, linear-oblong samara with the seed in the centre.

1. **A. excelsa,** *Roxb.* Pirinim, Ghorkaram (in Palamau f. Manson). Ghorkaranj, *Kharw.*

A tree with light-coloured bark, stout hoary tomentose branchlets, large pinnate leaves with 10-13 pairs of very coarsely toothed leaflets and large panicles of small flowers.

Along the Brahmini River in Gangpur.* Satbarua Fort, *Wood.* Palamau, frequent. Hazaribagh (Chorparan jungles).

Fls. *Jany.-March.* Fr. *May.* Sub-deciduous *May.* Renews leaves *May-June.* (According to Brandis, it is leafless in the early part of the cold season, but I have found it in full leaf in November and January.)

Smell fœtid. *Twigs* $\frac{1}{2}$-1" diam. with large leaf scars. *L.* 2-3 ft. long with hoary tomentose rachis. *Lflts.* opp. or alt., 3½-6" by 2-3", densely pubescent beneath and pubescent above when young, acute or acuminate with a very oblique base, sec. nerves about 12-20 pair *Petiolule* slender 1-2". Two hairy glands occur near the base of the petiole and sometimes also in the place of the lower leaflets. *Panicles* 10-20". *Fls.* yellowish. *Samaras* usually solitary, 1¾-2" by $\frac{1}{2}$", strongly veined with a twisted base.

The bark, ground, is used as a horse medicine "when horses fall down."

Fam. 27. ZYGOPHYLLACEÆ.

1. Balanites, Delile.

1. **B. Roxburghii,** *Planch.* Ingun, *Kharw.*; Hingux, *H.*

A very thorny grey-green shrub with alt. coriaceous, pinnate leaves of only 1 pair of leaflets, yellowish-green fragrant flowers in axillary cymes or fascicles, and fruit an ovoid drupe $1\frac{1}{2}$-2" long.

Palamau, esp. in the extreme west near the Sone. In the Journals in describing that part of the Grand Trunk road in Hazaribagh lying between Dumri and Baghoda, Sir J. D. Hooker, says "Balanites was not uncommon, forming a low thorny bush, with Ægle Marmelos and Feronia Elephantum."

Fl. *March-April.* Fr. Nov. Also found in flower Nov.

Thorns stout axillary, often elongated and bearing leaves. *Lfts.* entire ell. or obovate puberulous $\frac{3}{4}$-$1\frac{1}{4}$". *Petiole* hardly any. *Sep. and Pet.* 5 hairy. St. 10 at the base of the prominent disc which is 10-lobed. Ovary 5-celled, by abortion 1-celled with 1 pendulous ovule. *Drupe* yellow, slightly 5-groved with a very offensive smell and with very hard 5-angled 1-celled and 1-seeded stone.

Fam. 28. BURSERACEÆ.

Trees or shrubs secreting oleo-resins in the cortex. *L.* alternate, impari-pinnate, usually with opposite leaflets, stipulate or (in all the following) exstipulate. *Fls.* regular, small often polygomous in axillary or terminal racemes or panicles. *Calyx* often minute, lobes 3-6 imbricate or valvate. *Petals* 3-6 imbricate or valvate. *Disc* free or adnate to the base of the calyx. *St.* twice as many as the petals inserted on the margin of or underneath the disc. *Anthers* 2-celled dehiscing longitudinally. *Ovary* free, 3-5-celled. *Ovules* 2 in each cell axile pendulous anatropous. *Fruit* a drupe with 1-5 free or united pyrenes or stones or dry and dehiscent, each pyrene 1-seeded. *Albumen* 0. Cotyledons generally twisted or crumpled.

A Flowering before the new leaves.

L. lobulate or coarsely crenate. Disc fleshy annular. Fr. capsular . . . . 1. *Boswellia.*

L. shallowly crenate. Disc thin lining the calyx tube. Fr. drupaceous . . . . 2. *Garuga.*

B. Flowering on the new shoots.

L. sub-entire or serrate. Disc small annular. Fr. drupaceous. . . . . 3. *Bursera.*

1. Boswellia, Roxb.

1. **B. serrata,** *Roxb.* Salga, Sali, *K.*; Salga, *S.*; Salai, Sali, *H.*, *Kharw.*

A pretty tree with green, grey or reddish bark peeling off in thin flakes, large exstipulate impari-pinnate leaves 12-18″ long with numerous *opposite* sessile coarsely crenate-serrate leaflets and numerous racemes of smallish white flowers at the tips of the branches, usually appearing when the tree is bare.

Very common on dry hills, where it commonly attains 5 ft. girth. Rarer in the S. P.

Fl. *Jany.-March.* Fr. *May-June.* Deciduous *Jany.-May or June.*

Branches drooping, L. approximated at their ends. *Lflts.* 1½-3″ by ¼-¾″ opp. or sub-opp. 9-16 prs. lanceolate or ovate-lanceolate glaucous beneath and pubescent on the nerves above sometimes sub-lobed. *Racemes* 4-8″ pubescent, sometimes with short branches, crowded but not really terminal, the apex of the branch growing through them, so that they are below the new leaves in fruit. *Calyx* cupular 5-6-lobed villous. *Petals* 5-6, ¼″ oblong-ovate with thickened base. *St. 10.* inserted on the outside of the scarlet fleshy annular papillose disc. *Filaments* short subulate. *Anthers* dorsi-fixed sagittate introrse. *Ovary* free 3-celled with a 3-ridged style and capitate stigma. *Fruit* 3-gonous ½″ long with 3 valves and 3 winged hard pyrenes.

The wood is used for charcoal. The tree yields the Indian Olibanum, a golden-yellow gum-resin (luban, loban, *S.*) very fragrant and transparent. The leaves hung up in a cattle shed are said to keep away flies. Can be grown from large cuttings.

2. Garuga, Roxb.

1. **G. pinnata,** *Roxb.* Armu, *K.*; Kandwer, *S.*; Kekur Kenkar, *Kharw*; Karur, *Bhumij*, Kosromba, *Mal Pah.*

A mod.-sized handsome tree when in full foliage, with impari-pinnate leaves 12-18″ long, opp. leaflets 4½″ by 1½″ caudate-acuminate, crenate, shortly pubescent both sides. The yellow campanulate flowers ¼″ long are borne when the tree is leafless in numerous panicles 4-6″ long from the leaf scars at the tips of the branches.

Chiefly in the valleys, and on the ghats, frequent throughout the area.

Fls. *March-April.* Fr. *June-Aug.* Leafless *March-May.* Old leaves turn red before falling.

Twigs stout pubescent. *Lflts.* ovate-lanceolate with 12-16 prs. sec. n. lowest pair of lflts. usually very short reflexed. *Petiolules* $\frac{1}{12}$-⅛″. *Calyx-tube* very hairy, *sepals* half as long as the erect linear-oblong petals. *Filaments* hairy. *Fruit* globose yellowish-green ¾″ diam. with 2-4 stones.

A good tree for reclaiming grass tracts subject to fire, it may be classed among "fire-hardy" species. "Grows readily from cuttings," *Brandis.* Fr. eaten.

3. Bursera, L.

1. B. serrata, *Colebr.* Kandior, *K.*; Armu, *S.* (It will be seen that the Kols and the Santals reverse the names of these two trees); Sari, *Mal Pah.*

A mod.-sized tree with impari-pinnate leaves 6-12″ long, opp. leaflets 3″ by 1″ to 5½″ by 1¾″ caudate, entire or more or less serrate, pubescent on the nerves beneath. The very small green flowers ⅛″ diam. (and as long) are borne when the tree is in leaf in lax panicles 1½-3″ long from the leaf axils or below the leaves.

Common along ravines, and among rocks on the cool sides of hills.

Fl. *April.* Fr. *May.* Evergreen or nearly so. New leaves in *April.* *Twigs* pubescent. *Lflts.* 3-4 prs. only, oblong with 6-12 prs. sec. n. *Petiolules* ¼-½″. *Calyx-tube* very shallow with small lobes. *Petals* spreading above. *Disc* small free from calyx crenate with the stamens alternately on and between the crenatures. *Style* 0, or very short. *Fr.* globose red when ripe about ½-¾″ diam. with 1-3 stones.

Fam. 29. RUTACEÆ.

Tree or shrubs abounding in pellucid glands filled with essential oil,[1] with opp. or alternate, simple or compound

[1] Easily seen by holding a leaf up to the light.

exstipulate leaves. *Flowers* regular and usually 2-sexual in cymes or panicles. *Calyx* of 4-5 lobes or sepals. *Petals* 4-5 (or more in Citrus) valvate or imbricate. *Stamens* hypogynous, diplostemonous, *i.e.* 8 or 10, rarely (Citrus, Ægle) numerous. Filaments usually free and anthers 2-celled introrse. *Disc* within the stamens, crenate or lobed, sometimes large or long. *Ovary* entire or lobed 4-5-celled, or more celled (in many Aurantieæ). *Styles* as many as carpels or united with terminal stigma. *Ovules* usually 2 in each cell, sometimes numerous. *Fruit* very various. *Seeds* usually solitary in the cells, never winged, albumen fleshy or 0. *Embryo* straight or curved, radicle superior.

An order usually readily distinguished by its glandular leaves and flowers, closely allied to the Meliaceæ through Chloroxylon of that order, which also has glandular leaves and distinct stamens, but is retained in Meliaceæ on account of its fruit and winged seeds.

All the Chota Nagpur representatives of the order belong to the tribe Aurantieæ in which the fruit is baccate. L. alt. in all.

I. Ovules 1-2 in each cell.
- A. Unarmed.
  - 1. Style very short persistent, not jointed. Lflts. 1-5 . . . . 1. *Glycosmis.*
  - 2. Style jointed on the top of the ovary and deciduous.
    - *a.* Petals valvate. Lflts. over 3″ long (at least the upper) . . . . . 2. *Micromelum.*
    - *b.* Petals imbricate, Lflts. mostly under 3″
      - Fls. in cymes or corymbs. Filaments linear-subulate . . . . . . 3. *Murraya.*
      - Fls. in elongate panicles. Filaments dilated below . . . . . . 4. *Clausena.*
- B Armed . . . . 5. *Limonia.*

II. Ovules more than 2 in each cell. Trees or shrubs usually armed.
- Leaves 1-foliolate . . . . . . 6. *Citrus.*
- Leaves 3-foliolate . . . . . . 7. *Ægle.*
- Leaves impari-pinnate . . . . . . 8. *Feronia.*

1. Glycosmis, Corr.

1. G. pentaphylla, *Corr.* Ashaura, *Beng.*

A shrub 2-4 ft. with pinnately 1-5-foliolate leaves and large leaflets. Flowers small white in axillary pubescent panicles.

Parasnath, *Anders.*; Santal P. from Burio northwards, near rivers, gregarious. Fls., Fr. *Oct.-Feby.*

Twigs minutely puberulous. *Lflts.* usually 5 alternate (rarely opp.) very variable, usually ell. or ell.-oblong 2-5" by 1-2½" entire or obscurely toothed, glabrous. *Sepals* broadly ovate obtuse puberulous. *Pet.* 4-5 imbricate ⅛" oblong-obovate erect gland dotted. *St.* 8-10 free filaments linear flattened suddenly pointed. Anthers with an apical gland. *Ovary* 5-rarely 3-4-celled glabrous, mamillate with glands, style very short and stout, persistent. *Ovules* 1 in each cell, pendulous. *Berry* ⅓-½" diam. depressed globose pinkish glassy 1-seeded.

2. Micromelum, Blume.

1. M. pubescens, *Blume.* Exsira, *Vern.* (Wood).

A small tree attaining 25 ft. with pinnate leaves, very large leaflets and terminal large corymbs of white flowers which are succeeded by fœtid ovoid yellow or scarlet berries ½" long.

Shady valleys in Singbhum. Hazaribagh (Baragaon, *Wood*). Fl. *Jany.-March.* Fr. *May-July.* Evergreen.

L. 8-18". Lfits. 5-11 ovate to lanceolate attaining 8" by 3½", lowest sometimes only 1½" slightly pubescent, acuminate, base rounded oblique, rarely acute sometimes cordate. Corymbose *panicles* pubescent or tomentose. *Flowers* ⅓-½" diam. *Petals* narrow oblong, valvate. *St.* 10, alternate shorter. *Ovary* 2-7 usually 5-celled; cells with 2 superposed ovules. *Berry* fleshy very fœtid. *Cotyledons* crumpled.

3. Murraya, Linn.

Unarmed small trees or shrubs with impari-pinnate leaves and small alternate leaflets with oblique base. Fls. in axillary or terminal corymbose cymes rarely sub-solitary. Petals 5 imbricate. St. 10, inserted round an elongated disc, filaments linear-subulate, alt. shorter. Ovary 2-5-celled, narrowed into a long deciduous style. Ovules 1-2. Berry 1-2-celled oblong or ovoid, 1-2-seeded.

1. **M. exotica,** *Linn.* . Vern. Otli *K.*; Athel, *S.*; Kamini, *H.*, *Beng.* The Chinese Myrtle. China Box.

A handsome small tree or shrub with pinnate leaves 4-5″ long, small shining dark green leaflets $\frac{3}{4}$-2″ long and white fragrant flowers in corymbs or few-fid. loose cymes.

Wild (var. sumatrana) and not uncommon in rocky ravines (and on Parasnath) in Hazaribagh, Santal P., and Singbhum where it sometimes attains 25 ft. Commonly cultivated in gardens where it is usually a compact shrub.

Fls. *April-July.* Fr. *Dec.-Jany.* Evergreen.

Leaflets 3-8 rigid glabrous, entire. *Fls.* campanulate, very fragrant, with petals $\frac{1}{2}$″ long, oblong lanceolate. *Ovary* 2-celled. *Berry* red $\frac{1}{3}$″ apiculate, sometimes $\frac{5}{8}$″ by nearly $\frac{1}{2}$″ and spindle-shaped 1-2-seeded.

Var. sumatrana *Roxb.* is distinguished by its few-fid. cymes or subsolitary flowers, larger leaflets often 4 by $1\frac{3}{4}$″ and subulate sepals. One Santhal P. form has obtuse sepals, and petals $\frac{7}{8}$″ long.

2. **M. Kœnigii,** *Spreng.* Vern. Barsanga, *H.*

A shrub or small tree with pinnate leaves 5-16″ long, very oblique lanceolate or ovate leaflets 1-3″ long and terminal short peduncled pubescent corymbs of odorous white flowers $\frac{1}{2}$-$\frac{5}{8}$″ diam.

Often near gardens, but not seen truly wild in C. N.

Fls. *March-May.* Fr. *July-Aug.* A second flowering sometimes occurs in August. Evergreen.

Twigs pubescent. *Leaflets* entire or crenulate usually acuminate, lowest much smaller, 6-15 pairs, opposite or alternate. *Petals* linear oblong, $\frac{1}{3}$″ long. *Fruit* succulent ovoid or ellipsoid, $\frac{1}{3}$-$\frac{1}{2}$″ long, pink then black. *Seed* large.

The leaves are used in curries and as a stomachic.

4. Clausena, Burm.

1. **C. excavata,** *Burm.* Vern. Ote-armu, *K.*

An *undershrub* of which the shoots attain $1\frac{1}{2}$-2 ft. only and die down annually, with alternate 10- or more-foliolate leaves and terminal panicles of green flowers with 8 yellow stamens.

Singbhum, common in Sal forests. The new shoots appear in *April*. Fls. *May-June*. Fr. *July-Aug*.

Strongly scented. *Branches* tomentose from a perennial rootstock erect. *Leaf-rachis* tomentose 6-12″ long. *Lflts*. 1½-3½″ ovate to oblong or lanceolate with very oblique base, acuminate, hairy especially beneath when young and with large marginal pubescent glands. Branches of panicle cymose. *Fls*. ¼″ diam. hairy. *Sepals* 4 minute. *Petals* 4, 3-nerved. *Ovary* 4-celled, villous. Style stout deciduous. *Ovules* 2 in each cell. *Fruit* ⅜″ ellipsoid.

The dried and powdered rootstocks are used by the Kols for decayed teeth. In the Himalayas this plant becomes a large shrub or small tree.

2. C. Wampi, *Blanco*. Vern. Wampi (from the Chinese).

A small tree occasionally cultivated for its edible berries which are greenish and about ½″ diam. The leaves are 5-9-foliolate, 8-13″, glabrous. Lflts. 3-5½″ obliquely ovate. Rind of fruit full of glands.

Fls. *May*. Fr. *July*.

5. Limonia, L.

1. L. acidissima, *L*. Belsain, *Khar.*; Beli, *H*.

A small straight tree attaining 30 ft. with 1-2 axillary spines,[1] pinnate leaves with winged rachis and usually 5-7 leaflets, the small pale-yellowish white flowers in very short close racemes and the small globose fruits black when ripe and intensely bitter (not acid).

Frequent in valleys in Palamau (Betlah Forest, etc.) The Belsain Pir in the Ranchi district appears to be named after it. Santhal P. (Ghormara, in the south).

Sub-deciduous at the time of flowering. Fl. *May-June*. Fr. ripens *Nov.-Dec*.

Shoots pubescent. *Lflts*. opposite ell. or elliptic-ovate crenate 1-2″ long with cuneate base and usually obtuse notched apex. Wings narrowly obovate. *Racemes* ½-1″, mostly from leafless axils. *Fls*. ⅓″ diam. long-pedicelled, 4-merous. *St*. 8. *Ovary* 4-celled, sub-globose. Cells 1-ovuled. *Style* short very stout. *Berry* ½″ diam. green until ripe.

6. Citrus, Linn.

Small trees or shrubs, usually with axillary spines.[1] L. 1-foliolate with often winged petiole. Inflorescence lateral, flowers rather large, not greenish or yellow. Petals variable in number, imbricate. St. numerous with more or less connate filaments. Ovary many celled. Ovules 4-8 in each cell. Berry many-celled succulent with coriaceous or fleshy rind (Orange, Lemon and Citron).

1. C. Aurantium, *L.* The wild orange.

A small tree usually much branched from near the ground with green angular twigs and simple scented leaves. Fruits orange shaped globose or oblate not mamillate, juicy, 2-2½" diam.

Rocky secluded valleys in Singbhum (esp. near Bonai State.) Fruit ripens *April-June.*

Young shoots pale green. *Branchlets* mostly armed with straight axillary spines ¼-¾" long. *L.* ell. acute or somewhat acuminate and narrowed at base, sometimes faintly crenate 2½-5" by 1-2". *Petiole* ¼-½" narrowly winged or not. *Fls.* not seen. *Fr.* resembling a sweet lime in flavour, rind green not thick.

This is a rare plant and quite unlike the wild forms of the orange or lemon hitherto described. Flowers are required.

2. C. Aurantium, *L.* The orange: Narangi, *H.*

The ordinary form of C. Aurantium is cultivated on the Ranchi plateau and to a small extent in other places. It is a small tree with pure white flowers. L. 3-6" with petioles winged or not.

3. C. medica, *L.* Jamira, *K.*; Jambir, *S.*; Nimbu, *H.*

Usually a very spinous bush, young shoots purplish, L. 3-6". Flowers 1-sexual, more or less pink, fruit mamillate at the apex.

---

[1] The spines in the last four genera are often found laterally to a leaf or fascicle of leaves. In the leaf axils there usually arise 1-3 buds. Frequently one of these develops into a spine, sometimes the two lateral develop as spines, in other cases one lateral bud develops as a spine and the other as a branch bearing one, or a fascicle of leaves, when the original subtending leaf falls the spine thus becomes lateral to a leaf or fascicle.

Petals 3-5 thick, concave, white . . . . . 11. *Amoora.*

Petals 5 concave, yellow. Shoots lepidote . . 12. *Aglaia.*

N.B. – The length and shape of the staminal tube is usually correlated with that of the petals: concave petals = urceolate tube, oblong petals = cylindrical tube, etc.

1. Chloroxylon, D.C.

1. **C. Swietenia,** *D.C.* Sengel-Sali, *K.*; Bharhul, *Kharw.*; Bhira, *H.* Indian Satinwood.

A small or mod.-sized tree with thick corky bark, pretty, greyish or glaucous-green pinnate foliage, leaflets 10-20 pairs, about 1″ long, gland-dotted. Fls. white $\frac{1}{4}$″ diam. on the cymose branchlets of pubescent 3-5″ long panicles which are clustered towards the ends of the branches from the leaf scars.

Singbhum, usually on northern slopes and local; Gangpur; Palamau (woods near the Urunga R., etc.), frequent. Fl. *March-April* when leafless. Fr. *May-June.* Deciduous *Feby.-April.*

Lflts. rhomboid-oblong with rounded apex, petiolule $\frac{1}{12}$-$\frac{1}{10}$″, rachis with petiole 8-12″ long. *Pet.* with slender claws. *St.* 10 from the sinuses of the prominent disc. *Ovary* pubescent, 3-celled and -lobed. *Capsule* 3-gonous, oblong-ovoid, 1-1$\frac{1}{4}$″, 3-celled with winged seeds.

The wood is eagerly sought after, hence the scarcity of large trees. It is often found on the sides of hills in the form of coppice. The leaves blister the skin if rubbed on it, hence the Kol name Sengel-Sali (Sengel = fire), and cattle will not browse on it.

2. Cedrela, L.[1]

Trees. L. pinnate. Fls. short-oblong white in terminal, and sub-terminal panicles, 4-6- usually 5-merous. St. often with alternating staminodes, inserted on the fleshy disc, which is more or less adnate to the base of the ovary. Ovary 5-celled. Cells with several 2-seriate pendulous ovules. Capsule septifragally 5-valved, globose when young, then ellipsoid or oblong. Seeds many imbricate winged at one or both ends.

1. **C. Toona,** *Roxb.* Katangai, Roronga, *Ho.*; Katangari, *M.*; Tun, *H.* The Toon tree.

---

[1] *Vide* Records, Botanical Survey of India, III, 4, on the Indian Species of Cedrela by C. De Candolle.

A mod.-sized tree with large spreading leaves 1-2½ ft. long with 5-12 prs. of alt. or opp. lanceolate or oblong-lanc. finely acuminate glabrous or pubescent entire or faintly undulate lflts. with oblique acute bases. Fls. $\frac{1}{6}$-$\frac{1}{5}$″ long in drooping or sub-erect panicles on the new shoots. Seeds winged both ends.

Valleys in Singbhum, and Santal P.; Parasnath in Hazaribagh but not attaining large size and rather scarce. Lohardaga 2,500 ft., *Gamble.* I have not seen it wild elsewhere, but it is largely planted in all the districts. Fls. *March-April.* Fr. *June-July,* but the capsules often remain a whole year on the tree. Deciduous *Dec.-Feby.*

The typical C. Toona has quite glabrous leaves, panicles glabrous long and drooping, usually as long as or exceeding the leaves, *fls.* without staminodes. *Anths.* minutely apiculate. *Capsules* ¾″ smooth. This is rarely, if ever, found in Chota Nagpur, certainly not wild.

Var. α = C. Hainesii, *C. D.C.* sp.

L. 18″ long glabrous except the petioles and the axils of the sec. n. of the lflts. *Panicle* puberulous 8-9″ only, *erect. Fls.* $\frac{1}{5}$″. *Staminodes* 5 filiform. The fruit is *believed* to be that of the type and about ¾″ long. Truly wild in the valleys. It may be a distinct species, but a larger series of specimens is required.

Var. β (This is also included in C. Hainesii by De Candolle ? but it appears to me not to differ from C. Toona, var. pubescens, *Franch*). *L.* sometimes 2 ft. in length with 10-12 prs. of lflts. more or less *permanently pubescent* both sides. Sec. n. 14-16 prs. with pubescent pits in their axils. *Fls.* not seen, and it is possibly the same as α. Chiefly in village lands.

Var. γ Haslettii. *Lflts.* opp. 6-10 prs. under 4″. *Panicles* erect 6″ glabrous. *Fls.* $\frac{1}{8}$″. *Anthers* with a tail ½-¾ths as long as themselves. *Stmds.* 0. *Capsule* under $\frac{2}{3}$″ with small white lenticles. *Seeds* as in type. Santal P. Khatikhund, *Haslett* !

The fact that the young leaves appear at the commencement of the hot weather make the Toon a most desirable avenue tree.

3. Soymida, A. Juss.

1. **S. febrifuga,** *A. Juss.* Rohini, *K.*; Ruhen, S.; Rohan, Rohana *H.*, *Khar.*

A large or moderate straight tree with dark brown bark

thick wrinkled branchlets and pari-pinnate leaves 9-18″ long, usually red when young. Fls. greenish white in large terminal panicles. Tree often conspicuous from the large ellipsoid or obovoid pendent fruits, woody and septifragally 5-valved when ripe.

Singbhum rare, (at Chirubera); Gangpur, common; Manbhum, common in the Tundi forest, *Camp.*; and in other parts (*e.g.* along Barakka R.); Hazaribagh, frequent; coppiced on the Topchanchi hills. Palaman, frequent. Small stunted specimens a few feet high are very common in ruined forests; the young leaves are easily recognized by their red veins and petioles.

Fl. *April-May.* Fr. *May-June* (ripe ?) when nearly bare of leaves, and new shoots appear in the same months.

Lflts. 3-6 pair, distant opp. or alt., 2-4″ long, broadly oblong or elliptic obtuse with very oblique base, sprinkled when young with small sessile glands otherwise glabrous. *Sep.* 5 short imbricate. *Pet.* 5 obovate. *St.-tube* cupular, 10-cleft, lobes again 2-toothed, anthers between the teeth. *Ovary* 5-celled. *Capsule* 3″ by 2″ (1-2″ long only according to Brandis) with a large 5-rayed central axis and numerous large-winged seeds.

The bark is bitter and astringent. Among the Santals a decoction is given for rheumatic swellings, *Camp.* Wood used for oil mills, etc., very hard. Kundur (gunpowder) is prepared from its wood in Gangpur.

Chukrasia tabularis *A. Juss.* (sometimes spelt Chickrassia).

In a pamphlet entitled "On the Flora of Behar and the mountain Parasnath" by Thomas Anderson, formerly Superintendent of the Royal Botanic Gardens, Calcutta, it is stated that Chickrassia tabularis occurs on Parasnath from base to summit! This is the only record, and I suspect an error as I have failed to find it on Parasnath or anywhere else in Chota Nagpur. C. tabularis has 5-12 prs. of leaflets. White flowers ½″ long with erect oblong petals and a woody capsule about 1½-1¾″ long.

5. Azadirachta, A. Juss.

1. **A. indica,** *A. Juss.* Syn. Melia Azadirachta, *L.* Nim, *H.*, The Neem tree.

A handsome tree with pinnate leaves, 5-9 pair of coarsely-serrate unequal-sided leaflets and axillary panicles of white scented flowers.

Not indigenous, but occurs wild in jungles in Hazaribagh and frequently self-sown near gardens and villages throughout Chota Nagpur. Fl. *March-May*. Fr. *June-July*. The seed germinates the same season. Evergreen.

Fls. $\frac{1}{3}''$ diam., St.-tube $\frac{1}{3}''$ long, 10-toothed and anthers opposite the teeth. *Ovary* 3-5-celled. *Drupe* $\frac{1}{2}$-$\frac{3}{4}''$ ellipsoid, yellow when ripe, 1-celled and 1-seeded.

A most valuable germicide and the ripe fruits are largely collected by the Kols for the oil which is especially useful in parasitic skin diseases in both man and animals.

Brandis speaks of the fruits becoming purple when ripe, this is certainly not the case in Chota Nagpur.

6. Melia, L.

1. **M. Azedarach,** *L.* Bokom baha, *S.*; Bakain, *H.*; The Persian Lilac.

A small tree with 2-pinnate leaves and axillary panicles of small sweet-scented lilac and purple flowers. Ovary 5-6-celled. Drupe fleshy $\frac{1}{2}$-$\frac{3}{4}''$ yellowish with a bony 5-6-celled stone, each cell with 1 long narrow seed with brown testa, thin albumen and fleshy linear-oblong cotyledons.

Common in gardens and villages, not wild. Fls. *May-June*. Fr. ripens *Nov.-Dec.*, but often remains on the tree throughout the cold weather.

A pretty tree in flower but it is more or less leafless from Dec. to April.

7. Cipadessa, Blume.

1. **C. fruticosa,** *Blume.*

A small tree or a large shrub with long weak sub-sarmentose branches, leaves with 7-11 opposite variously toothed leaflets and axillary or extra-axillary small cymose panicles of small white flowers.

Valley forests in Singbhum, frequent in Saranda and Porahat; Parasnath, *Anders.* Fl. *April-May* with the new shoots. Fr. *May-Nov.* Deciduous in *March.*

Variable. Whole plant usually more or less pubescent. *L.* 5-12″. *Lflts.* from $\frac{3}{4}''$ (at base of leaf) to 5 by $2\frac{1}{4}''$, from entire to coarsely serrate or sub-lobed, acute or acuminate. *Petiolules* $\frac{1}{8}$-$\frac{1}{2}''$. *Panicles* narrow 3-4″ long including the long peduncle. *Calyx* 5-toothed. *Petals* 5, valvate strap-shaped. *St.* 10 loosely cohering into a tube, fil. villous within, forked, and anthers in the fork. *Ovary* 5-celled. Cells 2-ovuled. *Fruit* nearly dry under $\frac{1}{4}''$ diam. 5-gonous.

8. Heynea, *Roxb.*

1. H. trijuga, *Roxb.*

A small tree with pinnate leaves usually 12-18" long, large opposite entire leaflets and small white flowers in lax, corymbose panicles on slender peduncles 7-12" long.

Valleys in Singbhum. Kolomda 2,000ft. (Lohardagga) *Gamble*! Wood gives Laragaon (Hazaribagh) as a locality, but as he states that the vernacular is Ban-Simar, a name often given to Heptapleurum venulosum, and as also it is described as a large climber, there is probably some mistake.

Fl. *March-May.* Fr. *July-Sept.* Evergreen.

Lflts. 5-9 ovate acuminate, end one attaining $6\frac{1}{2}''$ by 3", paler and sometimes pubescent beneath, base straight, obtuse or rounded, petiolule $\frac{1}{4}$-$\frac{3}{4}''$ or of end leaflet 1", slender. *Panicles* (excluding peduncle) 2-4" only. *Fls.* short-oblong $\frac{1}{8}''$ long. *Sepals* short broad pubescent. *Petals* 4-5 oblong. *Fil.* cohering into a tube about half way, pubescent or villous within, forked, anthers apiculate within the fork. *Ovary* sunk in the disc 2-celled, cells 2-ovuled. *Fruit* ellipsoid $\frac{1}{2}''$ by $\frac{6}{16}''$, coriaceous with fleshy endocarp, ultimately 2-valved. *Seed* 1 with a white thin fleshy aril and large fleshy cotyledons.

9. Walsura, Roxb.

1. W. piscidia, *Roxb.*

A bushy tree with chartaceous pinnately 3-foliolate leaves 4"-6" long, oblong or somewhat ovate-oblong leaflets 3" by 1" to 5" by $2\frac{1}{4}''$ pale glaucous beneath and very shining above. Fls. yellowish $\frac{1}{8}''$ long in panicles 3"-5" wide composed of several long-peduncled partial panicles from the upper leaf scars.

Under the shade of immense gneiss rocks at the tops of the highest hills in Koderma. Fls. *May-June.* Partially deciduous at the time of flowering.

Innovations brown tomentose. *Lflts.* rounded both ends with about 0 prs of slender sec. n., very finely reticulate between. Lateral petiolules $\frac{1}{8}$-$\frac{3}{16}''$, terminal $\frac{3}{4}$-1". *Peduncles of panicles* $1\frac{1}{2}$-3" thickened upwards. *St.-tube* half length of petals cleft for two-thirds of its length into 10 bifid segments. *Ovary* 2-3-celled, and fruit brown-tomentose.

10. Dysoxylum, Blume.

Trees with large pinnate leaves and quite entire leaflets. Fls. panicled. Calyx 4-5-fid or sub-entire, deciduous. Petals 4-5 oblong valvate or slightly imbricate. St.-tube cylindrical, mouth usually toothed or crenulate. Anthers oblong 6, 8 or 10. Disc long tubular. Ovary 3-4-celled. Ovules 2 in each cell, superposed rarely solitary (*e.g.* D. Hamiltonii) Capsule coriaceous 1-4-celled, loculicidal. Seeds arillate or not, plumule sometimes hairy.

1. D. procerum, *Hiern.* ?[1]

A tall tree with light bark and very large pinnate leaves 3 ft. long crowded at the ends of the branches. leaflets attaining 12-14″ by 4″ decreasing in size towards the base of the leaf.

Karampoda forest in deep valleys with running water. Young fruit in *April*.

Lflts. 5-9 pair, opposite, oblong acute or acuminate with oblique usually rounded base, lower often only 4½″ by 2½″ and somewhat reflexed, sec. nerves 12-20 pair, distinct strong, straight then curved upwards to near the margin. *Rachis* grey microscopically tomentose, with minute scales and a few minute brown scales on the nerves beneath. *Petiolule* ¾″.
Frt. (unripe) ¾″ tomentose in axillary panicles on short pedicels, 3-celled, 3-seeded. *Calyx* 3-fid, tomentose.

11. Amoora, Roxb.

Trees with large pinnate leaves and entire leaflets. Fls. globose sometimes diœcious, panicled, or (A. Rohituka) female spicate. Calyx 3-5-fid or sepals nearly free. Pet. 3-5, concave, sometimes crenate. Anths. 6-10 included

---

[1] N.B.—Only once found and the fruiting-specimen with the remains of the perianth, sent to Calcutta where it was identified with D. procerum, but could not again be found on my visit. The species requires further investigation as the above description, taken from field notes, points to this tree being a species of *Amoora* rather than of *Dysoxylum*. It, in fact, closely resembles A. Wallichii, *King.*, a tree whose range is much more extensive than is supposed, having been found by me both in the Bhotan Duars and Sikkim Terai.]

in the tube. Disc obsolete. Ovary 3-5-celled. Cells 1-2-ovuled. Capsule 3-4-celled and -seeded, loculicidal. Seeds in a fleshy aril.

The juice is sometimes *milky*.

1. **A. Rohituka,** *W. & A.* Sikru, *Ho.* Sikaroru, *M.* Pitraj, *Beng.*

A handsome mod.-sized tree with a low spreading crown of large leaves 1-3 ft. long with 4-7 pair of large leaflets 3-9″ by $1\frac{1}{2}$-4″ decreasing in size towards the base of the leaf and small white flowers in lax simple (female) or branched (male) spikes.

Along river banks in Singbhum, chiefly in Saranda. Ravines in northern Santal P. Fl. *Aug.-Sept.* Fr. *May-June.* Evergreen.

Diœcious. *Branchlets* stout, shoots brown pubescent glabrescent. *Rachis* of leaves grey, but not microscopically pubescent, with scattered brown microscopic scales. *Petiolule* $\frac{1}{4}$″. *Lflts.* much as in last but base more oblique and nearly always acute, at least on one side. *Panicles* or *spikes* mostly extra axillary and shorter than the leaves. *Calyx* 5-partite lobes obtuse. *Petals* 3. *Anth.* 6. *Ovary* 3-celled. *Capsule* 3-valved, flesh coloured or yellowish $1\frac{1}{2}$″ diam. *Seeds* with scarlet arillus.

2. **A. Wallichii,** *King.* See note under Dysoxylum procerum.

12. Aglaia, Lour.

1. **A. odoratissima,** *Blume.*

A moderate tree with impari-pinnate leaves 3-7″ long with 1-3 pair of leaflets 2-5″ long and very small yellow flowers in elongate scaly panicles.

Pitorea, *Wood.* I have not seen this tree. Pitorea is close to Ranchi. Shoots, young leaves and inflorescence with ferruginous scales. *Fls.* $\frac{1}{12}$″. *Calyx* 5-lobed. *Petals* 5 concave. *Anthers* 5. *Ovary* 1-3-celled. *Fr.* $\frac{1}{4}$″ diam., indehiscent velvety. *Seeds* with a white edible arillus.

Fam. 31. ANACARDIACEÆ.

Trees or shrubs with alternate simple or compound exstipulate leaves. *Fls.* small regular often polygamous, sometimes diœcious, usually panicled. *Calyx* of 3-5 sepals or lobes *Petals* as many as the calyx lobes, imbricate or sub-valvate. *Disc* rarely absent. *St.* normally twice as many as the petals, but usually fewer, sometimes only 1 perfect, inserted under or on the margin of the disc. *Ovary* superior, of 1-more, rarely of 2-5, united or (in Buchanania) free carpels. *Carpels* with 1 ovule, either pendulous from the axis or from an ascending basal funicle. *Fruit* usually a 1-seeded drupe, rarely drupe with a 1-5-celled stone (Spondias), exalbuminous. *Embryo* straight or curved, *cotyledons* plano-convex.

Resin passages in the bark often filled with a caustic juice.

A. Carpels solitary or 3-4 united in a 1-celled ovary or if 2-celled, with one cell early suppressed.

I. Ovule pendulous from the top of the cell or from above the middle.

L. pinnate. Fls. before leafing, fascicled on numerous simple or branched racemes. Styles 3-4, rarely 6 . . . . 1. *Odina.*

L. simple. St. 5. Drupe on a swollen receptacle. Styles 3 . . . . 2. *Semecarpus.*

II. Ovule pendulous from a basal funicle. L. simple. St. 5-1. Style lateral. The Mango . . . 3. *Mangifera.*

B. Carpels 5 distinct, one only perfect. L. simple. St. 10. Drupe small, not on a swollen receptacle . 4. *Buchanania.*

C. Ovary 2-5-celled. L. pinnate.

Fls. before leafing white in a large terminal panicle . . . . 5. *Spondias.*

1. Odina, *Roxb.*

1. **O. Wodier**, *Roxb.* Nanam, *K.*; Doka, *S.*; (Dhauuk, doka, also used by the Tantis and other Hindu castes); Genjan, *Kharw.*; Parmi, *Ghatw.*; Jhingan, *H.*; Jial, *Beng.*

A small or large tree with stout soft branchlets, odd-pinnate glabrescent leaves clustered at the ends of the branchlets with 3-4 pairs of leaflets. Small yellowish-green diœcious flowers fascicled on the rachis of numerous racemes towards the ends of the bare twigs, succeeded by curved oblong compressed red drupes $\frac{1}{3}''$ long.

Very common in all the districts especially in dry forests, where it is one of the first trees to lose and one of the last to regain its leaves. Fl. *March-April.* Fr. *May-June.* Dec. *Nov.-May*, but seedlings keep their leaves till *January*.

Branchlets with a large pith, thin wood and thick tough white bark. Young shoots, leaves and inflorescence with scattered *stellate* hairs. *Lflts.* $2\frac{1}{2}$-$5\frac{1}{2}''$ ovate opposite mostly acuminate with oblique unequal base, lower smaller shortly petiolulate, upper sometimes sessile, terminal petiolule 1-2″. *Racemes* very numerous at the ends of the twigs or from upper leafless axils, never truly terminal, erect or ultimately drooping. *M.* 3-8″ often with slender branches. *Sep.* 4 (-5), ovate ciliate, $\frac{1}{20}$-$\frac{1}{18}''$ imbricate. *Pet.* as many $\frac{1}{8}''$ oblong acute. *St.* 8 on the margin of the annular disc. *Pistillode* 4-5-grooved clavate truncate. *F. racemes* 3-6″ elongating in fruit to 8″, not or very shortly branched. *Pet.* 4-5 oblong obtuse $\frac{1}{6}''$. Staminodes 8 on a small disc at base of the 4-6-grooved oblong ovary. *Styles* 3-6 short thick with a papillose stigma. *Ovule* on a long pendulous funicle. *Drupe* with a thin fleshy epicarp and large stone, seated on the persistent somewhat enlarged ($\frac{1}{10}''$) calyx.

The tree contains an abundance of starch and is therefore easily raised from cuttings and good for fodder. It yields a clear gum in considerable quantities The bark is astringent and gives a coarse fibre. The fruit is largely eaten by birds.

2. Semecarpus, Linn. f. The Marking Nut.

1. S. Anacardium, *L.* Soso, *K., S.*; Bhelwa, *Kharw., H.*; Bhela, *Beng.*

A small tree with large simple oblong or obovate strongly-nerved leaves 8-18″ long clustered at the ends of the branches, and small subsessible fasciculate dull greenish-yellow male or polygamous flowers on the branches of a terminal panicle. Fruit an oblong or obliquely ovoid drupe, black when ripe, seated on a fleshy orange cup (formed of the swollen accrescent calyx-base and disc).

Fairly abundant throughout the forest, but scattered.

Fl. *June-Sept.* Fr. *Dec.-March.* Dec. *March-May.*

Branchlets stout, young pubescent or tomentose. *L.* hairy on the nerves beneath and grey between the nervules with a close-felted layer of microscopic papillæ, apex rounded. *Sec. n.* 16-25 pairs reticulate within the *thickened* margin. *Petiole* 1-2″. *Panicle* stout pubescent as long as or longer than the leaves. *Fls.* ¼″ diam., polygamo-dioecious. *Calyx* ⅛″ long with 5 small teeth, tube accrescent with the receptacle. *Petals* oblong with rounded apex, greenish-yellow. *St.* 5 inserted outside and at the base of the disc. *Ovary* 1-celled tomentose with 3 styles. *Drupe* 1″ coriaceous.

The juice causes blisters and woodmen therefore object to felling the trees. The ripe orange cup of the fruit is eaten and also, it is said, the kernel of the fruits but the pericarp is full of a black juice which is a powerful vesicant and is used for marking clothes. The fruits form an important ingredient in some native medicines for dyspepsia, piles and skin diseases. They probably give the active principle in the mixture used for "chobing" elephants' feet.

3. Mangifera, L. Mango.

Trees. Fls. small, polygamous in terminal panicles, pedicels articulate. Calyx 4-5-partite. Pet. 4-5, only 1-2 usually perfect, inserted within the tumid lobed disc. Ovary sessile 1-celled, oblique, style lateral, ovule pendulous from a sub-basal funicle. Drupe large fleshy; stone compressed, fibrous.

1. M. indica, *L.* Uli, *K.*; Ul, *S.*, and the fruit Amsi; Am, *H.*

The wild mango is very similar to the cultivated one and is a fine largo tree 60 ft. high and up to 8 ft. or more girth. The fruit is 3-4″ long with a very large stone, thin rind and very abundant pleasant juice but little flesh.

Along rocky valleys and banks of streams, common in Singbhum. Also in Manbhum and on Parasnath. Possibly wild and indigenous throughout Chota Nagpur, certainly so in Singbhum. Fl. *Jany.-March.* Fr. *May-June.* Evergreen, renews leaves in *June.*

An important food in times of famine; large baskets of the fruit are boiled and the liquid drunk, while the kernels, after being steamed, are also eaten.

4. Buchanania, Roxb.

1. B. latifolia, *Roxb.* Tarub, *K.*; Tarop., *S.*; Piar, *Kharw.*; Piar, Pial, *H.*

A small straight tree with rough bark, stiff entire strongly nerved oblong simple leaves 6-10″ long and axillary and terminal panicles of small sessile white flowers $\frac{1}{6}''-\frac{1}{4}''$ diam. Drupes globose black $\frac{1}{2}''$ diam.

Very common, but rarely more than a small tree of $3\frac{1}{2}''$ girth. Especially abundant in dry forests. Fl. *Jany.-March.* Fr. *April-May.* Nearly evergreen, but sometimes leafless *April-May* in dry years. Renews leaves in *June.*

Innovations pubescent or villous. *L.* pubescent beneath rounded at the tip somewhat resembling oblong forms of Semecarpus, and nervation very similar but without the grey or white felt between the nerves. *Petiole* $\frac{1}{4}-\frac{1}{3}''$ stout pubescent *Panicles* pyramidal densely pubescent. *Sepals* 5 nearly free. *Pet.* triangular or oblong. *St.* 10, erect as long as the spreading petals, inserted on the base of the fleshy lobed disc. *Carpels* 5 (very rarely 6) of which 4 are rudimentary, hairy.

The fruit is largely eaten, the flesh is very palatable and the kernels somewhat like pistachio nuts.

5. Spondias, L. The Hog-plum.

1. S. mangifera, *Willd.* Ambo ; *Ho.*; Amburo, *M.*; Amra, S., *H.*; Amara, *Kharw.*; Katambolam *Mal. P.*, Ambra, *Beng.*

A moderate or large tree with stout branchlets, odd-pinnate glabrous sweet-smelling leaves clustered at the ends of the branchlets with 4-6 pairs of strong-nerved leaflets. White flowers $\frac{1}{4}-\frac{3}{8}''$ diam. sessile in small cymes on the branches of a large panicle terminal on the bare branches, succeeded by large plum-like drupes.

Wild in the lower lying forests especially near rivers, often planted. Easily recognised by its characteristic mango-like smell.

Fl. *Feby.-March.* Fr. ripens in the following *Jan.* when the tree is leafless. Dec. *Jany.-May.* Renews leaves *May-June.*

All parts quite glabrous. *Lflts.* opp. oblong acuminate 2-9″ by 1-4″ shortly petiolulate with 10-30 pairs of horizontal sec. nerves joined by a strong intra-marginal one. *Panicle* fleshy pyramidal 1-2 ft. *Calyx* salver-shaped with 5-6 ovate acute lobes. *Petals* white ovate-oblong. *St.* 10 inserted under the large cushion-shaped lobulate disc, with short subulate filaments. *Carpels* 4-6 free above united below into a 4-6 celled ovary, each with a very short style. *Drupe* $1\frac{1}{4}''$ long, yellow ellipsoid with a hard somewhat fibrous and grooved 2-6-celled stone, usually 1-3-seeded.

Fruit very astringent, greedily eaten by deer and other animals and is occasionally palatable when quite ripe.

FAM. 32. SAPINDACEÆ.

Trees or shrubs rarely herbs with alternate exstipulate simple or compound leaves. *Fls.* small usually polygamous, regular or usually more or less irregular. *Calyx* 4-8-lobed or sepalous, valvate or imbricate in bud. *Petals* as many as, or fewer than, the calyx lobes or 0, often bearded or squamate at the base. *Stamens* 4-10, very commonly 8, inserted inside rarely outside the disc, often declinate; anthers 2-celled basifixed or versatile. *Disc* sometimes unilateral, rarely 0 in male flowers. *Ovary* entire or lobed, often excentric usually 3- (4-2) celled; cells 1-2- rarely more-ovuled. *Ovules* axile ascending. *Fruit* capsular or indehiscent, sometimes bladdery, entire, lobed or winged. *Seeds* often arillate, usually exalbuminous. *Embryo* stout, sometimes spiral or plicate.

St. inserted inside the disc. L. compound.
- Trees. Pet. 4-5. St. 8-10 . . . 1. *Sapindus.*
- Tree Pet 0. St. 4-8 . . . . . 2. *Schleichera.*
- Climbing herb . . . . . 3. *Cardiospermum.*

St. inserted outside the disc in Herm. H. Disc 0 in M. L. simple A shrub . . . 4. *Dodonæa.*

To this family also belongs the Litchi (Nephelium Litchi, *Comb.*), in which only 1 lobe of the ovary usually develops fruit. The part eaten is the aril.

1. Sapindus, Plum.

Trees with pari-pinnate leaves and entire leaflets. Fls. sub-regular with 4-5 imbricate sepals and 4-5 petals which are furnished with a scale at the base. St. 8-10. Filaments usually pilose. Ovary 2-4-angled or lobed, 2-4-celled. Style with a 2-4-lobed stigma. Ovule 1 in each cell. Fruit fleshy or coriaceous, of 1-3 more or less distinct indehiscent carpels. Seed without arillus.

Neither of the following two species are indigenous. A saponaceous principle is contained in the pulp of the fruit which is largely used in the place of soap, and to which it is preferred for the washing of certain fabrics.

- Ovary tomentose. Leaflets 2-3 pair . . . 1. *trifoliatus.*
- Ovary glabrous. Lflts. 5-8 pair . . . 2. *Mukorossi.*

1. S. trifoliatus, *L.* Bor-ritha, *Beng.*

A handsome tree with leaves 5-12″ long, acuminate leaflets 3-6″ long usually pubescent beneath with pale raised nerves, and large terminal panicles of small dull-white flowers $\frac{1}{6}$-$\frac{1}{5}$″ long.

Occasionally cultivated. Chatra, Hazaribagh, *Wood.* "Appears to be wild, but very rare in Chota Nagpur," *Prain.* Fl *Dec.* Fr. *April.*

St. 8. Ovary 3-lobed. *Fruit* of three slightly united yellowish-green drupels, $\frac{1}{2}$-$\frac{3}{4}$″ long.

2. S. Mukorossi, *Gaertn.* (Syn. S. detergens, *Roxb.*) Ritha, *H.*, *Beng.*

A handsome tree with leaves 6-18 inches long clustered about the ends of the branchlets, acuminate leaflets 2-6″ by $\frac{3}{4}$-2″ glabrous with numerous close secy. nerves, and terminal pyramidal panicles of white or purplish flowers $\frac{1}{10}$″ long. Occasionally cultivated. Fl. *May-June.* Fr. *Sept.-Dec.* Deciduous. Renews leaves in *April.*

Sep. and *pet.* ciliate. *St.* 8 (rarely 6). Filaments wooly. *Ovary* 3-angled. *Fruit* of usually only one sub-globose smooth yellow drupel $\frac{3}{4}$-1″ diam.

2. Schleichera, Willd.

1. Schleichera trijuga, *Willd.* Baru, *K.*, *S.*; Kusum, *H*, *Kharw.*

A handsome dense-foliaged large tree with pari-pinnate leaves 8-16″ long 2-4-pairs of opposite entire leaflets 3-10″ long, the basal ones smallest, and inconspicuous greenish-yellow flowers in numerous lateral racemes appearing with the deep red new foliage.

Throughout Chota Nagpur. Fairly common in the Singbhum forests, but the finest trees are usually those in village lands. Fl. *Feby.-March.* Fr. *June-July.* Nearly evergreen. The new leaves appear *Feby.-March.*

Trunk attaining 7-8 ft. girth but not a great height. Crown rounded. *L.* ultimately dark green, rachis 3-6″. *Lflts.* sessile, ell. or oblong, glabrous, rarely repand or sub-lobed usually entire, with 10-16 pairs of distinct pale slender secondary nerves and intermediate shorter ones finely reticulate between. *Inflorescence* tomentose. *Fls.* 1-sexual or polygamous fascicled on racemes 2-6″ long which are axillary or below the leaves and often on special abbreviated branchlets. *Sepals* $\frac{1}{25}$-$\frac{1}{20}$″, 4-6 pubescent. *Petals* 0. *Disc* annular. *St.* 4-8 with long slender glabrous filaments $\frac{1}{8}$-$\frac{1}{6}$″ long. *Ovary* glabrous 3-celled. *Fr.* mostly 1-celled, toughly-coriaceous, 1-1½″, ovoid, usually with a sharp point, sometimes slightly prickly. *Seed* entirely enveloped in the aril with a thick smooth brown testa. Embryo large horse-shoe shaped, the short radicle in a fold of the testa:

The timber is good but the tree is rarely cut in the village lands, being left for the cultivation of lac, which yields twice the price of lac grown on any other tree. Both the aril and the kernel of the seeds are eaten and a good oil for cooking is expressed from the seeds. Campbell says that the oil is used also for the treatment of certain skin diseases.

The tree is very readily raised from seed sown as soon as ripe. The young plants should be put out in the second year, *i.e.*, exactly one year from the time of sowing.

Cardiospermum Halicacabum. *L.* Galphul, *Kharw.*, is a slender elegant climber with deltoid ternately divided and toothed leaves, and small white flowers in long peduncled axillary cymes, the lowest pair of pedicels developed as recurved tendrils. Capsule inflated membranous, 3-celled.

Common.

Fl. *Aug.-Sept.* Fr. *Nov.*

4. Dodonaea, L.

1. D. viscosa, *L.* Mehndi, *Vern.*

A light-green large shrub often 10 ft. high with simple oblanceolate glabrous sub-sessile leaves 1-3½″ long and short cymes of greenish flowers. Capsule membranous 2-4-winged compressed.

Often grown in gardens, and apparently naturalized about Koderma, but not native in Chota Nagpur.

Young leaves and flower-buds in *Dec.* Fl. *Jan.-Feb.*

Shoots and *Leaves* somewhat resinous. Sec. n. numerous. *Fls.* polygamous. *Sep.* 5 (or fewer). *Pet.* 0. *Ovary* 3-4-celled.

Fam. 33. SABIACEÆ.

Trees or shrubs with simple or pinnate alternate exstipulate leaves. *Fls.* small, with 5-3 sepals and petals or apparently only 3 petals, the other two being reduced to scales *St.* as many as the petals and opposite to them, but frequently only two fertile and the others variously modified, inserted on or at the base of the usually small annular disc. *Ovary* 2-3-celled, compressed or 2-3-lobed; *styles* distinct or connate often lateral in fruit. *Ovule* 1 or 2 in each cell, axile. *Fruit* drupaceous or of 2-3 drupels.

Meliosma, Blume.

1. M. simplicifolia, *Roxb.*

A small tree with large simple oblanceolate entire shining leaves 6-12″ by $1\frac{3}{4}$-$4\frac{1}{2}$″ and rusty-pubescent panicles as long as the leaves, of small yellowish white flowers or small keeled drupes.

Deep ravines with a perennial water supply at 2,000-2,500 ft. in the Karampoda forest, Singbhum. Fl. *Dec.-Feby.* Fr *March-June* Evergreen.

Twigs with prominent lenticels puberulous *L.* glabrescent and shining both sides, oblanceolate to obovate acuminate with base tapering into a slender pubescent petiole 1-$1\frac{1}{2}$″ long which is thickened at its base. *Sec. n.* 12-16 pairs oblique curving up inside the margin, prominent. *Fls.* minute sessile. *Sep.* 3-4 larger and 2 smaller (bracteoles ?) ciliate. *Pet.* 3 outer large orbicular concave the 2 inner bifid scale-like. *Drupe* $\frac{1}{4}$″ diam.

Fam. 34. MALPIGHIACEÆ.

Climbing shrubs with opposite simple entire leaves and regular or irregular flowers. *Sepals* 5 connate, one or more furnished with a large gland. *Petals* 5 imbricate often fimbriate. *Stamens* 10, one or more sometimes larger than the others. *Ovary* 3-celled. *Ovules* solitary in each cell. *Fruit* of 1-3, 1-more-winged samaras.

Hiptage, Gært.

1. H. Madablota, *Gært.* Sang Karla, S.; Madulata, *Beng.*

A large climbing shrub with elliptic or ovate-oblong or oblong-lanceolate shortly acuminate leaves from 4″-7″ by

$2\frac{1}{3}''$ and showy white flowers with one yellow petal in axillary pubescent racemes or leafy panciles.

Santal Parganahs in ravines (Morjhora, Sahebganj, etc.).

Fl. *Feb.-March.* Fr. *May.* Evergreen.

Branches pale. *Leaves* shining penninerved with 4-6 prs. arched secy. nerves and numerous very faint intermediate, base obtuse. *Petiole* $\frac{1}{4}''$. *Flowers* $\frac{3}{4}$-1″ across. *Pet.* fimbriate. Each carpel in fruit with one large central erect wing and two smaller lateral.

Fam. 35. POLYGALACEÆ.

1. Polygala, L.

Herbs or undershrubs with small alt. simple entire exstipulate leaves and irregular small green or coloured flowers. *Sep.* 5 of which the 2 inner are much larger than the others and are called *wings*, they are often coloured. *Pet.* 3 one forming a lip and often crested. *St.* 8 more or less united into a split sheath. *Ovary* 2-celled. *Capsule* usually herbaceous or membranous, flattened and 2-seeded. *Seeds* usually strophiolate.

1. P. glomerata, *Lour.*

A twiggy undershrub 1-2 ft. high with pubescent branches, ovate or ovate-lanceolate sub-distichous leaves 1-$1\frac{3}{4}''$ rarely 2″ by $\frac{1}{3}$-$\frac{3}{4}''$ and greenish inconspicuous flowers in extra-axillary racemes $\frac{1}{3}$-$\frac{1}{2}''$ long.

Valleys in the Latua forest under shade, very rare, but locally abundant.

Fl. *Dec.-Jany.* Fr. *Jan.-Feb.* Deciduous in the hot weather.

L. ciliate and somewhat hairy both sides acute with rounded base and 3-5 prs. fine rather obscure sec. n. *Petiole* pubescent $\frac{1}{10}''$. *Raceme* pubescent close flowered. *Calyx* persistent, wings $\frac{1}{5}''$ by $\frac{1}{10}''$ falcately-oblong apiculate with narrow scarious margins, nearly $\frac{1}{4}''$ in fr. ciliate. *Pet* white oblong with a small scale near base, lip $\frac{1}{4}''$ sub-saccate with small fimbriate crest. *Ovary* pubescent on margin. *Capsule* obcordate. *Seeds* with 3-lobed strophiole silky.

Several herbaceous species are common. **P. chinensis** *L.* Gaighura, *S.* is a branched herb 3-10″ with oblong, oblanc. or obovate L. $\frac{1}{3}$-$1\frac{1}{4}''$ and greenish fls. in short sub-capitate racemes or sub-solitary. The root is given in fever. Common in grassy ground. Fl., Fr. chiefly *August.*

Fam. 36. CELASTRACEÆ.

Trees or shrubs with simple alternate or opposite leaves; and stipules small caducous or 0. *L.* entire or crenate, more rarely serrate. *Fls.* small 2-sexual or polygamous in cymes or axillary clusters. *Calyx* 4-5-lobed, persistent, lobes imbricate. *Petals* 4-5, inserted outside the disc rarely continuous with its margin, imbricate. *St.* 3-5, inserted either on the disc or on its margin or arising from its inner side in which case the filaments are often connate as a membrane closely investing the ovary (*e.g.* Salacia sp.). *Anthers* 2-celled. *Disc* usually well developed. *Ovary* sessile free or somewhat sunk in the disc, 3-5-celled (sometimes 2-celled in Elæodendron cells *very many* in Siphonodon). *Style* short or 0. *Stigma* simple rarely 3-5-lobed. *Ovules* 2 in each cell, anatropous, erect (1 in each cell in Siphonodon, or more than two or pendulous in genera outside our area). *Fruit* various, often only 1-celled and 1-seeded. *Seed* arillate, sometimes winged, with or without albumen. *Embryo* usually large with flat foliaceous cotyledons.

L. alternate. Fruit dehiscent (Tribe Celastreæ)—
- Scandent shrub. Fls. in elongate panicled cymes . . . . 1. *Celastrus.*
- Erect shrub. Fls. in small dichotomous cymes 2. *Gymnosporia.*

L. mostly opposite and sub-opposite. Fr. indehiscent—
- A tree. Fls. in lax dichotomous cymes . 3. *Elæodendron.*
- Anomalous genus. L. alt. Ovary with numerous cells . . . . 4. *Siphonodon.*

1. Celastrus, L.

1. **C. paniculata,** *Willd.* Kujri, *K.*, *S.*; Konjri, *Kharw.*; Chiron, *Mal. Pah.*; Mal Kangni, *Beng.*

A scrambling or climbing shrub with long lenticellate branches, alternate obovate serrulate leaves, green flowers ½" diam. in terminal panicles and yellow 3-lobed capsules with red-arilled seeds.

Common, especially in hedges, throughout the area. Fl. *April-June* with the new leaves. Fr. *Oct.-Jany.*

L. $1\frac{1}{2}''$ by $1''$ to $5''$ by $2\frac{1}{2}''$ sometimes elliptic or oblong, always with a short sudden acumination, young (and young branchlets) pubescent and bright green, base acute, sec. nerves slender 4-7 pairs, *petiole* $\frac{1}{4}$-$\frac{1}{2}''$, *stipules* minute, deciduous. *Panicles* 2-6" lanceolate. *Bracts* minute. *Sepals* orbicular. *Pet.* ovate-oblong obtuse. *St.* 5 on the margin of the disc. *Ovary* not sunk in the disc usually 3-celled with 2 erect ovules in each cell. *Stigma* 3 lobed (simple according to *F.B.I.*). *Capsule* globose or obovoid $\frac{1}{3}''$ 3-valved, 3-6-seeded.

The seeds are used medicinally, and from them are obtained two valuable oils by expression and distillation respectively. The former method is the one usually employed in Chota Nagpur, and the oil so obtained is used for burning as well as for external and internal use. but is not so valuable as the so-called Oleum nigrum, obtained by distillation. The fruit is eaten before the seeds ripen.

2. Gymnosporia, W. and A.

1. G. montana, *Roxb.*

A shrub with slender spinescent branches, sub-orbicular crenulate leaves 1-3" long, divaricating dichotomous cymes of small white flowers $\frac{1}{4}''$ diam. and globose black 1-3-celled capsules. The cymes are axillary or borne fascicled on the spinose branchlets.

Parasnath. Fl Oct.—Dec.

L. grey coriaceous sub-sessile. *Petals* 4-5 spreading. St. 4-5 inserted under the disc. *Capsule* $\frac{1}{6}$-$\frac{1}{3}''$ usually 2-valved, seeds 1, 2, rarely 3, with or without an arillus, *Brandis.*

3. Elaeodendron, Jacq.

1. E. glaucum, *Pers.* Miri, *K.*; Niuri, *S.*; Ratan-garur *Ghatw.*; Thanki, *Asrur.*

A small tree with opposite (or alternate on some shoots), crenate or serrulate leaves 5" by $2\frac{1}{2}''$ and lateral divaricate lax cymes of small white or brownish flowers which are succeeded by nearly dry oblong or obovoid drupes $\frac{1}{2}''$ long.

Throughout the area usually in dry forests where it occurs as a small tree only. Fl. *Sept-Dec.* Brandis however says *Feby.-June*, so there may be two periods. The fruits may be found at most times of the year and appear to ripen about *Feby.* Nearly leafless *March-April* and new leaves appear in *May.*

L. deep green glabrous 2-6″ by 1-3″ ell., ovate to obovate, acute or acuminate, coriaceous, nerves slender. *Petioles* ½-1″ grooved above. *Cymes* 2-4″ with long slender peduncles. *Sep.* unequal orbicular. *Petals* oblong ⅛″ dorsally pubescent brownish with a white thinner margin. *St.* inserted on the lobes of the disc near the margin recurved with subglobose 2-celled anthers. *Ovary* conical, base only confluent with the disc, 2-celled, (or 3-celled, *Brandis*) with 2 linear ovules in each cell apex tapering into the stigma. *Fr.* 1-seeded crowned with the style.

A preparation of the bark is given in cholera.—*Campbell.*

4 Siphonodon, Griff.

1. S. celastrineus, *Griff.*

A small erect tree with coriaceous somewhat distichous ellip.-oblong more or less crenate leaves somewhat resembling those of Croton oblongifolious, white flowers ½-⅝″ diam. in 3-fld. axillary cymes or in several-flowered cymes from the branches. Fruit broadly pyriform 1¼-2″ long by 1-1½″ with coriaceous pericarp, firm mesocarp and numerous pyrenes with woody endocarp.

Ravines in the Rajmehal hills, not common. Fls. *April-June.* Fr. *ripens Feby.* Evergreen.

Glabrous. *L.* 4″ by 1½″ to 8½″ by 3½″ very shining above, acute or acuminate with rounded rarely acute base, sec. n. slender about 8 prs. depressed above. *Calyx* with broad rounded lobes. *Petals* on the calyx-tube broad-oblong. *Disc* filling and adnate to the calyx-tube with a lobed margin bearing the stamens between the lobes. *Filaments* broad, flattened arching over the pistil, with very broad connective bearing the oblique anther lobes on the margin, anthers laterally dehiscent. Ovary sunk in the disc hollowed out at the apex into a flask shaped cavity from the base of which rises what looks like a stout style and capitate stigma. This style-like organ is surrounded by a collar of 5 minute appendages of the ovary (opp. the petals) which are said to be the stigmas. There are also 5 still smaller points alternating with these. The *ovary* contains some 20-30 lenticular cells radially disposed, but otherwise showing no other arrangement, each with one ovule with funicle directed towards the axis. Irregularly arranged *pyrenes* laterally compressed. Testa very thin. *Cotyledons* large, thick caulicle directed to the axi.

A very remarkble tree on account of the structure of the pistil hitherto only reported from Sikkim, Burma and Java.

Fam. 37. RHAMNACEÆ.

Trees or shrubs, often scrambling or climbing furnished with tendrils in Gouania and Helinus (and rarely in Ventilago). Frequently spinous or prickly. *L.* simple, alternate, frequently basal-nerved. *Stipules* small, deciduous or changed into prickles. *Fls.* small, green or yellowish, in axillary cymes or running out into cymose panicles. *Calyx* 4-5- merous, lobes triangular, valvate, often keeled within. *Petals* 4-5, rarely 0, inserted on the margin of the disc or on the throat of the calyx-tube (hypanthium) which is usually filled or lined with the disc, usually *very small* and often hooded over the small *stamens*, which are always inserted *opposite to* the petals under or on the margin of the disc, and are hence frequently perigynous. Anthers 2-celled. *Ovary* free or sunk in the disc, usually superior in fruit, but inferior in tribe Gouanieæ, 3-rarely 2-4-celled. *Style* short simple, rarely cleft. Ovule 1 in each cell, erect anatropous. *Fruit* capsular or drupaceous, sometimes winged 3- rarely 1-4-celled. Albumen fleshy, rarely 0. Embryo large erect.

A. Trees, shrubs or woody climbers with some of the stipules converted into prickles. Young fruit superior drupaceous . . . . 1. *Zizyphus.*

B. Climbing shrubs without prickles.
   1. Branchlets rarely circinate. Fruit superior or half inferior, with a terminal narrow wing . 2. *Ventilago.*
   2. Some of the branchlets always ending in slender tendrils. Frt. inferior.
      L. with strong secondary nerves. Fruit 3-winged and 3-valved . . . . . . 3. *Gouania.*
      L. with few slender secondary nerves. Fruit not winged . . . . 4. *Helinus.*

1. Zizyphus, Juss.

Small trees or shrubs, sometimes scandent, usually with stipulary solitary or paired prickles; when paired, one member of the pair is generally straight and the other hooked. L. sub-bifarious entire or toothed, basal-nerved. *Fls.* in axillary fascicles or cymes, or cymes forming terminal panicles. Calyx 5- rarely 4-6-fid; lobes spreading triangular keeled within. Pet. very small hooded over the stamens ultimately deflexed, sometimes 0 (Z. rugosa). Disc more or less filling the calyx tube and often raised as a cushion above it or with a thin free margin under which the stamens are inserted. Ovary immersed in the disc 2-4-celled. Styles 2-4, free or partially united. Fruit drupaceous rarely dry when mature, with a 2-3- rarely 1-or 4-celled stone. Albumen very little or 0.

A. Cymes or fascicles axillary. Petals present.

1. Peduncles of cymes 0 or shorter than the pedicels. Fruit fleshy.
   - L. densely tomentose beneath. Drupe yellow or red. Tree . . . . . . 1. *Jujuba.*
   - L. densely tomentose beneath. Drupe yellow or red. Shrub . . . . 1a. *Var. fruticosa.*
   - L. densely silky beneath. Drupe black . 2. *Œnoplia.*
   - L. glabrous on both sides . . . . . . 3. *vulgaris.*
2. Peduncles of cymes stout, mostly longer than the pedicels. Fruit dry when ripe or flesh mealy 4. *xylopyra.*

B. Cymes in terminal panicles. Petals 0. Drupe white . . . . 5. *rugosa.*

1. Z. Jujuba, *Lamk.* Janumjan, *Ho.*; Dodari, M. Dedaori-janum, Jom-janum, *S.*; Dhani, *Kharw.*; Bair, *H.*; Ber, Bor, *Beng.*

A small tree with pendulous branches and oblong or ovate dark green leaves $1\frac{1}{2}$-3″ long densely tomentose beneath, small green flowers in dense axillary tomentose cymes or fascicles, and yellowish fleshy drupes $\frac{1}{2}$-$\frac{3}{4}$″ diam.

Not indigenous, largely cultivated and self-sown near villages. Fl. *March-June.* Fr. *Jany.-March.* Renews leaves *March-April.*

Branchlets tomentose, with geminate thorns or often unarmed. *L.* with a white or red tomentum beneath, glabrous above, usually minutely serrulate, or apex distinctly toothed, obtuse, rarely acute, with an oblique 3-nerved base. *Cymes* $\frac{1}{2}$-$\frac{3}{4}$″ long, sometimes with a short peduncle under $\frac{1}{4}''$ long. *Fls.* $\frac{1}{5}$-$\frac{1}{4}''$ diam. on pedicels longer than the peduncle. *Petals* minute spathulate reflexed white concave. *Ovary* cells 2 and style 2-fid. *Fruit* globose or sometimes (in gardens) ellipsoid with a 2-celled stone, yellow, shining.

The fruit is eaten and a drink is prepared from the sun-dried fruits.

Var. **fruticosa**, (Sp ?) Janumjan, *Ho.*; Bakura (in the Bible translation 'Bakula') *M.*; Kurit-rama (Vulture's talons), *S.*

A densely branched thorny shrub 3-4 ft. high. L. often symmetrical $\frac{3}{4}$-$1\frac{1}{2}''$ elliptic to sub-orbicular minutely serrulate or with 3-more coarse teeth near the apex. Fruit globose yellow or red shining $\frac{1}{3}$-$\frac{1}{2}''$ diam.

Common, sometimes gregarious. Singbhum, Manbhum, usually in waste open places, railway embankments, etc.

Fl. *Aug.-Sept.* Fr. *Dec.-Febr.* Evergreen. In some respects it appears to come very near to Z. nummularia, with which it is sometimes confounded.

Thorns geminate, one straight slender $\frac{1}{3}$-$\frac{1}{2}''$ long, the other much shorter curved. *Petioles* $\frac{1}{10}$-$\frac{1}{8}''$. *Cymes* sessile. *Flowers* $\frac{1}{8}$-$\frac{1}{5}''$ diam. rarely 4-merous. In other respects exactly as in the tree form.

Largely used for fencing. The fruit is eaten, but after being dried and pounded is chiefly used for a sherbert in the hot weather.

2. **Z. Œnoplia,** *Mill.* Dathora, *Kharw.*; Makai, *H.*; Siakul, *Beng.*

A straggling shrub or a large climber with single hooked (or rarely geminate) spines obliquely ovate or oblong-ovate leaves 1-$2\frac{1}{2}''$ with copious brown silky addressed hairs beneath, few-flowered axillary cymes and small black succulent fruits. Stone rugose compressed 1-seeded.

Not very common in Singbhum. Frequent in Gangpur, where it often festoons large trees, also in Manbhum, Hazaribagh, Ranchi, Palamau and the Santal Parganas.

Fl. *June-July.* Fr. *Nov.-Dec.* Evergreen or nearly so. Renews leaves *March-April* according to Brandis.

Branchlets brown-tomentose. *Spines* usually solitary small and hooked, if geminate 1 nearly straight. *L.* acute and cuspidate or sub-acuminate entire or faintly crenate with a very oblique 3-5-nerved base and very slender oblique silky sec. nerves. *Petioles* slender $\frac{1}{8}$-$\frac{1}{4}''$. *Cymes* under $\frac{1}{2}''$ long. *Pet.* cucullate. *Ovary* 2-celled. *Fruit* edible $\frac{1}{4}''$ diam.

A monstrous form is common bearing dense fascicles of small branches and tiny leaves, probably due to fungus attack.

3. Z. vulgaris. *Lamk.*

A small thorny tree with ovate-lanceolate quite glabrous leaves and dark red or black ellipsoid drupes $\frac{1}{2}$-$\frac{3}{4}$" long.

The only record of this from Chota Nagpur is in Wood's list, where he gives "Santalia" as a locality. He also gives, however, the Santal name "Kuritrama" for it, quoting Campbell and Watt as the authority. As a matter of fact, however, this name is given by Campbell and Watt for Z. oxyphylla. *Edgew.*, to which species the shrubby form of Z. Jujuba was referred. I think it very probable therefore that Z. vulgaris does not occur in our area. It is certainly not wild there.

4. Z. xylopyra, *Willd.* Karkata, *K.*; Karkat. *S.*; Kankor, *Kharw.*; Kat-ber, *H.*; Ghont, *Mal. P.*; Goit. *Bhumij.*

A small usually straggling and thorny tree (old trees nearly thornless) with broadly elliptic or ovate leaves 1$\frac{1}{2}$-3" long more or less permanently pubescent beneath. The small peduncled cymose clusters of green flowers are borne in the axils of the bright green leaves of the new shoots or are panicled on lateral branches. Ripe fruits globose 1-1$\frac{1}{2}$" diam., flesh dry and mealy.

An exceedingly common small tree especially on the drier hills on a clay soil.

The young plants are very bushy and very thorny with small leaves and sharp geminate spines.

Fl. *April-June* with the young shoots (so far as I have observed), but many herbarium specimens bear dates from *November* onwards. The fruits ripen in *January* or up to a year after flowering. Deciduous and renews its leaves *April-May.*

New leaves and shoots tomentose often unarmed. *L.* glabrescent above or somewhat permanently pubescent on the nerves, obtuse, serrulate, rounded or subcordate at the somewhat oblique 3-nerved base. *Cymes* $\frac{1}{2}$-1" tomentose, or leafless flexuous panicles up to 4". *Fls.* $\frac{1}{5}$-$\frac{1}{4}$" diam. sometimes 4-merous. *Pet.* spathulate hooded. *Disc* flat persistent. *Style* shortly 2-4 fid, very minute at first, ovary quickly rising above the disc on fertilization and style elongating *Fruit* sometimes tomentose, 2-4 usually 3-celled. Roxburgh says that the three valves of the nut separate when this has been for sometime exposed to the weather.

The fruit and bark are employed in tanning The kernel of the fruit is eaten. The wood is said to be hard and durable and is one of the woods used for obtaining fire by friction.

5. Z. rugosa, *Lamk.* Sirka (or Tsirka) *K.*; Sekra, S.; Pituar, Karail, *Kharw.*; Hohnoi, *Mal. P.*

A large shrub or small tree with long pendent or (in favourable localities) scandent branches, large elliptic 3-5 nerved serrulate leaves and large tomentose panicles of greenish-yellow flowers arranged in peduncled cymes (or lower cymes axillary forked).

Valleys in Singbhum, Manbhum, *Camp.*; Ranchi and Jashpur, *Wood*; Palamau, *Haslett*; Hazaribagh; Santal P., common.

Fl. *Feb.-March.* Fl. *May-July.* Evergreen. New shoots *Jan.-Feb.*

Young parts tomentose. *Prickles* usually solitary (a caducous triangular stipule on other side). *L.* minutely serrulate 2-6″ long (attaining 6″ by $4\frac{1}{2}$″) apex usually rounded and base sub-cordate. *Fls.* $\frac{1}{5}$-$\frac{1}{4}$″. *Sep.* 5-6 whitish within. *Petals* 0. *Disc* yellow lobed. *Ovary* pubescent 2-celled. *Frt.* $\frac{1}{3}$-$\frac{1}{2}$″ diam. white fleshy, with a thin 1-celled and 1-seeded stone.

The fruit is eaten. "The powdered bark mixed with ghee is applied to the swollen cheek in tooth-ache and for ulcers in the mouth," *Camp.*

2. Ventilago, Gaertn.

Scrambling or climbing shrubs occasionally with some of the *branchlets* circinately coiled into woody tendrils. L. penninerved entire or toothed, sub-bifarious, stipules caducous. Flowers small greenish, 5-merous, 2-sexual, in terminal and axillary panicles. Calyx lobes keeled within. Petals cucullate or conduplicate over the stamens which are incurved in bud. Anthers short, shortly horned (always ?). Disc filling the calyx-tube below and lining it above, with a short free margin. Ovary sunk in the disc, 2-celled with a short thick 2-fid style, which develops in fruit into a large linear or oblong wing surmounting the globose nut.

1. V. maderaspatana, *Gaertn.* Bonga-sarjom. (The Demon-sal) *K. S.*; Ter, Keonti, *Kharw.*; Rai-dhani, Pitti, *H.*; Raktapita. *Beng.*

A large scandent shrub with bifarious elliptic or oblong acuminate glabrous leaves (young somewhat pubescent) about 5″ long, and tomentose or pubescent fascicles of small yellow-green flowers 1/8" diam. arranged in interrupted panicles. The winged fruit is seated upon the disc-like remains of the calyx.

Chiefly along streams in Singbhum; Santal P. Fl. *Sept.-March.* Fr. *March.* Evergreen.

L. 3-5½' by 1½-2½", often crenate or crenate-serrate, with 6-8 pairs of very slender, but distinct sec. nerves and very fine numerous parallel tertiary nerves. *Petiole* ¼". *Calyx-lobes* shorter than the tube. *Petals* obovate-spathulate embracing the stamens 1/30", mid-rib produced. Wing of fruit linear oblong 1-2" long coriaceous, glabrous.

Bark yields a good cordage fibre. The seeds are said to be eaten when cooked and the oil expressed from them is used in cooking. The circinate woody tendrils are worn as charms by the Santals, *Campbell.*

Var. **calyculata,** *Tulasne* (sp.).

This has been united with the last by King and the vernacular names are the same. The leaves are often ovate with an acute base, crenate and permanently pubescent. Panicles densely pubescent. Nut girt about the middle by the rim of the adnate calyx-tube. Wing often ½" broad oblong pubescent surmounted by the two arms of the style.

Frequent in Singbhum, Manbhum, Palamau, Santal P.

Fl. *Sept.-Nov.* (*Feb.-March* on some authorities). Fr. *March-April.*

3. Gouania, L.

1. G. leptostachya, *D.C.* Bitkil-chand, *S.*

A rambling or climbing shrub with green branches, often ending in tendrils, green flowers fascicled on the rachis of simple or panicled terminal racemes, and 3-winged capsular fruits.

Valleys in Singbhum, not very common; Dalbhum, *Gamble* !; Jaspur, *Wood*; Santal P. (Barhait).

Fl. *Aug.-Sept.* Fr. *Nov.-Dec.* Nearly leafless and renews leaves *March-April.*

L. broadly ovate cordate coarsely crenate 2½-5" by 1½-4½" shining above nearly glabrous except on the 6-7 pairs of strong nerves. The lowest pair basal, crenatures glandular. *Petiole* 1-2½". *Racemes* 6-18" pubescent. *Petals* hooded over the stamens. *Ovary* sunk in the disc 3-celled. *Fruit* inferior, coriaceous, ⅓-½" long, broader than long, top emarginate crowned by the calyx, splitting through the wings into 3 cocci each with a black shining compressed broadly ovate-oblong seed ⅛".

4. Helinus, E. Meyer.

1. H. lanceolatus, *Brandis.*

A bright green slender climbing shrub with some of the branchlets modified into tendrils, ovate or lanceolate acute entire leaves about $2\frac{1}{2}''$ by $1\frac{1}{4}''$ and very numerous small yellowish flowers in slender peduncled cymes which are axillary or paniculate by reduction of the leaves. **Fruit a 3**-celled drupe.

Singbhum in Rolahamsada Gara, Jate Road, etc., rare; Neterhat, 3000 ft., *Gamble* !; Santal P. (Chandna).

Fl. *Jany.-March.* Fr. *March-April.*

Branches finely ridged, puberulous. *L.* glaucous beneath, those on inflorescence much reduced, 3-nerved with 1-2 pairs of sec. nerves and reticulate nervules. *Stipules* $\frac{1}{20}''$ deciduous. *Fls.* $\frac{1}{8}$-$\frac{1}{4}''$ diam. shallow. *Petals* 5 oblong folded round the filaments whitish. *St.* inserted on the free margin of the disc. Anthers exserted. *Ovary* sunk in the disc 3-celled. Style 3-fid. *Fruit* $\frac{1}{4}''$ diam.

Fam. 38. AMPELIDACEÆ.

Erect or climbing herbs or shrubs with the branches often transformed into tendrils in the vines (Vitis). *L.* alternate, simple or compound, stipulate. *Fls.* small in compound inflorescences, regular, often polygamous. *Calyx* small 4-5-lobed or truncate. *Petals* 4-5, valvate, sometimes falling off in a cap without expanding (calyptrate). *St.* equal in number to the petals and opposite to them, sometimes united. Anthers 2-celled, introrse. *Disc* large. *Ovary* free or the base sunk in the disc, 2-6-celled with 1-2 ascending anatropous ovules in each cell. Style usually very short or 0. Stigma simple or sub-lobed. *Fruit* a berry. Seeds with copious endosperm.

N.B.—Both the tendrils and the inflorescence in Vitis are morphologically main axes which get thrust aside with the growth of the stronger axillary shoots and so appear leaf-opposed.

Climbers usually with tendrils. Ovary usually 2-celled . . 1. *Vitis.*
Erect without tendrils. Ovary 3-6-celled . . . 2. *Leea.*

1. Vitis, L. (Vine).

Herbs or shrubs climbing by means of a modification of the stem or branches into simple or branched tendrils, which sometimes bear the inflorescence. L. simple and palmately nerved or digitate or pedate. Fls. 4-5-merous. Petals often calyptrate. Stamens free. Ovary 2-celled surrounded at the base or to the top by the disc. Ovules 2 in each cell. Berry 1-4-seeded.

Fls. 4-merous. L. not lobed, deeply cordate . 1. *repanda.*
Fls. 5-merous. L. not lobed, cordate, wooly . 2. *lanata.*
Fls. 5-merous. L. simple palmately lobed. Inflor. on the tendrils.
  Glabrous (except inflorescence) . . . 3. *latifolia.*
  Tomentose . . . . 4. *tomentosa.*
Fls. 4-merous. L. compound.
  L. 3-foliolate. Petioles 1½-3" . . . 5. *trifolia.*
  L. digitately 5-(3) foliolate. Petioles 3½-7" . 6. *auriculata.*
  L. pedately 5-foliolate. Glabrous . . 7. *lanceolaria.*
  L. pedately 7-foliolate. Pubescent . . 8. *pedata.*

1. V. repanda, W. & A. Bod-lar nari, *S.*; Harjarwa, *Kharw.*

A large climber with a soft stem, corky bark, large deeply cordate simple denticulate leaves and tomentose long slender-peduncled umbellate cymes of small flowers.

Valleys in Singbhum, rare; Manbhum, *Campbell*; Santal P., rare; Paraenath, *Anderson*; Palamau. Fl. *May-June* on the new shoots *Fr. r. s.* Deciduous *Feby.-May.* *L.* turn yellow in *Dec.*

New shoots and inflorescence tomentose and hairy. *L.* sub-orbicular or broadly ovate 5-8" diam. with large basal auricles (from the deep cordation), sometimes repand, with the strong secondary nerves running out into small teeth, finally glabrous. *Petioles* 6-12" long. *Stipules* oblong obtuse. *Inflorescence* terminating the new shoots and becoming leaf opposed, on slender erect peduncles elongating to 2-5", 3-5-rayed, and rays with umbelled pedicels ¼-⅓" long, or again rayed. *Petals* calyptrate as a very obtuse constricted cone sometimes slit at the top. St. 4.

The stem yields a large quantity of water, when cut in two places which is useful for quenching thirst. "The root, powdered and heated is applied to cuts and fractures. The bark and stalk yield a good cordage fibre." *Campbell.*

The localities given above by Campbell and Anderson, as well as Campbell's note on the root and fibre (which also apply to V. repanda), all refer in the original to *V adnata.* On the grounds that I have never seen specimens of V. adnata from Chota Nagpur, nor does Col. Prain in "Bengal Plants" give Chota Nagpur as a locality, I have, perhaps wrongly, applied the references to V. repanda.

2. **V. lanata,** *Roxb.* Kolo-nari, *S.*

A large climber with simple cordate serrate membranous leaves wooly beneath, small green flowers in thyrsoid paniculate cymes and round purple berries the size of a pea.

Tundi Hills, *Campbell.*

L. cordate-ovate shortly acuminate 3-6" by 1¾-3". Peduncle with a simple or forked tendril. Petals green calyptrate.

3. **V. latifolia,** *Roxb.* Oteron, *K.*; I'c-ewer, *S.*; Khopri, *Kharw.*; Govila, *Beng.*

An extensive but scarcely woody climber, glabrous, or nearly so, everywhere except the rachis of the inflorescence, with simple palmately-lobed leaves 4-8" long and broad, deep brown-red flowers and black succulent berries.

Very common especially in low scrub jungles in Singbhum, Manbhum, Hazaribagh and Palamau. Probably throughout Chota Nagpur. Fl. *June-July.* Fr. *Sept.-Oct.* The stems die down annually to the perennial rootstock which sends out long bare shoots in May and June sometimes to a height of 10 ft. before the leaves expand, and it flowers before the leaves are fully developed.

New stems glaucous or quite blue, hollow and often producing the inflorescence before the leaves. *L.* 3-7-angled or lobed mealy when very young, cordate or retuse at the base, lobes crenate-serrulate or dentate, *Fls.* rarely 4-merous in pyramidal panicled cymes borne on a very stout peduncle together with a forked tendril. *Petals* $\frac{1}{16}$" small oblong red expanding, saccate at the apex. *Disc* prominent lobed becoming adnate and often showing as a ring on the fruit. *Style* 0. *Berry* $\frac{1}{3}$" diam., sweet and juicy.

4. **V. tomentosa,** *Heyne.* Oteron, *K.*; Ghora-lidi, *S.*

A climber with the same habit as the last, but densely tomentose and with 3-5-lobed leaves often attaining 10" both ways.

In similar situations to the last and nearly as common. Fl. *July-Sept.* Fr. *Sept.-Nov.*

Shoots covered with a dense cottony tomentum. *L.* with a dense brown tomentum beneath, very deeply cordate with rounded basal lobes, serrate or serrulate. *Petioles* 3-6". *Fls.* sessile red in divaricate cymes on a peduncle under 1" long which again is borne together with a tendril on a common woody peduncle 3-6" long. *Pet.* free. *Berry* black ⅓" diam.

5. V. trifolia, *L.* (Syn. V. carnosa, *Wall.*)

An herbaceous climber with succulent compressed stems springing from a stout perennial rootstock, with 3 foliolate leaves, crenate leaflets and small greenish flowers in lax divaricate long-peduncled cymes.

On trees, or adhering to rocks by the tips of the tendrils, in valley in Singbhum and Palamau. Lohardaga, *Gamble* ! Not common Parasnath, *Anderson*.

Fl. *June-July*. Fr. *Nov.-Dec.* The stems die down in *Jany.* and *Feby.*

Stems weak or 1" diam. with a corky bark, *branches* brittle, young striate pubescent. *Lflts.*, terminal elliptic or obovate coarsely crenate and denticulate attaining 3" rarely 4" by 2½" shortly pubescent, lateral usually broadly ovate and somewhat cordate at base. *Petiole* fleshy 2-4". *Tendrils* slender branched, often tipped with sucker discs. *Petals* white saccate at tip. *Disc* surrounding the whole ovary except the conical tip, 4-lobed. *Berries* black, depressed globose, ⅓" diam. 2-seeded.

6. V. auriculata, *Roxb.* Baiang, *K.*; Amar-lata, *Kharw.*

A large sub-succulent climber with digitate 5-foliolate leaves, long-petioluled crenate-serrate leaflets, and large divaricating cymes on long succulent peduncles, with or without a tendril. Fruit the size of a cherry, red when ripe.

Valleys, usually near watercourses in Singbhum ; Mata in Manbhum, *Wood.*; Koderma, *Haslett* ! Palamau. Fl. *r. s* Fr. *Oct.-Dec.* Perennial? The fruit is said to be eaten.

Young parts pubescent. *L.* with a petiole 4-7" long and with auriculate stipules. *Lflts.* broadly elliptic to obovate 2-5" shortly acuminate with petiolules ½-2" long. *Tendrils* 2-3 fid. *Seed* 1.

7. V. lanceolaria, *Wall.*

An extensive climber with pedately 5-foliolate somewhat fleshy leaves, large coarsely crenate-serrate elliptic leaflets and small very shortly peduncled cymes of small yellowish flowers.

Parasnath, *Prain.*; Santal P. near Sahebganj. Fls. *Jany.-March.*

Shoots glabrous except the large oblong ½″ stipules. *Tendrils* simple. *Lflts.* acuminate up to 6½″ by 4″ with 1 fine sec. n. to each tooth. *Petiole* 2-6″. *Petiolules* stout. *Cymes* forked pubescent axillary sessile or sub-sessile on the old shoots, or sometimes rarely (on same plant) terminating long (2-4″) leaf-opposed peduncles (taking the place of tendrils). *Bracts* paired at the forks oblong to ovate pubescent ⅛-⅓″. *Fls.* papillose pubescent in stalked umbelled heads on the cymes. Buds oblong truncate each sepal with a spreading cusp. *Pet O.* *Ovules* 2 in each cell.

8. V pedata, *Vahl.*

A large weak climber with pedately 7-foliolate usually softly pubescent leaves, petiole 4-6″ long and large sub-corymbose cymes as long as the petioles. Whole plant softly pubescent or glabrate. Lflts. 4-8″ by 1½-3″, oblong-lanceolate acuminate, serrate. Frt. sub-globose, the size of a currant.

Chota Nagpur, *Prain.*

The description has been taken from the *F. B. I.* and " Bengal Plants ."

2. LEEA, L.

Stout herbs, shrubs or small trees, usually with herbaceous branches, erect and without tendrils. L. simple or pinnately-compound or -decompound. Peduncles leaf-opposed. Fls. in corymbose cymes distinguished from those of Vitis by the marked staminal-tube. Ovary cells 3-8. Berry 4-6-seeded or fewer by abortion.

A. Petals and inflorescence red. L. 1-pinnate . . . . 1. *alata.*

B. Petals greenish-white.

I. Herbaceous. Lowest one or more leaves very large and simple . . . . 2. *macrophylla.*

II. Suffruticose. L. 1-2-pinnate. Sec. n. close and parallel as many to half as many as the teeth.

Nerves 1 to each tooth. Corymbs sub-sessile . . 3. *crispa.*

Nerves less than 1 to each tooth. Corymbs peduncled.

Lflts. often setose between the nerves, base cordate. . . . . 4. *aspera.*

Lflts. not setose, base rhomboid or rounded . 5. *herbacea.*

III. Shrubby. L. 2-3-pinnate. Sec. nerves much fewer than the teeth.
L. glabrous . . . . 6. *sambucina.*
L. pubescent, at least on the nerves beneath . 7. *robusta.*

Numbers 4 and 5 probably form one variable species and should be united. I keep them distinct in accordance with Clarke's "Revision of the Indian Species of Leea" published in the Journal of Botany, Vol. X.

1. **L. alata,** *Edgew.*

A shrub 2-5 ft. high with pinnate leaves and narrow oblong sharply serrate leaflets sometimes broader upwards. Easily recognized from the other species by the leaflets being sessile or sub-sessile and the inflorescence scarlet.

Manbhum, *Campbell!* Occasionally found in first class sal forests. *Gamble* and *Manson.* Fl. *June-Aug.* *Fr.* ripens *Sept.*

L. with several serratures between each nerve. *Peduncle* of inflorescence long and slender. *Fruit* red.

2. **L. macrophylla,** *Horn.* Hatkan, *S.*; Dholsamudra, *Beng.*

A robust herb 1-3 ft. high, annual from a perennial stock, with large ovate-cordate leaves, very large stipules, and white flowers in sessile corymbs. Fr. black succulent $\frac{1}{3}''$ diam.

Singbhum, Manbhum and Rajmehal hills but not common.

Fl. *June.* *L.* turn yellow in *Jany.*, and plant dies down in *Feby.* *Lowest leaf* 1-2 ft. diam. A very distinct species.

The root is applied externally to allay pain, *Campbell.*

3. **L. crispa,** *L.* Ban-chalita, *Beng.*

Erect, 4-5 ft. suffruticose, stems annual from a perennial stock. Stems, petioles and peduncles often winged. L. pinnate. Lflts. with very parallel sides, coarsely serrate with one sec. n. carried right into each serrature. Corymbs sub-sessile stout. Ripe berry blue-black.

Singbhum, near Camaria (south of Chaibassa). Fl. *July Aug.* Fr. *Sept-Oct.* The winged form does not occur in Chota Nagpur.

Sec. n. of lflts. often 17 prs., only $\frac{1}{8}$-$\frac{1}{4}''$ apart. *Lflts.* not caudate.

4. **L. aspera,** *Edgw.* Hom, *Ho.*; Horom, *M.*

Erect spreading 5-10 ft. stems annual or perennial never winged. Lower leaves 2-pinnate. Lflts. mostly elliptic or ovate caudate with a rounded or cordate base most of the sec. n. bifurcating near the margin and giving a branch to each pair of teeth.

The commonest species in our area, and occurring in every district, chiefly under shade in the valleys. Fls. *July-Sept.* Fr. *Nov.-Dec.* The leaves turn red after fruiting and the stems break off at a node close to the ground.

Lflts. pubescent on the nerves beneath as in 3 and 5, also frequently hirtellous between the nerves above, often dotted. Teeth coarse. *Peduncles* sometimes slightly winged, usually long and slender, often geminate. *Berries* depressed of a green-slatey colour, finally black.

5. **L. herbacea,** *Ham.* Hom. *Ho.*; Horom, *M.*

Stems usually several from the root, attaining 2″ diam. and 15-20 ft. high, soft-wooded with very large pith, often longitudinally banded and with minute microscopic tomentum. Lower leaves 3-pinnate up to 3 ft. long and 2 ft. broad. Serratures often shallow.

Ravines in Singbhum. Santal P. *Gamble Herb.*? Fl. *June-Aug.* and Fr. same time as last, of which I believe it to be merely a robust form. Deciduous in *Dec.* and sometimes dies down like the last.

Lflts. from ovate to obovate-oblong not usually exceeding 7″ by 2½″, punctate, sec. n. about 8-9 prs. above the 4-6-nerved *base* which varies from cuneate to sub-cordate. *Cymes* from the forks or leaf-opposed sessile or peduncles 2½″ nearly always bifurcate and branches compressed winged. *Berry* glaucous.

6. **L. sambucina,** *Willd.*

A very large woody shrub with 2-pinnate leaves and leaflets (on terminal rachis) 3-4 prs. very large, oblong or lanceolate acuminate coarsely doubly serrate with sec. n. much curved within the margin and 3-5-times as many teeth as nerves. Fls. green with yellowish staminal-tube, in subsessile corymbs 3-6″ diam, Berries succulent black pruinose.

Santal P., in ravines in the Rajmehal hills. Fl. *June-Aug.* Fr. *Sept.* The most woody of the Leeas and not dying down.

Lflts. up to 12″ by 3½″ (Clarke gives 4″ by 2½″ only, but there is absolutely no doubt of the identity of the two. He transfers the arboreous Sikkim form to a new species *umbraculifera*). Base rounded or cuneate. Sec. n. 7-15 prs. much raised beneath united by very fine parallel tertiaries. *Petiolules* ⅓-1″.

7. **L. robusta**, *Roxb.* Hom, Horom, *K.*; Haramda, batkan, *S.*

A large sub-woody shrub 4-6 ft. with more or less tomentose branchlets, large 2-3-pinnate leaves with lflts. pubescent beneath and large branched usually geminate corymbs 7-15″ diam. The plant somewhat reminds one of an Elder bush.

In ravines or along nalas or on cool aspects, not unfrequent in Singbhum, and S. P.; Hundrugagh, *Prain*! Fl. *Aug.* Fr. *Nov.-Dec.* Apparently dies down annually.

L. 2-3 ft. *Lflts.* oblong to oblong-lanceolate or ovate-lanceolate, acuminate, attaining 11″ by 3½′ with several serratures to one nerve, pale beneath, sec. n. about 11 prs. above the 5-7-nerved base, oblique with numerous strong parallel tertiaries. *Cymes* 2-3 chotomously branched, brachiate *Peduncles* pubescent. *Berry* purple-black ⅓″ diam. depressed. *Bracts* not persistent.

Series B. (*vide* p. 51).

Fam. 39. CACTACEÆ.

Usually succulent shrubs with thick, fleshy often jointed stems, and leaves reduced to spines. Fls. regular, often very large, 2-sexual, torus sometimes sunk in the stem. *Sepals* and *petals* merging into one another. *Stamens* very numerous springing from the tube. *Ovary* inferior with several parietal placentæ. *Style* one hollow, with as many stigmas as there are placentæ. *Fruit* a berry.

The structure of the Cactaceæ is generally remarkably adapted to periods of drought, and the similar conditions have led to similar fleshy stems in some other groups of plants (*e.g.* spp. of Euphorbia) which are sometimes confounded with them.

The following (probably) Mexican species are more or less naturalized :—

1. **Cereus hexagonus,** *L.* Bonga-daru, *K.*

With erect columnar 6-ridged fleshy stems 4-6 ft. high covered with clusters of sharp spines. Very large solitary white flowers. Much grown in hedges. Fls. *Aug.-Sept.*

2. **Opuntia Dillenii,** *Haw.* Sapin, *S.* Prickly Pear.

Branched with short oblong compressed joints and long straight thorns from tufts of sharp bristles. *Fls.* large bright yellow, often variegated red.

Fls. esp. *January*, but more or less all the year round. Occasional near villages.

Roxburgh considered this indigenous in India.

Fam. 40. ROSACEÆ.

Herbs, shrubs or trees with stipulate alternate simple or compound leaves. *Fls.* regular, 2-sexual. *Calyx* lobes imbricate in bud, sometimes an epicalyx present. *Floral-axis* more or less hollowed out into a cupular or flask-shaped receptacle (" hypanthium " or " calyx-tube ") lined above, or entirely, by the disc and bearing the *petals* and usually numerous *multiseriate stamens.* *Carpels* 1 or more, more or less free at the bottom of the calyx-tube or adnate to its sides, 1-2-ovuled. *Fruit* very variable.

A large order, to which belong the plum, apple, pear, hawthorn, etc., but poorly represented in Chota Nagpur. The Peach (*Prunus persica*) and the Loquat (*Eriobotrya japonica*) are sometimes cultivated.

Carpel solitary, not included in the calyx-tube when ripe. Fr. a drupe. Leaves simple . . . . *1. Pygeum.*

Carpels several, included in the flask-shaped fleshy calyx-tube when ripe. Leaves compound . . . . 2. *Rosa.*

1. Pygeum, Gærtn.

Trees or shrubs with simple entire or toothed leaves with small fugagious stipules and sometimes a pair of flat, circular glands at the base below. Fls. small racemose. Calyx-tube campanulate or cupular. 5-6-toothed. Petals minute villous. St. 15-40. Carpel 1. Fr. a transversely-oblong obscurely didymous drupe with usually scanty flesh.

1. **P. acuminatum**, *Colebr.*

A small evergreen tree with coriaceous elliptic or oblong acute or cuspidate leaves 4″ by $1\frac{1}{2}$″ to 6″ by 3″, yellowish-green flowers and drupes $\frac{3}{4}$″ diam.

Along streams in the most shady valleys of the Saranda forests, *e.g.*, Rangan-gara, very rare. Fls. *Aug.* Fr. *April-June.*

Twigs brown. *L.* with rounded base or acute on the petiole which is $\frac{1}{2}$″ long and grooved above. *Sec. nerves* 6-8 prs. impressed above. Glands present or not (on the same tree). *Racemes* about 2-5″. *Pedicels* very short. *Calyx* and *corolla* pubescent.

2. **P. lucidum**, *And.* (P. Andersoni, *Hook f.*)

A rigid shrub somewhat resembling a Symplocos, quite glabrous except the margins of the petals. *L.* $2\frac{1}{2}$-$3\frac{1}{2}$″ by 1″ coriaceous oblong or oblong-lanceolate acuminate with sub-acute or obtuse base crenate-serrate eglandular (except the serratures) with 8-12 prs. of nearly straight ascending sec. nerves. *Petiole* $\frac{1}{3}$″. *Racemes* 1″ dense-fld. *Pedicels* very short. *Calyx-tube* hemispheric glabrous within, lobes broadly ovate, obtuse. *Petals* twice the calyx-lobes, ell. with densely ciliate margins. St. 15 with transversely oblong 2-celled anthers. Ovary in the herb, specimen minute imperfect.

This is a very interesting plant inasmuch as nobody seems to have found it except Anderson, on the summit of Parasnath. And he only found a solitary tree on the northern side of the central peak.

Fl. and renews its leaves in November.

2. Rosa, L. Rose.

1. R. involucrata, *Roxb.*

A pretty plant with arching branches, pinnate leaves of 3-4 prs. of finely serrate leaflets, and white flowers 2″ diam., solitary or in short corymbs.

Along the banks of the larger rivers. Fl. *Feby-May*. Fr. *r. s.*

Branchlets and inflorescence tomentose. *L.* 3-4″. *Lflts.* $\frac{1}{4}$-$1\frac{1}{2}$″. *Bracts* large lanceolate pectinately gland-serrate. *Sepals* deciduous in fruit. *Styles* distinct. *Fr.* globose, tomentose.

Fam. 41. MIMOSACEÆ.

Trees or shrubs, rarely (Mimosa pudica) undershrubs. *L.* often sensitive,* 2-pinnate (pinnæ and leaflets sometimes reduced to one pair). *Fls.* small regular, collected into dense spikes or globose heads with prominent stamens, but small 4-5-merous perianth. *Calyx* tubular or campanulate, truncate or valvately toothed or lobed, sometimes minute. *Petals* valvate, free or more or less connate into a tubular or funnel-shaped corolla. *St.* as many or twice as many as the petals or numerous, hypogynous to perigynous, free or monodelphous. *Ovary* 1-carpellary, 2-many-ovuled. *Fruit* a dehiscent or indehiscent sometimes curved pod.

I. Stamens definite, 4, 5, 8, or 10.
- *a.* Fls. spicate. An immense climber . . . 1 *Entada.*
- *b.* Fls. in globose heads.
  - Small tree. St. 10 . . . 2. *Leucæna.*
  - Shrubs or undershrubs. St. 4 or 8 . . . 3. *Mimosa.*

II. Stamens numerous.
- *a.* St. free. Erect or scandent prickly trees or shrubs . . . 4. *Acacia.*
- *b.* St. monodelphous. Erect, rarely thorny or prickly trees.
  - Pod thin ligulate, not twisted, not or tardily dehiscent . . . 5. *Albizzia.*
  - Pod twisted and dehiscent . . . 6. *Pithecolobium.*
  - Pod fleshy and indehiscent, septate between the seeds . . . 7. *Enterolobium.*

* Exhibiting sleep movements or otherwise irritable.

1. Entada, Adans.

1. E. scandens, *Benth.* Karu *K.*; Kari, *Kharw.*; Bidhanta, *S.*; Gila, *Beng.*

An immense woody climber with 2-pinnate leaves ending in a 2-fid tendril, solitary or fascicled axillary or extra-axillary spikes 4-9″ long of very numerous small green flowers. Conspicuous in fruit by the immense woody torulose pods, septate within and containing large discoid chesnut seeds $1\frac{1}{2}$-2″ diam.

Valleys in Singbhum (*e.g.*, Samta and Poradih garas), not common Baragai hills, *Wood*; Palamau, *Haslett*; Rajmehal hills, common. Fls. *April.* Fr. *March-April* of following year. Deciduous *March.*

Stem attaining 3-4 ft. girth. *Branches* green. *Pinnæ* 2 prs. opp. ending in an abortive lflt. *Lflts.* 3 prs. 2″ long, narrow-ellip. to obovate, apex emarginate. *Stipules* $\frac{1}{4}$″. *Spike* pubescent. *Calyx* $\frac{1}{8}$″ campanulate truncate. *Corolla* lobes valvate green $\frac{1}{8}$″ oblong-lanc. acute. *St.* 10. *Bracts* minute linear. *Pod* 1-2 ft. The powdered seed mixed with ghee is eaten as an anodyne during parturition.

NOTE.—The germination is hypogeal and the seedling concentrates all its energy in getting to the light, so that at first the whole of the leaves are converted into 2-fid. tendrils, the rachis ending in a mucro. At the base of the tendrils are two minute stipules. The tendrils gyrate very fast, describing many complete circles in the course of the day.

2. Leucæna, Benth.

1. L. glauca, *Benth.*

A small tree with 2-pinnate leaves, 4-8 prs. of pinnæ, 10-15 prs. of linear glaucous lflts. $\frac{3}{8}$-$\frac{1}{2}$″ long. Small white *fls.* $\frac{1}{8}$″ sessile in dense heads on fascicled peduncles, or the upper panicled. *Pet.* free from the calyx-tube and twice its length. *Pod* about 6″ by $\frac{5}{8}$″ flat dehiscent with transverse ovate seeds.

Ch. Nagpur, *Prain*; Planted about Ranchi, *Wood*; Introduced from America, and naturalized in parts of India. Fls. *May-June. Fr.* ripens following year.

3. Mimosa, L.

More or less prickly herbs or shrubs with digitate-pinnate or 2-pinnate leaves, and numerous small sensitive lflts. Fls. very small in dense globose heads, mostly 4-merous. Calyx campanulate, teeth small. St. as many or twice as many as the petals, much exserted. Pod flat dry breaking up into 1-seeded joints separating from the sutures.

1. **M. pudica,** *L.* Lajak, *Beng.* The Sensitive Plant.

A well-known small undershrub with weakly-prickly stems, and compound leaves with digitate pinnæ and pinnate leaflets. Peduncles 1-2 axillary. Fls. pink. St. 4. Pod with weak prickles on the sutures.

Sandy damp ground on the *plateaux,* not common in the hotter drier parts. Said to have been introduced from Trop. America, now naturalised. Fls., Fr. *r. s.*

2. **M. rubicaulis,** *Lamk.* Kundaru, *K.*; Sega janum *S.*

A weak very prickly shrub 6-12 ft., with many branches from the root with 2-pinnate leaves, 4-12 prs. of distant pinnæ 1-2½" long and 8-20 prs. of small close-set lflts. $\frac{1}{6}$-$\frac{1}{2}$" long with the rachises beset with small recurved prickles. Fls. pink or whitish in dense heads $\frac{1}{2}$" diam. on clustered long axillary peduncles, and running out into terminal racemes and panicles. Pod rather falcate 3-4", 6-10-seeded.

Very common in the forests, esp., in glades and on waste ground, in the valleys. Fls. *Aug.-Oct.* Fr. *Nov.-Jany.* Branches die down or shed their leaves in the hot season.

Branches grooved downy. *Lflts.* pubescent oblong one-sided. *Corolla* $\frac{1}{24}$", lobes 4. *St.* 8.

The powdered root given for vomiting from weakness, *Camp.* The square joints of the pod easily distinguish it from the Acacias when in fruit.

4. Acacia, Willd.

Erect or climbing armed shrubs or trees, with 2-pinnate leaves and small lflts. (exc. 8). Flowers very small in spikes or globose heads. usually 5-merous. Petals united below. St. inserted on a small hypogynous disc numerous, free, far exsert. Pod usually flat and dry (turgid in spp. 1-3) dehiscent or not, not septate or jointed (moniliform in A. arabica). The rachis often bears one or more glands.

A Fls. in globose heads.

1. Erect trees or shrubs.
   Spines stipular only. Pod swollen . . . 1. *Farnesiana.*
   Spines $\frac{1}{4}$-2″ long on stem and branches. Pod moniliform . . . . 2. *arabica.*
2. Prickly climbers. Heads panicled.
   Lflts. 15-25 prs., $\frac{1}{3}$-$\frac{5}{8}$″ long. Pod fleshy . . 3. *concinna.*
   Lflts. 10-40 prs. $\frac{3}{16}$-$\frac{5}{16}$″ long. Pod flat dry . 4. *Cæsia.*
   Lflts. 40-60 prs. $\frac{1}{16}$-$\frac{3}{16}$″ long. Pod flat dry . 5. *pennata.*

B. Fls. in spikes. Erect trees.

1. Lflts. small ligulate.
   Bark white. Corolla scarcely exceeding the calyx . . . . 6. *Suma.*
   Bark black. Corolla $1\frac{1}{2}$-3-times as long as calyx 7. *Catechu.*
2. Lflts. oblong $\frac{3}{4}$-$1\frac{1}{3}$″ . . . . . . 8. *lenticularis.*

1. A. Farnesiana, *Willd.* Gabur, *S.*

A shrub or small tree 12-20 ft. with 4-8 prs. of pinnæ and 10-20 prs. of minute crowded leaflets. A pair of stipular spines $\frac{1}{8}$-$\frac{1}{2}$″ long at base of each leaf. It bears very fragrant heads of deep yellow fls. on axillary penduncles $\frac{1}{2}$-1″ long. Pod 2-3″ brown thick with somewhat pulpy mesocarp.

Common, planted and semi-naturalized. Fls. *Aug.-March.* Fr. *Jany.-July.* Evergreen.

2. A. arabica, *Willd.* Babla, Babur, *K.*,*S.*; Babul, *H.*

A shrub or small black-barked tree armed with long straight white thorns (often thornless, when old), with 3-6 prs. of pinnæ, 10-20 prs. of crowded leaflets $\frac{1}{9}$-$\frac{1}{4}$″, and heads $\frac{1}{2}$″ diam. of yellow fls. on short axillary fascicled peduncles. Pod whitish tomentose 3-9″ long.

Waste ground, ry. embankments. etc., occasional. Often planted and naturalized on cotton soil in S. E. Fls. *Aug.-Dec.* Fr. *Jany.-March.* Evergreen. Yields a Gum-arabic. Pods form a good cattle fodder.

3. **A. concinna,** *D.C.* Kundaru, Kunduru, *K.*

A scrambling climber with 4-8 prs. of pinnæ and 15-25 prs. of oblong oblique lflts. $\frac{1}{3}$-$\frac{5}{8}$″ long by $\frac{3}{16}$″ broad and yellowish-white panicled heads of flowers. Pod thick fleshy, somewhat constricted between the seeds, 2-4″ long.

Valleys in Singbhum, rare. Fls. *April-July?* Fr. *Jany.-March.* Evergreen.

Branches nearly white, armed as well as the leaf rachis with copious small recurved prickles. *Pinnæ* $\frac{3}{4}$-1″ apart. This and the large leaflets easily distinguish it in leaf from the next two species.

4. **A. cæsia,** *W. and A.* A. Intsia, var. Cæsia. *F.B.I.*; Kundaru, *K.*; Kondro-jamun *S.*; Arar, *Kharw.*

A scrambling climber with 6-10 prs. of pinnæ and 20-40 (rarely as few as 10 on some pinnæ) prs. of oblong oblique lflts. $\frac{3}{16}$-$\frac{5}{16}$″ long by $\frac{1}{10}$-$\frac{1}{8}$″ broad, and white copiously panicled heads of flowers. Pod thin flat dry with strong sutures, 3-5$\frac{1}{2}$″ by $\frac{5}{8}$-1″, cuneate both ends, rarely obtuse, light brown.

All the districts in forest and waste ground. Fls. *May.-Sept.* Fr. *Jany.-March.* Evergreen. New leaves in *March.*

Stem angled and fluted. *Branches* brown pubescent or tomentose with minute prickles, those on the ràchis often absent. *Pinnæ* only $\frac{1}{3}$-$\frac{1}{2}$″ apart spreading stiffly, usually pubescent beneath.

5. **A. pennata,** *Willd.* Kundaru, *K.*; Arar, *Kharw.*

A scrambling climber with 8-20 prs. of pinnæ and 40-60 prs. (sometimes only 20 prs. on short basal pinnæ) of linear lflts. $\frac{1}{16}$-$\frac{1}{4}$″ by $\frac{1}{20}$″, and white copiously panicled heads of flowers. Pod thin flat dry with strong sutures, 3-6″ by $\frac{3}{4}$-1″, suddenly tapering at the apex, deep brown or purple, margins occasionally sinuate.

Frequent in Singbhum and Gangpur; Jaspur, *Wood*; !Hazaribagh, *Gamble*; S. P near nalas very common. Probably also in other districts. Fls. *May-Jany.* Fr. *Jany.-April.* Evergreen.

Stem rounded with 5 lines of very small prickles even when old. *Branches* grey or brown glabrescent with few and small prickles, which are usually absent on rachis. *Pinnæ* ¼-⅓" apart feathery. *Rachis* pubescent, *lflts.* glabrous or nearly so.

N.B.—The *flowers* of all these Acacias turn *yellow* on drying; hence they are often described as yellow in descriptions drawn from herbarium specimens.

6. A. Suma, *Buch. Ham.*

The following description is taken from *Indian Trees*:—

"A large or middle-sized tree; *bark* white; branches stiff, flexuose; branchlets and petioles downy, with soft pubescence. *Prickles* in pairs, infra-stipular, conical, downy while young, brown shining afterwards. *Petiole* 4-10" long (includes rachis?), unarmed, with a large cup-shaped gland above the base. *Pinnæ* 10-20 prs., lflts. 20-50 prs., linear, approximate, imbricate, generally ciliate. *Fl.* white or pale yellow; spikes lax. Petals not much longer than the calyx. *Pod.* 3-5" by ¾", pubescent when young."

Chota Nagpur, *Prain.* I have not met with it there, but see remarks under A. Catechu. Fl. r. s. *Roxb.*

7. A. Catechu, *Willd.* Khair, *H.*, *S.*

A small or mod.-sized tree with dark coloured bark and slender branches armed with geminate hooked prickles. Pinnæ 4-24 prs. Lflts. (30-50 prs. or only) 25-30 prs. (rarely more in Ch. Nag.). Petiole with rachis usually 3-4". Spikes axillary on the young shoots 2-3½" dense, *nearly white.* Petals 1½-2-*times as long as the calyx* densely hairy and greenish with membranous margins like the calyx. Ovary glabrous, stalked.

Manbhum; Hazaribagh (esp. on sandstone), often with sal; Palamau common, where it is found mixed with the sal, both on clay and sandstone S. P. on cotton soil. Fls. *May.-Oct.* Fr. *Nov.-Feby.* remaining till the new flowers appear.

Twigs pubescent. *Rachis* densely hairy, 2-6" rarely 8", pinnæ ½-1¼" a gland below the pinnæ and one between the uppermost 1-6 pinnæ. *Lflts.*, $\frac{1}{10}$-⅛" imbricate, hairy. *Peduncles* ½", sometimes paired. *St.* in 5 bundles at base of corolla with long glabrous filaments. *Pod.* 3-3½" dehiscent, like that of Suma, but thinner and darker brown, sometimes only 1-2½", by ½" and 1-3 seeded.

Baker, Brandis and Prain state that the corolla in Catechu is 2-3-times the length of the calyx (and give the number of pinnæ and lflts. as very much greater). Baker also states that the flowers of Catechu are of a darker yellow than those of A. Suma. The specimens examined by me in Hazaribagh and the S. P. do not agree in either of these particulars and are in fact, in many respects, *intermediate* between the two species. The corolla of the S. P. specimens is exactly *twice* the calyx.

Kath is manufactured from the wood in Manbhum and Hazaribagh but not apparently *Catechu*.

8. A. lenticularis, *Ham.*

A pretty tree, 20-40 ft. high, at first sight much resembling an Albizzia, with rough brown-grey bark and bright green foliage with large leaflets. Pinnæ 2-4, more rarely 5, prs., 3-5″ long. Lflts. 7-12 prs. oblong or obovate-oblong sub-sessile glabrous or nearly so $\frac{3}{4}$-1$\frac{1}{2}$″ by $\frac{5}{8}$″. Spikes *pure white* 4-5″ by $\frac{3}{4}$″ stout dense. Rachis hairy. Pod flat 5-9″ by 1-1$\frac{1}{2}$″.

Hazaribagh, frequent, esp. on quartzite (*e.g.*, Tatijheria.); on clay slates near the Damuda. Kumandi Reserve (Palamau), *Gamble*; Rajmehal hills, not common. Fls. *May-June*. Fr. *Dec.*

Armed with slightly recurved geminate compressed spines $\frac{1}{8}$-$\frac{3}{16}$″ long. *L.-rachis* 5-7″ glabrous or slightly hairy with a gland below the pinnæ. *Lflts.* margined with rounded apex and oblique base, mid-rib nearly central. *Calyx* slightly hairy, teeth nearly as long as tube. *Pet.* greenish nearly twice the calyx

This is probably the tree called *Kanta Siris* in Campbell's list of which he says "the wood is very hard." If so, Manbhum, *Camp.* should be added to localities.

5. Albizzia, Durazz. Siris.

Unarmed trees with 2-pinnate leaves. Flowers very small in globose heads, usually 5-merous. Corolla gamopetalous. St. numerous, united at the base into a tube, far exsert. Pod flat dry strap-shaped, indehiscent or late in dehiscing, not septate.

The fls. are always sessile; the so-called pedicel in A. Lebbek is a contracted part of the calyx-tube and corolla and staminal-tube and includes the pedicel of the ovary. Most species have a gland on rachis below the pinnæ and on between the one or more uppermost pinnæ and sometimes glands on the pinnæ between the lflts.

A. Fls. pedicelled. Heads (without stamens) over ½" diam.
  Lflts. wider on lower side of mid-rib . . . 1. *Lebbek.*
B. Fls. sessile. Heads (without stamens) under ½" diam.
  Lflts. over ½" broad, wider on upper side of rib . 2. *procera.*
  Lflts. under ½" broad, wider on lower side of rib . 3. *odoratissima.*
C. Fls. sessile. Heads ½" diam., more or less. Lflts. numerous, small, obliquely lanceolate, with mid-rib along the upper edge . . . . 4. *stipulata.*

1. A. Lebbek, *Benth.* Siris, *H.*; East Indian Walnut.

A large or mod.-sized tree with grey bark. Pinnæ 2-4 rarely 5 prs. with a gland below the 2-5 upper prs. of lflts. Lflts. 5-13 prs. oblong ¾" by $\frac{5}{16}$" to 2¼" by 1" mostly about 1½" by ¾" and always some over 1" long. Mid-rib not less than ⅓rd diam. of leaf from, and parallel to, its upper edge. Peduncles stout 1½-4" long, 1-3 together in the axils of the leaves of the young shoots, sometimes appearing sub-corymbose from the late development of these. Fls. with stamens 1½" long. Corolla exserted to twice the length of the calyx. Pod oblong attaining 12" by 1½-2".

"A large forest tree common on the Tundi hills," *Campbell.* I have found it apparently wild on the Damuda Ghats and the Kuru Ghats but, as it is frequently planted in stations and along roadsides, it may have been introduced. Dalbhum and Palamau, (cult.) *Gamble*! Wild near Silingi (*in a ravine*) in the Santal Parganahs.

Fls. *April-June* with the new shoots. The pods ripen *Jany.* and remain on the tree till *March or April* and make it conspicuous when leafless.

Shoots young leaves and inflorescence densely (often yellow-) pubescent. *Stipules* ⅛" linear deciduous, 2 minute stipellæ above the thickened petiolule when young. *Base of leaflet* 4-5 nerved. *Fls.* in a capitate raceme, scented. *Pedicel* $\frac{1}{10}$-⅛". *Calyx* ⅛", teeth short erect, pubescent. *Corolla* $\frac{5}{16}$"-⅓" tubular-ventricose, slightly hairy above, lobes nearly ⅛".

2. **A. procera,** *Benth.* Pandrai, *K.*; Safed-siris, *H.*; Garso, *Khar.*

A large tree with characteristic greenish-white or white bark. Pinnæ 3-6 prs. with a gland below the upper 1-3 prs. of lflts. or not. Lflts. 5-11 prs. broadly-oblong or rhomboid-oblong 1″ by ½″ to 2⅓″ by 1⅛″. Mid-rib nearer to the *lower edge* except at the tip. Peduncles ½-1″ copiously panicled 1-4-nate, bracts caducous. Fls. with stamens ½-⅝″. Exserted part of corolla 1–1½-times length of calyx. Pod 4-8 by ½-1″ thin strap-shaped.

In all the districts. Chiefly in the valleys. Campbell does not include it, so possibly his A. Lebbek is this. Fls. *Aug.-Sept.* Fr. *Dec.-May.* In May and June it may be nearly, or quite leafless for a very short time. There may be a second flush of new leaves in August growing through the panicle.

Youngest leaves silvery hairy, quickly glabrescent. *Inflorescence* nearly glabrous. *Panicles* large or only 3-4″. *Calyx* 1/10-⅛″, glabrous teeth unequal. *Corolla* greenish-white nearly ¼″ and lobes about ⅓rd as long, pubescent above. *Fil.* white, anthers yellowish. *St.-tube* exceeding the corolla.

3. **A. odoratissima,** *Benth.* Kiachalom, Pandrai, *K.*; Jang Siris, *S.*

A large or (usually in Ch. Nag.) a small tree, graceful with drooping foliage. Bark grey or sand-coloured. Pinnæ 2-5 prs. 5-10″ long with a gland below the upper 1-2 prs of lflts. rarely absent. Lflts. 6-24 prs. oblong or narrowly oblong rarely falcate, ⅝″ by ¼″ to 1¼″ by ½″ but mostly under 1″. Mid-rib about ¼th diam. of leaf from the upper margin. Peduncles ¾-1¼″ long, 1-3-nate in the axils of the young leaves and of bracts, and hence shortly panicled (or, forming ample deltoid terminal panicles *vide F.B.I.*) Fls. with stamens ¾-1″. Exserted part of corolla 4–5 times as long as the small calyx. Pod 5½″ by 1″ to 12″ by 1¼″, often contracted at the apex.

In all the districts, frequent, chiefly in the valleys. Fls. *May-July.* Fr. *Dec.-Feby.* Evergreen.

Shoots and inflorescence densely pubescent. *Rachis* pubescent, *lflts.* pale beneath, hairy or nearly glabrous except the margins and mid-rib.

Basal nerves 5-6 *Calyx* campanulate $\frac{1}{20}''$ pubescent scarcely toothed. *Corolla* hairy all over funnel-shaped, with lobes as long as tube, whitish.

There may be two vars. differing in the panicle and indumentum and shape of the leaves and pods. The new shoots usually grow through the panicle.

4. **A. stipulata,** *Boiv.* Japud, *K.;* Chapot, Keraserom, *S.*

A large handsome tree with feathery foliage. Pinnæ about 14 prs. 3-5″ long. Lflts. about 35-40 prs. $\frac{1}{4}$-$\frac{5}{16}''$ by $\frac{1}{16}''$ with the mid-rib close to the upper margin. Fls. with stamens 1-$1\frac{1}{4}''$ long on stout 1-3-nate peduncles in the axils of large cordate deciduous bracts. Pods dehiscent $3\frac{1}{2}''$ by $\frac{5}{8}''$ to $5\frac{1}{2}''$ by $\frac{3}{4}''$.

Valleys in Singbhum. Occasional in S. P., *Gamble.* Fls. *May-June.* Fr. *Oct.-April.* Evergreen.

Very distinct from the other Chota Nagpur species. Nearly all parts *densely pubescent. Lflts.* falcate, pubescent on ribs and margin when old, whitish beneath. Peduncles in simple racemes or panicled. *Large stipules* and *bracts deciduous,* or shortly persistent.

Pithecolobium dulce, *Benth.* Syn. Inga dulcis, *Roxb.*

A pretty tree cultivated and deserving to be more widely so. *Pinnæ* 1 pair. *Lflts.* one pair, oblique, small, 1-2″. *Stipules* spinose. *Heads* white $\frac{1}{2}''$ diam. in narrow panicles. *Pod* twisted. Seeds 6-8 with a white pulpy edible aril.

Fls. *Jany.-Feby.* Fr. *April-June.* Pods form a good fodder. Native of Mexico. If repeatedly cut back, it forms a good hedge.

Enterolobium Saman, *Prain.* Syn. Pithecolobium Saman, *Benth.* The Rain Tree.

A mod.-sized tree with large spreading crown and dark-grey bark. Often forked from the base. Pinnæ 3-7 prs. Lowest with 2-3 prs. of lflts., larger with 8-10 prs. Lflts. rhomboid, the mid-rib diagonal. Heads rose-coloured, axillary or appearing racemed from arising in the axils of very young leaves. Pod 5-9″ fleshy with firm sutures.

Very commonly planted in stations. Fls. *May-June.* Fr. *March-April.*

Shoots and rachis pubescent. *Petiole* eglandular, but often a small gland between one to all the pairs of pinnæ. *Lflts.* usually 1″ by $\frac{1}{2}''$ to 2″

by 1″ acute or obtuse and mucronate, somewhat hairy beneath esp. on the nerves. *Peduncles* 1-3-nate 2-3″ long. *Fls.* distinctly pedicelled with a bract on the pedicel. *Calyx* ¼″. *Corolla-tube* rather longer than the calyx, lobes ⅛″ and *filaments* pink.

Fam. 42. CÆSALPINIACEÆ.

Trees, shrubs or herbs. *L.* sometimes sensitive 1-2-pinnate, or if (Bauhinia) simple then palmately-nerved. *Fls.* large or small, zygomorphic, usually racemose. *Calyx* sometimes spathaceous, usually 5-merous and perigynous with a long or short tube (hypanthium), *sepals* imbricate rarely valvate. *Petals* 5, rarely fewer or 0, free, imbricate, posterior innermost in bud. *St.* 10 or fewer by abortion, perigynous. *Ovary and fruit* as in Mimosaceæ.

I. L. simple, usually 2-lobed, basal-nerved . . . 1. *Bauhinia.*

II. L. once pinnate. (Leaflets only 2 in Hardwickia).

A. Calyx-tube short, disc sub-basal.

Petals 0 . . . . 2. *Hardwickia.*

Petals 5 . . . . 3. *Cassia.*

B. Disc at the top of an elongated hypanthium (calyx-tube).

Petals 0. Calyx petaloid scarlet . . . 4. *Saraca.*

Petals 3 perfect. Flowers not showy . . . 5. *Tamarindus.*

III. L. 1-2 pinnate on the same tree. Trunk with branched thorns . . . . 6. *Gleditschia.*

IV. L. 2-pinnate. (Rachis much reduced in Parkinsonia)

A. Calyx-lobes imbricate, the lowest cucullate.

Erect trees or shrubs or prickly climbers. Fls. bracteate, at least in bud. Pod wingless 7. *Cæsalpinia.*

Prickly climber. Fls. ebracteate, calyx very oblique. Pod winged. . . . . . . 8. *Mezoneuron.*

B. Calyx lobes valvate.

A tree, not prickly. Fls. showy . . . . 9. *Poinciana.*

small tree, main rachis abbreviated, prickly 10. *Parkinsonia.*

1. Bauhinia, L.

Trees, shrubs or climbers with broad basal-nerved 2-lobed, rarely entire, leaves with rounded or cordate base, mid-rib (rachis) usually ending in a bristle. Fls. mod.-sized or large and showy in simple or panicled sometimes corymbose racemes (only 2-3 axillary in tomentosa). Hypanthium (calyx-tube) usually thickened and tubular, limb lobed or spathaceous. Petals clawed, with the posterior lobe usually different from the others. Stamens normally 10, often reduced, occasionally only 1-3 perfect. Ovary stipitate, stipes free or adnate to the side of the hypanthium. Pod linear to oblong, coriaceous or woody, dehiscent, rarely indehiscent.

I. Fertile stamens 10. Calyx with short tube and spathaceous or 5-cleft limb.
  A. Fls. not showy. Small or medium-sized trees.
    L. mostly under 2″ diam. Racemes simple. Pod swollen . . . . . . 1. *racemosa*.
    L. mostly exceeding 2″. Racemes branched. Pod flattish . . . . 2. *malabarica*.
  B. Fls. showy. Shrubs.
    Fls. 1-3 axillary, yellow . . . . . 3. *tomentosa*.
    Fls. in axillary racemes, white. Buds beaked 4. *acuminata*.
II. Fertile stamens 3-5. Calyx with an elongated base.
  A. Large climbers with large flowers . . . . 5. *Vāhlii*.
  B. Trees, rarely in B. purpurea only shrubby.
    a. L. not lobed. Fls. under 1½″ diam . . 6. *retusa*.
    b. L. 2-lobed or cleft. Fls. large and showy.
      L. mostly 11-nerved. Buds acutely 5-angled . 7. *purpurea*.
      L. mostly 13-nerved. Buds not angled . 8. *variegata*.

1. B. racemosa, *Lamk.* Kaimu, *K*; Katmouli, Kathul, *Kharw*; Ghatouli, *Oraon.*

A small tree with pubescent branches, small leaves broader than long, tomentose or pubescent especially on the nerves beneath, and simple racemes 2-3½″ long of small whitish flowers with spathaceous calyx and linear-oblanceolate petals. Pod 4-7″ rarely 10″ long, thick and slightly torulose, septate.

In mixed forest, Manbhum and Hazaribagh, (Tatijheria, foot of Parasnath, Koderma, etc.) ; Ranchi on the ghats, (Damuda and Kuru); Palamau, (Betlah forest, etc) frequent ; S. P. (Ghormara, Bokhraband). Fls. *April-June.* Fr. *Nov.-Dec.*, but persisting till *April*. Evergreen.

L. 1-1½″ by 1½-2½″ (rarely larger in Ch. Nag. specimens), pale-glaucous beneath, lobed ⅓rd, way down, lobes obtuse, base shallowly cordate 7-9-nerved *Corolla* scarcely exsert. *Pet.* . oblanceolate. *Anthers* densely villous. *Seeds* ⅛″.

2. **B. malabarica,** *Roxb.* Laba, *K.* ; Jhinjit, *S.* ; Koinar, *Turia.*

A small tree, attaining 4 ft. girth with a bushy crown and dark green leaves 1-4″ diam. broader than long, glabrescent and grey beneath. Fls. sub-regular whitish on slender pedicels in tomentose racemes 2-3″ long which are mostly in a *corymbose* panicle. Pod 7-12″ by about ¾″ flattened, curved, rostrate.

Singbhum on northern slopes and along valleys, common. Manbhum and Hazaribagh, (lower Parasnath hills, etc.) Santal Parganahs.

Fls. *Sept.-Nov.* Fr. *Jan.-March.* Evergreen.

Shoots pubescent or tomentose. *L.* lobed ⅛th-¼th way down, sometimes permanently minutely pubescent beneath. Base cordate 7-11-nerved. *Peti.* 1-2″ usually black at the thickened tip. *Calyx* ¼-½″ limb shortly 5 lobed *Petals* slightly exserted, oblong-spathulate. *Pod* usually described as reticulato-venose, but this only appears when dry.

In Ch. Nag. the smaller leaves of B. racemosa and its more delicate and pubescent nervation easily distinguish that species in leaf from B. malabarica. A very pubescent form of the latter, however, occurs in the U. P., and Kanjilal employs the acid taste of the leaves to distinguish it from racemosa. This taste is very characteristic.

3. **B. tomentosa,** *L.* is an ornamental shrub frequently planted. Wood, however, cites Tamar, 500-1,000 ft. as a locality.

4. **B. acuminata,** *L.*

A small tree or a shrub 15-20 ft. high, with new shoots sparingly pubescent, small leaves 1¼-2½″ and nearly as broad, pale and pubescent beneath, lobed about half-way down, and lobes very acute. Fls. pure white handsome.

Rajmehal hills. Wild according to a native collector. Frequent in gardens. Fls. *May*. Fr. ripens following *April*. Nearly deciduous in *May* and *June*.

Well characterized by the long acuminate or beaked *spathaceous calyx* and *beaked buds*. *Fls*. 2½-3″ diam. in racemes 1-3″ long. *Pods* 5″ by ⅝″.

5. **B. Vahlii,** *W. & A.* Rung, *K.*; Jom-lar, Lamak'lar, *S.*; Maholan, *Kharw.*; Maljan, *H.*

An immense climber attaining 2-4 ft. girth with deeply 2-lobed deeply cordate leaves from 3″ to 18″ diam. and corymbs of large white or cream-coloured flowers. Pod woody 6-12″ long by 1½-2″, flat.

Throughout the area, especially on the hills and in stony ravines. Fls. *April-June*. Fr. *Dec.-March*. Sub-deciduous. Renews its leaves in *May*.

The most destructive climber of the Ch. Nagpur forests but fortunately of considerable value to the people. The bark yields a strong fibre (chop, *K.*, lamak'lar, *S.*) used for ropes. The leaves are used as plates (kalu: *K.*) and cups (pu: *K.*). The pods are known as lama, *K.*, in Santal the small-seeded variety being *cihri lamak*, and the large seeded variety *dhalka lamak*. These pods are opened by means of heat, and as the operation is carried on in the forests, it is a fruitful source of forest-fires. The seeds are an important article of food.

6. **B. retusa,** *Ham.* Laba, *K.*; Birnju, Bunju, Jhinjit *S.*; Katmaun, Katmauli, *Kharw.*; Twar, *Oraon*; Kanla, *H.*

A mod.-sized tree with entire or emarginate leaves 4-7″ broad, rather broader than long with a cordate or straight 7-11-nerved base and ample terminal panicles of white flowers 1″ diam. in corymbose racemes. Pod straight oblong or usually rather broader upwards, 5-7″ by 1¼-1¾″ deep-red till ripe, thin.

Common especially on northern slopes in Singbhum. Frequent also in the other districts. Very common on quartzite along the Konor nadi (Hazaribagh). Fls. *Sept.-Dec.* Fr. *Feby.-March*. Evergreen.

L. green beneath, easily distinguished from the other species by its entire or scarcely divided apex. *Calyx-tube* scarcely any. *Petals* long-clawed, 3 upper purple-mottled. *St.* 3. perfect. *Buds* ovoid apiculate.

The bark yields a fibre and a gum, the latter is used in sweetmeats. Campbell says that the leaves have a bitter disagreeable taste.

7. **B. purpurea,** *L.* Singara, *M.*; Singa; *Ho.*; Sinhara, *S.*; Koinar, *Kharw.*; Kundrau, *Mal Pah.*

A mod.-sized tree (but not unfrequently flowering as a shrub) with very deeply-lobed leaves, cordate base 9-11-nerved and lobes with usually angular tips. Large purple fls. in terminal panicled racemes with *acutely 5-angled buds.* Pod 6-12″ by $\frac{3}{4}$-1″ flat, twisted and dehiscent when ripe with coriaceous thin valves.

Frequent in all districts, esp. in valleys, and often grown in the villages throughout Ch. Nagpur. Fls. *Sept.-Dec.* Fr. *Jan.-March.*

Twigs glabrous. *L.* 5-7″ long and about as broad (though quite little leaves may often occur on the same shoot) split from $\frac{1}{3}$rd of the way down (seldom less) often to near the base, glabrous or minutely puberulous on the nerves beneath, green scarcely glaucous, much more membranous than in B. variegata. *Petiole* 1-1$\frac{1}{2}$″. *Calyx* spathaceous, limb $\frac{3}{4}$″, the turbinate tube $\frac{1}{4}$-$\frac{3}{8}$″. *Petals* oblanceolate 1$\frac{1}{4}$-2″ long, often variegated white, long-clawed. *Stamens* 3-2 perfect and filamentous staminodes. *Pod* narrow below, nearly always broadening upwards.

The bark gives a fibre. The leaves are eaten as vegetables.

Var. α A small form with smaller pink flowers with darker center. On limestone, Naga Untari (W. Palamau) Fls. *Dec.*

This is probably Roxburgh's B. triandra, which should perhaps be maintained as a distinct species. The leaves are broader with broader sinus, the petals cuneate obtuse.

8. **B. variegata,** *L.* Buj, Buruju, Burunga, *K.*; Jhinjhir, *S.*; Kachnar, *Kharw.*, *H.*; Kundol, *Bhumij.*

A mod.-sized tree with leaves lobed $\frac{1}{4}$-$\frac{1}{3}$rd of the way down, cordate base 13-15-nerved (few L. only 11) and lobes rounded at the tips. Large pink or pure white flowers mostly in short racemes from leafless axils with *buds terete.* Pod 6-12″ by $\frac{3}{4}$-1″ flat, dehiscent.

On the hills in Singbhum (*e.g.*, Birda forest). Common in the Tundi forests (Manbhum, *Campbell*); Hazaribagh (near Bogoda); Palamau *Gamble!* S. P. occasional and generally distributed wild and cultivated. Fls. *Feby.-March* and the upper part of the tree leafless at the time. Fr. *April.*

Twigs pubescent *L.* 2¼" by 3" to 6" by 6½", usually about 5½" by 5¾" pubescent especially on the nerves and grey-glaucous beneath. *Petiole* ½-1¾" pubescent stout. *Calyx* spathaceous, tube 1-1¼", limb broad ovate. *Petals* obovate 2-2½" long, pure white (usually cultivated) or purple with one petal variegated with yellow, long-clawed. *Perfect stamens* 5 (5-3, F.B I.) without staminodes. Pod very venose when dry (more so than in B. malabarica). Stalk 1".

"The bark yields a fibre and is both eaten and used medicinally; *Campbell.* The flowers and flower-buds are sometimes eaten.

2. Hardwickia, *Roxb.*

1. H. binata, *Roxb.* Anjan, *H.*, *Kharw.*

An elegant tree with pendulous branches and leaves resembling those of a Bauhinia (in which the two lobes have separated to the base as distinct leaflets) with palmate nerves. Flowers small in axillary and terminal lax panicled racemes. Calyx-tube hardly any. Sepals 5 sub-petaloid, persistent. Petals 0. St. 10 alternate shorter. Ovary 2-ovuled. Pod thin, 2-3" long, oblong-lanceolate, with one seed near the end.

Palamau, especially towards the Sone, on the other side of which, in the Kymore Hills, it is frequent and attains 120 ft. (*Vide* Himalayan Journals). "Gregarious in patches south of the Sone River," *Brandis.* Fls. *July.* Fr. *Feby.-March.* Evergreen. New shoots in *April.*

Lflts. ovate-rhomboid, oblique 4-5-nerved 1-3" long. *Fls.* greenish-yellow.

Wood very hard and heavy, sometimes nearly black. Much lopped for fodder. Large trees are now very scarce but coppice shoots are frequent in the west of Palamau. The bark yields a fibre.

3. Cassia, L.

Trees, shrubs or herbs with pari-pinnate leaves and usually showy-yellow flowers in axillary racemes or terminal panicles, rarely small in axillary pairs. Calyx-tube short, sepals 5 imbricate. Pet. 5 usually somewhat zygomorphous. St. 10, frequently unequal or some reduced to staminodes, anthers dehiscing by a terminal pore or by a short slit. Ovary many-ovuled. Pod variable, septate, dehiscent or not.

A large genus with several species cultivated in gardens not here referred to. Many possess purgative properties, "Senna Tea" is the leaves of two species of Cassia.

A. Trees. St. 10 with anthers, 2-3 lower larger. Pods large, terete.
  - Flowers yellow in long lax racemes . . . 1. *fistula*.
  - Flowers rose pink in dense corymbs with persistent bracts . . . . . . 2. *javanica*.

B. St. 7 antheriferous, 2-3 lower larger, 3 posterior reduced to staminodes.
  1. Tree. Leaf-rachis without glands . . . 3. *siamea*.
  2. Shrubs or herbs. Leaf-rachis with glands.
     - Lflts. 3-5 prs. ovate-oblong acute . . 4. *occidentalis*.
     - Lflts. 6-12 prs. lanceolate acute . . . 5. *sophera*.
     - Lflts. 3 prs. obovate obtuse.
       - Glands between each of the two lowest pairs of leaflets . . . . 6. *tora*.
       - Gland between the lowest pair of leaflets only . . . . 7. *obtusifolia*.

C. Herbs. Sepals narrow. St. 4-10 all perfect without staminodes.
  - Lflts. 2 prs. St. 4 . . . . 8. *absus*.
  - Lflts. very numerous small. St. 5 . . . 9. *pumila*.
  - Lflts. very numerous small. St. 10 . . . 10. *mimosoides*.

1. **C. fistula**, *L.* Hari, *K.*; Mirju-baha Nuruc', *S.*, and the pod Bandor-lauri, *S.*; Dhanrach, *Kharw*; Bonurlati, *Oraon*; Amaltas, *H.*; The Indian Laburnum.

A small or mod.-sized tree very handsome in flower, with large leaves and large closely veined leaflets, long *pendulous racemes* of large *bright*-yellow flowers which are followed by long cylindrical drooping pods 1-2 ft. long.

In all situations but scattered in the forests, often planted.

Fls. *May-Aug.* Fr. *Jany.-Feby.*, but the pods may be found on the tree nearly all the year round and fall about *April*. Deciduous *March-April*.

Lflts. 4-8 prs., 2-6″ long ovate or ovate-oblong acuminate with close strong secondary nerves. *Racemes* 1-2 ft. *Fls.* $1\frac{1}{2}$-$2\frac{1}{2}$″ diam. *Pod* indehiscent with numerous transverse septa and flat seeds.

The flowers are eaten. Decoctions of the leaves and fruit are used as laxatives. The pulp surrounding the seeds is the Cassiæ Pulpa of the British Pharmacopœia. It is made into a sherbert in Chota Nagpur. The wood is strong and durable.

C. javanica. *L.* is a low tree with long spreading and weeping branches pubescent branchlets and oblong leaves 6-8″ long tomentose. *Lflts* 8-12 prs. $\frac{3}{4}$-$1\frac{1}{2}$″ long, minutely pubesent above, silky below, oblong obtuse or truncate, apiculate. *Pod* about 9″ by $\frac{1}{2}$″ (unripe), terete *Seeds* transverse embedded in flesh, and separated by septa. Allied to C. fistula, flowers and ripe pods not seen. Planted in Dumka station, esp. in front of the Circuit house. It may be C. marginata, *Roxb.*? Fls. not seen.

3. C. siamea, *Lamk.* Often called Siris locally.

A mod.-sized tree with leaves 6-12″ long, 6-14 prs. of oblong leaflets $1\frac{1}{2}$-$2\frac{1}{2}$″ long and numerous very large erect panicles of bright-yellow flowers.

Not indigenous, but very commonly planted and often self-sown. It is a wonderfully rapid grower attaining 20 ft. in 2-3 years, but is short-lived, and very little else will grow in its vicinity. The heart-wood is deep-brown but useless. Fls. *Sept.-Dec.* Evergreen.

Lflts. emarginate with a small bristle. *Panicles* of numerous corymbiform racemes. *Pods* flat 6-9″ long.

4. C. occidentalis, *L.* Kain, *K.*; Kasondi, *H.*

An erect stout herb or undershrub 2-4 ft. high with leaves 6-12″ long and about 5 prs. of ovate or ovate-oblong lflts. $1\frac{1}{2}$-4″ long. Flowers yellow $\frac{1}{2}$-$\frac{3}{4}$″ diam., in axillary and terminal short racemes, sometimes panicled. Pod 4-5″ long, flattened, septate slightly falcate with numerous seeds.

Annual. Very common in waste ground during the rains. Fls. *Sept.-Nov.* Fr. *Dec.-Jany.*

Fœtid. Stems grooved. Petiole with a gland just above the base.

5. C. sophera, *L.*

A shrub 6-7 ft. somewhat resembling the last but leaflets 5-12 prs. oblong-lanceolate or lanceolate, finely acute or acuminate, mostly 1-3″ long. Fls. 1-$1\frac{1}{2}$″ diam. in short axillary and terminal panicles. Pod less flattened than in occidentalis.

Not nearly so common as the last, usually near villages. Fls. *Aug.-Nov.* Fr. *Nov.-Dec.*

6. **C. tora,** *L.* Jomai-Kaiu *K.*; Bheda-deren, chakaoda, *S.*; Chekor, *Kharw.*; Chakunda, *H.*

An erect herb 1-2½ ft. high with 3 prs. of obovate leaflets increasing in size from the base of the rachis upwards. Fls. ⅛″ diam. solitary or paired axillary. Pods sub-terete or 4 angular slender, falcate 6-12″ long, incompletely septate with numerous brown oblong seeds ⅛″.

Very common and sub-gregarious in waste ground in the rains. Fls. *Sept.-Oct.* Fr. *Nov.-Dec.* Annual.

The young leaves (Chakaoda ara, *K.*) and fruit are eaten. The plant has usually a fœtid smell.

7. **C. obtusifolia,** *L.* Syn. Senna toroides, *Roxb.*

Like a tall variety of C. Tora with only one gland between the lowest pair of leaflets, while typical C. Tora has a gland between the *two* lowest pairs. Prain agreeing with Roxburgh considers that it should be reckoned as a distinct species from C. Tora as the leaves are less prominently veined, not glaucous and the flowers larger and pedicels longer. It is said to lack moreover, the fœtid smell of C. Tora, and its pod is less quadrate. I have grown plants with leaves fœtid and glaucous beneath, and only bearing 1 gland except on the lowest one or two leaves which had two and such plants may also be discovered in a wild state.

8. **C. absus,** *L.*

An erect viscous-hairy herb with only *2 prs.* of *leaflets* and terminal racemes of small *yellow or red* flowers with only *4 perfect stamens.*

L. with petiole 1½-2″. *Lflts.* 1-2″ unequal-sided. *Pod* 5-6 seeded.

In somewhat open stony jungles and waste ground, frequent.

Fls. *Aug.-Sept.* Annual.

9. **C. pumila,** *Lamk.* and **C. mimosoides,** *L.* Ot-kondro, *S.* are easily distinguished by their very numerous small lflts., the latter is often an erect undershrub, but C. pumila diffuse and prostrate. The latter is common in forest land and the former in waste land.

C glauca, *Lamk.* Var. suffruticosa is mentioned by Campbell as occurring in Manbhum. It is a shrub with 10 perfect equal stamens, and pale yellow flowers in axillary corymbs. Probably only cultivated.

4. Saraca, L.

1. S. indica, *L.* Husangid-ba, *K.*; Asoka, *Beng.*

A strikingly beautiful tree when in flower with dense corymbs 3-4" broad of a brilliant orange-scarlet, each flower with 3-8 exserted stamens. The flowers are well set off by the dark-green pari-pinnate leaves of 6-12 large acuminate leaflets attaining 9" by 2½".

Indigenous in the valleys of Singbhum along watercourses, esp. in the ravines of Porahat. There used to be some fine specimens near Kendbai village in the Leda forest. Fls. *March-April.* Fr. *Sept.* and seeds germinate in *Dec.* Evergreen. The new leaves are red and drooping. Rarely exceeding 30 ft. with a low dense crown. *L.* sub-sessile. *Lflts.* oblong or oblong-lanceolate acute (or obtuse, *F.B.I.*). *Sepals* scarlet $\frac{1}{4}$-$\frac{1}{3}$". *Petals* 0. *Ovary* many-ovuled stipitate. *Pod* 4-10" by 1½-2", 4-8 seeded.

"When this tree is in full blossom, I do not think the whole vegetable kingdom affords a more beautiful object," *Roxb.*

5. Tamarindus, L.

1. T. indica, *L.* Jojo, *K.*; Jojos *S.*; Tetar, *Kharw.*; Imli, Amli, H. The Tamarind.

A very large and very handsome tree with abruptly pinnate leaves with 10-20 prs. of small close oblong obtuse or retuse leaflets, about ½" long, and small red and yellow flowers in lax racemes, only the three upper petals and three stamens fully developed.

Commonly planted in the villages and sometimes found in the forest on old deserted village sites, but it suffers much from fires. Naturalized among granite rocks near Kuru. Fls. *April-June* also in *October.* Fr. *Dec.-April.* Evergreen.

Pod curved fleshy and fibrous, with a brittle thin epicarp.

Gleditschia sinensis, *Lamk.*, is a tree commonly planted on railway platforms. It has the trunks and branches armed with copiously branched thorns, 1-2-pinnate leaves, and small greenish flowers in dense spikes.

7. Cæsalpinia, L.

Trees or shrubs, often scandent and prickly, with large abruptly bi-pinnate leaves and (usually) showy flowers in copious axillary racemes. Calyx-lobes imbricate, the lowest much the largest and cucullate, tube very short. Petals spreading (erecto-patent in coriaria), usually orbicular and clawed, the posterior smallest. St. 10, free, declinate. Fil. often woolly. Ovary few-ovuled. Pod dehiscent or not.

I. Unarmed tree. Lateral petals small whitish, sub-erect . . . . 1. *coriaria.*
II. Prickly tree Pinnæ and leaflets 10-15 prs. . . 2. *Sappan.*
III. Prickly erect or diffuse shrub. Pinnæ 6-9 prs. . 3. *pulcherrima.*
IV. Scandent prickly shrubs. Petals broad, Pods unarmed.
  a. Leaflets 2-3 prs. on each pinna . . . 4. *Nuga*
  b. Leaflets 6-12 prs. on each pinna.
    Leaflets $\frac{1}{4}$-$\frac{1}{2}$″. Pod indehiscent, sub-fleshy. Stipules subulate . . . . 5. *digyna.*
    Leaflets $\frac{1}{2}$-1″. Pod sub-dehiscent, dry. Stipules semi-sagittate . . . . 6. *sepiaria.*
V. Scandent prickly shrub. Petals narrow. Pod echinate 7. *Bonducella.*

1. C. coriaria, *Willd.* Divi-divi. The American Sumach.

A mod.-sized tree with a low-spreading crown and elegant 2-pinnate leaves with very numerous close-set leaflets $\frac{1}{8}$-$\frac{1}{3}$″ long. Pinnæ 13-17, 1-2″ long. Fls. small whitish sweet-scented panicled. Pods spirally twisted.

Introduced from Central America and often cultivated, esp. in S. P. There are some trees about 30 ft. high at Chaibassa. Seed was sent to Singbhum and Palamau for experiment. They germinated well in about a week, but it would probably be scarcely worth while growing it on a larger scale; Brandis says that the pods of C. digyna are said to be as rich in tannin.

Fls. *May-June.* Fr. *Aug.* Evergreen.

2. C. Sappan, *L.*

A small tree with small and few or no prickles. Pinnæ 10-12 prs.

Planted at Ranchi and Hazaribagh. Fls. *r. s.*

Leaflets sessile close $\frac{1}{2}$-$\frac{3}{4}$" oblong oblique, 10-20 prs. *Fls.* yellow. *Pod* 3-4" by $1\frac{1}{2}$", polished, indehiscent, wider and beaked above.

3. C. pulcherrima, *Swartz.* Peacock-flower.

A large erect shrub, handsome when young, but becoming straggling and unsightly when old, glabrous, with 6-9 prs. of pinnæ and 10-12 prs. of leaflets $\frac{1}{2}$-$\frac{3}{4}$" long and gaudy terminal panicles of yellow or scarlet flowers. Pod thin strap-shaped. A common garden plant. Fls. *r. s.*

4. C. Nuga, *Ait.* Syn. C. paniculata, *Roxb.*

In the Him. Journals Sir J. D. Hooker writes: "On the way I found the C. paniculata, a magnificent climber, festooning the trees with its dark glossy foliage and gorgeous racemes of orange blossoms." This was in Hazaribagh, not far from Parasnath, but it is the only record of this species in Chota Nagpur. Fls. *c. s.* and *h. s.*

5. C. digyna, *Rottl.* Umul-kuchi, *Beng.*

A large scrambling prickly shrub with 5-10 prs. of pinnæ and 7-10 prs. of close oblong leaflets $\frac{1}{4}$-$\frac{1}{2}$" long appressed hairy beneath and slightly above. Flowers showy yellow in simple axillary or extra-axillary racemes. Pod oblong 1-2" thick fleshy 1-4-seeded, stipitate, crowned by the long style.

Dhipa (Singbhum), *Gamble*; Gangpur near the Brahmini R.; ravines and hedges in northern Santal Parganahs. Fls. *July-Oct.* Fr. *Jany.-March.*

L. rachis 5-8" fulvous hairy with geminate prickles. *Pinnæ* $1\frac{1}{2}$-2" with a distinct stalk $\frac{1}{8}$-$\frac{1}{4}$" long. *Peduncle* 3-7". *Pedicels* 1-$1\frac{1}{4}$" long with very oblique spreading truncate calyx-tube in fruit.

6. C. sepiaria, *Roxb.* Uchay, *K.* (*f. Gamble*).

An extensive shrub rambling or climbing by means of the recurved prickles on the stems and leaf rachis with 8-10 prs. of opp. pinnæ each with 6-12 prs. of broadly oblong leaflets $\frac{1}{2}$-1" long, and simple racemes of showy sulphur-yellow flowers $\frac{3}{4}$-$\frac{7}{8}$" diam., the smaller 5th petal often with red lines. Pod $2\frac{1}{2}$-$4\frac{1}{2}$" rigid, tardily dehiscent, cuspidate with the long hard style, the upper suture very narrowly winged.

Rare, Saranda Forests in Singbhum, *Gamble.* Occasional in gardens and hedges near Ranchi. Fls. *Dec.-May.* Fr. *May-Oct.* Evergreen.

Branchlets somewhat 5-angled and downy. *L. rachis* about 12″ pubescent. *Pinnæ* about 3-5″. *Leaflets* contiguous, puberulous both sides or nearly glabrous above, with rounded or retuse tip. *Stipules* caducous semi-sagittate. *Racemes* axillary several superposed, of which the uppermost is the first developed; young pubescent with deciduous lanceolate recurved bracts $\frac{1}{3}$″ long.

7. **C. Bonducella,** *Fleming.* Bagni, *S.*; Katkaranj, *H.*; Nata, *Beng.* The Fever-nut.

An extensive climbing shrub covered with short straight sharp prickles, those on the leaf rachis reflexed. Pinnæ 6-8 prs. and leaflets 8 prs. oblong or ovate-oblong $\frac{1}{2}$-1″ by $\frac{1}{2}$″. Racemes simple of palc-yellow flowers $\frac{1}{2}$″ by $\frac{3}{4}$″ across, the smaller erect 5th petal marked with orange. Young pods softly echinate, old broad oblong, 2-3″ long prickly, dehiscent, 1-2-seeded.

I have only seen it in hedges, where it is frequent in the S. P.

Fls. *Aug.-Oct.* Fr. *Dec.-Feby.* Evergreen.

Branchlets fulvous hairy. *Leaflets* not contiguous, slightly downy beneath, with obtuse mucronate tip. *Stipules* persistent large foliaceous compound or pinnatifid. *Racemes* often above the axil, very elongate with age, lower flowers only fertile. *Bracts* long linear reflexed over the buds deciduous, $\frac{3}{8}$-$\frac{3}{4}$″.

The seed is a powerful tonic, *Roxb.* It is also used as an antiperiodic in fever.

8. Mezoneuron, Desf.

Differs from Cæsalpinia chiefly in its very oblique calyx-tube, and its flat thin indehiscent pod broadly winged down the upper suture, and by the complete absence of bracts to the flowers.

1. **M. cucullatum,** *W. & A.* Baghin janum, *S.*; Koko-botur, *K.*

A large woody glabrous shrub scrambling or climbing by the numerous small black sharp prickles on branches and leaves. Leaves ample 2-pinnate with deep-green shining ovate leaflets $1\frac{1}{2}$-$3\frac{1}{2}''$ long. Fls. articulate on pedicel bright-yellow in numerous panicled racemes mostly from the old wood. Pod 2-4" long, 1-seeded.

Valleys, esp. in the Saranda Forests; Dalbhum, *Gamole*; Santal P. along streams. Fls. *Sept.-Feby.* Fr. *Feby.*

Stems with large conical bosses tipped by a prickle. *L.* rachis 6-12". *Pinnæ* distant 2-5 prs. *Lflts.* 3-5 prs. opp., ovate to narrow elliptic. *Calyx-tube* shallow-cupular thick persistent, two anterior sep. and ant. median petal produced into a foot receiving the base of the anterior filaments. *Ant. pet.* fleshy purple folded, deeply 2-lobed. Other petals and usually calyx, pedicel and rachis, yellow.

Poinciana regia, *Bojer.* The Gold Mohur tree, is a beautiful well-known tree with feathery 2-pinnate leaves, numerous small lflts., and large scarlet flowers in terminal corymbs. Often planted. The narrow-oblong seeds have a bony testa and often take two years to germinate.

Fls. *May-June.* Fr. *March-April.*

10. Parkinsonia, L.

1. P. aculeata, *L.* Bilaiti Kikar, *H.*

A small tree armed with sharp thorns which represent the abbreviated main rachis of a bi-pinnate leaf and bear 2-6 pinnæ, with a much flattened rachis, at their base, and often 2 recurved stipulary thorns. Lflts. numerous linear oblong $\frac{1}{4}''$ or very small or obsolete (the rachis performing the leaf functions). Flowers yellow in lax axillary racemes. Calyx-tube short. Petals 5 sub-equal. St. 10. Pod turgid dry moniliform, tardily dehiscent, 3-6" long.

Apparently naturalized in waste ground in many parts, esp. on well-drained soil and growing very fast. Banks of the Sone (Palamau) *Haslett*! Fls. *Sept.-Oct.*

Fam. 43. PAPILIONACEÆ.

Trees, shrubs or herbs with simple, 1-foliolate or compound leaves and strongly zygomorphic flowers. *Calyx* equally or usually unequally lobed, often 2-lipped, usually somewhat perigynous. *Petals* 5, imbricate, posterior (uppermost, *standard*) exterior in bud; 2 lateral (*wings*) more or less declinate free or adhering to the keel; 2 lowest usually more or less connate into a *keel* with an up-curved tip. *St.* rarely somewhat adherent to the petals, on the disc lining the very short hypanthium, monodelphous, or diadelphous (5+5 or 9+1), or the 10th absent, very rarely all free (Sophora); alt. ones sometimes shorter or reduced to staminodes. *Ovary* as in Mimosaceæ. *Pod* very various, sometimes coiled up and included in the calyx, or of 1-seeded joints, etc.

I. L. simple or digitately 3-foliolate.* Pod dehiscent turgid, not septate.

Herbs or shrubs. St. monodelphous . . . 1. *Crotalaria.*

Shrubs or undershrubs, usually gland-dotted. St. 2-adelphous . . . . 2. *Flemingia.*

II. L. pinnately 3-foliolate gland-dotted. Pod turgid 1-2-seeded. Climbers . . . . 3. *Rhynchosia.*

III. L. pinnately 3-foliolate gland-dotted (exc. Atylosia sp.). St. 2-adelphous. Pod with depressed lines between the seeds, 2-6-seeded.

Twiners. Seed with a large grooved strophiole . 4. *Atylosia.*

Erect, cultivated. Seeds without a strophiole . 5. *Cajanus.*

IV. L. pinnately 3-foliolate, not gland-dotted. Pod dehiscent throughout, rarely with depressed lines (Pueraria) or septate (Teramnus, Glycine, Phaseolus, Vigna).

A. Climbers (except Erythrina and Glycine sp.) Style beardless.

1. Nodes of inflorescence not tumid. St. 2-adelphous (exc. Teramnus).

Petals little-exserted. St. 1-adelphous . 6. *Teramnus.*

As in Teramnus, but sub-erect and st. 2-1-adelphous. Cultivated . . . 7. *Glycine.*

---

* Rarely 5-foliolate in Crotalaria.

Standard not spurred exceeding the wings and keel . . . . . 8. *Shuteria.*

As in Shuteria, but standard spurred . 9. *Dumasia.*

2. Nodes of inflorescence tumid.

Climbers. Petals sub-equal. Fls. showy. Wings free . . . . . 10. *Canavalia.*

Climbers. Petals sub-equal. Fls. showy. Wings adnate to keel . . . . 11. *Pueraria.*

Climbers. Petals very unequal . . 12. *Mucuna.*

Trees or dwarf shrubs usually prickly . 13. *Erythrina.*

B. Style bearded below the stigma. Climbers or sub-erect herbs.

Keel and included style spiral. Pod more or less septate . . . . . . 14. *Phaseolus.*

Keel and style not or partially spiral. Pod septate . . . . 15. *Vigna.*

Keel not spiral. Pod not at all septate . 16. *Dolichos.*

V. L. pinnately 3-foliolate, not gland-dotted. Pod only 1-seeded and only dehiscent at the apex. Ovary 2-ovuled. St. 2-adelphous.

Trees or climbers. Fls. large scarlet . . 17. *Butea.*

Woody climbers. Fls. smallish, white . . 18. *Spatholobus.*

VI. L. pinnate with opposite leaflets, the rachis usually ending in a tendril or bristle. St. 2-adelphous or the tenth absent. Pod dehiscent not septate or jointed. Slender climbers (exc. Cicer and Lens).

A. L. with usually a terminal leaflet. St. 9+1.

Fls. large showy. Petals very unequal . 19. *Clitoria.*

Fls. small. Lflts. toothed . . . . 20. *Cicer.*

B. L. ending in a point or tendril. Style hairy.

a. Staminal sheath oblique at mouth. Ovules 2 . . . . 21. *Lens.*

b. Staminal sheath truncate.

St. 9+1. Style dilated above . . . 22. *Lathyrus.*

As in 22 but style with reflexed margins and laterally compressed . . . 23. *Pisum.*

St. 9 . . . . 24. *Abrus.*

VII. L. odd-pinnate with alt. or opp. lflts. Pod flat indehiscent. St. 9, 9+1 or 10 or 5+5.

A Trees.

Fls. pink. Lflts. opp. Pod almost woody, wingless . . . . 25. *Pongamia.*

Fls. yellow. Lflts. alt. Pod thin at the margins, orbicular . . . . . . 26. *Pterocarpus.*

Fls. white pink or pale yellow. Pod thin, oblong . . . . 27. *Dalbergia.*

B. Woody climbers.

Pod usually thin. Lflts. alternate . . 27. *Dalbergia.*

Pod firm, winged, Lflts. opposite . . 28. *Derris.*

Pod hard, almost woody, not winged . . 29. *Millettia.*

VIII. L. odd-pinnate* (even-pinnate in Sesbania) with usually opposite lflts. Pod dehiscent, not jointed, septate (not or obscurely septate in 29 and 30). St. 9+1.

Woody climber . . . . 29. *Millettia.*

Undershrubs. Anthers obtuse. Hairs basifixed 30. *Tephrosia.*

Herbs or undershrubs. Anthers apiculate. Hairs usually laterally fixed . . . . 31. *Indigofera.*

Herbaceous or woody. L. even pinnate with numerous lflts. . . . . 32. *Sesbania.*

IX. Pod breaking up into 1-seeded joints, margin indented between the joints (only 1 joint in Lespedeza, and continuously dehiscent along the ventral suture, not breaking up, in two species of Desmodium).

A. Herbs, shrubs or undershrubs.

L. pinnate with numerous lflts. St. 5+5. Pod straight . . . . 33. *Æschynomene.*

L. pinnate. St. 9+1. Pod twisted up . . 34. *Uraria.*

L. 1-and 3-foliolate often intermixed. Pod twisted up . . . . 34. *Uraria.*

L. pinnately 3-foliolate. Pod of 1 flattened joint . . . . . 35. *Lespedeza.*

L. pinnately 1-3-foliolate. Pod flattened not twisted up . . . . . . 36. *Desmodium.*

B. Trees. L. pinnately 3-foliolate. Pod not twisted up . . . . 37. *Ougeinia.*

X. St. free. L. odd-pinnate. Pod dehiscent moniliform . . . . 38. *Sophora.*

---

* 3-1-foliolate in some Indigofera.

NOTE.—The genera with free stamens and pinnate leaves, being those most nearly related to other families of the order Leguminosæ, should logically have been placed first. The above key is somewhat artificial.

1. Crotalaria, L. Sakesing, *K.*; Jhunka, *S.*

Herbs or shrubs with simple or 3- rarely 5-foliolate leaves. Flowers yellow in terminal or leaf-opposed racemes. Corolla equalling or exceeding the calyx with a characteristic up-curved beaked keel formed of the connate anterior petals. Keel as long as the wings. St. 1-adelphous with dimorphous anthers. Pod inflated, continuous within, linear or oblong, usually many-seeded.

Most of the genus yield a strong fibre.

I. L. trifoliolate or 5-foliolate.

- Undershrub 2-4 ft. high. L. 3-foliolate . . . 1. *striata.*
- Annual 2-4 ft. high with 5, rarely 3 linear lflts. . 2. *quinquefolia.*
- A diffuse weed with sub-globose 2-seeded pods . *medicaginea.*

II. L. simple or 1-foliolate.

A. Fls. in long terminal (and lateral) leafless racemes, bracts minute (exc. in sericea)

1. A stout quite glabrous herb with glabrous pods and showy fls. . . . . . . 3. *sericea.*

2. More or less silky.

- Shrubby. Calyx $\frac{1}{2}$-$\frac{3}{4}$″, pods velvety . . . 4. *juncea.*
- Slender 1-3 ft. Calyx $\frac{1}{3}$″, upper calyx-lobes distinct . . . . 5. *albida.*
- Slender $\frac{1}{2}$-2 ft. Calyx under $\frac{1}{4}$″, upper calyx-lobes connate . . . . 6. *linifolia.*

B. Fls. in short terminal (and lateral) few-fld. or capitate racemes. Bracts sometimes foliaceous.

- Calyx $\frac{3}{4}$-1″ long. Stipules minute deciduous . 7. *calycina.*
- Calyx under $\frac{3}{4}$″ long. Stipules persistent linear $\frac{1}{8}$-$\frac{1}{3}$″ . . . . 8. *mysorensis.*
- Calyx under $\frac{1}{2}$″ long. Stipules 0 . . . . 9. *hirta.*

C. Fls. in short ultimately leaf-opposed racemes, sometimes sub-solitary.

1. Stipules decurrent as a wing on the branches 10. *alata.*
2. Stipules small or 0, not decurrent.
   - L. ovate, stipules small acuminate . . 11. *hirsuta.*
   - L. oblong, stipules 0 . . . . . . 12. *prostrata.*
   - L. oblong, often very small, stipules small linear reflexed . . . . 13. *acicularis.*

1. C. striata, *D.C.* Sakesing, *K.*; Son-jhunka, *S.*

An undershrub 2-4 ft. high with long-petioled trifoliolate leaves and terminal and lateral elongate racemes of yellow flowers $\frac{3}{4}''$ long, usually streaked with purple. Pods $1\frac{1}{2}$-2″ long by $\frac{1}{4}''$, 30-40-seeded, glabrous or very finely downy.

Occasional in waste ground and along road-sides, sometimes cultivated for its fibre. Annual. Fls. and Fr. *Oct.-Jany.*

Lflts. 1-$2\frac{1}{2}''$ broadly elliptic or obovate, with sparse appressed hairs beneath, base cuneate, tip rounded. Petiole 1-2″.

2. C. quinquefolia, *L.*

An erect annual 2-4-ft. high with 5, rarely 3, linear leaflets 2-4″ long. Chota Nagpur, *Prain.*

3. C. sericea, *Retz.* Sakesing, *K.*

A suffruticose herb 3-4 ft. high with often hexagonal waxy stems, oblanceolate to obovate leaves 3-6″ long with persistent stipules, long terminal paniculate racemes of bright yellow flowers and glabrous pods $1\frac{1}{2}''$ long.

A handsome plant frequent in grass under light shade and along nalas in Singbhum, Hazaribagh and S. P. Fls. *Sept.-Feby.* Fr. *Dec.-May.* Biennial.

L. appressed silky beneath with short stout petioles. *Racemes* often 1 ft. with persistent spreading or reflexed ovate acuminate leafy bracts $\frac{1}{2}''$ long. *Fls.* over 1″ long. *Fruiting-calyx* $\frac{3}{4}''$.

4. C. juncea, *L.* Jiri (the fibre Jiri-bair), *M.*; Ji., *Ho.*; Son, *S.*; San, *H.*; The Sun Hemp.

A shrub 4-5 ft. high with slender erect sulcate branches, linear or oblong leaves $1\frac{1}{2}$-3" long, bright-yellow flowers about $\frac{3}{4}$-1" long in loose long racemes. Pod sessile velvety 1-$1\frac{1}{4}$" long, stout.

Cultivated and sometimes apparently wild in Singbhum. Sili, Jonha jungles (Ranchi scarps), *Wood.* Fls. *Dec.-Jany.* Fr. *Jany.*

Beaked sepals, pedicels and pods all softly closely pubescent or velvety, usually brown. *Corolla* slightly exserted, standard 1" broad and long, veined red, silky without.

5. C. albida, *Heyne.*

An erect undershrub or herb 1-3 ft. sparingly branched with erect appressed-hairy or silky branches, narrow leaves and yellow flowers $\frac{1}{3}$-$\frac{1}{2}$" in terminal leafless 10-25-fld. racemes with a scarcely exserted corolla.

One of the commonest forest crotalarias, very abundant on hard clay soil on hilly ground. Fls., Fr. *Sept.-Jany.* Apparently annual.

L. linear-oblong, oblong or oblanceolate 1-3" by $\frac{1}{4}$-$\frac{3}{8}$" obtuse mucronate pubescent above glaucous and silky beneath, base narrowed to a very short petiole. *Stipules* 0. *Calyx* very silky, two upper lobes oblong obtuse. *Pod* glabrous $\frac{1}{2}$" slightly exserted, 6-8-seeded, on pedicels $\frac{1}{4}$" long.

6. C. linifolia, *L. f.*

An annual $\frac{1}{2}$-2 ft. high somewhat resembling the last, but with the upper lip of the calyx emarginate, not deeply lobed, leaves usually shorter and pod as long as the calyx.

Chota Nagpur, *Prain.*

7. C. calycina, *Schrank.* Mota bir-jhunka, *S.*

A herb 1-2 ft. high with brown silky branches and lanceolate or long linear leaves. Easily recognised by the pale-yellow corolla being shorter than the very large $\frac{3}{4}$-1" long calyx which is densely clothed with long brown hairs. Pod included. Seeds white. Frequent. Fls. in the rains Fr. *Nov.*

8. C. mysorensis, *Roth.*

A herb 3-4 ft high with erect branches covered with long spreading hairs, sessile linear-oblong or linear leaves 2-3" below, smaller upwards, with long linear foliaceous stipules up to $\frac{7}{8}$″ long. Fls. few in few-fld. bracteate terminal racemes.

Hills, Singbhum and Santal Parganahs. Fls. *Aug.-Oct.* Fr. *Dec.-Jany.*

Lower *sepals* linear acuminate $\frac{1}{2}$-$\frac{5}{8}$″ villous with brown hairs, upper broader lanceolate, the two linear bracteoles similar. *Pod* exserted 1″ by $\frac{1}{3}$″ grooved above, shining glabrous with 40-50 small shining black seeds.

9. C. hirta, *Willd.*

A diffuse undershub somewhat resembling the last. Branches densely clothed with *short* patent brown hairs. L. linear or linear-oblong, hairy, exstipulate. Fls. only 2-4 sub-capitate with lanceolate foliaceous bracts. Calyx $\frac{1}{4}$″ with teeth all linear acuminate.

Tirilposi savanah. Fls. *March.*

10. C. alata, *Ham.* Marang jhunka, *S.*

A herb or undershrub 1-2 ft. with sub-sessile elliptic usually oblique-based leaves 1-2″. Easily recognized by the large decurrent stipules forming wings on the branches. Racemes at first terminal, ultimately becoming leaf-opposed, 3-4″ in fruit.

Frequent. Fls. *Aug.-Sept.* Fr. *Sept.-Oct.*

11. C. hirsuta, *Willd.*

An erect herb 2-3 ft. with broadly-ovate leaves about $2\frac{1}{2}$″ by $1\frac{1}{2}$″ acute and sometimes slightly oblique, racemes few-fld. ultimately leaf-opposed. Stipules linear-subulate reflexed slightly longer than the very short petiole.

Common in rocky jungles. Fls. *Aug.-Sept.* Fr. *Sept.-Oct.*

Stems with soft spreading hairs. L. soft, usually mucronate. Sepals linear acuminate. Pod $\frac{3}{4}$-1″ with spreading hairs, about 6-seeded.

12. C. prostrata, *Roxb.* Nanha jhunka, Katic' jhunka, *S.*

A silky herb with spreading or long trailing branches, close oblong obtuse silky leaves attaining $1\frac{1}{4}$″ by $\frac{5}{8}$″, glaucous beneath. Racemes soon leaf-opposed 2-4-fld.

Very common on clay in open Sal forests, etc. Fls. r. s. Fr. Dec.

L. oblique at base. Stipules 0. Racemes attaining 3″. Calyx-lobes short densely villous ⅛″ long. Pods ½-⅝″ glabrous, shortly stipitate.

Used in certain disorders of the stomach, *Campbell*.

13. C. acicularis, *Ham.*

A procumbent very hairy weed, with a woody rootstock, often very conspicuous on cold mornings from the dew adhering to the hairs and giving it a silvery appearance. Fls. ¼″. Small black pods ¼-⅓″. Fls., Fr. *Dec.-Jany.*

2. Flemingia, *Roxb.*

Shrubs or suffruticose herbs, with 1-or digitately 3-foliolate leaves usually gland-dotted below. Fls. small or medium, white or pink, in small cymes racemes or panicles with often conspicuous bracts, ebracteolate. Corolla included or only slightly exsert; petals equal in length. St. 2-adelphous. Ovary 2-ovuled. Pod oblong turgid, usually 2-seeded.

I. L. simple.

A. Fls. enclosed in large persistent folded bracts, which are arranged in simple or branched racemes.

L. narrow. Shrub 4-6 ft. Branches not prominently angled . . . . 1. *strobilifera.*

L. narrow. Shrub 1-3 ft. Branches angled, shaggy 2. *bracteata.*

L. very broad . . . . 3. *Chappar.*

B. Fls. in fascicled or panicled racemes with small bracts . . . . 4. *paniculata.*

II. L. 3-foliolate. Fls. in dense subspicate racemes.

A tall scarcely branched erect annual shrub 5-6 ft. . 5. *stricta.*

A branched shrub 4-5 ft. . . . . . . 6. *congesta.*

A diffuse undershrub 1-2 ft. with narrow leaflets . 7. *prostrata.*

A dwarf undershrub with very broad leaflets . . 8. *nana.*

1. F. strobilifera, *R. Br.*

A bushy shrub 5-8 ft. high with appressed silky terete or slightly angular branches, lanceolate or ovate-lanc.

acuminate leaves 2-6″ by ¾-3″ with rounded base and numerous axillary and terminal racemes 2-3½″ long of small white flowers $\frac{5}{16}$″ long in short few-flowered cymes in the axils of folded membranous cordate bracts.

Beds of ravines in the Porahat forests. Shady forests, Saranda. Ranchi, 1,500-2,000 ft., *Wood.* Parasnath. Santhal Parganahs near streams (Banjhi, etc.) Fls. *Jany.-April.*

L. densely covered with small red glands beneath, and fulvous hairy on the nerves. Sec. n. 10-13 prs. strong straight. *Petiole* slender ½-¾″. *Stipules* linear ½-¾ as long as the petiole. *Bracts* (unfolded) ovate-cordate acuminate or apiculate puberulous, ½-1¼″, usually about 1⅓″ broad by ⅘″ long, puberulous. *Calyx* hairy and glandular, lower tooth linear nearly as long as flower.

2. **F. bracteata,** *Wight.* Syn. F. strobilifera, Var. bracteata of F.B.I. Sim-busac' *S.*

A shrub 1-3 ft. high with shaggily pubescent angled branches, lanceolate or oblong-lanceolate acuminate leaves 3-7″ by 1-2½″ with sub-cordate base and mostly terminal panicled racemes 2-5″ long of large folded deeply cordate bracts broader than long.

Singbhum, in forests and usually in drier places than the last; Manbhum.

Fls. *Jany.-April.*

L. with very few or no glands beneath. *Petiole* densely pubescent ¼″ only. *Stipules* linear setaceous with a filiform tip ½-1″ much longer than the petiole. *Bracts* (unfolded) very broadly orbicular and deeply cordate pubescent, ¾″ by 1⅓″. *Racemes* usually with a zig-zag rachis. *Fls.* ¼″ pinkish.

The above two species were united in the F.B.I. They were again separated by Col. Prain in "Bengal Plants." The two Chota Nagpur forms appear to differ even more than is indicated in that work which states for *both*: "Axis of racemes zig-zag, bracts hardly broader than long" and proceeds to discriminate them by the number of sec. nerves (which I do not find holds good in my specimen) and as follows: "*strobilifera*:—bracts 1″, finely puberulous, usually all obscurely cuspidate, sometimes the highest slightly emarginate; *bracteata*:—bracts ¾″, softly hirsute with long hairs, usually all slightly emarginate, sometimes the lowest, obscurely cuspidate."

Roots sometimes given for epilepsy, *Camp.*

3. **F. Chappar,** *Ham.* Ulu, *K.*, *S.*

An erect shrub 5-10 ft. with pubescent branches, strongly-nerved orbicular-ovate cordate cuspidate leaves and several axillary racemes of secund 2-seriate large folded bracts enclosing the small cymes of white flowers.

Singbhum forests, often forming a dense undergrowth. Manbhum; Hazaribagh.

Fls. *Jany.-March*, but the bracts are well-developed in *Oct.* Fr. *April-May* when the bracts are brown and dry. It is deciduous in *April*; new leaves appear *May or June.*

Petioles 1¼", thickened both ends. *Bracts* ¾-1" by 1¼-1½" (when unfolded), cordate emarginate. *Fls.* ⅜-½", opening one at a time successively and then becoming visible between the parted margins of the bract, few in an umbel, pedicelled.

4. **F. paniculata,** *Wall.*

A shrub 4-6 ft. high with rusty downy branches, rather large ovate-cordate simple cuspidate membranous leaves and small white or reddish flowers about $\frac{5}{16}$" in short rather dense axillary and terminal panicles or fascicled.

Valleys in Porahat and Saranda, rather rare. Valleys in S. P. (Morjhora). Fls. *Feby.-March.*

L. about 5½" by 3⅓", base sometimes nearly straight and oblique. *Petiole* ¾-1½". *Stipules* caducous. *Racemes* densely hairy sometimes very short solitary and axillary or in the same plant forming terminal panicles 6" long. *Bracts* dry ovate or lanceolate strongly nerved ⅓-¼". *Calyx-teeth* hairy with filiform tips. *Pods* ⅓".

5. **F. stricta,** *Roxb.*

A tall very distinct scarcely shrubby species 6-8 ft. high with large 3-foliolate leaves and dense axillary racemes of purplish flowers, conspicuous in *bud* by their densely imbricating brown linear-lanceolate bracts.

Valley-forests in shade, Singbhum, rare. Ranchi, 1,500-2,000 ft., *Wood.* Fls. *Jany.-Feby.* Shoots annual.

Branches triquetrous. *Lflts.* lanceolate or ell.-acuminate 6-10" long with numerous parallel nerves hairy below. *Petiole* 3-quetrous, sulcate, 5-6." *Stipules* and *lower bracts* 1-3½" acuminate. *Upper bracts* ½" brown deciduous when the flowers expand, finely acuminate. *Fls.* ⅓".

6. **F. congesta,** *Roxb.* Var. semialata. Syn. F. semialata, *Roxb.* *Bir-but, S.*

A shrub 4-6 ft. high somewhat resembling F. stricta, but much more branched and woody with densely pubescent or villous angular branches, 3-fol. leaves with narrowly winged petiole. Fls. purple $\frac{1}{3}''$ in densely bracteate axillary spikes, bracts brown silky, scarcely acuminate caducous.

Valleys in Singbhum, rare. Manbhum *Camp*. Parasnath. Fls. *Oct.-Jany*. Ripe fr., also found in *Dec.*

Petiole $1\frac{1}{2}$-4". *Lflts.* elliptic acuminate 4-$8\frac{1}{2}''$ by $1\frac{1}{2}$-$4\frac{1}{2}''$ with red glands below and very silky on the nerves. Base 3-nerved. *Spikes* 1-3", sessile, or shortly-stalked often fascicled or sub-panicled. *Bracts* $\frac{1}{4}''$. *Calyx* silky. Lower sepal as long as the flower.

7. **F. prostrata,** *Roxb.* Syn. F. congesta, Var., *F.B.I.* Bir-but, *S.*

A diffuse undershrub with a woody rootstock, brown tomentose angular branchlets, 3-foliolate leaves with lanceolate leaflets $4\frac{1}{2}''$ by 1" and fls. in dense sub-spicate axillary racemes about 1" long with sub-persistent brown bracts and very slender silky calyx lobes, the lowest equalling the oblong pod.

Singbhum forests frequent. Manbhum, common in the dry forests of the Gobindpur sub-division. Fls. *Aug.-Oct.* Fr. *Oct.-Dec.*

Petiole 1-2" not winged. *Lflts.* brown hairy or pubescent beneath esp. on the raised nerves. *Stipules* linear-lanceolate $\frac{1}{4}$-$\frac{1}{2}$." *Inflor.* much as in last. *Pod* and lower sepal $\frac{1}{2}$-$\frac{5}{8}''$. Pod pubescent.

The ground root is applied to ulcers and swellings, mainly of the neck. The fruit is eaten, and the pods are said to yield a dye. *Camp.*

8. **F. nana,** *Roxb.*

A dwarf undershrub 1 ft. high with a very short brown tomentose stem springing annually from a woody rootstock, very large (or sometimes small) 3-foliolate leaves with long winged petioles and congested racemes or panicles of small reddish flowers shooting out before the leaves.

Forests in Singbhum, under shade or on fire-lines. Manbhum. Fls. *March-April.* Fr. *April-May.* The leaves do not, however, appear until the rains, and they last until the succeeding *Feby.* The plant leaves a deep orange stain on the hand, esp. in fruit, from the numerous red glands.

Lflts. broadly-elliptic or rhomboid, 5½-6½″ by 3½-5″ (1-2″ only *F.B.I.*) not acuminate, lateral very oblique. *Petiole* sometimes 10″ long. *Petiolules* tomentose ¼″. *Racemes* 3-4″ densely pubescent. *Bracts* caducous. *Corolla* exsert ¼″. Lowest *sepal* ¼″. *Pods* ⅓-½″

3. Rhynchosia, Lour.

Twining herbs or shrubs with pinnately 3-foliolate leaves gland-dotted beneath. Fls. axillary or racemed with often very large sub-equal calyx lobes. Corolla included or exsert. St. 2-adelphous. Ovary 1-2-ovuled. Pod 1-2-seeded.

1. R. rufescens, *D.C.*

A scarcely-woody rusty-pubescent often glandular-hairy climber with slender whip-like branches, rhomboid or ovate scarcely-acuminate leaflets 2½″ by 1½″, long petioles, and innumerable lax few-flowered racemes of smallish yellow flowers, the corolla and the pod included in the large deeply 5-fid calyx.

Nalas in Singbhum, rare. Koderma forest among rocks, common. Fls. *Jany.-Feby.* Fr. *Feby.* Ripe fruit also found *Dec.*

Stems woody below, glandular-pubescent above. *Lflts.* gradually smaller upwards pubescent both sides, base 3-nerved, other nerves raised reticulate, sessile glands microscopic. *Peti.* 2½-3″. *Stipellæ* minute. *Racemes* 1½-2½″ laxly 3-5-fld. *Calyx* ⅓″ in fl., ½″ in fr., segments broad-oblong. *Ovary* silky 1-ovuled. *Pod* sub-quadrate flattened hairy beaked. *Seed* with a large grooved strophiole.

2. R. minima, *D.C.* Var. laxiflora.

A very slender annual climber with glabrescent stems and leaves, rhomboid leaflets 1-2″ long, and lax elongate racemes of small yellow flowers with the corolla twice as long as the calyx.

Lflts. acute or obtuse. *Racemes* 2-4″ long. *Pod* ⅓-⅜″, glabrescent, turgid, mostly 2-seeded.

Chota Nagpur, *Prain*

4. Atylosia, *W. & A.*

Twining herbs or shrubs with leaves *usually* gland-dotted beneath. Fls. yellow or reddish in axillary clusters or racemes. Corolla more or less exsert, keel not rostrate. Ovary sessile ; ovules 3-6 rarely more ; style filiform, glabrous or pubescent not bearded, stigma capitate. Pod linear or oblong, with depressed lines between the seeds, which have a conspicuous 2-fid strophiole.

1. **A. crassa,** *Prain.* Bir rambara, *K.* ; Bir malhan, *S.*

A suffruticose climber with downy stems, gland-dotted strongly-nerved leaves and moderate-sized yellow flowers in pedicelled pairs on short axillary racemes or panicles. Buds varnished. Pod 1-$1\frac{1}{4}$″ by $\frac{5}{8}$″ with oblique depressions between the seeds.

Not unfrequent in the damper Singbhum valleys ; Manbhum ; Ghats between Manbhum and Ranchi ; Sirguja, *Wood.* Fls. *Jany.-Feby.*

Branches striate. Terminal *leaflet* usually rhomboid attaining 4″ by $3\frac{3}{4}$″, sec. nerves 2-3 prs. above the 3-5-nerved base and with strong cross nervules, brown pubescent. *Petiole* 1-4″. *Racemes* usually in panicles shorter than the leaves 1-4″ long with large deciduous concave oblong parallel-nerved bracts $\frac{1}{2}$-$\frac{3}{4}$″ long ; the leaves on long flowering shoots are sometimes suppressed. *Fls.* $\frac{3}{4}$-1″. *Calyx* $\frac{3}{8}$″, teeth 4, $\frac{1}{2}$-$\frac{3}{4}$ths as long as tube, the upper two combined into one obtuse or emarginate. *Standard* and wings auricled. *Ovary* yellow glandular on sides with pubescent margins. *Style* bent at a right angle and pubescent all round above the flection. *Seeds* 3-5.

2. **A. scarabæoides,** *Benth.* Gaisani, *K.* ; Bir horec', *S.*

A copiously branched slender twiner with small strongly-nerved leaflets 1-$1\frac{1}{3}$″ long, smallish yellow or reddish flowers, the corolla not much exceeding the densely grey silky calyx and small oblong hairy pods $\frac{3}{4}$- 1″ long.

On clay soil, very common, esp. in scrub jungle. Throughout the area. Fls., Fr. *Aug.-Dec.*

Terminal leaflet elliptic or obovate-oblong, pubescent, base 3-nerved. *Peduncles* $\frac{1}{4}$-$\frac{3}{4}$″ slender, few-flowered. *Fls.* $\frac{5}{16}$″.

The seeds are said to be eaten. Campbell says that the plant is given to cattle for diarrhœa.

None of my specimens have the leaves glandular, though this character is always given as generic.

Çajanus indicus, Spreng. Arhi, *K.*; Arhar, *H.*; The Pigeon Pea or Dal.

An erect shrub 4-8 ft. high with slender grey silky grooved branches, hairy leaflets 1½-2½" long and yellow flowers ¾" long in axillary racemes or terminal panicles. Pod 2-3", 3-5-seeded with oblique depression between the seeds. Generally cultivated, but not on a large scale.

Teramnus labialis, *Spreng*. A slender climbing shrub with sparsely hairy stem and 3-fol. leaves. *Lflts.* ell. or rhomboid acute 1½-2" appressed hairy beneath. *Fls.* ⅛" reddish in slender racemes 1-4" long. *Pods* linear falcate 1½-2" beaked, twisted when ripe. *Seeds* red oblong.
Palamau, frequent. Parasnath. Fl. *Sept.-Oct.* Fr. *Nov.*

Glycine hispida, *Maxim.* Hende disum Horec', *S.*; Gari-Kalai, *Beng.*, is a sub-erect annual herb distinguished from Teramnus by the alternate anthers being abortive. It is occasionally cultivated

8. Shuteria, *W. & A.*

Climbers with 3-foliolate stipellate leaves and conspicuous persistent bracts and bracteoles. Flowers small or middle-sized racemose. Calyx-tube gibbous; teeth shorter. Standard not spurred exceeding the wings and united keel petals. Pod flat linear usually recurved.

1. S. vestita, *W. & A.* Var. densiflora. Syn. S. densiflora, *Benth.*

A slender twiner with pubescent stems, very slender petioles, membranous leaves and small white and purple flowers in dense axillary fascicled racemes remarkable by their persistent brown striate bracts.

In the damper valleys of Singbhum. Rare. Fl. *Dec.-Feby.* Fr. *Jany.-March.*

Lflts. nearly glabrous 1-2½" attaining rarely 3" by 2", terminal ovate or rhomboid, obtuse or emarginate, apiculate. *Rachis* very slender. *Racemes* ¾-1¾", sessile with hairy rachis. *Pedicels* ⅛" mostly geminate. *Bracteoles* lanceolate striate as long as calyx ⅛-⅙". *Corolla* ⅕" much longer than the wings and keel. *Pod* strap-shaped thin 6-8-seeded.

Prain (Journal, Asiatic Society of Bengal) says that this species is very distinct from S. vestita and that it is easily recognized by its glabrous pods and by the more horizontal, early-forking secondary nerves of its larger leaflets.

Dumasia villosa, *D.C.*

A slender twiner with stems densely clothed with grey or ferruginous hairs.

Fls. racemed, 3″ long. Calyx with obliquely truncate mouth. *Corolla* $\frac{1}{2}$-$\frac{3}{4}$″ yellow or purplish. *Pod* $1\frac{1}{2}$″ velvety, 3-4-seeded.

Only reported from Parasnath.

10. Canavalia, *D.C.*

Stout twining herbs with stipellate 3-foliolate leaves and showy flowers fascicled on a nodose rachis. Calyx 2-lipped. Wings shorter than the large rounded standard, equalling the incurved obtuse keel. Pod large with a distinct rib on either side of the upper suture.

1. C. ensiformis, *D.C.* Tihon, *S.*; Makhan sim, *Beng.*

Wide-rambling and twining. *Lflts.* glabrous or with few adpressed hairs above, 4-6″ ovate acute. Peduncles and racemes each 3-6″ or peduncle attaining 12″ and raceme few-flowered. *Fls.* geminate $1\frac{1}{4}$″. Pedicels very short. *Calyx* $\frac{1}{2}$″ with short teeth of which 2 upper larger projecting rounded and 3 lower acute. Standard 1″ broad red-purple retuse, strongly reflexed, claw 0, base auricled. Wings waved auricled. *Pod* 6-9″ by 1-$1\frac{1}{4}$″.

Cultivated and often apparently wild. Fls. *Aug.-Oct.* Fr. *Sept.-Nov.* The pods are used as vegetables.

2. C. virosa, *W. & A.* (Syn. C. ensiformis var. virosa).

This is regarded by Baker merely as the wild form of the last, but is kept distinct by Prain who distinguishes it by the leaflets being obovate and by the pod being narrower, only $\frac{1}{2}$-$\frac{3}{4}$″ wide and fewer-seeded, seeds 4-6 instead of 8-12.

Chota Nagpur, *Prain* (in Wood's list).

11. Pueraria, *D.C.*

Twining shrubs or herbs with stipellate 3-fol. leaves and often showy flowers fascicled on the swollen nodes of long often panicled racemes. Two upper teeth of calyx connate. Standard as long as the obtuse wings and keel. Pod linear, flattish (usually under ½" broad).

1. **P. tuberosa**, *D.C.* Jan tirra, *S.*; Shimia batraji, *Beng.*; Tirra, *H.*

A handsome large woody climber, flowering when leafless, with simple or branched fascicled racemes of blue-purple flowers ⅝" long.[1] Standard, wings and keel ½" spurred or auricled. St. diadelphous (always?).[2] Pod 2-3" bristly (or young densely brown hirsute), somewhat depressed between the seeds.

Chiefly on the banks of streams. Tandi forest, common, *Campbell*; Palamau, *Gamble*; Jaspur, *Wood*; Parasnath. Fls. *Feby.-April.* Fr. *r.s.*

Branches downy. *Lflts.* roundish 6-12", whitish with adpressed hairs beneath. Racemes 6-10" long. *Fls.* dense geminate or in threes, 2-bracteolate beneath the calyx. Node often with an abortive tip. *Calyx* brown silky $\frac{5}{16}$-⅜", limb spreading. Standard emarginate clawed. *Ovary* silky. Style glabrous. *Ovules* about 10.

The tuberous root is eaten. It sometimes attains an enormous size. Campbell mentions one from the Gobindpur district nearly 2 feet long and 2¼ ft. in circumference. He also states that it is used in renal complaints and to kill fish.

12. Mucuna, Adans.

Large twiners. L. usually stipellate. Stipules deciduous. Flowers large rather leathery, black when dry, on the tumid nodes of long often fascicled racemes. Calyx widely campanulate, two upper teeth connate, lowest longest. Standard much shorter than the wings and long rostrate keel. Anthers dimorphous. Ovary sessile hairy. Pod leathery or woody, usually covered with irritating bristles. Prain is inclined to reconstitute the following sub-genera as genera :—

Subgen. 1. Zoophthalmum, *P. Br.* Perennial climbers. Seeds large flat with a circumferential hilum.

Pods winged and plaited . . . . . 1. *imbricata.*

---

[1] Measured from tip of standard to keel.

[2] They are usually described as monadelphous.

Subgen. 2. Stizolobium, *P. Br.* Stems dying down annually. Seeds small ovoid with a small lateral hilum.

A. L. silky beneath.
  Pod grey with deciduous bristles. Fls. purple 2. *pruriens.*
  Pod black with velvety persistent tomentum. Fls. purple . . . . 2*a*. *utilis.*

B. L. glabrescent beneath.
  Pod as in 2*a*. Fls. white. L. glabrescent beneath . . . . 2*b*. *nivea.*
  Pod shortly velvety, glabrescent . . . . 2*c*. *capitata.*

1. **M. imbricata,** *D.C.* Marang atkir, *K.*; Itikar or Etka, *S.*

A large climber with slender sparsely hairy branches, 3-foliolate stipellate leaves sparsely shortly yellow-hairy beneath, dull purple flowers in pendulous few-flowered lax racemes about 6-12″ long, and pods 5″ by 2″, easily recognized by the two wings on each suture and the obliquely plaited faces of the pods.

Ravines in Singbhum, *e.g.*, those north of Longa Buru in Porahat. Rare. Parasnath. Santal Parganahs (Narganj). Fls. *r.s* Fr. *Decr.-Feby.* Pods remain long on the plant and were found on Parasnath in *May.*

Rachis of leaves exceedingly slender 3-5″ long including the petiole. *Petiolules* stouter $\frac{1}{4}$″. *Lflts.* membranous, the end one 4-6″ ell.-lanc. all cuspidate. *Pod* oblong, the plaits with ferruginous bristles. Style persistent as a hard slender beak.

2. **M. pruriens,** *D.C.* Alkusi, Atkir, *K.*; Etka, *S.*; Kivach, *H.*, whence the English name of Cowhage.

A slender climber with stipellate 3-foliolate leaves silky beneath, drooping short peduncled racemes 6-12″ long of purple flowers $1\frac{1}{4}$-$1\frac{1}{2}$″ long. Pod turgid, not plaited, 2-3″, densely clothed with brown or grey intensely irritating bristles.

Chiefly in scrub and grass jungles, frequent. Fls. *Sept.-Nov.* Fr. *Jan.-Feby.*

Branches with few appressed hairs. *Lflts.* membranous, apiculate, terminal rhomboid 3-5″ by $2\frac{1}{2}$-3″, lateral larger with lower side very produced and rounded, *Petioles* often 10". *Racemes* usually elongate. *Pod* curved at the ends.

Various medicinal virtues are ascribed to the plant, some probably imaginary. Campbell states that the root is given for delirium in fever and that a paste made from the powdered root is applied for dropsy. The hairs of the pods are anthelmintic and were at one time included in the British Pharmacopœia. Both the root and seeds are included in the Hindu Materia Medica. An intoxicating liquor "Khasuna" is said to be prepared from the plant in Palamau.

The following appear to me to be only varieties of M. pruriens:—

α. **M. utilis,** *Wall.* Alkushi, *Beng.* A cultivated variety with a black velvety pod which (like M. pruriens) is eaten as a vegetable when young. "In badly grown plants the racemes are often short and few-flowered, sometimes only 1-2-fld." *Prain.* Chota Nagpur, *Prain.*

β. **M. nivea,** *D.C.* Khamach, *Beng.* Cultivated in Ch. Nagpur, *Wood.* Fls. white.

γ. **M. capitata,** *W. & A.* The flowers are usually in short-peduncled few-flowered corymbs and the pod is 5-6" long, with the bristles much shorter than in M. pruriens. The leaves also are glabrescent. Prain ("Some additional Leguminosæ") says:—"The racemes of this are not always short, nor are the racemes of M. pruriens always elongate; the species are only distinguishable by their pods." Ch. Nagpur, *Prain.*

13. Erythrina, L.

Trees or (resupinata) undershrubs with large showy scarlet flowers in dense racemes, usually produced before the large 3-fol. stipellate leaves. Calyx spathaceous, campanulate or turbinate, oblique or 2-lipped, when spathaceous spliting to the level of the thickened disc. Petals very unequal, standard usually narrow and far exceeding the other petals Upper st. nearly free or connate half-way up. Ovary stipitate many-ovuled. Pod linear more or less torulose, stipitate, dehiscent.

1. **E. suberosa,** *Roxb.* Piri, *K.*; Buru Marar, *S.*; Pharar, *Kharw.*

A small very prickly tree with thick corky bark, leaves covered with white-brown tomentum beneath, and scarlet flowers in capitate racemes.

Dry hills, common in Singbhum; Tundi Hills (Manbhum); Hazaribagh (Sitagarh hill, etc.); Damuda Ghats (between Hazaribagh and Ranchi). Fls. *March-May.* Fr. *r.s.* Leafless up to *June.*

Innovations brown-tomentose. Trunk, branches and sometimes petioles prickly. *Prickles* usually straw-coloured. Terminal *leaflet* 6-8″ broad, broader than long, lobed and sinuate with truncate or cuneate, but not rounded base. *Petiole* 6-7″ tomentose. *Racemes* capitate only 1½-3″ long (excluding the peduncle). *Calyx* turbinate 2-lipped. *Standard* 3-4-times as long as broad and twice the keel. *Upper st.* nearly free. *Pod* 4-6″.

Bark gives a fibre, and see note under E. indica.

2. **E. indica,** *Lamk.* Marar, *S.*; Pharar, *Kharw.*; Hadhad, *Ghatw.*; Palita Mandar, *Beng.*

A prickly tree with the prickles small and black. L. glabrous beneath, the base of the terminal leaflet rounded. Racemes much longer than in the last, often 6″ excluding the peduncle. Calyx split spathaceous with very oblique mouth. Pod torulose stalked.

Ranchi, planted, *Wood*; Palamau, *Haslett*; Pokhuria and Tundi hills, *Campbell.*

Campbell says "common on the lower slopes of the Tundi hills. The bark yields an excellent cordage fibre of a pale straw colour. The wood, ash and the bark are used as dyes; the latter and the leaves are also used medicinally." Part of this may, however, refer to the last species, which is not given separately in Campbell and Watt's list.

3. **E. resupinata,** *Roxb.*

An interesting undershrub with a perennial rootstock which sends up annually racemes of bright scarlet flowers without any leaves, the herbaceous shoots succeeding them.

Parasnath. *C. B. Clarke.* Fls. *April-May.*

14. Phaseolus, L. (French and Kidney Bean).

Twining or sub-erect herbs with stipellate leaflets, small or mod.-sized flowers on the tumid nodes of axillary racemes. Corolla much longer than the campanulate calyx, characterized by the keel being long and spirally twisted, and enclosing the filiform style. Stigma very oblique. Pod usually linear, more or less septate.

1. P. calcaratus, *Roxb.* Sutri, *S.*, *H.*

A slender twiner with that part of the stem bearing the racemes often leafless, stems and petioles with reflexed brown hairs. Small yellow flowers in very short often long-peduncled racemes. Pod $1\frac{3}{4}$ by $\frac{1}{8}''$, puberulous.

Wild (or an escape) in Sal forests in Singbhum (*e.g.*, between Nakti and Tebu), Santal P., *Wood*, (wild or cult.?). Fls. *Aug.-Sept.* Fr. *Sept.-Oct.*

Lflts. softly hairy both sides, broad-ovate or rhomboid acuminate, or upper narrow-oblong, usually more or less lobed, base straight or obtuse, larger 4 by 3″. *Stipules* oblong $\frac{1}{2}''$, base produced rounded. *Peduncles* 2-4″. *Racemes* $\frac{1}{4}''$ elongating to 1″. *Fls.* $\frac{3}{8}''$ broad. *Bracteoles* setaceous. *Pod* 9-12-seeded.

2. P. aconitifolius, *Jacq.* Mung, *K.*; Bir-moch (The wild form) *S.*; Moth, *H.*

Procumbent with long spreading hairs. Easily recognized by its leaflets being deeply cut into 3-5 linear or linear-oblong segments $1\frac{1}{2}$-3″ long, hairy. *Stipules* $\frac{3}{8}''$ lanceolate acuminate, attached above the base. Stipellæ setaceous. Lower *petioles* 4-5″. *Peduncles* 3-$3\frac{1}{2}''$. *Racemes* 3-6-fld. *Bracts* setaceous $\frac{3}{16}''$. *Calyx* minute, tube $\frac{1}{16}''$, teeth 5 equal about half as long. *St.* $\frac{1}{4}''$ broad. *Pods* about 8-seeded.

Wild in dry situations in Manbhum, *Camp.*; Santal P., *Wood*, wild? Often cultivated on a small scale in the other districts.

3. P. trilobus, *Ait.* Mugani, *Beng.*

Very similar to the last but stems nearly glabrous, the central lobes of the 3-lobed leaves spathulate instead of linear-oblong and stipules oblong. Said to be wild in all the provinces of Bengal, *Prain.*

4. P. sublobatus, *Roxb.* Syn. P. trinervius, *F.B.I.* Ghora mung, *Beng.*

A climber similar to P. calcaratus, but pods, like the stems, densely beset with rusty hairs, slightly compressed, septate. Racemes subcapitate.

Ch. Nagpur, *Prain* ("Bengal Plants").

Several species of this genus are cultivated as field and garden crops :—

5. **P. Mungo,** *L.* Var. Roxburghii, *Prain* (P. radiatus, *Roxb.*) Ramra, *K.*; Bir san, *S.*; Urid, *H.*; Mash-kalai, *Beng. Not* Mung, *Beng.*

6. **P. radiatus,** *L.* (P. Mungo, *Roxb.*) Mugi, *K.*; Mung, *Beng.* The Green Gram.

P. vulgaris is the French or Haricot Bean and **P. multiflorus** the Scarlet Runner.

For an elucidation of the synonomy of the Phaseoli *vide* Prain, Journal of the Asiatic Society, LXVI, II, 2.

15. Vigna, Savi.

Habit and characters of Phaseolus, but the keel not spiral (except in V. vexillata which is intermediate). Ovary many-ovuled. Style long, filiform, bearded along the inner face below the oblique stigma as in Phaseolus.

1. **V. vexillata,** *Benth.* Bir ghangra, *S.*

A slender twiner with tuberous roots, scabrid stems, narrow leaflets, and large flat pale purple flowers in few-fld. capitate racemes on very long peduncles.

Especially the higher Porahat forests in Singbhum; Manbhum, *Camp.* Fls. *July-Oct.*

Lflts. lanceolate $6\frac{1}{2}''$ by $1\frac{3}{4}''$ often flushed with white near the mid-rib, minutely scabridly hairy above and on nerves beneath, base rounded. *Petiole* 2-3″. *Peduncle* 6-9″. *Racemes* 2-4-fld. *Fls.* $1\frac{1}{4}''$ diam. keel nearly spiral. *Pods* narrowly linear straight 4″ by $\frac{3}{16}''$ with short brown hairs, 20-more seeded.

The roots are eaten as well as the beans.

2. **V. Catjang,** *Endl.* Galjaramba, *Ho.*; Rambara, *M.*; Ghangra, *S.*; Barbati, *Beng.*

An erect herb with long trailing branches 2-3 ft., or a climber (var. sinensis, *Prain*). Terminal leaflet rhomboid or sub-hastate acute with obtuse base. Fls. 1″ geminate on the swollen nodes of few-fld. axillary racemes, usually pale yellow tinged with purple or pale blue and white (in the var.) Pod long linear 8-12″ and 15-seeded or (in the twiner), 1-2 ft. and 23-seeded, with intervals between the seeds.

Commonly cultivated. Fls., Fr. *Aug.-Nov.*

Nearly glabrous.– *Terminal leaflet* $2\frac{1}{2}$″ by $1\frac{1}{2}$″ to 5″ by $3\frac{1}{4}$″. *Rachis* $\frac{3}{4}$-$1\frac{1}{4}$″, and petiole 3-5″ chanelled or sub-alate. *Stipules* $\frac{1}{2}$-$\frac{2}{3}$″, rarely only $\frac{1}{3}$″, oblong acuminate with a lanceolate often curved auricle. *Peduncles* exceeding the petioles. *Standard* sub-orbicular, with 2 ridges and 2 small callosities above the claw (? absent in the erect form). Stigma sub-capitate in the twiner, very oblique in the erect form.

16. Dolichos, L.

Sub-erect or twining herbs with minute sub-persistent bracts bracteoles and stipules. Fls. several axillary, or racemose with sharply bent obtuse or rostrate keel. Ovary many-ovuled. Styles bearded down the inner face (D. Lablab) or round the terminal stigma (D. biflorus). Pod flat recurved.

1. **D. Lablab,** *L.* Sim, Sirmi, *K.*; *H.*; Malhan, malal, *S.*, *M.*; Shim, *Beng.*

A twiner with rather stout puberulous branches and red-purple flowers $\frac{3}{4}$″ long in terminal racemes 3-6″ long on long peduncles. Pod $1\frac{1}{2}$-$2\frac{1}{2}$″, often only slightly recurved, wider upwards and tipped with the style, frequently white with the margins slightly crisped.

Very commonly cultivated by the Kols and Santals on sticks or bushes near their houses. Fls. *Oct.-Dec.* Fr. *Nov.-Jany.* Perennial, but cultivated as an annual. One variety is sub-erect.

Lflts. slightly pubescent esp. on the nerves, terminal 2-3″ long and broad, broadly ovate or deltoid, shortly finely acuminate, base 5-nerved. *Peti.* 3″. *Brctls.* closely adpressed to calyx $\frac{1}{16}$″. *Calyx* $\frac{1}{4}$″. *Seeds* 2-4.

2. **D. biflorus,** *L.* Hore, *M.*; Hoe: *Ho.*; Horec, *S.*; Kurti, Kulti, *H.* The Horse Gram.

Erect with twining branches, pubescent or hairy all over. Fls. 3-4 together, axillary on a very short peduncle, yellow.

One of the commonest field crops in Singhbum and general throughout Chota Nagpur. Fls. *Oct.-Nov.* Fr. *Nov.-Dec.*

Lflts. 2″ by 1″ or smaller, ovate-oblong acute. *Stipules* $\frac{1}{3}$″ lanceolate.

Standard $\frac{3}{5}$ by $\frac{3}{10}$″. *Keel* oblong falcate. *Pod* $1\frac{1}{2}$-2″, hairy, falcate, 4-6 seeded.

Eaten by the natives but said to be inferior, chiefly grown as a cattle and horse food.

17. Butea, Roxb.

Trees or climbing shrubs with large 3-foliolate stipellate leaves and large showy red flowers fascicled in axillary or terminal racemes or panicles. Calyx broadly campanulate with short teeth. Petals nearly equal. Standard recurved. Keel much curved. St. diadelphous. Ovary 2-ovuled. Pod coriaceous splitting round the single apical seed.

1. **B. frondosa,** *Roxb.* Morud, *K.*; Murup', *S.*; Paras, *Beng.*, *Kharw.*; Dhak, *H.*

A small or mod.-sized tree with crooked trunk and black nodose branchlets, with handsome flowers which are produced in great profusion on the thickened nodes of the branches; and are $1\frac{1}{2}$-2″ long.

One of the commonest trees in Chota Nagpur and often gregarious in cultivated and waste lands, especially in Hazaribagh and Palamau. Fls. *Feby.-April.* Fr. *May-June.* Dec. *Feby.-May.*

Young shoots tomentose. *Lflts.* 4-8″ strongly veined and silky beneath with a peculiar greyish hue when seen from a distance. *Pedicels* and *calyx* brown-velvety. *Pods* 4-7″ by $1\frac{1}{2}$-2″.

On blazing the tree a red juice issues which hardens into a red astringent gum used in diarrhœa. The seeds are anthelmintic. The leaves are used as fodder and for manure. The bark of the roots gives a fibre for ropes, and the flowers a dye. Lac is sometimes cultivated on it.

2. **B. superba,** *Roxb.* Morud, *K.*; Nari-murup', *S.*; Dorang, *Kharw.*

A large woody climber with very large leaflets and the branches crowded when leafless with gorgeous orange-scarlet flowers 2-2½" long.

Common in the dry forests of Singbhum, and Manbhum. Common on the Damuda Ghats and in the Urunga River valley (Palamau). Hazaribagh. Probably throughout Chota Nagpur. Fls. *March-April.* Fr. *June-July.* Deciduous *Feb.-May.*

The leaves are sometimes confused with those of Spatholobus, but the leaflets are very much larger usually 12-18" and attain sometimes 20" in young plants, subrugose and dull above and more strongly nerved beneath with the nervules raised and distinctly pubescent while the areoles are nearly glabrous. *Racemes* 12" long. *Pedicels* 3-times as long as calyx. *Pod* like that of B. frondosa.

The economic properties are very similar to those of B. frondosa.

Roxburgh remarks that "the colours are so exceedingly vivid that my best painter has not been able, with his utmost skill, to imitate their brightness. When in flower, I do not think the vegetable world offers a more gaudy show."

18. Spatholobus, Hassk.

Large woody climbers, twining (at least in S. Roxburghii) *from right to left.* Stipules small, lflts. stipellate. Fls. small fascicled at the nodes of panicled racemes, nodes tumid or only slightly so. Calyx campanulate. Corolla exsert, petals sub-equal or standard largest. Keel nearly straight, obtuse. St. 2-adelphous. Ovules 2. Pod like that of Butea.

1. **S. Roxburghii,** *Benth.* Bandu, Bandan, *K.*; Cihut, *S.* The fruit 'Bando'; Bendo in Jaspur, *Wood;* Bibri, *Kharw.*; Maula, *H.* (The Kol name *Moru* sometimes quoted arises from confusion with Butea).

Trunk attaining 2-3 ft. girth, bark smooth. Wood with deep-red concentric bast bands. Lflts. 4-9" by 3-6½", obtuse or shortly acuminate cuspidate shining above strongly-nerved (but tertiaries not very prominent), minutely silky beneath. Fls. cream-cold., $\frac{5}{16}$" long 2-3 together on the nodes of the dense racemes. Pods 3-4″ by $\frac{3}{4}$-1$\frac{3}{4}$″, brown velvety, stipitate.

Common, especially in the Sal forests in the valleys. Fls. *Aug.-Dec.* Fr. *Decr.-Jany.*

The seeds give an oil used for cooking and for anointing. The bark gives a fibre. The red gum resembles that of Butea. Lac is sometimes collected from both it and the Butea.

Clitoria ternatea, *L.* The Mussel-shell creeper.

A very pretty slender climber with large blue flowers 1$\frac{1}{2}$-2″. Usually near houses, not indigenous.

Cicer arietinum, *L.* Moraijam, *K.*; Bhut, *S.*, *H.*; Chana. *Beng.* The Gram, Chick-pea. A pretty much branched viscous herb 6-9″ high. The rachis with pinnate leaves 1-2″ long, toothed leaflets and single axillary bluish-purple flowers $\frac{3}{8}$-$\frac{1}{2}$″. Pod oblong $\frac{3}{4}$-1″, 2-seeded.

A common cold-weather crop. Fls., *Jany.-Feby.*

Horses are largely fed on it as well as sheep.

Lens esculenta, *Moench.* (Cicer Lens, Ervum Lens, *L.*) Masur, Masut, Masuri-dal, *H.* The Lentil. Has a somewhat similar habit, 1-2 ft. high. The rachis of the leaves ends in a bristle or small tendril, as also does the short axillary peduncle which bears about two small white or pale-blue flowers. Lflts. pubescent narrow. Pod 2-seeded. Fls. *Jany.-March.* Occasionally cultivated.

Lathyrus sativus, *L.* Kansari, *K.*, *H.* is a very pretty little plant with winged stems, L. with 2 linear lflts. and a tendril, and solitary bright blue flowers $\frac{3}{4}$″. Cultivated on a small scale and apparently wild. The dal if eaten largely produces paralysis both in cattle and human beings.

Lathyrus Aphaca, *L.* is a small herb very interesting morphologically from the entire reduction of the leaves to tendrils, and the large development of its stipules which assume the leaf functions. Fls. yellow. Not uncommon in fields.

Pisum arvense, *L.* Batura, *K.*; Batui, *Ho.*; Mata, *H.* The Field Pea is often cultivated. Fls. *March.*

24. Abrus, L.

Shrubby or suffruticose twiners with pari-pinnate leaves, numerous lflts. and rachis ending in a point. Fls. small pedicelled fascicled on the swollen nodes of axillary racemes or short axillary branchlets. Calyx campanulate with very short teeth. Standard ovate short clawed slightly adnate to the staminal tube. Stamens 9 tube slit above. Ovary sub-sessile, ovules several. Pod flat or turgid.

1. **A. precatorius,** *L.* Kawet, *S.;* Karjain, *Kharw.;* Rati (The seeds) *H.;* Karjani, *Oraon?, M.;* Indian Liquorice, Crabs-eyes (The seeds).

An elegent twining slender shrub with leaves 2-3½" long of 10-20 pairs of leaflets ½-⅝" by ⅙-⅕", small reddish or white flowers ⅓" in crowded racemes 1-3" long. Pods about 1½" long turgid. Seeds polished round scarlet or white with a black eye.

Hedges and waste ground on bushes, in all the districts, frequent. Fls. *Sept.-Oct.* Fr. *Nov.-Dec.* Ripe seed also found in *May*. Deciduous.

Very pretty in ripe fruit when the pods open and disclose the scarlet seeds. The seeds contain a powerful poisonous alkaloid and are said to be used for poisoning cattle by hypodermic injection. They are used for nervous affections and externally in skin diseases, alopecia, etc.

25. Pongamia, Vent.

A tree with impari-pinnate leaves and opposite exstipulate lflts. Fls. pink in fascicles on the rachis of axillary racemes. Calyx campanulate, nearly truncate. Cor. exserted. Keel obtuse with petals cohering at tip. St. monadelphous, or upper fil. free at the base. Ovary sub-sessile 2-ovuled. Pod flattened woody, indehiscent, oblong with a short curved point.

1. **P. glabra,** *Vent.* Karanj, *K.;* Kuruinj, *S.*

A small or mod.-sized tree with leaves 8-14" long with 5-7 shining leaflets 3-8" long and lilac flowers ½", 2-4-nate with pedicels ½-⅝" in fruit. Calyx brown. Pod 1-seeded 1½-2" long.

Frequently self-sown and apparently wild along nalas in Singbhum. Seldom, if ever, found wild in Manbhum, *Camp.* Very commonly planted throughout Chota Nagpur. Fls. *May-June.* Fr. *Dec.-Jany.* Dec. *May* and renews leaves at the end of the same month.

The pods are very largely collected by the natives for the valuable oil which is largely used for skin diseases and for burning.

A wonderful tree for adapting itself to diverse conditions, growing well with its roots in salt water, or fresh water, or exposed to the hot dry winds of Chota Nagpur on road embankments.

26. Pterocarpus, L.

Large trees. L. with alt. exstipellate lflts. Fls. yellow in copious panicled racemes. Calyx turbinate curved in bud, teeth short. Corolla exserted. Petals crisped, keel obtuse, petals not or slightly connate. St. 10, monadelphous, or 9+1 or 5+5. Ovary stipitate 2-ovuled. Pod flat orbicular, winged all round, seed 1 rarely 2.

1. **P. Marsupium,** *Roxb.* Hid, *K.;* Murga, *S.;* Bia, *Kharw.;* Bija-sal, Paisar, *H.*

A large or mod.-sized tree with 5-7 close parallel-veined lflts. and terminal and axillary crisped yellow flowers.

Valleys and north aspects near valleys. Singbhum, frequent Manbhum; Hazaribagh; Ranchi; Palamau; S. P. (Gumra Protected Forest). Fls. *Oct.* Fr. *Dec.-Feby.* Evergeen or nearly so, the leaves are renewed *May-June.*

Lflts. oblong obtuse both ends, or apex retuse, 3-5" long, glaucous beneath. *Racemes* dense flowered in panicles 6-10" long and broad. *Calyx* brown-green, longer than, and articulate with, the pedicel. *Corolla* twice the calyx, $\frac{1}{2}$". Staminal-sheath 2-fid. *Pod* 1-1$\frac{3}{4}$" diam.

A red juice exudes on blazing the tree similar to that of Butea. It soon hardens and forms the Gum Kino of European medicine, an astringent, valuable in diarrhœa. The leaves are a good fodder.

Var. **acuminata,** *Prain.* Lflts. ovate acute or acuminate. Pods much larger than in the type. Rajmehal hills, *Prain.*

The best tree for planking in Ch. Nagpur and deserves to be largely planted as the supply is very limited.

27. Dalbergia, L. f.

Trees or shrubs, sometimes scandent. L. with alt. exstipellate leaflets. Fls. small in axillary or terminal panicles.

Corolla usually only shortly exserted. Wings oblong as long as the broad standard, keel obtuse, petals joined at the tip. St. 9-10, monadelphous or diadelphous 9+1 or 5+5 Ovary stipitate few-ovuled.. Style short, stigma capitate Pod flat, usually oblong, thin and veined opp. to the seeds, indehiscent, seeds 1-4.

Root-suckers are very common in this genus. The pods usually remain long on the tree, and the seeds germinate within it after it has become softened by the first monsoon rains, the radicle penetrating the pericarp close to the suture.

Trees. St. 9, sheath split along the top. Lflts. large roundish.

Lflts. 3-5 cuspidate. Corolla yellowish . . . 1. *Sissoo.*

Lflts. 5-7 orbicular obtuse or emarginate. Fls. white . . . . . . 2. *latifolia.*

Trees. St. diadelphous, 5+5.

Fls. pedicelled. Corolla pale-pink. Upper calyx-lobes obtuse . . . . . 3. *lanceolaria.*

Fls. sub-sessile. Corolla bluish-white. All calyx-lobes acute . . . . . . 4. *paniculata.*

Climbing shrubs.

St. 5+5. Lflts. 1" and more long . . . 5. *volubilis.*

St. 9+1. Lflts. ½-1" long . . . . . 6. *tamarindifolia.*

1. D. Sissoo, *Roxb.* Shisham, *H.* The Sissu.

Lflts. usually 5, broadly ell., ovate or obovate or orbicular cuspidate, 1-3". Panicles dense, densely pubescent, 2-3" long. Cor. yellowish, twice the calyx or less. Pod strap-shaped stipitate with cuneate base 1-3", 1-3 rarely 4-seeded.

This well-known tree is not native in Ch. Nagpur, and is never seen to great advantage there, though commonly planted. Miserable specimens put into heavy clay, a soil entirely unsuited to it, are often seen along road-sides. Fls. with the new leaves in *March-April.* The pods ripen in next cold weather and usually remain on the tree until the flowering season. Seeds germinate *June-July.*

2. D. latifolia, *Roxb.* Kiri, *K.*; Mahle, Satsayar, *S.*; Sitsal, *H.*; Blackwood, Rosewood.

A small tree. Lflts. sub-orbicular with round or emarginate tip, 1-4", glabrous. Fls. pure white in very numerous lax axillary and terminal panicles 2-4" long. Pod relatively broader than in Sissu 1-3-rarely 4-seeded.

Not uncommon as a small tree. esp. on cool aspects and along streams, but it has been largely cut out in Singbhum. A large tree, common in the Tundi forests, *Campbell*; Hazaribagh (Topchanchi, Sitagarah hill); Palamau (Kuru-Chandwar, etc.); S. P. scarce.

Fls. *Sept.*, when the tree is in full leaf, often from the old leaf scars. Fr. *Jany.-Feb.* A valuable wood.

Lflts. usually very unequal on the same rachis. Petiolules $\frac{1}{3}$-$\frac{1}{2}$". Pedicels $\frac{1}{8}$"-$\frac{1}{5}$". Calyx white $\frac{1}{8}$-$\frac{1}{4}$". Corolla twice as long. Pods $1\frac{1}{2}$-3" by $\frac{3}{8}$"-$\frac{3}{4}$" stipitate.

3. D. lanceolaria, *L.* Koiad, Kiachalom, *K.*; Chapot Siris, *S.*; Hardi, *Kharw.*

A mod.-sized tree somewhat resembling a 'Siris', but leaves simply pinnate reaching 1 ft. with 9-12 (or on the smaller leaves fewer) oblong, ell. or obovate-oblong lflts. Fls. white or tinged with pink with a purple calyx on unilateral racemes arranged in axillary fulvous-pubescent panicles 2-4" long. Pod 2-4" by $\frac{1}{2}$-$\frac{3}{4}$", 1-3-seeded narrowed both ends and often sinuate between the seeds.

Valleys in Singbhum and Gangpur, usually near water. Manbhum and Hazaribagh, frequent on the hills. Ranchi, esp. on ghats. Palamau. S. P. (Silingi, *Gamble*). Fls. *April-May* with the new leaves. Fr. *Sept.-Jany* Nearly evergreen.

Innovations yellow-silky. *Stipules* linear-oblong caducous. *Lflts.* reaching $2\frac{1}{2}$" by $1\frac{1}{2}$" emarginate with few short scattered hairs both sides, base obtuse rarely acute. Sec. n. numerous oblique, reticulate between. *Fls.* $\frac{1}{3}$" articulate. *Calyx* $\frac{3}{16}$". *Stalk* of *pod* $\frac{1}{3}$-$\frac{1}{2}$".

A young forest of suckers springs up around this tree subsequent to the trampling of the surface roots by cattle.

There are two forms:—α. *Panicles* and *racemes* lax. *Fls.* nearly $\frac{1}{3}$" *Calyx* hairy with the anterior-lobe about $\frac{1}{2}$-$\frac{3}{4}$th length of tube.

β. *Racemes* very dense in very numerous close panicles. *Fls.* $\frac{5}{16}$"-$\frac{3}{8}$". *Calyx* densely hairy with the anterior lobe as long as tube. S. P.

4. D. paniculata, *Roxb.*

The only record of this from Ch. Nagpur, or indeed from Bengal, is by Gamble in a list at the end of a Forest Report (1885). It is so like D.

lanceolaria in leaf that it is quite possible that a mistake was made in identification; on the other hand it is possible that it has been mistaken for *lanceolaria* by other observers. In addition to the characters given in the key, it is easily recognized by the bands of phloëm in the wood (*vide* Brandis in Indian Trees). Gamble (Ind. Timbers) states that it is easily recognized by its tall grey stem.

5. D. volubilis, *Roxb.* Nari Siris, *K.*, *S.*

A sarmentose and scandent shrub with long green branches, 7-13-foliolate leaves and pale-purple flowers in ample terminal panicles.

Valleys Singbhum, Gangpur, Manbhum, S. P. Fls. *Feby.* Fr. *May-June.*

L. 3-10″ long. *Lflts.* oblong attaining $3\frac{1}{4}$″ by $1\frac{1}{2}$″ but usually only $\frac{3}{4}$-$1\frac{1}{4}$″ on flowering branches, obtuse or retuse, apiculate, nearly glabrous. *Panicles* rusty pubescent or tomentose up to 20″ long, lateral branches 3-5″. *Fls.* $\frac{1}{4}$-$\frac{1}{3}$″ pedicelled, dense. *Pods* oblong 2-$3\frac{1}{2}$″ by $\frac{5}{8}$-$\frac{3}{4}$″, stipitate, tip rounded. *Seeds* 1-2, ellipsoid slightly reniform $\frac{5}{16}$″.

6. D. tamarindifolia, *Roxb.*

A large shrub scrambling or climbing by means of its recurved peduncles, with the branchlets and leaf-rachis fulvous pubescent. L. 4-7″ with 12-20 prs. of oblong leaflets $\frac{5}{8}$-1″ long. Fls. white in brown-pubescent panicles. Pod $1\frac{1}{2}$-3″, 1-3-seeded, linear-oblong.

Ravines in the northern Santal Parganahs (north of Banjhi). Fls. *March-April.* Fr. *April-May.*

Lflts. sub-sessile oblong with oblique base somewhat gibbous on the upper side, appressed fulvous-hairy beneath, apex rounded or retuse. *Fls.* in congested sessile axillary panicles with corymbose branches (*F.B.I.*), or in lateral short ovate dense racemes (*Roxb.*). The old inflorescences in the S. P. appear to have been large and terminal, probably due to the falling of the upper leaves.

28. Derris, Lour.

Derris is very closely allied to Millettia, the habit is identical, and except for the greater adhesion of the wing and keel the flowers are similar. The pod differs by always being winged either on one or both sutures and is usually thin. The pod is always indehiscent.

Lflts. lanceolate 1-3″. Pod $\frac{1}{2}$″ or less broad . . . 1. *scandens.*

Lflts. oblanceolate $1\frac{1}{2}$-$7\frac{1}{2}$″. Pod over $\frac{1}{2}$″ broad . . . 2. *cuneifolia.*

1. D. scandens, *Benth.*

A very large evergreen climber with leaves 3-6″ long, 3-6 prs. of lanc. or ell. lanceolate lflts. 1-3″ long and rose cold, fls. with slender pedicels fascicled on the nodes of slender axillary racemes 6-10″, *i.e.*, much longer than the leaves.

Pods narrow 1-3″ by $\frac{1}{3}$-$\frac{1}{2}$″ winged along the upper suture, 1-4-seeded.

Prain states that this is found in all the Bengal provinces, but I have no record of it from Ch. Nagpur. It occurs, however, in Bankura. Fls. *July*. Fr. c. s.

2. D. cuneifolia, *Benth.*

A large woody climber with tubercled branches. Leaf-rachis 3-10″ long, thick at base. Lflts. 4-5 rarely 3 prs., oblanceolate, oblong-obovate or narrow-ell. attain 7$\frac{1}{2}$″ by 3″, but may be only 1$\frac{1}{2}$″ by $\frac{3}{4}$″ at the base of the rachis. Racemes very short, 1-4″ only.

Ravines in the Santal P. near Banjhi. Fls. *April-May*. Fr. *Nov.-Jany.*

L. odd or even-pinnate. Young *lflts.* slightly ferruginous-pubescent, base rounded, sec. nerves 8-10 prs., slender, finely reticulate between. *Petiolule* $\frac{1}{4}$″ blackish. *Fruiting calyx* $\frac{1}{5}$″ diam. *Pod* about 2$\frac{1}{2}$″ by 1″ very thin, very narrowly winged down both sutures (or, down the upper suture only, *F.B.I.*), venose, sessile in the calyx.

29. Millettia, *W. & A.*

Large woody climbers or sub-erect in youth, with odd-pinnate leaves and opp. leaflets. Fls. in axillary or terminal simple or panicled racemes. Petals with long claws, standard broad, keel not beaked. St. mon- or di-adelphous. Ovary sessile linear few-ovuled. Style filiform incurved glabrous. Stigma capitate. Pod linear or oblong, 1- or few-seeded.

Standard not auricled. St. diadelphous. Pod torulose, dehiscent . . . . 1. *racemosa.*

Standard auricled. St. monadelphous. Pod flat, very tardily dehiscent . . . . 2. *auriculata.*

1. M. racemosa, *Benth.*

A large climbing shrub with leaves about 1 ft. long and 5-7 prs. of nearly glabrous lflts. Fls. $\frac{1}{2}''$ close in axillary, and terminal panicled racemes. Pods 4-8$''$ by $\frac{1}{3}$-$\frac{5}{8}''$ linear, torulose with 2-4 tapering segments, black and readily dehiscent when ripe.

Valleys, Santara Forest, rare; Rajmehal hills in ravines, rare.

Fls. *April-May.* Fr. *Nov.-Jany.* Dec. in *March.*

Innovations tomentose. *Lflts.* oblong-obovate shortly often obtusely cuspidate sometimes wavy, brown-silky beneath along the midrib, terminal largest about 3$''$ by $1\frac{1}{2}''$, or 4$''$ by 2$''$. *Petiole* thinly silky. *Stipellæ* setaceous exceeding the petiolule. *Corolla* (*vide F.B.I.*, I have not seen it) $\frac{3}{8}$-$\frac{1}{2}''$ whitish.

2. M. auriculata, *Baker.* Hel, *K.*; Hehel, *S.*; Gurar, *Kharw.*

A large shrub sub-erect or climbing with leaves 1-2 ft. long and 3-4 prs. of strongly nerved leaflets thinly silky beneath. Fls. $\frac{3}{8}$-$\frac{1}{2}''$ cream-cold, fascicled on numerous racemes 4-9$''$ long which are often clustered on short stout axillary peduncles. Pod flat woody tomentose, 4-6$''$ by $\frac{3}{4}''$ with thickened sutures.

Often erect and in this state forming a dense undergrowth in many of the valley forests of Singbhum. Sal forests and valleys throughout Chota Nagpur. Fls. *April-June.* Fr. *Jany.-March.*

Innovations silky-tomentose. *Lflts.* obovate-oblong cuspidate 3-8$''$ long, terminal longest. Sec. n. 8-12 prs. *Stipellæ* minute. *Racemes* dense silky. *Fls.* fascicled.

Cut as a fodder. The root, like some other species of Millettia, is used to kill fish. It is also used for killing insects on cattle sores.

30. Tephrosia, Pers.

Shrubs or herbs with odd-pinnate leaves and opposite lflts. exstipellate. Fls. fascicled axillary or on racemes which are usually leaf-opposed. Calyx teeth 5 sub-equal. Standard sub-orbicular distinctly, clawed. Keel incurved not spurred.

St. 9+1, anthers oblong, obtuse. Pod linear compressed, several-seeded, not or obscurely septate within.

1. **T. purpurea,** *Pers.* Sarphuka, *Kharw.*

Shrubby 2 ft. high with downy angled branches, leaves 2-6″ long with 4-9 prs. of oblong to oblanceolate lflts. $\frac{3}{4}$-1″ by $\frac{1}{4}$-$\frac{1}{2}$″ appressed silky beneath and purple or purple-grey flowers in terminal or leaf-opposed racemes.

Waste ground, very common and often gregarious.

Fls. *July-Jany.* Fr. *Oct.-June.*

Lflts. obtuse apiculate with distinct parallel oblique nerves. *Calyx* $\frac{1}{8}$-$\frac{3}{16}$″ canescent, teeth subulate=tube or two upper rather shorter. *Corolla* $\frac{1}{4}$″ silky. *Pod* 1$\frac{1}{2}$-2″ slightly curved flat 6-12-seeded.

2. Var. pumila, *Pers.* (sp.). Stems *prostrate. Lflts.* seldom more than 4-6 prs. This is kept distinct in "Bengal Plants," but there appears to be no distinction except the habit, the other characters given are variable. Common.

3. **T. candida,** *D.C.*, is a handsome shrub with racemes of white flowers. Rānchi, *cult.* Fls. r. s.

31. Indigofera, L.

Herbs or shrubs with usually adpressed forked hairs (I. hirsuta has simple basifixed hairs) and odd-pinnate rarely 1-3-foliolate leaves. Fls. reddish bracteate in axillary racemes or spikes. Calyx teeth 5 usually many times longer than the tube, sub-equal. Standard ovate or orbicular. Keel petals gibbous or spurred. St. 9+1, anthers apiculate. Pod various, usually more than 1-seeded and narrow, septate.

I. L. 5-or more-foliolate (rarely fewer in 3).

a. Shrubs.

Fls. $\frac{3}{8}$-$\frac{1}{4}$″. Lflts. 13-17 oblong or obovate-oblong . . . . 1. *arborea.*

Fls. $\frac{1}{8}$″. Lflts. 9-13 obovate . . . . 2. *tinctoria.*

b. Suffruticose or herbaceous.

Racemes lax 2-4-fld. . . . . . 3. *glabra.*

Racemes very dense, spiciform . . . 4. *hirsuta.*

Racemes capitate. Branches trailing . . 5. *enneaphylla.*

II. L. 3-foliolate.

Erect 2-3 ft. End leaflet sessile . . .	6. *trita.*
Branches trailing or sub-erect. End leaflet stalked	7. *trifoliata.*

III. L. simple.

Small weeds only, of which I, linifolia has a small quite globose 1-seeded pod. The roots are often copiously tubercled.

1. **I. arborea,** *Roxb.* (Syn. *I. pulchella* of the F.B.I. and the better known name, but *vide* Prain "Bengal Plants" p. 1274). Hutar, Utar. *K.*; Dare hutar, *S.*; Jirhul, Jirul, *Kharw.*

A much-branched shrub 4-8 ft. high with impari-pinnate leaves 3-6" long, usually 6-8 prs. of oblong or oblong-obovate opp. and sub-opp. lflts. $\frac{3}{4}$-1" long and numerous rather dense racemes of bright pink flowers. Caducous silky bracts only covering the very young buds. Pods straight slender $1\frac{1}{4}$-2" long, sutures thickened.

Very common in forests on the hills. Fls. *Nov.-Feby.* Fr. *Feby.-April.* Quite deciduous in very dry seasons, usually partially so.

Branches sulcate with grey appressed hairs, glabrescent. *Lflts.* $\frac{1}{2}$" by $\frac{1}{3}$" to $1\frac{1}{4}$" by $\frac{5}{8}$", obtuse or emarginate apiculate appressed hairy both sides. Base rounded. *Racemes* axillary and from leaf scars 1-4" with oblong cuspidate *bracts* $\frac{1}{7}$-$\frac{1}{8}$". *Fls.* $\frac{1}{2}$-$\frac{5}{8}$" pink. *Calyx* small cup-shaped oblique subpetaloid 5-toothed pubescent. *Standard* broadly elliptic $\frac{1}{3}$" broad, not clawed or spurred.

The flowers are eaten. "A decoction of the root is given for cough," *Camp.*

A form is found in Manbhum with black scales in addition to the ordinary hairs.

2. **I. tinctoria,** *L.* Ceylon Indigo. Nil, Lil, *H.*

An erect shrub with thinly-hairy branches and leaves 2-3" long. Pods nearly straight 8-12-seeded.

Prain distinguishes I. tinctoria and I. sumatrana. They are united in the F.B.I. I have no specimens. It is said to occur wild in Chota Nagpur, and Wood says that it is cultivated in Manbhum.

3. **I. glabra,** *L.* Syn. I. pentaphylla, *F.B.I.*

A common plant about 1-2 ft. high with very numerous branches. Pods very slender 1-1½″ long. Often only a dwarf weed. Chiefly on sandy soil. Fls., Fr. *Aug.-Jany.*

4. **I. hirsuta,** *L.*

Erect 2-3 ft. high. Whole plant with spreading pubescence or on the leaves *adpressed* hairs. *Racemes* 1-2″ long. *Pods* terete strongly reflexed ½-¾″ long hairy. Frequent. Fls. *Aug.* Fr. *Dec.-Jany.*

5. **I. enneaphylla,** *L.* and 7. **I. trifoliata,** *L.* are mere weeds of waste ground.

6. **I. trita,** *L.* is a rare woody undershrub. Ch. Nagpur, *Prain.*

32. Sesbania, Pers.

Slender soft-wooded trees or shrubs of quick growth and short duration, more rarely herbaceous. L. pari-pinnate, with numerous usually ligulate leaflets. Fls. in axillary racemes. Corolla much longer than calyx with long-clawed petals. Ovary linear stipitate many-ovuled. Style filiform incurved. Pod very slender, dehiscent, septate between the very numerous seeds.

1. **S. aculeata,** *Pers.* Chaipijan, *K.*

An annual shrub 3-6 ft. high obscurely muricate or with weak prickles, pinnate leaves with 20-40 prs. of lflts. 1-1½″ long and yellow flowers dotted with black on slender racemes 4-6″ long.

In damp open grassy ground, common. Fls. *Aug.-Sept.* Fr. *Sept.-Oct.* *L.* 6-12″. *Fls.* ½″. *Pod.* straight or curved 6-9″.

2. **S. ægyptiaca,** *Pers.* Var. bicolor, *W. & A.* Jainti, *Beng.*

A large shrub or small tree with leaves 4-6″ long ending in a point, 12-21 prs. of close-set linear-oblong leaflets ¾-1¼″ long and lax axillary racemes of orange and deep red flowers.

Gardens and waste ground. Often coming up in a curious spontaneous-like way. Fls., Fr. *Nov.-Jany.*

Racemes shorter than leaves 2-8-fld. *Fls.* 1″ long, standard ¾-1″ broad. *Pod* twisted 6-9″

3. **S. grandiflora**, *Pers.* Agati, *Vern.* is a handsome very short-lived small tree with very large white flowers often seen in gardens.

Æschynomene indica, *L.* and **Æ. aspera**, *L.* both occur in wet places, the former is common but the latter, the pith of which gives 'sola,' is very rare. They are both soft-wooded undershrubs with small linear leaflets, the former with the habit of Sesbania, the latter very much stouter. The pods somewhat resemble those of Desmodium and split up into 1-seeded joints, those of aspera being usually scabrous opposite the seed.

The genus **Smithia** may be distinguished by the joints of the pods being folded together and included in the calyx.

34. Uraria, Desv.

Undershrubs, often with the habit of Desmodium, but leaves 1-9 foliolate, stamens often exserted from the keel. Pedicels and setaceous lower calyx-teeth hairy or bristly or plumose. Pod of 2-6 small turgid 1-seeded indehiscent joints which are often abruptly bent on one another so as to be placed face to face.

L. 1-3-foliolate often both on the same plant.
- Branches prostrate and ascending . . 1. *lagopoides*.
- Erect. Racemes very dense 2-4″ . . 2. *alopecurioides*.
- Erect. Racemes lax 4-8″ . . . . 3. *hamosa*.

L. 5-9 foliolate, or with 1-foliolate intermixed . 4. *picta*.

1. U. lagopoides, *D.C.*

Branches from a perennial woody rootstock about 1 ft. L. orbic. or oblong 1-2″. Heads dense oblong with plumose persistent calyx teeth. Joints oblong $\frac{1}{8}$″.

Common in forest and waste ground. Fls., Fr. *Aug.-Oct.*

2. U. alopecurioides, *Wight.* (U. repanda, *F.B.I.*). *Vide* Prain in Jour. As. Soc.

L. ovate obtuse 2-4″, often clouded. Racemes very similar to last with the cuspidate bracts closely imbricate in bud and the racemes conspicuous in flower and fruit from the hairy pedicels and calyx lobes.

Common. Jungles in Hazaribagh. *Wood.* Fls. *r. s.*

3. U. hamosa, *Wall.*

A shrub 3-5 ft. with brown-pubescent branches, ell. ovate or oblong lflts. 2-5½" by 1-2½" and purple fls. in rather lax racemes 4-8" long.

Valley forests, esp. Kundrugutu block, elev. 2,000 ft. Fls. *Sept.-Oct.* Fr. *Dec.*

Lflts. acute or obtuse apiculate, base acute or rounded. Sec. n. about 13 pairs strong beneath parallel up to margin with parallel cross nervules, shortly pubescent. *Stip.* ⅜" setaceous. *Petiole* ½-¾". *Racemes* sometimes glandular, hairy. *Fls.* $\frac{5}{16}$-⅜". *Calyx-teeth* longer than tube $\frac{1}{12}$". *Bracts* orbicular-obovate cuspidate $\frac{3}{16}$-¼". *Pod* ⅓", 6-7-jointed (4-6 *F.B.I.*) joints $\frac{1}{16}$" brown.

4. U. picta, *Desv.*

An undershrub 2-4 ft. with the upper leaves 5-9-foliolate and with linear leaflets usually clouded along the centre. Fls. in dense cylindrical racemes.

Waste ground in Singbhum, common. Probably in all the districts (but it is not mentioned in Wood's list). Fls. *Sept.-Nov.*

Stems pubescent. *L.* very variable on the same plant, the first are usually small and orbicular; these are succeeded by 3-5-foliolate leaves often intermixed with large simple oblong-lanceolate leaves up to 6" by 1½"; the leaflets of the upper leaves are usually 5 in number, 4-8" by ¼-1". The *inflorescence* is sometimes clothed with golden-yellow hairs (in the Duars). *Calyx-segments* plumose.

35. Lespedeza, Mich.

1. L. sericea, *Miq.*

An undershrub 2-3 ft. high with long erect slender branches and close-set very shortly-petioled 3-foliolate leaves with linear-cuneate leaflets in the axils of nearly all of which are abbreviated bracteolate racemes of 2-4 small white-purplish flowers. Pod of one small oblong 1-seeded indehiscent joint.

Higher hills of Chota Nagpur, *Prain* Fls. *r. s.* Fr. *Dec.-Jany.*

Sulcate *stems* and strongly-nerved leaflets silky. *Fls.* ⅛-¼".

36. Desmodium, Desv.

Herbs or shrubs with pinnately 1-3-foliolate stipellate leaves, dry usually striate stipules and small white yellow or usually red flowers in umbels, fascicles, racemes, or panicles. Corolla exsert with broad standard and wings more or less adnate to the keel. Upper stamen connate with the others or free. Style incurved. Stigma minute capitate. Pod crenate at one or both sutures, ultimately dividing into one-seeded joints at the indentations, or in one section continuously dehiscent along the indented suture.

A genus well represented in Chota Nagpur. The following *key* is taken almost verbatim from Prain's "Bengal Plants."

I. Pods breaking up into 1-seeded joints.

A. Leaves trifoliate

a. Stems diffuse, prostrate

1. Lflts. not exceeding ½". Stems slender trailing.
   - Fls. 1-3 axillary . . . . 1. *triflorum.*
   - Fls. 6-10 in lax racemes . . 2. *parviflorum.*
2. Lflts. 2-3". Stems stout. Fls. racemed and panicled . . . 3. *diffusum.*

b. Stems erect or sub-erect.

1. Racemes with large 2-foliolate foliaceous bracts . . . . 4. *pulchellum.*
2. Bracts small simple deciduous
   - † Fls. in short-peduncled axillary umbels. Shrub . . . 5. *Cephalotes.*
   - †† Fls. in more or less elongate racemes.
     - Joints of pod dehiscent, not longer than broad . . . . . 6. *polycarpum*
     - Joints of pod indehiscent, much longer than broad . . . 7. *laxiflorum.*

B. Leaves 1-foliolate.

a. Stems diffuse (or erect in Chota Nagpur). L. rounded cordate. Racemes dense . 8. *brachystachyum.*

b. Stems erect or sub-erect.

Lflts. longer than broad. Racemes lax. Pods glabrescent . . . . 9. *gangeticum.*

Lflts. broadly ovate. Racemes dense. Pods very pubescent. . . . 10. *latifolium.*

II. Pods continuously dehiscent along the ventral suture.

Undershrubs. Lateral lflts. very small or 0, linear . . . . 11. *gyrans.*

Large shrub. Lateral lflts. small, oblong or ovate . . . . 12. *gyroides.*

Spp. 1-3 are frequent in pastures, waste-land and on roadsides. They flower chiefly in the cold and rainy seasons.

4. **D. pulchellum,** *Benth.* Bir kapi, *S.*

A shrub 3-5 ft. high with grey-hairy branches, easily recognised by the inflorescence which far exceeds the leaves and bears double rows of pinnately-2-foliolate coriaceous bracts (the rachis of which ends in a filiform point), which bear in their axils fascicles of small yellow flowers.

Valleys not uncommon. All the districts. Fls. *r. s.* Fr. *Nov.-Dec.*

Lflts. shortly grey-hairy beneath and on the nerves above, end one ell. or ovate-oblong 3-5″, often sinuate. Sec. n. 7-10 prs. with parallel cross nervules. Side leaflets about half as large. *Bracts* orbicular strongly nerved on a short rachis ending in a filiform point. Joints of *pod* 1-3, usually 2.

5. **D. Cephalotes,** *Wall.* Ramdataon *Kharw.* (Bir jhawar, *S.* is almost certainly an error).

A shrub 3-6 ft. high with much the habit of the last. Branches distinctly 3-cornered, shaggy. Bracts minute deciduous. Fls. numerous yellow (red. *F.B.I.*) in dense axillary short-peduncled umbels, often running out into leafless racemes.

Valleys, not uncommon in Sal forests in Singbhum; Manbhum; Ranchi, *Wood*; and Palamau, *Haslett.* Fls. *Aug.-Oct.* Fr. *Dec.-Jany.*

Lflts. silkily hairy on the nerves beneath, nearly glabrous above, end one ell. acuminate 3-6″. Sec. n. fine strong 13-20 prs. with indistinct parallel cross nervules. Side *leaflets* half to $\frac{3}{4}$ths as long. *Pod* $\frac{1}{2}$-$\frac{3}{4}$″ very silky, joints 2-5, usually 3.

6. D. polycarpum, *D.C.* Bæphol. *S.*

A shrub 2-4 ft. usually with very numerous stems. Branches with appressed pubescence. Lflts. densely appressed silky beneath or glabrescent except on the nerves. Fls. purple $\frac{1}{4}''$ in dense terminal often panicled racemes, conspicuous in bud by the densely imbricating $\frac{1}{4}''$-long bracts. Pod brown hairy 5-7-jointed.

Common, especially on the edges of Sal forests in Porahat; Manbhum; Hazaribagh (Chorparan jungles). Fls. *Sept.-Oct.* Fr. *Nov.-Dec.*

Lflts. 1-3″ long, end one about $1\frac{1}{2}$-twice as long as the side ones usually 2″ by 1″ broadly ell.-oblong or obovate, tip rounded. *Bracts* with a setaceous tip. *Pedicels* $\frac{1}{8}''$. *Pods* $\frac{3}{4}$-1″, suture indented about $\frac{1}{4}$th way down. Joints $\frac{1}{8}$-$\frac{1}{6}''$ long and broad, indehiscent.

7. D. laxiflorum, *D.C.*

An undershrub with thin twiggy angled branches clothed with short hairs. Long lax often branched racemes of small flowers with yellowish-white standard and keel, and wings edged with purple, Pod linear 3-7-jointed, joints about 3-times as long as broad.

Shady banks in the forests *e.g.,* Latua Block, rare; Hazaribagh (common on Parasnath); S. P. (Ghormanra). Fls. *Sept.-Oct.* Fr. *Dec.*

Rootstock woody but stems often sub-herbaceous 2-3 ft. End *lflt.* $3\frac{1}{2}$-6″ by $1\frac{1}{2}$-3″ rhomboid or ell. acute, silky beneath, side ones about half as long. *Racemes* reaching 8-10″. *Pedicels* $\frac{1}{4}$-$\frac{1}{2}''$, distant. Joints of *pod* with minute tubercle-based hairs.

The elastic stamens are enclosed in the keel petals and wings, and shoot the pollen to a distance when the latter are depressed.

8. D. brachystachyum, *Benth.*

Undershrub 1-2 ft. stems adpressed hairy, often erect. L. usually strongly reflexed on their petioles 1-$1\frac{1}{2}''$ by $\frac{3}{4}$-$\frac{7}{8}''$ broadly-oblong to sub-orbicular with rounded or sub-cordate base. Fls. small deep-purple in axillary and terminal dense racemes $\frac{3}{4}$—1″ long.

Under light cover in open jungles, Porahat, esp. near Hesedi in Singbhum. Fls. *Sept.-Oct.* Fr. *Dec.*

Lflt. with long adpressed hairs beneath, slightly hairy above, tip rounded or retuse. *Bracts* ovate acuminate $\frac{3}{16}''$ persistent. *Pedicels* not quite as long, the end sharply deflexed after flowering. *Standard* $\frac{1}{8}''$ diam. *Pod* 1-3-jointed. Joints $\frac{1}{10}''$ by $\frac{1}{16}''$ widely dehiscent when ripe, slightly hairy. *Seed* shining yellow peppered red.

9. **D. gangeticum,** *D.C.* Tandi Bhidi Janetet', *S.*

An undershrub or sub-herbaceous with sub-erect or erect or trailing stems 3-4 ft. long. Lflts. oblong or ovate-oblong 3-6″ long. Fls. $\frac{1}{8}$-$\frac{1}{6}''$ white or red in ascending lateral and terminal lax often somewhat branched racemes 6-12″ long. Pod falcate, $\frac{1}{2}$-$\frac{3}{4}''$ long, 6-8-jointed.

Common in forest and waste-land.

Fls. *March-Oct.* Fr. *June-Jany.* Probably flowers most of the year.

Lflt. with rounded base and gradually tapering at the acute tip, with thin adpressed hairs beneath. A very variable plant.

10. **D. latifolium,** *D.C.*

An erect shrub 3-6 ft. high with densely brown-pubescent branches. Lflts. sub-coriaceous broad-ovate 3-6″ by $1\frac{1}{2}$-$3\frac{1}{2}''$. Fls. $\frac{1}{6}$-$\frac{1}{5}''$ purple in numerous axillary and terminal often panicled dense spiciform racemes 2-7″ long.

Frequent in shade, Singbhum; Ranchi; Hazaribagh (Parasnath, Damuda valley); Palamau, common, *Haslett!*; S. P., frequent. Fls. *Aug.-Sept.* Fr. *Oct.-Jany.*

Lflts. often sub-repand with rounded or acute tip and truncate or cordate base densely brown pubescent beneath and appressed hairy above. *Pod* $\frac{1}{2}$-1″, 4-6-jointed, clothed with minute hooked hairs.

11. **D. gyrans,** *D.C.* Gora Chand, *Beng.* The Telegraph Plant.

Perennial 3-4 ft., branches often sub-herbaceous glabrous. Terminal leaflet oblong lanceolate 3-4″ by 1-$1\frac{1}{4}''$, side lflts. 0, 1, or 2 about $\frac{1}{2}$-1″ very narrow. Fls. $\frac{3}{8}$-$\frac{1}{2}''$ in axillary terminal racemes 2-6″ long, with large bracts concealing the flower-buds and forming a terminal club.

Common on damp shady banks in Singbhum. Tamar. Tori and Sirguja, *Wood.* Fls. *Aug.-Nov.* Fr. *Oct.-Dec.*

Lflts. nearly glabrous, sometimes flushed with white, obtuse, and base rounded. Sec. n. distinct but fine, tertiaries very inconspicuous. *Stipules* $\frac{1}{4}''$ setaceous from a broad base. Terminal *raceme* often branched. *Pod* 1-$1\frac{1}{2}''$ shortly pubescent, slightly indented.
The small side-leaflets move by jerks in warm damp weather.

12. **D. gyroides,** *D.C.* Jatangsing, *M.*

A shrub 6-20 ft. high with softly hairy branches. Lfts. 1-3 drooping, end one obovate obtuse attaining $3\frac{1}{4}''$ by $1\frac{3}{4}''$, side leaflets rarely $1\frac{1}{2}''$. Fls. $\frac{1}{2}''$ deep purple in short axillary and terminal racemes 1-2″ long, with large deciduous bracts as in the last.

Valleys on the Porahat plateau. Fls. *Aug.-Nov.* Fr. *Oct.-Jany.*

Lfts. appressed-hairy both sides, sec. n. 6-8 prs, and tertiaries distinct. Terminal *raceme* often branched rarely elongating to 4″. *Bracts* large ovate $\frac{5}{16}''$ by $\frac{1}{4}''$. *Pod* $1\frac{1}{4}$-2″, hairy, 6-10-seeded, lower suture indented.

37. Ougeinia, Benth.

1. **O. dalbergioides,** *Benth.* Ruta, *K.*; Rot, *S.*; Sandan., *H.*; Pandan, *Kharw.*; Panan, *H.*

Usually a small and crooked tree with slender grey branchlets, pinnately 3-foliolate leaves and copious smallish white or pink flowers in fascicled racemes appearing before the new leaves.

Common in the hills but seldom above $3\frac{1}{2}$ ft. girth in Chota Nagpur. Fls. *Feby.-April.* Fr. *May-June.* Dec. *Feby.-April.*

L. often sub-tomentose beneath. Terminal *lflt.* ovate, orbicular or obovate 3-6″ long, obtuse, entire or crenate with 5-10 pairs strong sec. nerves. *Fls.* 2-3 together on slender pedicels. *Calyx* $\frac{1}{8}$-$\frac{1}{6}''$ campanulate, teeth distinct. *Corolla* far exsert, standard sub-orbicular, keel obtuse. *Ovary* linear, many-ovuled. *Pod* linear or linear-oblong 2-5-jointed, or joints obscure.

Large pieces are prized for the "patura" or hubs of the sugar wheels and it is in request for agricultural implements. On being blazed a red gum exudes resembling that of Butea, and a decoction of the bark is used when the urine is too dark coloured. The leaves form a good fodder.

38. Sophora, L.

1. **S. Bakeri,** *Clarke.*

An erect shrub 4-5 ft. with tomentose impari-pinnate leaves 5-8″ long, sub-opposite leaflets 1-$1\frac{1}{4}''$ or up to 2″ by $\frac{3}{4}''$

and leaf-opposed racemes of purple flowers with 9 very loosely cohering or free stamens. Pod 3-4″ moniliform beaked, dehiscent, hairy.

Dry ridges in Singbhum *e.g.* Louri Buru; Parasnath *Anders.*, *Clarke*; Manbhum, *Camp.* Fls. *May-June.* Fr. *Oct.-March.*

Lflts. oblong sub-sessile mucronate silky about 5-7 pairs, glabrescent above. *Racemes* 2-3″. *Calyx* campanulate purple pubescent $\frac{1}{4}$-$\frac{1}{3}$″, teeth short. *Standard* narrow-oblong deep-purple notched. Wings narrow-oblong, long-clawed. *Keel* purple-veined auricled.

Fam. 44. MYRTACEÆ.

Trees or shrubs with opposite and gland-dotted leaves (more rarely alternate or without glands) which are simple, entire penni-veined and usually with an intramarginal nerve. *Stipules* 0 or small and caducous. *Flowers* regular. *Calyx* superior. *Petals* rarely 0, inserted on, or on the margin of the epigynous disc or disc lining the hypanthium. *St.* usually indefinite inserted on the disc, sometimes with filaments more or less combined. *Anthers* small with longitudinal dehiscence. *Ovary* inferior 2-many-celled with axile placentation. *Style* 1 and stigma simple. *Fruit* various 1-many seeded usually crowned by the calyx. Albumen 0.

N. B.—Barringtonia and Careya are not typical Myrtaceæ, and are sometimes placed in a distinct family Lecythidaceæ.

L. opposite. Often gland-dotted. Fr. a berry.

- Fls. (in Ch. Nag. sp.) cymose. Seeds few large . 1. *Eugenia.*
- Peduncles axillary 1-3-flowered. Seeds many, small 2. *Psidium.*

L. alternate, not gland-dotted. Fr. angular or berry-like.

- Fls. in elongate racemes . . . . . . 3. *Barringtonia.*
- Fls. large, 1-3 in short spikes . . . . . . 4. *Careya.*

1. Eugenia.

Usually glabrous trees or shrubs with often quadrangular branchlets and opp. rarely alternate leaves. Fls. usually white, axillary or racemose or more usually (always in Ch. Nag. species) in trichotomous cymes. Calyx-tube or hypanthium obconic or globose truncate or with 4-5 calyx lobes, and prolonged above the ovary. Petals 4 rarely 5, sometimes falling off as a calyptra on the stamens expanding. St. many with small versatile anthers. Ovary 2-rarely 3-celled; style filiform, stigma small. Ovules many in each cell. Fruit a berry with few seeds. Embryo thick, radicle short, cotyledons large fleshy.

A. Venation fine close and parallel.

- Tree. L. ovate or broadly oblong. Berry ½-¾″ oblong . . . . . . 1. *Jambolana.*
- Tree. L. ovate-lanc. or lanc. acuminate Berry pisiform . . . . *Var. caryophyllifolia.*
- Shrubby. L. narrowly oblong or lanc. Berry oblong or ovoid ½″ . . . . . 2. *Heyneana.*

B. Secy. nerves 10-15 prs, distinct.

- L. broadly elliptic or ovate . . . . 3. *operculata.*
- L. oblanceolate or oblong-lanceolate . . *Var. obovata.*

1. E. **Jambolana**, *Lam.* Kuda, *K.*; So-Kod, *S.* Jamun, *H.*, *Kharw.*; Jambun, *Oraon.*

A large or mod.-sized tree with dense crown, dark-green broadly-oblong or ovate usually acuminate leaves about 6″ by 2½-3″ with close sub-parallel venation. Fls. white sessile in threes in 3-chotomous panicles mostly from the leaf scars. Berry ½-¾″ long oblong.

This is the form commonly found in the villages. Fls. *May.* Fr. *July-Aug.*

Var. *α. L.* ovate-oblong tapering 4½-5″ by 1½-2¼″. *Panicles* 2-2½″. *Calyx* $\frac{5}{32}$″ truncate with small glands. *St.* eglandular.

Along rivers. Fls. *June.* Evergreen.

Var. *β* = Var. **caryophyllifolia**, *Lamk.* (sp.) ? Buru-Kuda, *K.*; Bir-Kod, *S.*

A small tree with bright green *lanceolate* or *lanceolate-ovate* acuminate leaves 3-5 by 1-1½″. Calyx-tube ⅛″ truncate. Connective of anther *gland-tipped. Berry* pisiform.

A very common hill form and perhaps as distinct a species as E. Heyneana.

Singbhum, Palamau, Manbhum. Fls., Fr. with the others.

The fruit is eaten and is said to be useful in dysentery.

2. **E. Heyneana,** *Wall.* Gara-Kuda, *K.*; Chuduk' Kud, or Kod, *S.*; Kat-jaman, *Kharw.*

A shrub or small bushy tree 8-20 ft. high with narrowly-oblong-elliptic or lanceolate acuminate leaves 3-5″ by ½-1″ and lateral cymes of capitate white flowers from the old leaf scars.

Along streams. Common in Singbhum, common about Dumri (Hazaribagh); Manbhum; Palamau; and probably other districts not specifically noted. Fl. *May-June.* Fr. *July-Aug.*

L. with the glands more numerous and pellucid than in Jambolana and usually longer-peduncled *cymes* 2-3″ with brachiate branches. *Fls.* sub-sessile. usually several in a head, calyx-lobes small, *petals* calyptrate as in 1. *Berry* ½-⅔″ oblong, crowned by the cup of the hypanthium.

The fruit is eaten.

3. **E. operculata,** *Roxb.* Topa, *K.*; Totonopak', *S.*; Paiman, *H.*

A low tree with broadly elliptic or ovate leaves 5-7 by 3—3½″ and sessile flowers in threes in brachiate panicles 3-6″ long mostly from old leaf scars. Berry globose ¼-½″.

Forests in Singbhum but not as common as the next. Usually in grassy glades; Hazaribagh (along Konor nadi); S. P. (Silingi). Fls. *April-May.* Fr. *June.* The leaves turn red before falling.

Twigs usually quadrangular. *L.* obtuse or shortly bluntly acuminate base acute or sub-obtuse, sec. n. 8-12 prs. arcuate. *Petiole* ½-¾″. *Calyx* obconic about $\frac{3}{10}$″ long and broad. *Sepals* 4 transversely oblong $\frac{1}{10}$″ broad glandular. A large gland also on the tip of the connective.

Var. **obovata,** *Kurz.*

Very different in general appearance and perhaps a distinct species. L. oblanceolate or obovate about 7″ by 1¾-2.″

More evidently glandular, esp. on the flowers. Petals sometimes expanding.

Valleys in Singbhum, Manbhum, S. P. (rare), etc. Fls. *April-May.*

Campbell says that the fruit is eaten for rheumatism, the root boiled down (the extract?) to the consistence of gur is applied to the joints by rubbing, the leaves are much used in dry fomentations.

Psidium Guyava, *L.* The Guava. Ambaru, *K.*

A small tree largely cultivated. Indigenous in Mexico.

3. Barringtonia, Forst.

1. **B. acutangula,** *Gærtn.* Dundi, Saparung, *K.* Hinjor, *S.*; Ingan, *Kharw.*; Hijal, *Beng.*

A small, or large tree (in Manbhum), with alt. obovate or oblanceolate denticulate leaves reaching 9″ by 4″ clustered at the ends of the branches, and long drooping racemes of flowers conspicuous from their bright red stamens. Fruit blong quadrangular truncate about 1″.

In nalas in Singbhum; Tundi Forests, Manbhum, *Camp.*; Gangpur. Fls. *May.* Fr. *Sept.*

Rarely over 25 ft. in C. N. *L.* narrowed into the $\frac{1}{3}$″ petiole. *Racemes* attaining 2 ft. glabrous. *Pedicels* $\frac{1}{4}$″. *Calyx* $\frac{1}{4}$″, tube acutely 4-angled. *Petals* pale pink very caducous. *Ovary* 2-4-celled. Ovules 2-8 in each cell. *Fruit* 1-seeded, exalbuminous.

4. Careya, Roxb.

1. **C. arborea,** *Roxb.* Asanda, *K.*; Kumbir, *S.*; Kumb. Kumbi, *Kharw.*, *Beng.*

A small tree with large obovate or obovate-oblong leaves clustered at the ends of the branches, large white and pink flowers in few-fld. dense spikes succeeded by large globose green fruits $2\frac{1}{2}$-3″ diam. crowned with the persistent calyx.

Valleys in Singbhum; Manbhum; Hazaribagh (Bagodar and Damuda valley); S. P., scarce, *Gamble*; Sarjuga, *Wood.* Fls. *April-May.* Fr. *July.*

L. 6-15″ long, glabrous, slightly crenate-denticulate, sec. n. 10-12 prs. not very strong. Fls. 3″ with large bracts and bracteoles, sessile or scarcely pedicelled. Sep. 4 ovate obtuse. *Pet.* 1¾″ white. Fil. pink, very numerous, the middle ones alone fertile. *Ovary* 4-celled. *Ovules* numerous. *Seeds* in a fleshy pulp.

The bark gives a fibre suitable for rough ropes. Campbell says that the fruit is eaten. The root is used to kill fish in Gangpur.

Fam. 45. LYTHRACEÆ.

Trees, shrubs or herbs with often 4-angled branches. *L.* usually opposite and entire, exstipulate. *Fls.* 2-sexual, regular or zygomorphous. *Sepals* 3-6 with sometimes intermediate smaller ones, valvate. *Petals* perigynous as many as the sepals, rarely 0. *St.* definite or indefinite, nearly hypogynous or perigynous (epigynous in Punica). *Ovary* 2-6-celled. Stigma capitate. *Ovules* very many axile (or parietal in Punica). *Fruit* coriaceous or membranous, dehiscent or not. *Seeds* many, albumen 0.

Punica is better placed, as is done by Engler, in a separate family.

A. Trees or shrubs.
- Fls. zygomorphous with declinate stamens . . 1. *Woodfordia.*
- Fls. regular.
  - Petals 5-8, rarely 4. Capsule 3-6-valved . . 2. *Lagerstrœmia.*
  - Petals 4. Capsule irregularly breaking up . 3. *Lawsonia.*
  - Ovary completely adnate to the hypanthium, cells 1-3-seriate . . . . 4. *Punica.*

B. Herbs of wet ground with minute flowers . . 5. *Ammannia.*

1. Woodfordia, Salisb.

1. **W. floribunda,** *Salisb.* Icha: *K.*; Ichak', *S.*; Phul-dawai, Dhai-phul, *Kharw.*; Dadki, *Bhumij.*

A bushy shrub 4-6 ft. with simple sessile or sub-sessile linear-lanceolate distichous acuminate leaves 2½-4″ long, silvery finely pubescent and gland-dotted beneath, and scarlet showy tubular flowers ½-¾″ long in fascicled cymes, axillary and from the old wood.

A very common shrub, especially on clay in open places, and as second growth. Fls. *Jany.-April.* Fr. *April-May.* Nearly leafless in March when in brilliant flower, and leaves often not renewed till end of May.

Hypanthium petaloid slightly curved and oblique with 6 outer greenish tooth-like sepals, 6 very small scarlet petals, and 6 linear hair-tipped scales. *St.* 12 exserted. *Capsule* enclosed in the remains of the hypanthium, very thin, splitting irregularly. The stamens are trimorphic.

It is a favourite flower of the Kols who often mention it in their songs. The flowers yield a dye.

2. Lagerstrœmia, L.

Trees or shrubs with opp. or sub-opp. distichous entire leaves and flowers (usually showy) in axillary and terminal panicles. Sepals and petals 6-9 on the margin of the tubular hypanthium; petals very long-clawed, wrinkled, erose or crisped. St. very many, hypogynous with long, often curled and barren, filaments. Ovary 3-6-celled. Capsule girt by the persistent calyx 3-6-valved and celled partially adnate to the calyx-tube. Seeds winged.

Hypanthium strongly ribbed. Fls. large dark mauve . 1. *Flos-Reginæ.*
Hyp. not ribbed. Fls. ½″ white . . . . . . 2. *parviflora.*
Hyp. not ribbed. Fls. 1½-2″ white, pink or purple . . 3. *indica.*

1. L. **Flos-Reginæ**, *Retz.* Kwiri, *M.*; Gara Sekre, *Ho.*; Jarul, *Beng.*

A large or mod.-sized but usually crooked tree and often flowering when only 20 ft. high. L. ellip. to lanceolate 4-8″. Very handsome when covered with flowers which are 2-3 diam.

Along the larger rivers in Singbhum and Gangpur and in the muddy side nalas. Fls. *May-June.* The old capsules remain on the tree till the next flowering season.

L. glabrous with 6-12 prs. strong sec. n.: base usually rounded. Petiole very short. Hyp. strongly ribbed, whitish, woody in fruit. *Capsule* septifragally 5-6 valved, sub-globose, 1-1½″ woody.

2. L. **parviflora**, *Roxb.* Sekre, *K.*; Sekrec', *S.*; Sidha, *Kharw.*, *H.*, *Beng.*

A tree, or in Ch. Nag. a shrub or small tree, with narrow ell. or oblong or ovate-lanceolate acute or acuminate distichous leaves and delicate white flowers in trichotomous panicles with petals under $\frac{1}{4}''$.

Common, usually in poor valley forest and on clay soil, often as a scrub jungle (in the forests of the sub-Himalaya it is a large tall tree). Fls. *April-May*. Fr. *Dec.-Jany*. Deciduous *Feby.-March*, and flowers on the young shoots.

All the Ch. Nag. specimens belong to the var. majuscula with *leaves* 3-5″ long and axillary panicles often simply racemose and *capsule* ellipsoid or oblong 1-1½″ long.

L. coriaceous when old pale or glaucous, glabrous or shortly pubescent beneath with 6-10 prs. sec. nerves. Peduncle and pedicels slender, bracts linear. Hypanthium woody in fruit, partially embracing the capsule. *St.* few long and many short. *Capsule* 3-4-valved.

Used for agricultural implements.

3. **L. indica,** *L.* A handsome shrub, largely cultivated in gardens. Fls. *May-Aug.* A native of China.

Lawsonia alba, *Lamk.* Mehnde, *H.* The Henna is a small tree or large shrub somewhat resembling a Myrtle, often cultivated, with lanceolate or narrow-rhomboid leaves, and very fragrant small cream-coloured, red or white *fls.* $\frac{1}{4}''$ diam. *Capsule* $\frac{1}{4}$-$\frac{5}{16}''$ diam. depressed globose irregularly dehiscent with very numerous angular seeds. Fls. and Fr. at various seasons.

Punica Granatum, *L.* Anar, *H.* The Pomegranate. Is a well known handsome shrub with deep green foliage and large scarlet flowers. The structure of the flower is peculiar, by the infolding of the wall of the ovary, the cells come to lie in tiers and Punica is sometimes placed in a separate order, the Punicaceæ.

Ammannia is a genus of herbs, some minute, others 2 ft. or more. At least eight species occur in Ch. Nagpur. Petals 3-5 or 0. St. 2-8. Septa of the ovary sometimes quickly absorbed so that the placenta becomes free central.

Fam. 46. ONAGRACEÆ.

A family usually easily recognized by the floral-whorls being in multiples of 4 (rarely 5), and the wholly inferior ovary with many axile ovules in each cell. **Trapa** is somewhat exceptional.

1. Trapa, L.

1. **T. bispinosa**, *Roxb.* Singhara, *H.*, *K.* The Water-chestnut.

A pretty floating herb with pinnati-partite submerged leaves, and a rosette of long-petioled rhomboidal floating leaves. Fls. solitary axillary, pure white, $\frac{3}{4}''$ diam. Ovary 2-celled, half-inferior. Ovule 1 in each cell. Fruit hard spinescent.

Tanks. Fls. *Aug.-Sept.* Fr. *Nov.-Dec.*

Segments of submerged leaves capillary. *Petiole* swollen in the middle, villous above. *Blade* $1\frac{1}{2}$-2″ diam. sharply dentate on the two anterior margins, villous beneath.

The kernel of the fruit is largely eaten.

Jussiea suffruticosa, *L.* Dak' ichak', *S.*; Parsati (Jaspur, *Wood*); is an erect herb 2-4 ft. high. common in wet places. It has lanceolate leaves about 3″ long and yellow flowers. Wood says that a decoction of the root is drunk for fever.

J. repens, *L.* is a smaller prostrate plant with 5-6 petals, also common.

Fam. 47. MELASTOMACEÆ.

Sub-fam.—Melastomeæ.

Herbs or shrubs. *L.* opp. entire with basal nerves exstipulate. *Fls.* regular or slightly zygomorphous, 2-sexual. *Calyx-tube* or hypanthium united by vertical walls to the ovary, with 4-7 usually deciduous sepals. *Petals* as many as the sepals. *Stamens* perigynous as many or twice as many as the petals, *anthers* opening by pores and connective often appendaged. *Ovary* 3-7-celled. Style simple. Ovules very many, axile. Fruit capsular or berried. Seeds minute, very many, albumen 0.

Shrubs. Alternate anthers unequal and dissimilar . . 1. *Melastoma*

Shrubs or herbs. Stamens equal or sub-equal, all similar 2. *Osbeckia.*

47. *MELASTOMACEÆ.*

1. Melastoma, L.

1. **M. malabathricum,** *L.* Indian Rhododendron (a misnomer).

A beautiful bushy shrub with 4-angled branches, 3-7-basal-nerved rough broadly lanceolate or elliptic leaves 3-4″ long, and numerous bright mauve-purple fls. 1-1½″ diam. in terminal clusters with conspicuous yellow dimorphous stamens.

Along water-courses in Singbhum, not common. S. P. (stream near Kuskira) *Gamble!* Fls. *March-May.* Fr. *r.s.* Evergreen.

Stems 4-6 ft. strigose. *L.* with adpressed hairs. *Petiole* ½″.

2. Osbeckia, L.

1. **O. chinensis,** *L.*

A perennial-rooted erect herb 1½-2½ ft. with 4-angled sparsely adpressed hairy stems, linear or rarely oblong basally 3-nerved leaves and handsome mauve flowers 1″ diam. in terminal capitate cymes.

Usually on clay soil and common in grassy forest. Singbhum; Santal P.; Parasnath; Palamau (Neterhat). Fls. *Aug.-Oct.*

Larger *L.* 2-2½″ by ⅜″, acute, margin very obscurely serrulate. *Sepals* 4 with alternating stellate scales. *St.* 8 yellow, awned.

2. **O. truncata,** *Don.* A small variety of this species (Kurzii) only 2″ high occurs on Parasnath. Anthers not awned.

Fam. 48. RHIZOPHORACEÆ.

Trees or shrubs with opposite usually coriaceous glabrous leaves with interpetiolar caducous stipules. Fls. usually in axillary cymes or clusters. rarely solitary or spicate. *Calyx* superior, 4-14-usually 4-8-lobed, lobes valvate persistent.

Petals often small, free, caducous, alt. with the sepals. *St.* twice as many as the petals. *Ovary* inferior or half-inferior, 5-1-celled (in Carrallia usually 4-celled), styles connate stigma capitate lobed. *Ovules* two in each cell, pendulous (in Carallia from the axis). *Fruit* coriaceous, usually indehiscent 1-celled and -seeded. Albumen fleshy or 0.

In the Mangroves which belong to this family, the seed germinates on the tree.

A tree. Fls. small shortly cymose Ovary inferior . . 1. *Carrallia.*

1. Carrallia, Roxb

1. **C. lucida**, *Roxb.* Syn. C. integerrima, *D.C.* Jur, Aramata, *K.*[1]; Kierpa, *Beng.*

A small tree with opp. shining leathery oblong elliptic or obovate shortly acuminate leaves and stout dense 2-3-chotomous cymes of small greenish sessile flowers, with inconspicuous white erose petals.

Singbhum, frequent along the banks of streams and dry nalas. *S. P.* Fls. *Dec.-April.* Fr. *r.s.* Evergreen. New leaves in *March* and *April.*

Branchlets somewhat quadrangular. *Buds* $\frac{1}{2}$-$\frac{3}{4}$" long acuminate enclosed in the caducous stipules. *L.* 3" by 1$\frac{3}{8}$" to 6" by 3$\frac{1}{4}$" with numerous close fine oblique parallel nerves reticulating within the margin, base acute. *Petiole* $\frac{1}{3}$-$\frac{1}{2}$". *Cymes* stout dense 1-2" long. *Fls.* $\frac{3}{16}$" long obconic. *Hypanthium* produced above the ovary. *Sepals* 6-8. *Petals* sub-orbicular or quadrate, equalling the sepals, shortly clawed. *Disc* epigynous, lobulate. *Ovary* (3-) 4-celled. Stigma (3-) 4-lobed. *Fr.* $\frac{1}{4}$" globose, coriaceous, crowned by the persistent sepals and style.

Fam. 49. COMBRETACEÆ.

Trees or shrubs, sometimes scandent, with opp. or sub-opp., more rarely quite alternate simple exstipulate leaves. *Fls.* generally small, sometimes 1-sexual, usually in spikes or

---

[1] There appears to be no specific Kol name, the names given belong properly to two other trees, *viz.*, Canthium and Antidesma.

racemes or heads, generally sessile. Hypanthium enclosing the ovary and often prolonged above it into a beak carrying a more or less tubular or campanulate 4-5-lobed limb or 'calyx-tube.' *Petals* between the lobes, or 0. *St.* 2-seriate, twice as many as the lobes or one series reduced or absent, sometimes doubled. *Ovary* inferior 1-celled with few pendulous ovules. *Style* simple. *Fr.* 1 seeded usually dry and indehiscent generally 2-5-angled or winged. *Seed* exalbuminous.

All parts usually rich in tannin.

A. Trees. Petals 0.
- Fls. in spikes or racemes, often panicled . . 1. *Terminalia.*
- Fls. capitate . . . . 2. *Anogeissus.*

B. Shrubs, often sarmentose or climbing. Petals 4-5 rarely 0.
- Fls. small greenish, bracts sometimes petaloid . 3. *Combretum.*
- Fls. showy. Calyx-tube above ovary very long . 4. *Quisqualis.*

1. Terminalia, L.

Trees with opp. sub. opp. or alt. leaves sometimes clustered at the ends of the twigs and often bearing large glands on the petiole or base of the blade. Small greenish *fls.* in the axils of caducous bracts, in simple or panicled spikes 4-6-merous. Hypanthium not beaked above the ovary, "calyx-tube" campanulate. *St.* twice as many as the calyx-lobes inserted above the hairy disc. *Ovules* 2-3. *Fruit* drupaceous or dry, endocarp 4-5-angled, or when dry the pericarp produced into wings (5 in our species).

A. Fr. drupaceous, not winged.

I. L. alt. and clustered at the ends of the twigs. Spikes simple.
- Petioles very short. Fr. glabrous compressed elliptic . . . . 1. *Catappa.*
- Petioles 1″ and more. Fr. tomentose, globose or pyriform . . . . 2. *belerica.*

II. L. not clustered at the ends of the twigs, petioled. Spikes panicled.

Fr. glabrous ellipsoid, 5-angled when dry. L. alt. to opp. . . . . 3. *Chebula*.

B. Fr. with 5 (-4) sub-equal wings. Spikes panicled. Petioles very short or L. sub-sessile.

Bark pale. L. glabrous, smaller ell., larger oblong 4. *Arjuna*.

Bark dark. L. tomentose beneath ell. or ovate . 5. *tomentosa*.

Bark dark. L. very large oblong tomentose beneath, and bark dark, L. ell. or ovate glabrous beneath are varieties of *tomentosa*.

1. **T. Catappa,** *L.* Badam, *Beng.* The Indian Almond.

Frequently planted, but the tree does not succeed well in Ch. Nag., the climate is not sufficiently humid.

2. **T. belerica,** *Roxb.* Lupung, *K.*; Lopong, *S.*; Behra Bahera, *Kharw, H.*; Bohera, *Beng.* The Beleric Myrabolan.

A large tree with broadly ell. or obovate leaves clustered at the ends of the branchlets (they may be alt. and distant on some branches) on petioles 1-2½″ long and solitary axillary spikes 4-6″ long of small greenish-white or -yellow fls. $\frac{3}{16}$-$\frac{1}{4}$″ diam. Fr. ¾″ diam. grey-tomentose, only showing faint furrows when quite dry, usually pyriform.

Rather common, chiefly in the valley forests. Fls. *Feby.-May.* Fr. *Jany.-April.* Dec. *Jany.-Feby.*

Trunk usually straight and tall. *L.* with cuneate base and acute or rounded tip. 3-8″ long generally dotted above, eglandular.

The fruits have scarcely any market value in Singbhum, their sale in Calcutta only just covers the cost of export. The kernels are eaten, but are said to produce vertigo if taken in excess, they are a favourite food of monkeys and cattle. "It yields a gum which is eaten by the Santals," *Camp.*

3. **T. Chebula,** *Retz.* Rola, *K.*; Rol *S.*; Hadra, *Oraon*; Hara, Hari-taki (the fruit), *H.*, *Beng.* The Chebulic Myrabolan.

A small or mod.-sized tree with a rounded crown, usually sub-opposite ovate or elliptic entire leaves 4″ by 2¼″ to 7½″ by 4″ and whitish flowers in spikes from the upper axils and in small terminal panicles. Fr. a drupe, ellipsoid $\frac{3}{4}$-$1\frac{1}{4}$" long glabrous, 5-ribbed when dry.

Common on the lower hills, and especially in the protected forests of the low plateaux, frequent on a hard clay. Fls. *April-May.* Fr. *Nov.-Feby.* New shoots *April-May.*

Young leaves usually beautifully silvery-hairy, adult nearly glabrous, acute or obtuse with a rounded rarely acute base and 7-9 pairs prominent sec.-nerves. Often 2-glands at the top of the $\frac{1}{2}$-1" long petiole. *Spikes* 2-$3\frac{1}{2}$". *Bracts* linear as long as the young flowers, caducous. *Fls.* very densely white villous within.

Much used as a tanning material and in Hindu medicine

A variety on the top of Parasnath occurs with the leaves very shaggy beneath and small fruit only $\frac{3}{4}$" long. *C. B. Clarke.*

4. **T. Arjuna,** *Bedd.* Kowa, Gara-Hatana, *K.*; Kauha, *S.*; Kahua, *Kharw.*; Arjun, *H.*

A large tree with a pale bark, long inclined branches with opp. or sub-opp. oblong leaves 2-3-times as long as broad (smaller ones only at bases of shoots are elliptic) sub-sessile, soon glabrous. Fls. $\frac{3}{16}$" diam. white in shortly panicled spikes. Fruit 1-$1\frac{1}{2}$" long, wings less than $\frac{1}{2}$" wide usually premorse above, with ascending striations.

Common along nalas where it sometimes attains an immense size. All districts. Fls. *March-July.* Fr. *March-April.* Evergreen.

L. 5-8" with 2 glands at base or on the very short petiole (under $\frac{1}{2}$") entire or crenate but nerves not excurrent as teeth. Seedlings may have toothed leaves.

5. **T. tomentosa,** *W. & A.* Hatana, atana, *K.*; Atnak', *S.*; Asan, Sain, *H.*

A large tree with dark cinerous rough bark, opp. or sub-opp. ell. or ell.-obovate or oblong leaves subsessile or petioled, with distinct tertiary nerves, permanently pubescent beneath or in one variety glabrescent. Fls. as in 4 but panicles often larger. Fruit $1\frac{1}{2}$-2" long sometimes attaining 3 by $2\frac{1}{2}$" wings over $\frac{1}{2}$" broad with horizontal striations.

Common in the forests, especially in the damper valleys. Very common in the village lands where it is pollarded for the Tusser Silkworm which is reared on it. Fl. *May-June.* Fr. *Feby.-March.* Deciduous *March-May.*

L. 5-9″ with 2 glands beneath near the base or on the short petiole, entire or the nerves excurrent as teeth. *Petiole* sometimes ½″.

The young ovaries are attacked by a cynips so that panicles of galls are very common on the tree and are sometimes mistaken for fruits.

N. B.—The glabrous variety which is not uncommon in Ch. Nagpur is sometimes difficult to distinguish from T. arjuna in herbarium specimens. The pubescent form has the leaves usually green beneath. I do not remember in C. N. the peculiar grey form common in the Sub-Himalayas. There may be differences in the timber between these varieties. Hybrids occur between this and Arjuna.

2 Anogeissus, Wall.

Trees or shrubs with opp. or sub-opp. and alternate entire petioled leaves and small greenish flowers in globose axillary peduncled heads. Ovary inferior and hypanthium produced above it into a beak and then into a campanulate 5-lobed "calyx-tube." Petals 0. St. 10 in two series adnate to the campanulate tube. Disc crenate hairy at the base of the tube. Ovules 2 pendulous. Fruits small indehiscent compressed 2-winged beaked, in densely packed heads.

Bark smooth pale. Old L. glabrous 1½-3½″ . . 1. *latifolia.*
„ „ „ „ tomentose „ . *var tomentosa.*
Bark rough dark. Old L. hairy beneath 1-3″ . . . . 2. *acuminata.*
Bark light. Old L. silky beneath 1-2″ . . 3. *sericea.*

1. **A. latifolia,** *Wall.* Hesel, *K.*, *S.*; Dhaunta, *Kharw.*; Dhaura, *H.*

An erect mod.-sized or large tree with whitish bark and alt. to opp. ovate or ell. leaves 2-4″ long usually obtuse both ends and becoming glabrous with age. Peduncles mostly in short axillary racemes.

Very common, especially on the drier hills, where it forms a large proportion of the growing stock. Also frequent in second growth. Fls. *June-Sept.* Fr. *Dec.-Jany.* Dec. *Feby.-April.* Leaves turn red or brown in *December.*

L. sometimes acute or emarginate with 8-14 prs. of sec. nerves. *Petiole* $\frac{1}{4}$-$\frac{3}{4}$″. *Heads* $\frac{1}{3}$″ diam. *Fruit* (excluding beak) about as long as broad rarely $\frac{1}{4}$″. Beak at length usually deciduous, equalling or rather shorter than the diameter of the fruit.

It yields a copious gum "used by the Santals in cholera," *Camp.* The leaves contain much tannin. The very strong wood is largely used for agricultural implements and carts.

Var. *tomentosa*, twigs and leaves, esp. beneath, persistently tomentose. Near the Barakar river in Manbhum; on the hills in the extreme east of Palamau, and west of Hazaribagh (about Barwadih). Ripe fruit in December.

2. **A. acuminata,** *Wall.* Parsia, Gara-hesel, *K.*; Chakwa, *Beng.*

An erect straight large beautiful tree with slender drooping branches, or flowering as a small tree. Bark dark. L. mostly sub-opp. narrowly ell. acute at both ends, more rarely broadly ell. and very obtuse and mucronate, esp. when young, always densely silky pubescent when young and more or less so beneath when old with 4-10 prs. fine distinct sec. nerves. Heads and peduncles rusty tomentose, mostly from the previous year's shoots solitary axillary or from leaf scars or several together. Wings of fruit not jagged.

In valleys in Singbhum, esp. along water courses.
There seem to be two or three different forms of which complete material (in all stages) is wanting:—

(*a*) Small tree in full leaf and flower in *April*. *L.* narrowly ell. 1$\frac{1}{2}$-2″ by $\frac{5}{8}$—$\frac{3}{4}$″ acute at both ends, thinly pubescent beneath. *Peduncles* solitary. *Branchlets* very slender.

(*b*) A tree in flower with new leaves in *April*. Branchlets stouter. *Innovations* very villous or silky-pubescent. *Old L.* broadly ell. 2$\frac{1}{4}$″ by 1$\frac{1}{4}$″ more densely pubescent beneath, acute both ends or obtuse and mucronate. *Peduncles* usually clustered and branched.

(*c*) A tree 6-7 ft. girth with very slender branches, flowering in *March* and fruiting in *April*. *Frt.* $\frac{3}{20}$″ long and $\frac{1}{4}$″ broad with a beak $\frac{3}{20}$″ long, top of fruit villous pubescent. *L.* as in (*a*).

Wood used for cart wheels and ploughs.

3. **A. sericea,** *Brandis.*

Described in the Indian Forester Vol. XXV, p. 287 as follows:—"A mod.-sized tree, branchlets and underside of leaves clothed with long silky hairs. *L.* 1-1½" long, elliptic, shortly acuminate, on short petioles. Sec. nerves 4-6 prs. *Flower-heads* ¾" diam. single, on long peduncles, which frequently bear a number of leafy bracts. *Fr.* tomentose, with the wings broader than long, wings jagged. Calyx often persistent, at the end of the long tube."

One of the vars. above, of which I have only incomplete specimens, *may* be referable to this species.

3. Combretum, L.

Usually large sarmentose shrubs (C. nanum is a dwarf shrub) with opp. or sub.-opp., more rarely alt., entire leaves. Fls. small in panicled spikes or racemes, sometimes with white petaloid bracts, polygamous. Hypanthium or receptacle constricted above the ovary, urceolate or tubular above and bearing 4-5 small sepals and as many, or 0, petals and twice as many stamens in two series. Ovules 2-5 pendent. Fr. with 4-5 angles or wings. Seed 1.

A. Fls. 5-merous. Fr. 5-winged . . . . . 1. *decandrum.*

B. Fls. 4-merous. Fr. 4-winged . . . . . .

  a. Hyp. not produced into a narrow tube above the ovary.

    Large sarmentose shrub . . . . . . 2. *ovalifolium.*

    Undershrub . . . . 3. *nanum.*

  b. Hypanthium produced into a cylindrical tube above the ovary . . . . 4. *extensum.*

1. C. decandrum, *Roxb.* Phalando, Palandu, *K.*; Aten, *S.*; Rateng, *Kharw*; Gorunda, *Oraon*?

A large scrambling climber, sometimes covering the highest trees and conspicuous from the large white bracts on the inflorescence.

Very common especially along nalas. Fls. *Nov.-Feby.* Fr. *April-June.*

Innovations densely rusty villous. *L.* coriaceous oblong shortly suddenly acuminate 3-5" rarely attaining 6" by 3", shining above, somewhat appressed hairy or with tufts of hairs in the axils of the strong nerves beneath. *Spikes* rusty villous ½-1" in large axillary and terminal panicles. *Hypth.* urceolate ⅛" diam. densely pubescent, sepals ultimately reflexed. *Pet.* ovate acuminate hairy. St. 10. *Fr.* 1-1¼", oblong or elliptic.

The leaves on the panicle turn white in *Nov.*, while the buds are unopened.

2. C. ovalifolium, *Roxb.*

Habit of last; with or without the white bracts. L. ovate to lanceolate from an acute base usually about 4½″ by 3″, shining, glabrous or slightly hairy on midrib beneath. Racemes lateral and terminal panicled. Calyx-tube glandular and slightly pubescent. Fr. ¾″ long and about as broad nearly glabrous, 4-winged.

Ch. Nagpur, *Prain.* Rare. Fl. *Feby.-Mar.* L. turn dark red before falling. *Dec.-Feby.*

3. C. nanum, *Ham.* Phirtol-rel, Andaika, *K.*

An undershrub with woody rootstock, 1-2 feet high with numerous erect branches 1-2 feet high, opp. or alt. leaves and rather dense racemes of white flowers. Fr. 1-1½″, 4-winged, of a pretty pink or red colour.

Dry burnt jungles, fire-lines, etc., Singbhum, Manbhum, *Camp.*, Hazaribagh, Ranchi, Palamau and probably in the other districts. New shoots and flowers *April-May.* Fr. *June-Aug.* L. turn brilliant red in *Dec.* before falling.

L. young red then bright green, orbicular obovate to lanceolate retuse or obtuse 2½″ by 2″ to 4″ by 3½″. *Petiole* ⅓″. *Racemes* 4-8″. C.-tube obconic. *Petals* far exceeding the sepals.

4. C. extensum, *Roxb.*

A scandent shrub. L. 4-8″ ovate or ell. acute, glabrous or nearly so, punctate when young. Racemes dense lateral rarely divided, terminal, sub-paniculate usually elongate 4-6″ long. Calyx-tube funnel-shaped. Petals narrow obovate. Fr. 1¼″ long and nearly as broad.

Chota Nagpur, *Prain.* I have not seen it. Fls. *c. s.*

Quisqualis indica, *L.* is a rambling sub-scandent shrub often found in gardens. Fls. in spikes showy rose or scarlet with a very long slender hypanthium 1½-2½″ long. Fr. dry 5-angled.

Fam. 50. UMBELLIFERÆ.

Herbs with fistular stems, compound (simple and kidney-shaped in the creeping Hydrocotyle asiatica, L.) leaves with a sheathing petiole, and small white or yellow, often polygamous flowers in simple or compound umbels, the exterior flowers sometimes irregular with the outer petals larger. *Sepals* superior, very small or 0. *Pet.* 5. *St.* 5 in the male and herm. fl., epigynous. *Disc* large. *Ovary* 2-celled. *Ovules* 1 in each cell. *Fruit* of 2 cocci (mericarps) separating from a columella (carpophore.)

Bracteoles 3-4. Fruit strongly dorsally compressed . 1. *Peucedanum.*
Bracteoles 0-2. Fruit didymous, broader than long . 2. *Pimpinella.*

1. Peucedanum, L.

1. P. nagpurense, *Prain.* Enondom. oponom, *K.*; oponom, *S.*

An erect stout herb 3-4½ ft. high with a fusiform root, polished striated stems, and twice ternately-compound leaves. Bracts 0 or 1. Bracteoles 3-4 lanceolate below long caudate, spreading and reflexed in fruit. Umbels terminal 2-3″ diam. Fls. 1/8-1/6″ diam.

Forests, frequent in Singbhum, Manbhum, Palamau and S. P. Fls. *Oct.-Nov.* Fr. *Dec.*

Lower petioles 8-12″. *Lflts.* ovate or rhomboid attaining 6″ by 3¼″ coarsely serrate glabrous except the ribs beneath, upper very narrow. *Sepals* minute. *Petals* green or brownish, oblong lanceolate with an inflexed tip. *Mericarps* ⅓″ elliptic-oblong truncate both ends, winged, brown with the ridges white, 4 vittæ (oil channels) on the outer and 3 on the inner face. *Carpophore* 2-fid to the base.

The stems are used for shepherd's pipes (rotu). The root is used as a stomachic.

2. Pimpinella, L.

1. P. Heyneana, *Wall.*

A slender erect branched herb 1-3 ft. high with glabrous striated stem, and 1-2-ternately compound leaves. Bracts 0. Bracteoles 0 or 1, rarely 2, setaceous, ¼″ or less long.

Umbels leaf-opposed $1\frac{1}{2}$-3″ diam. Fls. minute, scarcely $\frac{1}{10}$″ diam.

Damp places, common. Fls. *Oct.* Fr. *Dec.-Jany.*

Lower petioles 2″. *Lflts.* rarely 2″, finely doubly-serrate, lanceolate or ovate-lanc. shortly pubescent both sides. *Sep.* 0. *Pet.* white, with an inflexed tip. *Mericarps* $\frac{1}{16}$″ smooth. Vittæ 8.

Root used in fever, *Wood.*

Fam. 51. ARALIACEÆ.

Trees or shrubs, often scandent, with usually palmately-nerved and lobed or digitate more rarely 1-3 pinnate leaves, *petioles* with a sheathing base, stipulate or not. *Fls.* small regular, 2-sexual or polygamous. *Sepals* small superior or 0. *Petals* 5 rarely 6-7, valvate or sub-imbricate. *St.* alt. with the petals, inserted outside the epigynous disc. *Ovary* inferior 2-several-celled. *Styles* as many as the cells or united. *Ovule* 1 in each cell, pendulous. *Fruit* usually drupaceous with 1 or more cells and seeds. *Albumen* sometimes ruminated.

Small tree. L. palmate (or young digitate) . . 1. *Trevesia.*
Climbing shrub. L. digitate . . . . . 2. *Heptapleurum.*
Small tree. L. 2-3-pinnate . . . . . 3. *Heteropanax.*

1. Trevesia, Vis.

1. T. palmata, *Vis.*

A small erect scarcely branched soft-wooded prickly tree with hairy shoots, large palmate sub-orbicular leaves 1-2 ft. diam. and white flowers in large panicles composed of numerous umbels.

Valleys in Singbhum (*e.g.*, Leda Block, Jui gara), rare. Fls. *Jany.-Feby.* Fr. *May-June.* Evergreen

Attaining 15 ft. Lobes of leaf sharply harshly serrate. *Panicles* 18. *Sepals* minute. *Petals* 8-10.

2. Heptapleurum, Gærtn.

1. **H. venulosum,** *Seem.* Sukriruya; Sukrirun, *K.*; Sunum jur, *S.*; Ban Simar, *Beng.*

A large climbing or epiphytic shrub attaining 3 ft. girth[1] with digitate 5-7-foliolate leaves, and pale or yellow flowers in panicled umbels.

Valleys in Singbhum; Hazaribagh; S. P.; Kurughat (Palamau). Fls. *May-June.*

Lflts. unequal 2-6″ by 1·2″, glabrous, acuminate. *Petioles* 3-6″, *Petiolules* 1-2″. *Stipules* connate within the petiole. *Umbels* ⅓″ diam. racemed on the 5-8″ long branches of the short panicle. Bracteoles 0. *Calyx* truncate. *Pet.* 5-6, 3-nerved. *Ovary*-cells as many. Styles 0.

3. Heteropanax, Seem.

1. **H. fragrans,** *Seem.* Rengebanam, *K.*

An erect small tree up to 2 ft. girth with enormous tri-pinnate leaves 3-4 ft. long and 2-3 ft. across, elliptic or ell. ovate glabrous entire leaflets 3-7″ long and small yellow flowers in umbels on the branches of large panicles. Fruit a laterally compressed 2-seeded berry.

Valleys in Singbhum and S. P. near streams. Very common on north aspects on the trap of the Rajmehal hills near Dharampur and Morjhora. Fls. *Dec.* Evergreen.

Pinnæ sometimes 4-5 often together with a single leaflet, at the nodes of the main rachis. *Lflts.* with a short acumen, 1-7 on the ultimate branches of the leaf, base usually rounded.

Fam. 52. CORNACEÆ.

Trees or shrubs with opp. or alt. simple exstipulate leaves often basal-nerved. *Fls.* regular in cymes or panicles,

---

[1] Clark says (Journal L. S. XXI, 252) "I noticed that Heptapleurum commences its life here (*i.e.*, on Parasnath) as a scandent epiphyte, but subsequently reaching the ground, it grows to a large size as a tree, and shows no signs of its early history."

sometimes capitate. *Sepals* 4-10 superior or calyx-limb truncate, persistent. *Petals* 4-10 or 0. *St.* epigynous 1-3-times as many as the petals. Epigynous *disc* usually conspicuous. *Ovary* inferior 1-4 celled. Style 1. Stigma capitate or branched. *Ovule* 1 in each cell pendulous (rarely 2-3). *Fruit* generally a berry or drupe. Albumen copious fleshy and embryo large with flat cotyledons. The endocarp, sometimes infolded as a plate into the seed.

L. alt. St. 2-3-times as many as the petals. Ovary 1-celled. 1. *Alangium.*

1. Alangium, Lamk.

1. A. **Lamarckii,** *Thwaites.* Ankol, *K.;* Dhela, *S. Kharw.;* Kumri, *Mal Pah.;* Akar-kanta, *Beng.*

A small bushy tree attaining 25 ft. usually thorny, with oblong or elliptic leaves 3-6″ by 1-2″ pubescent when young, moderate-sized white flowers in axillary fascicles or from leafless axils. Petals 5-10. Stamens 20-30. Fr. $\frac{1}{3}$-$\frac{3}{4}$″ ellipsoid, black, succulent, with bony endocarp, crowned by the calyx, appearing ribbed when dried. Albumen not ruminate.

A very common tree in waste ground and on the hills. Fls. *March-May.* Fr. *June-July.* More or less leafless at the time of flowering. New leaves appear *May-June.*

L. with unequal base, first pair of sec. n. at or near the base, upper surface with pubescent nerves, beneath sparsely hairy and with gland pits, or tufts of hairs in the axils of the sec. nerves. *Sec. n.* about 6 prs., tertiaries more or less parallel. *Petiole* $\frac{1}{4}$″. *Calyx-limb* minutely toothed. *Anthers* very long and slender. *Disc* hirsute. *Cotyledons* flat with 3-nerved base.

The fruit is eaten. The bark and root are used in jaundice. The wood is strong.

Fam. 53. OLACACEÆ.

Trees, shrubs, undershrubs or climbers, sometimes root parasites, with alt., simple, exstipulate entire leaves often several-nerved at the base. *Fls.* regular, 1-2-sexual or diœcious. *Calyx* (hypanthium) small, 4-6-toothed, or obsolete, base free or adnate to the disc or ovary, in fruit often enlarged and enclosing the fruit. *Petals* 4-6 free or connate, valvate in bud, rarely imbricate. *St.* as many as the petals (often only 3 fertile) and opposite to them or 2-3-times as many. Anthers 2-celled with longitudinal dehiscence. *Ovary* free at the base or enclosed in the torus, 1-celled, or 2-5-celled at the base. *Placentæ* usually free axile from which 1 rarely 2 long anatropous ovules depend into each loculus, or ovary 1-celled with 1 pendulous or erect ovule. *Style* with small stigma. *Fruit* 1-seeded usually drupaceous, the placenta often embedded in a cleft of the seed. *Seed* with a thin testa and copious albumen. Embryo usually small and apical.

Stamens more than the petals, calyx accrescent . . . 1. *Olax.*
Stamens isomerous with the petals alternating with staminodes or disc glands.
Bracts orbicular caducous. Fls. slender pedicelled . . 2. *Opilia.*
Bracts minute subulate. Fls. sessile . . . . . 3. *Cansjera.*

1. Olax, L.

Calyx very small in flower, truncate, greatly enlarging in fruit and more or less enclosing it. Petals or perianth leaves 5-6. Stamens 9-12, occasionally fewer, usually 3 fertile, the rest staminodes. Ovary free, 1-celled or at the base 3-celled. Ovules 3, linear pendulous from the apex of the free central placenta, two soon abortive. Drupe surrounded by the accrescent fleshy calyx(or hypanthium). Embryo minute.

(The fertile ovule pushes the central placenta to one side, so that the latter appears as an ascending basal funicle in fruit).

A considerable shrub usually scandent . . . . 1. *scandens.*
A dwarf undershrub . . . . 2. *nana.*

1. **O. scandens,** *Roxb.* Rimil, Rimil-biri, *K.*; Hund, *S.*; Koko aru, *Beng.*

Sometimes an erect shrub,[1] usually scandent with woody trunk attaining 1 ft. diam. with pubescent branchlets and white flowers in short axillary racemes. Fruit yellow fleshy, $\frac{1}{3}''$ diam. more than half enclosed in the truncate calyx.

Stony ground, especially near ravines, common. Singbhum, Manbhum and throughout Ch. Nagpur. S. P. Fls. *April-June*. Fr. *Oct.-Dec.* Evergreen.

Rarely thorny. *L* somewhat distichous, coriaceous elliptic or ell.-ovate or oblong, obtuse, with rounded base, attaining 3″ by $1\frac{1}{2}''$, rarely $4\frac{1}{2}''$ by $1\frac{3}{4}''$. Sec. n. slender, not raised, lowest close to the base. *Petioles* $\frac{1}{2}$-$\frac{1}{3}''$ pubescent. *Fls.* on short pedicels, often distichous sometimes panicled from leaf suppression. *Calyx* ciliate. *Petals* narrow, $\frac{1}{4}$-$\frac{1}{3}''$ long. St. 7-10 at base of corolla, only 3-5 fertile, staminodes 2-fid. Disc thin, cupular.

The fruit is eaten. It is insipid and somewhat viscous. A sherbert is made from it in Hazaribagh.

2. O. nana, *Wall.* Merom-met', *S.*

A suffruticose perennial with a woody rootstock, sending up annually erect strict herbaceous shoots 1-2 ft. high with sub-sessile oblong-lanceolate or linear-oblong leaves and solitary axillary small white flowers.

Open places, and scrub jungles, Manbhum. Fls. *May.* Fr. *May.*

Shoots striate. *L.* glabrous, reaching 3″ by $\frac{1}{2}$-$\frac{3}{4}''$ obtuse. *Peduncles* $\frac{1}{8}''$ long. *Fls.* $\frac{1}{3}''$ white when expanded, buds oblong. *Calyx* rudimentary in flower, growing up and enclosing the fruit with a fleshy scarlet covering. *Petals* 3 linear-oblong. Fertile St. 3, Stmnds. 3, white 2-fid. *Fruit* (with calyx) $\frac{1}{2}''$ diam., oblong or obovoid.

2. Opilia, Roxb.

1. O. amentacea, *Roxb.*

A scandent shrub with fulvous-tomentose branchlets and lanceolate or lanceolate-ovate leaves. Fls. very small greenish slender-pedicelled in threes, racemose, concealed when young by orbicular-rhomboid ciliate bracts which are arranged in catkin-like axillary and extra axillary spikes $\frac{3}{4}$-$1\frac{1}{2}''$ long.

---

[1] A root parasite. *Vide* Studies in Root Parasitism by C. A. Barber, Memoirs of the Department of Agriculture in India, Botanical Series, Vol. II, No. IV.

Calyx-tube nearly obsolete, annular. Filaments 5 very slender alternating with 5 large green fleshy disc lobes. Fr. globose or ellipsoid, tomentose (at least when young).

Singbhum, Saranda forest in open grassy places. Santal Parganahs (Kuskia, *Gamble*). Fls. *April-May*. Fr. *July*.

L. 1½-4" long mostly acuminate, rather coriaceous, with distinct fine and irregular sec. n. usually over 5 pairs, tertiaries distinct reticulate. *Petiole* $\frac{1}{10}$-⅛". *Racemes* solitary or clustered with pubescent or tomentose rachis. *Pedicels* ⅛". *Tepals* 5 yellowish. *St.* opposite the tepals. *Anths.* versatile. *Drupe* about ⅓" pedicelled.

3. Cansjera, Juss.

1. C. Rheedii, *Gmel.*

A large, usually scandent, shrub[1] with pubescent, sometimes very green and lenticellate, branches and shining ovate or lanceolate-ovate leaves. Fls. very small yellowish sessile tomentose, subtended by minute subulate bracts on tomentose spikes ½-1" long. Calyx-tube obsolete. Filaments 4-5 slender slightly adnate to the perianth-tube, alternating with 4-5 subulate staminodes (or disc lobes). Fr. a fleshy scarlet ellipsoid drupe with thin hard endocarp.

Along ravines and near water. Singhbhum and S. P. (east of Chandna). Monghyr. Fls. *Nov.-Dec.* Fr. *April-May*.

L. 1⅓" by ⅞" to 4½" by 2", mostly acuminate, often minutely translucent-dotted, somewhat puberulous beneath when young. Sec. n. rarely over 5 pairs, of which the first 1 2 prs. close to the often oblique base, tertiaries very indistinct. *Petiole* $\frac{1}{10}$-⅛". *Fls.* 2-sexual. *Perianth* tubular-campanulate ⅛" long with 4-5 recurved lobes. *Drupe* ⅓-½" sessile (it often appears long-peduncled from only a single terminal flower at the end of the spike developing fruit).

Fam. 54. LORANTHACEÆ.

Green parasitic shrubs attaching themselves by means of haustoria to the branches of other woody plants, with opp. or alt. simple entire leaves, or leaves reduced to scales and

---

[1] A root parasite, *vide* loc. cit. Vol. II, No. 5.

their functions assumed by the flattened green branches. *Fls.* from very small, regular and inconspicuous, to brightly coloured and with a tendency to zygomorphy, 1-2 sexual. *Ovary* completely sunk in the floral axis and united with it, the axis sometimes growing up as an entire or toothed ring ("*calyculus*"). *Perianth* sepaloid or petaloid of 4-6 leaves free or on a perianth tube. *Stamens* as many as the per. leaves and opp. to them. *Ovule* and placenta not differentiated, completely filling the ovary, with usually 1 rarely 2-3 embryo sacs. *Fruit* baccate, rarely drupaceous with a viscid inner layer, by means of which it becomes adherent to the future host.

Calyculus present. Fls. 2-sexual, often conspicuous . 1. *Loranthus.*
Calyculus 0. Fls. 1-sexual, inconspicuous . . . 2. *Viscum.*

1. Loranthus, L.

L. opp. or alternate usually broad. Perianth usually more or less tubular with free or connate tepals, St. epiphyllous. Anthers adnate or versatile.

A. Fls. in tomentose fascicles or sub-racemose. Bracteoles 0. (Bracts present in all).
  L. under 3″ broad, base rarely sub-cordate usually cuneate . . . . 1. *scurrula.*
  L. over 3″ broad, base cordate or rounded . . . 2. *cordifolius.*
B. Fls. distincly racemed.
  Bracteoles 0. Calyculus tubular toothed . . . 3. *longiflorus.*
  Bracteoles 2 connate. Calyculus entire . . . 4. *globosus.*

1. L. scurrula, *L.* Huring sum, *K.*; Banda, *S.*, *H.*

A tufted epiphytic shrub, young parts with a brown stellate or scaly tomentum. L. ovate-oblong or elliptic 2″ by 1″ to 4″ by 2½″, young rusty, mature often glabrous. Fls. in sub-racemose fascicles or contracted racemes axillary and clustered at the old nodes. Perianth tomentose ½-⅝″ long green split with 4 linear lobes $\frac{1}{8}$-$\frac{3}{16}$″ long, filaments bright red. Fr. clavate $\frac{1}{3}$″ stellate.

Common throughout the area, chiefly on Woodfordia and Wendlandia.

Fls. *Nov.-Jany.* Fr. *Dec.-Jany.*

L. obtuse or sub-acute, base usually cuneate and decurrent on the $\frac{1}{3}$-$\frac{1}{2}$″ long petiole. Sec. n. 4-5-prs. faint. *Peduncles* up to $\frac{1}{4}$″ long. *Bract* minute ovate-acuminate. *Calyculus* minute entire. *Per.-tube* inflated below.

(When quite ripe the outer covering of the fruit consisting of an epidermis, a parenchymatous tissue with little chlorophyll and an inner sheath of very fine cells becomes detached leaving a somewhat 4-gonous clavate body probably corresponding to the seed. This has an outer transparent very small celled layer and an inner thicker tissue very rich in chlorophyll which secretes the mucous).

2. L. cordifolius, *Wall.* Ichac' banda, *S.*

As Sir J. D. Hooker remarks, this is scarcely more than a variety of L. scurrula, differing in its greater size, more rounded and cordate leaves and the copious white tomentum, which gives it a very different aspect from the ordinary state of L. scurrula.

Hazaribagh; Manbhum, *Camp.*? (Campbell's plant L. buddleioides, a synonymn for this, may be L. scurrula, which he does not mention. The vernacular name means the Loranthus which grows on the Woodfordia.)

Fls. *Dec.*

3. L. longiflorus, *Desr.* Sum, *K.*; Banda, *S.*, *H.*, etc.

A shrub, glabrous (exc., sometimes the puberulous racemes). L. variable in shape and size, usually about 3-7″. Fls. in axillary and extra axillary racemes 1-4″ long. Perianth 1-2″ long slender red and orange with 5 linear-oblong often green lobes. Fruit oblong $\frac{1}{2}$″ glabrous crowned with the calyculus.

The commonest Loranthus, found on a large variety of trees including the Sal. Fls. *Nov.-Feby.*

4. L. globosus, *Roxb.*

A quite glabrous shrub with elliptic-lanceolate sub-acute or acuminate leaves, very obscurely nerved and 3-7 fls. $\frac{1}{2}$″

long in short axillary racemes, and from the leaf scars. Perianth-tube oblong 5-6 angled inflated even in bud with 5-6 linear spathulate lobes nearly as long as the tube. Fr. globose.

Manbhum, *Camp.*! Fls. *April.*

2. Viscum, L. Mistletoe.

L. opp. sometimes reduced to scales. Fls. small or minute, solitary or fascicled. Perianth leaves 3-4. Anthers sessile adnate to the perianth leaves, opening by pores.

A. Branches leafly.
  L. lanceolate or elliptic acute. Fruit oblong . 1. *monoicum.*
  L. obovate to oblong obtuse. Fruit globose . . 2. *orientale.*
B. Branches flattened, leafless . . . . . . 3 *articulatum.*

1. V. monoicum, *Roxb.*

A shrub with slender terete branches compressed at the ends, narrowly elliptic often oblique (or obliquely ovate, *Prain*) leaves $1\frac{1}{2}''$ by $\frac{1}{2}''$ to $3''$ by $1\frac{1}{4}''$ rarely attaining $5''$, and minute greenish flowers in sessile, or very shortly-peduncled fascicles at all the nodes. Fr. oblong $\frac{1}{4}''$ green polished with white veins.

Manbhum, on Helicteres Isora, *Camp.* (The Santal name quoted by Wood, *viz.*, Pet chamra Banda merely means this); Pitorea (Ranchi) *Wood*; Santal P. Fls. *Nov-Dec.* Fr. *Jany.*

2 V. orientale, *Willd.*

A shrub with terete greenish 2-3-chotomous or sub-verticillate branches, obovate or ell.-oblong (or, linear-oblong, *F.B.I.*) leaves about $1\frac{1}{2}''$ by $\frac{5}{8}''$ or less, with a mat surface, and usually slightly crimped margins. Small yellowish flowers $\frac{1}{12}''$ long sessile in axillary and terminal sessile or stalked fascicles. Fr. globose nearly $\frac{1}{4}''$ diam.

Singbhum (on Zizyphus, Croton and other trees). Hazaribagh at Lunkta, *Wood*; also in the Damuda valley, Manbhum, *Camp.* Fls. *May-June.* Fr. *Nov.*

Branchlets ridged and grooved. L. rarely $2\frac{1}{4}''$ subsessile. *Peduncles* $0\text{-}\frac{1}{6}''$. *Heads* usually 3-5-fld. subtended by 2 boat-shaped bracts connate at base sometimes heads compound and bracts in decussate pairs. Per. leaves 4, $\frac{1}{30}''$ long.

Campbell says this plant is believed to derive its medicinal properties from the tree on which it grows, and these are therefore as numerous as its hosts.

3. **V. articulatum,** *Burm.* Katkom janga, *S.*

A leafless shrub with sap-green striate often sub-verticillate flattened branches contracted at the nodes. Internodes $1\text{-}2''$ by $\frac{3}{16}''$(up to $\frac{1}{3}''$ in one form which I have not seen in our area). Fls. minute, fascicled at the nodes with cup-shaped bracts, 3-4-merous.

Common, Singbhum; Hazaribagh, esp. on Diospyros; Manbhum, very common on Bassia and Diospyros and several other trees, *Camp.*; Kurwandi reserve, Palamau, *Gamble. Fls. Dec-Jany.*

Fam. 55. SANTALACEÆ.

1. Santalum, L.

1. **S. album,** L. Sandal-wood.

A small glabrous evergreen tree, a hemi-parasite-like Loranthus, but terrestrial with haustoria attached to the roots of trees. L. opp. $1\text{-}2\frac{1}{4}''$ long elliptic or ovate-lanceolate acute or sub-acute. Fls. small in terminal trichotomous panicles perianth $\frac{1}{6}''$ diam. at first pale then deep red rotate. Fr. a fleshy globose shining black drupe.

Collected by the Revd. A. Campbell on Parasnath. Fls. *March.* Fr. Nov.

Fls. regular 2-sexual. *Perianth* campanulate with 4-5 spreading lobes, with a tuft of hair behind the stamens which are inserted opp. the lobes on the margin of the disc which lines the tube. *Ovary* perigynous at first, ultimately half inferior with long style and short 2-4-lobed stigma, 1-celled. *Ovules* 2-4 inserted below the summit of a long free central placenta.

Fam. 56. PORTULACACEÆ.

1. Portulaca, L.

Diffuse succulent herbs with alt., opp. or (below the inflorescence) whorled leaves and small yellow (brilliantly coloured in cult. species) solitary or clustered fls. *Sep.* (or bracts ?) 2 connate below, the free part deciduous. *Pet.* 4-6 perigynous. St. 8-12 inserted with the petals. *Ovary* half-inferior 1-celled. Style 3-8 fid. *Ovules* ∝ central. Capsule transversely dehiscent.

Two common herbs largely used as vegetables are 1. **P. oleracea,** *L.* Dalia : , *Ho.*; Mota uric 'alang, *S.* 6-12″ high with alt. cuneate truncate leaves $\frac{1}{4}$-$1\frac{1}{2}$″ whorled above.

2. **P. quadrifida,** *L.* Suni a : , *Ho.* Diffuse with ovate or ovate-lanceolate opp. leaves $\frac{1}{5}$-$\frac{1}{3}$″ and terminal solitary fls.

The beautiful little garden plant known as **Portulaca** is a Brazilian species.

Fam. 57. AMARANTACEÆ.

Herbs, rarely shrubs with opposite or alternate simple, exstipulate leaves and small white or green, dry, regular flowers in simple or panicled spikes, cymes or clusters, some of the flowers frequently more or less rudimentary or altered. *Bracts* and 2 *bracteoles* scarious. *Perianth-lobes* inferior 5 free (rarely 1-3) persistent, hyaline or scarious imbricate in bud. *St.* 1-5 opposite the lobes, sometimes with alternating staminodes, filaments connate below. *Anths.* 1- or 2-celled. *Ovary* 1-celled ; styles 1-3 ; ovules 1 or more, often amphitropous, basal with capillary funicle. *Fruit* usually a utricle, rarely a berry or capsule, seated on or inclosed in the perianth. Seed erect compressed, with annular or horse-shoe-shaped embryo surrounding a mealy albumen.

Ovules few or many. Rambling shrub with red berries . 1. *Deeringia.*

Ovule 1 erect.

- Herbs with alt. leaves and 1-sexual fls. . . . 2. *Amarantus.*
- Herb with alt. leaves and 2-sexual fls. . . . 3. *Digera.*

Ovule 1 suspended from a basal funicle.
Fls. clustered with rudimentary one reduced to hooked awns . . . . 4. *Pupalia.*
Fls. all perfect. Perianth lobes spinescent . 5. *Achyranthes.*
Fls. all perfect. Perianth lobes soft . . . 6. *Aerua.*

Celosia cristata, L. often with a cockscomb-shaped inflorescence is common in gardens, and **Celosia argentea**, L. with white or pink scarious flowers in spikes, is a common weed (Sirgit arak' S.) whose leaves are eaten. There are also other weeds of the order not described here, *e.g.*, Alternanthera.

1. Deeringia, R. Br.

1. D. celosioides, *Br.* Latman, *H.*; Gola mohani, *Beng.*

A rambling or sub-scandent shrub with arching branches alt. petioled leaves, and small greenish white flowers in panicled spikes. Conspicuous in fruit by the numerous small scarlet berries $\frac{1}{4}$-$\frac{1}{6}$″ diam., containing small black seeds.

Only seen by me, in Chota Nagpur, in the low lands of Palamau near the Sone. Fls. *Sept.* Fr. *Dec.-Jany.*

L. ovate or ovate-lanceolate acuminate. *Fls.* $\frac{1}{8}$″ diam. 2-sexual. *Stamens* 5 (4-5, *F.B.I.*) connate at the base. An annular hypogynous *disc* also present. *Stigmas* 2-4.

2. Amarantus, L.

Herbs with alt. leaves and small greenish 1-sexual flowers in axillary or panicled-spiked clusters. Sepals 2-5, and st. as many without staminodes. Stigma 2-3. Utricle compressed. Embryo annular.

1. A. spinosus, *L.* Januma:, *Ho.*; Janum Ara, *M.*

An erect glabrous copiously branched weed armed with sharp axillary spines and bearing axillary clusters and long terminal often panicled spikes of green 1-sexual flowers.

A very common weed. In all districts. Fls. and Fr. most of the year.

Stems green, red or striped 1-3 ft. L. $\frac{1}{4}$-4″ long narrowed into the slender petiole.

The leaves are eaten. The ash of the plant is used as a dye.

The numerous species of Amarantus are known generically as Leper ara (or a: in Ho.) in *Kol*, and Gandhari arak', in *S. e.g.*, **A. giganteus,** *Konig* is marang leper a:, **A. gangeticus,** *L.* is ara leper a:, or naguri leper a:, according to variety, etc., etc.

Digera arvensis, *Forsk.* Kari Gandhari, *S.* is an erect or prostrate herb with long-petioled ovate leaves and axillary long spikes of small pink flowers. Fls. distant ⅛" long, 2 outer tepals cymbiform, 3 inner deep-magenta broadly-oblong. Bracteoles with forked green fleshy scales in their axils (imperfect flowers ?). Very common, used as a pot-herb. Fls., Fr. r. s.

4. Pupalia, Juss.

Herbs or undershrubs with opposite leaves and small greenish flowers in spiked clusters. Outer fls. in the cluster reduced to awns bearing stellately spreading hooked bristles. St. 5. Staminodes 0. Style slender, stigma capitellate.

1. P. lappacea, *Moq.* Kuya-duya, *Beng.*

A pubescent or tomentose undershrub with long straggling branches, shortly petioled softly pubescent ovate-oblong leaves. Chiefly noticeable from the barbed heads of fruits ½" diam. which tenaciously adhere to the clothes.

Rocky places in Palamau. Fls. *Sept.-Oct.* Fr. *Nov.-Dec.*

L. 2-4" with acute base. The *heads* consist of perfect flowers with densely wooly 3-nerved sepals, and stalked stellate spines in threes with a persistent bract from below their point of origin, the whole on a tough peduncle. The number of such spines is 4-7 in a whorl.

2. P. atropurpurea, *Moq.*

A herb with long straggling branches, distant pairs of petioled shining leaves and green flowers, about 2 perfect in globose clusters ¼-⅓" diam. along a spike, with a number of sterile ones, which develop in fruit into stellately spreading *red* hooked bristles.

Waste ground, esp. edges of fields and jungles in grassy places frequent. Singbhum, etc. Fls., Fr. *Nov.-Jany.*

Branches glabrous or roughly pubescent. *L.* 1-4" ovate or ell. acute apiculate, narrowed into the petiole. *Spikes* reaching 1 foot, globose sessile clusters distant. *Bracts* pungent. *Sepals* 3-nerved wooly at base and sides, sparsely hairy on back, pungent.

Achyranthes aspera, *L.* Sitir Kedn, M.; Chipchirit', *S.*; Apang, *Beng.*, is a common weed with opp. leaves and long spikes of flowers, which are soon deflexed and very troublesome in fruit from the spinescent bracts, bracteoles and perianth segments running into the hand and adhering to the clothes.

Var. porphyristachya is sub-scandent and common in the forest. Fls., Fr. *Oct.-Jany.*

6. Ærua, Forsk.

Herbs or undershrubs, sometimes climbing, with alt., opp. or whorled leaves and small or minute flowers in solitary or panicled dense spikes. Perianth segments 4-5, short membranous, all or the 3 inner wooly, Filaments connate at base into a cup with intervening staminodes. Stigmas 1 capitellate or 2. Fruit a utricle or circumscissile capsule with coriaceous apex.

1. A. scandens, *Wall.* Nuriya, *Beng.*

Stem woody below with branches 2-4' ft. high or sub-scandent, pubescent or hoary-tomentose. L. alt., or opp. and alt., elliptic or ell. lanc., lower attaining 6" by $2\frac{1}{4}$", upper often only 1". Fls. white in dense oblong axillary, terminal and panicled spikes $\frac{1}{4}$-2" long.

Forests, not unfrequent, Singbhum, Hazaribagh, etc., Fl., Fr. *March-Dec.*

Stems striate. *L.* sub-acuminate, base decurrent on the short petiole. Sec. n. about 8 prs. *Fls.* 4-5 on short branches of the spike, each subtended by a hyaline shortly awned bract $\frac{1}{18}$" long exactly resembling the wooly or villous softly aristate sepals. Capsule thin rupturing irregulary transversely. Seeds black smooth.

2. A. lanata, *Juss.*

Branches many from a woody rootstock, erect or prostrate, hoary tomentose about 1 ft. with small alt. elliptic to orbicular *leaves* $\frac{1}{2}$-1" and numerous axillary *spikes* $\frac{1}{4}$-$\frac{1}{2}$" long of small wooly flowers.

A common weed. Fls., Fr. *Nov.-Jany.*

3. **A. Monsonia,** *Mart.* is a small plant with opposite or 3-nately whorled filiform leaves ½-1" and solitary or sub-panicled peduncled spikes ½-1" long of rose-coloured flowers. Hazaribagh in Sal forest. Fls. *Nov-Dec.*

Fam. 58. CHENOPODIACEÆ.

Herbs or shrubs with alt. simple exstipulate leaves and small usually regular 1-2-sexual flowers. *Calyx* herbaceous or membranous of 3-5 free or connate sepals or 2 or 0 in the female. *Pet.* 0. *St.* usually 5 opposite the sepals nearly always free at base, hypogynous or perigynous, anths.; 2-celled. *Ovary* 1-celled, stigmas 2-4. *Ovule* 1 basal or lateral campylotropous. *Fr.* a utricle enclosed in the often enlarged fleshy calyx. Seed alb. or exalb. Embryo curved, annular or spiral.

The cultivated Beet and Spinach belong to this family, and two or three weeds which are used as pot herbs.

1. Basella, L.

1. **B. rubra,** *L.* Utu a:; *Ho.*; Pui, *H.*

A fleshy twining much branched herb with ovate shining rather fleshy leaves and small sessile pinkish fleshy flowers in distant spikes, succeeded by ovoid pointed black 1-seeded berries (utricle enclosed in the fleshy perianth) ¼" diam.

Grown on trellises and hedges in all Ch. Nag. villages. Fls., Fr. *March-Dec.*

Stems often red. *L.* 1½" by 1¼" to 3" by 2" slightly acuminate with straight or rounded base. *Spikes* ½-3" long with fleshy rachis. *Fls.* 2-sexual, urceolate, with a small green bract and 2 adnate coloured bracteoles. *Perianth* 5-fid, fleshy with deep purple juice in fruit. *St.* 5 perigynous. *Styles* 3.

A pot-herb.

Fam. 59. POLYGONACEÆ.

1. Polygonum, L.

Herbs or rarely undershrubs with alt. simple, entire rarely lobed sometimes gland-dotted leaves and *ocreate* stipules. *Fls.* small 2-sexual clustered, clusters axillary or in spiciform racemes, with ochreate bracts and bracteoles. *Perianth* 4-5-partite, more or less enlarged or sometimes fleshy in fruit which it encloses. *St.* 5-8 rarely fewer, free, often wider at the base and adnate to the perianth base or an annular disc. *Ovary* free with 2-3 free, or more or less connate, styles and 1 erect orthotropous ovule. *Fr.* compressed or 3-quetrous, with a hard pericarp.

Ten species of the genus occur in Chota Nagpur, but they are of no forest importance. Several, however, are used as pot-herbs, and medicines. Among them—

P. plebejum, *Br.* Munia, Muni ara *K.*; Muic', *S.* A very common diffusely branched prostrate herb with pink flowers in the axils of the leaves, is eaten both by human beings, as a sag, and by horses. It resembles in appearence our English Knot-grass.

P. glabrum, *Willd.* Sauri arac', *S.* An erect species 3-4 ft. high growing in marshy places $\frac{1}{2}''$ thick and woody below, with lanceolate acuminate leaves about $5\frac{1}{2}''$ by $\frac{3}{4}''$ (attaining 10″ by 2″ in luxuriant plants) dotted glabrous shining narrowed into a very short petiole. *Stipules* truncate not ciliated. *Spikes* dense pinkish $1\frac{1}{3}$-3″ long about 2-5 in a panicle. *St.* 6-8. Style 2-fid. Fls. *Dec.-Jany.* Eaten as a sag.

To the Polygonaceæ belongs the beautiful Mexican climber **Antigonon leptopus,** *H.* and *Arn.*, with palmately-nerved leaves which at the ends of the shoots are often modified into tendrils. Fls. bright pink. Three outer tepals accrescent in fruit. Common in gardens.

Fam. 60. PIPERACEÆ.

1. Piper, L. Pepper.

Shrubs or herbs sometimes scandent, with swollen nodes, simple alt. entire often unequal-sided aromatic basal-nerved gland-dotted stipulate leaves and minute diœcious flowers in leaf-opposed or terminal spikes. *Spikes* usually with thick rachis and peltate bracts sometimes adnate to and decurrent on the rachis. *Perianth* 0. *Stamens* usually 2-3, rarely 1, 4 or 6. *Ovary* 1-celled, with 2-5 stigmas. *Ovule* 1 erect orthotropous. Fruit fleshy.

1. **P. longum,** *L.* Narjom red, Ralli red, *K.*; Ralli, *S.* Long pepper.

A creeping and ramblimg herb with distant alt. long-petioled or sessile cordate shining leaves with a seven-nerved base. M. spikes yellow about 3″ long. F. spikes $\frac{1}{2}$-$\frac{3}{4}$″.

Moist places under dense shade in Singbhum (Saranda and Porahat) Manbhum, *Camp.*; S. P., (Silingi) not common. Fls. *Aug.-Dec.* Fr. *Jany.-Feby.*

Quite glabrous, or pubescent above. Lower *leaves* 4″ by 4″ deeply cordate acute with petiole 3″. Upper smaller and narrower nearly sessile and amplexicaul. *Peduncles* 1-1$\frac{1}{4}$″. *Bracts* stalked peltate. Fruiting *spikes* sub-erect with berries $\frac{1}{10}$″ diam.

Both the root and fruit are used medicinally. They are stimulant and carminative, and used for cough. Campbell says that the root is used to ferment rice beer.

Piper Betle, *L.* The Pan is occasionally cultivated in grass green houses in Palamau.

Fam. 61. ARISTOLOCHIACEÆ.

1. Aristolochia, L.

Climbing herbs or shrubs with simple entire alternate exstipulate leaves, usually palmi-nerved with cordate base. Base of petiole dilated or decurrent on the stem. *Flowers* 2-sexual very zygomorphic, haplostemonous with petaloid gamopetalous perianth tube inflated at the base and constricted above the staminal column, hairy within. *St.* 6 fused into a column (gynostenium)with the style above the inferior 6-celled ovary. *Placentas* parietal meeting in the axis. *Ovules* many horizontal. *Fruit* capsular, usually dehiscing from the base.

1. A. indica *L.* Gad, *S.*

A glabrous shrub with a woody rootstock, slender sulcate branches, membranous, panduriform leaves (L. variable from linear to obovate-oblong, *F.B.I.*), and greenish flowers usually 2 or more on a peduncle with slatey-purple (*C. B. Clarke*) or brownish (*F. B. I.*) lip. Capsule 1½-2″ long, oblong, grooved. Seeds winged.

Santal Parganahs, Sundarpahari, *Haslett*! Fls. *June-Aug.* Fr. *Dec.*

L. 2-4″ by 1-2″, always broadest above the middle, mostly acuminate. Basal nerves 1 or 2 on each side of the mid-rib. *Petiole* slender ¼-⅓″. *Perianth* straight, tube shortly funnel-shaped with oblique trumpet-shaped mouth and short oblong obtuse lip.

Roxburgh says the root is nauseously bitter. Haslett says that it is used as a cure for snakebite. This is probably from a fancied resemblance of the flower to the head of a serpent, and is interesting inasmuch as several species have enjoyed a similar reputation in both North and South America (f. Solereder).

2. A. bracteata, *Retz.*

Stem slender decumbent or trailing with a long slender rootstock and striate branches 12-18″ long, reniform or broadly-cordate leaves 1½-3″ both ways and petiole 1-1½″. *Fls.* solitary on a bracteate peduncle; lip erect linear dark-purple with revolute edges. *Fruit* 1″ ovate grooved.

Chota Nagpur according to Wood's list (without locality), but I have seen no specimens from our area.

Fam. PROTEACEÆ.

A large non-Indian family of which there are some 590 Australian species, the remainder being chiefly African. To it belongs Grevillea robusta, *A. Cunn.*, which is often planted though not growing well in Chota Nagpur. It bears golden-yellow spikes of flowers in April-May.

Fam. 62. URTICACEÆ.

Herbs, shrubs, or small trees without milky juice, sometimes with stinging hairs. *L.* alt., rarely opposite (spp. of Boehmeria and others not of C. N.) with usually 3-nerved base and often marked by opaque dots (due to cystoliths). *Stipules* usually membranous, sometimes intrapetiolar. *Fls.* 1-sexual in cymes or clusters which are sometimes spicate. *Sep.* 4-5 free or united into a tube in the female, sometimes 2-3-merous or 0. *St.* one opposite each sepal. *Ovary* 1-celled, 1-carpellary with 1 erect orthotropous ovule. *Fr.* a utricle, sometimes enclosed or girt by the enlarged fleshy perianth.

Fls. cymose 2-5-merous.

F. calyx campanulate 4-lobed. L. (in C. N. sp.) entire or nearly so . . . . 1. *Laportea.*

F. perianth tubular 2-3-toothed. L. distinctly serrate . 2. *Girardinia.*

Fls. fascicled, clusters sometimes spicate.

Shrubs. Fls. clusters spicate. L. toothed . . . 3. *Bœhmeria.*

Herbs. Fls. clusters axillary. L. entire . . . 4. *Pouzolzia.*

1. Laportea, Gaud.

1. L. crenulata, *Gaud.*

A soft stemmed shrub 3-8 ft. with white stout branches, large shining elliptic penni-nerved leaves and greenish flowers in divaricate cymes. Utricle inflated white.

Deep shady ravines in the Karampoda forest. Evergreen. Fls. *Sept.-Oct.* Fr. *Nov.-Dec.*

L. 12" by 4½" or more, quite entire in C. N. specimens, minutely pustular and with few scattered hairs. *Inflorescence* covered with hairs. The sting of this nettle is most virulent, the effects sometimes lasting for days and producing sleeplessness and fever. It has been noted, however (Hook. Him. Jour. and by others), that it is worst in the autumn, and indeed I have often found it quite innocuous at some times of the year. This is due to the fact that the hairs are deciduous, and they are especially abundant on the inflorescence. While cutting coupe lines in Nov. in the Sikkim Terai where the plant is abundant, the coolies have been attacked with sneezing, catarrh and ultimately vertigo from, apparently, inhaling the numerous minute hairs.

2. Girardinia, Gaud.

1. G. zeylanica, *Decaisne.* Syn. G. heterophylla, var. zeylanica, *F.B.I.* Nettle.

A suffruticose herb 4-6 ft. high covered all over with stout stinging bristles, with coarsely lobed and serrate leaves 4-8″ long and broad, and clustered flowers, the M. mostly in sub-cylindric spiciform cymes from the lower axils, the F. in somewhat reniform compact panicles from the upper axils.

Chota Nagpur, *Prain*. Fls., Fr., in the cold season.

"The bark abounds in fine, white, glossy, silk-like, strong fibres." *Roxburgh*.

3. Bœhmeria, Jacq.

Shrubs or small trees with opp. or alt. toothed leaves 3-nerved at the base and flowers in clusters which are axillary or spiked *or* the spikes panicled. Sep. 3-5 in M., calyx tubular 2-4-toothed in the F. Stigma filiform persistent.

L. very long, narrow-lanceolate . . . 1. *macrophylla*.
L. broadly ovate or elliptic . . . . 2. *scabrella*.

1. B. macrophylla, *Don*.

A large shrub easily recognized by its long opposite narrow serrulate leaves and globose clusters of flowers in long drooping spikes.

Deep shady ravines in Saranda, very rare. Fls. *Sept.*

Twigs strigose. *L.* 6″ by 1″ to 15″ by 3¼″, strongly 3-nerved, caudate, reticulate nervules depressed above raised beneath. *Petiole* ¾-3″. *Spikes* about as long as the leaves.

2. B. scabrella. *Gaud.* Syn. B. platyphylla, *Don.* var. scabrella, *Wedd.**

---

* *Fide* Bengal Plants, but the Saranda form is rather B. platyphylla var α of Weddel's monograph, and var. macrostachya of Kew Herb. Weddel's var. macrostachya has pendulous spikes. The very rugose leaved form (scabrella of C. B. Clarke) is chiefly confined to Parasnath.

A shrub 4-10 ft. with sub-strigose branches large elliptic or ovate obtuse to acuminate leaves 4-8″ by 3-6″ and minute clusters of flowers in erect or inclined spikes attaining 1 ft. in length.

Ravines on the Porahat plateau as well as in Saranda, not common, Parasnath in Hazaribagh. Fls., Fr. *Sept.-Jany.*

L. opposite 3-nerved scaberulous both sides, crenate-dentate, dotted with cystoliths. *Base* obtuse to sub-cordate. *Petiole* 2-6″.

Yields a good fibre.

The Parasnath plant has the leaves very areolate beneath and relatively shorter petioles.

4. Pouzolzia, Gaud.

Pouzolzia differs from Bœhmeria by the leaves being usually (always in our species) entire and the style articulate to the ovary and deciduous. The M. sepals have often abruptly inflexed tips, so that the buds appear abruptly truncate or shouldered.

1. **P. indica,** *Gaud,* is a perennial herb with creeping rootstock and long weak branches found on moist banks and sides of rivers. It has scabrid stems and alt. small basally 3-nerved leaves (with only 1 pair above the basal) and minute axillary greenish fls. M. buds globose and apiculate, strigose.

2. **P. pentandra,** *Benn.,* is suffruticose with trailing stems and ascending often bright red slender branches and numerous close alt. small ovate floral leaves barely ¼″ long upwards. M. buds truncate. The achene is samaroid with two lateral concave wings and a dorsal fleshy lobe. River banks.

3. **P. auriculata,** *Wight.,* is a tall erect perennial with alt. leaves 1-5″ long, several-nerved above the base and buds not truncate.

4. **P. hirta,** *Hassk.,* is a slender sub-erect or decumbent herb or sub-scandent, with opp. leaves and truncate buds. Both the last are very rare.

Fam. 63. ULMACEÆ.

Trees or shrubs without milky juice with alt. simple distichous stipulate leaves. *Fls.* small 1-2-sexual with a 4-9-lobed perianth. *St.* as many as and opposite to the perianth obes, rarely twice as many. *Ovary* 1-rarely 2-celled Styles 2 free, or connate, or stigmas two sessile. *Ovule* 1 in each cell, pendulous. *Seeds* exalbuminous.

1. Fls. appearing before the leaves. L. entire. Fr. a samara . . . . 1. *Holoptelea.*
2. Fr. drupaceous. Fls. in the axils of developed leaves, cymose . . . . 2. *Trema.*

1. Holoptelea, Planch.

1. H. integrifolia, *Panch.* Chilbil, *Kharw.*; Charha. *S.*; Churla, *Mal Pah.*

A large or small tree (according to locality), in some states somewhat resembling a beech. L. ell. or ovate entire (or toothed or crenate in very young trees) usually 2″ by $1\frac{1}{2}$″ to $4\frac{1}{2}$″ by $2\frac{3}{4}$″. Fls. green in very numerous fascicles or short racemes on the leafless branches. Samara broadly elliptic 1″, on a slender articulate pedicel, notched between the two stigmas.

Usually in valleys, Manbhum and Hazaribagh scarce; Santal Parganahs; Palamau, common. Occurs also on the hills in Palamau in a stunted form. It flowers *March* or *April*, the flowers only last a few days, and the fruit is ripe by the end of *May* when the tree is in full leaf. The small hill form does not produce its leaves till *June*.

Twigs white. Young shoots and leaves beneath tomentose. *L.* usually glabrescent shortly acuminate or cuspidate, base rounded, oblique or slightly cordate, sec. n. 5-7 prs. raised beneath, very reticulate between the lowest 2-5 usually quite close to the base. *Petiole* $\frac{1}{2}$-$\frac{3}{4}$″. *Stipules* linear caducous, scarcely leaving a scar. *M.* and *F. fls.* in the same cluster. *Sep.* and *St.* 4-8.

There are three, if not four, very distinct forms which require further examination in different stages. They may be distinct species :—

α. Branchlets with raised round lenticels, puberulous. L. under $3\frac{1}{2}$″ long, quickly glabrous (May), base oblique or rounded or only in few sub-cordate. Petiole slender $\frac{1}{3}$-$\frac{1}{2}$″.

β. Branchlets with few scarcely raised lenticels, glabrous or puberulous. L. mostly up to $5\frac{1}{2}$″ or 6″ rather membranous, pubescent beneath (at least up to July). Base sub-cordate, or unequal. Petiole only $\frac{1}{4}$-$\frac{1}{3}$″. This closely corresponds to Thwaites No. 2381 from Ceylon. called var. tomentosa in Kew Herb γ. Twigs very pubescent hiding the lenticels. L. rather coriaceous 3-4" long, base distinctly cordate, beneath tomentose with stout raised nerves and tip very obtuse or with very obtuse short cusp. Petioles ½-¾" stout. It has somewhat the facies of a Cordia, from which, however, the L. can at once be distinguished by the nerves looping within the margin, while in Cordia they run into the margin or are excurrent.

Eastern Palamau and Western Hazaribagh.

δ. The shrubby form of the Palamau hills has not been collected in mature leaf. It has a very white bark, and some of the twigs have circular raised lenticels. The young leaves are very tomentose.

2. Trema, Lour.

Usually small trees with the leaves serrate, 3-7-basal-nerved and often oblique, small green flowers in axillary cymes, and fruit a small drupe seated on the persistent calyx. Fls. diœcious, monœcious or polygamous, 4-5-merous. Ovary 1-celled, 1-ovuled. Style 2-fid. Fruit a small ovoid drupe.

L. silky beneath, base oblique. Twigs adpressed-pubescent. Cymes lax . . 1. *orientalis.*

L. tomentose beneath or silky, base oblique. Twigs with spreading pubescence, cymes dense . . . . *Var. amboinensis.*

L. scabrid beneath, base sub-regular . . 2. *politoria.*

1. **T. orientalis,** *Bl.* Roronga, *K.*; Jhawar, *S.*; Rukni, *Kharw.*; Kokoara, *Mal. Pah.*

A fast-growing tree attaining 35 ft. marked with stipular scars, with bifarious ovate or ovate-lanceolate caudate leaves 3-6" long, mostly very oblique at the base, more or less white or silvery beneath with silky hairs and scabrid or not above. Panicles usually much branched and ultimately longer than the petioles.

Throughout the area, chiefly in moist valleys. Fls., Fr. *Nov.-April.* Var. α = T. amboinensis, *Bl.* There are two specimens so named from C. N. in the Cal. Herb., one from Manbhum, and one from Parasnath collected by Clarke. These only differ from T. orientalis by the somewhat more spreading pubescence and smaller denser cymes, which are, however, still young. Another specimen found by me on Parasnath, and otherwise similar had large laxer cymes (⅜"). Singbhum, Valleys in Saranda. It can be distinguished from the type by the beautiful whiteness of the leaves beneath (T. orientalis is green or silvery beneath) and by the shagginess of the pubescence. The veins are sometimes red.

2. **T. politoria,** *Planch.* Kaksi (from the rough leaves), *K.*; Tila, *Kharw.*

A small tree attaining about 25 ft. with pubescent twigs, stiff oblong or ovate-lanceolate serrulate leaves 2-4" long, scabrous both sides, and compact cymes usually shorter than the petiole.

Frequent, often on roadsides. Fls. *Aug.-Sept.* Fr. *March.* Evergreen.
L. with a rounded or cordate base acute or somewhat acuminate, thinly hairy on the secondary and tertiary nerves, not silky between, and reticulations not raised beneath as usually in T. orientalis. Stipules longer than the ¼-½" petiole.

The rough leaves are sometimes used for polishing wood, and the fruits are made into an acid jam.

Fam. 64. MORACEÆ.

Trees or shrubs usually with milky juice, sometimes climbing or epiphytic, with alt. (rarely opp. eg. Ficus hispida) simple, frequently dotted,[1] stipulate leaves. *Stipules* in some genera sheathing and caducous leaving a permanent circular nodal scar. *Fls.* small greenish, usually in dense inflorescences, often crowded on or inside (as in the figs) a fleshy receptacle formed of the aggregate axes, unisexual, mon- or di-œcious. *Sep.* usually 4, seldom 2-6 in the male, free or connate. *St.* isomerous opp. the sepals or only one (in Artocarpus and some Ficus). *Ovary* 1-celled of 2 carpels with one pendulous anatropous or amphitropous ovule. *Fr.*

[1] Dots due to cystoliths and not therefore pellucid.

small, an achene or drupe, frequently aggregate into large fleshy pseudocarps from the growth of the axis or perianth.

Fls. not enclosed in, nor on, broad fleshy receptacles.

M. . in peduncled heads. F. 1-few, peduncled . . 1. *Streblus.*

M. and F. fl. in catkin-like spikes . . . . . 2. *Morus.*

Fls. crowded on, or enclosed in broad fleshy receptacles.

Fls. on the outside of globose or clavate receptacles . 3. *Artocarpus.*

Fls. enclosed in the receptacles (Recepts, Figs) . . 4. *Ficus.*

1. Streblus, Lour.

1. S. asper, *Lour.* Kakasa (rough), Ote, Ripi-chum, K.; also Soor, *Ho.*[1]; Sahra, *S.*

A small tree with tough stringy bark, rigid very scabrid rhombic ell. or obovate leaves 2-4″, male capitula $\frac{1}{4}$-$\frac{1}{3}$″ diam. F. fl. long-peduncled inconspicuous with 2 very long styles, perianth yellow fleshy in fruit.

Not uncommon in valleys, throughout the area. Evergreen, new L. in March. Fls. *March-May.* Fr. *May-June.*

Juice very slightly milky in the cold weather. *L.* slightly toothed, acuminate, scabrid both sides, sub-sessile. *Peduncles* $\frac{1}{4}$-$\frac{1}{2}$″ in both sexes axillary and from leaf-scars, 1-4 together. *F. fl.* usually surrounded at the base by 3 bracts, and the ovary enclosed in the perianth. *Fruit* with a thin coriaceous pericarp, $\frac{1}{8}$″ diam. including the succulent perianth.

Often grazed down by goats.

Morus indica, *L.* Indian Mulberry and **M. lævigata,** *Wall.*, are both sometimes cultivated; the latter is a tree with a slender cylindrical spike of pale *yellow* fruits. The fleshy part is the enlarged perianth.

---

[1] This is the same word as "Soroa" *M.* applied to Garcinia Cowa, but as it is apparently allied to the Santal name and to the "Sahora" of the Currakpur hills, it probably belongs to Streblus. Hara saijang, Sukri saijang, sometimes quoted mean bullock's ribs, pig's ribs respectively and are names often applied to Anogeissus acuminata, and to many trees with prominent side nerves.

3. Artocarpus, Forst.

Trees with large coriaceous leaves, those of seedlings often quite different from the adult, being usually deeply lobed or pinnatifid while the adult are usually entire. Stipules leaving a circular scar, very large and coriaceous and sheathing the inflorescence on flowering shoots, or small in some species. Perianth of male 2-4-lobed or -partite, of F. tubular, sunk in the receptacle.

1. **A. Lakoocha,** *Roxb.* Daho, Dahu *K., S., H.*

A mod.-sized tree with large ell. or ovate obtuse or shortly acuminate leaves 6-10″. M. inflorescence ellipsoid or globose 1″ diam. deciduous. F. inflor. irregularly sub-globose 2-4″.

Frequent in villages throughout the area; truly wild in the Saranda hills, Singbhum; in the Manbhum forests, *Camp.*; Ranchi (Damudaghats); Hazaribagh (Parasnath). Sub-deciduous *March.* Fls. and new leaf *April.* Fr. *May* and *Oct.-Nov.* (There appears to be two periods).

Branchlets tomentose. *L.* pubescent or tomentose beneath with 8-12 prs. of sec. n. *Petiole* ½-1″. *Stipules* ½″, lanceolate. The fruit is eaten.

2. **A. integrifolia,** *L.* Poros, *K.* (*fide* Gamble); Kathal, *H.*; Kauthar, *M., S.* The Jack-fruit.

Cultivated throughout the area, but not growing well in the drier parts of Singbhum and Palamau; abundant on the plateaux and the S.P. The wood largely used for the large native drums (dumung). Fls. *Decr.-Feby.* Fr. *r.s.*

A native of the Western Ghats.

On flowering shoots each pair of large conduplicate stipules bears a naked inflorescence, a lateral bud, and the succeeding leaf and its stipules, the bud continues the branching in a similar manner, and so does the succeeding leaf, so that the Jack fruits are complicately panicled.

4. Ficus, L. Fig.

Trees or shrubs, often epiphytic when young, sometimes scandent. Stipules sheathing the bud and leaving a circular scar on falling. Mouth of recept closed by bracts. Fls. mon-rarely di-œcious and recepts usually androgynous.

Sep. 2-6 more or less connate in male, sometimes imperfect in fem. St. 1 or 2 rarely 3-6. Style often lateral with entire or 2-fid. stigma.

Note.—Special fem. fl. (Gall fls.) with reduced styles are used by certain Chalcididæ in which to lay their eggs. The mature insects in escaping from the recepts brush against the M. fl. which frequently occupy a zone near the mouth of the recept, and so carry away the pollen.

I. Recepts cauline or rameal, clustered or on special scaly more or less leafless branches; rarely also a few among the leaves.

- *a.* Shrub. L. narrow-lanceolate . . . 1. *lanceolata.*
- *b.* Trees. Recepts mostly on short leafless cauline branches.
  - L. under 4″ broad, more or less ovate or oblong, alt. . . . . 2. *glomerata.*
  - L. 4-12″ broad, broadly ovate or sub-orbicular, alt. . . . . . . 3. *Roxburghii.*
  - L. under 4″ broad, some or all opposite. Recepts fascicled . . . . . . 4. *hispida.*
- *c.* Recepts usually on long leafless branches.
  - L. ½-sagittate . . . . . . 5. *Cunia.*

II. Recepts 1-2 (sometimes more in gibbosa) axillary, or from the leaf scars just below the foliage.

1. Recepts distinctly stalked (sometimes sessile in glabella).
   - *a.* More or less scabrid or tomentose. Sec. n. 3-5 prs. above basal.
     - L. broad sub-rhomboid. Bracts at base of peduncle . . . . . . 6. *gibbosa.*
     - L. ell. or ovate. Bracts at base of peduncle . 6*a. cuspidifera.*
     - Scandent shrub often rooting at the nodes. Bracts near top of peduncle . . . 7. *scandens.*
   - *b.* Glabrous (or young parts pubescent in glabella) and smooth. Sec. n. over 5 prs.
     - Bracts at base of peduncle. L. oblong . 8. *nervosa.*
     - Bracts at base of recept. Petiole under 1″. Sec. n. close, over 10 prs. . . . 9. *glabella.*
     - Bracts at base of recept. Petiole, over 1″. Sec. n. distant, rarely 10 prs. . . . 10. *infectoria.*

2. Recepts sessile.

a. Petiole 1-3" long, or ⅓rd length of leaf. L. glabrous.

† Stipules ½" or less.

L. narrow-ovate or oblong-ovate . . . . 10. *infectoria.*

†† Stipules over ½".

L. ovate gradually tapering; base not cordate . 11. *Rumphii.*

L. ovate suddenly acuminate or cuspidate, base often cordate . . . . . . 12. *Arnottiana.*

L. caudate acuminate with tail half as long as rest of blade . . . . . . 13. *religiosa.*

b. Petiole short, less than 1"

i. Glabrous. Sec. n. very fine and numerous, or intermediate nearly as strong.

L. oblong or ell.-oblong, base narrowly sub-cordate 9. *glabella.*

L. broad, obtuse or obtusely cuspidate, base cuneate . . . . 14. *retusa.*

L. broad, cuspidate or acuminate, base obtuse or rounded . . . . 15. *Benjamina.*

ii. Pubescent or tomentose, or if glabrescent sec. n. few and strong.

L. beneath and recepts permanently tomentose . 16. *tomentosa.*

L. beneath and recepts glabrescent or puberulous . . . . 17. *bengalensis.*

1. **F. lanceolata,** *Ham.* Gara Loa, *K.* (but this name is also applied to Trewia).

A glabrous shrub 3-5 ft., usually with prostrate branches lanceolate acuminate leaves $3\frac{1}{2}$-7" by $\frac{1}{2}$-$1\frac{1}{2}$" dotted beneath, Recepts 5-6 clustered on short lateral branches, $1\frac{1}{2}$-2" diam.

In the rocky beds of streams, Singbhum and S. P., not common. Fr. *June.*

L. sometimes remotely toothed narrow-lanceolate or narrow-oblong, base 3-nerved rounded. *Petiole* $\frac{1}{4}$-$\frac{3}{4}$". *Recepts* reddish flattened at top, young more or less ribbed and warted. *Ped.* 1" much swollen at top in ripe fruit.

Fruit very palatable.

2. **F. glomerata,** *Roxb.* Loa, *K.*; *S.*; Gular, *Kharw.*; Jagidambar, *Beng.*

A mod.-sized. tree with ovate, ovate-lanc., or ell. dark-green leaves 4-7½" by 1¾-3¼" narrowed to an obtuse or sub-acute tip. Recepts 1-1½" diam. globose or pyriform pubescent on cauline and rameal branches which may be 2 ft. long, occasionally axillary recepts are found as well.

A common fig in valleys and northern slopes throughout the area Recepts ripen *May-June.* It is deciduous *Oct.-Nov.* and renews its leaves in *Decr. or Jany.* !

Buds pubescent *L.* pale beneath and pubescent on the nerves, base rounded rarely acute, 3-nerved, sec. n. 4-7 prs. *Peti.* ¾-1¾" pubescent. *Stipules* ½-1".

Fruits eaten.

3. **F. Roxburghii,** *Wall.* Gara Sosokera, *Ho.*; Kota, *M.*

A handsome low spreading tree with very large cordate leaves reaching 18" by 12" pubescent beneath with a 5-7-nerved base. Recepts 2" diam. with peduncles 2-3" clustered on cauline knobs or short leafless branches.

Along streams above 1,500 ft. in Saranda (Kumbia Jhora) and on the Porahat plateau. Kochang, *Wood* and *Gamble.* Fr. *April-Sept.* Evergreen.

L. usually more or less repand-toothed.

A good fodder, and fruits eaten.

4. **F. hispida,** *L.* Sosokera, *K.*; Kotang, *M.*; Seta Podo, *S.*; Dumar, *Kharw.*; Poroh, *Mal Pah.*

A tree 10-25 ft. high with thick hollow branchlets, easily distinguished by always having some or all of its leaves opposite. Recepts numerous fascicled on both the trunk and branches or on leafless drooping branches or also axillary.

Along nalas, throughout the area, not very common. Fr. *Jany.-Feby.*

L. ovate-oblong 4-12" by 2-5½" scabrid above and hispid beneath. *Recepts* 1" diam. yellowish and hispid when ripe. *Fr.* eaten.

Bark yields a fibre.

5. **F. Cunia.** *Ham.* Aie, *Ho.*; Podho, Ari, *M.*; Hor Podo, *S.*

A small or mod.-sized tree easily recognized by its short petioled leaves with a semi-sagittate base. Recepts in pairs or clusters on long (often several feet) usually leafless drooping branches, especially near the root.

Common, esp. near nalas and on cool northern slopes. Recepts borne most of the year, ripe *May-June*. Evergreen, or leafless in *May*.

L. 6-15" long, ell. or oblong-lanceolate, entire or serrate. *Stipules* $\frac{1}{4}$-1". *Recepts* $\frac{1}{2}$-$\frac{3}{4}$", red-brown or quite white, eaten.
Lac is often cultivated on the branches, sold at As. 2 per seer in Singbhum.

6. **F. gibbosa,** *Bl.* Sub-sp. **parasitica.**

A large epiphyte frequently becoming an independent tree, with large sub-rhomboid leaves $2\frac{1}{2}$-8" very hispid above and paler pubescent beneath with 4-5 prs. prominent sec. n. above the 3-nerved base. Recepts $\frac{1}{4}$-$\frac{1}{3}$" diam. fascicled or in pairs densely hispid, with prominent umbo.

Chiefly on the Porahat plateau in Singbhum; on gneiss rocks at Tatijheria (Hazaribagh); Kuru ghat (Palamau).

Fr. *Feby.-April.*

L. with few large reticulations and inconspicuous ones between. *Peti.* $\frac{1}{4}$-$\frac{1}{3}$".

Sub-sp. **cuspidifera,** *Miq.* (Sp.) Var.

A large epiphyte, or erect with obovate or ell. leaves up to 8" by $3\frac{1}{4}$" very stiff, hispidulous beneath, cuspidate or acuminate, base cuneate. *Recepts* $\frac{1}{4}$", 1-2 axillary or from leaf scars, pyriform, puberulous, narrowed into slender pubescent pedicels $\frac{1}{5}$-$\frac{1}{3}$" long which have 3 minute connate bracts at their base. S. P., January.

7. **F. scandens,** *Roxb.* Madhur lata, *S.*

A shrub creeping or climbing on rocks or trees with ovate acute leaves 2" by 1" to 4" by $2\frac{1}{4}$". Recepts $\frac{1}{3}$" by $\frac{5}{16}$" yellowish-brown, puberulous or hispid, umbo small depressed at top, pedicel $\frac{1}{3}$".

Valleys in Singbhum; Manbhum *Campbell*; and S. P., but rare; Parasnath, on northern side, common. Recepts *Jany.-May.*

New *shoots* rusty. *L.* pale beneath between the very reticulate sub green nervules; base rounded 3-nerved, about 2-5 prs. sec. n. above the basal, looping within the margin. *Petiole* $\frac{1}{4}$-$\frac{3}{4}$".

8. F. nervosa, *Roth.*

A usually straight tree about 30 ft. Twigs mouse-coloured with appressed tomentum. L. oblong or oblanceolate cuspidate very dark and shining above attaining 10″ by 4″, but usually smaller. Recepts sub-globose $\frac{1}{3}$-$\frac{7}{16}$″ diam. axillary and from leaf scars on slender pedicels $\frac{1}{3}$-$\frac{1}{2}$″ long.

Chiefly along nalas, Singbhum, S. P. Recepts *Jany.-April.* Evergreen.

L. somewhat bullate, glabrous except some fine hairs along the mid-rib. Sec. n. 5-11 prs. looped within the margin.

9. F. glabella, *Bl.* var. affinis. Putkul, *Ho.*

A tree with oblong or ovate-lanceolate acuminate or cuspidate leaves with close sec. n. and intermediate nearly as strong, and small white or yellowish (ripe purple? *F.B.I.*) recepts solitary or in pairs sub-sessile or on slender pedicels chiefly from the leaf scars.

Rocky ravines (Komsai Lor, Oraiburu valley, etc.) in Singbhum. Recepts *Jany.-May.*

Larger *leaves* 5$\frac{1}{2}$ by 2″, base acute or obtuse, sec. n. 7-14 prs. with intermediate scarcely finer, parallel and reticulate, and fine reticulations raised above between the loops and the fine cartilaginous margin. *Peti.* $\frac{1}{2}$-$\frac{3}{4}$″. *Recepts* $\frac{1}{4}$-$\frac{1}{3}$″ diam. umbonate with deciduous basal bracts. *Peduncle* $\frac{1}{16}$-$\frac{1}{4}$″.

10. F. infectoria, *Roxb.* Baswesa, Pepe Hissa, Jojo Hissa, *K.*; Pakare, *S.*, Pakar, *H.*; *Beng.*

A tree with long-petioled glabrous oblong or oblong-ovate sharply acuminate or cuspidate leaves 3″ by 1$\frac{1}{8}$″ to 7″ by 3$\frac{1}{2}$″ with distant distinct sec. n. above a 3-nerved obtuse rounded rarely sub-cordate base. Recepts $\frac{1}{3}$-$\frac{1}{2}$″ diam.* globose or sub-pyriform whitish sessile or pedicelled.

Form 1. Chiefly in rocky ravines, Singbhum. S. P. (Silingi jhora). Recepts *Jany.-Feby.*

---

* ·25″ fide King in Annals of Calcutta Botanic Gardens. Gamble's Koderma specimen has L. 3$\frac{1}{2}$-5$\frac{1}{2}$″ with sub-cordate base and 5-6 prs. sec. n. Petioles 2-2$\frac{1}{2}$″. Recepts $\frac{1}{3}$″ subsessile. This is nearly typical.

A small tree. *L.* about $4\frac{1}{2}''$ by $2\frac{1}{2}''$ abruptly shortly caudate, margins undulate, sec. n. about 9 prs. looped within the margin, very reticulate between. *Petiole* slender whitish $1\frac{1}{2}$-$2\frac{1}{4}''$. *Recepts* $\frac{3}{8}$-$\frac{1}{2}''$ diam. subglobose with 3 short orbicular bracts at base. *Pedicel* very stout $\frac{1}{4}$-$\frac{1}{2}''$ pubescent. *Fruits* eaten.

Form 2. Chiefly in cultivated lands and villages. Recepts *Decr.-June.* More or less deciduous, new leaves appear in the hot weather.

A large tree. *L.* up to $7\frac{1}{2}''$ by $3\frac{3}{4}''$ oblong to ovate-lanceolate with petioles $1\frac{1}{2}$-$3\frac{1}{2}''$. *Recepts* white globose-pyrifom $\frac{5}{8}''$ diam. *Pedicel* puberulous. The leaf base is sometimes cuneate on the petiole on rapidly growing shoots.

The Kol name is uncertain, sometimes it is called Barsa Hesa. The fruit is eaten.

11. F. Rumphii, *Bl.* Duraoga Hesa, *K.*

A spreading mod.-sized. tree with ovate or broadly ovate leaves gradually tapering to the acuminate tip and with straight or obtuse not cordate base. Recepts oblong-obovoid $\frac{1}{2}''$ long sessile from a very broad base, in pairs axillary and from leaf scars.

Along nalas frequent, Singbhum, Hazaribagh, etc. Often in village lands and planted along roadsides where it does well, and is frequently mistaken for the Pipal, than which it is a much smaller and less handsome tree. Recepts *Jany.-March.*

Twigs often puberulous. *L.* about 5-6" by 3-4" often confused with the next from which it may be distinguished by the base hardly ever cordate, by its longer gradual acumination, the nervules not areolate with fine reticulations, and by the surface being minutely punctulate. *Petiole* $\frac{1}{3}$rd to $\frac{2}{4}$ths as long as the blade, much stouter and stiffer than in the true Pipal.

12. F. Arnottiana, *Miq.* Ganjar, (f. Gamble) Duranga Hesa, *K.*; Sunum jor, *S.*

A small tree or sometimes a shrub with broadly ovate leaves abruptly acuminate or cuspidate and with a cordate base. Recepts 1-2 chiefly from leaf-scars globose $\frac{5}{16}$-$\frac{1}{2}''$ diam. globose or pyriform sub-sessile or stalked faintly verrucose.

Chiefly on dry rocks or in rocky places on dry hills, Singhbhum, Hazaribagh, etc.

Leafless *April*, new leaves in *May* reddish. Recepts *March-June* black when ripe.

L. about 6″ by 4-4½″ with cusp only ½-⅜″, base with 3 strong and 2-4 much weaker nerves and 5-8 prs. of strong translucent straw-coloured sec. n. above the basal, looped within the cartilaginous margin, very minutely reticulate between and outside the sec. n. *Petiole* about half as long as leaf or rather longer. *Stipules* 1-2″ acuminate.

13. **F. religiosa,** *L.* Tepe Hesa, *K.*; Hesak,' *S.*; Pipal, *H.* The Pipal Tree.

A large tree, epiphytic when young, with broadly ovate caudate-acuminate leaves with the long slender tail ⅓rd to half the entire length of the leaf, slender petiole 3-4″ Recepts in axillary pairs depressed-globose ½″ diam.

Very common and often planted. Nearly deciduous. Recepts *March-June.*

The bark is peculiarly pitted when old.[1] The branches are much lopped for fodder and the fruit is eaten.

14. **F. retusa,** *L.* Buti Hesa, Chuman Hesa, *K.*; Jir, *Beng.*

A small or very large tree, epiphytic when young, with rotund, obovate, oblanceolate or ell. leaves, always with a cuneate 3-nerved base and very slender sec. n. about 5-12 prs. with intermediate nearly as strong. Recepts in axillary pairs sessile divaricate sub-globose ¼-½″ diam. with 2-3 basal bracts.

Form *a.* *L.* 2″ by 1″ to 3″ by 2¼″ obovate or broadly ell. with shortly cuspidate obtuse apex and sec. n. few. *Petioles* ¼-⅓″. *Recepts* red to purple when ripe ½″ diam.

Valleys in Singbhum, and Santal P. Recepts *Oct.-Nov.*

Form *β.* *L.* 2″ by 1″ to 5″ by 2½″ mostly ell. with acute, sub-acuminate or obtuse tip and 5-12 sec. n. *Petiole* ¼-⅓″. *Recepts* ¼-⅓″ diam. whitish sub-verrucose, usually only 2-bracteate, often clustered above the leaves as well as axillary. Usually in ravines or epiphytic, Singhbhum, Hazaribagh, and Santal P. Recepts *Feby.-May.*

15. **F. Benjamina,** *L.* Pokaha, *S.*

A very handsome large tree with slender drooping branches, broadly ell. or ovate abruptly acuminate or caudate

---

[1] The bark is said by Mr Innes to be ground, made into flour and eaten in times of famine (at Balrampur, Oudh).

leaves with a rounded or obtuse base and very numerous fine parallel sec. n. spreading from the mid-rib, those at the base quite similar to the others. Recepts divaricate globose $\frac{5}{8}$-$\frac{3}{4}$" diam., yellow or reddish when quite ripe, in axillary pairs, sessile with a narrow base.

In valleys, Singbhum, Hazaribagh, and Santal. P., but not common. Evergreen. Recepts ripen *Jany.-May.*

L. 2" by 1" to 3½" by 2". Main sec. n. are about 12 prs. scarcely stronger than the numerous intermediate ones. *Petiole* ⅓-1". *Bracts* 2 almost concealed by the base of the recept.

16. **F. tomentosa,** *Roxb.* Janapa Hesa, *K.*; Capakia bare, *S.*; Barun, *Kharw.*

A large or small tree with tomentose or wooly branchlets and frequently with thin aërial roots. L. very variable in size, easily recognized by the more or less persistent tomentum and very prominent venation beneath, by the cordate base and a curious longitudinal glandular depression on the mid-rib a little above the base beneath. Recepts white or grey tomentose $\frac{1}{3}$-$\frac{1}{2}$" diam. globose sessile.

Among dry rocks, often on the most rocky and arid hills, throughout the area, occasionally on old buildings as on the Palamau Fort. Evergreen. Recepts appear in the axils of the new leaves in *June* and remain over a year, the old ones being at the leaf scars.

L. ell., oblong, ovate or somewhat obovate, 2½" by 2" to 8½" by 4½", or 7" by 5½", sec. n. 5-8 prs. above the many-nerved base.

17. **F. bengalensis,** *L.* Bai, *Ho.*; Bare, *M. S.*; Barh, *Kharw.*, *H.*; Bor, *Beng.* The Banyan.

A large tree with the shoots pubescent when young, branches sending down aërial roots which in favourable localities become as thick as the parent stem. L. ovate to elliptic obtuse with rounded or sub-cordate 3-5-nerved base, old glabrous or slightly pubescent beneath. Recepts sessile in pairs $\frac{1}{2}$-$\frac{3}{4}$" diam. scarlet when ripe puberulous.

Wild in the damper valleys of Singbhum and the S. P. Recepts may be found all the year round; they ripen about *April-May* and again *Dec.-Jany.* and are eaten. Nearly evergreen. Renews leaves *May-June.* The tree may be propagated by large cuttings.

Fam. 65. SALICACEÆ.

1. Salix, L. Willow.

Trees or shrubs with simple alt. stipulate leaves and fls. in dense spikes (catkins), each in the axil of a small bract, diœcious (very rarely 2-sexual in solitary specimens). *Perianth* 0, but 1 or 2 fleshy glands or scales situated posteriorly, or post. and anteriorly, at the base of the flower may represent a perianth. (In S. tetrasperma 2 smaller lateral glands are often added in the male). *St.* 2 or several, fil. often connate at the base. *Ovary* of 2 rarely 3 combined carpels and the same number of stigmas, 1-celled. *Seeds* few or many parietal, with a pencil of hairs from the base.

1. S. tetrasperma, *Roxb.* Nachal, *K.*; Gada sigric', Sunu..ikui (*vide* Homonoia), *S.*; Chihur, *Kharw.*

A tree, or in one form a shrub, with silkily-pubescent shoots, lanceolate or oblanceolate to ovate-lanceolate acuminate leaves sparsely hairy and pale-glacuous beneath. Catkins terminating the short lateral shoots, $1\frac{1}{2}$-4″ long pubescent. Disc. glands very broad.

Along rivers and streams, in all the districts, but nowhere very common. Fls. *Oct.*, on the new shoots. Seed ripens *Dec.-Jany.* Deciduous in *Sept.* In some districts of Bengal it flowers in the hot season!

L. about 4″ by $1\frac{1}{2}$″ in the broader forms, but often only $1\frac{1}{2}$″ by $\frac{3}{8}$″ on the flowering shoots, entire or crenate with rounded or acute base Sec. n. very slender 10-19 prs. *Petiole* $\frac{1}{3}$-$\frac{1}{2}$″. *Bracts* almost wooly $\frac{1}{16}$-$\frac{1}{12}$″ much shorter than the 5-10 very slender filaments. *Disc* glands in the male usually of a large anterior and posterior lobe and two small lateral side lobes, of the female (sometimes also of the male?) 1 semi-circular. *Capsules* $\frac{1}{4}$″ pubescent or glabrous, on pedicels nearly as long as themselves. *Style* hardly any. *Stigmas* 4, or two 2-lobed.

There are two varieties well marked by habit. One a tree, with narrow leaves, and sec. n. scarcely visible beneath. Growing chiefly along river banks. The other, a small tree or a *shrub*, with broader more crenate leaves, and sec. n. fine but raised beneath. This also has the semi-circular disc. Found along small streams, often in thick forest.

Sub-class II.—Sympetalæ.

Fam. 66. PLUMBAGINACEÆ.

Herbs or undershrubs with alt. leaves and fls. in terminal heads, spikes or panicles. *Bracts* usually sheathing the flowers and with scarious margins. *Calyx* inferior, tubular, 5-10-ribbed, scarious. *Petals* 5, polypetalous or gamopetalous. *St.* 5 opp. the petals. *Ovary* superior 1-celled, 5-angular above; *styles* 5, free or only connate below. *Ovule* 1, pendulous from a basal funicle, anatropous. *Fruit* membranous or the apex hardened, circumsciss or rupturing or apex 5-valved.

Calyx glandular, fls. spicate, styles connate except above . . . . 1. *Plumbago.*

1. P. zeylanica, *L.* Citar Kathi, Jog Kathi, *S.*

A shrub with long rambling green branches very glandular above, pale green clustered leaves and long panicled spikes of pretty long-tubed white flowers $\frac{1}{2}$-$\frac{3}{4}''$ diam.

Among rocks on the Ranchi plateau; Manbhum, *Camp.* Fls. *Sept.-Nov.* Fr. *Nov.*

L. ovate or ovate oblong, the base suddenly narrowed into a short amplexicaul petiole. *Calyx* persistent $\frac{1}{2}''$ densely covered with stalked glands. *Filaments* slender free the whole length of the tube, with purple anthers. *Fruit* as long as the calyx included 5-angled. Seed large albuminous.

P. rosea, *L.*, with red flowers, and **P. capensis,** *Thunb.*, a very pretty plant with blue flowers, are often cultivated.

Fam. 67. MYRSINACEÆ.

Shrubs or small trees with alt. simple exstipulate leaves often with minute *glands* (generally red) on the leaves and flowers. *Fls.* reg. often polygamous or diœcious. *Calyx* hypogynous or perigynous (Mæsa), persistent and often enlarged in fruit. *Corolla* polypetalous (some Embelia), or usually gamopetalous with 4-5 petals and as many stamens opp. the petals. *Ovary* 1-celled with few or many ovules on a swollen central placenta; style slender, stigma simple or rarely lobed. *Fruit* usually a berry and 1-seeded or more rarely many-seeded. *Seed* generally with an excavate base, albumen pitted or ruminate, embryo transverse.

Calyx half perigynous. Corolla small gamopetalous. Berry many-seeded . . . . 1. *Mæsa.*

Calyx hypogynous. Fruit 1-seeded.

Corolla nearly or quite polypetalous, very small white or greenish . . . . 2. *Embelia.*

Corolla gamopetalous, small or mod.-sized, pink . . . . 3. *Ardisia.*

1. Mæsa, Forsk.

1. **M. indica,** *Wall.* Syn. M. montana, A.R amjani *Beng.*

A shrub 4-8 ft. high with markedly lenticellate branches ell. ovate or ovate-lanceolate coarsely serrate leaves $3\frac{1}{2}$-6″ by $1\frac{1}{2}$-3″ and small white flowers in simple or compound racemes 1-3″ long. Berry $\frac{1}{10}$-$\frac{1}{8}$″ diam. almost entirely enclosed in the calyx-tube, ultimately sub-coriaceous.

Valleys on the Porahat and Ranchi plateaux. Kochang, *Gamble*! Fls. *March-April.* Fr. *Aug.-Dec.* Evergreen.

L. acute to caudate-acuminate, shining above, pale beneath and nearly glabrous with 6-7 prs. of sec. *n.* Fls. $\frac{1}{8}$″ diam. *Calyx-lobes* sub-orbicular, ciliate, lineate.[1] *Petals* veined sub-orbicular. *Fil.* very short on the corolla-tube. *Pedicels* $\frac{1}{8}$″ bracteate.

2. Embelia, Burm.

1. **E. robusta,** *Roxb.* Gointa mata, *K.*; Bhabri, *S.*

A shrub or small tree with light grey lenticellate branches, ell. or obovate acuminate or obtuse leaves pale beneath and small diœcious greenish-white flowers in axillary and extra-axillary racemes $\frac{1}{2}$-$1\frac{1}{2}$″ long. Fr. red sub-globose $\frac{1}{8}$-$\frac{1}{4}$″ diam.

[1] In the Kochang specimen, but only microscopically ciliate in other Singhbhum specimens, and not lineate. The Singhbhum plant, however, appears to come nearest to M. indica as defined by Mez in his monograph than to any of his other species.

with a crustaceous epicarp and fleshy endocarp, tipped by the style.

Rather common througnout Chota Nagpur, esp. in open scrub jungles. The branches in the type are glabrous. Fls. *May-July*. Fr. *Dec.-Jany*.

Twigs rusty pubescent or tomentose. *L.* very variable on the same plant $1\frac{1}{4}$-6", entire or denticulate above, with a very short rusty sometimes stellate pubescence esp. beneath, narrowed at base into the $\frac{1}{3}$-$\frac{1}{2}$" long pubescent petiole, sec. *n.* 5-9 prs. *Pedicels* $\frac{1}{8}$". *Bracts* shorter linear. *Calyx* pubescent without $\frac{1}{16}$-$\frac{1}{12}$" diam. deeply 5-lobed, glandular. *Corolla* $\frac{1}{6}$-$\frac{1}{8}$" diam. puberulous.

The fem. fl. has short imperfect epipetalous stamens.

3. Ardisia, Sw.

Small trees or shrubs. Fls. racemed or in umbels with small deciduous bracts. Calyx persistent, sometimes accrescent in fruit. Corolla 5-partite, often fleshy, petals acute twisted to the right in bud. Fil. very short with acute ovate-lanc. anthers. Ovules few. Berry with a large globose seed.

A shrub or small tree. Fls. over $\frac{1}{2}$" diam. . . . . . 1. *solenacea*.
A shrub. Fls. under $\frac{1}{2}$" diam. . . . . 2. *depressa*.

1. A. solenacea, *Roxb.* Syn. A. humilis, *(F.B.I.)* Gara boi (the stream earring) *K.*

A small tree or shrub attaining 25 ft. with large bright green rather fleshy leaves clustered towards the ends of the branchlets and moderate-sized rose-cold. waxy flowers with yellow stamens in peduncled axillary often contracted racemes. Berry $\frac{1}{3}$-$\frac{1}{2}$" diam., depressed-globose, black when ripe.

Along the sides and beds of streams under shade, common. Fls. *April-May*. Fr. *Oct.-Jany*. Evergreen.

L. 4-8" obovate-oblong narrowed into a petiole $\frac{1}{4}$" long. *Peduncles* 1-3" stout, and *raceme* often 2-3". *Fls.* $\frac{3}{4}$-1".

2. A. depressa, *Clarke.*

A shrub 6-8 ft. with dark green obscurely-nerved wavy leaves and small pinkish flowers in racemed umbels

Deep valleys in the Karamonda forest, near streams. Very rare.

• Fls. *March-May.*

Twigs rusty tomentose as also to some extent are the petioles and inflorescence. *L.* lanceolate or oblong-lanc. acuminate 2-4″, beneath with numerous scattered rusty scales or glands and few above, sec.*n.* very fine numerous. *Umbels* cymose on peduncles ½-1″ long, axillary or clustered on small shoots. *Pedicels* ⅛-¼″. *Calyx-lobes* spreading pubescent acute. *Petals* waxy white with pink or brown scales, ⅛″ long. *Berry* globose ⅛″ diam. (fide *F.B.I.*)

Fam. 68. SAPOTACEÆ.

Trees or shrubs often with milky juice, with the innovations often rusty pubescent. *L.* alt. coriacious entire; *Stipules* 0 or caducous. *Fls.* small or mod.-sized axillary (often from leafless axils) and fascicled, bracts and bracteoles minute or 0. *Calyx* persistent, lobes 4-8 imbricated, or 2-seriate with the outer series valvate. *Petals* as many as, or 2-4-times as many as, the calyx lobes. *St.* on the corolla-tube as many as the petals and opp. to them or 2-3 seriate, if isomerous with the petals then with alternating staminodes, Fil. short. *Ovary* superior, 2-8-celled; style linear, stigma a point, *ovules* solitary in each cell usually axile. *Berry* indehiscent, 1-8 seeded. Testa usually crustaceous. Embryo straight, exalbuminous with large cotyledons, or albuminous; radicle inferior.

Calyx-lobes and petals each 5 and imbricate . . . 1. *Sideroxylon.*
Calyx-lobes 4, 2-seriate, petals 6-12 . . . . 2. *Bassia.*
Calyx-lobes 6-8, 2-seriate, petals 16-20, 2-3-seriate . 3. *Mimusops.*

1. Sideroxylon, L.

1. S. tomentosum, *Roxb.*

A small tree with tomentose twigs, and branches often armed with straight spines ½-¾″ long, with elliptic obovate or oblanceolate leaves, tomentose or very hairy beneath, smallish white flowers solitary or fascicled from the old leaf scars and yellowish sub-globose or ovoid fruit 1-1¼″ diam.

Valleys in the Latua and the Saranda forests, but not common; S. P. (stream near Bokra-band, Karcho, etc.) Fls. *May-June,* Fr. ripens the following *April.*

L. 3-6″ by 1½-2½″, obtuse or suddenly acute, glabrescent above, base narrowed into the ¼-⅓″ long petiole, *sec. n.* 9-12 prs. straight strong. *Pedicels* ultimately reflexed. *Calyx* campanulate, 2 outer lobes pubescent or tomentose ovate-oblong, inner narrower. *Corolla* tubular-campanulate ¼-⅓″ long, petals twice as long as the tube. *St.* 5 alternating with a corona of 5 ovate petaloid staminodes with filiform tips. *Ovary* tomentose, 5-celled. *Fr.* with very bitter flesh. Seed 1 large deep brown compressed with a very thick testa, long hilum and copious albumen.

2. Bassia, L.

1. B. latifolia, *Roxb.* Madkom, Matkom, Mandukam, *K.*, *S.*; Mahua, *H.* The Mohwa.

A large or *m. s.* tree with low dense crown, pubescent or tomentose twigs, large leaves clustered at the ends of the branches with petioles 1-1½″ long and numerous ovoid-campanulate cream-coloured flowers on long rusty-tomentose pedicels clustered at the ends of the branches, from the leaf-scars. Berry ovoid 1-2″ long.

A well-known tree common throughout Chota Nagpur, but in the forests chiefly confined to the hills. Fls. *Feby.-April.* Fr. *June-July.* It is more or less leafless at the time of flowering and the new leaves appear about *May.*

L. 5-8″ by 2½-3½″ shortly acuminate with 10-12 prs. of strong sec. nerves, tertiary *n.* strong. *Corolla* ⅝″ fleshy with 7-14 short erect teeth. *St.* 20-30 3-seriate sub-sessile *Seeds* large 1-4 with thick fleshy cotyledons and no albumen.

Corollas eaten raw and cooked and are also eaten largely by animals. A spirit (daru, *H.*; arki, *K.*) is also distilled from them. The fruit is eaten. A cooking and lighting oil (Kuindi sunum, *S.*; dola, *K.*) is expressed from the seeds (Kuindi, *S.*) The wood is good and used for oil-mills, but living trees are never felled by the Kols.

3. Mimusops, L.

1. M. Elengi, *L.* Bokul, *Beng.*

A tree often cultivated, with shining glabrous broadly-oblong finely-nerved leaves about 4″ long with petioles ½-¾″. *Fls.* white about 1″ diam. in fascicles with pubescent pedicels about as long as or shorter than petiole. *Calyx segments* 8 acuminate. *Corolla-lobes* 2-seriate, inner 8-10, obovate-oblong, outer linear-oblong. *St.* 8 alternating with lanceolate staminodes, anthers acuminate hirsute. *Berry* narrowly ovoid or ellipsoid, 1″ long, orange, 1-seeded. Flesh eaten, very astringent when unripe. Fls. *April-May.* Evergreen.

Fam. 69. EBENACEÆ.

1. Diospyros, L.

Trees, rarely shrubs, with alternate (or sub-opp. or opp. in D. tomentosa) entire *leaves* with alt. sec. n, and small or m. s. green, white, or yellowish, diœcious flowers; the *males* in 3-more flowered cymes, the *females* usually solitary. *Calyx* 3-5-lobed, often nearly to base, persistent and usually enlarged in fruit. *Corolla* tubular, salver-shaped or campanulate with lobes twisted to the right. *M. fl.* with 8-64 stamens, often in pairs, hypogynous, anthers linear, pistillode present. *F. fl.* with 0-16 staminodes. *Ovary* 4-10-celled, alternate dissepiments sometimes imperfect. Cells 1-ovuled. Styles short 2-4. *Fr.* a berry, sometimes nearly dry, 2-8-seeded with usually remains of the suppressed cells. *Seeds* oblong. Albumen ruminate (D. tomentosa and sometimes D. sylvatica) or not.

L. oblong or oblong-lanceolate under 4" pubescent, base cordate	1. *cordifolia.*
L. ell. glabrous or glabrescent 3-6", acute or obtuse, finely reticulate between the 7-11 prs. sec. n. .	2. *montana.*
L. ell. 4-8" glabrous narrowed or acuminate both ends, not finely reticulate between the 4-8 prs. slender inarching sec. n.	3. *sylvatica.*
L. oblong or narrow-oblong 5-9" glabrous, not acuminate, base rounded, sec. n. not raised . . .	4. *Embryopteris.*
L. oblong or ell.-oblong 7-10" glabrous base subobtuse or cuneate, sec. n, distinct raised beneath .	5. *variegata.*
L. in shape and size much as in 5, silvery silky beneath	(*discolor*).
L. broadly-ell. to sub-orbicular with rounded base 4-12", more or less hairy or tomentose beneath. Nerves strong. Reticulations impressed above .	6. *tomentosa.*
As in 6, but L. narrowed both ends Reticulations raised above	7. *melanoxylon.*

1. **D. cordifolia,** *Roxb.* Syn. D. montana of *F.B.I.* (part). Bangab, *Beng.*

A small tree, sometimes spinose, with very rugose dark bark, pubescent twigs and small oblong pubescent leaves 1-3" long with cordate or rounded base. M. cymes usually 3-fld. F. fls. solitary on slender peduncles $\frac{1}{4}$-$\frac{1}{3}$″ long. Sepals triangular-ovate usually acuminate.

Purulia, Manbhum, *C. B. Clarke*! Monghyr. Fls. *April*. Fr. ripens following *March-April*. Deciduous. New leaves *April*. This tree is easily separable in the forest from D. montana, *Roxb.* and indeed usually also in the herbarium. It is rare in Chota Nagpur, but occurs also at Monghyr close by.

L. rarely attain 3$\frac{1}{4}$″ by 1$\frac{1}{4}$″, lanceolate or mostly oblong-ovate or ovate-lanceo. Very small ones at base of twigs often obtuse. Sec. n. weak, usually 1-3 prs. near base and 4-5 prs. above base. *Peti.* $\frac{1}{8}$-$\frac{1}{4}$″. *M.* in 3-rarely more-fld. cymes, buds conical $\frac{1}{4}$″. *St. about* 8 prs. *F.* white, turning brown below whitish above on drying, not black. *Ped.* $\frac{1}{4}$-$\frac{1}{2}$″. *Calyx* $\frac{5}{8}$″ diam. lobes twice as long as tube, enlarged to $\frac{1}{2}$″ not hardened in fruit. *Staminodes* variable 9-13. *Berry* yellow globose not at all apiculate, about 1-1$\frac{1}{3}$″ diam. Flesh very bitter. Albumen somewhat corrugate.

2. **D. montana,** *Roxb.* (includes D. Kanjilali, *Duthie*)* Sakamhara, *M.*; Sara tiril, *K.*; Gada terel, *S.*; Patwan, *Kharw.*

A small or *m. s.* tree rarely spinose, with smooth reddish flaky bark, glabrous shoots and twigs, and ovate-oblong, ell. or ell.-ovate glabrescent leaves 2-6″ with obtuse rounded or sub-acute base. M. fls. green in 3-5 or often more-fld. cymes. Buds conical. F. fls. $\frac{1}{2}$-$\frac{3}{4}$″ diam. solitary on peduncles which rarely attain $\frac{1}{4}$″ (exceptionally however $\frac{1}{3}$″), sepals 4 broadly- or ovate-oblong with rounded apex coriaceous in fruit.

Along rivers and nalas, frequent in Singbhum, Palamau and Santal Parganahs; Manbhum, *Camp.*; also near Topchanchi, Hazaribagh (Sitagarh hill, etc.); Ranchi, *Clarke*; Ranchi ghats above Ramgarh; Gangpur; Santal Parganahs (Ghormanra, etc.)

Fls. *April-June*. Fr. *Dec.-Feby*. Deciduous.

Twigs sometimes puberulous in the form with pubescent leaves. *L.* quickly glabrous or with a permanent minute pubescence beneath, at first membranous ultimately coriaceous, obtuse or suddenly acute, more rarely shortly acuminate, base rarely cordate or retuse, sec. n. 7-11 prs. from a very broad mid-rib, raised beneath when old, the first 2-3 prs. usually close to base, very finely and evidently reticulate between. *Petiole* $\frac{1}{8}$-$\frac{1}{4}$.″ *M.* buds conical. St. *about* 16. *F. Calyx* flat without a distinct tube in fruit, sep. 4 pubescent or puberulous, $\frac{1}{2}$″ in fruit sub-coriaceous ovate-oblong spreading or reflexed. *Petals* purple-black when old. *Ovary* 8-celled. Styles 4. *Fr.* 1″ globose to somewhat oblong or with short conical tip, seeds 4-8 rarely 2. Albumen equable.

This tree attains 4 ft. girth, but is not much used. The leaves contain much tannin and are used to kill fish. The form with leaves pale or minutely pubescent beneath is found in drier places as on shady sides of hills.

*(Note.—There may be two species included here, but D. Kanjilali as described and figured in Ind. For. XXXI, 307, appears to Dr. Hiern and myself as almost *typical* montana of Roxburgh's figure and description. The only positive characters that differ are in the number of staminodes, but I find both number of stamens and esp. of staminodes a most variable character, the latter may be 2, 4, or 8, the number of flowers in a cyme is also very variable. D. cordifolia on the other hand is quite distinct as Roxburgh described it. (*Vide* also Addenda.)

3. **D. sylvatica,** *Roxb.* Gada tiril, gara tiril, *K.*; *S.*; Maka kend, *S.* (but the true Maka kend is No. 4).

A tree sometimes large (60 ft. by 5 ft. girth) with smooth black and white bark, twigs usually tuberculate or pustulate with lenticels, narrow elliptic or ell.-oblong generally acuminate glabrescent leaves 4″ by 2″ to 8″ by $3\frac{1}{2}$″ with cuneate or sub-acute rarely obtuse base. M. fls. in small dense cymes, cymes racemed, buds globose. F. fls. 1-3 together very numerous, sub-sessile on a short very stout peduncle under $\frac{1}{8}$″ long. Clusters often racemose. Calyx in fruit with a short but distinct campanulate tube, sepals often only 3, sometimes 5, about $\frac{1}{3}$″ long, broadly oblong obtuse, very coriaceous, usually with reflexed margins. Fr. only $\frac{1}{2}$-$\frac{5}{8}$″ diam.

Singbhum, along streams, rather scarce. Santal Parganahs in similar situations, frequent. Fls. *April*. *Fr. Jany.-Feby.*

Crown large and low. *Twigs* pubescent or glabrous. *L.* glabrous, or puberulous on the ribs. *Sec. n.* 4-8 prs. slender arching some distance from margin, not finely reticulate between, first 2-3 prs. usually close to base. Leaf-buds linear tomentose. *Petiole* $\frac{1}{4}$-$\frac{3}{4}$″. *St.* about 20. *Fr.* olive-green globose or oblong glabrous or nearly so with broad base, very rarely attaining $\frac{3}{4}$″, usually very numerous below the leaves, the *calyx* circumsciss at base leaving the short nobbed pubescent peduncles. *Seeds* 1-4, testa with a *crimson juice.* Albumen ruminated or nearly equable.

4. **D. Embryopteris,** *Pers.* Gara tiril, Kendu, *K.*; Makar kenda, *S.*; Tend, *Kharw.*

A handsome tree with low spreading branches almost to the ground, with smoothish black bark, coriaceous oblong or narrowly oblong glabrous shining leaves 5″ by $1\frac{1}{2}$″ to 8″ by $2\frac{1}{4}$″

or more, acute or obtuse with rounded base. M. fls. white fragrant in axillary usually 4-fid. umbellate cymes, buds ovoid-oblong with 4 small silky patches. F. fls. 1″ diam. solitary. Fruit covered with a deciduous red tomentum, globose, $2\frac{1}{2}$-3″ diam.

Common along streams in the Singbhum valleys, rarer in Manbhum and Palamau. Very rare now in the Santal Parganahs and chiefly in the northern valleys. Fl. *April-May.* Fr. ripens the following *April.* Evergreen, the new leaves which are bright crimson appear about *April.*

Buds lanceolate silky. Sec. n. scarcely raised, soon inclined very obliquely forward, very reticulate. *Petiole* $\frac{1}{2}$-$\frac{5}{8}$″. *M. peduncles* $\frac{1}{3}$-$\frac{1}{2}$″ pubescent. *Calyx* urceolate silky. *Corolla* nearly $\frac{1}{2}$″ campanulate or urceolate with short sub-orbicular lobes. *St.* 20-35 or more, fil. in pairs from near the base, pubescent. *F. peduncles* stout $\frac{1}{2}$″. *Sepals* $\frac{1}{2}$″ broadly ovate or sub-orbicular, 1″ in fruit foliaceous. *Cor.-lobes* 4-5, $\frac{1}{3}$″ diam. *Seeds* about 8 large in pulp which is largely eaten by monkeys, sometimes by human beings, but is said to produce great thirst. I find that it burns the throat.

5. **D. variegata,** *Kurz?*

A tree with smooth bark and pink blaze, very large oblong or elliptic-oblong leaves mostly 10″ by $3\frac{3}{4}$″, easily distinguished from the last by the prominent 7-8 prs. of sec. n. raised beneath, first spreading then more or less arched within the margin, raised and reticulate nervules, and by the sub-obtuse or cuneate base.

Found in ravines in the northern Santal Parganahs in January, but I have been unable to procure flowers. It compares exactly with specimens in the Sibpur Herbarium of D. variegata, *Kurz*, from Assam. Time of flowering probably *April-May.*

The M. fls. of D. variegata are described as in very short sparingly pubescent cymes with a salver-shaped corolla nearly glabrous without and with about 16 stamens.

D. **discolor,** *Willd.* A specimen, from Ranchi, probably cultivated, collected by *Gamble* has leaves 9″ with numerous slender nerves, easily recognised by being silvery-silky beneath. Bears a large red velvety edible fruit. Fls. *April.* Fr. *Dec.*

6. **D. tomentosa,** *Roxb.* Terel, Tiril, *K., S.*; Tend, *Kharw.*; Kend, *H., Beng.*

A small or sometimes a large tree with black rugose bark, rusty-tomentose shoots and large broadly ovate leaves mostly with a rounded base, which are permanently more or less tomentose pubescent or hairy beneath. M. fls. in peduncled tomentose simple and branched cymes with narrow-ellipsoid buds $\frac{1}{4}''$ long. F. solitary, the calyx, with wavy reflexed margins to the short broad lobes, 1″ diam. in fruit. Fr. $1\text{-}1\frac{1}{2}''$ diam. smooth and yellowish when ripe.

One of the commonest trees throughout the area, often small in scrub jungle, sometimes attains 6 ft. girth with a long clean bole in virgin forest. It reproduces itself copiously from root-suckers on cultivated lands, and coppices freely. Fls. *May*. Fr. ripens the following *May*. Evergreen.

L. 4″ by $2\frac{1}{2}''$ to 8″ by 5″ vary from elliptic to orbicular on the same tree tip obtuse or rounded, old coriaceous with usually impressed tertiary nerves and rugose appearance above, rarely glabrescent. Sec. *n.* 9-12 prs., often branched and irregular. *M.*, *Calyx* funnel-shaped, acutely-toothed ; *St.* about 16, connective pilose. Fr. solitary axillary sub-sessile, globose to ovoid, densely hairy when young, 3-4-seeded. Albumen ruminate.

The black heart-wood is used for carving in the S. P. G. Mission school at Chaibassa. The wood emits showers of sparks when burnt. The fruit is excellent eating when just ripe.

7. **D. melanoxylon,** *Roxb.* Is included in Wood's list and said to be common in scrub jungle. All the specimens in the Cal. Herb. labelled D. melanoxylon from Chota Nagpur appear to me to be D. tomentosa. Brandis, however, unites the two in his Forest Flora and, I think, correctly.

At Kew there is a specimen labelled D. melanoxylon collected by C. B. Clarke from Ranchi 2,000 ft. dated 22nd Oct. 1873. *L.* ell. to very broadly-elliptic 5-7″ tomentose to glabrescent beneath. Sec, n. 9-10 prs. *Petole* $\frac{1}{2}\text{-}\frac{3}{4}''$. The tertiary nerves are *scarcely raised* above, and the fact that they are not depressed above appears to be *the only reason* for including *this* in D. melanoxylon.

A specimen of D. melanoxylon collected by R. Thomson in the Central Provinces has elliptic-oblong leaves 12″ long and petiole under $\frac{1}{2}''$ and in nervation *very closely resembles* D. variegata (see above) but is *very pubescent* beneath. This is quite a *different looking plant* from the Chota Nagpur specimens called D. melanoxylon.

Fam. 70. STYRACEÆ.

1. Symplocos, L.

Trees or shrubs with alt. exstipulate leaves and 2-sexual regular white or yellowish flowers in axillary spikes or racemes, bracteate and with 1-3 bracteoles at the base of each flower. *Calyx* with 4-5 small imbricate sepals persistent superior. *Petals* 5 imbricate, usually connate only at the very base into a very short tube bearing the numerous stamens, rarely quite free. *Anthers* shortly oblong. *Ovary* inferior, 3- rarely 2-4-celled; style slender, stigma small sub-3-lobed. Ovules 2, pendulous from the inner angle of each cell. *Drupe* ellipsoid, endocarp 1-3-seeded. *Seeds* oblong, albuminous, straight or curved; embryo straight or curved.

L. 2-5″. Fls. pedicelled, sepals minutely pubescent. Fr. oblong . . . . 1. *racemosa*.
L. 4-7″. Fls. sessile, sepals glabrous. Fr. globose . . 2. *spicata*.

1. **S. racemosa,** *Roxb.* Ludam, *K.*; Lodam, S.; Lodh *H., Beng., Oraon.*

A small tree with oblong, elliptic or ell-lanceolate coriaceous shining leaves which are entire, crenate or serrulate, and white flowers, turning yellow with age, in axillary simple or compound racemes 2-3″ long. Drupe oblong $\frac{1}{3}$-$\frac{1}{2}$″ by $\frac{1}{6}$-$\frac{1}{4}$″ crowned by the calyx. (Diseased globose drupes occur.)

Throughout Chota Nagpur and Santal Parganahs abundant, esp. in poor open forest. Fls. *Oct-Jany.* Fr. *Dec.-May.* Evergreen.

L. $3\frac{1}{2}$″ by $1\frac{1}{2}$″ to $5\frac{1}{2}$″ by $2\frac{1}{3}$″ glabrous or slightly pilose on the mid-rib acute or obtuse both ends, or acuminate, nerves slender irregular. *Petiole* $\frac{1}{4}$-$\frac{1}{2}$″. *Racemes* pubescent or hairy, pedicels $\frac{1}{20}$-$\frac{1}{8}$″, sepals broadly oblong connate below. *Corolla* $\frac{1}{8}$-$\frac{1}{4}$″ diam.

The bark is used in conjunctivitis. A concoction of the leaves is used as a mordant for the Chaili (Al) dye. Campbell states that the bark is used as a dye and the wood-ash as a mordant.

2. **S. spicata,** *Roxb.* Marang Ludam, *K.*

A small tree with very shining elliptic or oblong serrate or serrulate acuminate leaves often attaining 9″ by 3″, and white flowers in simple or branched axillary spikes 1-$3\frac{1}{2}$″ long. Drupe globose ovoid $\frac{1}{4}$″ diam. crowned by the small glabrous calyx. Seed and embryo curved.

Deep valleys near streams in the Saranda foresst, rare. Fls. *Dec.* Fr *May.* Evergreen.

L. pale beneath, narrowed at the base, often sinuately or sharply serrate above the middle, glabrous, sec. n. fine distinct 7-9 prs. oblique. *Spikes*, small ovate *bract, and bracteoles* rusty pubescent.

Fam. 71. OLEACEÆ.

Trees or shrubs, sometimes scandent, with opposite simple or pinnate exstipulate leaves. *Fls.* regular usually 2-sexual, usually in 3 chotomous cymes or panicles. *Calyx* small truncate or 4-lobed or sometimes 5-9-lobed. *Corolla* 4-9-petalous rarely 0. *St.* 2 hypogynous or on the corolla-tube. *Ovary* 2-celled, style 1, stigma simple or 2-lobed. *Ovules* 1-2 in each cell, axile. *Fr.* dehiscent or indehiscent. *Seeds* 1 or 2 in each cell, erect or pendulous; albumen present or not, embryo straight.

I. Corolla ½" diam. or more, lobes imbricate. Fr. capsular or a berry.

Shrubs sometimes scandent. Corolla-tube white. Fruit baccate . . . . 1. *Jasminum.*

Small tree. Corolla-tube yellow. Fr. a coriaceous capsule . . . . 2. *Nyctanthes.*

Tree. L. pinnate. Fls. brownish. Fr. a pyriform woody capsule . . . . 3. *Schrebera.*

II. Corolla under ½" diam., lobes valvate. Fr. a drupe.

Petals in pairs, distinct or nearly so. Panicles axillary . . . . 4. *Linociera.*

Corolla tubular. Panicles terminal . . . . 5. *Ligustrum.*

1. Jasminum, L. Jasmine.

Shrubs often scandent or with sarmentose branches, with simple leaves (in the Chota Nagpur spp.) articulate petioles and white or pinkish flowers in 2-3-chotomous cymes. Calyx with 0 or 4-9 linear teeth. Corolla salver-shaped with narrow tube and 4-10 spreading petals. Ovules 2 in each cell near the base. Berry simple or didymous, seed one in each carpel, erect, exalbuminous.

I. Cymes lax.

(*a*) Cymes about 1-7-fld. Calyx lobes ¼." Ripe carpels globose . . . . 1. *Sambac.*

(b) Cymes 7-many-fld. Calyx-lobes under $\frac{1}{4}''$. Ripe carpels oblong.

L. glabrescent. Calyx-lobes $\frac{1}{16}$-$\frac{1}{8}''$ . . . 2. *arborescens.*

L. softly hairy both sides. Calyx-lobes under $\frac{1}{10}''$ . . . . 3. *Roxburghianum.*

II. Fls. sub-sessile in dense sub-capitate cymes. 4. *pubescens.*

1. **J. Sambac,** *Ait.* Mallika, *K.*; Chameli, *H.*; Bel, *Beng.*

A climbing or, in cultivation, sometimes an erect shrub with pubescent branches sub-sessile nearly glabrous leaves and white very fragrant flowers in usually about 3-fld. pubescent cymes. Ripe carpels 1-2, globose $\frac{1}{4}''$ diam. black

Saranda forest, *Gamble* (but as this is the only Jasmine in the list, it may be an error); Chota Nagpur, *Wood's list* (without locality). I have only seen it in cultivation where it is very variable and often double.

Fls.—*May-July* and also at other times.

L. 2-3″, sometimes 1·5″, ell. rotund or usually ovate, shortly and obtusely acuminate. *Calyx-lobes* 5-9 linear or subulate half the length of the corolla-tube or more, hairy. *Corolla-tube* $\frac{1}{2}''$, petals $\frac{1}{2}''$ oblong.

2. **J. arborescens,** *Roxb.* Hundi, *K.*; Gada Hund Baha, *S.*

Sub-erect with thick trunk and long drooping branches or scandent, with young branches, leaves and cymes pubescent, nearly glabrous in fruit. L. ovate-lanceolate to very broadly ovate, acute or usually acuminate, petioled. White flowers in lax 7-many-flowered 3-chotomous cymes. Ripe carpel usually solitary oblong or ellipsoid often curved nearly $\frac{1}{2}''$ long black.

The commonest Jasmine in Chota Nagpur but not abundant. Usually by the sides of rocky nalas. In all the districts.

Fls. *April-May.* Fr. *June-July.* Deciduous. New shoots in *March* and *April.*

L. $1\frac{1}{2}$-3″ in flower, sometimes with two very small ones at base of shoot, often attaining 5″ by $3\frac{1}{2}''$ (sometimes 7″ by 5″) in fruit and then quite glabrous; sec. n. 4-8 prs.; *petiole* $\frac{1}{4}$-$\frac{1}{2}''$ in fl., up to $\frac{3}{4}''$ in fr. *Cymes* rarely with only 3-5 fls. glabrescent. *Calyx-lobes* linear $\frac{1}{16}$-$\frac{1}{8}''$, or $\frac{1}{8}$-$\frac{3}{16}''$ in fruit. *Corolla,* tube $\frac{1}{2}''$, lobes $\frac{1}{2}$-$\frac{5}{8}''$ narrow-oblong.

3. J. Roxburghianum, *Wall.* Hundi, *K.*

A large climbing shrub or sub-erect as in the last, with tomentose-pubescent branchlets, ovate strongly-nerved leaves, tomentose beneath, softly shortly pubescent above, and tomentose cymes of white flowers much as in the last.

Forests of the Porahat plateau, not common.

L. 2-4" by $1\frac{3}{4}$-$2\frac{1}{2}$" acute, base obtuse straight or sub-cordate. Sec. n. 6-9 prs. reticulate some distance from the margin. *Petiole* $\frac{1}{4}$-$\frac{1}{3}$". Inflorescence much as in the last but calyx-lobes even smaller.

Fruit said to be eaten.

4. J. pubescens, *Willd.* Chameli, *H.*

A sub-scandent shrub with drooping densely pubescent or tomentose branches, ovate or ovate-lanceolate acute or sub-acuminate leaves 1" by $\frac{5}{8}$" to $3\frac{1}{2}$" by $1\frac{3}{4}$" and white flowers in capitate cymes on 2-bracteate axillary peduncles or terminating short axillary branches, dimorphic. Fr. ellipsoid $\frac{1}{2}$-$\frac{5}{8}$" long (globose according to *Prain* and *F.B.I.*) surrounded by the long hairy erect sepals.

Santal Parganahs, along ravines. Jaspur and Sirguja, *Wood.* Fls. *Jan.-March.* Fr. *May.*

L. puberulous beneath and pubescent on the nerves, nearly glabrous above, base usually rounded, slender sec. n. 3-4 prs. of which the first pair is from the base. *Petiole* $\frac{3}{16}$-$\frac{1}{3}$". Bracts same shape as the leaves. *Larger flowers* up to $1\frac{3}{4}$" diam. shortly pedicelled, *calyx* fulvous hairy, *teeth* 7-9 setaceous $\frac{1}{2}$"-$\frac{9}{16}$", *Cor.-tube* $\frac{3}{4}$" long. Anthers apiculate. *Smaller flowers* $\frac{5}{8}$" diam. sessile, calyx-teeth $\frac{1}{8}$-$\frac{1}{3}$", cor.-tube $\frac{3}{8}$-$\frac{1}{2}$" long.

There appears to be no difference in the length of style or position of the stamens, both forms occur closely associated.

2. Nyctanthes, L.

1. N. Arbor-tristis, *L.* Saparom, *K., S.*; Kula marsal, *K.*; Snamshihar, *Kharw.*; Harsinghar, *H.*; Sephalika, *Beng.*

A small tree with usually weeping 4-angular branches, very scabrous ovate entire or somewhat toothed acute leaves, and white salver-shaped flowers with yellow tube in bracteate heads which are disposed in ample terminal 3-chotomous cymes. Capsule orbicular compressed papery or leathery 2-celled.

Very common esp. on steep northern aspects. On some slopes of sliding hæmatite schists layered parallel with the slope, it is sometimes nearly the only tree, and as it coppices readily is useful for fuel. Common as second growth on the Rajmehal trap.

Fls. *Sept.-Oct.* Fr. *Dec.-Jany.* Deciduous *April-May.*

Branches scabrous. *L.* about 4½″ by 2½″ and *petiole* ⅓″.

The seeds yield a medicinal oil and a preparation from the roots is given for rough skin, *Campbell.* The root is eaten, *Diller.*

3. Schrebera, Roxb.

1. **S. swietenioides,** *Roxb.* Sandapsing, *K.*; Jarjo, *K.* (fide Watt); Akasara, *S.*; Gæ ka lundi, *H.*; Chapsing, *Kharw.*; Ghanto, *Oraon.*

A mod.-sized tree with opp. impari-pinnate leaves with 3-7 leaflets, and terminal panicled 2-3-chotomous cymose panicles of salver-shaped flowers ½-⅝″ diam. Capsules with small worts, usually few with the fully developed foliage, pyriform 2½″ by 1″, 2-celled with 2-4 large angular seeds in each cell.

Fairly common on the hills in Singbhum. Also in Manbhum, Hazaribagh and Palamau. On the trap in the Santal Parganahs. Fls. *May-June* with the young leaves. Fr. *Oct.-March.* Deciduous *Feby.-March.*

L. 9-12″ pubescent when young. *Lflts.* articulate, opp., 3-5″ by 2-3″ oblong to ovate-lanceolate sub-acuminate, finely reticulate and pale beneath, base narrowed into a short or very short *petiolule* or petiolule of terminal lflt. 1-2″, rachis finely pubescent. *Inflorescence* pubescent. Fls. with minute brown scales. *Calyx* irregularly lobed persistent. *Corolla-tube* ½″. *Anthers* slightly exserted. *Ovules* 4 in each cell. Albumen 0. Cotyledons large crumpled.

4. Linociera, Swartz.

1. **L. intermedia,** *Wight.* Suli-Udi Kuda, *K.*; Deorkuda, *K.* (f. Gamble).

A small glabrous tree with ell.-oblong or obovate leaves 3½″ by 1¼″ to 8″ by 3″, axillary pyramidal panicles 1½-4″ long of small white flowers and broadly-oblong or ovoid drupes about $\frac{1}{2}''$.

Singbhum near streams, not common; Kochang; Neterhat, *Gamble*; Parasnath; Santal Parganahs, along streams. Fls. *Feby.-March.* Fr. takes over a year to ripen. Evergreen, renews leaves in *Feby.*

L. chartaceous acute obtuse or shortly acuminate narrowed at base into the $\frac{1}{2}$-1″ petiole; sec. n. about 10 prs. distinct. *Fls.* in subsessile clusters on the opposite branches of the short panicle. *Calyx* $\frac{1}{16}''$. *Petals* 4 nearly distinct $\frac{1}{8}$-$\frac{1}{6}''$ long oblong with incurved margins. *Ovary* 2-celled. Ovules 2 in each cell, pendulous from the apex. Albumen 0.

Var. Roxburghii, *C. B. Clarke.*

A small gnarled tree very common on the top of Parasnath, not collected in flower, is this, according to exactly similar specimens, in the Cal. Herb. and at Kew.

Flowers just over in *Dec.* Ripe fruit *May.*

Quite glabrous with erecto-patent oblong shortly suddenly acuminate leaves about $4\frac{1}{2}''$ by $1\frac{1}{4}''$ with weak sec. nerves reticulate within the margin. *Fruit* a blue glaucous broadly oblong obtuse drupe $\frac{1}{2}''$ long. Seed *with* endosperm.

I doubt this being a variety of L. intermedia, *Wight.* From the albuminous seed it should be an Olea.

Prain (*Bengal Plants*) includes all Chota Nagpur specimens in var. Roxburghii.

5. Ligustrum, L.

1. L. robustum, *Blume.*

A small tree with bifurcate curly-pubescent twigs, and opp. lanceolate acuminate very shortly-petioled distichous eaves $1\frac{1}{2}$-$3\frac{1}{2}''$. Fls. small white in terminal pubescent panicles 3-8″.

Ravines in the Rajmehal hills, very rare.

Fls. *June.* Fr. *Dec.-Jany.* (I have only seen old inflorescence.)

Lenticellate pale branchlets compressed at the nodes. *L.* glabrous (at least when old), narrowed at base. Sec. n. about 6 prs. rather obscure. *Petiole* $\frac{1}{8}''$ articulate at base, the two first bracts of the axillary buds often simulating intrapetiolar stipules. *Calyx* shortly 4-toothed. *Corolla-tube* as long as the calyx. *Drupe* $\frac{1}{4}$-$\frac{1}{3}''$ oblong.

Fam. 72. LOGANIACEÆ.

Trees, shrubs or herbs with opposite simple leaves with or without stipules. *Fls.* regular, cymose, cymes often sub-capitate in spikes or panicled. *Calyx* inferior, small, 4-5-toothed or lobed. *Corolla* gamopetalous. *St.* 4-5 on the tube and alternate with the petals. *Ovary* free 2-celled, style simple, stigma capitate or 2-partite. Ovules 1 or more in each cell, axile or basal in the inner angle. *Fruit* capsular septicidal or indehiscent and baccate, 1-many-seeded. Albumen copious; embryo straight, long or short.

Shrub. L. penni-nerved. Fr. a small capsule . . 1. *Buddleia.*
Trees. L. 3-5-nerved or sub-penni-nerved. Fr. a berry . 2. *Strychnos.*

1. Buddleia, L.

1. B. asiatica, *Lour.* Nimda, *Beng.*

A pretty shrub 3-7 ft. clothed on the branchlets and often on the leaves with a hoary or grey tomentum, with lanceolate acuminate leaves and small white flowers $\frac{1}{6}$-$\frac{1}{4}$" in small cymose clusters on axillary or terminal spikes which are often panicled.

Near streams in Singbhum, not common; Santal Parganahs, rare. Fls. *Dec.-Feby.* Fr. *March.* Evergreen.

L. 3-6" narrowed at the base into a short petiole, exstipulate. *Spike* 3-6". *Fls.* 4-merous. *St.* 4 on the corolla-tube, anthers sub-sessile. Stigma clavate. *Capsule* $\frac{1}{4}$" reflexed when ripe, septicidally 2-valved. Seeds very many ellipsoid.

2. Strychnos, L.

Scandent shrubs or (in Chota Nagpur) trees with 3-5-basal-nerved leaves (or in S. potatorum sometimes sub-penni-nerved) exstipulate, but with stipular lines. Fls. 4-5-merous in terminal or lateral cymes. Petals valvate. St. 5. on the tube. Berry 1-2 or many-seeded. Seeds often large, embryo small.

L. petioled 5-nerved. Cymes terminal . . . 1. *Nux-Vomica.*
L. subsessile sub-3-5-nerved. Cymes lateral . . 2 *potatorum.*

1. **S. Nux-vomica,** *L.* Kuchila, *H.* The Strychnine tree.

A mod.-sized rather handsome tree with shining green shoots, short-petioled shining leaves about $3\frac{1}{2}''$ by $2''$ to $4''$ by $3''$ and small greenish-white flowers $\frac{1}{3}$-$\frac{1}{2}''$ long in small terminal corymbose cymes. Barry globose with a coriaceous pericarp orange when ripe and a white pulp. Seeds several discoid $\frac{1}{2}''$ diam. with a grey satiny lustre.

Dalbhum, *Wood*; Occasional in Singbhum and Palamau; Megatura (Hazaribagh), *Haslett!* but always near villages, and I do not think indigenous. Parasnath, *Camp. Herb!*

Fls. *Jany.* Fr. *Dec.* Evergreen.

L. elliptic to sub-orbicular rounded both ends, reticulate beneath, two lateral basal nerves fine. *Petiole* $\frac{1}{4}$-$\frac{3}{4}''$.

The dried ripe seeds are the Nux-Vomica of the Pharmacopœia. Merely powdered, they are a valuable tonic and useful in atonic dyspepsia both in human beings and horses. They are the chief source of Strychnine.

2. **S. potatorum,** *L. f.* Nirmali, *H.*; Kuchila, *S.* The Clearing Nut.

A small tree with elliptic to ovate sub-sessile glabrous leaves united by a stipular ridge and white (or greenish-yellow, *Roxb.*) fragrant flowers $\frac{1}{8}$-$\frac{1}{4}''$ long in lateral sub-sessile cymes. Berry sub-globose black when ripe $\frac{1}{2}$-$\frac{3}{4}''$ diam. Seeds 1-2, $\frac{1}{4}$-$\frac{1}{3}''$ diam.

Chota Nagpur, *Prain.* Manbhum, *Camp.* whether wild or not is not stated. I have not seen it in C. N. It occurs along the Sone, *Hook.* (Him. Journals). Fls *h. s.* Fr. Nov.

L. 2-3″. *Corolla-tube* campanulate hairy within.

The seeds rubbed round the inside of a vessel are used to clear muddy water. The pulp is eaten.

Fam. 73. GENTIANACEÆ.

Herbs usually glabrous with opposite entire exstipulate often basal-nerved leaves. *Fls.* regular or irregular usually in ebracteate cymes. *Calyx* inferior, lobes 4-5 imbricate in bud. *Corolla* funnel-shaped or rotate. *Stamens* on the tube, as many as the petals and alternate with them, all equal or some smaller than the others or altogether suppressed, anthers dehiscing longitudinally or by apical pores. *Disc* 0 or of glands. *Ovary* free 1-celled or more or less 2-celled, style simple, stigmas 2. *Ovules* numerous. *Fr.* capsular. Seeds numerous. Albumen copious.

I. Flowers regular

Ovary 1-celled. Fls. white with 1-2 glands at base of petals . . . . 1. *Swertia.*

Ovary 2-celled. Fls. blue (rarely white). Petals eglandular . . . . 2. *Exacum.*

II. Flowers irregular

Ovary 1-celled. Fls. white or pink. Stamens unequal 3. *Canscora.*

1. Swertia, L.

Erect herbs with 1-5-basal-nerved leaves and 4-5-merous flowers in panicled cymes. Corolla rotate, tube very short. One or two orbicular glands at the base of each petal often covered by a scale or with a fimbriate margin. Style 0 or very short, stigmas 2. Capsule 2-valved.

1. S. angustifolia, *Ham.* Var. pulchella, *Burkill,* Chiretta, *H.*

A pretty erect herb 1-3 ft. high with stems 4-angled above, linear-lanceolate sessile 3-nerved or sub-3-nerved leaves and white or very pale-blue 4-merous flowers $\frac{1}{2}$-$\frac{2}{3}$" diam. in numerous panicles.

Frequent in grassy glades in the valley forests, Singbhum, Manbhum, Hazaribagh and Palamau. Fls. *Oct.-Dec.*

Petals usually with black or purple streaks or dots and each with 1 orbicular gland near the base.

The above includes the two species of the F.B.I. S. pulchella *Ham.* and S. affinis, *Clarke.* I have adopted Burkill's nomenclature (Journ. As. Soc. II, 8), especially as I had already noted a Singhbhum variety as being intermediate between S. angustifolia, *Ham.*, and S. pulchella. An infusion of the plant is used like that of the English Centaury" as a tonic and stomachic.

2. Exacum, L.

Erect herbs with ovate or lanceolate 3-5-nerved leaves and 4-5-merous blue or white flowers in terminal or axillary cymes. Calyx-lobes often winged. Corolla rotate. Style long, stigma small sub-capitate. Capsule globose, septicidal y 2-valved. Seeds very many, minute.

Fls. blue, petals ½-¾″. Stem 1-4 ft. . . . 1. *tetragonum.*
Fls. blue, petals ¼-⅓″. Stem 3-12″ L. 1¾ by ½″ . . 2. *pedunculatum.*
Fls. white or very pale blue. Stem 3-12″. L. 3 by 1¾″ 3. *petiolare.*

1. E. tetragonum, *Roxb.* *Kuchuri, Beng.*

A lovely plant with 4-angled stems, sessile 5-nerved leaves about 5″ by 1½″ and panicles of azure-blue flowers with broadly-elliptic or ovate petals and erect large yellow lanthers.

Grassy glades not uncommon. Singbhum, Ranchi. Fls. *Oct.-Dec.*

Root given in fever, *Wood.*

The other species are small plants of damp places.

3. Canscora, Lamk.

Herbs with flowers in terminal dichotomous cymes. Calyx often keeled or winged 4-toothed. Corolla more or less irregular, St. 4 one larger perfect, three shorter smaller barren or nearly suppressed. Capsule 2-valved.

Calyx winged, Fls. white . . . . 1. *decussata.*
Calyx not winged, Fls. small rose-coloured.
Cyme branches with small subulate bracts . . . . 2. *decurrens.*
Cyme branches with broadly-ovate foliaceous bracts . 3. *diffusa.*

1. C. decussata, *Roem.* Kalmeg, *K.*; Sankhahuli, *H.*

Stem 4-20. inches high, 4-winged. L. 1-2″ oblong-lanceolate.

Common on clayey ground in the forest. Fls. *Sept.-Nov.*

Used as a tonic, laxative and in fever.

2. C. decurrens, *Dalz.*, is a small plant 6-1 ft. high with lanceolate leaves somewhat decurrent on the stem and small flowers,

trichotomous panicles. 3. **C. diffusa**, *Bar.* is a pretty little plant 6-18 high and has dichotomous panicles with foliaceous bracts at the forks. They are both frequent on wet banks.

Fam. 74. APOCYNACEÆ.

Trees, shrubs or herbs, often climbing, with opposite or whorled (alt. in the cultivated Thevetia and Plumeria) quite entire simple exstipulate leaves and usually milky juice. *Fls.* regular, 2-sexual, cymose or axillary. *Calyx* inferior with 5 imbricate lobes. *Corolla* usually rotate or salver-shaped (funnel-shaped in Thevetia). *St.* 5 rarely 4, on the corolla, not connate as in the Asclepiadaceæ but with their anthers usually conniving over the stigma and sometimes adhering to it. *Pollen* granular. *Disc* often large. *Ovary* 2-celled or usually of two more or less distinct carpels united by the style, the top of which is usually enlarged. *Ovules* 2 to many in each cell, rarely 1 only. *Fr.* of follicles, more rarely a berry or drupe. Seeds often with a coma of silky hairs or winged. Albumen present or not.

I.—Anthers not adhering to the stigma.

(*a*) Ovary 2-celled. Fr. a berry or drupe

A spinous shrub. L. opposite . . . . . 1. *Carissa*.

A large unarmed shrub with narrow alt. leaves . 2. *Thevetia*.

(*b*) Ovary of 2 distinct (sub-connate in 4) carpels united by the style—

A small tree or shrub with alt. large leaves . . 3. *Plumeria*.

A shrub with 3-4-nately whorled leaves. Fr. a drupe 4. *Rauwolfia*.

A tree with whorled leaves, Fr. of follicles . . 5. *Alstonia*.

A small tree or shrub, L opposite. Fr. of follicles 6. *Holarrhena*.

II.—Anthers adhering to the stigma by a point. Ovary of distinct carpels united by the style. Fruit of 2 free or united follicles.

(*a*) Mouth of corolla with scales—

1. Anthers exserted. Small tree. Follicles connate 7. *Wrightia*.

2. Anthers included—

Erect shrub. L. whorled . . . . . . 8. *Nerium*.

Climbing shrubs. L. opposite. Petals caudate. 9. *Strophanthus*.

(*b*) Mouth of corolla without scales. All climbing shrubs.

1. Anthers exserted. Fls. white ¼″-⅜″ diam. . . 10. *Vallaris.*
2. Anthers included—
   - (i) Corolla very large, tubular-campanulate . 11. *Beaumontia.*
   - (ii) Corolla small or medium-sized. Petals overlapping to the right in bud—
     - Petals nearly straight in bud. Cymes tomentose . . . . 12. *Aganosma.*
     - Pet. sharply twisted to the left in bud. Cymes glabrous . . . . . . 13. *Anodendron.*
     - Pet. as in 13 but the tips inflexed. Cymes pubescent . . . . 14. *Ichnocarpus.*

1. Carissa, L.

1. **C. Carandas,** *L.* (Including C. spinarum, *A.D.C.*) Kannwan, *K*, (*f.* Gamble,) *Oraon* (*f.* Watt); Karwak, janum, Karwat', *S.*; Karaunda, *H.*

A rigid dichotomously branched small or large shrub, or small tree, with pairs of divaricate simple or branched thorns at the nodes, elliptic ovate or rounded coriaceous leaves ½-1½″ and small white or pale-pink flowers. Fr. a globose or ellipsoid berry first red then black.

Very common over the northern parts of the province, chiefly frequenting sandy soils and rapidly diminishing on clay, while it is absent from the forest tracts of Singbhum and Gangpur. Chiefly in the north-west of the S. P., *Gamble.*

In full flower *April-May,* but also flowering up to *Sept.* Fr. ripens *Nov.-Dec.* and onwards to *March.* Evergreen, the new shoots appear in *March.*

There are two species recognized in the F.B.I. of which **C. spinarum** is said to be sub-erect and shrubby, tip of leaves mucronate or apiculate spines more slender, corolla only ½″ long and berry ¼″ diam. sub-globose, while **C. Carandas** is large and erect, often arboreous, tip of leaves rounded or obtuse, corolla ¾-1″ long, and berry ellipsoid ½-1″. Brandis suggested that the latter is a form of the former, and as the Chota Nagpur plant is often a small tree 25 ft. high with most of the other characters of C. spinarum, and the large berried form is usually only seen in cultivation, the forms are better united. A small variety "hirsuta" with branches and cymes and leaves beneath pubescent is also found in Chota Nagpur.

The fruit is eaten.

Thevetia neriifolia, *Juss.* Borenjo, *S.*, is a very common large evergreen shrub in gardens, of quick growth, with crowded 1-nerved linear leaves and large yellow funnel-shaped corollas. Fruit a large green drupe with a very hard usually 2-celled stone.

Plumeria acutifolia, *Poir.* Champa pungar, gulanj baha, *S.*, is another small tree very commonly cultivated. It has very thick round branches, leafless in the hot weather and large narrowly elliptic leaves with strong horizontal parallel sec. nerves which are crowded at the ends of the branchlets. Fls. about 2″ diam. fragrant white with a yellow eye in terminal cymes. Fruit follicular.

4. Rauwolfia, L.

1. R. serpentina, *Benth.* Chandra, *Beng.*

A pretty glabrous undershrub 1-2 ft. high with bright green shining opposite or 3-4-nately whorled oblong or obovate acute leaves 5-7″ by 2-2½″ and small white flowers with pink tubes in peduncled bright red cymes.

Valleys esp. in grass lands, rare. Fls. *May-July.* Fr. *July-Aug.*

L. narrowed into the ½-¾″ petiole. *Pedicels* red. *Drupes* ¼-⅓″ diam. black.

The root is a reputed cure for snake-bite.

5. Alstonia, R. Br.

1. A. scholaris, *R. Br.* Kunumuug, *K.*; Chatni, *S.* Chatawan, *H.*

A usually straight handsome tree with the branches and leaves whorled and greenish-white flowers in umbellately branched cymes. Fruit of two slender follicles 1-2 ft. long, pendulous.

Valleys in Singbhum, not common; Tundi hills in Manbhum Hazaribagh, rare; S. P. (Silingi). Fls. *Nov.-Jany.* Fr. *r.s.* Evergreen.

L. 3-7 usually 6 in a whorl, 4-8″ by 1-2½″ oblanceolate or obovate glabrous whitish beneath, base narrowed into the ⅓-½″ petiole. Sec. n. numerous close horizontal. *Inflorescence* puberulous sessile or stalked, branches 2-4″ with often 2-3 whorls of sec. branches ¼ 1″ long bearing the sub-capitate umbels. *Corolla* ⅓-½″ diam. throat with reflexed hairs. *Follicles* terete only ⅓″ diam.

6. Holarrhena, R. Br.

1. H. antidysenterica, *Wall.* Kuar, Tuar, *K.*; Hat, *S.*; Kurchi, *H.*, *Beng.*; Koraiya, *Kharw.*; Korkoria, *Oraon.*; Kurdu, *Mal Pah.*

A large shrub or small tree with somewhat distichously spreading sub-sessile leaves 6-12″ by 1½-5″- strongly nerved beneath and terminal corymbose cymes of sweet-scented white flowers ¾-1½″ diam. Follicles slender 8-16″ divergent.

Very common, esp. in open glades in the valleys and in waste ground. Fls. *May-July.* Fr. *Dec.-Feby.* Dec. *Feby.-April*, it flowers with the new shoots.

New shoots pubescent. First pair of leaves on a twig broadly elliptic 3″ long, others ovate-ell. or ell.-oblong shortly acuminate with obtuse base, glabrous or pubescent beneath. Sec. *n.* 5—13 prs. *Cymes* 3-6″ diam. *Corolla-tube* slender ⅓-½″ with stamens low down in the tube. Disc 0. *Seeds* (Inderjao, *H.*) linear-oblong with long brown coma.

An excellent cure for bad dysentery. A case in Chaibassa of nearly a year's standing was cured in a few weeks by a native practitioner. The patient was a European, who gave me a few of the seeds for identification. " The leaves are distasteful to cattle and goats," *Gamble.*

7. Wrightia, R. Br.

1. W. tomentosa, *Roem.* Tuar, *K.*; Buru machkunda, *S.*; Khirna, Kherua, *Kharw.*

A small tree with slender pubescent branches and distichous elliptic shortly caudate-acuminate tomentose leaves with 8-14 prs. of strong sec. nerves and greenish-orange or cream-cold. Fls. with deep-orange ór scarlet coronal-scales in tomentose corymbose cymes. The follicles are connate into a compressed grooved pendant cylinder, greenish with white tubercles.

Valleys in Singbhum but not common; Manbhum and Hazaribagh, occasional; Palamau; Santal Parganahs, occasional. Fls. *April-July*. Fr. *Dec.-Feby*. Dec. *Feby.-March*.

Milk yellowish-white. *L.* 3-5" by 1½-2½" base acute. Sec. n. strong 10-14 prs. *Petiole* ¼". *Fls.* 1" diam.; coronal scales 10, toothed. *Fr.* 6-12" by ½-⅜". Seeds slender with white coma.

Nerium odorum, *Soland.* Raj baha, *S.*; Kaner, *H.*; Oleander *Eng.* is a common handsome shrub often cultivated (and as if wild, *Prain*) in Chota Nagpur. The leaves are linear or linear-lanceolate in whorls of three, and it bears handsome white or rose-cold. flowers 1-1½" diam. in terminal cymes. Follicles connate till ripe. Seeds tomentose and with a brown coma.

9. Strophanthus, D.C.

1. S. Wallichii, *A.D.C.*

A climber with lenticellate branches, oblong cuspidate glabrous leaves with minute stipules and terminal 2-chotomous cymes of pale-coloured flowers remarkable from their long twisted caudate petals.

Ravines in Singbhum. Fls. *April-May*.

Juice watery. *L.* 3 by 1" to 4" by 2½" with about 6-10 prs. of fine nerves reticulate within the margin. *Petiole* ⅛-¼". *Cymes* 3-4" with recurved linear bracts at the forks, lax. *Calyx-lobes* linear-subulate ½". *Corolla-tube* constricted in the middle ¾" with lobes nearly 2", veined purple within and throat with 5 deeply 2-fid. scales. *St.* with long filiform appendages.

10. Vallaris, Burm.

1. V. Heynei, *Spreng.* Adaka red, *K.*

A climber with light grey tough lenticellate cord-like stems, oblong or ell. acuminate nearly glabrous leaves and cymes of pretty white flowers ½-¾" diam. with broad roundish spreading petals and exserted stamens, conspicuous by the large dorsal gland and basal spurs. Fruit 6" by 1½", terete, of perfectly united carpels, ultimately dehiscent.

Valleys in Singbhum and Gangpur. Pochra (Palamau), *Wood*.

Fls. *April-May*. Fr. *Nov.-Jany*. New leaves in *March*, a light bright green.

L. 1½" by ⅝" to 4" by 1½" membranous, sometimes distinctly pellucid punctate, with 5-9 prs. of arching fine but distinct sec. *n.*; base acute or obtuse somewhat decurrent on the ⅓-½" petiole. *Fruit* sub-truncate at base, tapering above the midde to a blunt apex. Seeds 2-seriate ovate flat with a silky coma.

Bark very bitter, and astringent, chewed by the Kols for fixing loose teeth.

Beaumontia grandiflora, *Wall.*, an immense climber often grown in gardens. It has rusty-pubescent shoots, large obovate-oblong abruptly acuminate leaves and very large handsome white flowers. Tubular portion of the corolla short campanulate above with large rounded lobes.

12. Aganosma, G. Don.

1. A. caryophyllata, *G. Don.* Raten, *S.*

A large climber with ovate or ell. acute, obtuse, or shortly acuminate leaves 3-5½" by 1½-3" and lax pubescent cymes of Jasmine-like white flowers 1½" diam. with broad falcate petals ½" long. Follicles densely yellow tomentose when young, spreading, or recurved, or cornute and cohering by their tips.

Pandra (Manbhum), *Camp.*! Rocky ravines in the Santal Parganahs, frequent on trap rocks; Monghir, *Hamilton.*

Fls. *Aug.* Fr. *Jany.-Feby.*

Young *shoots* densely tomentosely hairy. *L.* glabrous or tomentose beneath, base rounded; sec. n. 2-5 prs. often red very oblique minutely reticulate between. *Petiole* ¼-¾". *Sepals* ⅜" tomentose about equalling the pedicels, *Cor.-tube* ⅓" first very narrow then wider with villous ridges, *petals* twisted to the right in bud. *Anthers* almost awned, bases sagittate. *Follicles* very variable in size 4-14" long and ⅓-⅔" diam. tapering gradually to the tip. *Seeds* flat ⅝-1" long and coma rather longer.

13. Anodendron, A.D.C.

1. A. paniculatum, *A.D.C.*

A large climber with stout green stems ½-1" diam., coriaceous 'Sal'-like lower leaves and small pale-yellow salver-shaped flowers in very lax slightly branched axillary and terminal brachiate panicles.

Along streams in Singbhum but very rare. Fls *March-April* and fruit takes a year to ripen.

Lower *leaves* 7-8" by 4-5", very coriaceous, entire or slightly waved and with slightly reflexed margins, shortly cuspidate with 12-13 prs. of strong nearly straight nerves, shining above, quite glabrous, or puberulous beneath, *petiole* ¾". *Upper leaves* narrow-oblong 4-5" by 1½", cuspidate. *Panicles* 3-6". *Fls.* 3-nate. *Corolla* ⅛" long. Mouth contracted, lobes narrow ¼", throat villous. Anthers sagittate and shortly spurred. *Follicles* spreading 5-6" by ¾" at base, narrowed to an obtuse base. Hairs of coma 2" long.

Said to produce rubber.

14 Ichnocarpus, Br.

Climbing shrubs with small salver-shaped flowers in axillary and terminal panicled cymes. Corolla throat contracted, lobes overlapping to right, narrow with the upper half inflexed in bud. St. at or below the middle of tube, anthers sagittate adhering to the stigma, sometimes spurred. Disc 5-lobed. Carpels pubescent with about 10 ovules. Follicles very slender divaricate. Coma deciduous.

1. **I. frutescens,** *R. Br.* Onol-sing, *K.*; Dudhi-lota, *S.*; Saon-lar, *Kharw.*

Large rambling shrub woody below with rusty-tomentose branches, ellip. or broadly-oblong acute or shortly acuminate glabrous leaves and narrow panicles of small white flowers ⅓" diam. with narrow twisted bearded lobes.

Common, especially in hedges in moist localities. Fls. *Sept.-Dec.* Fr. *Jany.-March.* The leaves turn brown or reddish in *Feby.* and are probably deciduous.

L. 1½" by 1" to 4½" by 2" pale and finely reticulate beneath, base rounded or acute, sec. n. about 5 prs. *Petiole* ⅛-¼". *Panicles* usually leafy with short branches. *Pedicels* $\frac{1}{16}$-⅛". *Calyx* with 5 linear glands alternating with the small erect sepals within. *Follicles* 3-6½" linear divaricate slightly flattened, $\frac{1}{10}$" broad only with a brownish thin tomentum. Seed about ½" linear, or with coma ¾", grooved, pale-brown.

Is much used for tying.

2. **I. ovalifolius,** *A.D.C.*

Said to occur in Chota Nagpur. The distinguishing characters are described as the corolla-tube pubescent and the mouth puberulous, while in the last the corolla-tube is said to be glabrous and the mouth villous; the leaves are also described as much larger and broader. The corolla, tube of I. frutescens, however, is usually pubescent.

Chota Nagpur, *Prain*. A specimen from Jhirjoi (Santara forest) may be this, which I consider only a variety of I. frutescens.

Fam. 75. ASCLEPIADACEÆ.

Usually climbing shrubs or herbs. rarely erect. Differing from the Apocynaceæ chiefly in respect of the androecium. The *stamens* are sometimes free, but more usually connate into a fleshy column surrounding the pistil and generally bear dorsal processes collectively termed the "*staminal corona*" (to distinguish it from the scales or processes which are sometimes present on the corolla and which are termed the "*coralline corona*"). The pollen forms 1 or 2 masses (*pollinia*) in each anther lobe, and these pollinia are united to a gland (*corpuscle*) lying between the several anthers so that the pollinium (or pollinia) of the left-hand lobe of one anther is connected with the pollinium (or pollinia) of the right-hand lobe of the next anther. *Carpels* 2 distinct. *Styles* united in the stigma. *Fruit* normally of 2 follicles. Albumen copious and embryo large.

I. Filaments free. Pollinia granular. Staminal corona 0.

Fls. in lax cymes. Petals overlapping . . . 1. *Cryptolepis.*

Fls. very small in dense axillary cymes. Petals valvate . . . . 2. *Hemidesmus*

II. Filaments connate into a column. Pollinia waxy. Anthers with an inflexed membranous tip (except in Ceropegia). . . . . . .

A. Erect shrubs or herbs. Corona staminal only.

L. broad. Coronal processes fleshy laterally compressed . . . . 3. *Calotropis.*

L. lanceolate. Fls. red. Coronal processes erect spathulate . . . . . . 4. *Asclepias.*

Leafless. Fls. white . . . . . 5. *Sarcostemma.*

B. Climbers. Pollinia pendulous, *i.e.*, the corpuscle is above the pollinia which are attached to it by stalks (sometimes very short) Corona staminal.

1. Corolla campanulate 1-1¼″. Coronal processes slender ligulate . . . . 6. *Raphistemma*.
2. Corolla salver-shaped ⅜″ diam. Coronal processes subulate . . . . 7. *Dœmia*.
3. Corolla rotate.
   - Corolla 1-1½″ diam. Corona 10-lobed . . 8. *Holostemma*.
   - Corolla ¼-⅓″ diam., green or purplish. Corona toothed . . . . 9. *Cynanchum*.

C. Climbers. Pollinia erect, *i.e.*, *their stalks* usually reflxed.

1. Corona corolline only. Fls. small. Petals overlapping . . . . . . 10. *Gymnema*.
2. Corona staminal only.
   - Corolla campanulate. Fls. green, under ½″ diam. . . . . 11. *Marsdenia*.
   - Corolla salver-shaped. Fls. yellowish over ½″ diam. . . . . 12. *Pergularia*.
   - Corolla rotate. Petals overlapping. Fls. green 13. *Dregea*.
   - Corolla rotate. Petals valvate. Fls. white, waxy 14. *Hoya*.
   - Corolla 1¼-2″ long with a long tube. . . 15. *Ceropegia*.

1. Cryptolepis, R. Br.

1. C. Buchanani, *Roem.* Utri dudhi, *S.*; Dudhla lar, *Kharw.*; Karanta, *H.*

A large twining shrub with glabrous oblong or elliptic entire leaves shining above and very pale-glaucous beneath, and axillary 2-chotomous cymes of pale yellow flowers with petals contorted in bud. Follicles 2½-4″ long, ½-¾″ diam. in the middle.

Valleys in Singbhum, occasional. Common in Manbhum. Hazaribagh, Damuda valley, frequent. Ranchi, Palamau, and Santal Parganahs.

Fls. *May-June.* Fr. *Dec.-Feby.* Evergreen.

With copious milky juice. *L.* 3½″ by 1½″ to 4½″ by 2″ rarely 6″ long, with very numerous slender nearly horizontal nerves united within the margin, and reticulate nervules; base and tip rounded or latter cuspidate. *Cymes* panicled with opp. divaricate bracteate fleshy branches constricted at the nodes, 1-2" long and broad. *Pedicels* $\frac{1}{8}$".. *Sepals* ovate $\frac{1}{10}$". *Corolla-tube* $\frac{1}{10}$-$\frac{1}{8}$", lobes $\frac{1}{3}$" linear-lanceolate. *Coronal-scales* clavate fleshy in the tube. *Pollinia* very minute linear.

Campbell says that a preparation of the plant is given to children as a cure for rickets. It is also given to nursing mothers when the supply of milk fails. The remedy is apparently suggested by the milky juice, species of Euphorbia being given in the same way.

2. Hemidesmus, R. Br.

1. **H. indicus**, *R. Br.* Dudli, *Kharw.*; Annantamal, *Sans.*, *H.*

A slender twining shrub with oblong to linear-lanceolate rarely obovate acute or acuminate or obtuse leaves whitish beneath and small greenish-purple flowers in opposite dense sub-sessile cymes. Follicles glabrous often purplish slender, divaricate 4-5" long, sometimes 6" by $\frac{3}{16}$".

Rather common, usually in fairly dense shade, but also in scrub jungle. Fls. *r.s.* Fr. *Oct-Dec.* Evergreen.

New shoots pubescent. *L.* very variable from 1-4" long and $\frac{1}{3}$-1$\frac{1}{2}$" broad, very frequently with a white central streak above, base rounded, sec. n. few. *Petiole* $\frac{1}{8}$-$\frac{1}{4}$". *Sepals* glandular within. *Coronal-scales* on the throat alternate with the corolla-lobes. *Pedicels* with ovate imbricating bracts. *Calyx* in fruit spreading $\frac{1}{4}$" diam.

The roots which have a pleasant smell are taken to relieve fever and also in skin diseases. In Hindoo medicine it is sometimes used in conjunction with the roots of Ichnocarpus frutescens, which it often much resembles.

3. Calotropis, R. Br.

Erect herbs or shrubs with broad sessile or sub-sessile leaves and mod.-sized bluish or reddish flowers in umbelliform or sub-racemose cymes. Calyx 5-partite, glandular within; sepals lanceolate. Corolla campanulate or sub-rotate, petals valvate. Staminal-column with 5 radiating fleshy compressed dorsally spurred or tubercled coronal processes. Pollinia flattened. Follicles very stout.

Corolla 1-1$\frac{1}{2}$" diam. with spreading petals . . . . . 1. *gigantea.*
Corolla under 1" diam. with erect petals, about $\frac{1}{2}$" long . 2. *procera.*

1. C. gigantea, *R. Br.* Palati, *K.*; Akaona, *S.*; Akaon, *Kharw.*; Madar, *H.*; Akanda, *Beng.*

Sometimes a small tree with trunk 1 ft. girth, usually a shrub with oblong-obovate coriaceous leaves white felted beneath as also are the branches and peduncles. Fls. reddish or light-purple or lilac, coronal processes shorter than the tall column, tips with two small fleshy lateral tubercles and base with a fleshy curved spur. Fr. much as in the next.

Waste ground, railway embankments, etc., common. Fls. *Dec.-July*. Fr. *Feby.-June.* Evergreen.

Yields the well-known Madar fibre. Various medicinal virtues are ascribed to the plant. The Kols use it as a drastic purgative and fever medicine, but they prefer the Euphorbia. The Santals give a decoction of the root in infantile convulsions and delirium during fever, *Campbell.* Mahouts use the leaves as warm fomentations in treating abscesses on elephants.

2. C. procera, *R. Br.* Vernacular names as above.

A shrub 3-4 ft. closely resembling the last when not in flower.

Waste ground, chiefly in Palamau; Manbhum, *Camp.*; Common from Barhi to Koderma (Hazaribagh); Santal Parganahs (Morjhora, etc.). Fls. and Fr. periods much as in last and uses the same. Fls. esp. *Dec.-Jany.*

L. usually suddenly often sharply acute or sub-mucronate, old glabrous beneath. *Peduncles* numerous, often 2 from an axil 1·3″ long, tomentose. *Fls.* with *erect* petals which are white with a deep purple blotch on the upper half within and acute. *Coronal-procs.* with a purple obtuse tip and fleshy dorsal upturned white spur. *Follicles* 3″ by $1\frac{1}{2}$″ obtuse, somewhat sausage-shaped, outer and inner coats with fibrous tissue between. *Seeds* obovate densely imbricate $\frac{1}{4}$″ flattened.

Asclepias curassavica, *L.* Is a pretty erect perennial with lanceolate or oblong-lanceolate glabrous leaves and many-flowered umbelliform cymes of scarlet flowers with reflexed corolla and 5 erect spoon-shaped coronal-scales adnate to the stipitate column. A native of the West Indies often found in village lands.

5. Sarcostemma, R. Br.

1. S. brevistigma, *Wight.* Kula-tuar, *K.*

A leafless jointed shrub with terete green straggling branches and terminal sessile umbels of white waxy sweet-smelling flowers $\frac{1}{3}$-$\frac{1}{2}$″ diam.

On arid rocks in Singbhum. Fls. *Sept.*

Occasionally bears small linear-oblong *leaves* $\frac{1}{4}$-$\frac{3}{4}$" long in the rainy season. *Column* short and stout with slits between the anthers. *Coronal-processes* large fleshy obtuse. *Pollinia* linear, stipitate.

The milk is used in the same way as that of Calotropis, it is said to be 'very powerful' (the name signifies Tiger's milk), in fact Europeans would usually call it a rank poison.

6. Raphistemma, Wall.

1. R. pulchellum, *Wall.*

A very large twining shrub with cordate ovate leaves 3-7" and handsome pure-white or cream rather fleshy campanulate flowers 1-1$\frac{1}{2}$" long in long-peduncled axillary umbelliform cymes.

Evergreen forest near streams in deep valleys, Singbhum. Fls. *Aug.-Sept.*

L. with 5-7 strong primary nerves, a wide basal sinus and glandular at the base of the mid-rib. *Fls.* well marked by the thick white coronal scales at the back of the anthers being produced into slender tails and meeting over the stigma. *Follicles* 6" by 1$\frac{1}{4}$", fusiform (*F.B.I.*).

7. Dæmia, R. Br.

1. D. extensa, *R. Br.* Chagul-bati, *Beng.*

A slender subhispidly hairy or glabrate fœtid climber with membranous orbicular or broadly ovate deeply cordate acuminate leaves 2-4" long and broad, and green, or yellowish-green, and red salver shaped flowers $\frac{5}{8}$-$\frac{2}{3}$" diam. in long-stalked corymbose drooping panicles. Follicles 1$\frac{1}{2}$-2" lanceolate, clothed with long soft spines.

Palamau, not general. Chiefly in hedges. Fls. *Oct.-Dec.* Fr. *Dec.-Jany.*

L. pubescent beneath, basal lobes rounded incurved. *Petiole* about as long as leaf. *Peduncles* 2-6". *Pedicels* capillary, $\frac{1}{2}$-2". *Sepals* short erect $\frac{1}{8}$" with 2 small glands within, pubescent. *Cor.-tube* slightly longer with spreading densely villous-ciliate linear- or ovate-oblong green petals with reflexed margins. *Corona* (outer) adnate to cor.-tube slightly exceeding it with 5 oblong truncate petaloid lobes and (inner) small intermediate inflexed lobes carrying long white fleshy acuminate processes adnate to the anthers and meeting over the stigma, dorsally spurred below.

8. Holostemma, Br.

1. H. Rheedei, *Wall.* Apung, *K.*; Morou arak', *S.*

A twining glabrous shrub with membranous triangular ovate or oblong-ovate cordate leaves 3-6″ long, the large basal lobes of which are often incurved and meet, sub-globose purple and white large flowers 1-1½″ diam. and short thick smooth acute follicles.

Common in Manbhum, *Campbell.* Ravines in Singbhum, rare. Chakulia (Dalbhum), *Gamble.* Fls. *July-Sept.* Fr. *Jany.*

L. sometimes faintly puberulous, basal lobes rounded spreading or incurved. *Petiole* 1-3″, glandular at the base of the mid-rib above. *Cymes* umbelliform or in irregular racemes, peduncles and pedicels 1-2″. *Anthers* very large oblong, horny, shining, cohering into a 10-winged column.

Leaves eaten as a pot-herb. A decoction of the root is given for cough, *Camp.*

9. Cynanchum, L.

1. C. Callialata, *Ham.*

A glabrous or sparsely hairy twiner with acuminate leaves glaucous beneath, with a contracted cordate base spreading obscure nerves and shortly peduncled axillary umbels of glabrous flowers ⅓″ diam. Corona short-cupular irregularly 5-toothed and crenate. Follicles 2-winged.

Top of Parasnath, *Hooker.* I have not seen it.

10. Gymnema, Br.

Fls. small in crowded umbelliform cymes. Calyx 5-partite. Corolla sub-rotate with thick lobes, and fleshy coronal processes on the throat which are produced downwards on the tube as double villous ridges. Follicles slender, smooth, acuminate.

1. G. sylvestre, *Br.*

A rather slender woody climber with densely appressed hairy branchlets and broadly ell. to oblong, acute or acuminate leaves 2⅓-3″ by 1⅓-1½″ with rounded or sub-cordate base. Calyx hairy ⅛″ diam. in fruit.

Palamau, and common on the low hills beyond Akbarpur. Only seen in fruit and may be the same as the next. Fr. *Dec.*

L. somewhat pubescent both sides esp. on the nerves beneath, not pronouncedly basal-nerved, sec. n. about 5 prs. *Petiole* $\frac{1}{4}$-$\frac{1}{3}$". *Follicles* 2-2½" poniard-shaped, only $\frac{1}{5}$" broad. *Peduncle* of cyme only $\frac{1}{5}$-$\frac{1}{4}$".

[This plant is intermediate between the "G. hirsutum" collected by Sir J. D. Hooker in the same locality, and typical G. sylvestre. The two are probably only varieties of one species as he suggests.]

2. G. hirsutum, W. & A.

A twiner with all parts densely softly pubescent, broadly ovate or cordate acute or acuminate leaves 1½-2½" and flowers $\frac{1}{4}$" diam. in 2-nate sub-sessile cymes. Petals ciliolate. Follicles 2-3 by $\frac{1}{3}$".

Tundi hills, Manbhum, *Camp. Herb* !

Var. **Decaisneanum**, *Wight.* Moronarak, *S.* *L.* oblong or ovate with wide cordate base 3½" by 2" but much smaller at base of shoot, those quite at base sub-orbicular ½" only. *Cymes* simple forked or 3-nate ½-1" diam. dense sub-sessile. Tundi Hills. Fls. *July.*

11. Marsdenia, Br.

1. M. tenacissima, W. & A. Jiti, chiti, (Pal. and Rajmehal); Siti (Koderma) *H.* ?; Kongat, *S.*

A stout tough twiner with very milky juice, all parts densely softly pubescent or tomentose, broadly ovate suddenly shortly finely acuminate leaves about 5" by 4" with deeply cordately lobed base, and green flowers $\frac{1}{3}$" diam. sub-campanulate with spreading lobes in dense corymbosely-branched cymes. Follicles 4½-5½" by 1½-1$\frac{3}{5}$" finely pubescent, or velvety.

Tundi hills opposite Topchanchi; Manbhum; Singbhum very rare; Palamau, common, thence extending sporadically in scrub jungles through Hazaribagh to the Rajmehal Hills. Fls. *April-June.* Fr. *Jany.-March.*

L. 3" by 2½" when in flower, adult 4-7" by 3-5" occasionally even 9" by 8½" velvety above softly pubescent and pale beneath, basal lobes rounded sometimes incurved; base 4-5-nerved, one pair sec. n. usually close to base and 1-2 other prs. above. *Petiole* 1½-3". *Calyx* $\frac{3}{16}$" long, 5-partite, sepals oblong. *Petals* oblong about as long as the tube. *Coronal-processes* erect adnate to the stamens and extending above them, ligulate, grooved and thickened below. *Follicles* thickest a little above the obtuse base then tapering to a blunt apex, solitary, slightly grooved on one side. *Seeds* flat margined, with a coma 2″.

It has a very strong fibre used for bow-strings, and which Roxburgh refers to as one of the strongest he had met with in the vegetable kingdom (Fls. Ind. II, 56). It has been several times recommended for cultivation.

12. Pergularia, L.

Differs from Marsdenia chiefly in the much larger flowers with a distinct tube, and the transversely-bifid or 2-lamellate large coronal scales. These are often described as simple in P. pallida, but as a fact the two lamellæ though often connate are distinguishable, the long ligule extending to above the anther evidently being the inner lamella. The coronal scales are only shortly adnate to the anthers.

1. P. pallida, W. & A. Kongat, *Kharw.*, *S.*

A twining shrub with *sub-watery* juice, ovate or ovate-cordate acuminate leaves, and greenish or yellowish-white flowers $\frac{3}{4}$-1″ diam. in axillary umbelliform cymes. Follicles deeply grooved solitary about 4″ long acuminate.

Palamau and Santal Parganahs, chiefly in nalas and scrub-jungle. *Fls. May.* Fr. *Dec.-Jany.* Renews leaves at time of flowering.

Stems somewhat furrowed and pustular glabrous when old. Young *leaves* seldom deeply cordate, old usually deeply cordate with nerves beneath shortly pubescent but otherwise nearly glabrous. *Petioles* $1\frac{1}{2}$″ (often only $\frac{1}{2}$″ when in flower).

The three species Marsdenia tenacissima, Dregea volubilis and this are frequently mixed up in the forest, and without flowers are somewhat difficult to distinguish. Marsdenia is usually known from its dense pubescence. Dregea is more pubescent than the Pergularia and may be known from both by its almost invariably paired follicles. Its leaves too are less cordate, or even acute at base.

13. Dregea, E. Meyer.

1. D. volubilis, *Benth.* Marang Kongat, *S.*

A stout twiner with often pustular branches, ovate or broadly-ovate leaves more or less acuminate, with rounded or rarely cordate but scarcely lobed sometimes acute base, green rotate flowers $\frac{1}{2}''$ diam. and stout follicles 3-4″ by 1-$1\frac{1}{2}''$ diam.

Manbhum, Palamau, in scrub jungle. Fls. *June.*

Usually hoary with a fine curled pubescence, and *L.* 3-6″ by 2-$4\frac{1}{2}''$ strongly nerved, often glandular at the base of the mid-rib above; *petiole* 1·3″ with generally a curved thickened base. *Fls.* in dense umbels which are sometimes several on short branches, pedicels $\frac{1}{2}$-1″, peduncles 1-3″. *Calyx* 5-partite, sepals $\frac{1}{10}''$ ovate oblong obtuse. *Petals* broadly oblong, longer than the tube, pubescent outside. *Column* very short truncate, coronal-processes sub-globose horizontal.

This also yields an excellent fibre.

14. Hoya, Br.

1. H. pendula, *Wight.*

A climber with twiggy pendulous branches oblong fleshy smooth shining leaves with the venation not visible, and white flowers $\frac{2}{3}''$ diam. with a truncate stellate corona in short-peduncled pendulous umbels.

Parasnath, *Anders.* A Singbhum Hoya, not collected, may be this.

15. Ceropegia, L.

1. C. hirsuta, *W. & A.*

A hirsute climber with pale spreading hairs, lanceolate leaves up to 5″ by $1\frac{1}{2}''$ with rounded base and tubular flowers $1\frac{3}{4}''$ long with a ventricose base and sub-erect oblong obtuse ciliate petals.

Manbhum, near Pokhuria, *Camp.Herb.*! Fls., Fr. *Aug.*

Fls. greenish blotched with purple. *Follicles* erecto-patent 3″.

Fam. 76. SOLANACEÆ.

Herbs or shrubs with alternate simple, entire lobed or pinnatifid (pinnate in Lycopersicum) exstipulate leaves. *Fls.* regular 2-sexual in lateral or terminal axillary or often extra-axillary cymes, sometimes with additional solitary flowers, more rarely all the flowers solitary or clustered; bracts and bracteoles 0. *Calyx* inferior usually persistent and often larger in fruit. *Corolla* funnel-shaped, rotate or campanulate, limb sometimes sub-entire, petals usually 5. *St.* 5 on the tube, anthers dehiscing by apical pores or longitudinally. *Ovary* normally 2-celled; style linear; *ovules* very many on prominent peltate placentæ. *Fruit* baccate or capsular, usually 2-celled (4-celled in Datura) and many-seeded. *Seeds* compressed, embryo curved round the albumen (straight in Tobacco).

Besides those described, the following well-known plants belong to this order:—**Solanum tuberosum**, *L.*, the Potato; **Lycopersicum esculentum**, *Mill.*, the Tomato, which often has numerous placentæ in cultivation; several varieties of **Capsicum**, Chillies and Nepal pepper, some of which are naturalized; **Physalis peruviana**, *L.*, the Cape Gooseberry; **Physalis minima**, *L.*, a wild plant, can be recognised by its similarly inflated calyx; **Nicotiana Tabacum**, *L.*, the Tobacco, is cultivated in Chota Nagpur on specially manured plots of land near the homestead only, or down near the edges of rivers. Its Kol name "*sukul*" merely means smoke. The wrapper of the Kol cigarette or "*fikr*" is a Sal leaf.

Corolla rotate. Anthers opening by pores. Fruit a berry. 1. *Solanum.*
Corolla tubular-funnel-shaped. Fruit capsular . . . 2. *Datura.*

1. Solanum, L.

Shrubs or herbs, rarely small trees, often spinous, pubescence often stellate. L. sometimes in sub-unilateral pairs. Fls. in dichasial or sympodial cymes. Calyx 5- or 10-lobed. Corolla rotate, limb usually 5- rarely 4-6-merous, plaited in bud. Anthers conniving in a cone, opening by pores or short slits. Seeds discoid.

I. Unarmed, Fls. sub-umbellate or corymbose.
  Herbaceous or suffruticose, glabrous or nearly so 1. *nigrum.*
  A large shrub, densely stellate-tomentose . . 2. *verbascifolium*
II. Armed, rarely unarmed in S. Melongena, cymes sympodial, or fls. sub-solitary.
  A diffuse very prickly herb . . . . . 3. *xanthocarpum.*
  Shrubs or undershrubs

Fls. white. L. not prickly on the nerves . 4. *torvum*.
Fls. blue. Nerves prickly. Peduncles usually 5-many-fld. . . . . 5. *indicum*.
Fls. blue. Nerves prickly or not. Peduncles 1-5-fld. . . . . 6. *Melongena*.

1. **S. nigrum**, *L.* Makoi, *H.*; the Black Nightshade.

An erect herb 1-4 ft. high with ovate or oblong sinuate toothed or lobed leaves, small white *flowers* $\frac{1}{3}$-$\frac{1}{2}$″ diam. in cymose umbels on extra-axillary peduncles and small black *berries* $\frac{1}{4}$″ diam.

A common weed. Fls. and fr. more or less all the year round.

The berries are said to be eaten.

2. **S. verbascifolium.** *L.* Bondu, *M.*; Arosa, Urusa, *Beng*.

A large shrub 6-15 ft. densely stellately tomentose all over, with corymbose cymose panicles of white flowers $\frac{1}{2}$′ diam. and globose yellow berries $\frac{1}{3}$″ diam. seated on the persistent campanulate tomentose calyx.

Waste ground and scrub jungle. Porahat plateau. Fls. *Aug.-Nov.* Fr. *Oct.-Dec.* Evergreen.

L. ovate to ovate-lanceolate acute or acuminate 6-12″ by 3-6″ softly tomentose. *Corymbs* 3-5″ diam. *Peduncles* stout 1-4″ in fl., 3-4″ in fr. *Calyx* in fl. $\frac{1}{4}$″ with teeth half as long as tube, enlarged in fr.

3. **S. xanthocarpum,** *Schrad.* Rangaini janum, *S.* Ringni, *H.*; Kantakari, *Beng.*

A procumbent very prickly rather pretty herb with glabrescent bright-green very prickly leaves copiously armed with straight $\frac{1}{2}$″ long spines. Fls. deep-blue 1-1$\frac{1}{2}$″ diam. with bright-yellow anthers.

Common in open waste ground. Fls., Fr. *Dec.-June.*

L. sinuate or sub-pinnatifid. *Berry* $\frac{1}{2}$-$\frac{3}{4}$″ diam. green or yellow when ripe, often variegated with white or green.

The fruit, boiled in ghee, is given for cough and toothache, *Campbell.*

4. **S. torvum,** *Swartz.* Hanjád, *K.*; Bengar-betahet', *S.*

A tomentose shrub 4-8 ft. high with entire or shallowly lobed leaves not prickly on the nerves and lateral dense usually bifurcate cymes of white flowers.

Waste ground, but not nearly as common as the next. Fls. Fr., nearly all the year round.

L. usually with rounded or sub-cordate base and shallow lobes. *Fls.* ¾-1″ diam. *Berry* yellow ⅓″ diam. exceeding the unarmed calyx.

The fruit is said to be eaten.

5. **S. indicum,** *L.* Hanjád, Anjed, Hanjid, *K.*; Barhanta, *H.*; Baiakur, *Beng.*

A stellately tomentose shrub or undershrub 3-6 ft. high with usually deeply lobed leaves always more or less prickly on the nerves beneath, and with lateral usually simple cymes of blue flowers.

Waste ground, very common. Fls., Fr. nearly all the year.

L. with acute, uneven or straight rarely rounded base, 3-6″, usually acuminate. Inflorescence usually and calyx-lobes sometimes spinous. *Fls.* ¾″ diam. rarely nearly white. Fruiting-pedicels often 7 or more, erecto-patent. *Berry* yellow ⅓″ diam. exceeding the calyx.

The berries are rubbed on the forehead for headache.

6. **S. Melongena,** *L.* Dhoko (wild form), Bengar, *K.*; Baigan, *H.* The Brinjal (when cultivated) Var. insana, *Prain* (S. insanum, *Willd*) Erect herbaceous 2-6 ft., branches stellate tomentose, covered with straight straw-coloured prickles on stems, leaves, inflorescence and calyx. *Fls.* blue 1½″ diam. Fruiting-peduncles stout with 1-4 or 5 reflexed pedicels. *Berries* globose or oval 1-2″ diam. yellow.

Waste ground, occasional, and supposed to be an escape from cultivation. Fls., Fr. *Jany.-June.*

Each calyx-lobe has usually a long recurved spine.

2. Datura, L.

Large coarse sub-shrubby herbs with large simple leaves and very large tubular-funnel-shaped flowers. Calyx tubular circumscissile above the base in fruit. Corolla limb plaited entire or shortly lobed. Ovary 2-, or by further partitions, 4-celled. Capsule 4-celled, 4-valved or opening irregularly, spinous.

1. **D. stramonium,** *L.* Var. Tatula. Dhatura, *H.*, *K.* Thorn-apple

A large annual 2-4 ft. high with ovate toothed or sinuate leaves 6-8″ long and large purple flowers 3-6″ long with 5 linear teeth. Capsule 4-valved ovoid seated on the swollen calyx base.

Waste ground near villages. Fls., Fr. *c.s.*

Yields the well-known poison. The powdered seeds are *said* to be used in the Kolhan for stupefying coolies whom it is desired to take to Assam.

2. D. fastuosa, *L.* Dhatura. *H., K.* Thorn-apple.

A large annual 2-6 ft. high with ovate glabrous entire or toothed leaves 6-8″ and large white flowers usually 7″ by 5″. Capsule irregularly dehiscent sub-globose seated on the swollen calyx base.

Gardens and waste ground near villages.

Same properties as the last.

Fam. 77. BIGNONIACEÆ.

Trees (exotic species often large woody climbers) with opposite usually 2-3-pinnate, more rarely 1-pinnate or simple, exstipulate leaves. *Fls.* large or showy, irregular, 2-sexual, in racemes or panicles. *Calyx* campanulate, sometimes spathaceous, lobes valvate. *Corolla* tubular-ventricose, lobes sub-equal. *St.* 4, with the 5th. often rudimentary or suppressed, rarely perfect. *Disc* pulvinate or annular. *Ovary* 2-celled; style long, stigma 2-lobed. *Ovules* numerous, anatropous, usually many-seriate. *Fruit* pod-like, loculicidally or septicidally 2-valved. Seeds flattened winged, exalbuminous.

Species of Tecoma and Bignonia, erect shrubs or climbers, with handsome yellow, orange or red flowers, are common in gardens. Anderson quotes " Heterophragma Roxburghii, D.C.," a tree with 1-pinnate leaves and woolly panicles as occurring on Parasnath !

I. St. 5 perfect, Small tree with 2-3-pinnate leaves. 1. *Oroxylum.*

II. St. 4 perfect, L. 1- or 2-3-pinnate.

L. 1-pinnate. Septum of pod thick subterete . 2. *Stereospermum*

L. 2-3-pinnate, Septum of pod flat . . . 3. *Millingtonia.*

III. St. 4 perfect L. simple . . . . 4. *Tecoma.*

1. Oroxylum, Vent.

1. O. indicum, *Vent.* Rengebanam, *K.*; Bana hatak', *S.*; Sonpatta, *Kharw.*; Sona, *H.*; Dantkura, *Mal Pah.*

A small tree rarely over 25 ft. in Chota Nagpur, with but few branches and terminal clusters of very large ternately 2-pinnate leaves 2-4 ft. long and broad. Flowers large fleshy purple, but not showy, in terminal stout racemes. The tree is easily recognized when leafless by its large leaf scars and immense flat pods with woody valves and flat-winged seeds 2-3" diam.

Common, chiefly in ravines. Fls. *July-Aug.* Fr. *Dec.-March.* Deciduous *Dec.-June.*

Lflts. about 5" by 3" acuminate, *Corolla* 2-3" long and broad. Fifth *stamen* rather shorter than the others. *Capsule* 1-3 ft.

Seeds purgative *Wood.* They are, however, sometimes eaten. Mr. Innes says that in times of famine they are parched and ground into flour ! [1]

2. Stereospermum, Cham.

Trees with pinnate leaves and entire or toothed leaflets. Flowers mod.-sized, in lax terminal panicles. Corolla bilabiate with 5 sub-equal orbicular more or less toothed lobes. Capsule long terete or obscurely angular with a much thickened septum. Seeds (in Chota Nagpur species) sub-trigonous. winged each side.

1. S. suaveolens, *D.C.*, Hussi, *K.*; Pader, *S.*; Panrar, *Kharw.*; Paroli, *Mal Pah.*; Parul, *Beng.*

A handsome large or mod.-sized tree with young parts tomentose, large odd pinnate pubescent leaves with 5-9 lfits., and dull crimson fragrant flowers $1\frac{1}{2}$" long in large glandular pubescent panicles. Pod 18" by $\frac{2}{3}$", terete, often cork-screw-like, the thick corky septum occupying most of the cavity, seeds embedded in notches.

Frequent in the valleys in Singhbhum. Manbhum, not abundant, *Camp.* Ranchi, Hazaribagh, Palamau. Fls. *April-May.* Fr. *Sept.-Jany.* Deciduous *March.*

---

[1] Appendix to "Indian Forester" for Feb. 1908, p. 5.

Lflts. broadly-elliptic or oblong shortly suddenly acuminate 3-7″ by 2½-3″, in young plants harsh and spinous-serrate (in quite young seedlings simple, as they also are in Oroxylum and numerous other pinnate-leaved plants). Venation beneath strong. *Petiolule* $\frac{1}{18}$-¼″. *Calyx* ⅓-½″ glandular-hairy, lobes 3-5 short broad. *Corolla* yellow within, *petals* crisped-crenate.

2. S. chelonoides, *D.C.*

A large tree glabrous except the flowers, with odd-pinnate leaves with 5-9 lflts., and pale rose-cold. and yellow or light-purple flowers ¾-1″ long in very lax glabrous panicles. Pod 12-20″ by ⅓-½″, somewhat angled.

Rare. Valleys in Saranda. 'Parasnath?' *Anders.* Fls. *April-May.* Fr. *Dec.*

Lflts. elliptic caudate-acuminate. *Petiolules* ½-¾″. *Calyx* ¼″ with 3 short teeth. One of the most difficult woods to split.

Millingtonia hortensis, *L.*, sometimes called the Indian Cork tree, is a tall very handsome tree with 2-3-pinnate leaves and pendent panicles of fragrant white flowers with long corolla-tubes. The tree is shallow rooted and apt to be blown down. Fls. *Nov.-Dec.*

4. Tecoma, Juss.

1. T. undulata, *G. Don.*

A shrub or small tree with narrowly oblong undulate leaves and orange red flowers in terminal corymbose racemes.

Palamau, wild? Fls. *April.* Specimens of this shrub were collected by Dr. J. P. Hendley on waste land in Palamau, and had every appearance of being indigenous or naturalized.

Young *shoots* grey puberulous. *L.* about 6″ by 1½″ short-petioled. *Calyx* tubular-campanulate, 5-toothed. *Corolla* 1½″ tubular-ventricose with 5 rounded sub-equal lobes. *Capsule* 8″ by ⅓″.

N.B.—The cultivated species of Tecoma have compound leaves.

Fam. 78. PEDALIACEÆ.

Herbs or undershrubs with opposite leaves, or the upper alternate, often deeply lobed or pinnatifid. *Flowers* irregular axillary ebracteate or bracts very small. *Corolla* tubular ventricose, lobes imbricate. *Stamens* 4 didynamous.

Ovary 1-2-celled, or 4-celled by the growth of a second septum, not lobed. Style slender with a 2-lobed stigma. *Ovules* few, or if many in one series, not scattered all over a broad placenta (as in Scrophulariaceæ). *Fruit* capsular or indehiscent. Seeds wingless, exalbuminous.

Ovary 1-locular with 2 parietal placentæ. Fr. with indehiscent endocarp . . . . 1. *Martynia.*

Ovary 2-spuriously 4-locular. Capsule dehiscent . 2. *Sesamum.*

Martynia diandra, *Glox.* Bilai sarsar, *K.*, is a handsome stout viscidly-hairy herb with broadly ovate cordate sinuate-toothed leaves 3-6″ both ways on long petioles, and drooping purplish flowers $1\frac{1}{2}$″ long in short racemes with pink bracteoles. Fruit sub-drupaceous but the outer fleshy pericarp 2-valved. Endocarp armed with 2 sharp curved claws.

An American weed, now abundant in waste ground.

Fls. *r. s.* Fr. *c. s.*

Sesamum indicum, *D.C.* Tilming, *K.* The Gingeli oil plant is a herb widely cultivated, 1-2 ft. high, more or less fœtid and glandular, with the opp. lower leaves often lobed, pedatisect or toothed, upper narrow sub-entire or toothed. Fls. purple or white drooping $1\frac{1}{4}$″ long. Capsule 1″ long, narrow erect hairy. Fls. *Oct.-Dec.* Fr. *Dec.-Jan.*

Fam. 79. ACANTHACEÆ.

Shrubs or herbs or often undershrubs with opp. exstipulate simple, rarely aromatic leaves, often with slender raised nerves and lineolate with raphides. Leaf scars usually conspicuous. *Fls.* irregular in heads, spikes, cymes, or panicles, rarely solitary, bracteate and 2-bracteolate, rarely either bracts or bracteoles absent. *Corolla* lipped or lobes sub-equal. *St.* 4 or 2 inserted on the corolla-tube ; anths. 2- or 1-celled. *Disc* often large. *Ovary* superior 2-celled never lobed, usually linear or oblong with 2 or more *superposed* ovules in each cell (very rarely 1 only, *e.g.*, Blepharis, or collateral, Thunbergia) *Capsule* loculicidal. *Seeds* (exc. in Thunbergia) ceated in the axils of upcurved hard supports (retinacula), often hairy. Albumen 0.

I. Calyx inconspicuous annular or 10-15-toothed. Climbers . . . . 1. *Thunbergia.*

II. Calyx distinct, 4-5-partite. Corolla subregular or two-lipped.

A. Petals twisted in bud. Anthers with 2 cells parallel, level, or one only a little above the other (Tribe Ruelliæ).

1. Ovules 2 in each cell. Corolla not distinctly lipped

Cor.-tube long slender. St. 2. Anths. muticous . . . . 2. *Dædalacanthus*

Cor. tubular ventricose. St. 2 or 4. Anths. muticous . . . . 3. *Strobilanthes.*

St. 4. Anthers distinctly spurred. Fls. large white . . . . 4. *Petalidium.*

2. Ovules 3-12 in each cell.

Cor. not distinctly lipped. Bract 0. Bracteoles large leafy . . . . . 5. *Ruellia.*

Cor. not distinctly lipped. Bracts large. Brateoles 0. . . . . 6. *Hemigraphis.*

Cor. distinctly 2-lipped. Herbs with narrow leaves . . . . 7. *Hygrophila.*

B. Petals imbricate in bud. Anths. with 1 or 2 cells. When 2-celled, one cell often placed considerably above the other (Tribe Justicieæ).

1. Ovules 2 in each cell Corolla not distinctly, or rarely, lipped. Sepals 4, the two outer much the larger.

Fls. yellow or blue. Anths. 2-celled . . . 8. *Barleria.*

Fls. orange. Anths. 1-celled . . . . . 9. *Crossandra.*

2. Ovules 2 in each cell. Corolla distinctly 2-lipped.

a. Stamens 4.

Upper anthers with only one cell perfect. Fls. blue . . . . 10. *Neuracanthus.*

nthers all 2-celled. Fls. usually white or purple. 11. *Lepidagathis.*

b. Stamens 2.

i. Corolla large 1½″ white. Stout shrub . 12. *Adhatoda.*

ii. Corolla under 1½″ or with very slender tube.

† Lower anther-cell with a white spur.

Spur minute. Spikes terete or 2-4- ranked . 13. *Justicia.*

Spur very evident' Spikes short unilateral. 14. *Rungia*

†† Anthers muticous.

Bracts paired unequal, one or both longer than calyx, fascicled in reduced axillary and terminal dense cymes	15. *Dicliptera.*
Bracts paired unequal, one or both longer than calyx, 2-4 prs. only, terminal . .	16. *Peristrophe.*
Bracts and bracteoles minute $\frac{1}{12}$"long or 0.	17. *Rhinacanthus.*
3. Ovules 3-10 in each cell. Corolla 2-lipped. Stamens 2.	
Herbs or undershrubs. Corolla small with slender tube	18. *Andrographis.*
Shrub with showy curved brick-red corolla .	19. *Phlegacanthus.*
III. Calyx distinct. Corolla 1-lipped only, the upper lip obsolete.	
Herbaceous. Ovules 2 in each cell . . .	20. *Blepharis.*

1. Thunbergia *L. f.*

Climbers with axillary or racemed flowers, and large bracteoles enclosing the flower buds. Corolla large with a ventricose curved tube and 5 rounded petals. St. 4 didynamous. Disc conspicuous. Ovary cells 2-ovuled. Capsule very characteristic, being globose with a flat hard sword-shaped beak.

1. T. fragrans. *Roxb.* Var. lævis.

A slender climber with ovate or oblong leaves 1-3" by $\frac{1}{2}$-$1\frac{1}{2}$", lower with cordate or hastate base, and white flowers $1\frac{1}{4}$" long solitary or paired in the leaf axils. Calyx teeth 14-20 lanceolate $\frac{1}{16}$-$\frac{1}{10}$".

Singbhum on Porahat plateau. Fls. Fr. *Oct.-Nov.*

. Glabrous, puberulous or hairy. *Pedicels* 1-2" thickened upwards in fruit. Fls. not fragrant (they are fragrant in the type). *Calyx-teeth* hard in fruit and then $\frac{1}{8}$" long. *Fruit* puberulous depressed globose with 4 rounded excavate seeds. Beak with grooved edges.

2. T. tomentosa, *Wall.*

Similar but calyx-teeth in flower filiform much longer than the tube often $\frac{1}{4}$", hairy, and capsule villous. Fls. $1\frac{1}{2}$".

Chota Nagpur, *Prain.*

T. alata, *Boj.* with winged petioles and yellow corolla with a brown or purple eye, and **T. grandiflora**, *Roxb.*, with blue flowers in racemes, are often cultivated.

2. Dædalacanthus, *T. And.*

Shrubs or undershrubs with the leaves marked with raphides. Fls. showy, red or blue, in spikes with large usually prominently nerved, often imbricating, bracts. Corolla with slender tube and spreading rounded lobes. St. 2. Ovary glabrous, cells 2-ovuled. Style long, stigma simple.

1. D. nervosus, *T. And.*

A shrub 2-6 ft. with ovate acuminate entire glabrous leaves attaining 9″ by 4″, very handsome in flower with blue flowers 1-1¼″ long and ¾″ diam. in ternately panicled terminal spikes with white green-veined imbricating bracts.

Ravines in Singbhum, not uncommon. Fls. *Jany.-March.*

L. with very tapering base and about 7-12 prs. of rather strong sec. n. *Petiole* ½-1½″. *Spikes* 1-3″. *Petals* ⅓″ elliptic. *Bracts* ½″ concave-elliptic. *Anths.* exserted, *Capsule* ½″.

2. D. purpurascens, *T. And.* Gulsham, *H.*

Similar to last but smaller, 2-4 ft. Spikes solitary and ternate, axillary and terminal but not usually panicled. Corolla lilac or rose-purple 1-1¼″ long, tube pubescent. Bracts similar but ovate or rhomboid, long-acuminate, pubescent beneath and margins long-ciliate.

Associated with the last, but also in drier valleys and much more common. Singbhum; Manbhum; Sirguja, *Wood*; Hazaribagh; Palamau, in ravines; S. P. Fls. *Jany.-March.*

Stems shortly pubescent, 4-angled. *L.* ovate and base decurrent on the petiole, rarely exceeding 6″ by 4″ and with 6-8 prs. sec. n. *Spikes* long or short peduncled, oblong, dense 1¼-2″ often very numerous. *St.* scarcely exserted.

There is a form without the long ciliæ to the bracts.

3. Strobilanthes, Blume.

Shrubs or herbs with leaves often unequal in the pairs, and often bearing raphides. Inflorescence various, but always close and spicate in the Chota Nagpur species. Calyx deeply 5-fid. Corolla tubular-ventricose with 5 sub-equal spreading rounded petals. St. 4 didynamous. Ovary cells 2-ovuled. Style long, stigma simple.

1. S. auriculatus, *Nees*. Hutid, *K.*; Gada Kalha, *S.*

A shrub 2-6 ft. with usually unequal leaves, hairy above, with auriculate base, and axillary and terminal linear spikes of blue flowers, spikes 1-3″ long with densely imbricate obovate obtuse bracts with recurved margins, velvety pubescent or usually with spreading white cilia $\frac{1}{4}$″ long. (Var. Edgeworthiana).

This plant often forms a dense undergrowth under Sal in the Singbhum forests, it flowered in 1898 and flowers gregariously every 6 years. The seedlings were 2-3 inches high in Jan. 1899 but there were also a few old plants flowering. Jaspur, rocky hill tops, *Wood.* Manbhum, "very common on the banks of nullahs" *Campbell.*; Hazaribagh (Koderma forest, etc). Fls. *Dec.-Feby.* Fr. *March-April.*

L. sessile oblong or ovate or lanceolate crenate, the larger one of a pair sometimes attaining 10″ by $2\frac{1}{4}$″, sometimes sub-equal. Sec. n. 10-13 prs. *Corolla* blue 1″ long slightly curved. *Bracts* densely covered with stalked glands beneath. *Bracteoles* 0. *Capsule* $\frac{1}{3}$″ glabrous.

The pounded leaves are rubbed on the body during the cold stage of intermittent fever, *Camp.*

2. S. scaber, *Nees.*

A herb with creeping rootstock, rather stiff entire or crenate leaves and yellow flowers 1″ long in bracteate capitate spikes.

Along watercourses in Saranda forests and Santal Parganahs. Fls. *Jany.-April.*

L. ell. or ovate $2\frac{1}{2}$-5″ with raphides above, scabrous beneath. *Spikes* 1-$1\frac{1}{2}$″ from upper axils and in short terminal panicles. *Bracts* $\frac{3}{4}$-$1\frac{1}{4}$″ lanceolate caudate, hairy or glandular. *Corolla* tubular for $\frac{1}{4}$″ then ventricose, 1″ long and $\frac{5}{8}$″ diam. villous within. *Capsule* $\frac{1}{3}$″ downy. *Seeds* 2 (sometimes 3 !) in each cell with broad, membranous margins and long silky hairs.

4. Petalidium, Nees.

1. Petalidium barlerioides, *Nees.*

A straggling shrub with largish white flowers sub-solitary or in opp. decussate pairs in dense or sub-capitate spikes, (abbreviated lateral branches). Leaves (very few at time of flowering) 2-4″ ovate toothed or crenulate, acuminate, sometimes attaining 6″ by 4″.

Singbhum, in Sal jungles (Bera forest, Ankua forest, etc.); Hazaribagh (Chorparan, Koderma, etc.); Parasnath, *Anders.* Palamau, *Gamble* ! S. Parganahs. Fls. *Feby.-April.* Fr. *April.* Nearly deciduous *March—April.*

Twigs straw-coloured. L. puberulous suddenly decurrent on the 1-2″ long petiole.

Readily recognised by the large green-veined pairs of bracteoles ¾″ long, strongly ribbed lower lip of corolla and the long fulvous hairs within it. Anths. 4, with long spurs. Capsule ½″.

5. Ruellia, L.

Herbs or undershrubs with sessile or sub-sessile, solitary or clustered, large or m. s. flowers subtended by two leaf-like bracteoles, with tubular-ventricose more or less oblique corolla. St. 4 didynamous. Anther-cells muticous, glabrous. Ovary-cells 3-10-ovuled. Stigmas simple. Capsule clavate ellipsoid with solid base. Seeds imbricate, hairy.

Stems prostrate or rambling. L. ovate, not very lineolate . . . . 1. *prostrata.*

Stems erect, or sometimes 0 in suffruticosa. L. very lineolate.

L. oblong-lanceolate, acuminate. Fls. 1½-2″ . 2. *cernua.*

L. elliptic acute. Fls. 3″ . . . . . . 3. *Beddomei.*

L. oblong or elliptic obtuse. Fls. 2″ long . . 4. *suffruticosa.*

1. R. prostrata. *Lamk.*

Creeping or rambling, often rooting at the nodes, scarcely shrubby, with ovate leaves 1″ by ¾″ to 1¾″ by 1″ (or up to 3″ in var. dejecta) and axillary solitary purple flowers ¾″ diam. and about 1″ long.

Shady banks, common. Fls. *July-Sept.*

Stems nearly glabrous except at the nodes. L. obtuse or sub-acute (or acute in var. dejecta) slightly hispid or hairy above, more so on the veins beneath, with 6 prs. distinct oblique nerves. Fls. caducous, falling before mid-day, very shortly pedicelled, tube about 3″. Sepals linear, ciliate. Ovary downy with about 6 ovules in each cell. Stigma tongue-like.

2. R. cernua, *Roxb.* (see however note under R. Beddomei).

A strict erect herb or undershrub 1-2 ft. high, from a slender woody rootstock, with lanceolate or oblong-lanceolate acuminate leaves 3-5″ by 1-1¼″ Fls. 1½″ light purple with petioled elliptic acute or acuminate leafy bracts.

Frequent in valleys among the Singbhum mountains; Parasnath. Fls. *Aug.-Sept.* Fr. *Dec.*

Stems obtusely 4-gonous and often grooved (as also in the following species), strigose with adpressed hairs. L. hairy above hairy and strigose on the nerves beneath. Petioles slender. Capsule ⅝-1″ slightly beaked.

3. R. Beddomei, *Clarke.* (R. cernua partly of Anderson and Prain).

A branched erect herb or undershrub 1-2 ft. high, from a slender woody rootstock, with elliptic or ovate-lanceolate acute, not acuminate, leaves 1½-3″ long. Fls. 3″ purple with petioled ovate acute leafy bracts.

Valleys in Singbhum. Fls. *Aug.-Sept.*

Stems minutely strigose. L. somewhat hairy above, with only a few hairs beneath. Bracteoles ovate, less acute than in *cernua,* of which it is sometimes considered a form. If so, the name of both forms should be R. Beddomei rather than cernua, in view of the great dissimilarity of both Roxburgh's figure and description of R. cernua to any form of this plant. Roxburgh's R. cernua was a *glabrous* plant with small pale-pink flowers in the leaf axils.

4. R. suffruticosa, *Roxb.* Brunaia, Charpatu, *K.*; Chaulia, *S.*

A perennial herb or dwarf undershrub with many long fleshy tuberous roots, stems 0 to 18″ high, both stem and leaves with many white hairs. Leaves broadly elliptic or oblong obtuse 2-5″. Fls. white or purple 2″ long.

Singbhum and Manbhum, common in dry jungles; Hazaribagh; Santal Parganahs; probably general. Fls. *May-Sept.* Fr. *Aug.-Oct.*

Often forming a rosette on the ground with scarcely any stem in May; the stem frequently elongates in the rainy season. The plant is very much more hairy than are the preceding species. L. 1½-2″ only when first flowering, petioles ⅛-⅓″. Peduncles shorter than or exceeding the leaves in fruit. Sepals ¼″. Petals rounded ⅓″. Capsule ⅝″-¾″ with 12-14 thinly discoid marginate seeds.

It is one of the herbs known collectively as Ili-rann (Rice-beer medicine) by the Kols, by whom it is used in the fermentation of rice-beer (Ili, *K.*; Handi, Handia, *S*, *Oraon*). Campbell says that the root is used in gonorrhœa, syphilis and renal affections.

6. Hemigraphis, Nees.

1. H. latebrosa, *Nees.*

A softly hairy diffuse undershrub about 12-18″ high with long petioled coarsely crenate-dentate leaves and pretty bright blue flowers $\frac{2}{3}$-$\frac{3}{4}$″ long with curved tubular corolla and subequal spreading petals.

Frequent in rocky jungles in Singbhum, Palamau, Hazaribagh and probably throughout Chota Nagpur and Santal Parganahs. Fls. *Nov.-Jany.*

Fls. opposite in sub-capitate spikes. *St.* 4. Cells of ovary 4-ovuled.

7. Hygrophila, Br.

1. **H. salicifolia,** *Nees*, and 2. **H. spinosa**, *T.*, *And.*, are conspicuous ditch or *marsh* herbs with lipped flowers in axillary whorls and didynamous stamens. The former attains 3 ft. and the latter 4 ft. or more, though both are often dwarf. H. spinosa, gokhula janum, *S.*; Kanta Kalia, *H.*, has long willow-like leaves and dense spiny whorls of handsome purple flowers, the lower lip $\frac{1}{2}$-$\frac{5}{8}$″ broad with a yellow palate. Spines usually 6, often 1″ long. Fl. *Nov.-Dec.* The former is unarmed with linear leaves and has about 22 seeds in its linear $\frac{1}{2}$″ capsule. Fls. *Sept.-Nov.*

8. Barleria, L.

Herbs or undershrubs, sometimes prickly, with entire leaves and showy sessile flowers, axillary or in spikes, the latter sometimes very dense and unilateral. Sep. 4, the 2 outer much larger than the inner. Corolla-tube long. Pet. 5 sub-equal. St. 2 perfect and 2 or 3 rudimentary. Disc large. Seeds with silky hairs.

Fls. yellow. A prickly shrub . . . . 1. *Prionitis.*
Fls. blue or red. Unarmed . . . .
Fls. few or clustered or spikes capitate, not secund. . . 2. *cristata.*
Spikes secund . . . . 3. *strigosa.*

1. **B. Prionitis,** *L.* Kanta phul, *S.* Kanta jati, Beng.

A prickly undershrub 2-5 ft. high with elliptic leaves 1½" by ½" to 4" by 1¾" and yellow flowers, one to three together, in the axils and in terminal spikes with elliptic spine-tipped bracts ½-1" long.

Gangpur near the Brahmini River. Manbhum, grown as a hedge plant, *Camp.*; S.P., near villages (Jurmoondee, etc.). Fls. Fr. *Dec.-June.* Doubtfully wild.

L. acuminate both ends, narrowed into the ½-¾" petiole or upper subsessile, mostly with axillary spines. *Corolla* 1¼". *Capsule* ⅝" beaked.

2. **B. cristata,** *L.* Raila baha, *S.*; Jati, *Beng.*

An erect or diffuse undershrub 1-3 ft. high with narrow leaves and bright rose-coloured flowers solitary or paired in the leaf axils (in shade) or forming dense capitate spikes on the branchlets (in sunny places).

Very common on rocky hills in Singbhum and occurs throughout Chota Nagpur, often covered with flowers and then very handsome. The colour of the flowers is quite different to that of the Himalayan plant.

Fls. *Sept.-Nov.* Fr. *Oct.-Jany.*

Stems sub-terete strigose. *L.* ell. to oblong-lanceolate 2-5½" by ½-1½" sub-acuminate both ends, rarely obtuse, sparsely adpressed hairy above. Sec. n. about 4-6 prs. *Petiole* ⅓-¼". Outer *sepals* ell. or rhomboid ¾", pectinate, strongly nerved, with adpressed yellowish hairs. *Cor.-tube* 1½" long. Upper lip 4-lobed, lower ½-¾" long. Perfect and imperfect *st.* each 2. *Capsule* ⅝" glabrous shining compressed.

3. **B. strigosa,** *Willd.* Raila baha, S.; Dasi, *Beng.*

An undershrub 2-4 ft. high with ovate acuminate leaves 4-8" by 2-5" decurrent on the petiole and large handsome azure blue flowers 2" long and 1¼" wide in dense bracteolate 1-sided spikes.

In shady places only. Singbhum. Fls. *Oct.-Nov.* Fr. *Dec.*

Easily recognized by the two larger sepals being imbricate in a row on the upper side of the spike and the bracteoles in two lateral rows.

Crossandra undulaefolia, *Salisb,* is an undershrub 2-4 ft. high occurring in hedges about Chaibassa under shade, with narrow leaves 2½-5" with wavy margins and pale beneath. *Flowers* deep orange-red, in linear-oblong spikes with imbricating bracts. *Cor.-tube* curved slender ¾" long and 1" diam. Fls. *July-Oct.*

10. Neuracanthus, Nees.

1. N. tetragonostachyus, *Nees.*

Suffruticose 1-2½ ft. with perennial creeping root, subterete stems with two lines of hairs, membranous ell.-acuminate leaves about 3½″ by 1½″ and bright blue 2-lipped flowers ⅓″ long by ¼″ diam. in 4-ranked axillary and terminal sessile spikes 1-1½″ long with imbricate ell. white-hirsute veined bracts $\frac{5}{16}$″ long.

Frequent on trap - rocks in the Rajmehal hills. Previously only reported from Burma. Fls. *Jany.-Feby.*

L. narrowed into a very short petiole hispid-pubescent on the nerves beneath. *Calyx* ¼″ lobes linear 2 larger than the other 3, with long white hairs. *Bracteoles* 0. *Corolla tube* conical, then suddenly ventricose. *St.* 4 in the throat didynamous with very short filaments. Upper anthers with only 1 perfect cell. *Ovules* 2 in each ovary cell. *Stigma* linguiform.

11. Lepidagathis, Willd.

Herbs or undershrubs with sessile flowers in heads or spikes, usually secund and with bracts longer than the sepals. Sepals unequal, two anterior more or less connate. Corolla small 2-lipped, very swollen at base or in the middle, lower lip 3-lobed usually spotted. St. didynamous. Capsule 2- or 4-seeded.

1. L. fasciculata, *Nees.* Serendri dumbu, Bile-mata a:, *K.*

A small highly aromatic viscous hairy herb 1-2 ft. much branched from the creeping rootstock, with *crenate* ovate acuminate leaves and small white lipped flowers in numerous bracteate sub-capitate spikes *rarely exceeding* ½″ *long.*

Common among rocks in the Sal forests of Singbhum, also in grass near nalas. Fls. *Jany.-April.* Fr. *March. April.*

Stems with 4 raised green lines. *Leaf-blade* suddenly tapering into the winged petiole, larger 5″ by 2″ including the petioles. Bracts ¼″ *3-nerved herbaceous.* *Calyx* sub-2-lipped ⅛-¼″, lower sepals linear, lateral acicular. *Cor.* $\frac{5}{16}$″ Anther-cells beaked or mucronate at base, nearly level. Seeds 4. The leaves are eaten.

2. **L. hyalina**, *Nees.* A branched herb 1-2 ft high with root of fleshy fibres. Stems with short curly pubescence above and 2 green lines decurrent from the petioles.

L. lanceolate, ell.-oblong or ovate *entire*, decurrent on petiole as in last, attaining 7″ by $2\frac{1}{4}$″ *including* the petiole, upper narrow-lanceolate subsessile, hairy both sides. *Fls.* $\frac{1}{3}$″ in 1-sided clustered spikes $\frac{1}{2}$-$1\frac{1}{2}$″ long with lanceolate or linear finely-acuminate *1-nerved bracts* $\frac{3}{8}$-$\frac{7}{16}$″ long, with long white cilia.

Similar localities. Fls. *Nov.-Feby.*

3. **L. purpuricaulis**, *Nees.* Very closely allied to last, often with purple stems. Bracts striate lanceolate mucronate.

4. **L. trinervis**, *Nees.*, has linear or linear-lanceolate glabrous leaves, ovate or obovate sub-spinescent bracts and flowers sometimes conglomerated near the root. The sepals are not spinescent.

5. **L. Hamiltoniana**, *Wall.*, with linear leaves is a common herb on dry slopes, remarkable from its flowers being always conglomerated in spinescent cushions on the ground. The bracts and sepals in this are both spinescent. Fls. *Dec.-Feby.*

12. Adhatoda, Nees.

1. **A. Vasica**, *Nees.* Vasaka. *Beng.*, is a bushy shrub or undershrub often occurring in compounds and near villages but with no claim to be considered indigenous in our area. It has large minutely pubescent elliptic leaves with a fœtid smell, acute both ends, and with many strong sec. n. The large white lipped flowers are borne in dense terminal spikes. Evergreen.

An insecticide.

13. Justicia, L.

Shrubs or undershrubs or usually herbs with small lipped flowers usually sessile in bracteate spikes. Sep. 4 or 5. St. 2, anths. 2-celled, lower cell with a small white appendage. Seeds 4, compressed, not hairy but more or less tubercled or glochidiate.

1. **J. Betonica**, *L.* Hád-pát, *K.*

Shrubby below with many stems 2-4 ft. high from a perennial rootstock, ovate-lanceolate leaves acuminate both ends and small white rose-spotted flowers in mostly terminal 1-3-nate spikes conspicuous from the closely-seriate white green-veined ovate mucronate bracts.

Singbhum forests common. Rocky ravines in Hazaribagh and Palamau. Jaspurnagar, *Wood*. Probably in all districts. Fls. Fr. *Nov.-Jany.*

Stems swollen above the nodes, terete striate (sub-tomentose in Var. villosa). *L.* pubescent both sides or glabrous, larger 4¼″ by 1¾″, margin sometimes faintly toothed, sec. n. 6-8 prs. fine raised. *Petiole* ⅓-½″. *Spikes* 2-6″. *Bracts* ½-⅔″ and bracteoles similar, *sepals* ¼″ subulate. *Capsule*, ½″ clavate pubescent. *Seeds* with a corrugated testa.

Used in diarrhœa.

2. J **Gendarussa,** *L.* f. Jagat madan, *Beng.*, is an erect undershrub 2-4 ft. sometimes cultivated and occurring as an escape. It has narrow leaves, interrupted spikes 2-5″ long and *linear* bracts.

Four other species of Justicia occur, they are only herbs.

Rungia parviflora. *Nees.* Var. pectinata. Bir lopong arak', *S.* is a herb 6″-2½ ft., the stems with dense recurved pubescence at the 4 angles, narrow leaves, and very small blue flowers in 1-sided spikes ½-⅔″ long with white-margined bracts. Very common esp. in rocky ravines.

Fls. *Nov.-Jany.*

The root is given in fever.

15. Dicliptera, Juss.

Herbs or undershrubs. L. ovate, one of each pair sometimes deciduous. Inflorescence fascicled. Fls. 3-5 of which 1 or 2 only are perfect in a contracted cyme, each cyme in a pair of *unequal* posterior and anterior bracts of which the posterior are larger. Cymes often in one or more transverse *series*, each *series* within a pair of lateral bracts, and the whole in the axil of a floral leaf. Each flower of a cyme has also its own bract, with or without bracteoles, and 5 linear sepals, or sepals lanceolate in perfect flowers. Corolla rose, purple spotted within with a narrow upper lip and a sub-equal recurved 3 toothed lower lip. Anth.-cells superposed.

The Cor.-tube is often twisted so that the anterior lip becomes superior.

1. D. Roxburghiana, *Nees.* Var.

A tufted undershrub about 2 ft. with 4-angled striate stems and swollen nodes, pubescent, especially on two sides.

Rocky jungles, Singbhum. Pitorea (Ranchi District, *Wood.* Type ?)

Fls. Fr. *Nov.-Dec.*

L. acuminate 3½″ by 2″, base cuneate, shortly densely hairy beneath and hairy above, nerves oblique strong. Petiole ½-1½″ hairy. Heads of flowers terminal and on leaf-opposed branchlets ½-1″ long. *Cor.-tube* 3/16″, upper lip ligulate, lower ⅛″ broad minutely 3-toothed. *Capsules* 3/16-¼″ pubescent and with long hairs. *Seeds* densely papillose.

N.B.—D. Roxburghiana is described in the F.B.I. as having leaves *obscurely* pubescent or *glabrous*. In the C. N plant the proper bracts of each flower are setaceous ¼″, the larger cyme bracts (which are perhaps those referred to in the F.B.I.) oblanceolate ½″, and the smaller ⅜″ long.

2. **D. micranthes**, *Nees.*, is a diffuse herb with a corolla only ¼″ or less.

16. Peristrophe, Nees.

1. **P. bicalyculata**, *Nees.* Barge Khode baha, *S.*; Nasa bhaga, *Beng.*

A laxly paniculately branched herb 3-6 ft. high with swollen nodes and sharply 6-angled stems, ovate leaves and smallish light purple 2-lipped flowers in lax axillary and terminal divaricate panicled clusters of two flowers.

Very common in hedges, also under light shade in waste ground where not browsed. Fls., Fr. *Nov.-Jany.*

Lower *leaves* 4¼″ by 2½″, floral often lanceolate, hairy, base somewhat decurrent on the 1½-2″ slender petiole. *Panicles* with setaceous ⅙″ bracts. Each cluster (or pair) terminal with an *outer* linear or linear-spathulate *bract* 1½ times as long as the calyx and an *inner* smaller one, *bracteoles* 2 prs. but one *flower* sometimes abortive. *Sepals* ⅙″ connate at base. *Cor.-tube* ⅕-¼″ *twisted.* Posterior lip (lower) elliptic obtuse entire ¼-5/16″, anterior ¼″ long very shortly 3-lobed or divided into 3 linear petals. *Capsule* ⅓″ solid below. Seeds glochidiate.

It is hardly separable generically from Dicliptera.

L. acuminate 3½″ by 2″, base cuneate, shortly densely hairy beneat and hairy above, nerves oblique strong. Petiole ½-1½″. Heads of flower terminal and on leaf-opposed branchlets ½-1″ long. Corolla hairy, tub 3/16″, upper lip ligulate, lower ⅛″ broad minutely 3-toothed.

17. Rhinacanthus, Nees.

*1. **R. communis**, *Nees.*

A slender divaricately branched shrub with elliptic obovate, or ovate-oblong leaves 3-7″ by ¾-3¼″ and white flowers 1″ long with a slender pubescent corolla-tube. Calyx $\frac{1}{10}$″ deeply 5-partite longer than the minute clustered bracts.

Rocky ground under shade. Karampoda and Porahat forests, Keonjhur boundary. Palandu (Ranchi), *Wood.* Koderma, *Gamble.* Fls. *Jany.-April.*

L. narrowed both ends. *Petiole* slender. Upper lip of *corolla* shortly 2-fid, lower with 3 broad lobes $\frac{1}{3}$″ long.

18. Andrographis, Wall.

Herbs or small undershrubs with small 2-lipped pubescent flowers in axillary and terminal often 1-sided racemes with small bracts, and bracteoles 0 or minute. Anther cells parallel, base bearded. Capsule 6-12-seeded. Seeds glabrous, not compressed.

1. **A. paniculata,** *Nees.* Kalmeg, *S.*, *H.*; Chiretta, *Beng.* (The true Chiretta, however, is a Swertia.)

An erect herb 1-3 ft. with square stems glabrous below, lanceolate glabrous leaves about $2\frac{1}{2}$″ and flowers $\frac{1}{2}$″ long vertical on spreading panicled racemes.

Common, often seen on fire-lines before they are cleared. Fls. *Sept.-April.* Fr. *Dec.-May.*

L. narrowed both ends. *Petiole* 0-$\frac{1}{4}$″. *Inflorescence* glandular-hairy. Capsule narrow $\frac{5}{8}$-$\frac{3}{4}$″.

Used in fever (a decoction of the whole plant). Also given "in diarrhœa, convulsions, and epilepsy," *Camp.*

2. **A. echioides,** *Nees.* Bir Kubet, *S.*

Erect herb 8″-2 ft. with pubescent stems, sessile oblong leaves $1\frac{1}{2}$″ by $\frac{1}{3}$″ to $3\frac{1}{2}$″ by $1\frac{1}{4}$″ pubescent or somewhat hairy both sides, and flowers vertical on spreading simple or branched (but not panicled) racemes from all the axils.

Similar localities. Girga Forest, etc. Fls. *July-Nov.* Fr. *Sept.-Jan.*

Sepals slender $\frac{1}{5}$-$\frac{1}{4}$″. Capsule ellipsoid.

19. Phlogacanthus, Nees.

1. **P. thyrsiflorus,** *Nees.*

A handsome shrub with entire dark green elliptic leaves 6-8″ long and widely tubular 2-lipped curved brick-red flowers in terminal thyrses. Bracts linear. Bracteoles 0. St. 2.

Damp ravines in Singbhum, rare. Fls. *April.*

(I find that I have no specimen or note of occurrence of this familiar shrub, and memory may be at fault in quoting it from the Singbhum forests.)

20. Blepharis, Juss.

1. B. boerhaaviæfolia, *Pers.*

A herb or undershrub about 2 ft. high with a creeping rootstock. Stems pubescent. L. in unequal pairs or 3-4-nately whorled 2″ by $\frac{3}{4}$″ to $3\frac{1}{4}$″ by $1\frac{1}{4}$″ elliptic with cuneate base, with a few small teeth. Fls. nearly $\frac{3}{4}$″ long solitary axillary and terminal on many-bracteate reduced branchlets. Corolla with a white narrow-urceolate tube $\frac{1}{6}$″ long with a truncate rim on one side and one narrowly-obovate 3-toothed lip pubescent with pink veins.

Among rocks in Palamau jungles. Fls. and Fr. *Nov.-Dec.*

L. acute or very acute and apiculate, sparsely hairy both sides. *Petiole* $\frac{1}{10}$-$\frac{1}{4}$″. *Bracts* with retrorsely hispid awns obovate. *Bracteoles* spathulate.

2. B. molluginifolia, *Pers.*, is somewhat similar but with obtuse leaves and with the 2 seeds shaggy, whereas in the last they are densely covered with thick fleshy compound hairs (described as spinous in Bengal Plants) and are viscous when young. Chota Nagpur, *Prain.*

Fam.—80. CONVOLVULACEÆ.

Usually twining herbs or shrubs, sometimes with milky juice (Cuscuta is parasitic). *L.* alternate (0 in Cuscuta) exstipulate. *Fls.* regular usually cymose. *Sepals* 5 imbricate, often persistent and accrescent. *Corolla* campanulate or funnel-shaped, rarely rotate, petals often very short *Aestivation* usually plicate and usually also contorted. *St.* 5 on the tube. *Ovary* 2- (rarely 3- or 1-) or 4-celled. Style 1 (rarely 2 or 0), stigmas 2 (rarely 1, 5-lobed). *Ovules* 4 altogether (*i.e.*, 2 in each carpel), erect, anatropous

Fruit dehiscent or indehiscent, sometimes fragile. *Seeds* 2-4 rarely only 1. Albumen 0 or scanty. Cotyledons generally plicate.

I. Climbing shrubs. Ovary 1-celled. Fr. a 1-seeded berry	1. *Erycibe.*
II. Climbing shrubs. Ovary 2-celled. Fr. dry 1-seeded, sepals enlarged into wings in fruit	2. *Porana.*
III. Climbing or prostrate herbs. Stigmas linear, oblong or ovate oblong. Fr. dehiscent.	
Ovary 1- (or incompletely 2-) celled, hirsute . .	3. *Hewittia.*
Ovary 2-celled. Style 1. Fls. white . . .	4. *Convolvulus.*
Ovary 2-celled. Styles 2. Fls. blue	5. *Evolvulus.*
IV. Erect or climbing. Stigmas linear-oblong. Ovary 4-celled. Frt. indehiscent	6. *Rivea.*
V. Stigmas 2, globose	
(*a*) Fruit indehiscent. L. tomentose or adpressed hairy beneath, not lobed.	
Ovary 4-celled	7. *Argyreia.*
Ovary 2-celled	8. *Lettsomia.*
(*b*) Fruit dehiscent. L. not tomentose or strigose beneath. Ovary 2-, 3-or 4-celled . . .	9. *Ipomæa.*
VI. A filiform yellow-green parasite without leaves . .	10. *Cuscuta.*

Prain's division of Ipomæa in "Bengal Plants" into several genera is more natural and consistent with the separation of Argyreia and Lettsomia, but it involves many unfamiliar names. This classification has been indicated under Ipomæa.

1. Erycibe, Roxb.

1. **E. paniculata,** *Roxb.* Urumin, Hurmi, *K.*; Kari, *S.*

A large climbing shrub with conical protuberances on the trunk, rusty-tomentose shoots, entire oblong, rarely oblanceolate or obovate, acuminate leaves about 5 by $1\frac{1}{2}''$ and terminal rusty-tomentose cymose panicles of yellowish-white flowers $\frac{1}{2}''$ diam. with crisped emarginate petals. Berry black $\frac{5}{8}''$ with dark-purple flesh, seated on the spreading persistent calyx.

Generally near nalas, frequent, Singbhum; Dalbhum, *Gamble*! Manbhum; Hazaribagh (common in Koderma forest): Sirguja, *Wood*; Palamau; and Santal Parganahs. Fls. *May-June*. Fr. ripens following *May*. Evergreen.

L. 3-6″ tomentose when young, long- or shortly-obtusely acuminate shining and glabrous when old, sometimes punctulate beneath, with 4-6 prs. of oblique not prominent nerves, base narrowed into a ¼″ reddish petiole. *Panicles* narrow 6-7″ long. *Corolla-tube* as long as calyx. *St.* 5 at base of corolla included *Stigma* sessile sub-globose *5-lobed* (2-lobed according to F.B.I.) Ovules 4 erect. Seeds ellipsoid ⅓.″

The fruit is sweet and is eaten.

2. Porana, Burm.

1. P. paniculata, *Roxb.* Era-bair, *K.*; Panjot nari, *S.*; Bhuria lar, *Kharw.*; Bridal creeper.

A beautiful climber forming large pure white patches in the jungle with innumerable, panicled, small white flowers, and softly white-tomentose ovate-cordate leaves.

Singbhum, in stony nalas and banks but not very common. Hazaribagh, (Parasnath, Barwadih, etc.); Chutupalughat and Jaspur, *Wood*; Palamau, *Haslett*; Santal Parganahs. Fls. *Oct.-Dec.* Fr. *Jany.*

L. 1″ by ½″ to 5″ by 3″ rarely lower leaves 6″ diam., acute or acuminate, base 5-6-nerved. *Corolla* ¼″-⅓″ campanulate. *Fruiting-sepals*, three ¾″ by ¼″, two ¼″ linear, or all enlarged in fruit. *Capsule* membranous globose hairy or tomentose ½″ diam.

3. Hewittia, W. & A.

1. H. bicolor, *Wight.*

A twiner with pubescent stems, peduncles, petioles and nerves, cordate ovate simple or somewhat lobed acute or cuspidate leaves and pale yellow flowers 1-1⅛″ diam. with purple throat.

Hedges, etc., Porahat. Fls. *Jany.-Feby.*

L. 3½″ by 3″ to 5″ by 4″ shining both sides. *Peduncles* 1-3-fld. Outer *sepals* ovate ½″. *Ovary* villous.

Convolvulus pluricaulis, *Choisy*, is a diffuse hairy perennial with white flowers. Sirguja, *Wood*.

Evolvulus alsinoides, *L.*, is a small diffuse perennial with very pretty small bright blue flowers. Common in sandy places.

6. Rivea, Choisy.

Erect or climbing shrubs. Peduncles axillary 1-7-fld. Corolla large hypocrateriform. Ovary 4-celled. Capsule thinly woody breaking transversely a little above the base and exposing a central white spongy endocarp with 4 seeds, the septa remaining as 4 persistent vascular bundles in pairs, 2 outside and 2 inside the endocarp.

1. R. hypocrateriformis, *Chois.* Kalmi lata, *Beng.*

A climber with silky stems orbicular-cordate cuspidate leaves, 2-3½″ diam. often broader than long, white with adpressed silky hairs beneath and long-tubed white flowers 2″-diam., solitary axillary or terminal, jointed on the peduncle, rarely peduncles 3-fld.

Scrub jungles in Singbhum, not common. Sirguja, *Wood.* Hazaribagh (Koderma forest, etc.); Palamau and Santal Parganahs.

Fls. *Sept.* Frs. *Nov.-Dec.*

L. with rounded or cuspidate tip. Petioles about as long as the leaves. *Sepals* ovate ⅓″. *Corolla-limb* glabrous or puberulous without, tube 2″ long tubular. *Capsule* sub-globose apiculate ⅜″ seated on the 1″ diam. calyx.

2. R. ornata, *Chois.*

Erect, otherwise very similar. *L.* 3-5″ diam. much more tomentose beneath. *Peduncles* 3-7-fld. *Sepals* lanceolate, ½-¾″. *Corolla-limb* silky without.

Jaspur, 12 ft. high, *Wood.* In the Duars it is usually about 5-6 ft. and fls. in the rains.

7. Argyreia, Lour.

Climbing shrubs with silky hirsute or pubescent leaves. Flowers showy in capitate or corymbose cymes. Sepals adpressed to, and often somewhat enlarged in fruit. Corolla funnel-shaped, very shortly lobed. St. included. Ovary

4-celled, Disc annular often large. Fr. baccate or dry, 4-1-seeded.

1. **A. speciosa,** *Sweet.* Kedok' arak', *S.*; Bistarak, *Beng.* The Elephant Creeper.

A large twiner with ovate-cordate leaves white silkily tomentose beneath and large light-purple flowers 2-3" diam. sub-capitate on stout peduncles 3-10" long.

Manbhum, *Camp.*

Stems tomentose. *L.* 3-12" glabrous above, long petioled. *Bracts* up to 1½" ovate-lanceolate acute woolly. *Sepals* ovate woolly. *Fr.* ½" diam., brown-yellow nearly dry.

The plant yields an oil. "The root is applied to the running sores on the legs and feet known in Santali as *rasphutao.* The leaves are eaten as a pot-herb," *Camp.*

2. **A. Daltoni,** *Clarke.*

A large handsome climber with large ovate-oblong leaves with adpressed yellowish hairs beneath and bright red-purple flowers over 2½" diam. in 3-7-flowered cymes on stout peduncles 1-5" long.

Porahat plateau (in Singbhum) on the highest ridges; Jaspur, *Wood.*

Fls. *Sept.-Oct.*

Stems adpressed-pubescent. *L.* reaching 8½ by 4" or even larger, base rounded, not, or very slightly, cordate, petiole 1-2". *Cymes* rather dense with foliaceous persistent spathulate or linear-oblanceolate bracts ½-¾" long. *Pedicels* short. *Sepals* ½-⅝" outer oblong, inner smaller lanceolate, silky. *Corolla-tube* 1½" with long soft hairs outside. *Berry* ½" diam.

8. Lettsomia, Roxb.

More or less hairy climbing shrubs with usually cordate-based leaves and tubular-funnel-shaped flowers in axillary bracteate peduncled densely corymbose or capitate cymes. Sepals often somewhat enlarged in fruit. St. included or exserted. Ovary 2-celled, disc annular often large. Fr. indehiscent baccate or sometimes dry and papery, 4-1-seeded, usually more or less enclosed in the persistent calyx.

1. L. aggregata, *Roxb.*

Branches, and leaves beneath, white-tomentose or woolly. Fls. $\frac{2}{3}''$ long rose, capitate with orbicular woolly sub-persistent bracts $\frac{1}{3}$-$\frac{1}{2}''$ long and ovate white tomentose sepals. Fr. dry $\frac{1}{3}''$ red and fruiting sepals red within.

On the ghats Tainmara to Bundu, *Wood.*

L. glabrous above. *Peduncles* 0-2". Closely allied to next.

2. L. bella, *Clarke.* Jamu chalum, *K.*

Branches and leaves beneath silkily white-tomentose. Fls. $\frac{3}{4}$-1" long funnel-shaped white with a crimson border, capitate with spathulate or oblong bracts $\frac{1}{4}$-$\frac{1}{3}''$ long. and oblong or elliptic densely white villous or hirsute sepals $\frac{1}{3}$-$\frac{1}{2}''$ long in flower and in fruit. Fruit dry $\frac{1}{3}''$ diam. scarlet subtended by the spreading hardened calyx which is deep red within and white silky without.

Grassy glades in Singbhum, not uncommon. Gurhma, *C. B. Clarke!* Palamau, *Gamble!* Sirguja, *Wood.*

Fls. *Aug-Sept.* Fr. *Dec.-Jan.*

A very pretty plant both in flower and in fruit. *L.* sub-orbicular or ovate cordate 2½-5" diam., obtuse to cuspidate, softly hairy above. *Petiole* 2½-3½" *Peduncles* 1-3". *Corolla* villous outside. *Anthers* exserted. *Seeds* black glabrous.

(The fruit breaks up irregularly like many Ipomœas, the epicarp is papery, and the endocarp a white dry papery or pithy substance extending between the seeds.)

3. L. setosa, *Roxb.*

A large handsome climber with milky juice, stems and leaves beneath covered with adpressed hairs, flowers funnel-shaped 1-1¼" diam with a short spreading purple limb, in dense regularly branched long-peduncled corymbiform cymes. Fruit an ovoid berry, 4-2-seeded.

Bichia Buru and other mountains in Singbhum 2,000-3,000 ft.; Kochang *Gamble!* Jaspur, *Wood*: Sirguja, *Clarke!* Fls. *Oct.-Nov.*

L. cordate-ovate to cordate-oblong acute or acuminate 4" by 2" to 5" by 8", slightly hairy above, sec. n. 8-10 prs. *Peduncles* stout 3-5" and cymes 1½-3" diam. covered with adpressed hairs. *Bracts* silkily-hirsute large persistent oblong or broadly elliptic obtuse $\frac{1}{3}''$. *Sepals* $\frac{1}{3}$-$\frac{1}{2}''$ oblong obtuse outer $\frac{1}{3}''$ broad, fleshy and accrescent in fruit. *Corolla* $1\frac{3}{4}''$ long, white except the short light-purple petals, densely hairy without. *Fil.* with enlarged woolly base curving over the ovary. *Fruit* globose orange $\frac{5}{16}''$ diam. 2-celled and seeded.

9. Ipomea, L.

Prostrate or climbing herbs rarely shrubs, with palmi-nerved or palmately-divided (pinnatisect in I. Quamoclit) leaves usually cordate at base. Fls cymose, or on 1-fld. peduncles. Sepals often unequal. Corolla funnel-shaped or campanulate, scarcely lobed, limb plaited in bud. St. unequal. Ovary 2-celled with 2 ovules in each cell, more rarely 4-celled (3-celled in I. Nil), style slender with 2 globose stigmatic lobes. Capsule valvular or irregularly dehiscent, epicarp and endocarp often separately dehiscent, dry often papery.

The following sections are conterminous with the separate genera adopted in Prain's " Bengal Plants " (but *with the addition of Pharbitis*), and which are themselves old genera resuscitated.

A. Corolla campanulate tubular-campanulate, or funnel-shaped white, yellow or orange. Pollen not spinescent.

Sec. I. Merremia, *Dennst* (genus). Vertical bands on corolla usually with 5 purple lines. St. unequal. Anthers included or exserted, usually twisted. Ovary-2 or 4-celled. Capsule 4-valved.

1. Spaces between bands badly defined. No purple lines. Corolla 1-$1\frac{3}{4}''$.
   - Cymes compact sub-umbellate. Fls. pure white or cream . . . . 1. *cymosa.*
   - Fls. sub-racemose, yellow, shaggy without . . . 2. *petaloidea.*
2. Spaces between bands well defined. Lines usually present.
   - *a.* Corolla $1\frac{1}{2}''$ long. L. palmately lobed. Fls. yellow . . . . 3. *vitifolia.*
   - *b.* Corolla $\frac{1}{2}$-$\frac{3}{4}''$ long. Fls. pale yellow.
     - Prostrate. L. rarely over 1'' sessile hastate oblong . . . . 4. *tridentata.*
     - Twining. L. 1-2'' ovate-cordate. Peduncles $\frac{1}{2}$-3'' . 5. *chryseides.*
     - Creeping. L. $\frac{1}{3}$-$1\frac{1}{4}''$ reniform or ovate-cordate. Peduncles 0-$\frac{1}{2}''$ . . . . 6. *reniformis.*

Sec. II. Operculina, *Manso* (genus). Stems and peduncles winged. Fls. white tubular-campanulate. Anthers at length twisted. Ovary 2-celled. Capsule with epicarp circumsciss above the middle . . . . . 7. *Turpethum.*

Sec. III. Aniseia, *Choisy* (genus) Fls. white, solitary on the peduncle, outer sepals cordate much larger than inner. Ovary 2-celled. Cap. 4-valved . . . . 8. *martinicensis.*

B. Corolla usually funnel-shaped and purple, sometimes blue or white. St. included. Pollen spinescent.

Sec. IV. Ipomæa proper. Fls. usually cymose, rarely solitary, anthers straight or twisted. Ovary 2- or 4-celled. Capsule 4-valved.

1. Ovary 2-celled.

a. L. not distinctly lobed (sometimes sub-lobed in reptans.)

\+ Corolla 1″ long or less.

Peduncles short few-fld. Sep. very unequal in fr. . 9. *calycina.*

Fls. in sessile heads., Sep. sub-equal unaltered in fr. . . . . 10. *hispida.*

Peduncles long 1-3-fld. Corolla ochroleucous, purple at base . . . . 11. *obscura.*

\+ + Corolla 1½″ long or more.

Hirsute. Ped. 1-fld. Sep. ¾″ lanceolate, larger in fr. . . . . 12. *barlerioides.*

Nearly glabrous. Ped. 1-5-fld. Sep. ⅓″ ovate, unaltered in fr. . . . . 13. *reptans.*

Fls. sub-umbelled. Sep. ovate ⅓″ Pedicels clavate in fr. . . . . 14. *sepiaria.*

b. L. digitate, palmate or palmately lobed.

L. palmately-lobed. Fls. ¾-1¼″diam. only . 15. *pes-tigridis.*

L. palmate Fls. white 1½″ diam. Seeds glabrous, crested . . . . . 16. *quinata.*

L. palmate. Fls. purplish 2″ diam. Seeds villous . . . . 17. *pulchella.*

2. Ovary 4-celled. L. more or less lobed.

L. palmately 5-7-lobed. Seeds woolly . . . 18. *paniculata.*

L. angular or somewhat lobed. Seeds glabrous. Root tuberous . . . . 19. *Batatas.*

Sec. V. Pharbitis, *Chois* (genus). Corolla tubular-funnel-shaped. Anthers included.

Ovary 3-celled, 6-ovuled Capsule 3-celled. . . 20. *Nil.*

C. Corolla hypocrateriform. Pollen spinescent. Fls. scarlet or white rarely purple. Stamens exserted.

Sec. VI. Calonyction, *Chois* (genus). Stems often muricate. Peduncles 1-2-fld. only. Fls. purple or white. Ovary 2-celled.

Corolla tube 3″. Limb 3-5″ diam. white . . 21. *bona-nox.*

Corolla tube 1-2″. Limb 2-2½″ diam. rose-purple. . . . . 22. *muricata.*

Sec. VII. Quamoclit, *Mœnch* (genus). Fls. scarlet in few-fld. cymes. Ovary 4-celled.

L. ovate-cordate . . . . 23. *coccinea.*

L. pinnatisect with linear segments . . . 24. *Quamoclit.*

1. I. cymosa, *Roem.* Syn. Merremia umbellata, *Hallier.*

With oblong or ovate-oblong leaves with strong parallel nerves, and hastate or cordate base. Pure white (or tinged yellow, *F.B.I.*) flowers in shortly peduncled umbelliform cymes shorter than the leaves.

Usually near rivers or streams. Singbhum, rather common. Palamau.

Fls. *March-April.* Fr. *May.* The flowers open at noon. Evergreen. the new shoots appear in *June.*

Stems tough. Corolla pubescent towards the tip in bud and seeds very hairy. Bracts caducous, pedicels stout, about as long as peduncle.

2. I. petaloidea, *Chois.* Syn. Merremia crispatula, *Prain.*

L. ovate acute or upper lanceolate 5″ by 3½″ with rounded or sub-cordate base. Fls. yellow sub-racemose.

Chota Nagpur, *Prain.*

N.B.—Crispatulus (Convolvulus crispatulus; *Wall* No. 1403) is the older name, but does not appear to have been published until after petaloidea.

3. I. vitifolia, *Sweet.* Syn. Merremia vitifolia, *Hallier.*

A large hairy sub-herbaceous twiner with bright sulphur-coloured flowers and palmately 5-lobed leaves.

Valleys in Singbhum in the damper localities. Kewatbar, Palamau, *Wood & Gamble*! Fls. *Jany.-April.*

L. 2-6" diam. *Peduncles* 1-4", 2-7-fld. *Pedicels* swollen below the flowers. *Sepals* ½-¾", outer hairy hirsute, inner glabrous. *Filaments* dilated below. *Corolla* about 2" diam

Var. Sepals glabrous. Santal Parganahs.

4. **I. tridentata,** *Roth.* Syn. Merremia tridentata, *Hallier.*

A prostrate glabrous herb with a woody rootstock and narrow hastate lyrate or obovate-oblong leaves rarely up to 1¼" long, usually truncate with 2-3 teeth at apex and several sharp teeth at the base. Corolla small yellow.

Singbhum, damp places. Fls. Fr. *r. s.*

Peduncles sometimes far exceeding the leaves. *Capsule* ¼" diam. papery 4-seeded, sepals ¼" long in fruit.

5. **I. chryseides,** *Ker.* Syn. M. chryseides *Hallier.*

A twining herb. Cymes usually forked on very long peduncles. L. 1-2".

Singbhum, damp places and hedges. Fls. *Oct.-Nov.*

6. **I. reniformis,** *Chois.* Syn. M. emarginata, *Hallier.*

A prostrate creeping herb rooting at the nodes. Peduncles very short 1-3-fld. Corolla ½-¾" yellow campanulate.

Chaibassa. Fls. *Nov.*

7. **I. Turpethum,** *Br.* Operculina Turpethum, *Manso.* Bana etka, *S.*; Pitohri, *H.*; Tohri, *Beng.*

A climber with narrowly 3-4-winged stems, ovate cordate acuminate or acute leaves and 2-5-fld. cymes of white flowers 1½-2" diam.

Longabera in Singbhum, scarce; Kolhan, *Gamble* ! Manbhum, *Campbell* ; common about Garhwa (Palamau). Fls. *Oct.-Dec.* Fr. *Dec.-Jany.*

L 2½" by 2" to 5" by 4½" shortly pubescent as are the stems and inflorescence. *Petiole* ¾-3". *Cymes* about 3" long. *Pedicels* 1-1¼" lengthening and stouter in fruit. Outer *sepals* ¾" broadly elliptic, inner membranous, all enlarged in fruit. *Endocarp* of fruit quite transparent. Seeds 1-2.

The powdered root made into a paste is applied in rheumatism, *Campbell.* Roxburgh states that the bark of the roots is employed as a purgative.

8. **I. martinicensis,** *Mey.* Syn. I. uniflora, *Roem.* Aniseia martinicensis, *Chois.*

Creeping or twining. *L.* about 3″ by 1″. *Corolla* 1″ campanulate hairy without. Chota Nagpur, *Prain.*

9. I. calycina, *Benth.*

A villous twiner with ovate-cordate hairy or glabrate leaves 2-3″ and rose-coloured or white tubular-funnel-shaped flowers about ⅞″ long. Sepals enlarged in fruit ultimately cordate or sagittate.

Chota Nagpur, *Prain.*

10. I. hispida, *Roem.* Syn. I. eriocarpa, *F.B.I.*

A slender very hairy twiner with narrow lanceolate to deltoid or ovate acuminate cordate-based leaves and axillary dense capitate cymes of small purple campanulate or urceolate flowers.

Not uncommon in jungle and Arhar fields, Singbhum; Palamau, *Gamble*! Mahretta and Jaspur, *Wood.* Fls., r.s. Fr. *Sept.-Nov.*

L. 2-3″ *Cymes* ¾″ diam. sometimes with a peduncle ⅓-½″. *Sepals* very imbricate hairy 2 outer with long cusp. *Capsule* 2-4-valved globose hairy, ¼″ diam.

11. I. obscura, *Ker.*

A slender twiner with hairy stems, sub-orbicular or ovate deeply cordate leaves. Corolla ¾″ diam. yellow or white with the bands yellowish and always with a purple eye.

Rudia-Lotwa Tea Estate, *Wood*; Palamau, frequent in the west in hedgerows.

Fls., Fr. *Oct.-Dec.*

L. about 2½″ each way, hairy, petiole 1½″. *Peduncles* axillary 1-2-fld. ½-1″ long, pedicels nearly as long clavate upwards. *Capsule* ovoid ⅓″ 2 (-4) -valved with 4 brown velvety seeds.

12. I. barlerioides, *Benth.*

Hirsute. leaves ovate-oblong peduncles 1-fld. 1-4″ long. *Corolla* 2-3½″ long, 2½″ diam. purple or purplish-white.

Chota Nagpur, *C. B. Clarke.*

13. I. reptans, *Poir.* Syn. I aquatica, *F.B.I.*

" *Creeping* or *floating* with narrow hastate or cordate leaves 3-6″ long, long petole and pale-purple *fls.* 2″ long by 1½″, or *fls.* white with a purple eye. *Seeds* glabrous or minutely hairy.

Ponds and muddy places. Singbhum, Palamau, but not common in Chota Nagpur. Fls. *Nov.-March* and at other times. Tender shoots eaten

14. I. sepiaria, *Koen.* Ban Kalmi, *Beng.*

Twining. L. ovate-cordate. *Fls.* $1\frac{1}{2}''$ or more, pale-purple or white, with a dark-purple eye, sub-umbelled on long peduncles. *Pedicels* clavate in fruit. *Seeds* woolly.

Singbhum, occasional near streams. Sirguja, in similar situations, *Wood.*

15. I. pes-tigridis, *L.* Languli lata, *Beng.*

A *twiner* with spreading hairs and deeply palmate 5-9-lobed leaves with the lobes contracted at the base. *Corolla* funnel-shaped $1\text{-}1\frac{1}{4}''$ pink or pale mauve. *Sepals* $\frac{1}{3}\text{-}\frac{1}{2}''$. *Bracts* 1″.

Common everywhere esp. in fields. Fls. *r.s.* Fr. *Sept.-Nov.*

16. I. quinata, *Br.*

Usually twining with palmate or digitately 5-foliolate leaves with sessile or sub-sessile elliptic acuminate leaflets and white flowers $1\frac{1}{2}''$ diam.

Singhbhum, in open jungles, frequent. Manbhum, *Gamble* ! Fls. *Aug. Oct.*

Lflts. attain 4 by $1\frac{1}{4}''$ on the lower leaves with acute or cuneate base. *Petiole* hairy 2″ or shorter above. *Peduncles* solitary or paired usually 2-fld. $\frac{3}{4}\text{-}2''$ long.

17. I. pulchella, *Roth.* Syn. I. palmata, *F.B.I.* This is the well-known Railway-creeper. Often cultivated but not indigenous in Chota Nagpur.

18. I. paniculata, *Br.* Syn. I. digitata, *F.B.I.*

A large glabrous *climber* with large palmately 5-7-lobed *leaves* 3-7″ diam. with petiole 2-5″, and widely campanulate pink-purple *flowers* in dense long peduncled cymes, with peduncle attaining 6″.

Chota Nagpur, rare, *Prain.*

19. I. Batatas, *Lamk.* Uku Sangar, *K.*; Sakakanda, *H.* The Sweet Potato.

Prostrate, juice milky. *L.* simple or somewhat lobed. Fl. *Feby.*

Often cultivated, but I have never seen it flower in Chota Nagpur.

20. I. Nil, *Roth.* Syn. I. hederacea *F.B.I.*, Pharbitis Nil and P. hederacea, *Chois.*

A hairy climber with ovate cordate deeply 3-lobed leaves and handsome bright-blue or rose-coloured flowers on 1-5-fld. peduncles.

Common in hedges near villages only. Fls. *Aug.-Nov.*

Lobes ovate acuminate. *Sepals* hirsute ¼-1" linear acuminate above.

21. **I. bona-nox,** *L.* Syn. Calonyction bona-nox, *Boj.* The Moon-flower.

Easily distinguished by the very large white flowers. *L.* ovate with cordate base acute glabrous. *Capsule* 1".

Near stations and villages. Not seen wild in Chota Nagpur.

22. **I. muricata,** *Jacq.* Syn. C. muricatum, *Don.*

Stems muricate. L. cordate-ovate glabrous. Peduncle much swollen in fruit.

Surguja, in village jungle, *Wood*; Hazaribagh (Barwadih).

Fls. *Sept.-Nov.* Fr. *Dec.*

23. I. coccinea, *L.* and 24. I. Quamoclit, *L.* are both found more or less naturalized near stations and villages. The flowers are crimson or scarlet, sometimes white.

10. Cuscuta, L. Dodder.

1. **C. reflexa,** *Roxb.* Jansing, *K.*; Alaj-jari, *Kharw.* Algusi, *Beng.*

Slender yellowish-green or reddish thread-like branches adhering by means of haustoria. Fls. white or pinkish ¼-⅓" tubular-campanulate with short reflexed lobes, solitary or in 2- or few-flowered cymes or sub-spicate or racemose. Scales at the base of the corolla emarginate fimbriate. Ovary narrowed into a very short style with 2 lanceolate stigmas. Ovules basal on a very spongy thick placenta, erect, anatropous. Unripe fruit with black marks or warts. Seeds often only 1 or 2 (4 according to F.B.I.),

Especially common on Zizyphus. In all the districts. Duranta hedges are sometimes ruined by this parasite.

Fls. *Oct.-Dec.* Fr. *Dec.-Jany.*

2. **C. chinensis,** *Lamk.* Manbhum, on Guizotia abyssinica, *Camp.* Smaller, pale yellow. Fls. in dense racemes or cymes: Scales shortly fimbriate. Ovary and young fruit obtuse with 2 elongate styles and capitate stigmas.

Fam. 81. BORAGINACEÆ.

Trees, shrubs or more usually herbs, with alternate exstipulate simple leaves and regular flowers usually in dichotomous scorpioid cymes. *Corolla* gamopetalous often with scales in the throat, petals 4-6 imbricate or sub-valvate with the tips inflexed in bud. *St.* alternate with the petals. *Ovary* superior often lobed and style terminal or from between the lobes, 2-celled with each cell 2-ovuled or 4-celled, or 4-celled in fruit. Stigma capitate or 2-lobed or style twice bipartite. *Fruit* drupaceous or of 4 (or fewer) 1-seeded nutlets. Albumen present or not. Radicle superior.

A large number of herbs belong to this family with 4, often glochidiate, nutlets which adhere to the clothing. Cynoglossum denticulatum, *A.D.C.* especially, is a great pest.

Small trees or shrubs. Calyx shortly 4-8-lobed. Style twice 2-partite . . . . 1. *Cordia.*

Small trees. Calyx small sub-5-partite. Style 2-fid. . 2. *Ehretia.*

Shrub. Calyx 5-partite. Style undivided. Stigma 2-lobed . . . . 3. *Rhabdia.*

1. Cordia, L.

Trees or shrubs. Fls. in corymbose sometimes fascicled cymes, polygamous. Calyx tubular or campanulate with very short lobes or, sometimes (C. Myxa), lobes about as long as the tube, often unequal, accrescent in fruit. Buds often apiculate, corolla tubular or funnel-shaped with 4-8 recurved petals. St. 4-8 usually hairy at base, anthers large exserted. Ovary 4-celled. Drupe with a hard 1-4-celled stone. Albumen 0. L. often furnished with cystolith cells, which may appear as superficial discs (*old* leaves are required however for comparison).

A. Trees. L. over 3″ long.

L. oblong, ell., or obovate. Superficial discs absent or as small dots. Petiole slender usually $\frac{1}{4}$-$\frac{1}{3}$rd as long as blade . . . . 1. *Myxa.*

L. broadly ell. or ovate, not tomentose, usually repand-toothed. Discs visible superficially. Petiole stout not $\frac{1}{4}$th blade . . . . . 2. *obliqua.*

L. broadly ovate cordate, often tomentose beneath. Discs not very distinct. Calyx glabrescent below not ribbed . . . . 3. *Wallichii.*

L. broadly ovate cordate, and twigs densely white felted, sub-rugose above with discs distinct or not. Calyx tomentose, usually ribbed . . . 4. *Macleodii.*

B. Shrub. L. under 3″ long, scabrid above with white discs . . . . 5. *monoica.*

1. **C. Myxa.** *L.*, Hemrum, *K.;* Buch, *S.;* Bahnar *Kharw.*; Lahsowra, *H.;* Bohari, *Beng.*

A small tree, usually with drooping branches, with ashen twigs only hairy when young, orbicular, ell., oblong or obovate but never cordate leaves $2\frac{1}{2}$-5″ obtuse rounded or bluntly acuminate, rarely slightly sinuate; base 3-6-nerved or with 3-5 strong nerves from close to base which is cuneate or if rounded always acute on the slender petiole. Fls. in numerous terminal irregular or sub-corymbose cymes 2-4″ diam.

Common in valleys, often along streams. Fls. *March-April.* Fr. *July-Aug.*

L. usually permanently hairy in the axils of the nerves beneath otherwise glabrous, tetiary nerves not very straight, very reticulate between, with raised nervules. *Discs* often visible in old leaves as small white dots. *Calyx* saucer-shaped in fruit $\frac{1}{2}$-$\frac{3}{4}$″ diam. *Fruit* conical when young, old shining yellowish glassy with very viscous pulp 1-seeded.

The fruit is eaten.

2. **C. obliqua,** *Willd.?* Included in C. Myxa, *L.* in "Indian Trees."

A small tree with brown striate pubescent or puberulous twigs, broadly-ovate or ovate, rarely ovate-oblong, leaves 3-8″ by $5\frac{1}{2}$″ with rounded or sub-cordate base acute or sub-acuminate or blunt, always mucronate, usually sinuate or coarsely dentate; principal nerves above the base usually with 1-3 prs. below and 2-7 prs. above them. Base usually decurrent on the stout $\frac{1}{2}$-$1\frac{1}{4}$″ petiole on one side only.

Singbhum and Hazaribagh, esp. in dry nalas in the Koderma forest; Santal Parganahs (Chandna, etc.) I have unfortunately never collected the inflorescence, but the tree is quite distinct from the last and in some specimens rather resembles C. grandis. It requires further investigation.

L. not hairy in the nerve axils but puberulous between the straight prominent tertiary nerves beneath, nervules not raised or very distinct. *Discs* on old leaves usually yellowish, not distinctly raised.

3. **C. Wallichii,** *G. Don.* Syn. C. obliqua, *Willd.* var. Wallichii.

This is probably a variety of the last, but again I have never collected its inflorescence. The leaves are entire, broadly-ovate, sub-cordate, densely stellately pubescent beneath. *Petiole,* nervation, and discs as in last. According to Prain, the calyx is glabrescent beneath, villous but not ribbed upwards.

Singbhum, on the hills.

4. **C. Macleodii,** *Hook. f. & T.* Porponda, *Ho.*; Toraising, *M.*; Jugia, *S.*; Bharwar, Belwanjan, *Kharw.*

A small tree with twigs, leaves beneath and inflorescence covered with a dense felted white or tawny tomentum, broadly-ovate entire often deeply cordate obtuse or very shortly bluntly acuminate leaves about 7″ by 5½″ with venation as in *obliqua,* or nerves 3-5 quite basal. Petioles much longer 1½-3″. Discs usually numerous and in old leaves often giving the upper surface a rugose appearance.

Throughout the area, not uncommon on the hills. Fls. *March-April.* Fr. *May-June.* Evergreen or nearly so.

L. attain 10″ but usually 4-8″ appressed cottony glabrescent above. *Fls.* white in dense tomentose extra-axillary on leaf-opposed corymbs, *buds* clavate. *Calyx* in fruit broadly campanulate, ½″ diam. toothed or lobed, tomentose, usually distinctly ribbed but not always. *Petals* recurved. Young *fruit* very acuminate, ripe globose ¾″ long by ½-⅗″ diam. and yellowish somewhat tomentose, apiculate.

5. **C. monoica,** *Roxb.*

A shrub usually under 6 ft or a small gnarled tree with the flowers and new leaves fascicled on short shoots. L. hoary when young, old ell., ovate or obovate 1-3″ obtuse dentate or denticulate from the strong excurrent nerves, pubescent beneath scabrous above. Nervules strongly reticulate.

Gangpur, Hazaribagh and Palamau in dry jungles. Common on the Rhotas cliffs. Fls. *May-June.* Fr. ripens *Nov.-Dec.*

Calyx $\frac{1}{3}$-$\frac{1}{2}$" campanulate in fruit. *Berry* ovoid scarcely exceeding the calyx.

2. Ehretia, L.

1. E. lævis, *Roxb.* Pusi pan, *S.*; Bhairo, *Kharw.*; Chamror, datranga, *H.*

A small tree with white bark, or ovate glabrous broadly or narrowly ell. or elliptic oblong, rarely obovate, entire leaves usually with small tufts of hair in the axils of the nerves beneath, and small white sessile or sub-sessile flowers $\frac{5}{16}$-$\frac{3}{8}$" diam. in 2-chotomous and scorpioid pubescent corymbose cymes.

Frequent, chiefly near river beds. Throughout the area. Fls. *Feby.-March* with the old leaves, or when leafless or with the young leaves. Fr. *March-April*. Deciduous *Feby.* or *March.*

Innovations rusty pubescent or tomentose glabrescent. *L.* 4-6" by 2-3$\frac{1}{2}$" rarely 7" by 4" sometimes oblique, shining acute or acuminate with 5-6 prs. of sec. nerves. Base usually cuneate. *Petioles* $\frac{1}{2}$-1". *Inflorescence* axillary or sub-terminal 2-4" diam. *Calyx* very small pubescent, lobes longer than the tube, acute. *Petals* acuminate. *Ovary* 2-celled. Style long 2-fid. *Fr.* a sub-globose black drupe with 1-4 1-seeded, pyrenes.

The leaves are used for fodder, the fruit is eaten.

Var. *α* A form in Betlah forest (Palamau) has thinly hairy shoots, *flowers* under $\frac{1}{4}$" diam., and *calyx* 5-partite nearly to base with lanceolate sepals $\frac{1}{10}$". Fls. *June.*

3. Rhabdia, Mart.

1. R. lycioides, *Mart.* Tipa, *K.*

A shrub with very tough erect or prostrate and rooting branches, linear or oblong-oblanceolate leaves $\frac{1}{2}$-1$\frac{1}{4}$" by $\frac{3}{8}$", and small pink flowers $\frac{1}{4}$-$\frac{1}{2}$" diam. usually 2-3 at the ends of short lateral branchlets.

In river and stream beds but not very common, Singbhum, both in Saranda and on the Porahat plateau. Fls. *Oct.-Jany.* Fr. *Dec.-Feby.* Evergreen.

Twigs appressed hairy. *L.* acute and narrowed at the base into a petiole $\frac{1}{20}$" long, with very faint 2-4 sec. n. shining or almost silvery beneath. *Calyx* persistent 5-partite, sepals acuminate. *Ovary* 2-celled. *Drupe* $\frac{1}{8}''$ orange-red with 4 crustaceous 1-seeded pyrenes.

Fam. 82. VERBENACEÆ.

Trees or shrubs or more rarely herbs, often with stellate hairs and often with a characteristic fœtid or aromatic smell generally arising from small or miscroscopic peltate glands. *Branches* 4-angled or not. *L.* opposite or sometimes 3-nately whorled, simple or (in Vitex) digitately compound. *Stipules* 0. *Fls.* usually zygomorphic, never solitary. *Calyx* gamosepalous persistent sub-entire or 4-5-or (Symphorema) 4-8-toothed. *St.* usually 4 rarely 2 or more than 4 (Symphorema). *Ovary* superior 2-4-celled, 4-ovuled (but see Duranta). Style simple terminal, entire or shortly bifid. *Fr.* usually a drupe with 1-4 pyrenes, sometimes nearly dry. Albumen 0.

I. Inflorescence of lax, corymbose, or panicled cymes. Fr. a drupe with 1-4 pyrenes or a 1-4-celled stone, or of drupels, or nearly dry in Caryopteris.

A. Fls. regular. St. exserted spreading.

Panicles axillary, corymbose . . . . . 1. *Callicarpa.*
Panicles very large terminal . . . . . 2. *Tectona.*

B. Fls. irregular. St. didynamous.

L. digitate. . . . . 3. *Vitex.*
L. simple.
Trees or shrubs. Fls. very small white or greenish . . . . 4. *Premna.*
Shrubs. Fls. with a long slender corolla tube . 5. *Clerodendron.*
Shrub. Fls. blue with *short* corolla-tube. Fr. sub-capsular . . . . 6. *Caryopteris.*
Tree. Fls. over 1″ yellow, corolla tubular ventricose . . . . 7. *Gmelina.*
A woody climber with patelliform scarlet calyx . 8. *Holmskioldia.*

II. Inflorescence of capitate cymes, or contracted or elongate spikes.

Fls. in capitate spikes. Drupe succulent . . 9. *Lantana.*

Fls. as in Lantana but fruit dry . . . 10. *Lippia.*
Fls. in involucrate 3 9-flowered capitate cymes . 11. *Symphorema.*
Fls. in elongate spikes. St. 2. . . . 12. *Stachytarpheta.*
III. Fls. in pendulous racemes. Ovary 8-celled . 13. *Duranta.*

1. Callicarpa, L.

Trees or shrubs with the young parts stellately tomentose. Fls. small often glandular in axillary usually corymbose peduncled cymes. Calyx very small, 4-lobed. Corolla subregular, tubular with 4 (-5) lobes, purple or red. St. 4-5 exserted. Ovary imperfectly 2-celled. Style long, stigma capitate sub-entire or 2-lobed. Drupe small, with 1-4 free pyrenes.

1. **C. arborea,** *Roxb.* Bomud, Bodudn, *K.;* Dam Kotokoi, *S.;* Bagodi, *Kharw.;* Sakrela, *Mal Pah.*

A small or mod.-sized tree with compressed 4-angled tomentose branchlets, large ovate to ovate-lanceolate or ovate-oblong acute or sub-acuminate entire leaves, tomentose beneath (both sides when young), and small lilac-purple flowers in 2-chotomous corymbous cymes 3-5" diam. on peduncles $1\frac{1}{2}$-2" long. Drupe purple.

Valleys in Singbhum, but rare. Dhadka (Manbhum), *Wood.* Common on the northern slopes of the Parasnath range (Hazaribagh and Manbhum). Palamau, esp. on the ghats. Rajmehal hills, frequent.

Fls. *May-June.* Fr. *Aug.-Nov.*, rarely *Dec.-Jany.* Evergreen.

L. $5\frac{1}{4}$" by $2\frac{3}{4}$" to 12" by $5\frac{1}{2}$" usually about 9 by 4", rarely slightly toothed base rounded. Sec. n. 8-12 prs. with strong cross tertiaries. *Petiole* $\frac{3}{4}$-$1\frac{1}{2}$". Cor. $\frac{1}{8}$" diam. Fr. $\frac{1}{10}$-$\frac{1}{8}$" purple or black seated on the $\frac{1}{16}$"-broad calyx.

2. **C. macrophylla,** *Vahl.* Bundudn, *K.;* Buddhi ghassic', *S.;* Mathara, *Beng.*

A stout shrub with the branches leaves beneath and inflorescence densely woolly. L. large elliptic rarely ovate-lanceolate long-acuminate crenate or crenate-dentate. Fls.

rose-cold., in dense 2-chotomous cymes about 1″ long and 2″ diam. on peduncles $\frac{1}{3}$-1″ long. Drupe $\frac{1}{8}$-$\frac{3}{16}$″ diam. white.

Singbhum, Saitba forest, (Rangamati) ; Porahat plateau frequent ; Palamau, *Gamble* ! Manbhum, *Camp*. Nearly always in open jungle or waste land.

Fls. *Sept.-Nov.* Fr. *Nov.-Dec.* Evergreen.

L. 5″ by 1$\frac{3}{4}$″ to 10″ by 4$\frac{1}{2}$″, base usually rounded, upper surface more or less stellate. Sec. n. strong 10-15 prs. *Petiole* $\frac{1}{4}$-1$\frac{1}{4}$″. *Calyx* $\frac{1}{20}$″ with 4 minute teeth. *Corolla* $\frac{1}{16}$″.

Tectona grandis, *L.* The Teak, is planted at all the stations but its growth is slow and the tree does not thrive. *L.* very large, often over 1 ft. tomentose beneath. *Fls.* small white. *Fruit* with a 4-celled endocarp and spongey nearly dry pericarp $\frac{1}{2}$″ diam. enclosed in the much enlarged bladdery calyx.

Fls. *July-Aug.* Fr. *Nov.-Jany.* Renews its leaves in *May*.

3. Vitex, L.

Trees or shrubs often glandular with opp. or 3-nately whorled digitately 3-5-foliolate leaves and rather small lipped flowers in panicled or dichasial cymes. Calyx tubular-campanulate, usually enlarged in fruit, shortly toothed or truncate. Corolla 2-lipped, upper lip 2-lobed, lower 3-lobed with central lobe larger than the others. St. 4 didynamous. Ovary 2-4-celled. Stigma of 2 unequal subulate lobes. Drupe with a 1-4-celled bony putamen.

A. Shrubs or sub-arboreous (V. leucoxylon is a tree in *other* parts of India).
- Panicles mostly terminal dense. Lflts. 3-5 white tomentose below . . . . 1. *Negundo.*
- Panicles all axillary dichasial. Lflts. 3-5 under 5″ long . . . . 2. *leucoxylon.*

B. Trees. Panicles all axillary.
- Panicles dichasial. Lflts. mostly 5, attaining 8″. Petiolules over $\frac{1}{2}$″ . . . . 3. *glabrata.*
- Panicles narrow-oblong. Lflts. 3, 3-7″. Petiolules under $\frac{1}{2}$″. . . . . 4. *peduncularis.*

1. V. Negundo, *L.* Bigana, Sursing, *Ho.*; Huri, *M.*; Sindware, *S.*; Sinoar, *Kharw* ; Shivari, *H.*

A large strongly scented shrub 6-12 ft. sometimes sub-arboreous, covered with a fine hoary tomentum, with 3-5-foliolate leaves and white or lilac flowers in oblong panicles 2-8″ long.

Frequent in waste ground and hedges in all the districts. Fls. and Fr. most of the year, esp. *May-June*. Evergreen.

Lflts. lanceolate entire or crenate glabrate above 2-6″, lateral sessile or shortly petioluled, other petiolules $\frac{1}{2}$-1″. *Panicles* with short branches $\frac{1}{4}$-$\frac{3}{4}$″ long. *Fls.* $\frac{1}{4}$-$\frac{1}{3}$ greatest diam, puberulous outside, palate hairy, lobes of upper lip smaller and paler than the lateral. *Drupes* globose $\frac{1}{8}$″ diam.

It is used as a stomachic.

Var. with much smaller 3-foliolate leaves, petioluled leaflets and very dense contracted panicles of white flowers $\frac{1}{4}$″ across. Drupes 2-seeded.

Near the Sone mixed with the ordinary variety.

2. V. leucoxylon, *L. f.*

A large shrub 4-12 ft. with pubescent shoots, 3-5-foliolate nearly glabrous leaves, lanceolate leaflets, and white lipped flowers $\frac{1}{2}$″ across (greatest diameter) in divaricate peduncled cymes, often sub-sessile in the forks (but not so regularly dichasial as in V. glabrata).

Along rivers in Gangpur. Also near Pachamba in Hazaribagh. *Camp. Herb* ! (The latter a 3-foliolate variety with panicles exceeding the leaves).

Fls. *May-June.* Fr. *Oct.-Nov.* Evergreen ?

L. rarely reduced to one small leaflet. *Lflts.* entire or in very young plants serrate, 1″ by $\frac{1}{3}$″ to $4\frac{1}{2}$″ by $1\frac{1}{2}$″ acuminate coriaceous shining above pale beneath, often woolly on either side of the mid-rib beneath, otherwise glabrous. Mid-rib prominent, sec. n. scarcely raised, more distinct above, finely reticulate between. *Petiole* $1\frac{1}{2}$-3″. Petiolules $\frac{1}{2}$-1″. *Panicles* 3-6″ long peduncled with usually 2 linear bracts $\frac{1}{4}$″ long at the first fork only. *Calyx* $\frac{3}{16}$. *Cor-tube* nearly twice as long, corolla densely appressed hairy without. Mid-lobe of lower lip $\frac{1}{4}$″ villous. *Drupe* $\frac{1}{2}$-$\frac{3}{4}$″ seated on the enlarged scarcely lobed calyx.

3. V. glabrata, *R.Br.* Bhadu, *S.*

A tree, often large attaining 6 ft. girth, with thinly pubescent shoots and tomentosely-hairy buds, mostly 5-foliolate leaves sometimes resembling those of the Simal tree (V. bombacifolia was Wallich's very happy name for it) with large leaflets permanently sparsely appressed hairy beneath.

Fls. about $\frac{1}{3}''$ long with a bluish lip (Fls. purplish-blue, *Haslett*) in very regular dichasial panicles, each fork with a shortly pedicelled flower.

Rajmehal hills, usually along streams but ascending to the tops of the hills in favourable situations (*e.g.* Dhowdi, and between Narganj and Silingi). Very local.

Fls. *May-June*. Fr. *June-July*. Perhaps deciduous *March-April*.

Twigs light-grey somewhat 4-angled. *Lflts.* ell, broadly ell, or obovate $8\frac{1}{2}''$ by $2''$ to $8''$ by $4''$, usually suddenly acuminate glabrous shining above, nerve-axils glandular, base usually cuneate, sec. n. 8-14 prs. rather strong, others obscure. *Petioles* $2\frac{1}{2}$-$6''$. Petiolules $\frac{5}{8}$-$2''$. *Peduncle* 2-4″. Pedicels $\frac{1}{8}$-$\frac{1}{3}''$. Calyx $\frac{1}{8}''$ campanulate in flower, deeply saucer-shaped $\frac{1}{4}$-$\frac{1}{3}''$ diam. in fruit. *Corolla* densely grey-pubescent lobes rounded reflexed, mid-lobe of lower lip shortly quadrate then concave orbicular, throat hairy. *Drupe* oblong obovoid $\frac{1}{2}$-$\frac{3}{4}''$ long.

The timber of this tree is likly to prove useful, and it should be protected.

4. V. peduncularis, *Wall.* Simjanga, *K.*; Bhadu, *S.*

A tree sometimes attaining 5 ft. girth and 50 ft. high but usually small, with pubescent shoots and constantly 3-foliolate leaves, well distinguished when young and even sometimes in the adult (var. Roxburghiana) by the winged petiole. Panicles primarily monopodial, the shape much as in V. Negundo, 6-11″ long and exceeding the leaves.

Valleys in Singbhum and Gangpur, especially along streams, but also on northern rocky slopes; Manbhum and Hazaribagh, very common and attaining large size on the northern slopes of Parasnath; Koderma; Palamau, esp. in Ghat forests; Santal Parganahs, frequent. Fls. *May-June*. Fr. *Aug.-Sept.* Evergreen.

Lflts. narrowly ell. or lanceolate 3″ by $1\frac{1}{4}''$ to 7″ by 2″ acuminate glabrous concolorous, punctulate above. Sec. n. above 20 prs. very slender. *Petiole* $1\frac{1}{2}$-$3''$. *Petiolules* $\frac{1}{4}''$ or blade often decurrent on them. Lateral branches of panicle 1″ or less, cymose. *Calyx* $\frac{1}{8}''$ campanulate very shortly toothed with yellow glands. *Cor.* upper lip erect, mid-lobe of lower lip shovel-shaped with rounded tip. *Drupe* $\frac{1}{3}''$ diam. with a 3-4-celled stone.

Wood good for yokes. Bark applied externally to allay pain in the chest, *Camp.* All *young* plants have distinct wings.

4. Premna, L.

Trees or shrubs (P. herbacea, a herb) with opp. or ternately whorled entire, or toothed, often unequally paired, leaves with a fœtid or aromatic smell. Fls. small white or greenish, sub-regular or 2-lipped in pubescent usually corymbose cymose panicles. Calyx small 2-5-toothed or sub-entire, sometimes lipped. Corolla tubular, throat hairy, petals 4-5. St. 4 didynamous. Ovary 2-4-celled. Drupe small with a 1-4-celled, 1-4-seeded stone, seated on the usually cupular calyx.

Note.—The Chota Nagpur species of Premna require further investigation. Some flower in July, a month in which I have never been on tour. The following key is based therefore mainly on the leaves. A ? is appended to doubtful forms.

L. entire 2-6″, drying blue-black. Corymbs 2-5″ diam.	1. *latifolia.*
L. more or less serrate $2\frac{1}{2}$-8″, drying green, old nearly glabrous. Corymbs 1-$2\frac{1}{2}$″	2. *barbata.*
L. dentate ovate 6-12″, old minutely glandular and pubescent on nerves beneath	3. *sp.?*
L. entire ovate or elliptic 5-9″, old only stellate on nerves beneath. Corymbs 4-7″ diam . .	4. *bengalensis.*
L. entire ovate acuminate 4-6″, old stellately tomentose beneath. Corymbs $2\frac{1}{2}$-4″	5. *tomentosa.*
L. entire oblong to ovate 5-10″, pubescent or villous (not stellate) beneath. Corymbs 6″	6. *flavescens.*
Leaves as in flavescens but serrate	6a. Var.?
Dwarf with leaves appressed to the ground . .	7. *herbacea.*

1. P. latifolia, *Roxb.* Sande sabar, Dandra sea, *S.* Bakar, H.

A low bushy tree with trunk up to 4 ft. girth, or shrubby; with usually ovate, sometimes elliptic leaves attaining $6\frac{1}{2}$″ by $2\frac{5}{8}$″ entire acuminate, and small white flowers in terminal corymbose 3-chotomous panicles 1-5″ broad. Drupe black depressed globose $\frac{1}{4}$″ diam. Stone ridged, 4-celled, usually 1-seeded.

Gangpur, along banks of streams (tree form with usually elliptic leaves and cuneate base); Hazaribagh (Nemiaghat, Tatijheria); Manbhum, a common bush, *Camp.*; Rajmehal hills, frequent on trap (small tree or bush with leaves rounded at base but shortly cuneate on the petiole)

Fls. *April-May*, on the new shoots. Fr. *May-June.*

Shoots pubescent, often rusty. L. minutely hispidulous above when young, pubescent on the nerves beneath. Sec. n. 5-8 prs. *Petiole* $\frac{1}{4}$–$\frac{3}{4}$″. *Calyx* $\frac{1}{16}$″ in flower with 5 small sub-equal teeth, saucer-shaped $\frac{3}{16}$″-$\frac{1}{4}$″ diam. in fruit. *Cor.* $\frac{3}{16}$-$\frac{1}{4}$″ long, upper lip oblong obtuse entire, lower longer with spreading obtuse lobes.

2. P. barbata, *Wall.*

A small tree attaining 30 ft., with yellow-brown glabrous twigs (but new shoots hairy), ovate-lanceolate, ovate or obvate-oblong leaves 4-8″ by 2-4″ (or smaller at base of shoot) acuminate and usually coarsely toothed, never quite entire above. Nerves only persistently slightly hairy or puberulous beneath. Petioles $\frac{3}{4}$-$2\frac{1}{2}$″. Corymbs of small white flowers under 3″ diam. Drupe globose or pyriform, stone verrucose, 3-4-celled, 1-2-seeded.

Singbhum, in ravines. Rajmehal hills, common. Fls. *April-May.* Fr. *May-June.* Deciduous *March.*

Base of *leaves* usually rounded or obtuse with 3-5 nerves at or near the base and 4-6 prs. above, tertiary nerves not straight and parallel. *Calyx* minutely glandular lobed. *Corolla* $\frac{1}{8}$″.

3. P. nov. sp. ?

A tree sometimes attaining 3 ft. girth with large broadly-ovate opp. or 3-nate membranous acuminate dentate leaves 7-12″ by 4-8″ often with sub-cordate base, not, or only very shortly, acuminate. All nerves beneath minutely pubescent and with very minute glands between. Petioles 3-4″.

Rocky ravines in Palamau. Rajmehal hills. Especially on limestone. Fls. not seen.

Twigs same colour as in *barbata*, puberulous even when old, young tomentose and glandular. L. aromatic with small glands like those of a Clerodendron. Sec. n. 7-8 prs. very strong, two or three basal or close to base, tertiaries strong sub-parallel. *Petiole* 3-4″ straw-coloured, petioles joined by a densely villous and glandular line.

This interesting little tree might possibly be a new species, the glands and stipulary hairs and indeed the whole leaf remind one much of a Clerodendron. It was well matched with P. pinguis by Babu Janada of the Calcutta Herbarium, but its *habit* is different.

4. P. bengalensis, *Clarke.*

A small tree with large narrow-ell. to ovate acuminate leaves 5″ by 2¼″ to 9″ by 6″ closely stellately pubescent beneath when young and permanently stellate pubescent on the nerves. Panicles 6-8″ diam. of minute white 2-lipped flowers stellately pubescent. Drupe globose or obovoid.

Tundi hills, Manbhum, *Camp. Herb.*! Fls. *June-July.*

L. with 8-12 prs. strong sec. n. *Petiole* 1″. *Calyx* sub 2-lipped. Throat of *corolla* villous.

5. P. tomentosa, *Willd.*

A tree with branchlets, leaves and inflorescence densely clothed with a tawny stellate tomentum. L. ovate acuminate 2½-6″ by 2-3″ with rounded or sub-cordate base, permanently stellate tomentose beneath. Panicles compact 2-4″ diam. somewhat rounded or pyramidal with small greenish-yellow flowers. Drupe ovoid.

Rajmehal hills, *Gamble, Brandis.* I can find no specimens of it from our area either at Kew or Calcutta or in Gamble's Herb, and Brandis probably quotes Gamble (Indian Timbers).

Fls. *March-April* with the new leaves. Fr. *May.* Deciduous.

L. with about 7 prs. sec. n. *Petiole* 1-1½″. *Calyx* shortly 5-lobed. *Ovary* very hairy.

There are minute peltate glands between the hairs also in this species. Old L. in C. P. attain 10″.

6. P. flavescens, *Ham.* Aria Kasmar, *S.*

A small or mod-sized tree with grey or brown twigs, pubescent even when old, large oblong to ovate-oblong, more rarely ovate acute scarcely acuminate leaves 5″ by 2½″ to 10″ by 6″ with rounded sometimes oblique base, densely pubescent (but not stellate) esp. on the nerves beneath. Panicles 5-7″ diam. tomentose. Drupe globose ⅕″.

Singbhum in the valleys; Santal Parganahs along streams and rocky nalas in the hills; Gurhma (Lohardaga), *C. B. Clarke.*

Fls. *June-July.* Fr. *Aug.-Jany.* Evergreen? I have obtained many specimens in fruit and young bud but not in flower.

L. usually minutely hairy and pubescent on the nerves above. Sec. n. 6-8 prs. strong beneath as also are the sub-parallel tertiaries. There are glands between the hairs very similar to those of (3) and with a similar aromatic scent. *Petiole* 1¼-4½″. *Bracts* at the forks linear ⅛-¾″. *Calyx* glandular and somwhat pubescent, sub-2-lipped, lips scarcely toothed. *Stone* areolate.

Note.—A specimen of this collected by Gamble at Tatkora, Singhbhum, is placed under P. villosa in the Cal. Herbarium. *P. villosa, Clarke,* although widely separated in the Flora of British India, is very closely allied and only distinguishable by its completely truncate calyx and shorter bracts.

Var ? Almost exactly as in 6, but crenate-toothed much as in 3. From ills near Chandna, S. P. Coll. in *Jany.* without inflorescence.

7. P. herbacea, *Roxb.* Ote chamba, *K.*; Kāda met', *S.*

A curious little undershrub with herbaceous shoots 1-4" high from a woody stock. L. usually closely appressed to the ground, sessile, obovate, coarsely serrate, 2-4" sometimes 6" by 4" and repand. Fls. very small white, in small corymbs $1\frac{1}{2}$" diam. on a short peduncle. Drupe $\frac{1}{4}$" diam.

On clay in open ground, *e.g.* fire lines, etc., common. Fls. *May-June.* Fr. *June-July.*

A decoction of the root is given internally for rheumatism, *Camp.*

6. Clerodendron, L.

Trees or shrubs or sub-herbaceous with opp. or ternate, frequently palmate-nerved and gland-dotted aromatic or fœtid leaves, and usually conspicuous flowers in axillary cymes or terminal panicles. Calyx campanulate, often brilliantly coloured in fruit. Corolla tube slender with a more or less oblique 5-fid spreading limb. St. 4 exserted. Ovary imperfectly 4-celled. Drupe usually succulent, separating into 1-4 pyrenes.

L. under $2\frac{1}{2}$". Fls. white . . . . . . 1. *phlomoides.*

L. over 3" long.

L. ovate. Fls. white, or white and pink . . . 2. *infortunatum.*

L. oblong or elliptic, often ternate. Fls. blue. Cor.-tube $\frac{1}{3}$-$\frac{1}{2}$" . . . . 3. *serratum.*

L. narrowly or linear-lanc., 3-4-nate. Fls. white with tube 3-4" . . . . 4. *Siphonanthus.*

1. C. phlomoides, *L. f.* Panjot, *S.*; Urni, *H.*

A large shrub with somewhat hoary pubescent shoots puberulous ovate or sub-rhomboid crenate-serrate or sub-entire leaves about 2 by 1½", and axillary and terminal cymose panicles of white flowers ¾" diam. Odorous at night.

Usually in hedges and often introducing itself into gardens, but doubtfully indigenous. Singhbhum, Palamau, Santal Parganahs. Fls. *Sept.-Jany.*

Old *leaves* nearly glabrous, acute or sub-acuminate. *Petiole* ⅓-¾". *Cymes* 1½-3" 3-12 flowered. *Calyx* purplish ⅓-½" lobed half-way down into 5 triangular acute lobes. *Cor.-tube* 1". *Fruit* nearly dry ⅓-½", separating into 4 pyrenes.

Given to cattle for diarrhœa and worms.

2. C. infortunatum, *Gærtn.* Kula marsal, Chamgar, *Ho.*; Barni, Varni, *S.*; Gokhola, *Kharw.*; Bhant, *H.*, *Beng.*

A robust under-shrub or shrub 4-6 ft. with densely fulvous-hairy branches, large ovate usually cordate-leaves 4-8" long and broad and large terminal 3-chotomous corymbose panicles of white and pinkish flowers 1" diam. Conspicuous in fruit from its large red calyces and often reddening branches. Drupe bluish-black, at first enclosed by the calyx which however opens widely when it is ripe.

In all the districts, along streams and in shady places and edges of glades. Often gregarious. Fls. *Feby.-May.* Fr. *May-July.*

L. persistently hairy, entire or dentate with very strong sec. and tertiary nerves. Minute glands numerous. *Panicle* tomentosely-hairy, often leafy. *Calyx* lobes ½-1" long in fruit. *Cor.-tube* ⅔-¾" long. Lobes 1 posterior and 4 obliquely spreading. *Stamens* 1½-2" long.

3. C. serratum, *Spreng.* Saram lutur, *S.*; Barangi, *H.*

A shrub, usually with tall annual branches 3-6 ft. high from a woody stock, with opp. or 3-nate sub-sessile ell., obovate or oblanceolate leaves 3-6" by 1-2" and sub-pyramidal terminal panicles of blue flowers 1" or more across. Drupe of 1-3 succulent usually green pyrenes.

Singbhum, valleys and shady slopes, not common. Tundi hills common, *Camp.*; Palamau, *Gamble*! Fls. *April Nov.* Fruiting shortly after flowering. The stems do not always die down, and it is then an irregularly branched shrub with smaller fleshy leaves.

L. glabrous, coarsely serrate above. Petioles $\frac{1}{3}''$. *Panicle-branches* and pedicels shortly hairy with persistent ovate bracts. *Calyx* $\frac{1}{5}''$ very shortly lobed. *Corolla* with an anterior blue-oblong petal $\frac{3}{4}''$ long with a large nectary at base, other lobes obliquely spreading. Tube $\frac{1}{3}$-$\frac{1}{2}$.'' *St.* bluish very declinate.

Root given in fever, also used in the fermentation of rice-beer, *Camp.*

4. **C. Siphonanthus,** *Br.* Barangi, *H.*; Bananhati, *Beng.*

A shrub, or herbaceous with tall annual hollow stems 3-6 ft. high, with 3-5-nately whorled rarely opp. sessile or sub-sessile narrowly-lanceolate entire or sinuate glabrous leaves 5-8'' by $\frac{1}{2}$-$1\frac{1}{3}''$, and pretty white or cream-coloured flowers in axillary cymes forming a large terminal panicle. Drupe blue on the large red calyx.

Along river banks and in moist localities, Singbhum, Ranchi, Palamau, and probably in all districts. Fls. *June-Aug.* Fr. *Aug.-Nov.*

6. Caryopteris, Bunge.

1. **C. Wallichiana,** *Schauer.*

A laxly branched shrub with 4-angled sub-tomentose shoots, and lanceolate sub-entire or serrate leaves 2-4'' long. Easily recognized by the numerous yellow glands, and the spreading blue or light purple flowers in small cymes which are arranged in narrow axillary and terminal thyrses, somewhat as in Clerodendron serratum.

Santal Parganahs, *Gamble* (in Sonthal Parganahs list). The only record. Fls. *Dec.*

Peti. short. *Calyx* deeply 5-6-fid. *Ovary* 1-celled above. Placentæ 2 with incurved margins, ovules pendulous from a thickened funicle. *Fruit* dividing into 4 valves with incurved margins, embracing the 1-seeded slightly winged pyrenes.

7. Gmelina, L.

1. **G. arborea,** *L.* Kasmar, *K. S.*; Gambhar, Gamhar, *H.*

A mod.-sized or large tree with broadly ovate acuminate usually cordate leaves 4-9'' by $2\frac{1}{2}$-8'' usually glaucous beneath, petioles 2-6'' long, and large reddish or brown and yellow irregular flowers 1-1⅓″ long in lateral or terminal panicles. Fruit a succulent drupe 1″ diam. with a usually 2-celled stone.

Throughout the area, esp. on the cool sides of hills. Fls. *Feby.-April* when more or less leafless. Fr. *May-June.*

L. in the type stellately-hairy beneath, base 3-5-nerved and usually cuneate on the petiole, some or all with glands at the base between the primary nerves. Sec. n. 4-6 prs. above the basal, tertiaries more or less parallel. *Panicles* 3-4″ (or attaining 12″ fide *F.B.I.*). *Bracts* ¼-⅓″ linear-lanceolate. *Calyx* ⅛-¼″ campanulate with small teeth. *Corolla* tubular below, ventricose; anterior lobe shovel-shaped yellow.

The seedlings have oblong fleshy cotyledons, and the first leaves are strongly toothed. The wood is largely used for making drums, it is white, easily worked and does not warp or shrink. Cattle and deer are very fond of the fruit.

Var. α. glaucescens, *F.B.I. L.* large 6-10″ glabrous and *glaucous* beneath the glaucous appearance being due to dense microscopic glands or scales (these however are present also in the pubescent forms). *Tertiary nerves* not much raised or only slightly raised. *Panicle* usually large. *Commoner than the type.* In all districts.

Var. β. canescens. *L.* 3-6″ sub-coriaceous, grey-pubescent beneath with simple not stellate hairs. *Tertiary-nerves* strongly raised beneath. *Panicle* 3-4″ strict. Santal Parganahs.

8. Holmskioldia, Retz.

1. H. sanguinea, *Retz*, Jhimbria, *S.*

A large climbing shrub with angular drooping branches, ovate crenate-serrate or sub-entire leaves 2-6″ by 1¼-3½″ very handsome in flower. Fls. with a scarlet tubular curved corolla ¾-1″ long and an orange or scarlet patelliform calyx 1″ diam. which is persistent in fruit, arranged in short racemes ½-1″ long from the leaf axils and running out into terminal panicles.

Rocky ravines in Bandgaon and Porahat; Pitorea East hill (Ranchi), *Wood*; Manbhum; *Camp.*; Tatkora, 2,500 ft, *Gamble*; Chorparan ghats (Hazaribagh); Parasnath, *Camp.* Fls. *Nov.-Jany.*

L. slightly pubescent acuminate with 4-5 prs. oblique sec. n. *Petiole* ¼-2″. *Drupe* obovoid ¼-⅓″, with 4 spreading lobes.

9. Lantana, L.

Rambling pubescent scabrous or prickly shrubs with 4-angled branches, crenate, often rugose leaves, and small flowers in peduncled, often capitate spikes. Bracts exceeding the membranous truncate or sinuate-toothed calyx. St. 4 didynamous included. Ovary 2-celled. Drupe with 2 1-celled pyrenes.

1. L. indica, *Roxb.*

A shrub with adpressed scabrid-pubescent stems and branches, cordate serrate rugose leaves 3-4" by 2-3" and light-purple scentless flowers in numerous axillary ovate heads.

Chota Nagpur, *Wood's list.*

Fls. and Fr. chiefly in the rains.

2. L. aculeata, *L.* Syn. L. Camara, *L.*

A straggling or scandent shrub with small recurved prickles on the branches. L. much as in last or smaller. Fls. orange coloured with pink tube, strongly scented.

An American shrub widely spread in some parts of India, occasionally semi-naturalized in Chota Nagpur (*e. g.* about Chorparan).

Fls. and Fr. principally in the rainy season.

It makes an excellent hedge if continually cut back, and grows freely from cuttings.

Lippia geminata, *H.B.* and *K.*, occurs in Wood's list without remark or locality. It is an erect shrub "so closely resembling Lantana indica that without fruit it is difficult to distinguish," *C. B. Clarke.* Branches and L. softly strigose. *L.* ovate-oblong crenate. *Peduncles* mostly opposite, bracts ovate acuminate, softly hairy.

11. Symphorema, Roxb.

1. S. polyandrum, *Wight.*

A large sub-scandent shrub with ovate villous coarsely toothed leaves usually 4-5" long reaching 8-9" by 4". Easily recognized in flower by its whorls of grey involucral leaves surrounding a 7-flowered cyme of white flowers with a 12-16-partite corolla and an equal number of exserted stamens.

Dry Sal forests in Singhbhum. Fls. *April*. Deciduous at the time of flowering.

Petiole $\frac{1}{2}$-$\frac{3}{4}$". *Bracts* obovate 1-1$\frac{1}{4}$" long foliaceous, toothed above. *Corolla* $\frac{1}{2}$" long. *Fr.* included in the calyx, nearly dry, 1-seeded.

2. S. **involucratum**, *Roxb.*, which is found in the Monghyr hills, may very likely occur in the Rajmehal hills. It may be distinguished by its smaller size and the corolla only $\frac{1}{4}$" long and 6-8 lobed.

Stachytarpheta indica, *Vahl.* (Syn. S. jamaicensis), is a herb 1-2$\frac{1}{2}$ ft. high with spikes of blue flowers sunk in the rachis, a pestiferous weed in many gardens which have been under the plough.

Fls. *r. s.*

One or two other species of Stachytarpheta are garden shrubs with red or purple flowers.

Duranta is an American genus with an 8-celled ovary, and the drupe with 4 2-celled pyrenes. D. **Plumieri**, *Jacq.*, with panicles of pretty small blue flowers, and yellow drupes is frequently cultivated in hedges. D. Ellisii has white flowers.

Fam. 83. LABIATÆ.

Herbs, more rarely shrubs or undershrubs, usually *very aromatic* with oil glands. *Stems* often 4-angled. *L.* opposite, sometimes whorled. *Stipules* 0. *Fls.* sub-regular and 4-5-merous, or *usually* irregular and 2-lipped usually in contracted axillary cymes or whorled, more rarely solitary or few, cymes or whorls sometimes forming spikes and panicles from the reduction of the leaves or bracts. *Calyx* persistent, teeth 4-5 or 10, sometimes 2-lipped. *Corolla* tubular below. *St.* 4 or 2 more or less suppressed. *Disc* prominent. *Ovary* superior of 2 2-ovuled carpels, usually deeply 4-lobed, and each carpel ultimately dividing into 2 dry 1-seeded lobes (nutlets).

A. Fls. sub-regular, with flat corolla lobes, stamens straight diverging or ascending. Anther cells short, 1-celled.

Fls. in panicled sub-capitate cymes. Filaments bearded 1. *Pogostemon.*
Whorls in dense panicled spikes. Fls. minute, white 2. *Colebrookia.*

B. Fls. distinctly 2-lipped. Stamens declinate.

Whorls 6-3-fld. panicled. Lower cor. lip long boat-shaped . . . . 3. *Plectranthus.*
Fls. in dense oblong spikes. Lower cor. lip long concave . . . . 4. *Anisochilus.*
Cymes axillary and panicled. Lower cor. lip 3-lobed, mid-lobe saccate . . . . 5. *Hyptis.*

C. Fls. distinctly 2-lipped. St. 4 didynamous ascending under the erect, often hooded, upper lip of the corolla

Upper cor. lip nearly flat. St. exserted . . . 6. *Anisomeles.*
Upper cor. lip hooded, villous.
Fls. white. Bracts not spinescent . . . . 7. *Leucas.*
Fls. scarlet. Bracts spinescent . . . . 8. *Leonotis.*

1. Pogostemon, Desf.

1. P. plectranthoides, *Desf.* Jin, *Beng.*

An undershrub sometimes attaining 6 ft. high with large ovate acute coarsely crenate leaves and small white flowers conspicuous from the light-purple bearded stamens. Fls. in dense sub-capitate 1-sided bracteate cymes which are secund on the branches of a large panicle.

In damp localities, somewhat local. It sometime forms dense thickets, as in the Karampoda forest in Singbhum. Along rivers in Santal Parganahs. It also occurs in the hills. Fls. *Jany.-Feby.*

Stem with 4 rounded corners, glabrous or hairy. *L.* about $4\frac{1}{2}''$ by $3\frac{1}{2}''$, very sparsely hairy above and with a short mealy pubescence and minutely glandular beneath, but never hoary (as usually described). Sec. n. 4-6 prs. very oblique, strong. Crenatures serrate. *Cymes* sub-globose about $\frac{1}{2}''$ long with narrow-oblong white-villous bracts, on a raceme with elliptic obovate or rhomboid decussate bracts. *Calyx* tubular $\frac{1}{7}$-$\frac{1}{6}''$ glandular and hairy with 5 equal acuminate teeth. Upper lip of *corolla* with 3 rounded lobes, lower entire lanceolate acute, *St.* 4 declinate villous at base and with pink jointed villi in the middle. Style 2-fid.

The odour is strong, but chiefly from the inflorescence.

2. Colebrookia, Smith.

1. C. oppositifolia, *Sm*. Bhaiñsa, *S*.

A large spreading soft shrub 5-10 ft., with stout whitish branchlets, large white tomentose crenate leaves and very small white flowers densely whorled in panicled spikes. The calyx teeth elongate and become plumose in fruit.

Valleys; Singbhum; Ranchi (Pitorea), *Wood*; Hazaribagh (on Parasnath, and valleys in Koderma); Valleys in Santal Parganahs. Fls. *Dec.-Feby*. Fr. *Feby.-March*.

L. sometimes 3-nate, 4-8″ elliptic or elliptic-oblong acuminate with about 12 prs. oblique sec. n. *Petiole* ¼-1¼″. *Spikes* 2-4″. *Corolla* minute 4-lobed. *Nutlets* hairy.

A preparation of the root is given in epilepsy, *Camp*.

3. Plectranthus, L'Herit.

Herbs or shrubs. Fls. in 6-8-fld. racemed or panicled cymes. Calyx lobes 5 sub-equal or 2-lipped, Corolla 2-lipped, tube exserted from the calyx often decurved, upper lip usually short broad 2-4-fid recurved, lower much longer entire boat-shaped, narrow at the base. St. 4 declinate.

Fls. white densely crowded. Calyx equally 5-toothed . 1. *ternifolius*.
Fls. reddish lax. Calyx 2 lipped . . . . . . 2. *incanus*.

1. P. ternifolius, *Don*.

A shrub 3-5-ft. densely white tomentose all over. with strict erect branches, opposite, or usually 3-nately whorled shortly-petioled lanceolate acuminate serrate rugose leaves 3-7″ long and sub-sessile white flowers in dense cymes crowded in panicled racemes.

Parasnath in Hazaribagh, Fls. *Nov.-Jany*.

Corolla very short villous, tube inflated and lips very short. Upper lip 2-fid. with pink spots at the base.

2. P. incanus, *Link*.

An erect coarse herb or undershrub 3-4 ft. with square stems, long-petioled velvety ovate cordate crenate leaves with a strong smell, and terminal racemose panicles of small pale lilac lipped flowers ⅓" long, arranged mostly in opposite pairs in the axil of a small foliaceous bract.

Waste ground near villages in Singbhum. Common near Muhru, Ranchi. Sirguja, among dry rocks, *Wood*. Fls. *Sept.-Oct.*

Whole plant softly shortly pubescent. *L.* 2" by 1¾" to 4" by 4" acute glandular punctate beneath. *Petioles* up to 3-4". *Calyx* ⅛" enlarged in fruit with an upper broad ovate lobe, and lower 4-subulate-toothed lip. *Corolla-tube* slightly exsert. *Pedicels* ⅓-½".

Anisochilus carnosus, *Wall*. Gitil ran, *S.*, is a herb 1-3 ft. high with very stout stems below. Branches 4-angled villous. Lower leaves 4½" by 3¼", long petioled ovate crenate rather fleshy. Spikes 1-1½" 4-gonous in bud from the 4-ranked deciduous bracts, inflorescence with red glands. Corolla purple. Common on rocks Singbhum, Palamau, especially on *limestone*.

5. Hyptis, Jacq.

1. H. suaveolens, *Poit*. Ganga tulsi, *S.*

A tall coarse strong-smelling herb 4-5 ft. with patently hairy obtusely 4-angled stems often ½" diam., large ovate sinnate and crenate-denticulate leaves and small blue-lipped flowers in axillary stalked cymes running out into terminal panicles.

Waste ground. A native of America but quite naturalized and frequent throughout Chota Nagpur and the Santal Parganahs. Fls. *Oct.-Nov.* Fr. *Dec.-Jany.*

Glandular. Lower *leaves* 4½" by 3½" slightly cordate. *Calyx-tube* ¼" in fruit, 10-nerved with 5 sub-equal sub-spinose teeth, tube with a hirsute margin inflexed in fruit, hairy and very glandular outside. *Corolla* nearly ¼", upper lip shortly 2-lobed, lower 3-lobed, mid-lobe folded at base and saccate at apex. *Nutlets* compressed oblong-emarginate ribbed, pointed below ⅛" long.

The plant, pounded, is applied in parasitical cutaneous diseases, *Campbell*.

6. Anisomeles, R. Br.

1. A. ovata, *R.Br.*

A coarse strong-smelling softly pubescent herb 3-6 ft. high with ovate coarsely crenate acuminate leaves and purplish flowers in axillary dense flowered whorls and terminal spikes.

Waste ground, frequent. Ranchi plateau; S. P., common. Fls. *Sept.-Nov.* Fr. *Dec.-Jany.*

Calyx $\frac{1}{3}''$ hirsute within and without, with sub-equal acuminate teeth. *Corolla* upper lip pale or greenish nearly flat entire, lower purple spreading 3-lobed, mid-lobe longest vertically compressed notched. St. exserted *upper* pair slightly longer with 1-celled anthers, lower 2-celled. *Filament* purple bearded. *Nutlets* $\frac{1}{20}$-$\frac{1}{18}''$ black polished.

7. Leucas, R. Br.

Herbs or undershrubs, usually tomentose or villous with white flowers in axillary, more rarely terminal, whorls. Calyx 10-nerved, 6-10-toothed, mouth sometimes oblique. Cor.-tube included. Upper lip erect hooded villous, lower spreading 3-fid. with very large mid-lobe. Anthers conniving, cells divaricate, at length confluent. Style simple.

1. L. mollissima, *Wall* Gitil a:, *Ho.*; Gitil arak', *S.*

An undershrub or he with many annual branches 8"-2 ft. long from a perennial rootstock, with hairy or pubescent or almost tomentose short petioled ovate or oblong crenate-serrate leaves about 2" by 1" and white flowers $\frac{1}{2}''$ long in axillary 6-14-fld. whorls.

Very common in rocky jungles, also in waste ground. Fls. *Sept.-Dec.* Fr. *Nov.-Dec.*

Branches occasionally 4 ft. among undergrowth, 4-angled with reflexed appressed hairs. L. attaining $2\frac{1}{2}''$ by $1\frac{1}{3}''$, smaller upwards, acute or obtuse. *Petiole* $\frac{1}{8}$-$\frac{1}{3}''$. *Calyx-tube* $\frac{1}{4}$ $\frac{1}{3}''$ cylindric 10-ribbed, teeth 10 very short, hispid (var. scaberula) or woolly. *Cor.* upper lip small, lower with two small recurved side lobes and a broad spreading rounded mid-lobe.

The leaves are eaten as a pot-herb.

There are some 9 other species of Leucas in Chota Nagpur, mostly field weeds. Among these **L. Cephalotes,** *Spreng.* Andia durap arak', *S.*, is conspicuous from its large sub-globose terminal whorl with many large awned bracts. "The seeds of this yield a medicinal oil," *Campbell*, and the leaves are eaten as a pot-herb. Fls. *Dec.-Jany.*

Leonotis nepetæfolia, *R. Br.* Dare dhompo, janum dhompo, *S.*, is a tall herb 4-7 ft. high usually occurring near villages, sometimes also in rocky waste ground, with large ovate crenate leaves and scarlet flowers in dense globose axillary whorls with spinescent bracts and spinescent calyx teeth. Fls. *Oct.-Jany.*

"The ash produced by burning the flower-buds is applied to burns and scalds," *Camp.*

Fam. 84. RUBIACEÆ.

Trees, shrubs, or herbs of various habit with *opposite* simple entire leaves with *interpetiolar* stipules, more rarely whorled or with intrapetiolar stipules. (Stipules sometimes inconspicuous, esp. in fascicled leaves, or absent and replaced by leaves in Tribe Stellatæ.) *Calyx* superior, sepals usually 4-5 sometimes minute or 0. *Corolla* gamopetalous, petals usually 4-5. *St.* isomerous, on the corolla tube; anthers usually dorsifixed with lateral or introrse dehiscence. *Disc* epigynous. *Ovary* inferior 2- sometimes 5-10-celled, style simple; *ovules* either 1 or numerous in each cell, rarely 2 or few, on axile placentæ. *Fruit* various, 2-10-celled or of 2-more pyrenes. Albumen fleshy or horny.

A. Ovules numerous in each cell.

I. Fls. small in dense globose heads. Corolla funnel-shaped (Tribe Naucleæ.)

a. Bracteoles 0. Stipules and buds lanceolate.

Sepals 5. Peduncles solitary . . . 1. *Anthocephalus.*

b. Bracteoles between the flowers narrow.

Stipules connate by their edges over the broad bud.

Sepals subulate. Peduncles terminal solitary or panicled . . . . 2. *Nauclea.*

Sepals linear. Peduncles axillary mostly 3-nate . . . . 3. *Adina.*

Sepals 0. Peduncles 1-3-nate . . . 4. *Stephegyne.* (*Mitragyna*).

II. Fls. not in dense globose heads.

a. Fr. capsular 2-celled, or of 2-4 dehiscent or indehiscent cocci. Seeds small.

Fls. in drooping thyrsoid panicles. Tree . 5. *Hymenodictyon.*

Fls. in erect panicles, small, white. Small trees . 6. *Wendlandia.*

Fls. in close or capitate cymes. Herbs . 7. *Hedyotis.*

b. Fr. indehiscent, a berry or drupe, sometimes dry.

1. Petals valvate in bud. Fls. yellow, corymbose . . . . 8. *Mussaenda.*

2. Petals twisted in bud. (Tribe Gardenieæ) Stigma fusiform. Ovary 2-4-celled. Seeds many in each cell . . . . . . 9. *Randia.*

Stigma fusiform. Ovary 1-celled. Seeds many 10. *Gardenia.*

Style-branches 2 linear. Seeds few . . 11. *Hyptianthera.*

B. Ovule solitary in each cell.

I. Corolla lobes twisted in bud. Fr. a 2-4-celled berry or drupe, or with 2-4 pyrenes. (Tribe Ixoreæ.)

a. Fls. corymbose or panicled.

Style not twice as long as the corolla-tube . 12. *Ixora.*

Style twice as long as the corolla . . . 13. *Pavetta.*

b. Fls. axillary fascicled or solitary . . . 14. *Coffea.*

II. Corolla lobes valvate in bud.

a. Erect trees or shrubs.

1. Fls. small green or white, axillary, fascicled.

Ovary 2-celled. Stigma large mitriform. Fr. small black . . . . . . 15. *Canthium.*

Ovary 3-5-celled. Stigmas connate into a globose head. Fr. large green . . . 16. *Vangueria.*

Ovary 4-9-celled. Stigmas 4-9 short obtuse. Fr. small blue . . . . . . 17. *Lasianthus.*

2. Fls. m.-s. in dense globose heads . . 18. *Morinda.*

3. Fls. in terminal 3-chotomous panicled cymes . . . . 19. *Hamiltonia.*

b. Climbing fœtid shrub with small white fls . . 20. *Pæderia.*

c. Herbaceous or sub-herbaceous.

Tall herb . . . . 21. *Knoxia.*

Scrambling herb, with leaves in whorls (Tribe Galieæ) . . . . 22. *Rubia.*

1. Anthocephalus, A. Rich.

1. A. Cadamba, *Miq.* Sanko, *K.* Kadam, *S.*, *H.*

A large and (in the forest) very straight tree with spreading sub-whorled branches and large ell.-oblong or ovate, sometimes cordate leaves 5-10″ long, small orange coloured flowers in dense heads with prominent styles and stigmas becoming in fruit a fleshy orange globose pseudocarp 2-2½″ diam.

Valleys in Singbhum, chiefly on the Porahat plateau. Planted in Ranchi and elsewhere. Fls. *May-July*. Fr. *Aug.-Oct.* Evergreen.

L. shining above with usually sub-cordate base, or where base acute leaf widest below the middle, sec. n. 8-15 prs. usually 12. *Stipules* narrow, lanceolate ½-⅗″ long. *Sep.* 5. $\frac{1}{10}$-⅛″ linear-oblanceolate.. *Cor.* ⅓″. Anths. apiculate. *Fls.* without bracteoles. *Ovary* 4-celled above, 2-celled below, placentæ twice bifid. Each *fruit* consists of 4 horny cocci above, which are separable from the fragile lower part and contain most of the *numerous* angular punctulate seeds (seeds few, fide *F.B.I.* but I have counted over 50 from one fruit).

Pseudocarp is eaten.

2. Nauclea, L.

1. N. purpurea, *Roxb.*

A small tree with pale glabrous twigs and large oblong stipules ½-⅝″ long enclosing the terminal bud as in Adina. L. 5″ by 2½″ to 10″ by 4¾″ elliptic ell.-lanceolate or ell.-oblanceolate acute or sub-acute, quite glabrous, shining above, base narrowed into the petiole. Sec. n. prominent beneath with glandular pits in the axils of some, other nerves obscure. Petioles ¾-1¾″, rather slender.

Ravines in the Santal Parganahs, very rare.

Fls. not seen in the Santal Parganahs tree, hence there must, for the present, be some doubt of the identification. N. purpurea has not hitherto been recorded north of the Circars. The *stipules* at once distinguish it from Anthocephalus. *Glandular-pits* in the nerve axils are very rare and obscure in Sarcocephalus, absent in Anthocephalus and Cephalanthus, but frequent in Adina, Stephegyne and Nauclea.

The floral characters of N. purpurea, *Roxb.* are as follows :—

Heads 1½″ diam. terminal 1-3 together on peduncles 2-3″ long which are bracteate near the middle, the *receptacle* with conical bristle-like bracteoles between the flowers. *Calyx* silky 5-lobed. *Corolla* tubular-funnel-shaped glabrous with short *imbricate* lobes. *Fruit* of 2 dehiscent many-seeded cocci. *Testa* winged.

3. Adina, Salisb.

1. **A. cordifolia**, *Hook.* f. Kumba, *Ho.*; Kurumba, *M.* Karam, *S.*, *H.*

A large tree with broadly ovate or orbicular cordate leaves 4-8″ long and broad and sub-orbicular stipules enclosing the terminal bud. Heads long peduncled usually in a vertical axillary row of three. Capsules of 2 cocci dehiscent from below and towards a persistent columella.

Fairly common in all districts and attains 7-8 ft. girth with a straight clean trunk in some of the Singbhum forests, especially on the tops of some of the more sheltered hills.

Fls. *June-July*. Fr. *Feby.-May*. Dec. *Feby.-May*.

L. pubescent beneath with 5-8 sec. *n.*, usually shortly abruptly acuminate. *Petioles* 2-3″. *Peduncle* with 2 small bracts. *Heads* ¾-1″ diam. Bracteoles filiform slightly clavate. *Receptacle* hairy ¼-¾″ in fr. *Corolla-tube* ¼″ pubescent. Stigma sub-globose.

A fair timber, but planks are apt to split badly on drying.

4. Mitragyna, Korth (Stephegyne, Korth).

1. **M. parvifolia**, *Korth*; S. parvifolia, *Korth*; Sandekumba, *Ho.*; Guni, *M.*, *Kheria*; Guri, *Kharw.*, *H.*; Gore, *S.*

A mod.-sized tree with silver-grey twigs, broadly ell. obtuse leaves 4-6″ by 3-4″ and oblong keeled stipules covering the buds, deciduous. Heads of fls. 1″ diam. 2-3-together or solitary, each with 2 pale-coloured leaves (bracts) near the top of the peduncle. Capsules of 2 dehiscent cocci, as in Adina.

Frequent in all districts, chiefly in the villages. Fls. *May-June*. Fr following *March and April*, but ripe seed also collected in *Nov*. Deciduous *May*.

L. glabrous except near the axils of the 7-10 prominent nerves, base rounded. *Petioles* ½-1″. *Fls.* surrounded by palæaceous bracteoles. *Heads* ¾″ diam. in fruit.

It is sometimes pollarded for fodder.

5. Hymenodictyon, Wall.

1. **H. excelsum,** *Wall.* Borkunda, *K.*; Bhorkond, *S.*, *Kharw.*; Bhurkul, *H.*; Bharwar, *Gond.*

A large or mod.-sized tree with leaves at the ends of the branches ovate to very broadly elliptic 4-10″ by 3-6″. Fls. greenish, crowded in dense sub-erect or drooping tomentose panicles 3-6″ long, which are subtended by a pair of spreading long petioled leaf-like bracts. Capsules ⅔-¾″ long ovoid or ellipsoid loculicidal.

Common usually in dry rocky situations, but also in valleys. In all districts. Fls. *Aug.* Fr. ripens *Jany.*? It is leafless from *Nov.* to *May* when it may be easily recognized by its large pyramidal persistent panicles of small dry reflexed capsules and by the dry persistent pair of foliaceous bracts.

L. softly pubescent, abruptly acuminate, base acute, sec. *n.* 7-10 prs. *Stipules* deciduous. *Petiole* 1-4″. *Calyx-tube* with sepals $\frac{1}{16}$″. *Corolla* ¼″ with a very slender tube and small campanulate limb. *Ovary* 2-celled. Style slender exserted.

"The inner bark and root are given in fever of the tertian type," *Campbell.*

6. Wendlandia, Bartl.

Small trees or shrubs. Fls. small white in terminal dense panicles, 2-3-bracteolate. Sepals 4-5, small persistent. Corolla with long or short tube and 4-5 lobes imbricate in bud. Ovary 2-celled. Ovules on small globose axile placentæ. Capsule small globose 2-valved with minute compressed seeds.

1. **W. exserta,** *D.C.* Tilai, *K.*; Hundru, *S.* (The Kols and Santals reverse the names of these trees); Tirawa, *Mal Pah.*

A handsome small tree, hoary-pubescent or tomentose all over, with oblong- or ovate-lanceolate acuminate leaves, persistent recurved stipules, and panicles of very fragrant small white flowers.

Common, esp. in second-growth forest and on broken ground. Light demanding. Fls. *March-April.* Fr. *April-May.* Evergreen.

L. 4-8″ by 1-2½″ with 12-16 prs. of prominent sec. nerves. *Corolla-lobes* longer than the tube. *Capsules* hoary pubescent $\frac{1}{16}$″ diam.

2. **W. tinctoria,** *D.C.* Hundru, Undru, *K.*; Tilai, *S.*

A small tree or shrub, much branched, with nearly glabrous ell., oblong or obovate leaves 4-8″ by 2-3½″ acute, narrowed into the petiole. Stipules ½″ erect orbicular with laterally flattened acumen. Corolla $\frac{1}{5}$-¼″ long, lobes much shorter than the tube.

Very common in Sal forests. Shade-bearing. Fls. *Jany.-March.* Fr. *March-April.* Evergreen.

L. shining above, pubescent on the 8-12 prs. of sec. nerves beneath. *Petiole* ½-¾″. *Panicles* 6-8″. The flowers open before the corolla-tube lengthens. *Capsules* somewhat pubescent, brown, rather larger than in the last.

7. Hedyotis, L.

1. **H. vestita,** *Br.*

Diffuse herb 1-3 ft. from a slender twisted nodose tuberose rootstock with pubescent or sub-villous branches, elliptic soft pubescent leaves 2-3″ by ⅝-1″ and small flowers in axillary 3-5-nate cymes.

Sal forest, Latua block, etc., in the valleys. Fls. *Oct.-Nov.* Fr. *Dec.*

Petiole ⅛″. *Stipules* connate below with 1-3 excurrent setæ ⅛-¼″ long. *Cymes* ¼-½″. *Calyx-tube* globose. *Sepals* 4, $\frac{1}{16}$″. *Fr.* indehiscent.

H. hispida and **H. pinifolia** are small annual species common in Sal forest and open ground, but of very different habit.

8. Mussænda, L.

1. **M. incana,** *Wall.*

An undershrub 1-3 ft. densely clothed with appressed hairs, with ell. ovate or oblong hairy leaves 4½″ by 2½″ and sub-sessile corymbose cymes of chrome-yellow flowers, remarkable from one of the sepals being large foliaceous and cream coloured. Berry $\frac{1}{3}''$ diam., with adpressed hairs. Seeds minute.

Forests on the Porahat plateau, rare. Fls. *July-Aug.* Fr. *Sept.-Oct.*

L. pale beneath, acute or sub-acute, nearly sessile, base acute or rounded, nerves strong 9-10 prs.

M. macrophylla, *Wall.*, a considerable shrub, also conspicuous by its large white calyx leaves, is cultivated in gardens in Ranchi (fide *Wood.*) The species usually cultivated in the plains is **M. Roxburghii**, *Hook. f.*, which may be distinguished from M. macrophylla by its persistent sepals, those of M. macrophylla are deciduous in fruit.

9. Randia, L.

Small trees or shrubs, often armed with strong axillary thorns. L. often fascicled on short branchlets. Fls. large or m.-s. solitary or fascicled or in axillary or leaf-opposed cymes, white turning yellow. Often dimorphic. Anthers sub-sessile, linear or oblong. Ovary 2-rarely 3-4-celled. Stigma usually large, fusiform. Fruit a 2-celled many-seeded berry.

Calyx-lobes linear, L. ovate. Berry small, black . . 1. *fasciculata*.
Calyx-lobes ovate to obovate. L. obovate. Berry $\frac{3}{4}$-$1\frac{1}{2}''$. 2. *dumetorum*.
Calyx-lobes short sub-orbicular. L. obovate to oblong. Berry 2" . . . . 3. *uliginosa*.

1. R. fasciculata, *D.C.*

A shrub or small spreading tree with ovate or elliptic acuminate leaves 1-3", straight slender axillary thorns, white flowers $\frac{2}{3}$-$1\frac{1}{2}''$ diam. with a slender corolla-tube $\frac{1}{2}$-$1\frac{1}{4}''$ long, and small purple-black berries $\frac{1}{4}''$, slightly contracted upwards with a prominent disc.

Valleys in Singbhum. Fls. *April-May*. Fr. ripens following *Jany.-Feby.*

Twigs pubescent. *L.* nearly glabrous exc. mid-rib beneath, sec. n. 3-4 prs. *Petiole* $\frac{1}{4}''$. *Stipules* linear caducous. *Fls.* 1-few together axillary. *Calyx* hirsute.

R. tetrasperma, *Benth. & Hook. f.* Kota, *K.*, mentioned in Manson's list as occurring in Lohardugga, is probably R. fasciculata.

2. R. **dumetorum,** *Lamk.* Potu, *Ho*; Potab, *K.*; Portoho, *M.*; Loto, Boi bindi, *S.*; Mowan, *Kharw.*; Saro, *Mal Pah.*

A small tree or shrub with oblanceolate to obovate obtuse or shortly acuminate leaves, fascicled on the old branches and especially in young plants, armed with straight axillary thorns. Fls. white, $\frac{1}{2}$-$1\frac{1}{4}''$ diam. turning yellow, with a short campanulate corolla-tube $\frac{1}{4}$-$\frac{3}{8}''$ and ultimately reflexed obovate or oblanceolate lobes.

Common esp. in the valley forests. Fls. *April-June.* Fr. *Aug.-Jany.* Dec. *March-April.*

L. 1-3″ or sometimes up to 5″ by 2″ (including the petiole) glabrous or pubescent, narrowed into the short petiole. *Fls.* solitary terminal on new shoots or (in one variety in Singbhum) in 3-4-fld. sessile cymes, subsessile or with pedicels $\frac{1}{2}''$. Fr. yellow when ripe globose or ovoid $1\frac{1}{4}''$ diam. crowned by the calyx-tube.

The fruit is used to intoxicate fish. It is also occasionally eaten according to some authorities, but the Kols say that it is not edible, and though it has a pleasant smell, it produces a most uncomfortable burning in the throat.[1] Campbell states that it is applied externally in fever and that the bark is given internally and externally for fever, and that it is also used as a dye.

There are believed to be at least two very distinct varieties included under this name (Cp. Gamble, Manual of Indian Timbers, 2nd Ed., p. 415). It is possible, however, that the solitary and cymose flowers correspond with sexual forms, as in Gardenia spp.

3. R. **uliginosa,** *D.C.* Kumbikum, *K.*; Pinde, *S.*; Pindar, *Kharw.*; Mohwan (*Koderma*); Pindaro, *Mal Pah.*; Piralo, *Beng.*; Perar, *H.*

A small tree or a shrub with thick black branchlets, handsome when in flower, with large elliptic or obovate fascicled leaves 2-8″ by 1-4″ and numerous solitary pure white flowers 1-2″ diam. Berry large ellipsoid 2-$2\frac{1}{2}''$ green or yellowish.

[1] Since writing the above the reprint of Mr. Innes's Famine Foods (Ind. Forester, February 1908) has appeared. He states that the *unripe* fruit is boiled and eaten, but the ripe fruit is rather poisonous.

Valleys; Singbhum, Manbhum, Hazaribagh, Palamau, Santal Parganahs; not uncommon. Fls. *May-July.* Fr. *Dec.-Feby.* Deciduous. *Feby.-April.* L. turn colour *Dec.-Jany.*

Sometimes thorny. *L.* obtuse narrowed into the short petiole. *Fls.* dimorphic, large and sessile or small and peduncled, but *many* Randias vary considerably in these characters. Some flowers 1½″ have a peduncle over 1″. The corolla of the large flower has a ring of hairs inside and a fusiform 2-lobed stigma, that of the small form has a very short tube glabrous within and an entire stigma.

The fruit is eaten and makes a good vegetable when cooked.

10. Gardenia, L.

Trees or shrubs, armed with axillary thorns in a few species. L. opp. or 3-nately whorled, or sometimes fascicled in the thorny species. Fls. large or m.-s. usually solitary axillary, more rarely fascicled or terminal, often dimorphic, white, or turning yellow. Petals 5-12. St. as many, anthers sub-sessile, linear, included. Ovary 1-celled. Style stout, stigma clavate or fusiform, sometimes 2-cleft. Placentæ 2-3, fruit a berry or drupe, many-seeded.

A. Thorny. Small trees or shrubs. Fls. 1½″ or less in diam. dimorphic.
- A tree. Corolla salver-shaped. Endocarp bony . 1. *turgida.*
- Shrub. Corolla-tube campanulate. Endocarp not bony . . . . 2. *campanulata.*

B. Unarmed. Fls. 2-4½″ diam.
- L. 1½–3½″. Usually a shrub . . . . . 3. *gummifera.*
- L. 4-10″. Usually a tree . . . . 4. *latifolia.*

1. G. turgida, *Roxb.* Dudni, Durdi, *K.*; Dundukit', *S.*; Karhar, *Kharw.*, *Oraon*; Kharkar, *Mal Pah*; Dhanuk, *T.*

A straight erect small tree with white or pale-grey bark and rigid branches armed with sharp straight thorns. L. 1-4″ elliptic or usually obovate, glabrous or pubescent beneath, or (Var. montana) often orbicular and densely tomentose beneath, 1-4″ long. Male flowers sub-solitary or fascicled, ½-1″ diam.; female solitary, about ¾″-1″ diam. length of tube variable, fruit large globose 1½-3″ diam.

grey-green with fleshy pericarp and thin woody or bony endocarp, with 5 or 6 placentæ and densely packed with hard angular seeds.

Abundant in dry forests, esp. on slopes of clay and quartz-stones. Also frequent in second growth forest. Fls. *April-May*, mostly when leafless, but also at other times. Fr. takes about a year to ripen. Deciduous *March-May*.

L. narrowed into a short petiole. *Calyx* of male truncate, or with minute teeth, of female campanulate with lanceolate, ovate or foliaceous teeth.

Fruit sometimes eaten.

A membranous-leaved glabrous variety with elliptic or ell.-obovate leaves with the sec. n. all oblique and parallel (not sub-flabellate as in the common form) is indistinguishable from G. campanulata except by the flowers. F. *fl.* only $\frac{3}{4}''$ diam., tube not exserted. I suspect Roxburgh may have been right in making two species. The fruit is wrongly described by authors as always beaked, the beak may entirely disappear.

2. G. campanulata, *Roxb.*

Has only been recorded from Parasnath (by Sir J. D. Hooker and Anderson).[1]

L. membranous ell.-obovate or oblanceolate. *M. corolla* under $\frac{1}{3}''$ diam. campanulate. *F.* $\frac{1}{3}$-$\frac{1}{2}''$ diam. with very short lobes. *Calyx-teeth* linear-lanceolate. *Fr.* $\frac{3}{4}$-$1\frac{1}{4}''$ diam.

3. G. gummifera, *L.f.* Bururi, *M.*; Burui, *Ho.* Bruru, *Bhumij.*

A handsome shrub, sometimes 12 ft. with sub-sessile shining oblong to obovate leaves $1\frac{1}{2}$-$3''$ and, at certain seasons, a clear drop of gum completely covering the leaf-buds. Large white nearly sessile flowers with a tube 2-$2\frac{1}{2}''$ long and 5 oblong lobes 1-$1\frac{1}{2}''$ by $\frac{1}{2}$-$\frac{3}{4}''$. Fr. 1-$1\frac{1}{2}''$ beaked with the calyx.

In most of the districts, but peculiarly local. It occurs sub-gregariously on many of the dry hills with a clay soil covered with quartz fragments in Singbhum, Manbhum and Gangpur, but is absent from the Tundi hills and the Santal Parganahs. Fls. *March-May*. esp. in *April*, when the bushes are bare of leaves. Fr. *June-July*.

---

[1] Mr. Innes says boiled and eaten when *unripe* chiefly in *July August*. When ripe becomes rather poisonous.

L. often cordate at base with 12-16 prs. of sec. n. Stipules connate truncate. *Fls.* 1-3-together apparently terminal. *Calyx* with a tubular limb about $\frac{1}{4}$" long and triangular acute keeled teeth. Corolla-tube often pubescent. Endocarp hard thin.

It yields a clear yellow resin from wounds in the bark. The fruit is eaten.

4. G. latifolia, *Aiton.* Papa, *Ho.*; Papara, *M.*; Popro, *S.*; Papar, *Kharw.*; Pempri, *Mal Pah.*

A small tree with a round low crown of large opp. or 3-nate broadly-ellip. or orbicular obtuse leaves and large solitary white flowers 3-4" diam. Fr. $1\frac{1}{2}$-2" diam. crowned by the calyx.

On the hills, Singbhum; Manbhum; Hazaribagh (Sitagarh Hill); Santal Parganahs (often on trap hills). Fls. chiefly in *April* when leafless, and with new leaves in *May* but also at other times. Fr. young found at all times from *December* to *June*, ripens about 8 months after flowering? Chiefly in the rains. Deciduous *March-April.*

Bark whitish. Twigs very stout and buds gummy. *L.* sub-sessile, sec. n. about 12 prs. glandular-hairy in the axils beneath. *Stipules* large. *Calyx tube* mealy, limb campanulate with unequal teeth. *Corolla-tube* 2-3" pubescent. Petals 5-9, heavy-scented. Endocarp woody.

The tree is remarkably xerophytic. The seeds often germinate in the crevices of bare rocks, over which the stem forms a large cushion. Gamble states that it is frequently *epiphytic* on large trees.

The fruit is eaten.

11. Hyptianthera, W. & A.

1. H. stricta, *W. & A.*

A shrub, or small tree attaining 15-20 ft. with sharply 4-angled horizontal decussate branchlets (terete according to *F.B.I.*), spreading, lanceolate or oblong-lanceolate acuminate glabrous leaves 3-6" by $\frac{3}{4}$-$1\frac{1}{2}$", small white sessile flowers in axillary fascicles and black globose-oblong berries $\frac{1}{4}$-$\frac{5}{16}$" diam. crowned by the linear acute calyx lobes.

Cool valleys, rare, Singbhum; Morjhora, Bhera nadi (east of Chandna) and other ravines in Santal Parganahs. Fls. *April-May.* Fr. ripens *Feby.-March.* Evergreen.

L. often undulate glabrous and shining both sides, (or nerves beneath pubescent *F.B.I.*) sec. n. 5-7 prs. slender, others obscure. *Petiole* $\frac{1}{4}$-$\frac{1}{2}$''. *Stipules* acuminate persistent, hairy. *Corolla-tube* $\frac{1}{8}$'' hairy within, with 4-5 spreading lobes. Style included 2-fid. *Ovary* 2-celled. Seeds 4-5 in each cell, somewhat angled with a characteristic fibrous testa, about $\frac{1}{8}$'' diam. Flesh of unripe fruit viscous.

12. Ixora, L.

Small trees or shrubs with opp. or ternate leaves and flowers in terminal 3-chotomous often corymbose cymes, 4- very rarely 5-merous. Calyx-tube ovoid, limb persistent. Corolla-tube very long and slender with 4 spreading lobes. Stamens on the mouth with usually very short filaments and slender linear anthers. Ovary 2-celled style filiform, exsert; stigma slender fusiform with 2 branches. Fruit with 2 coriaceous pyrenes. Seeds peltate.

L. acuminate. Lower cyme-branches 2'' long or more . 1. *undulata*.
L. rounded at apex. Lower cyme-branches under 2'' long . 2. *parviflora*.

1. I. undulata, *Roxb.* Kota, *K.?*

A large shrub with oblong or lanceolate shining leaves 5-9'' by 1$\frac{1}{2}$-3'' and lax brachiate panicles with slender-peduncled branches of white flowers $\frac{5}{16}$'' long with linear petals. Fr. $\frac{1}{3}$'' diam. dull-purple or slate, with two plano-convex pyrenes.

Near streams; Saranda forests and also in Manbhum and Hazaribagh; Santal Parganahs common. Fls. *April-May*. Fr. ripens *Aug.-Sept.* Evergreen.

L. with undulate margins, glabrous, acute or acuminate. Petiole $\frac{1}{2}$-1''. Stipules broad with slender compressed cusps. *Panicles* pubescent with a pair of reduced leaves at their base, sessile or long peduncled, 6-8'' with lower internodes 2-3'' long. *Fl.-buds* $\frac{1}{2}$'' slender.

2. I. parviflora, *Vahl.* Pete, *K.*; Merom met', *S.*; Datranjin, *Kharw.*; Kholan, *Ghatw.*; Konthra, *Mal Pah*; Kota Gandhal, Loha jangia, *H.*; Rangan, *Beng.*

Usually a small tree with smooth very coriaceous oblong or elliptic sub-sessile leaves 3-6'' by 1$\frac{1}{2}$-2$\frac{1}{2}$'' and compact panicles of smallish white sessile scented flowers $\frac{1}{3}''$ long with 4-5 linear-oblong lobes $\frac{1}{8}''$ long. Fr. $\frac{1}{4}$-$\frac{1}{3}''$ diam. depressed globose black shining.

Common, often in Sal forest, Singbhum, Gangpur, Manbhum, Palamau, Santal Parganahs, etc., in drier localities than the last. Common on cotton soil.

Fls. *March-May*. Fr. *May-June*. Evergreen.

L. obtuse with rounded or cordate base, glabrous. *Panicles* 2-6". *Anthers* linear tailed.

The fruit is eaten. Brandis states that the green branches are used as torches. The fruit is described as didymous in the F. B. I.

13. Pavetta, L.

1. **P. indica**, *L.* Sikriba :, sikiba:, K. ; Buddhi ghasse' *S.* ; Burhi, *Kharw.* ; Jui, *Beng.*

A large shrub or small branched tree with ell. or obovate softly pubescent leaves 3-8" long and large trichotomous corymbose panicles of slender white flowers $\frac{1}{2}$-$\frac{3}{4}''$ long and very slender styles exserted $\frac{3}{4}$-1" beyond the corolla throat. Fruit globose black $\frac{1}{3}''$ diam., with 1-2 pyrenes.

Valleys and shady slopes in the forests, all districts, but not very common. Fls. *June-Aug.* Fr. *Oct.-Dec.* and shrivelled berries may be found later.

L. acute or obtuse, rarely acuminate in Chota Nagpur specimens, base cuneate, sec. n. 11-15 prs. strong ; petiole $\frac{3}{8}$-1", stipules broad. *Panicles* pubescent. *Petals* oblong $\frac{1}{4}''$.

A form found along the Konor nadi, Hazaribagh had leaves *tomentose* beneath.

14. Coffea, L.

1. **C. bengalensis**, *Roxb.*

A shrub 3-4 ft. high with bright green ovate acuminate leaves 3-4" by 2-2$\frac{1}{2}''$, setaceous stipules and pure white salver-shaped flowers 1-1$\frac{1}{2}''$ diam. with tube $\frac{3}{4}''$ long. Fr. an ovoid drupe $\frac{1}{2}''$, 1-2-seeded. Seed grooved.

Forming semi-thickets in damp low ground under dense shade, in Singbhum, but rare. Its habit in other parts of Bengal is rather that of a small undershrub in the open. Fls. with the new leaves *April-May*. Fr. *Feby.-April.* Dec. *Feby.-April.*

L. pubescent on the ribs beneath (at least when young). Base contracted. *Petiole* $\frac{1}{8}$-$\frac{1}{4}$". Fls. 2-3 in a terminal fascicle sessile. *Calyx-limb* obsolete or of several minute glandular teeth. Anthers slightly exserted, sessile, $\frac{1}{3}$" long, apiculate. Style short, stigma 2-fid.

2. **C arabica,** *L.* The Coffee is cultivated on the Ranchi plateau.

The leaves are 4-6" long, bifarious shining and the corolla funnel-shaped.

15. Canthium, Lamk.

1. **C. didymum,** *Roxb.* Jur, *K.*, Garbha gojha, *S.*

A small tree with spreading or drooping branchlets flattened above, bifarious dark-green ovate or lanceolate-ovate acuminate leaves 4-6" by 2$\frac{1}{2}$-3" and greenish flowers in very dense shortly-peduncled corymbose cymes. Fr. black globose $\frac{1}{2}$" diam. with two pyrenes.

A very common tree along the edges of dry watercourses, etc., in Singbhum; Manbhum; Santal Parganahs; Sirguia. *Wood*.

Fls. *Feby.-April.* Fr. *May*. Evergreen.

L. dark-green shining above pale beneath with 4 prs. distinct sec. n. with large axillary glands. *Petiole* $\frac{1}{3}$". *Corymbs* pubescent (always?) peduncle with 2 connate bracts. *Pedicels* $\frac{1}{8}$-$\frac{1}{3}$" in fruit. *Fls.* 5-merous. *Calyx* truncate or minutely toothed. *Corolla* $\frac{1}{4}$" diam. rotate with campanulate tube woolly within and lanceolate lobes. St. on the throat. Style long, stigma mitriform. *Ovary* 2-celled. Stones slightly rugose.

The fruit is eaten.

The Chota Nagpur variety appears to differ from the type in some of the leaves having glandular axils, and in the fruit (*vide* F.B.I.) *not* being didymous.

16. Vangueria, Juss.

1. **V. spinosa,** *Roxb.* Serali, Kataiara, *K.*; Boi-bindi; *S.* Monphal, *Kharw.*; Mainphal, *H.*

A small tree or shrub, often with long straight spines, ovate ell. or oblong acute or acuminate leaves 3-4" rarely few 6″ by 3″ (only $1\frac{1}{2}$-$2\frac{1}{2}$″ at time of flowering), small green sub-globose flowers in dense axillary cymes, and globose fruits 1-$1\frac{1}{2}$″ diam., marked with a large apical areola.

Singbhum, valleys, not very common; frequent in both Manbhum and Hazaribagh, often on the hills; Ranchi; Santal Parganahs. Fls. *April-May* with the new leaves. Fr. *Aug.-Oct.* Dec. *March-April.* L. turn yellow *Jany.*

Twigs nearly glabrous and leaves hairy or pubescent. L. often fascicled. Fl.-buds ovoid-oblong constricted, crowned with the cusps of the petals. *Calyx-tube* very short, teeth 5 linear, spreading. *Corolla-tube* $\frac{1}{4}$″ both ways, lobes triangular cuspidate, throat villous with white jointed hairs. Anthers introrse sub-sessile on the throat. *Ovary* 5-celled, free above. Style exsert. Stigma large globose. *Drupe* ($\frac{1}{2}$-1″ diam, *f.* Brandis) with 1-5 woody pyrenes.

The young leaves are eaten as a vegetable, the fruit is also eaten.

A form nearly resembling the glabrous type is found in the Santal Parganahs; the ordinary Chota Nagpur plant belongs to the var. mollis (F.B.I.) and is very pubescent and sometimes unarmed. Some spinous forms closely resemble the large-leaved variety of Randia dumetorum, and the fruit is sometimes said to kill fish, *possibly* through confusion with the Randia.

17. Lasianthus, Jack.

1. L. lancifolius, *Hook. f.*

A shrub 4-6 ft. somewhat resembling Hyptianthera, with appressed shortly-pubescent branchlets, lanceolate acuminate leaves about $5\frac{1}{2}$″ by $1\frac{1}{4}$″ and axillary fascicles of sessile inconspicuous white flowers. Fruit blue succulent ovoid downy surmounted by the calyx-tube, with 5-4 1-seeded pyrenes.

Deep shady valleys in the Tholokabad forest, Singbhum. Very rare.

Fl., Fr. *April-May.*

L. often undulate and variegated yellow, pubescent on the nerves beneath, narrowed both ends, with 7-9-prs. of oblique arched sec. n. strong beneath and numerous sub-parallel cross nervules. *Petiole* $\frac{1}{6}$-$\frac{1}{4}$″. *Calyx* 3-toothed or truncate in fruit. *Corolla* tubular, densely pubescent within with 5 sessile anthers, sometimes calyptrate. *Ovary* 4-5-celled. Ovule basal erect.

18. Morinda, L.

Trees or shrubs. Fls. in peduncled heads more or less coherent. Calyx-tube short truncate or with one foliaceous sepal. Corolla salver-shaped, petals 4-7, usually 5. Fil. short. Disc pulvinate. Ovary 2- rarely 4-celled. Style slender. Stigmas 2 narrow. Pseudocarp consisting of the connate succulent fruits of the several flowers each with 2-4 1-seeded pyrenes or a 2-4-celled putamen.

1. **M. tinctoria,** *Roxb.* Syn. M. citrifolia (Brandis, in "Forest Trees" ?) Chaili, *K.*, *S.*; Sali, *M.*; Al, ach, *H.*

A small tree 15-25 ft. with large ovate obovate or broadly elliptic leaves or upper oblanceolate and white flowers in solitary or 2-nate leaf- opposed or terminal stalked heads. Pseudocarp whitish-green.

Valleys in Singbhum and Santal Parganahs. Near villages in Manbhum. Fls. *May.-Sept.* Fr. *Jany.-Feby.*

Bark cracked. *Twigs* light brown, oblong in section.

L. 6-11″ by 4-6″ shortly suddenly acuminate and base suddenly narrowed into the 1″ petiole. Stipules acute or acuminate. Corolla ¾-1″ diam., tube ½—⅝″ long.

2. **M. tinctoria,** *Roxb.* Var. tomentosa. Syn. M. tomentosa, *Heyne*; Chaili, *K.*, *S.*

A large shrub or small tree with pubescent branchlets, elliptic tomentose or pubescent not shining leaves 4-5″ by 1½-2½″. Stipules caudate.

Valleys in Singbhum, undoubtedly wild. Fls. *May-June.*

A very different looking tree from the last, but usually united with it. The bark of the roots is collected for dyeing.

19. Hamiltonia, Roxb.

1. **H. suaveolens,** *Roxb.* Selauli, Sarkapi, *K.*; Kudia, *K.* (f. Gamble).

Shrub, fœtid when bruised, sometimes 6 ft. high (15 ft. in Santal Parganahs) with erect branches, stiff leaves 4-9″ by 1½-3″ and large terminal tri-chotomous panicles of small sweet-scented 4-5-merous lilac flowers. Fr. a 5-valved capsule, 1-celled from the absorption of the Septa, with 1-5 3-quetrous seeds.

Singbhum, on rocks on northern aspects, Manbhum; Hazaribagh; Ranchi; Santal Parganahs. Fls. *Aug.-Jany.*

L. elliptic-lanceolate or -oblong. or ovate acute, more or less pubescent beneath with 15-20 prs. strong sec. nerves and reticulate nervules. *Petiole* ¼-¾". *Fls.* capitate on the branches of the panicle ½-⅝" long pubescent. Calyx hairy with linear sepals. *Ovary* 5-celled. Style filiform, 5-fid above. *Ovule* basal erect in each cell.

The root is used in diarrhœa and cholera. The flowers are much frequented by Humming-bird Hawk moths.

20. Pæderia, L.

1. P. fœtida, *L.* Gandhali, *H.*; Gandha bhadulia, *Beng.* (in allusion to the smell).

A slender wiry climbing fœtid shrub with ell.-ovate acute or acuminate leaves 3-4" by 2", nearly sessile dingy-purple tubular-funnel-shaped fls. ½" long in axillary and terminal cymose panicles. Fruits dry compressed with a thin fragile veined epicarp separating from 2 oblong compressed winged pyrenes.

Mixed forest and scrub. Ranchi-Manbhum-ghats; Ranchi Hill near Pitorea, *Wood.* Fls. *Aug.-Oct.* Fr. *Dec.*

L. glabrous with rounded or sub-cordate base. *Petioles* 1-2" often twisted. *Panicles* 4-6" pubescent. *Calyx-lobes* 4-5 small obtuse. *Petals* ¼th as long as the corolla tube oblong with white incurved crisped margins, tube glandular hairy within. *St.* in the tube. *Ovary* 2-celled.

21. Knoxia, L.

Erect herbs or undershrubs, stems with 2 lines of hairs. Stipules connate with the petioles into an entire or bristly sheath. Fls. very small cymosely or spicately arranged on the branches of the corymbose cymose panicles. Sepals 4 minute. Corolla-tube long, throat villous, petals 4. St. in the tube. Ovary 2-celled. Fruit dry of 2 indehiscent cocci, which sometimes remain united, the whole fruit separating from a slender persistent columella which leaves a perforation through the axis, or columella deciduous.

1. K. corymbosa, *Willd.*

Erect sparingly branched 1-4 ft. with long narrow sessile or petioled leaves and minute white or purple flowers spicate on the cyme-branches. Fruit separating from the persistent columella.

Very common, attaining its largest size in damp ravines. Fls. *Aug.-Oct.* Fr. *Oct.-Dec.*

2. K. brachycarpra, *Bl.*

Erect strict herb 2-4 ft. with sessile linear-oblong obtuse leaves 2-4" by $\frac{1}{4}$-$\frac{3}{4}$." Cymes capitate or open. Fls. not spicate. Fruit falling away with the columella.

Parasnath, *Prain.*

22. Rubia, L.

1. R. cordifolia, *L.*

A herb scrambling by means of its scabrid stems and whorled ovate-cordate long petioled leaves. Fls. minute yellow in panicled cymes. Corolla rotate. Ovary 2-celled. Frt. $\frac{1}{8}$-$\frac{1}{6}$" diam. fleshy, didymous or globose from the suppression of one carpel.

Parasnath. *Anders.*

Fam. 85. COMPOSITÆ.

Shrubs or usually herbs, very rarely trees. L. usually alternate, generally simple, stipules 0, base of petiole sometimes sheathing. *Flowers* clustered into dense heads resembling single flowers, heads surrounded with an involucre of bracts. *Fls.* in a head all *similar, i.e.*, either all tubular or all ligulate or *dissimilar, i.e.*, either inner tubular and outer ligulate or outer of much more slender tubes (and sometimes with a different number of petals) than the inner. *Calyx* 0, or a pappus or scales. *Anthers* connate. *Ovary* quite inferior 1-celled. *Ovule* 1, basal, erect, anatropous. *Fruit* dry indehiscent.

Some 60 species occur in Ch. Nagpur, nearly all herbs, of which only a few of the most striking are here mentioned.

Heads with the fls. all tubular, similar and bisexual. Not spinous.

L. alt. Fls. purple. Pappus long . 1. *Vernonia.*
L opp. Fls. lilac. Pappus paleaceous 2. *Ageratum*

II. Heads with the fls. all tubular and similar, often diœcious. L. and invol. bracts spinous . 3. *Cnicus.*

III. Heads with the fls. all tubular, but outer filiform 2-3-toothed and much more slender than the inner which are 5-lobed or toothed.

a. Anther lobes without (or with short free) tails.

Style arms of center fls. terminated by a cone . 4. *Conyza.*

Style arms not terminated by a cone . . 5. *Laggera.*

b. Anther lobes each with a tail, the tails of adjacent anthers connate, so that there are 5 in all . . . 6. *Blumea.*[1]

IV. Heads with the outer fls. ligulate, inner tubular.

a. Receptacle not paleaceous. Pappus present . 7. *Vicoa.*

b. Receptacle paleaceous. Pappus 0 or of bristles.

5 outer invol. bracts large spathulate glandular . 8. *Siegesbeckia.*

Outer invol. bracts subequal, inner paleaceous. Fls. large yellow . . . . 9. *Guizotia.*

Outer invol. bracts small, inner membranous. Ray fls. white . . . . 10. *Bidens.*

1. Vernonia, Schreb.

Shrubs or herbs or (not in Chota Nagpur) small trees with alt. often toothed leaves and purple (sometimes white) flowers. Invol. ovoid, globose or campanulate, bracts many-seriate, inner longest. Receptacle naked or shortly hairy. Corolla slender tubular or narrow-campanulate above, lobes 5. Anther bases sagittate or tailed or obtuse (*F.B.I.*). Frt. striate, ribbed or angled, rarely terete. Pappus hairs copious often with an outer ring of short scales.

I. Heads solitary or few, axillary or terminal, subsessile . . . . 1. *teres.*

II. Heads panicled, ½-1″ long.

Involucre bracts all appressed . . . . 2. *Roxburghii.*

Involucre bracts free and spreading above often constricted . . . . 3. *anthelmintica.*

---

[1] The characters separating these genera are unsatisfactory. Conyza is widely separated from Blumea in the F.B.I. and included in the Asteroideæ, but it seems in some respects more naturally included in the Inuloideæ. The anther lobes are often tailed, and the style-characters not at all well marked.

III. Heads panicled, small, under ½″ long.

Shrubby; 4-8 ft. . . . . 4. *divergens.*

Herbaceous, 1-3 ft. . . . . 5. *cinerea.*

1. V. teres, *Wall.*

A rigid herb, somewhat resembling the English knapweed, scabrid, with harsh sub-sessile obovate or obovate- or ell.- or oblong-lanceolate acute serrate leaves, 2-5″ by 1-2″. Outer invol. bracts often squarrose. Fruit silky.

Common, esp. in open scrub jungles. Fls. *Oct.-Nov.*

2. V. Roxburghii, *Less.* Dora bohok', *S.*

Somewhat resembling the last, but larger 3-4 ft. and more branched and heads panicled. L. harsh sub-sessile or petioled acuminate serrate, up to 7″ by 2¾″. Invol. ½″ cylindric or ovoid of very numerous imbricating often reddish bracts, outer subulate or lanceolate, inner linear apiculate or pungent, not squarrose. Fr. ⅛″, ribbed. Pappus dirty white.

Waste places and jungles, common. Fls. *Oct.-Nov.* Fr. *Jany.*

3. V. anthelmintica, *Willd.* Syn. Centratherum anthelminticum, *O. Kuntze*; Saoraj, *S.*

A tall coarse annual 2-7 ft. high, with coarsely toothed sub-sessile ell. or obovate acuminate leaves tapering at the base, lower often 8″ by 3″, upper gradually smaller ell-lanceolate toothed. Heads with a short thick peduncle, oblong ⅝″ long. Easily recognized by its linear-oblong involucral bracts which are constricted beneath the free foliaceous green or coloured tips.

Especially common in waste land and near villages under the shade of trees. Fls. *Sept.-Dec.* Fr. *Nov.-Jany.*

Stems sometimes as thick as the thumb below, with tomentose branches. *Corolla* teeth sometimes 6, ⅓rd as long as the dilated part of the tube, anthers slightly exserted and often *tailed.*

4. V. divergens, *Benth.* Bara pathol, *S.*

Stout perennial 4-8 ft., leaves petioled serrate 2-5 by 1-4". Heads $\frac{1}{4}$". Fr. glabrous 10-ribbed. Pappus reddish-brown or dirty-white.

Common on Parasnath (= V. saligna of *Anders.* ?)

5. V. cinerea, *Less.* Bahu tuturi, Barangom, *S.*

An erect pubescent herb 1-$3\frac{1}{2}$ ft. with toothed ovate or lanceolate leaves 1-$2\frac{1}{2}$" decurrent on the petiole and terminal sub-corymbose panicles of small heads $\frac{1}{4}$" long of light purple flowers.

Very common everywhere. *Fls.* most of the year exc. the hot season.

Invol. narrowly campanulate. Outer invol. *bracts* very narrow, softly awned, much shorter than the linear 3-nerved inner. *Anthers* shortly tailed or sagittate apiculate. *Fr.* $\frac{1}{16}$" with adpressed pubescence.

The leaves are eaten.

Ageratum conyzoides, *L.*, is a very common hairy annual with petioled ovate crenate leaves and small lilac heads in dense terminal corymbs. The upper leaves are sometimes alternate.

Fl. *Oct.-Jan.* and also at other times.

Cnicus arvensis, *Hoffm.* This is a common European thistle often found in the fields of the cooler parts of Chota Nagpur, hardly ever in Singbhum. It is diœcious.

Echinops echinatus, *D.C.* with one flowered heads collected together in dense prickly balls like single heads, is found about Hazaribagh, etc. Balls 1-2" diam.

4. Conyza, Less. 5. Laggera, Sch. Bip. 6. Blumea, D. C.

Annual or perennial, usually glandular, pubescent or woolly herbs with entire toothed or lobed, sometimes rigid and decurrent leaves. Heads corymbose, panicled or fascicled, rarely racemed, heterogamous. *Outer* fl. female, filiform, 2-3-often minutely-toothed. *Disc fls.* hermaphrodite usually yellow, tubular, 5-toothed. *Involucre* ovoid or campanulate; bracts usually many-seriate, narrow, outer smaller. Receptacle usually flat and naked, rarely (in some Conyza) convex, pitted and fimbriate. Anther bases, obtuse and entire (some Conyza), or sagittate with auricles, tailed (most Blumea) or not (most Laggera). Fr. very small; pappus slender 1-seriate, often caducous.

There are 13 species in Chota Nagpur, mostly weeds of waste ground.

1. **C. viscidula,** *Wall.*

A stout herb 5-6 ft. high with very numerous obliquely spreading lateral pubescent or tomentose branches with lateral and terminal leafy panicles of pinkish flowers. Stems with a close curled pubescence, cauline leaves lanceolate or ell. acuminate attaining 8″ by 2½″ shallowly crenate, the sinuses mucronate, narrowed below into the very short half-amplexicaul petiole, puberulous beneath and on the nerves above. L. on the flowering branches lanceolate entire.

Grassy glades, Porahat and Hazaribagh. Fls., Fr. *Jany.-Feby.*

Heads ¼″ oblong, with slender pedicels ¼″ long, in loose corymbs. *Invol.* campanulate with about 20 3-seriate bristle-pointed 1-nerved green narrowly scarious linear *bracts* ⅛″ hairy and glandular. *Recept.* depressed, *Anther-cells* apiculate not tailed. *Achenes* compressed, puberulous.

2. **C. stricta,** *Willd.*

A stout herb excessively fastigiately branched and leafy with heads only ⅛″ in extremely numerous peduncled corymbs.

Pitorea and Jaspur, *Wood.*

Invol. bracts narrowly lanceolate without scarious margin. Pappus $\frac{1}{12}$″ reddish.

3. **L. flava,** *Benth.*

A herb 1-3 ft. erect with lower leaves amplexicaul auricled attaining 6″ by 2½″ irregularly toothed and denticulate. Heads very numerous *bright yellow* ⅛-¼″ long with green shining involucre.

Very common on clay soils in poor open forest. Fls. *Nov.-Jany.*

A very distinct species, glabrous. *Heads* campanulate in numerous cymous clusters on leafless branches, often 1-sexual.

4. L. aurita, *Sch. Bip.*

A coarse strong-scented grey-green villous and glandular weed 2-2½ ft. high, often much branched from the large tap-root. Stems densely clothed with deeply lobed or pinnatifid leaves and their decurrent basal lobes. Fls. pale-purple in ovoid heads ⅓-½" long.

Waste ground, common. Fls. *Jany.-March.*

L. 1½-2½", sharply lobed and toothed. The *anthers* are often shortly tailed and the tails of the adjacent anthers connate!

5. L. alata, *Sch. Bip.*

A stout leafy herb 2-4 ft. much branched pubescent or tomentose. Fls. purplish, heads drooping in fruit, racemed on short winged branches.

Fls. *Nov.-Jany.*

Easily recognized by the continuous wings of the stem.

6. B. lacera, *D. C.* Gada pachwani, *S.*

A herb 1-3 ft. with strong *camphorous* smell,* softly hairy or villous and more or less glandular hairy. L. obovate or upper oblong, dentate and spinulose-toothed or (var. glandulosa) very acutely serrate. Heads yellow, ¼" long and broad clustered in narrow panicles; invol. campanulate.

Waste ground, common. Fls. *Jany.-March.*

L. on robust plants often 8", on others only 2" often pinnatifid at base, sessile or petioled, silky-pubescent beneath. Gland-hairs very short. Here also the heads are frequently *functionally* female, the disc fls. have staminodes only, low down in the tube.

Vicoa auriculata, *Cass.* is a usually much branched annual with slender rigid stems, sessile lanceolate or oblong lanceolate leaves 1-3" and yellow heads of flowers ½-¾ diam. on slender peduncles.

Very common in open jungles and much resembling a "ragwort.".

Fls. *Nov.-March.*

L. with broad rounded auricled base. *Anthers* tailed. *Pappus* hairs slender.

---

* Camphor is prepared from some species of Blumea.

35. COMPOSITÆ.

Siegesbeckia orientalis, *L.* is a branched coarse annual 2-5 ft. with opp. leaves and pubescent branches and minute yellow flowers. It is easily recognised by the 5 spreading clavate or linear-spatulate glandular involucral bracts.

Fls. Fr. *Oct.-Dec.*

Guizotia abyssynica, *Cass.* Sargnja, *K.* This is a stout leafy herb with large yellow heads ¾-1″-diam. which is rather largely cultivated for its oil seeds, and forms beautiful golden yellow crops in Nov. and *Dec.*

Bidens pilosa, *L.* A tall erect herb 2-4 ft. with opposite 3-foliolate or 1-2-pinnatifid leaves and heads of yellow disc fls. and few white ray fls. or ray sometimes absent. Easily recognized by its angular long narrow fruits ½″ long and pappus of 3 rigid retrorsely hispid bristles by which it adheres to the clothes. Common. Fls. *Sept.-Oct.* Fr. *Nov.-Jany.*

CLASS II.—MONOCOTYLEDONEÆ.

Fam. 86. LILIACEÆ.

Usually bulbous or rhizomatous perennial herbs, more rarely tough climbing shrubs. *L.* usually parallel-veined, rarely net-veined (Smilax) or reduced to minute scales or spines (Asparagus) with the leaf function assumed by slender cladodes. *Fls.* usually 2-sexual (exc. Smilax) and regular. *Perianth* in two whorls of 3 members, usually similar and petaloid. *St.* in two whorls of 3 members, rarely more. *Ovary* superior of 3 carpels, 3-celled with usually many axile anatropous ovules. *Seeds* albuminous.

(Note.—A very distinct physiological type of Liliaceæ is represented by the fleshy or leathery often spiny leaved Aloes, Yuccas and some Dracænas. Some of these become arborescent and shew a secondary increase in thickness. The Agaveæ would appear to be closely allied, and are often called Aloes, but they are placed in the Amaryllidaceæ on account of their distinctly inferior ovary.)

I. Climbing usually prickly shrubs with inconspicuous flowers. Anthers introrse.

L. with several nerves from the base. Fls. umbelled . . . . 1. *Smilax.*

L. not evident. Cladodes acicular. Fls. racemed . . . . 2. *Asparagus.*

II. Erect or climbing herbs or undershrubs with a leafy stem, creeping or tuberous rootstock and conspicuous flowers. Anthers extrorse.

Climbing by the cirrhose leaves. Fls. handsome solitary . . . . . . 3. *Gloriosa.*

Erect branched. Fls. $\frac{1}{2}$-$\frac{3}{4}$″ in umbels . . 4. *Disporum.*

III. Herbs with bulbous or cormose rootstock, or fleshy roots, stem short or 0.

Rootstock very small with fleshy roots. Fls. racemed. Perianth spreading white . . 5. *Chlorophytum.*

Rootstock a bulb. Fls. racemed. Perianth spreading purple . . . . . . 6. *Scilla.*

Rootstock a bulb. Fls. racemed. Perianth campanulate . . . . 7. *Urginea.*

Rootstock a corm. Fls. erect corymbose. Perianth spreading . . . . . . 8. *Iphigenia.*

1. Smilax, L.

L. with several strong curved primary nerves reticulate between, base of short petiole sheathing often winged or auricled and usually bearing a pair of stipular tendrils. Fls. very small diœcious, umbelled. Umbels usually in bracteate cymes or panicles. Perianth leaves 6. St. 6, sometimes more. Staminodes in the F. fl. 3 or 6. Style 0, stigmas 3. Ovules 1 or 2 in each cell. Fruit a berry.

I. Umbels panicled with slender peduncles. Sheath often auricled . . . . . 1. *prolifera.*

II. Umbels 1-3.

a. Sheath without large auricles.

Branches terete. L. 6-18″, 5-7-nerved. Sep. $\frac{1}{4}$″ . . . . . . 2. *macrophylla.*

Branches angled. L. 5-7″, 3-5-nerved. Sep. $\frac{1}{8}$-$\frac{1}{4}$″ . . . . 3. *zeylanica.*

b. Sheath with large auricles often embracing the branch . . . . 4. *Roxburghiana.*

1. S. prolifera, *Roxb.* Atkir, *K.*

A stout prickly climber with stipular tendrils on the young shoots, and elliptic, rarely elliptic-ovate leaves, with sheath winged and wing more or less auricled one or both ends. Umbels in axillary and terminal panicles 3-6″ long with usually a zig-zag rachis and 3- (1-4-) nate slender peduncles about 1″ long. Bracts at the nodes inconspicuous, usually under $\frac{1}{8}$″.

A very distinct species (though apparently sometimes confused with S. macrophylla, *vide* F.B.I., p. 310) found in ravines in Singbhum.

Fls. *Feby.-April.* Fr. *Nov.*

Branchlets terete or angled, prickles under $\frac{1}{8}$″. *L.* 5″ by 2½″ to 7½″ by 4½″ obtuse with a short deflexed cuspidate tip, base rounded sub-acute or sub-cordate with 2 lateral basal nerves and two others connate with mid-rib to about $\frac{1}{3}$″ above the base. *Petiole* stout about $\frac{1}{2}$-$\frac{3}{4}$″ above the winged sheath, the cirrhi arising at the apex of the wings. Common *peduncle* 1-2″. M. special *peduncles* slender 1-1½″, *F.* $\frac{3}{8}$-1¼″. *Pedicels* $\frac{1}{4}$-$\frac{1}{3}$″. *M. sep.*, linear-oblong $\frac{1}{5}$″. *Petals* linear as long, 1-nerved. *F. sep.* rather broader about $\frac{1}{20}$″ broad, *petals* much broader than in the M. below, the upper half ultimately breaking off leaving the almost *ovate*-lanceolate base, often 2-nerved. Sepals and petals recurved in both sexes. *Staminodes* 3 filiform. *Berry* red $\frac{1}{4}$-$\frac{5}{16}$″ long, not quite as broad.

2. **S. macrophylla,** *Roxb.* Atkir, *K.*, *S.*; Raupawan, *Kharw.*

Habit of last but attaining a larger size sometimes 1″ diam. L. broadly ell. or orbicular, sheath not winged or auricled. Umbels 1-3 rarely 5, in axillary cymes rarely 3″ long on short peduncles less than the diam. of the umbel. Bracts at the nodes ovate or truncate over $\frac{1}{8}$″.

The common Smilax of Chota Nagpur, found in all the districts, frequent in the valley forests. Fls. *April-June.* Fr. *Nov.-Jany.* Subdeciduous in *May.*

Branches quite terete or with 4 lines. *Prickles* small. *L.* 6″ by 5″ to 12″ by 12″ with a short hard cusp as in *prolifera*, base rounded or subcordate or suddenly acute and decurrent on the petiole usually 7-costate, sometimes even 9-costate in the larger leaves, 3 often produced as ribs on the petiole. Base of petiole sheathing, triangular in section, enclosing a hard bud, sheath not broadly winged, but its edges infolded and meeting above at the base of the petiole proper where the two cirrhi thus arise almost base to base. *Common-peduncle* $\frac{3}{4}$-1″. M. special peduncles $\frac{1}{2}$-1½″. *F.* $\frac{1}{2}$-$\frac{3}{4}$″. *Pedicels* $\frac{1}{4}$-$\frac{1}{3}$″, or $\frac{1}{2}$″ in fruit. *Berry* $\frac{1}{3}$-$\frac{1}{2}$″ diam. globose, 1-3-seeded, seeds biconvex.

A preparation from the root is applied for rheumatism and pains in the lower extremities, *Camp.*

3. S. zeylanica, *L.*

Branches more or less 4-angled. L. 4″ by $1\frac{3}{4}$″ to 7″ by 4, elliptic usually 3-nerved from the base (or above the base, *F.B.I.*) with 2 fainter nerves. Petiole very shortly sheathing at the base.

Sirguja, *Wood.*

4. S. Roxburghiana, *Wall.*

Branches terete. L. acuminate *without* a hard cusp, and the sheaths with large auricles.

Parasnath, Santal Parganahs (see below).

A specimen from Chandna, Santal Parganahs, collected in fruit in May without leaves is probably this. It has branches of the panicle up to 3″, special peduncles $\frac{1}{8}$-2″ (on same plant) and fruiting pedicels $\frac{1}{4}$″, berry $\frac{1}{4}$″, seeds 1-2 biconvex, reddish.

The variability of the length of the special peduncles is characteristic of this species.

2. Asparagus, L.

1. A. racemosus, *Willd.* Huring Atkir, *K.*; Kedar nāṛi, *S.*

A slender climber with tuberous roots and annual woody prickly shoots with reflexed spines. Cladodes acicular $\frac{1}{2}$″ somewhat curved, 3-quetrous. Small white fls. $\frac{1}{8}$″ diam. on filiform articulate pedicels $\frac{1}{8}$-$\frac{1}{6}$″ long in very short racemes.

Common in the forests and scrub jungles. Fls. *Sept.-Oct.* Fr. *Dec.*

Var. α This is a very distinct plant from the ordinary A. racemosus in its very short cladodes. *Stems* with strong straight reflexed thorns $\frac{1}{3}$″ long below. *Branches* spreading short 3-quetrous. *Cladodes* in groups of 3, rarely 2- or 4-nate divaricate, tip with a minute white point and angles minutely scabrous. *Racemes* $\frac{1}{2}$-$1\frac{1}{4}$″ mostly 2-nate, simple or slightly branched, bracts minute. *Berries* $\frac{3}{16}$-$\frac{1}{4}$″ diam. scarlet. *Seed* usually only 1, black somewhat ellipsoid-globose.

β. *Branches* striate not 3-quetrous, *racemes* un ar $\frac{1}{2}$″ long. *Cladodes* as short as in the last slightly 3-grooved. The common form in Singbhum, and as Col. Prain remarks, a very puzzling form.

Roxburgh draws a distinction in the position of the embryo in the species racemosus and acerosus. As far as this is intelligible the embryo of Var. α is that of his acerosus: the radicle starts in the umbilical hemisphere low down and the filiform embryo ascends in a large semicircle remote from the "umbilicus" and down again to the equator the other side. The arch, however, is not in one plane but wavy. The *seedling* from the very commencement only shews scale-leaves and cladodes.

"A decoction of the root is given in fever," *Camp.*

3. Gloriosa, L.

1. G. superba, *L.* Bunum ki chuog, Bing ki chung, *K.*; Sinic' samanom, *S.*; Karihari, *Kharw.*

A well-known and beautiful plant 3-10 ft. high with a large torulose tuberous rootstock, sessile or sub-sessile lanceolate leaves 6" long with the tip more or less converted into a tendril, and large red and yellow flowers solitary, or sub-corymbose at the ends of the branches.

Hedges and thickets throughout the area. Fls. and Fr. in the *rains* and dying down in the *cold* season.

Perianth-leaves linear-lanceolate crisped reflexed. *Capsule* 2" long septicidal.

The root gives one of the 'seven minor poisons' of Sanscrit writers and is used medicinally. It is also said to yield a violent poison with which the Kols once used to poison their arrows, nevertheless it is eaten by them after preparation.

4. Disporum, Salisb.

1. D. pullum, *Salisb.*

A stout herb 3-4 ft. with tuberous rootstock and thick fleshy roots, stem often $\frac{1}{3}$" diam. dichotomously branched with opp. and alt. ovate-lanceolate leaves 3-5" by $1\frac{1}{4}$-$1\frac{3}{4}$". Fls. $\frac{1}{2}$" long about 5 in an umbel with very short peduncle. Fr. black succulent depressed globose and sub-trigonous $\frac{1}{3}$" diam.

Shady damp forests in Singbhum. Parasnath. Fls. *July*. Fr. *Dec*

L. acute or acuminate. Very short *petiole* decurrent as a line on the stem. *Peduncle* $\frac{1}{2}$" or less fluted, at first terminal, ultimately appearing lateral by growth of a lateral axis. *Pedicels* 1-$1\frac{1}{2}$" angled or fluted, decurved. *Seeds* 3 light-brown, rounded-oblong, under $\frac{1}{4}$" long.

Chlorophytum arundinaceum, *Baker,* is a pretty herb with fleshy roots, a tuft of lanceolate linear leaves about 6-9″ long and a simple or slightly panicled raceme 8-18″ high of pretty white flowers with sub-erect and spreading perianth leaves ½″ long. Common on fire-lines and in light forest in Singbhum and Santal Parganahs ; Jaspur and Sirguja, *Wood*. Probably occurs throughout the area. Fls. *April-June*.

Scilla indica, *Baker,* is a small herb with scaly bulbs which are said to have the properties of the Scilla or Squill of the British Pharmacopœia (Stimulant, expectorant, diuretic and cardiac tonic). It is not common.

Urginea indica, *Kunth,* is a common herb with globose-ovoid necked bulbs 1¼-1½″ diam. of connate fleshy scales without smell. It has long very slender scapes which rise above the ground in the hot season before any leaves appear, and bear distant oblong flowers ¼-⅜″ long on pedicels which are at first erect, then droop when the flowers open and again become erect and elongate to 1¼″ in fruit.

Perianth leaves greenish with a brown streak and pubescent at the tips.

The bulb is said to have the same properties as the last, and also to be used for sizing cloth.

Iphigenia indica, *Kunth.* Chutia chandbol, *S.*, has a globose corm ½″ diam. with a neck 1-2″ long, flexuous stems and reddish or purplish small erect flowers with clawed, spreading and reflexed linear-subulate perianth leaves. Manbhum, *Camp.*

The flowers are said to yield a red dye.

Fam. 87. AMARYLLIDACEÆ.

Herbs with a perennial tuberous or bulbous underground stem, rarely with a short stout erect stem. *Flowers* usually large and showy (small in Curculigo and Hypoxis) usually on a leafless scape and enclosed in bud by spathaceous bracts, sometimes (Agave) in an immense panicle. Fls. regular or slightly zygomorphic as in the Liliaceæ, except that the *ovary* is quite inferior and the *corolla* is often furnished with a petaloid corona. *Fruit* capsular or indehiscent, not baccate.

A. Bulbous plants with radical not plicate leaves and an unbelliform inflorescence enclosed by two or more spathaceous bracts on a leafless scape.

Filaments free . . . . 1. *Crinum.*
Filaments united by a cup-shaped membrane . . 2. *Pancratium*
B. Small rhizomatous plants with plicate leaves and yellow flowers . . . . 3. *Curculigo.*
C. Rhizomatous shortly caulescent suffruticose plants with many thick fleshy leaves and flowers in a large panicle.
Flowers erect. St. longer than the perianth . . 4. *Agave.*
Flowers drooping. St. shorter than the perianth . . . . 5. *Furcræa.*

1. Crinum, L.

Stout herbs with tunicate bulbs and narrow fleshy leaves. Fls. handsome white or blush-red umbellate with long linear bracts. Perianth funnel-shaped with a long tube, sometimes slightly zygomorphic. Anthers versatile, dorsifixed. Fruit bursting irregularly with a few large seeds.

Per. lobes linear to linear-lanceolate. Anthers linear ¾″ grey . . . . 1. *defixum.*

Per. lobes lanceolate to oblanceolate. Anthers black under ½″ long crescent-shaped. St. declinate . 2. *latifolium, Var.*

1. C. defixum, *Ker.*

L. 1″ broad. Perianth-tube 3½-4″, longer than the linear-lanceolate lobes Stamens not quite as long as the perianth lobes (much longer, *F.B.I.*). Fruit beaked with the tube.

Muddy banks of rivers, common. Fls. *Aug.-Sept.*

2. C. latifolium, *L.* Var. Campbellii. Sikiyom Baha, *S.*

L. attain 30″ by 4½″ (about half way up) or more, tapering gently to a sharp point, *Camp.* A beautiful species with stout compressed scapes and 8-10 drooping white or rosy flowers with a slightly curved tube 4-5″ and oblanceolate perianth lobes 4-5″ long. St. 3-4″ with linear-oblong black anthers curved into a semicircle.

Dry jungles. Singbhum, Gangpur, Manbhum and Hazaribagh (Tatijheria jungles). Fls. *May-June.* The leaves appear June.

Bulbs globose 5″ diam. *with a long neck* 3-5″. *Scape* 1 ft. by 1″ broad. Spathaceous *bracts* broadly-lanceolate 3-4″ by 1½″. Linear bracts 3″. *Ovary* ¾″ on the pedicel ¼-⅓″. Fr. 2-2½″ diam. with membranous epicarp striate with about 25 vertical lines. Seeds large but variable in same capsule, about 12 angular.

"A decoction of the root is given internally, and pounded and made into a paste, is applied externally in dropsy; also used for diarrhœa in cattle," *Campbell.*

This differs considerably from C. latifolium, *L.* and is probably a distinct species, but the whole of this section of Crinum requires elucidation.

There are two beautiful flowering plants of the genus **Pancratium** conspicuous in hill forest in May and June, these are:—

1. **P. verecundum,** *Ait.* Gering ba, *K.*, with stout compressed *scape* 12-18″ long, 3-5-fld with 2 spathes. *Fls.* with a tube 4″ long and narrowly oblanceolate apiculate lobes 2½-3″ long. *Tube* of the obconic staminal-cup about 1½″ with teeth ⅓-½″. The flowers only last for one day.

2. **P. biflorum,** *Roxb.* A smaller species but with longer filaments and an erose, not toothed staminal corona. Spathes 3-4.

3. Curculigo, Gærtn.

Flowers few or capitate on short, or sometimes very short and subterranean, scapes. Perianth rotate, on a more or less elongated beak like-hypanthium. Fruit indehiscent.

1. **C. orchioides,** *Gærtn.* Turam, *K.*

A small plant, first conspicuous after the jungle fires by its small bright yellow flowers which rise just a little above the soil, accompanied, or not, laterally, by the new leafy shoot.

Hill forests, common. Fls. *May-June.* Leaves appear *June.*

Plicate *leaves* about 10″, glabrous or hairy. *Scape* 2-3-fld. *Bracts* narrow colourless hairy about ¾″. *Fls.* thrust above the ground by means of the hypanthium (perianth-tube?) which is about ¾″ long. *Perianth-lobes* ¼-⅓″ or ⅓-½″ (perhaps according to sex) oblong, hairy without. *Anthers* green.

The long tuberous roots, about the thickness of a pencil, are boiled and eaten.

2. C. recurvata, *Dryand.*

A herb with palm-like leaves 2-3 ft. long and yellow fls. collected into a decurved head 2-4″ diam. on a scape 3-9″ long.

Shady marshy places. Fls. *May-June.*

Hypoxis aurea, *Lour.* differs from C. orchioides in the absence of any beak to the smaller flowers which are borne 1-2 together on a filiform scape. L. linear.

4. Agave, L.

Stout shrubby rhizomatous plants with a short aërial stem more or less concealed by the leaf bases, and with thick fleshy spine-tipped and often spinosely-toothed leaves. *Flowers* somewhat funnel-shaped, erect, paired or fascicled on the branches of the panicle which is terminal and usually very large. *Hypanthium* produced into a short tube above the ovary. *Tepals* narrow erect or slightly spreading. *Ovary* 3-celled. Stigma 3-lobed. *Capsule* loculicidal with many seeds.

The Agaves are usually propagated by bulbils, which are often formed in the place of the fruits. Wood relates a case of one plant producing over 3,000 bulbils. The following descriptions are taken from the "Notes on Agave and Furcræa in India" by J. R. Drummond and D. Prain (Bulletin No. 8 of the Agricultural Series, published by the Bengal Secretariat, 1906).

I. Perianth segments not constricted towards the tip.

a. L. broadest in the middle, tapering to both extremities.

L. oblong-lanceolate, neck sharply constricted . 1. *americana.*

L. linear-oblong, neck not constricted . . . 2. *Vera-Cruz.*

b. L. linear-lanceolate, hardly widened in the middle 3. *Cantula.*

II. Perianth segments narrowed from about the middle to the ligulate tip.

L. straight and narrow, often spineless . . 4. *sisalana.*

1. A. americana, *L.*

L. commonly variegated yellow, stout, sharply constricted above their swollen bases. *Margin* distinctly sinuate bearing the mostly reflexed prickles on the eminences. Apical-spine 1-2″ long.

Common in gardens. Not known to be of any economic value.

2. A. Vera-Cruz, *Miller.* Syn. A. Cantula, *Bengal Plants*; Moraba, *K.*, *S.*; Mordha and Murga are given as vernacular names in the Notes.

A stout plant usually producing numerous shoots from the rhizome, which render it polycarpic. L. very deep green and glaucous 4-6 ft. long and attaining 10″ in width, scarcely constricted above the base. Margins not, or only slightly, sinuate. Apical spine ½-1″ dark-brown.

More or less naturalized in Singbhum, *e.g.*, about Anjedbera; Hazaribagh, *e.g.*, Tatijheria, Daltonganj, etc., but all these citations require confirmation by comparison of the characters with those now given. Fls. *Sept.-Dec.*

L. often rather concave at the widest part (just above the middle) early curving upwards, ends more or less recurved. Interval between spines ½″ or less, rarely ¾″. Main branches of *panicle* 3-chotomous, curved or flattened. *Fls.* in pairs with a subsidiary bud laterally developed at a different level. *Tepals* linear-lanceolate pale amber tint. *Anths.* ½″ and upwards. *Capsules* rather turgid, oblong-cylindrical, tip rounded, seeds black shining.

3. A. Cantula, *Roxb.*

L. in a lax but even tuft from a short ascending rhizome, pale green, older darker, sometimes glaucous, attaining 4 ft. or more but usually only 2¼″ broad rarely over 3″ at the widest part (just above the middle). *Apical-spine* usually acicular ½-1″ long reddish or dark brown, cylindrical. *Marginal-prickles* conspicuous falcate pointing forwards ¼″ or more and very sharp. *Fls.* 1-2 together. *Tepals* 1½″ linear-oblong obtuse, greenish-yellow.

Cultivated at Hazaribagh Jail and elsewhere in Chota Nagpur, *Wood.* Wood's list, however, was compiled before the completion of Prain and Drummond's investigations and the plant referred to may be another species.

4. A. sisalana, *Perrine.*

Rhizome sometimes ascending, hidden by the leaf-bases. *L.* closely tufted, not at all constricted above the moderately thick base, deep-green glaucous or not, up to 6 ft., breadth up to 10″. *Prickles* 0, or if present weak, scattered and pale.

This species is cultivated in Chota Nagpur and is likely to be more extensively planted. It is stated that a somewhat poor land of a loose stony nature is best suited to produce a good fibre (*Cameron*, quoted in the Bulletin, p. 27).

Furcræa is easily distinguised from Agave by the hypanthium not being produced into a tube or cup above the ovary, and the stamens being much shorter than the tepals, with the lower part of the filament very much expanded. Although the hypanthium is not produced into a tube, it is however often (always ?) produced together with the adnate style or top of the ovary into a solid beak. Species of Furcræa, one of which yields the *Mauritius hemp*, are frequent in gardens. The leaves are usually unarmed or only slightly armed, green (not glaucous) and the flowers pendulous in immense panicles.

Fam. 88. TACCACEÆ.

Tuberous-rooted herbs with the inflorescence of Amaryllidaceæ but *leaves* partite or pinnatifid. *St.* broadly adnate to the perianth tube, one opp. each lobe, with decurrent wings, free portions completely hooded inflexed bearing the adnate linear anther lobes one on each side of the mid-rib on the upper (inside) surface of the hood, the lobed apex of which is slightly upcurved disclosing the tips of the anther-cells. *Ovary* 1-celled with 3 parietal placentæ and many ovules. *Stigmas* large petaloid.

1. Tacca, Forst.

1. T. pinnatifida, *Forest.* Dhai, *K.*, *S.*

A herb with a large globose tuber, and long petioled succulent tripartite and pinnatifid leaves 1-2 ft. wide, terminating in 2-3 large ovate lobes 4-9″ long. *Fls.* broadly campanulate greenish about $\frac{1}{3}$-$\frac{1}{2}$″ long. Bracts among the flowers very long and filiform. Fr. about 1", 6-ribbed yellow.

Singbhum, Manbhum, Hazaribagh, frequent among rocks in the forest and open jungles. Fls. *Aug.-Sept.*

The root which is acrid and poisonous when fresh yields a nutritious starch when macerated and repeatedly washed with cold water.

Fam. 89. DIOSCOREACEÆ.

1. Dioscorea, L.

Climbers with usually strong annual stems rising from a large perennial rhizome, or rhizome small with numerous long fleshy fibres bearing at their ends large tubers, or tubers rising directly from the base of the stem. *L.* alt. or opp. 3-5-foliolate or simple, and typically cordate ovate, basal-nerved. *Fls.* small regular diœcious, with a bract and oblique-bracteole, 3-merous, spicate. *Spikes* usually several together, often panicled. *Sep.* and *pet.* similar or dissimilar, united at base or nearly free. *M. fl.* with 6 stamens, or 3 inner sterile or 0 opp. to and adnate to the per. leaves, or central. *F. fl.* with a 3-celled *inferior* ovary and 3-6 or 0 minute staminodes, stigmas 3 usually 2-fid. *Ovules* 2 in each cell. *Capsule* sharply 3-cornered or winged. *Seeds* 2-winged.

Generally the deep tubers are the edible ones, those lying near the surface being acrid. The tubers are called *dhaka* in Kol.

I. L. simple. St. 6 fertile. Seeds winged all round exc. in 5 and 7.

A. M. spikes usually stiffly spreading under 3", clustered or whorled on an elongate rachis.

1. Buds oblong. Sepals oblong.

a. More or less pubescent all over. F. spikes panicled . . . . . 1. *anguina.*

b. Glabrous. L. glaucous beneath. F. spikes not panicled (exc. by the loss of the upper leaves).

L. pale glaucous. M. petals obovate. Cross-nervules obscure . . . . . . 2. *nummularia.*

L. dark-glaucous. M. petals ell.-oblong. Cross-nervules raised . . . . 3. *bellophylla.*

2. Buds globose Sep. ovate-oblong or orbicular (or lanceolate in alata). L. not glaucous beneath. Capsule broader than long.

M. spikes straight. F. panicled. Stem terete . . 4. *aculeata.*

M. spikes zig-zag. Stem angled. Seed winged one side. . . . . 5. *Hamiltoni.*

M. spikes zig-zag. Stem winged. Seed winged all round. . . . . 6. *alata.*

B. M. spikes very slender drooping and panicled. Sep. linear in both sexes.

Capsule oblong . . . . 7. *bulbifera.*

II. L. digitately compound. Capsule oblong.

L. 3-foliolate. Lflts. about 6″, 4-6-costate . . 8. *dæmona.*

L. 3-5-foliolate. Lflts. about 3,″ 1-2-costate . . 9. *pentaphylla.*

1. **D. anguina,** *Roxb.* Kukuri, *M.*; Kukui sanga, *Ho.*

Stem unarmed, soon thickening into a narrow cylindrical tuber 1-more ft. long, which is often palmately branched, stem branches densely pubescent. L opp.. pubescent even when old on the nerves beneath, very broadly cordate ovate, upper ovate, M. spikes pubescent $\frac{1}{2}$–$1\frac{1}{4}$″ long on a rachis 2-4″ long. Buds globosely oblong. Sep. broadly oblong, Petals membranous ovate, slightly imbricate in bud, glabrous. Capsules tomentose or old glabrescent, $\frac{3}{4}$″ by $1\text{-}1\frac{1}{8}$″.

Singbhum forests, common. Hazaribagh. Fls. *Sept.-Nov.* Fr. *Dec.-Jany.* *Bulbils* 1-2″ like potatoes with a thin greenish or grey-brown skin without conspicuous eyes. *L.* attain 10 by 10″ acute or acuminate, 7-costate with distinct cross nervules raised beneath. *Petiole* up to 4″ thickened below. M. fl. $\frac{1}{10}$″. St. about half as long as petals. *F. spikes* 4–6″ usually copiously panicled. *Bracts* ovate hairy. *Seeds* winged all round.

The tubers are eaten, but they are said to have an offensive smell when cooked. The bulbils are eaten.

2. **D. nummularia,** *Lamk.* Syn. D. glabra, *Roxb.* Unur Sanga, *K.*, Ato sang, alto sang, *S.*

Stem with numerous small prickles below, enlarged at the base into a perennial rhizome from which proceed long fibro-fleshy roots 2-more ft. long which enlarge into elongate fleshy tubers 5-12″ by 1-2″. L. opp., very rarely also alt., glabrous pale-glaucous beneath, usually ovate oblong, the base of the uppermost leaves often straight or rounded. M. spikes $\frac{1}{2}$-$\frac{3}{4}$″ long, on axillary rachides 1-3$\frac{1}{2}$″ long and finally whorled direct on the main axis in terminal more or less leafless panicles. Buds oblong. Base of the perianth tube very broad and pulvinate on the upper side. Sep. oblong, united below. Pet. fleshy obovate-spathulate. Capsule $\frac{5}{8}$-$\frac{7}{8}$″ long by 1-1$\frac{1}{4}$″ broad, base with a short obconic beak.

Singbhum, in the valley forests, esp. common on the Porahat plateau, Hazaribagh (Koderma forest, etc.) ; Manbhum, *Camp.* ; Jaspur and Kochang, *Wood.* Probably throughout the area. Fls. *Sept.* Fr. *Nov.* The plant in flower has a strong rather unpleasant smell perceptible to a considerable distance.

Bulbils 0. *L.* very variable, exceptionally sub-orbicular 7″ by 6″, or narrow very long 8$\frac{1}{2}$″ by 3$\frac{1}{2}$″, usually cuspidate, with base of lower leaves deeply cordate and 5-9-nerved, the sec. n. not scalariform between the costæ. *Petiole* slender, from half as long to as long as the blade. *St.* at the base of the perianth minute, less than one-third as long as the petals. *F. spikes* 3″-1 ft., several from each upper axil. Pistillode very minute. Bracteole much shorter than the acuminate bract. *Seeds* winged all round.

The tubers are largely eaten.

There are two forms, one with lax small flowers, the other with very dense larger flowers.

3. **D. belophylla,** *Voight.* Duri sanga, Hasa sanga, *K.* ; Mutur Sang, *S.* Included in D. glabra in F.B.I. from which it is, however, quite distinct, and easily recognized.

Stems quite smooth, enlarged at the base into a small rhizome bearing tubers at the ends of long fleshy fibres as in the last, the tubers sometimes 2 ft. long and very deep. L. opp. and alternate sap-green and dull above, glaucous beneath, usually ovate-and deeply cordate with well-marked cross nervules between the costæ beneath. M. spikes $\frac{3}{4}$-2″ long lax-fld., 1-3-nate sometimes branched, on rachis 4-6″ long, and running into leafless slender panicles. Base of perianth broad not pulvinate. Sep. nearly free oblong obtuse dotted and with scarious margins. Pet. ell.-oblong nearly as long, 2-ridged within. Capsule less broad than in last, less cordate at base.

Rocky valley forests in Singbhum, common, not on the hills. Fls. *Sept.-Nov.* Fr. *Dec.-Jany.*

Bulbils rather rare, narrow clavate or linear often 1-2" long, smooth with hard points. *L.* variable, rarely orbicular, often sagittate with rounded basal lobes, a much deeper green than in last and nervation very different, the sec. n. being distinctly scalariform. *Petioles* slender nearly always ridged in the upper portion and sometimes throughout with the decurrent primary nerves of the leaf. *St.* on a short column, about $\frac{3}{4}$ths as long as the petals. Cells adnate to and not much wider than the fleshy filament. Pistillode 3-gonous at top. *F. spikes* usually 1-3 in each axil, 3-5" long with angular rachis. Bracteole not much smaller than the ovate or cordate bract.

The most highly prized of the forest yams, but often impossible to obtain owing to the tubers being wedged in the crevices of rocks.

4. **D. aculeata,** *L.* Syn. D. Wallichii, *F.B.I.*; Kulu, Tungam sanga, *K.*

Stems very stout somewhat thorny below and characterized by the hard thick bases of the articulate petioles which are also sometimes thorny at the base. Tubers elongate 2-3 ft. and 2-4" girth rising directly from the base of the stem without the intervention of long roots. L. mostly alternate sub-orbicular or broadly ovate with a large basal sinus usually cuspidate. M. spikes $\frac{1}{2}$-1" long rather lax, 2-3-nate on the branches of a panicle $1\frac{1}{2}$-4" long. Buds sub-globose 3-lobed. Sepals nearly free, oblong-ovate concave. Petals similar. Anther cells very large broad, as long as the filament. F. spikes always racemed on a short rarely long axillary branch. Capsule $1\frac{1}{2}$" diam., tapering below (when ripe?).

Singbhum, esp. in the valley forests and on northern slopes, frequent. Hazaribagh. Fls. *Nov.-Dec.* Fr. *Jany.*

Bulbils not seen. *L.* cuspidate or caudate. Costæ about 9 with the lowest forked. Sec. n. scarcely visible above, scarcely raised beneath and only few straight and scalariform, finely reticulate between. (Translucent dots and dashes are usually visible both in this species and in nummularia). *Petioles* very long, usually as long as and often exceeding the blade, thickened and somewhat laterally compressed above rarely grooved, and only appearing ridged or striate when dry. *M. panicle* $1\frac{1}{2}$-4″ several-nate in each axil or on an abbreviated common peduncle. *St.* nearly as long as the petals, on a short central column surrounding a large grooved pistillode. *Bracteole* as large as the bract.

The tubers are said to require a large number of successive boilings before they are palatable.

5. **D. Hamiltoni,** *Hook. f.*

Superficially much resembling D. nummularia, but the stems distinctly angled. L. opp. narrowly ovate acuminate or caudate, base cordate or not with a slender petiole ridged or sub-alate above. M. inflorescence very easily recognized from all the other wild species by the zig-zag rachis of the spikes which bears a flower at each angle. F. spikes not racemed on lateral branches, sometimes appearing panicled in fruit from the absence of the leaves on the main rachis. Capsule with wavy wings when unripe, ripe $1\frac{1}{3}$-$1\frac{1}{2}$″ diam. by 1″ long (longer than broad, *F.B.I.*) base obconic.

Manbhum, *Camp*; Hundrughag (Ranchi), *Wood*!; Ranchi, *Clarke*! Hazaribagh (Parasnath), *Prain, Clarke*!

Brown when dry. *Bulbils* 0? *Petiole* about $\frac{3}{4}$ths as long as the blade almost winged above. Zig-zag *spikes* $\frac{1}{4}$-$\frac{3}{4}$″ simple or branched, 1-5-nate on the main stems or on an axillary rachis 3-5″ long, or appearing panicled from the suppression of the leaves. *Petals* -oblong-obovate. *St.* 6 with large anthers on a central disc, not half as long as petals. Bract acuminate, bracteole very minute. *F. spikes* 3-9″ long. (The F. fl., according to Wight's figure, is remarkable in having lanceolate-acuminate perianth leaves, but the perianth leaves in the specimens kindly lent me by Mr. Burkill are not specially characteristic.)

6. **D. alata,** *L.* Merom tuar sanga, *K.* (Goat's milk root, in allusion to its nutritive value).

Tubers (cult.) very large proceeding direct from the base of the stout stem, which has scattered prickles below and on the petiole-bases, and is compressed or 4-angled below, 4-many-winged above. L. usually opp. with the cross nervules not very pronounced. Bulbils geminate, often many on special branches, mostly oblong brown with a tesselated or longitudinally cracked corky surface, attaining 3" by 1-2". Not wild in Chota Nagpur.

The generally cultivated variety in Singbhum (var. rubella, *Prain*, "Bengal Plants") has largely irregularly clavate tubers ending in a narrow neck at the stem, white within and pinkish outside.

7. **D. bulbifera**, *L.* Pisika, *K.*; Bengo nari, *S.*

Stems smooth from a large brown sub-globose rhizome covered with roots and eyes, and not bearing tubers. L. alt. sub-orbicular or broadly ovate abruptly caudate and deeply cordate. M. fls. green or purple in numerous long very slender axillary and panicled spikes. Young buds ovoid. Sepals linear and pet. similar. F. spikes slender drooping several from each axil, sepals linear. Capsules oblong $\frac{3}{4}$" by $\frac{1}{2}$" reflexed. Seeds with an oblong wing above.

A common plant, throughout Chota Nagpur. Fls. *Aug.* Fr. *Nov.*

Bulbils are roundish brown with prominent eyes, exactly like the rhizomes on a small scale. *L.* with 7-11 costæ glabrous with very distinct straight cross nervules. *Petioles* shorter than the leaves. *St.* not $\frac{1}{4}$th as long as the petals. Bract and bracteole acuminate.

The rhizomes are said to be very acrid but sometimes eaten after much preparation.

Var. crispata, *Prain* (*Roxb.*, sp.). Stem with 10-15 small crispate wings. Chota Nagpur, *Prain*.

8. **D. dæmona**, *Roxb.* Kolo, *S.*

Stems with few small prickles on the stems from roundish rhizomes. L. 3-foliolate, leaflets about $7\frac{1}{2}$" by $3\frac{1}{2}$", 5-6-costate, central more or less obovate. M. fl. in very dense short oblong spikes $\frac{1}{4}$-$\frac{1}{3}$" long, in long narrow axillary pubescent panicles 6-8" long. F. spikes simple 8-12" long pubescent. Capsule large oblong $1\frac{1}{2}$-$1\frac{3}{4}$" long.

Manbhum, *Camp.* Santal Parganahs. Fls. *July.* Fr. *Sept.*

M. spikes on peduncles $\frac{1}{8}$-$\frac{1}{2}$" long. Bracts sub-orbicular as long as the flower, pubescent. Bracteole and petals exceeding the sub-orbicular pubescent sepals. *St.* 6 fertile.

According to Roxburgh the root is dreadfully nauseous even after boiling.

9. D. pentaphylla, *L.* Baiom sanga, Itulad sanga, *K.*

A much more slender plant than the last. Tubers oblong or clavate, direct from the stem. Stem with small prickles. L. 3-5-fol., leaflets about 4″ by 2-2½″ or less, rarely attaining 6″, 1-costate with another strong nerve from near its base, oblanceolate to obovate. M. fl. in linear spikes ¼-1¼″ long., in panicles 3-9″ long. F. spikes 6-8″. Capsules oblong ¾-1″.

Singbhum in valleys, frequent. Fls. *Aug.* Fr. *Nov.-Dec.*

Bulbils elongate or obpyriform. *M. spikes* on peduncles ⅛-¼″ long. Bracts usually acutely lobed nearly as long as the flowers pubescent, bracteoles much smaller. Sepals and petals sub-equal ovate. *St.* 3 only fertile, staminodes 3. Pistillode large.

The tubers are eaten.

Prain and Burkill distinguish two well-marked varieties, both of which occur in Chota Nagpur, *viz.*:—

Var. Linnæi. Silvery grey. Tuber white and soft

Var. Rumphii. Rusty-red. Root puce-coloured and stringy.

Fam. 90. COMMELINACEÆ.

Herbs rarely shrubby, with cymose often capitate or panicled, small more or less zygomorphic, rarely regular, flowers. *L.* sometimes broad, parallel-nerved. *Inflorescence* often enclosed in spathaceous often boat-shaped bracts. *Perianth* heterochlamydeous. Sep. 3 usually green. Petals 3, sometimes very unequal. *St.* hypogynous or epipetalous, all 6 perfect, or 3 or more reduced to staminodes, filaments often bearded with long coloured hairs. *Ovary* 3-2-celled, superior, with few ovules in each cell which are orthotropous. *Fruit* capsular. *Seeds* often broader than long with a minute embryo opposite the hilum, sometimes capped by a shield-like boss of the testa.

A. Stamens only 2 or 3 perfect.

Cymes restricted and included in a spathe, Petals unequal . . . . 1. *Commelina.*

Cymes not included in a spathe, often panicled. Pet. equal. . . . . 2. *Aneilema.*

B. Stamens 6 perfect.

Cymes scorpioid, fls. hidden by imbricating spathaceous bracts . . . . 3. *Cyanotis.*

1. Commelina, L.

Herbs with blue or white small irregular flowers in racemes or few fld. 2-nate cymes which are included in conduplicate or cucullate spathes, only one flower emerging at a time. Upper flowers usually male. Ovary 3 rarely 2-celled, 2 cells 1-2-ovuled, the third with only 1 ovule or empty.

1. C. bengalensis, *L.* Kana arak', *S.*

A herb with subsucculent branches often rooting below, ell.-ovate leaves 1-3″ suddenly contracted at the base or rounded, and bright-blue flowers which emerge singly from a cowl-like conduplicate spathe into which the fruit is again retracted by the reflexed pedicel.

Damp places, common, and on high ground in the rains. Fls., Fr. *July-Oct.* and also at other times.

Root with *tubers* ¼″ diam. *Stem* often pilose below the nodes, sheaths pubescent and with long setæ or ciliæ above. One fork of the *cyme* with usually a single pedicelled barren flower, the other with about 2 fertile flowers. *Capsules* 5-seeded.

The plant is eaten as a pot-herb.

2. C. suffruticosa, *Blume.* Dare orsa, *S.*

A much stouter herb than the last with large sessile lanceolate-acuminate leaves attaining 1 ft. long and 2″ broad with auricled sheaths. Spathes many small. Fls. white or blue in a 6-12-fld. raceme.

Jungles, not common.

L. roughly pubescent. *Spathes* ⅓-½″ conduplicate slightly cucullate villous, exceeding the short peduncle. *Capsule* 2-celled. Seeds rugose.

The root is applied to sores, *Campbell.*

There are several other species of Commelina in Chota Nagpur, but not, I believe, put to any use.

The genus **Aneilema** is easily distinguished from Commelina by the absence of the spathaceous conduplicate bracts. The fls. are bracteate and bracteolate with *equal* petals.

A. scapiflorum, *Wight*, is a very beautiful little plant which throws up its scapes of panicled purple-blue flowers ¾″ diam. in March and April. The ensiform *leaves* appear in May. The *sepals* are reddish, and the 3 ovary cells are each 3-6-ovuled.

The tuberous roots are credited with various medicinal properties.

3. Cyanotis, Don.

1. C. tuberosa, *Schul.* Merom chunchi, *S.*

A herb with the procumbent and ascending flowering stems 18″-2 ft. Cymes terminal in capitate corymbs, with densely imbricate villous or hairy falcately ovate-lanceolate bracts concealing the flowers except the exserted petals and stamens.

Among bushes. Fls. *July-Aug.* Fr. *Sept.*

Roots of numerous elongate fascicled tubers. *L.* tufted radical and cauline, linear-lanceolate or ensiform scaberulous and with few long silky hairs beneath, shining, often purplish beneath, margins and rest of plant villous or woolly. *Fls.* blue-purple, petals sub-equal. *Seeds* broadly conical on a flat base, rugose.

The roots are eaten. Under the Santali name Hodo jereng arak, Campbell states that "the root is given in long continued fevers and also for worms in cattle. The leaves are eaten as a pot-herb."

Fam. 91. MUSACEÆ.

1. Musa, L.

Stout often tree-like herbs with the stems composed of the convolute leaf-sheaths, large alternate *leaves* with pinnate-venation, the sec. n. spreading nearly at right-angles to the stout mid-rib. *Fls.* zygomorphic mostly monœcious, several in the axils of large leathery, often coloured, bracts. *F.* only at the base. *Bracts* arranged in a close spike terminating a peduncle which ascends from the rhizome through the middle of the stem. *Sepals* and 2 *petals* connate into a 3-5-partite split tube, posterior petal free. *Stamens*

5 fertile, posterior absent or reduced to a staminode. *Ovary* 3-celled inferior with many anatropous ovules. *Seeds* with hard testa, mealy perisperm and straight embryo.

1. **M. sapientum,** *L.* (Var. sylvestris, *Prain*) Kadal, Kadela, *K* ; Kæra, *S.* ; Kela, *H.* ; The Wild Plantain.

A tree-like herb 8-12 ft. high, the bracts deep red or purple arranged on an elongate drooping spike, the terminal forming a close club. Fls. many in the axil of each bract, fem. fls. occupying many of the lowest bracts. Odd petal shorter than rest of perianth. Fr. with a coriaceous rind and numerous black seeds.

Deep valleys in Singbhum, frequent. Northern slopes of Parasnath (Hazaribagh). Valleys in the northern Rajmehal hills.

Prain distinguishes the typical M. sapientum as being the *cultivated* variety, of which the fruit is edible uncooked (Banana). Var. paradisiaca, *F.B.I.* is the *Plantain* with firm pulp, only edible when cooked.

For a summary of information relating to Bananas and Plantains, see Kew Bulletin for August 1894.

2. **M. ornata,** *Roxb.* Syn. M. rosacea, *F.B.I.*

A stout herb 3-5 ft. high, the bracts bright rose-coloured or pink in a perfectly erect spike. Fls. 3-4 only in the bract, F. fls. occupying only the 4 lowest bracts.

A beautiful plant found growing in mud along streams in the wildest Singbhum valleys. Fl. *May-July.*

Stoloniferous. *Leaf* 4½ by 1 ft. *Petiole* 1-2 ft. The whole *inflorescence* is about 15-18″ from the base of the linear rose-coloured spathe, the tip only of which is foliaceous. Flowering part of spike 3-4″ only. *Rachis* glabrous. *Bracts* ovate-oblong 3″. *Perianth* 1½″ greenish, yellow upwards 5-toothed. Odd petal as long colourless. *Fruits* 2-4 only in a cluster, trapezoidal in section.

Fam. 92. ZINGIBERACEÆ.

Perennial herbs with an elongate or bulbous rhizome, and fleshy roots, with or without an aërial stem, which is sometimes composed of leaf-sheaths as in Musaceæ. *Leaves* large penni-veined distichous with long sheaths and short petioles and furnished with an ochrea or ligule. *Fls.* irregular

2-sexual. Perianth of two 3-merous whorls. *Calyx* tubular 3-toothed often spathaceous. *Corolla* with three equal or unequal segments. Outer whorl of stamens absent or of two often petaloid staminodes (lateral staminodes). Inner whorl of a single perfect posterior stamen and of two petaloid staminodes connate into a 'lip.' *Ovary* inferior 3-celled with many axile ovules, rarely 1-celled with 3 parietal placentæ. Style slender passing along a channel in the stout filament and connective, the large stigma projecting beyond the anther.

Three species of Globba with *parietal* placentation occur in Chota Nagpur, all the following have *axile* placentation.

1. Lateral staminodes developed, broad petaloid.

a. Stems very short or 0.

Fls. large showy, exsert from a very short spike . 1. *Gastrochilus.*

Fls. in dense spikes crowned by a coma of coloured bracts . . . . 2. *Curcuma.*

b. Flowering spikes terminating a well-developed leafy stem . . . . 3. *Hedychium.*

2. Lateral staminodes undeveloped or small. Leafy stems well developed.

a. Fls. in dense cone-like spikes, radical or terminating the stem.

Spikes radical sub-sessile. Connective with a dilated crest . . . . 4. *Amomum.*

Spikes peduncled or terminating the stem. Connective not dilated, usually tapering above . . 5. *Zingiber.*

Spikes terminal. Filament petaloid with the anther adnate . . . . . . 6. *Costus.*

b. Flowers panicled. Panicle terminating a tall leafy stem . . . . 7. *Alpinia.*

1. Gastrochilus, Wall.

1. G. longiflora, *Wall.*

A beautiful herb with oblong leaves 12-16" by 4-5½ pale and glistening beneath and large white lipped flowers variegated red with very long stalk-like perianth-tube, arising from a few flowered spike.

Singbhum jungles along muddy streams. Fls. *June-Sept.*

Petioles 12″ deeply channeled or almost winged above. *Spikes* very short lateral or from the centre of the leaves. *Perianth-tube* bright red 3-4″ long. Petals white glistening oblong 1-1¼″. *Lat. staminodes* as long, spathulate obtuse. *Lip* very large ventricose sub-orbicular entire 2″ long.

2. Curcuma, L.

Herbs with radical leaves or a short stem composed of leaf-sheaths. Rhizome often bearing tubers at the ends of long fleshy roots, or tubers sessile. *Comose* spikes independent of, or arising from the centre of, the leaf-sheaths. Lower bracts membranous bearing several flowers successively. Corolla-tube funnel-shaped. Lateral staminodes oblong connate with the short filament. Lip orbicular. Anther-cells spurred.

The tubers of many species are rich in starch and are used for food.

I. Bracts of coma pink or purple, sometimes very pale.
  A. Flowering spike distinct from the pseudostem, usually developed before it.
    Tubers yellow inside. Fls. shorter than the bracts. L. broad silky beneath . . . . . 1. *aromatica.*
    Tubers grey inside. Fls. as long or nearly as long as the bracts. L. oblong with a purple cloud, glabrous . . . . 2. *cæsia.*
    Tubers white inside. Fls. longer than the bracts. L. oblong "with dark-red mid-rib beneath" (*Prain*) glabrous . . . . . . 3. *rubescens.*
  B. Flowering spike central from the pseudostem.
    Tubers deep yellow inside . . . . . . 4. *longa.*
    Tubers pale yellow inside . . . . . . 5. *Amada.*
II. Bracts of coma orange or yellow . . . . . 6. *reclinata.*

The above key is mainly from Prain's "Bengal Plants." The species aromatica, longa and Amada are cultivated. **Curcuma aromatica**

Salisb, is called the *wild Turmeric*, **C. longa,** *L.*, being the Turmeric proper. **C cæsia,** *Roxb.* is called the Black Zedoary.

The following are the common *forest* species in Singbhum :—

3. **C. rubescens,**[1] *Roxb.* Dundir, *K.*

Whole plant from rhizome to tips of leaves 4-6 ft., rhizome small $\frac{3}{4}''$ diam. about 8″ below the surface. L. narrowly-oblong or oblong-oblanceolate 2-3 ft. by $3\frac{1}{2}$-4″ tapering into the very long petiole, acute with a short sharp acumen, glabrous. Spike with peduncle appearing before the leaves are fully developed 6″ to 12″ above ground, without peduncle $3\frac{1}{2}$-5″ by 2″. Fl.-bracts 1-$1\frac{1}{2}''$ by $\frac{3}{4}$-1″, from green to deep crimson, the margin adnate for about $\frac{1}{3}$-$\frac{1}{2}''$. Bracts of coma few magenta 2″ oblong or. ell.-oblong, inner surface puberulous.

Common in the Sal forests. Fls. *May.* L. appear end of *May*, and last till the autumn.

Fls. $1\frac{1}{2}''$ from bright sulphur-yellow with colourless corolla to a chrome yellow and a delicate pink-veined corolla. *Calyx* $\frac{1}{2}''$, usually with 2 distinct keeled pubescent obtuse lobes. *Corolla-tube* $\frac{1}{2}''$, upper lobe $\frac{3}{4}''$ ovate oblong mucronate above the involute margin. Lateral-lobes shorter. Staminodes exceeding the corolla obtuse obovate-oblong. *Lip* broadly oblong-obovate emarginate, sometimes 3-lobed.

5. **C. Amada,** *Roxb.* Paro, Dundir, *K.*; Mango Ginger.

Whole plant from rhizome to tips of leaves $2\frac{1}{2}$-$3\frac{1}{2}$ ft. L. elliptic or narrowly-elliptic $1\frac{1}{2}$-2 ft. by 3-7″ tapering into the petiole acuminate glabrous. Spike appearing from the centre of the leaves about $4\frac{1}{2}''$ by 2″ or, including the peduncle, about 12″ from base. Fl.-bracts white or greenish 1-$1\frac{1}{2}''$ oblong-obovate obtuse or truncate adnate about half-way then spreading. Bracts of coma very few pale pink or whitish about as long as the flowering.

Common in the Sal forests. Fls. *July.-Sept.*

Fls. $1\frac{1}{2}$-$1\frac{3}{4}''$ whitish with pale yellow lip. *Calyx* $\frac{3}{8}''$ truncate. *Corolla-tube* $\frac{5}{8}''$, lobes nearly as long as the staminodes and closely applied to them, posterior sometimes slightly mucronate, tip incurved, slightly longer than the others. Lateral *staminodes* pale oblong, lip a little longer nearly

---

[1] The specimens were identified by Capt. Gag at the Cal. Bot. Gardens.

straight with vertical pale side-lobes, mid-lobe emarginate yellow as is the palate.

The fresh root possesses the smell of green mango and is used as a condiment and vegetable. Medicinally it is described as cooling and useful in prurigo, *Dutt.*

6. C. reclinata, *Roxb.* Bundu, Dundir, *K.*

A small very pretty species with long petioled elliptic leaves about 10″ by 4″ with petiole 4-7″. Spikes 3-4″ with the bracts deep orange-yellow. Coma scarcely any.

On damp banks in the forests. Fls. *Aug.-Sept.*

L. acuminate with unequal base. *Bracts* 1½-2″ limb recurved rounded, bracts of coma only 1-3. *Fls.* yellow.

The globose *tubers* ¼-1″ diam. at the ends of the root fibres, like similar tubers in the other species, are called " da," and are cooked and eaten.

3. Hedychium, Kœnig.

1. H. coronarium, *Kœnig.*

A stout handsome leafy rhizomatous herb 3-5 ft. high with oblong or oblong-lanceolate distichous leaves 8-12″ and fragrant white flowers in a dense cone-like spike 6″ long at the top of the stem.

Chota Nagpur, *Prain.* Jonha, *Wood.* Rajmehal hills, in nalas near Dharampur (coll. *Jany.* without flowers, is *probably* this). A herb of watery localities.

Fls. *Aug.-Sept.*

L. usually pubescent beneath. *Spike* very dense spindle-shaped with imbricate oblong rounded 3-4-fld. bracts 1½-2″. *Corolla-tube* 3″ with reflexed linear lobes. *Lateral-staminode* petaloid ½″ diam. *Lip* 1-2″ broad exceeding the stamen, or somewhat shorter.

The flower in some varieties is yellowish, I have never seen the Chota Nagpur wild plant in flower. The species is often cultivated in gardens.

4. Amomum, L.

1. A. dealbatum, *Roxb.* Paro, *K.*

A very large herb with tuberous rootstock and stems 5-6 or 7 ft. high with distichous leaves 2-3 ft. by 4-6″. Spikes radicle 3-4″ long on a short stout peduncle. Bracts deciduous in fruit. Fls. 2" long with oblong-obovate lip 1½" by ¾" with crisped margins. Anther with a dilated sub-quadrate crest ¼" or more wide.

Watery shady places. Singbhum, Rajmehal hills and Parasnath, rare. Fls. *June*. Fr. *Aug.-Sept.* Leafy stem persistent.

L. glabrous in Singbhum, pubescent beneath in Santal Parganahs' specimens, oblong-lanceolate. *Calyx* ¾-1" minutely pubescent. *Lip* with a band of yellow or red down the centre passing into sulphur yellow near the tip otherwise pure white. Fruit oblong 1½" with 9 crenulate wings, densely packed on the radical spike.

5. Zingiber, Adans.

Tuberous herbs with leafy stems and flowers in dense bracteate spikes produced direct from the rootstock, rarely (Z. capitatum) terminal on the stem. Bracts persistent usually only 1-flowered. Lateral staminodes 0 or adnate to the obovate-cuneate lip. Fil. short, anther-cells contiguous, connective produced into a narrow or subulate appendage. Stigma small, sub-globose. Capsule not winged.

I. Spike produced direct from the rootstock.
  1. Peduncle very short, 1-2". L. pubescent beneath.
    Lip nearly as long as corolla, copiously spotted and streaked . . . . 1. *rubens*.
    Lip shorter than corolla, with or without light markings . . . . 2. *roseum*.
  2. Peduncles elongate clothed with bracts.
    a. L. glabrous beneath.
      Fl.-bracts sub-orbicular. Lip and St. purple 3. *officinale*.
      Fl.-bracts ovate. Lip and St. yellowish . 4. *Zerumbet*.
    b. L. pubescent beneath . . . . . . 5. *Casumunar*.
II. Spike terminal on the leafy stem . . . . . 6. *capitatum*.

1. **Z. rubens**, *Roxb.*, is not recorded in Bengal Plants from Chota Nagpur; it is, however, included in Wood's list but without comment or locality. 3. **Z. officinale**, *Rosc.* is the cultivated ginger. 4. **Z. Zerumbet**, *Smith*, is included in Wood's list without remark; Prain says "cultivated, and *as if wild*" in most of the provinces. The same remark is made in "Bengal Plants" against **Z Casumunar**, *Roxb.*; this species is, however, *undoubtedly* wild in both the Duars and Chota Nagpur, where indeed I

have never seen it in cultivation. The following are common Forest species:—

2. Z. roseum, *Rosc.*

Leafy stems $4\frac{1}{2}$ ft. L. oblong erecto-patent 16″ by $3\frac{1}{2}$″ minutely pubescent beneath with a filiform acumen. Ligule membranous $\frac{1}{2}$-$\frac{3}{4}$″ long. Fl.-heads oblong 3″. Outer bracts oblong, inner lanceolate $1\frac{1}{2}$″.

Sal forests in Singbhum, frequent in the valleys. Fls. *Aug.*

Bracts bright red, 1-2 barren bracts only on the short peduncle. *Corolla-segments* deep red. *Lip* oblong with a recurved crisped margin with broad short lateral segments and a sub-3-lobed terminal segment. *Stamen* bright yellow as long as the lip or somewhat shorter.

5. Z. Casumunar, *Roxb.* Paro, *K.*

Leafy stems 4-5 ft. L. narrow- or linear-oblong patent, larger 12″ by 2″ pubescent beneath and along the edges of the leaf-sheaths, finely acuminate. Ligule hardly any. Fl.-heads ovoid $2\frac{1}{2}$-5″. Bracts obovate $1\frac{1}{4}$-$1\frac{1}{2}$″.

Damper forests of Singbhum, common. Ranchi (Forests near Jonha). Palamau. Sirguja, *Wood.* Fls. *Aug.*

Peduncle 6-12″ clothed with bracts. *Fl.-bracts* deep red. *Fls.* large cream-coloured.

Tubers aromatic.

6. Z. capitatum, *Roxb.*

Leafy stems 3-4 ft. L. linear 12-18″ by 1-$1\frac{1}{2}$″ erecto-patent, more or less pubescent beneath. Ligule very short. Fl.-heads terminal oblong 3-6″. Bracts ell.-oblong below, oblong above, green with narrow brown margins.

Damper forests, probably throughout Chota Nagpur. Fls. *Aug.* Fr. as in the others often conspicuous by the bright red valves of the open capsule well into the cold season.

Corolla pale yellow. *Lip* yellow with orbicular lip and bright red basal auricles.

Tubers very aromatic.

6. Costus, L.

1. C. speciosus, *Smith*.

A handsome herb 2-6 ft. high, the stem usually spiral so that the distichous leaf arrangement is no longer apparent. L. oblong 6″-12″ thinly silky beneath. Fls. very large pure-white in terminal dense spikes 2-4″ long with scarlet ovate bracts 1-1½″ long.

Generally distributed, esp. in moist localities among undergrowth. Fls. *July-Sept.*

Calyx 1″. *Cor.-lobes* oblong 1-1½″. *Lip* sub-orbicular 2-3″ with the margins incurved and meeting. Connective oblong petaloid.

The rootstock is eaten.

7. Alpinia, L.

1. A. Galanga, *Sw.*

This is recorded in Wood's list without remark. It might possibly occur in the swampy tracts along the Ganges, or it might be only cultivated. The plant is common in the swamps of the Terai and has a leafy stem 6-7 ft. high terminated by compound pubescent panicles of flowers with a pretty obovate clawed emarginate white lip ½″ long veined with red or lilac. The fruit is globose and orange-red. It flowers *May-June.* The commonest of the Alpinias is, perhaps, **A. Allughas**, *Rosc.* with cuneate pink 2-fid lip and *black* fruits.

Fam. 93. MARANTACEÆ.

Habit much the same as in Zingiberaceæ, but petiole of leaf well developed above the sheath. *Calyx* of free sepals or sepals only slightly coherent. Outer *staminal-whorl* with generally two of its members converted into petaloid staminodes. Only *one cell* of the posterior anther of the inner whorl fertile, the other half-anther barren, usually petaloid. *Lateral-staminodes* of inner whorl not forming a lip, more or less petaloid or coriaceous, one enclosing the style and stigma. Ovary 3-1-celled. Cells 1-ovuled.

93. *MARANTACEÆ.*

1. Phrynium, Willd.

Herbs with creeping rootstock, and stem with a single large broad leaf and a lateral dense head or spike of flowers. Corolla-lobes linear-oblong spreading. Ovary 3-celled. Fr. globose indehiscent or tardily dehiscent.

1. P. capitatum, *Willd.*

A herb 4-5 ft. high with the large elliptic-oblong leaf 1-1½ ft. by 6-8″ and a solitary sessile hemispherical spike 3″ diam. of purple flowers. Bracts rigid, tip almost spinous. Capsule 3-lobed, 3-valved.

Gregarious in marshy places in dense shade, Singbhum. Not common. Fls. *March.*

2. P. parviflorum, *Roxb.*

Much resembles the last, but sessile spike 1-2″ diam., fls. white and fr. usually only 1-lobed and seeded.

Chota Nagpur, *Prain.*

Fam. 94. PALMÆ.

Trees, rarely shrubs, usually with an erect unbranched stem bearing a crown of large leaves, sometimes scandent naked or prickly, rarely stem 0. *L.* simple palmately or pinnately nerved, or palmately or pinnately divided, *petiole* sheathing. *Fls.* small regular (somewhat irregular in Areca) in spikes or panicles subtended by one or more spathes. *Perianth-leaves* usually dry and rigid free or connate, usually in two 3-merous whorls as also are the stamens, rarely *st.* 3, 9, or more (∞ in Caryota). *Carpels* 3 or by suppression 1, free or united, superior. *Ovule* 1 in each carpel. *Fr.* baccate or drupaceous. Seeds 1-3, with horny or stony albumen, sometimes ruminate.

I Erect Fan palms, (*i.e.* L. simple palmately-nerved)

- Large trees. L. flabelliform. Fls diœcious, F. large . . . . 1. *Borassus.*
- Small trees L. orbicular, deeply partite. Fls. 2-sexual, not large . . . . 2 *Licuala.*

II.	L. bi-pinnate. Lflts. flabellate or cuneiform . .	3. *Caryota.*
III.	L. pinnate. Lflts. narrow. Erect trees or shrubs.	
	Tree. Ovary 3-celled. Fruit a cocoanut . . .	4. *Cocos.*
	Trees or shrubs. Ovary of 3 free carpels. Fr. a berry	5. *Phœnix.*
	Tree. Ovary 1-celled. Fr. sub-baccate . . .	6. *Areca.*
IV.	L. pinnate. Scandent prickly shrubs . . .	7. *Calamus.*

1. Borassus, Schreb.

1. **B. flabelliformis,** *Willd.* Tale, *S.*; Tal or tali (the common vern. name derived from the Sanscrit *tala*). The Palmyra palm.

A beautiful and well-known tree with a smooth trunk attaining 60 ft. and a large crown of fan-shaped leaves with a prickly petiole. Spadices very large axillary. M. fl. very small sunk on small spikelets in the branches of the panicle. F. fl. large globose 1″ diam. with large coriaceous imbricating bracts surrounding the fleshy accrescent perianth. Drupe 6-8″ diam., 3-celled and seeded.

This palm is mostly confined to a belt in Chota Nagpur skirting the Gangetic plain from the Sone to the Ganges at Sahebganj. It is, however, common on the Palaman and Hazaribagh hills within this zone, esp. on gneissic rocks, and occurring quite naturalized in the jungles. Anderson speaks of semispontaneous Borassus and Phœnix between Raneegunge and the Barakur R. Elsewhere it is only occasional and near villages.

Fls. *May.* Fr. the following *May.*

2. Licuala, Thunb.

1. **L. peltata,** *Roxb.*

A small erect palm 6-20 ft. high with sub-orbicular digitately partite leaves with obcuneate segments and interfoliar erect spadices 6-8 ft. with simple drooping tomentose spikes 8-18″ long.

Swamps at the heads of springs and along sluggish streams in the Saranda forests, frequent. Fls. *Dec.-April.* Fr. *March-May.*

L. 3-5 ft. diam. with a deciduous rufous tomentum. *Lflts.* 4-10″ wide at top truncate, sharply plaited with rounded retuse or emarginate lobes. *Petiole* 3-4 ft. with stout lateral reflexed spines. *Spathes* 12″ with 3-4 sharp teeth. *Fls.* sub-sessile. *Calyx* obconic $\frac{1}{3}$-$\frac{1}{2}$″ toothed. *Corolla-lobes* hard spreading or erect ovate-lanceolate acute downy, lobes as long as calyx-tube. *St.* 6. *Ovary* of 3-1 nearly free carpels. Style as long. *Fr.* ellipsoid $\frac{1}{2}$″ orange.

Leaves used for mats, etc. Elephants feed on the lower parts of the stem.

3. Caryota, L.

1. C. urens, *L.* Mari, *H.*

A beautiful erect palm 30-40 ft. with trunk slightly ringed, immense bi-pinnate leaves 15-20 ft. with alt. obcuneate leaflets 4-8″, obliquely præmorse and much jagged. Fls. innumerable on the numerous branches of a drooping spadix many feet long.

Northern steep ravines. Once fairly frequent near Tuia in the Saitba forest, etc., but now unfortunately nearly extinct, having been cut down by the Kols for its sago. Fl. *May-Aug.*

The *flowers* are monœcious, 3-nate, a female between two males. *Sepals* rounded. *Petals* linear-oblong in M., rounded in F. *St.* many. *Ovary* 3-celled.

Cocos nucifera, *Willd.* Narial, *H.* The Cocoa-nut Palm is occasionally seen planted near villages. The fruit is described as a coriaceous drupe with a fibrous pericarp. Two of the three scars on the nut are said to represent the blind germ-pores of the two aborted carpels. The large leaves are pari-pinnate.

5. Phœnix, L. Khajur, H.

Trees, or almost stemless shrubs, with pinnate leaves of which the leaflets usually lie in different planes, the lowest often converted into spines. Diœcious. Fls. coriaceous, small. M. calyx 3-toothed, pet. 3, valvate ; st. usually 6. F. globose calyx accrescent, pet. rounded imbricate, stmdes. 6 or a 6-toothed cup ; carpels 3 free, of which one only develops into a berry with a more or less fleshy pericarp.

1. P. acaulis, *Buch. Ham.* Kita, *K.* ; Pind Khajur, *H.*

Stem hardly any, or thick and ovoid covered with the persistent leaf bases, lflts. fascicled, not in one plane, lowest reduced to long sharp spines, base thickened and decurrent on the rachis. Spadix 6-10″, elongating to 1-3 ft. in fruit. Berry ½″ red, finally black.

A common plant especially on poor clay soils in open grassy forest. On quartz in Eastern Palamau. The Kita buru in the Saitba forest which is almost entirely grass and Kita is composed of Serpentine.

Fls. *April.* Fr. *May-June.*

The fruits are much eaten by pea-fowl. The leaves are used for thatching, mats, etc. A Sago is prepared from the soft tissue of the stem.

2. **P. humilis,** *Royle.* Kita, *K.*

Stem attains 6-7 ft. L. much as in last but leaflets softer, the base not swollen or decurrent on the rachis. The spadix 1·3 ft. and usually exceeding the leaves in fruit.

Less common than the last. Chiefly on ridges esp. on white clay schists.

Fl. and Fr. the same time, and uses similar.

3. **P. robusta,** *Hook. f.* P. humilis, var. robusta, *Beccari.*

Stem attains 15 ft. or more, very stout "tessellated with short persistent rhomboidal leaf bases" ripe fruit brown. Reported by Hooker from Parasnath only.

4. **P. sylvestris,** *Roxb.* Khajur, *K., H.*

Stem tall and leaves 7-12 ft. Fr. 1-1½″ long, orange, ripens August.

Frequently cultivated for toddy, esp. between Chorparan and Barhi in Hazaribagh. The fruit is also eaten and the leaves used for mats.

6. Areca, L.

1. **A. Catechu,** *L.* Gua, *S., Beng.*; Supari, *H.*; The Areca or Betel-nut Palm.

A very graceful palm with a very slender trunk. L. pinnate below, pinnatifid or undivided above. Spadices from below the leaves, branched, with numerous spikes bearing the female flowers at their base, and many minute oblique male flowers above. St. 6. Ovule 1 basal erect. Fr. 1½-2″ with a fibrous mesocarp. Albumen ruminate.

Only very sparingly cultivated in Chota Nagpur, the climate of which is too dry for it.

7. Calamus, L. Cane.

1. C. viminalis, *Willd.* Bent, *H., K.*; Bĕt, *S.*

A very slender palm climbing in favourable situations by long slender thorny flagellæ (from the leaf-sheaths and spadix) which are armed with 2-3-fid claws. L. pari-pinnate 2-3 ft. long with fascicled or irregularly scattered linear-lanceolate leaflets with sharp bristles on the mid-rib, nerves and margin. Spadix very long much branched with several spathes, the first elongate-tubular, closely sheathing Fr. $\frac{1}{3}$-$\frac{1}{2}$" diam., pale-yellow, scaly, beaked.

Wild in rocky valleys in Singbhum, but rare, and I have never seen it in flower.

Fam. 95. ARACEÆ.

Usually stout herbs with a perennial rhizome, sometimes scandent, with sheathing often peltate simple or compound leaves, generally basal-nerved and with reticulate venation. Individual *flowers* inconspicuous but usually crowded on a cylindrical fleshy rachis (spadix) which is often subtended by a large green or brightly coloured spathe. *Fls.* ebracteolate 1-2-sexual usually monœcious (diœcious in some Arisæma), shewing a progressive reduction from complete flowers to 1-sexual flowers composed of a single stamen or pistil. *Spadix* often produced into a barren portion "*appendage*" above the flowers. *Fr.* a berry, rarely dry. Outer integument of the seed fleshy

From a forest point of view, the Aroids are important from their yielding nutritious or poisonous tubers. Many species possess laticiferous vessels and these are all more or less poisonous, but the poison may be dissipated by heat.

I. Perianth present.

A stout prickly herb . . . . 1. *Lasia.*

II. Perianth suppressed.

A. Fls. 2-sexual. Stamens distinct. A stout climber 2. *Scindapsus*

B. Fls. 1-sexual monœcious (sometimes diœcious in Arisæma)

Stamens synandrous. L. undivided. Ovary 1-celled.

Ovules many parietal. Limb of spathe spreading and reflexed . . . . . 3. *Remusatia.*

Ovules many parietal. Limb of spathe erect narrow . . . . 4. *Colocasia.*

Ovules few basal. Limb of spathe erect . 5. *Alocasia.*

2. Stamens free. L. deeply lobed or compound. Ovary 1-4 celled.

a. Ovary 1-celled. Ovules 1-2 basal erect. Appendage elongate.

Fls. with leaves. L. hastately 3-lobed or sub-3-partite . . . . 6. *Typhonium.*

Fls. before leaves. L. one pedatipartite . 7. *Sauromatum.*

Fls. with leaves. L. (in C. N. species) 2-3, pedatisect . . . . 8. *Arisæma.*

b. Ovary 2-4-celled. Ovule 1 in each cell. Appendage 0 or short.

Neuter flowers between the M. and F. Appendage 0. 9. *Plesmonium.*

Neuter flowers 0. Appendage short and very stout 10. *Amorphophallus.*

1. Lasia, Lour.

1. L. heterophylla, *Schott.* Kanta saru, Gola Kanta, *S.*

A very spiny stout herb with thick creeping rhizome and hastate pinnatifid prickly leaves with the lower lobes pedate. Spathe deep purple 1 ft. long, twisted, convolute, thick and rather brittle, deciduous.

Along muddy streams in Singbhum and the Santal Parganahs. Fls. Fr. *Dec.-Feby.*

Spadix 2″. *Fls.* densely packed 2-sexual, with 4 pink imbricate perianth leaves hooded over the stamens. *Fil.* flat broad, connective behind the 2-celled anthers very delicate. *Stigma* broad sessile. Head of fruits oblong 4-6″ by 2″ diam. Fr. more or less 4-sided muricate ¾″ long. *Seed* large with a coriaceous testa.

Fr. and rhizome used for sore or swollen throat.

cordate leaves with a tubular green thick accrescent lower portion of the spathe and a convolute yellow upper portion or limb. The male and female portions of the spadix separated by flat neuters.

Damp banks and among rocks frequent. Often cultivated. Fls. *Aug.-Oct.* Fl. with the leaves.

Very variable. Prain keeps C. nymphæifolia, *Kunth,* distinct, and characterizes it as having a bronze margin to the leaves and a dark yellow spathe, while C. Antiquorum has leaves quite green and pale yellow spathe. The following wild forms of the latter occur :—

a. L. green 10″ by 7″, petioles over 18″. Peduncle 6-10″, green tube 3″, limb 6″ yellow-white. F. portion of inflorescence 1″, neuter portion 2″ and M. 1″ with appendage 4″, some neuters also below the appendage. Root fibrous. Wet places.

b. L. 7″ rather glaucous beneath with a very fine green nervation petiole 10″. Peduncle $4\frac{1}{2}$″, tube $1\frac{1}{2}$″, limb 4″ yellow. F. portion of inflorescence only $\frac{1}{2}$″. Root tuberous. Among rocks.

c. L. deep purple beneath. Banks of streams in Saranda forests

The plant is eaten as a vegetable.

5. Alocasia, Schott.

Distinguished from Colocasia by the characters given in the key. The rootstock is more often sub-erect or erect and sometimes even forms a distinct stem.

Leaves distinctly peltate.
- L. sagittate with basal lobes connate about $\frac{1}{3}$rd their length . . . . . 1. *fornicata.*
- L. sagittate with basal lobes connate about $\frac{1}{10}$th their length . . . . . 2. *macrorrhiza.*

L. not or only slightly peltate . . . . . 3. *indica.*

1. A. fornicata, *Schott.*

A stout herb with strongly 3-nerved leaves 18″ by 10″ or larger, shining, cuspidate. Basal lobes not half as long as the terminal. Petiole 2-3 ft. Spathe $3\frac{1}{2}$″ only consisting of a green tube 1″ and an expanded whitish-green limb $2\frac{1}{2}$″ long, oblong cuspidate as long as the spadix.

Along muddy sluggish streams in dense forest. Fls. *July-Aug.*

Top of *staminal-column* crenulate, cells several opening by pores above. *Ovules* 3-5. *Style* short stout. Stigma capitate.

2. **A. macrorrhiza**, *Schott*, and 3. **A indica**, *Schott*, only occur cultivated and near villages. The former is remarkable for the enormous development of the stem, and the leaves in lower Bengal may attain 4 ft.

6. Typhonium, Schott.

1. T. trilobatum, *Schott.*

A herb with a sub-globose tuber, hastately 3-lobed leaves 4-7" long and broad, petiole 6"-1 ft. Spathe 3-8" purplish inside and nearly flat. Spadix produced into a bright red muricate appendage. Neuters long curved filiform.

Valleys in Singbhum, often in rocky places. Fls. *Aug.-Sept.*

7. Sauromatum, Schott.

1. S. guttatum, *Schott.*

A herb with a hemispherical tuber. Leaf solitary 6-12" broad pedati-partite. Spathe about 7" narrow-oblong with purple blotches, margin incurved and sinuate. Peduncle 0. Spadix rather shorter than spathe with long stalked clavate neuters above the ovaries, then a smooth purple striate space about $1\frac{1}{2}$" long with the males above. Appendage long and slender.

Fls. *April.* The leaf appears in *June.*

Arisæma tortuosum, *Schott*, has only been found on Parasnath in Chota Nagpur.

It is easily recognized by its erect stem with 2-3 pedate leaves and terminal green spathe with cymbiform limb. The spadix with its appendage is exsert erect but with an intermediate obliquely curved portion. Fls. *August*.

9. Plesmonium, Schott.

1. P. margaritiferum, *Schott.* Had, *K.*

A herb with a hemispherical tuber about 3" diam. Leaves 12-18" diam. ternate with the segments pinnatisect, the lateral forked. Lflts. 4-6" linear acuminate. Spathe tubular green leathery 4″ deep purple within at base, flushed purple above broadly ovate when unfolded.

Common. Fls. *June.* Leaves do not appear till the rains are well set in.

Petiole $1\frac{1}{2}$-2 ft. green. *Peduncle* about 15″ mottled brown below, bract at base 4″ narrow oblong cuspidate dry. *Spadix* 4-5″. F. portion about $\frac{3}{4}$″, above this yellow disciform neuters, then the male portion about 3″.

The tubers are eaten after much cooking.

10. Amophophallus, Blume.

Tuberous herbs, flowering before leafing. L. ternately compound with the segments simple or forked, pinnatisect. Limb of spathe various, marcescent. Spadix with a large but not elongate appendage. M. and F. contiguous without an intermediate space or neuters.

1. A. campanulatus, *Blume.* Ol, *K.*, *S.*, *H.*

A very stout herb with the leaf 1-3 ft. broad and petiole about as long, rarely leaves two. Lateral segments usually bifurcate with oblong leaflets 4-8″. Petiole mottled dark and light green very stout and *rough with small tubercles.* Peduncle very short, elongating in fruit. Spathe broad open campanulate 6″ across with sinuate and crenulate margin, appendage short thick sinuous, purple.

Usually near villages and often cultivated, doubtfully wild.

The large hemispherical or depressed globose bulbilliferous tuber is eaten.

2. A. bulbifer, *Blume.*

Similar but leaf not usually so broad and leaflets obovate or lanceolate. Petiole as long, green and pink mottled with black, *not* rough. Peduncle long with erect pinkish spathe with an ovate cymbiform obtuse limb. Appendage 3-4″ long.

Common in the forests. Fls. *May.* L. appear *June.*

The leaf usually bears a large bulbil at the forks, by which it is easily recognized.

Fam. 96. PANDANACEÆ.

1. Pandanus, L. f.

1. **P. fascicularis,** *Lam.* Keora, *H.*, Kia baha, *S.*; The Screw Pine.

A small tree with numerous thick aërial roots, and spirally 3-farious long narrow spinulose leaves in terminal crowns.

Ranchi Lake, *Wood*, but probably planted. Often cultivated. Fls. *r.s.*

L. 3-5 ft. long. *Fls.* diœcious small crowded on a spadix without perianth. M. with numerous stamens with connate filaments. F. in fruit of firm obconic drupes 1½″ long connate in groups in an oval cone-like head 6-8″ long.

The flowers, esp. the males, are very sweet-scented.

Fam. 97. GRAMINEÆ.[1]

Grasses or bamboos. Annual or perennial plants, if perennial usually with annual shoots with hollow internodes (solid in most Andropogoneæ), alt. distichous leaves and minute flowers concealed by imbricating bracts (*glumes*). *Leaf* with a split tubular sheath furnished with a ligule at the mouth, *ligule* sometimes of hairs only or, rarely, altogether absent. *Petiole* usually 0, except in the bamboos. *Glumes* imbricate in small spikes (*spikelets*), the lowest two and sometimes also the uppermost empty. Rachis of the spikelet (*rachilla*) sometimes articulate below the spikelet or above the two lowest glumes. *Spikelets* variously arranged in spikes or panicles. *Flowers* 1-2-sexual sub-sessile in the axils of the flowering glumes, usually with a bracteole (pale, palea) on the opposite side to the glume which frequently closely invests the ovary or fruit. *Perianth* 0 or perhaps represented by the *lodicules*, 2 rarely 3 minute hypogynous scales

---

[1] In the genera Andropogon and its allies considerable use has been made of the "Oil grasses of India and Ceylon," by Dr. Otto Stapf' (Published in Kew Bulletin, No. 8 of 1906.)

which usually become turgid at flowering, or may be absent. *St.* 2 or 3, rarely (Rice, some Bamboos, etc.) 6. Anthers versatile. *Ovary* with 2 (rarely 1 or 3) usually feathery stigmas. Ovule 1. Ovary wall adherent to the seed in fruit, frequently also to the pale and glume.

(*Note.*—The glumes in a *spikelet* are numbered in Roman figures from the base upwards.)

A. Each spikelet with only 1 or 2 *flowering* glumes, if 2 then only the upper one fruiting. Rachilla articulate on the pedicels (exc. in Arundinella, Pennisetum, and Isachne) below the *empty* glumes, deciduous (so that the whole spikelet falls off together when old), or deciduous with the pedicel in Pennisetum. Rachilla of the spikelets not articulate above the lowest glumes.

I. Spikelets, not geminate. Rachis of the spike not articulate.

a. Spikelets spicate.

1. Spikelets fascicled on the spike.

Spkts. sessile in deciduous fascicles with an involucel of bristles . . . . 1. *Pennisetum.*

Spkts. shortly pedicelled, involucel of bristles persistent . . . . 2. *Setaria.*

2. Spikelets not in fascicles. Fruiting glume and pale much hardened.

Glumes on one side of a flattened rachis, never awned . . . . 3. *Paspalum.*

Rachis of spike not flat . . . . 4. *Panicum.*

b. Spkts. panicled, not spicate

1. Glumes 4, two lowest, sometimes 3 empty.

Gl. I very small. III usually male, IV 2-sexual hardening . . . . 4. *Panicum.*

Gl. I and II minute. III empty, IV clothed with white hairs . . . . 5. *Thysanolæna.*

2. Glumes 4, III and IV usually awned and flowering. Spkts. not articulate on pedicel . . . . . 6. *Arundinella.*

3. Glumes 2-3, III much the largest and strongly nerved . . . . . . 7. *Oryza.*

II. Tribe Andropogoneæ. Spikelets geminate, usually one sessile and one pedicelled, terminal sometimes ternate. Inflorescence usually of spikes or panicled spikes, the rachis of the spike articulate (exc. Apluda). Flowering glume smaller than the empty ones, hyaline, usually awned or reduced to an awn base.

a. Spikelets all 1-sexual only the males 2-3-nate, in a separate inflorescence or part of inflorescence from the female.

Fruiting spkts. conspicuous by the large hard white bracts . . . . 8. *Coix*.

Fem. spkts. with long cottony stigmas. Frt. exposed (Maize). . . . . 9. *Zea*.

b. Spikelets 2-sexual (fls. often 1-sexual) or one of each pair 2-sexual.

1. Spkts. of each pair similar (subsimilar in Pogonatherum) and homogamous, if heterog. then fem. pedicelled. Spikes not subtended by spathes.

† Spkts. many in hirsute or silky spikes which are solitary digitate or fascicled (or sub-panicled in Ischæmum spp.)

i. Gl. I of sessile spkt. convex or dorsally flattened with narrowly inflexed margins.

Gl. IV very much reduced. Pale as short as the ovary 10. *Pollinia*.

Gl. IV distinct and its pale longer than the ovary . 11. *Ischæmum*.

ii. Gl. I of sessile spkt. laterally compressed. Awns two . . 12. *Pogonatherum*

†† Spkts. in a dense silvery-hairy thyrsus or spreading panicle.

Both spkts. of the pairs pedicelled. Stem 1-3 ft. . 13. *Imperata*.

Pairs of one sessile and one pedicelled spkt. Gl. IV awnless . . . . 14. *Saccharum*.

As in Saccharum but Gl. IV distinctly awned . 15. *Erianthus*.

2. Spkts. often dissimilar, always heterogamous, 1-fld. Sessile spkts. usually 2-sexual, pedicelled male or neuter (rarely 2-sexual in Apluda).

† Sessile spkts. all similar to one another. Spkts. 2-or 3-nate on the whorled articulate branches of simple or compound panicles, spikes not sheathed by spathes (*exc.* Andropogon spp., in which also the inflorescence is various).

Spkts. 1-few on a branch. Tips of articulations truncate, not bearded . . . . . . 16. *Sorghum.*

Spkts. 1 sessile and 2 pedicelled on a branch, tips of articulations obliquely truncate and bearded . . 17. *Chrysopogon.*

Spkts. many on a branch, or spike, or if few then joints and pedicels compressed with thickened margins and translucent centre . . . 18. *Andropogon.*

†† Lower sessile spikelets, differing from those above them. Spkts. in simple or geminate spikes, common peduncle of latter in a spathiform leaf sheath.

Spikes simple terminal . . . . 19. *Heteropogon.*

Spikes geminate in a leafy panicle . . . 20. *Cymbopogon.*

††† Spkts. in capitate or fascicled spikes with spathiform leaf sheaths, the whole in leafy panicles.

Clusters of 2 or more pedicelled bracteate spikes and empty glumes (reduced spikes) subtended by spathes. Spikes with one 2-sexual spkt. sessile on the bulbous base of the short rachis, 1 empty basal sessile spkt. and 1 male or neuter terminal spkt. . . . . 21. *Apluda.*

Clusters of one or few pairs of sessile and pedicelled spkts. surrounded by an involucre of empty ones . . . . 22. *Anthistiria.*

B. Each spikelet with 1-many flowering glumes. Spkts. not articulate on their pedicels or deciduous with their pedicels, but rachilla usually articulate above the two lowest glumes (so that when ripe these two glumes only remain attached to the pedicel).

Spkts. with only 3 glumes, 1-fld., unilateral on 3-6 digitate slender spikes . . . 23. *Cynodon.*

Spkts. with more than 3 glumes, 3-12-fld. sessile and 2-3-seriate in dense digitate spikes . . 24. *Eleusine.*

Spkts. few-fld. sessile solitary at the nodes of a spike, with the plane of the spkt. tangential to the rachis (Wheat) . . . 25. *Triticum.*

Spkts. 1-fld. sessile 2-3-nate at the nodes of a spike, with the plane of the spkt. tangential to the rachis (Barley) . . . 26. *Hordeum.*

Spkts. 2 many-fld., with long narrow glumes, in effuse large panicles, the flowering glumes with long silky hairs on the callus . 27. *Phragmites.*

C. The Bamboos. Spikelets. 1-many-fld. St. 6.

Spkts. in loose or dense not globose clusters not completely whorled round the stiff rachis. Auricles (of stem sheaths) large, or if small then branches prickly . . . 28. *Bambusa.*

Spkts. in very dense globose prickly heads entirely concealing the nodes of the stiff rachis. Stem sheaths only slightly auricled . 29. *Dendrocalamus.*

Spkts. in bracteate clusters on a very slender drooping rachis. Stem sheaths short with large fringed auricles . . . . . 30. *Cephalostachyum.*

1. Pennisetum, Pers.

Usually stout grasses, sometimes annual, with spiciforem inflorescence which is composed of clusters of 1-3 spikelets. in an involucel of scabrid or plumose simple or branched bristles, the whole cluster being articulate on the rachis. Glumes normally 4. but I very short or sometimes 0 ; IV only bearing an ovary.

A very tall stout cultivated annual . . . . . 1. *typhoideum.*

Involucel ciliate. Rachis of spike glabrous . 2. *setosum.*

Involucel densely villous. Rachis of spike glabrous . . . . 3. *pedicellatum.*

Involucel ciliate. Rachis of spike hairy . . . 4. *orientale.*

Involucel glabrous . . . . 5. *parviflorum.*

1. P. typhoideum, *Rich.* Tuti, *K.* ; Lendha, *S.* ; Bajri, *H.*

A striking grass 4-5 ft. high sparingly cultivated in Chota Nagpur, bearing very dense cylindrical spiciform inflorescences. Fls. *Stpt.* Fr. *Nov-Dec.*

2. P. setosum, *Rich.* Swati, *Beng.*

A handsome grass 3-4 ft. high (or only 1 ft.) fastigiately branched above with flaccid leaves $\frac{3}{4}$-$\frac{7}{8}''$ broad and reddish spikes $1\frac{1}{2}$-$2''$ long with tufts of barren filiform villous bristles and a sessile, or sessile and shortly pedicelled, spikelet. Some of the bristles $\frac{3}{8}''$ long, red, beautifully plumose except above.

Among rocks chiefly, rather local, abundant in Palamau. Fls. *Nov.-Dec.*

Spikelets usually solitary in the cluster. *Gl.* I shorter than the others, hyaline; II longest $\frac{1}{8}''$ 5-nerved shortly awned, both villous; III 5-nerved, 3-toothed with very minute bristles or ciliæ; IV and its pale both bristly at the tip.

2. Setaria, Beauv.

1. **S. italica,** *Beauv.* Erba, *S.*, is a cultivated grass (Italian Millet) but is not largely grown. 2. **S. glauca,** *Beauv.* Kukru, *K.*, *S.*, is a grass 18″-2 ft. high occurring among other crops spontaneously but of which the seed is gathered and eaten. It has inflated leaf-sheaths. *Ligule* of very short stiff hairs. *Spike* dense $2\frac{1}{2}$-$3\frac{1}{2}''$ by $\frac{1}{4}''$. *Involucel* of about 10 long stiff bristles $\frac{1}{4}''$ long which are barbed, whereas the bristles of S. italica are not, or very minutely, barbed. Gl. IV is very hard transversely rugose and closing round the hard pale and fruit.

3. Paspalum, L.

Paspalum has its spikelets on one side of a broad flat rachis; these secund spikes are usually racemed, or in a simple panicle. Gl. I is absent, the other three glumes correspond with II-IV of Panicum. The genus contains important fodder grasses, but some species are poisonous.

1. P. scrobiculatum, *L.* Gara Kode, *K.*; Janhe, *S.*

A grass 3-4 ft. high with a perennial creeping root, or annual, with lower sheaths inflated and compressed hairy at the edges and ligule of long hairs. Spikes about 3 distant spreading on an angular almost 2-winged rachis.

In ravines and wild. Also cultivated as a crop. Camp. says sown about beginning of rains on high lands and reaped in November. Fls. *Oct.-Nov.*

L. 18″ by $\frac{3}{8}''$ glabrous with scabrid margins. *Spikes* 3-$3\frac{1}{4}''$ base with ong hairs. *Spikelets* 2-seriate broad-elliptic oblong $\frac{1}{8}''$. Gl. II and III sub-equal membranous with one central and two marginal green nerves, IV crustaceous in fruit with inflexed margins.

The grain is eaten.

4. Panicum, L.

A large genus of grasses of various habit, a great number very common as meadow grasses in the rainy season. The genus is fairly easily recognized by its 4 glumes of which I is always very small and fewer nerved than the others, II and III usually sub-equal 3-many nerved, III sometimes with a M. flower. IV paleate and 2-sexual becoming *hard in fruit* and its edges usually wrapping round the hardened pale. One section closely resembles Paspalum, in another the inflorescence is a large effuse panicle. An awn is absent (exc. in P. Crus-galli) the branches of the panicle are however sometimes produced into an awn-like bristle.

The following are the most striking, common or useful :—

A. Spikelets arranged much as in Paspalum. Gl. I present but very small.

1. **P. flavidum,** *Retz.* A very common grass erect from a geniculate creeping base. *Stem* flattened. *L.* glabrous, ligule 0, represented by long hairs. *Spikes* on panicle erect distant much shorter than the internodes about 1″. *Spikelets* 2-seriate. *Gl.* IV minutely rugose.

2. **P. punctatum,** *Burm.*, is somewhat similar but *spikes* only ½″ and internodes not much longer, stem copiously branched from the creeping base. Tip of spike excurrent setiform. *Spikelets* sub-globose. *Glumes* sub-orbicular. IV granulate as also is the hardened pale.

3. **P. javanicum,** *Poir.* Creeping and ascending 1-2 ft. high with *leaves* 6-7″ by ¾-1″ broad with cordate base, ciliate sheaths, bearded ligule and conspicuous pubescent nodes. *Spikelets* 1-seriate or in unequally pedicelled pairs not closely appressed to the rachis. *Spikes* ¾-2″ long conspicuous from the long hairs on the pedicels of the spikelets. *Gl.* IV hard rugulose white apiculate.

4. **P. Crus-galli,** *L.* 1-3 ft. high, frequent in moist ground, with several secund *spikes* 1-3″ long and *spikelets* 3-4-nate on the rachis. Easily recognized by the awned Gl. III. Gl. IV shining white.

B. Spikelets very many crowded on a spike-like inflorescence (a panicle with very close reduced lateral branches).

5. **P. myosuroides,** *Br.*, is a very slender grass 3-4 ft. growing in marshes with shining striate stems, loose glabrous leaf-sheaths, short flat

leaves and very long slender tail-like *panicles* often 8 or more inches long, often purple. *Spikelets* innumerable ovoid $\frac{1}{18}''$ on pedicles $\frac{1}{30}''$.

6. **P. indicum**, *L.* Very similar but spiciform panicles only about 2″. *Stems* often red. *Spikelets* 1-2-nate oblong acute $\frac{1}{12}$-$\frac{1}{10}''$.

C. Spikelets on the branches of a decompound usually open panicle, or branches of the panicle sometimes erect.

(1) Panicle usually contracted with many erect slender branches.

7. **P. miliare**, *Lamk.* Gandli, Gundli, *K.*, *S.*, is a millet 1-3 ft. high, cultivated in Chota Nagpur rather frequently. *L.* hairy.

8. **P. repens**, *L.*, somewhat resembles it but the panicle is sometimes somewhat effuse, it is a grass of wet places with a creeping and ascending stem. *L.* glabrous or hairy with a ciliate rounded base and sheaths with ciliate margins. *Ligule* a narrow coriaceous ring. The short pedicels have a cupular tip. *Spikelets* erect. Gl. I truncate.

(2) Panicle usually large and effuse.

9. **P. maximum**, *Jacq.*, is the Guinea grass, a native of Africa. I grew this successfully in Singbhum, and it is a most useful fodder. It is a large perennial, easily propagated both by seed and division of the roots.

10. **P. montaum**, *Roxb.* A common forest grass 3-4 ft. with very slender stems, short broad *leaves* 5-6″ by $\frac{3}{4}$-1″ suddenly narrowed to a short ciliate base and terminal large effuse *panicles* 12″ both ways with capillary 1-3-nate branches usually with swollen axils. Minute *spikelets* $\frac{1}{12}''$ long terminating long capillary pedicels. Fls., Fr. *Nov.-Dec.* Stem glabrous striate. *Sheaths* minutely pubescent with ciliate margins, *ligule* very short truncate. Base of leaf with long ciliæ. Gl. I 3-nerved (or 5-nerved F.B.I.); Gl. II-III, 5-nerved; Gl. IV polished brown.

11. **P. plicatum**, *Lamk.* A very distinct perennial grass with broad plicate leaves somewhat resembling those of a Curculigo and large thyrsoid or effuse panicles of which the branchlets are often produced into a bristle. Moist valleys in the hilly forests, rare.

5. Thysanolæna, Nees.

1. **T. Agrostis**, *Nees.* Dodri, Gara jonor, *K.*; Karsar, *S.*

A very large grass 5-10 ft. high with stems often $\frac{1}{2}''$ diam., large broad flat leaves 18″ by 3″, and large decompound effuse panicles often 3 ft. by 2 ft. of innumerable minute spikelets.

On shady slopes, but especially along ravines and water-courses. Singbhum, Manbhum and probably in all the districts. *Fls. May.*

Glabrous. L. broadest at the base. *Ligule* truncate nearly obsolete. Branches of *panicle* rather flexuous swollen below and pubescent or tomentose on the swelling. Gl. I and II very minute nerveless, III and IV green sub-equal, IV clothed with white hairs.

Used for brooms. Campbell says that a decoction of the root is used for rinsing the mouth in fever.

6. Arundinella, Raddi.

Erect often perennial slender or stout grasses with narrow leaves and terete spikelets pedicelled and paired along the usually slender and ascending branches of a panicle. Spikelets usually inarticulate on the pedicels but with the glumes I and II sometimes separately deciduous. Gl. IV small thin articulate and bearded at the base and awned, sometimes 2-sexual. Gl. III male or neuter paleate equalling or rather longer than I; II lanceolate or ovate-lanceolate, acuminate or sub-aristate 5-7-nerved.

1. A. setosa, *Trin.* Jharu, Motamui jhar, *K.*

A cæspitose slender grass 3-3½ ft. with tufted stoloniferous rootstock, smooth glabrous stems, flat and involute setaceous-acuminate leaves 6-8″ (on the stem) and not over ¼″ broad. Spikelets ¼″ paired in unequally pedicelled pairs on slender racemes 3″ long, these racemed on a panicle 3-5″ long.

Very common and sub-gregarious on dry hills. Fls. *Sept.-Oct.*

L. ciliate with long rather rigid hairs. *Ligule* short truncate. Lower *spikelets* often reduced to empty glumes. Gl. I cymbiform strongly 3-ribbed awned; II 5-nerved long-beaked; III 3-nerved muticous membranous with hyaline pale; IV $\frac{1}{12}$″ with 2 slender tails and a slender $\frac{1}{3}$-$\frac{1}{2}$″ long awn. Used for brooms.

2. **A. brasiliensis,** *Raddi,* has stems 1-5 ft. and stout perennial rootstock, the *panicle* attains 18″ and the *spikelets,* which are $\frac{1}{8}$-$\frac{1}{6}$″ long, lack the slender lateral tails on glume IV which bears a solitary twisted awn.

It is less common than the last.

3. **A. tenella,** *Nees.*, is an annual grass with very small spikelets under $\frac{1}{10}''$.

4. **A. Wallichii,** *Nees.*, is a rather stout perennial 1-3 ft. very distinct from the others in the short stiff 1-3-nate branches of the panicle rarely exceeding 1″ long with an angled scabrous rachis, and in Gl. IV being nearly or quite awnless, or with a short stiff straight awn. *Spikelets* close ciliate.

Oryza sativa, *L.* Baba, *K.* (there are various names for different races), is the rice plant which occurs apparently (or truly?) wild in marshy localities. The Kols distinguish numerous distinct races but classify them generally into *Gora* or upland, and *bera* or lowland rice. The spikelets of Oryza are 1-fld., oblong and laterally compressed with only 2-3 glumes. Gl. III much the largest, strongly 3-5-nerved, sometimes awned. St. 6.

O. granulata, *Nees et Arn.*, is a forest grass with awnless spikelets in simple racemes and Gl. III glabrous and granulate.

Coix Lachryma-Jobi, *L.* Horeng, *M.*; Jargadi, Gargadi, *S.*

A stout very leafy grass easily recognised in fruit by the oval shining white or grey bodies which are $\frac{1}{4}$-$\frac{1}{3}''$ long and of almost stony hardness. These are *bracts* which enclose the fem. spikelets and through which the male portion of the spike projects, they are green and coriaceous in flower.

Common in watery places and also among rocks on northern slopes. Fls., Fr. *Nov.-Feby.*

L. 4-12″ by 1″ or more broad *M. spikelets* 2-3-nate at the nodes of the rachis, one sessile and two pedicelled with 4 glumes of which III and IV are 3-androus or empty.

Variable. Prain distinguishes **C. gigantea,** *Roxb.* (reduced to a variety in F.B.I.), as a separate species distinguished by the large size (sometimes 15 ft.) and the numerous male spikelets with Gl. I broadly winged.

Horses are fond of the leaves, but soon tire of it. A bad fodder.

Zea Mays, *L.* Jondra, *M.* Maize, Indian Corn, a native of America, is cultivated in the rains. The *spikelets* are unisexual, the males in terminal panicles, the *F. spikelets* are sessile densely crowded in vertical series on the thick rachis of axillary spikes which are enclosed by several bracts or spathes from the top of which the several very long styles and 2-fid stigmas project. The fruits become exserted from the small glumes as they enlarge.

2. Scindapsus, Schott.

1. S. officinalis, *Schott.* Dhare jhapak', *S.*

A stout epiphyte climbing by means of rootlets, with almost woody stems when old and large leaves with dilated petiolar sheaths. Spathe green, ultimately yellow within, terminating in a long acumen, deciduous. Spadix stout nearly as long, elongating to 6-9″ in fruit, with densely packed prismatic truncate ovaries grooved below, the short 4-celled anthers in the grooves.

In the damper valleys of Singbhum; Manbhum, *Camp.* Probably in all districts. Fls. *June-July.* Deciduous in the hot weather.

L. 8-10″ by 5-6″ broadly elliptic acuminate with rounded or cordate base. *Sheath* 6-7″ by 1″ or more, suddenly contracted into the very short petiole. *Peduncle* shorter than the sheath. The tissues of the spathe and ovary are crowded with raphides.

The fruit is applied for rheumatism, *Camp.*

3. Remusatia, Schott.

1. R. vivipara, *Schott.*

A herb with the habit of a Caladium with a bulb ½-1″ diam., smooth peltate shining leaves and a spathe 4-5″ long. Remarkable for its long shoots bearing clusters of bulbils with awned hooded scales.

On damp banks and among rocks. Singbhum, esp. on the Porahat plateau. Ranchi. It is said to flower and leaf in alternate years.

Bulbiferous shoots often 12″ long. The *leaves* which much resemble those of a Colocasia may be distinguished by being polished below as well as above, the nervules not clearly defined and the tip acuminate, they attain 12″ by 10″ but are usually smaller. Limb of *spathe* 2·3″ golden-yellow.

4. Colocasia, L.

1. C. Antiquorum, *Schott.* Pichigi, Bir saru, *K.*, *S.*; Kalhhu, *H.*

A stout or small herb with the habit of a Caladium with or without a distinct tuberous rhizome, smooth peltate ovate

10. Pollinia, Trin.

Annual or perennial not very large grasses closely allied to Ischæmum, with the basal sheaths of the stems often woolly or villous, leaves narrow or filiform; and the inflorescence densely hairy or silky. Pairs of spikelets in spikes which are usually clustered sub-digitate and erect. Gl. 4, I dorsally flattened or concave, with a narrowly inflexed margin throughout, rarely both I and II sub-convex (*vide* pedicellata); II keeled acute; III hyaline ciliate paleate usually flowering; IV very short hyaline or reduced to a dilated base of the long twisted exserted awn. Pale as short as the ovary. Stigmas long.

Section Dichanthium of Andropogon resembles Pollinia in habit, and may be distinguished by the sessile and pedicelled spikelets being dissimilar.

A. Glume II with a slender short awn. Gl. III obsolete.

- One spikelet sessile. Gl. I truncate; IV 2-toothed . . . . 1. *articulata.*
- Both spikelets pedicelled. Gl. I 2-toothed; IV entire . . . . 2. *pedicellata.*
- One spikelet sessile. Gl. I forked . . . . 3. *ciliata.*

B. Glume II not awned.

- Glumes I and II equal. Spikes 2-12 usually over 3″ long . . . . 4. *argentea.*
- Gl. I shorter than II. Spikes 2-4 distant under 3″ long . . . . 5. *Cumingii.*

1. P. articulata, *Trin.*

An erect tufted grass 1-2 ft. high, very slender with filiform leaves. Spikes 1-2½″ usually numerous. Spikelets $\frac{1}{12}$-$\frac{1}{10}$″ brown. Gl. I narrowly truncate, keels villous below with white hairs; II glabrous except the margins; IV narrowly oblong 2-fid or 2-toothed, awn very long ciliate, palea (sometimes described as Gl. III) short broad.

Common. Fls. *Oct.-Nov.*

2. P. articulata, *Trin.* **Var. pedicellata** (*F.B.I.*).

A very common erect tufted grass varying from 4-6″ to 18-30″ very similar in general appearance to the last with grey-brown spikes in a contracted raceme and pairs of pedicelled spikelets, $\frac{1}{16}$″ long ; both rachis and pedicels with long white hairs. Spikelets lanceolate brown. Gl. I coriaceous shining narrow lanceolate scarcely or not at all flattened, forked at the apex, dorsally hairy, margins ciliate ; II scarcely keeled slightly hairy, minutely 2-toothed at the apex with a very slender awn $\frac{1}{8}$″ long more or less.

Very common on half-bare soils of hard clay associated with Laggera flava, Vicoa, etc. Fls. *Oct.-Nov.*

Spikes 6-10, 2-2$\frac{3}{4}$″ long. Gl. IV reduced to the narrow base of he long twisted ciliate awn which is about $\frac{3}{4}$″ long. Pale oblong about $\frac{1}{40}$″ long.

The description of 1. P. articulata is taken from the F.B.I., it will be seen that this plant differs materially from that description and hence I have kept it quite distinct. The stem and leaf-sheaths in both are glabrous.

3. P. **ciliata,** *Trin.*, is a much-branched straggling grass which is not common. The base of the leaf is conspicuously constricted above the sheath. *Spikelets* $\frac{1}{8}$″ long narrow pale.

4. P. argentea, *Trin.*

A tall slender grass 4-5 ft. with flat leaves and spikelets in 4-10 shortly racemed (sub-digitate) brown spikes with long awns. Spikes usually 4-7″ long and spikelets subsecund. Gl. I $\frac{1}{8}$″ brown narrow-oblong, villous, with nerves obscure ; IV of two very slender hyaline lanceolate lobes and a long awn $\frac{5}{8}$″.

Common in open forest on dry and stony soil. Fls. *Nov.*

Perennial with short rootstock. *Stem* and *sheaths* shiny. *L.* 1-2 ft. by $\frac{3}{16}$-$\frac{1}{4}$″ with scattered long soft hairs towards the base, tip filiform. Gl. II as long as I, keeled, glabrous outside, ciliate on the incurved margins ; III (or pale of IV ?) nearly as long as II, linear with incurved margins and sparsely-villous above, brown.

5. P. Cumingii, *Nees.* Lopud Dumbu, *K.*

1$\frac{1}{2}$-2 ft. high with a perennial stout stoloniferous rootstock, very slender stems, short flat leaves and spikelets in slender rarely more than 2 terminal brown or yellow-brown spikes 1-3½″ long.

On damp soil, sites of deserted villages, etc. Fls. *Oct*.

L. 3-4″ by ⅛″. Ligule short truncate, glabrous. *Rachis* and *pedicels* compressed with long brown hairs on the edges. *Spikelets* nearly ⅛″. Gl. I brown silky, tip truncate with short hairs; III absent; IV reduced to a long bent awn with 1-2 short hairs at the base.

A good fodder grass.

11. Ischæmum, L.

Ischæmum differs from Pollinia in the usually very few spikes, sometimes solitary, and 1, rarely more than 3 on the common rachis (*vide* also P. Cumingii); in the pedicelled spikelet being usually dissimilar to the sessile spikelet, and in the much larger Gl. IV and its pale. The spikelets nearly always bear both a male and a 2-sexual flower. *I. angustifolium* is intermediate between the two genera, and should, I think, more naturally be in Pollinia, it differs only by the large pale of the Gl. IV.

A. Sessile and pedicelled spikelets alike. Spikes 1-4 on a peduncle. Sheaths at base of stem woolly. L. under ⅛″ broad . . . . . . 1. *angustifolium*.

B. Sessile and pedicelled spikelets more or less dissimilar (sometimes alike in rugosum). Sheaths at base of the stem not woolly.

1. Spikes 2-3 (rarely many in hirtum).

Gl. I dorsally hairy; II not winged. L. ¼″ broad . . . . 2. *hirtum*.

Gl. I glabrous or villous; keel of II winged . . 3. *ciliare*.

Gl. I glabrous at back, transversely rugose, broad . . . . 4. *rugosum*.

2. Spike solitary. Spikelets over ¼″ long, second . . . . 5. *laxum*.

1. I. angustifolium, *Hack.* Syn. Pollinia eriopoda, *Hance.* Barchon, *K.*; Bachkom, *S.*; Sabai, bhabar, *H.*

A tufted grass 1-2 ft. high with long drooping wiry leaves when old and clothed with wool at the base of the tuft. Spikes terminating filiform often branched peduncles, rachis glabrous but joints clothed with dense long yellow or brown hairs which almost conceal the spikelets which are $\frac{1}{3}$-$\frac{1}{6}$" long with a hard callus and 1 or 2 very fine awns. Both spikelets similar or only differing in the number of nerves and teeth of Gl. I, which is 5-7-nerved and with 2 or 3 small teeth, the back with a tuft of long brown hairs on the lower half, incurved or inflexed margins with brown ciliæ below and tip microscopically ciliate.

Common and often gregarious in open forest in Singbhum, less so in other districts, but largely cultivated on the northern slopes of the Rajmehal hills, esp. near Sahibganj. Fls. *Feby.-June.* Seeds *May-July.*

Rootstock stout. Very young *leaves* flat and erect, soon becoming concave or involute and harsh and often attaining 3 ft. in length, strongly-nerved, glabrous except at the ciliate mouth of the sheath. *Ligule* of hairs. Gl. II cymbiform with mid-rib excurrent into a small point or a short slender awn half as long as the glume, faintly 3-or sometimes 5-nerved, scaberulous on the keel above and margins ciliate towards the tip, dorsally hairy below. III wrapping round the M. fl., hyaline, elliptic $\frac{1}{6}$" long, sparsely ciliate above, its pale shortly stipitate oblong finely ciliate. *St* 2. IV narrowly lanceolate conduplicate about $\frac{1}{8}$" long including its very slender awn, its pale broad-oblong densely ciliate at the obtuse tip, nearly as long as the glume. St. 1-2, style-arms very long and slender.

Sabai grass is the most important economical grass in our area. It is used locally for string, ropes and mats, and is largely exported for paper making. It has been an important source of Forest revenue in Singbhum and from 1901 to 1903 yielded 42,000 rupees net revenue annually. Fire protection, and the improvement of the more valuable Sal crop, is however reducing the outturn from the reserves. It is entirely useless for fodder. It is easily grown either from seed or division of the roots.

The other species of Ischæmum are quite unimportant.

I. laxum, *Br.*, a forest grass 3-4 ft high is known in Kol as *raboga*, but I am not aware that it is put to any use.

I. hirtum, *Hack.*, is chiefly found on rocks in streams, and **I. rugosum**, *Salisb.*, in rice fields.

12. Pogonatherum, Beauv.

Spikes solitary terminal on slender peduncles. Spikelets sessile and pedicelled similar, except that the pedicelled is smaller, or sometimes Gl. III present in sessile and not in pedicelled. Glumes usually only I, II, and IV present in both. I, narrow oblong, obtuse tip with a tuft of hairs, membranous 2-4-nerved; II, longer $\frac{1}{10}''$ hyaline with stout mid-rib terminating in a very long slender awn, tip of glume ciliate; III (if present), hyaline, paleate. male; IV, very narrow 2-toothed with a very long slender awn, its pale broadly ovate-oblong hyaline wrapping round 2 stamens and the minute ovary which it much exceeds. Styles long slender, just exserted from the pale.

1. **P. saccharoideum,** *Beauv.* Bonga carec', *S.*

A tufted much branched and very leafy elegant grass 1-2″ ft. high with firm slender almost woody stems from a perennial rootstock. L. 1-2″ long linear sub-erect scabrid. Peduncles filiform very numerous narrowly sheathed, mouth of sheath ciliate. Spike $\frac{1}{2}$-2″ very slender terminating in the pencil of awns, 2 from each spikelet. Awns $\frac{5}{8}$-1″ long.

Very common and sub-gregarious along banks overhanging streams Fls. *April-May.*

13. Imperata, Cyrill.

Spikelets in pedicelled pairs in very close spiciform panicles silvery white from the long callus hairs exceeding the spikelets. Glumes 4 membranous awnless. I and II lanceolate hairy; III hyaline much smaller, IV smaller than III. St. 1-2.

1. **I. arundinacea,** *Cyrill.* Chero ghas, *S.*

A common grass 1-3 ft. high with erect flat leaves, conspicuous at the end of the hot weather especially after jungle fires by its silver-white spiciform panicles with the dark anthers and stigmas among the hairs. Stems thickened or tufted below, pubescent or almost woolly, glabrous above except at the bearded nodes. Panicle 3-6″ long.

Especially on open loamy ground where it may become gregarious.

Fls. *April-May.*

It can be used for paper-making.

14. Saccharum, L.

Tall perennial grasses with very long basal leaves and leafy stems and minute spikelets in very large dense decompound silky panicles, the branches erect in bud and fruit, spreading in flower, articulate. Spikelets awnless or Gl. IV shortly awned, geminate, sessile 2-sexual and pedicelled female, rarely both pedicelled and 2-sexual. Glumes 4, III empty; IV shortest flowering with a hyaline pale, or pale 0. St. 3. Lodicules cuneate. Stigmas laterally exsert.

(The awned glume IV in some varieties of S. arundinaceum breaks down the only distinguishing character between this genus and Erianthus.)

a. L. mostly ½" broad or more, margins not convolute.

L. very broad. Gl. I glabrous Cultivated only . 1. *officinarum.*

L. ¾—2" broad. Panicle branches 3-9" long, white or grey with Glume I finely pointed, its hairs about twice the spikelet . . . . . 2. *arundinaceum.*

L. ½" broad. Panicle branches 1-3" purple with Gl. I obtuse . . . . 3. *Narenga.*

b. L. under ½" broad, margins convolute. Hairs of spikelet many times as long as the spikelet . . 4. *spontaneum.*

1. **S. officinarum,** *L.* Ak. *H.*, *S.* The Sugarcane is sparsely cultivated on irrigated lands.

2. S. arundinaceum, *Retz.* Sar (arrow), *S.*

A very large stout grass attaining 20-30 ft. in favourable situations, with solid stems ½" diam. or more, glabrous below the panicle and with glabrous nodes. Panicle 1-2 ft. (2-4 ft. in the Duars) grey silvery with a glabrous rather angular rachis; rachis of spikes, pedicels of spikelets, and back of Gl. I with long dense silvery hairs 1-2 times as long as the spikelet which is $\frac{1}{8}$-$\frac{1}{6}$" long, narrow-lanceolate with acuminate or sub-aristate glumes.

In low ground in some of the larger river valleys, *e.g.*, the Sone in Palamau, the Ganges in Santal Parganahs, and the Fatlai R. in Koderma. Fls. Fr. *Sept.-Jany.*

L. sometimes 5ft. long with very stout mid-rib and serrulate cutting margins, ligule very short truncate. mouth of sheath with dense villous hairs. Pairs of *spikelets* rather distant. *Gl.* I 3 faintly 5-nerved acuminate or cuspidate ; II 1- or sometimes 3-nerved sparsely scaberulous and ciliate on the slightly excurrent nerve ; III hyaline very acute ; IV hyaline ciliate very shortly but distinctly awned.

The solid stems are used for making arrow shafts by the Santals, *Camp.*, and for the walls of houses. The leaf sheaths give a fibre.

NOTE.—This is Var. ciliaris of " Bengal Plants " which differs from typical arundinaceum in the less effuse (sub-fastigiate) panicle, and it might be added in the much shorter stouter internodes between the spikelets, but it appears to differ from Roxburgh's S. Sara in the absence of the long flagellum of the panicle-spathe, and in the shorter and less finely-acuminate spikelets, though Gl. I and II are sometimes sub-aristulate.

3. S. Narenga, *Hack.*

A stout grass 7-9 ft. high with a stout horizontal rootstock and numerous solid stems $\frac{1}{4}''$ diam. densely hairy at the nodes and silky below the panicle. Panicle 1-$1\frac{1}{2}$ ft. purple, the rachis scaberulous and bearded at the nodes, hairs on rachis of spikes and pedicel and callus not or only slightly exceeding the spikelet which is $\frac{1}{11}$-$\frac{1}{10}''$ long, glume I brown oblong obtuse not dorsally hairy.

In damp valleys both outside and inside the forests. Fls. *Aug.-Nov.*

L. 1-3 ft. by $\frac{1}{2}''$ with scabrid margins, sheaths hairy, ligule hard with long hairs from the base. L. below the panicle reduced to a brown sheath with villous margins and setaceous point. Branches of *Panicle* 1-4-nate, lower often compound, $\frac{3}{4}$-2 $''$ long. *Spikelets* quite awnless.

Used for rough mats, ceilings, etc., also for arrows.

4. S. spontaneum, *L.* Puyal, *K.*; Kariba, *M.*; Khans, *H.*, *Beng.*

A grass 5-7 ft. high with solid stems but much more slender than either of the preceding, easily recognised by its very narrow leaves with incurved or rolled up margins and the white silvery narrow panicles 1-2 ft. long with the callus hairs many times as long as the small spikelet.

Along water courses and swampy ground, common. Fls. *Aug.-Oct.* Fr. *Sept.-Dec.*

Stems silky below the panicle. Mouth of *sheath* woolly, ligule membranous. Branches of *panicle* 3-4″ more or less whorled on the silky rachis and articulate to it. *Glumes* usually 3 only, outer sub-equal hyaline hardened below, 3rd shorter, pale ciliate.

Used for thatching and brooms, and the panicle for decorating the hair at the Kol dances. The long callus hairs waft the seed to immense distances.

Erianthus fastigiatus, *Nees.* A grass 2-8 ft. high is recorded by Prain from Chota Nagpur.

16. Sorghum, Pers.

Tall grasses with broad flat leaves and spikelets in large terminal leafless panicles with sub-verticellate branches which are naked below, spikes peduncled on the branches or terminating them with few (rarely 7-8 prs.) large more or less dorsally compressed spikelets. Tips of the branches and joints of the spikes not bearded, the latter truncate. Pedicels filiform. Gl. I of sessile spikelets coriaceous with margin narrowly inflexed above, involute below; II awnless; III hyaline 2-nerved; IV entire or 2-fid and awned.

Perennial. Panicle lax, rachis of spike fragile. Spikelets reddish . . . 1. *halapense.*

Annual. Panicle dense, rachis of spike tenacious. *Cultivated* . . . 2. *vulgare.*

Perennial. Panicle lax. Sessile spikelets black shining . . . . 3. *fulvum.*

1. **S. halapense,** *Pers.* Syn. Andropogan halapensis. *Brot.*

A grass 3-6 ft. high with creeping rootstock, glabrous except above the ligule of the leaves. L. 6-10″ by $\frac{3}{4}$″. Panicle reddish 8-10″ with 1-3-nately whorled spreading branches 2-3″ long. Spikes with 3-4 prs. of spikelets. Pedicel half as long as the sessile spikelet.

Along rivers, not very common. Fls. *Nov.-Dec.*

Margin of leaf scabrid. *Ligule* very short or a row of short hairs, sheath hairy above the ligule. *Axils* of panicle-branches with a thickening and ciliate. Joints of rachis and pedicel margined ciliate. *Sessile spikelet* $\frac{1}{8}$-$\frac{1}{5}$", Gl. I appressed silkily-hairy; embracing the others, usually faintly 6- (5-11-) nerved, somewhat shining. II sub-coriaceous, keeled above; IV ovate obtuse, awned or not. *Pedicelled spikelet* narrow-lanceolate, Gl. I glabrous 5-9-nerved.

The grain is eaten, in fact, it is considered to be the wild ancestor of the cultivated S. vulgare. The spikes are sometimes reduced to a single fertile and two pedicelled spikelets.

2. **S. vulgare,** *Pers.* Syn. Andropogon Sorghum, *Brot*; Gangai, *K.*; Juar, *S.*

A very stout cultivated grass with broad leaves and a large usually white panicle, the latter usually sub-effuse in the Chota Nagpur form but the whorls of branches very crowded, pedicelled spkts. usually neuter, much narrower than the very broad female and their pedicels very short. *Joints* of the spikes not easily separated, leaving a ragged scar at the tip.

Sparingly cultivated. Usually reaped in *Nov.*

Spikes several on the flexuous branches which are whorled or not. *Rachis* compressed. *Axils* of spikes villous. *Scar* when spkt. is removed from its pedicel truncate hairy. Gl. I pale 10-nerved villous apiculate with incurved margins; II, 7-nerved; III, white-silky; IV, 2-fid, awn short $\frac{1}{4}$". Terminal spikelets ternate, 2 pedicelled.

3. **S. fulvum,** *Beauv.* Syn. Andropogon serratus, *Thunb.*

A tall tufted perennial grass 6 ft. high with sheaths villous on one side and villous at the nodes, leaves with long hairs at the base. Brown or black shining spikelets in short spikes at the ends of filiform sub-verticellate branches which are arranged in a sub-simple lax oblong panicle about 9" by 3".

Rocky shady forests in Singbhum and Santal Parganahs. Fls. *Nov.*

L. on stem 9"-2$\frac{1}{2}$ ft. by $\frac{3}{8}$-$\frac{1}{2}$" with prominent white mid-rib. *Rachis* and branches of panicle often flexuous. *Spikelets* 3-4 prs. about $\frac{1}{5}$", terminal with 2 pedicelled spikelets, rachis of spike compressed bearded with brown hairs. *Sessile* spkt. Gl. I coriaceous ell. obtuse polished 6-7-nerved; II polished somewhat keeled 7-nerved glabrous, margins involute; III hyaline nerveless, villous at the convolute tip; IV, small hyaline hairy, 2-toothed with a $\frac{1}{2}$" long bent awn or awn of lower spikelets obsolete. *Pedicelled* spikelet pale with brown hairs pedicels over half as long as the sessile spikelet bearded.

(*N. B.*—The Flora of India describes Gl. II as 1-nerved and IV as shortly awned or awnless.)

17. Chrysopogon, Trin.

A genus closely allied to the last (which usually has the terminal spikelets ternate) but with all the spikelets ternate, and with the tips of the branches of panicle and joints of spikes bearded. Spikes consisting of a central sessile hermaphrodite and two pedicelled male or neuter spkts., the triplets arranged on the articulate branches of a terminal panicle (occasionally 1-3 prs. of spikelets added on the lower branches). Spikelets more slender and less hardened than in Sorghum. Gl. I 3-many nerved ; II sometimes awned, keeled ; III smaller hyaline ; IV awned or reduced to an awn.

I. Pedicels of upper spikelets half as long as sessile spikelet or longer.

Slender grass under 2 ft., spikes solitary on panicle branches . . . . . 1. *aciculatus.*

Stout grass, spikes solitary on panicle branches, pedicel densely rusty villous 2. *lancearius.*

Stout grass, spikes 2-4 on the panicle branches, pedicel ciliate or glabrous . 3. *Gryllus.*

II. Pedicels less than half as long as the sessile spikelet.

Pedicels with villous margins. Panicle not secund . . . . 4. *monticola.*

Pedicels not villous on margin. Panicle secund . . . . 5. *polyphyllus.*

1. C. aciculatus, *Trin.* Syn, Andropogon aciculatus, *Retz.* Chora kanta, *Vern.*

A small grass 12-18″ high with creeping stem and short densely tufted leaves 1-5″ by $\frac{1}{8}$-$\frac{1}{5}$″. Panicle usually turning purple 1-3″ with capillary branches.

A weed of damp and heavily grazed lands, and a pest from the small awns sticking to the clothes. The leaves which lie close to the ground escape to a large extent the lips of cattle.

Fls. *Aug.-Nov.*

2. **C. lancearius,** *Stapf.* Syn. Andropogon lancearius, *Hook. f.* Korpo dumbu, *K.*

A large coarse grass 4-6 ft. high with very leafy stems minutely downy above, leaves 18"-2 ft. by 1-1½" broad (⅓-½" *F.B.I.*) with minutely spinnlose cutting edges, and oblong panicles 8-12" long with whorls of numerous capillary sub erect branches 2-4" long which exhibit the characteristic clavate oblique brown-bearded tips on the fall of the spikelets. Gl. I of pedicelled spikelet with a slender awn over ¼"; Gl. IV of sessile spikelet with an awn 1½-1¾" silky.

Usually in shady positions on rocky slopes. Fls. *Sept.* Fr. *Oct.-Nov.*

L. glabrous minutely scaberulous above with very broad white mid-ribs, *sheaths* compressed, ligule of short hairs. *Spikelets* ¼" long very narrow; *Sessile* with long (short *F.B.I.*) callus pungent with a barb of brown hairs, Gl. I convex with ciliate margins; II broadest but strongly laterally compressed with a mid-rib and hyaline margins, brown hairy on the upper half and with a slender hispid awn ⅓"; III sparsely silky. *Pedicelled-spikelet* with compressed pedicel about half as long as the spikelet, subterete; Gl. I 5-7-nerved convolute with awn over ¼"; II hyaline 3-nerved; III nerveless sparsely villous; IV similar but narrower. St. 3. A good fodder.

3. **C. Gryllus,** *Trin.*

A stout tufted grass with leaves up to ⅓" broad, glabrous or hirsute with serrulate margins, *panicle* 3-8" with branches 2-4", their axils bearded and with 2-4 *spikelets* ⅛-⅓" long. Awn of Gl. IV of sessile spikelet from minute to 1½" (*F.B.I.*) and Gl. I of pedicelled spikelet acuminate or aristulate, the pedicel glabrous or only thinly ciliate.

Jaspur, *Wood.*

Two other large grasses of this genus called Andropogon monticola. *Schult* Var. Trinii of F.B.I., and A. polyphyllus, *Hack* of F.B.I. occur in Chota Nagpur (*vide* Prain, "Bengal Plants"). The former varies from 1½—4 ft. high.

18. Andropogon, L.

Habit various. Pairs of spikelets (sessile and pedicelled dissimilar) similar to one another in many- rarely few-jointed spikes which are simple or branched and clustered solitary or half verticellate on the rachis of a diffuse panicle, rarely rachis abbreviated or spikes digitate (when it resembles Ischæmum), or panicle contracted. Sessile spikelet 2-sexual, glumes 4, outer largest muticous 3-many-nerved, median nerve sometimes evanescent, II empty keeled rarely with a straight awn; III much smaller hyaline empty; IV flowering often very narrow or reduced to the geniculate awn. St. 3, styles distinct.

I. Spikes solitary. Peduncle enclosed in a spathiform sheath. Internodes and pedicels villous.

Annual tufted slender 12-18″. Ped. spikelet smaller than the sessile one . . . 1. *exilis, Hochst.*

Perennial, branched upwards, 1-3ft., spike 1-2″. Sessile spikelet $\frac{1}{6}$-$\frac{1}{5}$″ smaller than the pedicelled . . . . 2. *fastigiatus, Sw.*

Densely tufted, 1-2 ft. Spike 1-1½″. Spikelets $\frac{1}{8}$-$\frac{1}{6}$″ sub-equal . . . 3. *foveolatus, Del.*

II. Spikes digitately 2-nate. Common peduncle with a spathiform sheath . . . . . 4. *apricus, Trin.*

III. Spikes sub-digitately fascicled. Pedicels and internodes compressed with translucent centre. Tufted rarely 1 ft. Spikes 1-2″ . 5. *pertusus, Willd.*

IV. Spikes racemed or panicled.

a. Pedicels and internodes of spikes compressed with thickened margins and translucent centre.

1. Spikes with more than 5 prs. of spkts. Joints cup-shaped. Base of panicle branches ciliate and bulbous . . . 6. *intermedius, Br.*

2. Spikes with fewer than 5 prs. of spkts. Joints truncate. Base of panicle-branches ciliate, not bulbous.

Herbaceous, not fastigiate, L. linear . 7. *micranthus. Kunth.*

Suffruticose, fastigiately-branched. L. linear-lanceolate . . . . . . 8. *assimilis, Steud*

b Pedicels and internodes of spikes terete.

Panicle 1-2″. Branches subsolitary, spikes $\frac{1}{4}$-$\frac{1}{2}$″ with spkts. almost to their base . 9. *fascicularis, Roxb.*

Panicle 6-12″. Branches many whorled naked below with a long slender terminal spike. Spkts. muricate . . 10. *squarrosus*, L.

Only apricus, intermedius, assimilis, and squarrosus are further dealt with.

4. A. apricus, *Trin.*

A cæspitose slender grass 3-6 ft. high branched above. Branches with slender peduncles sheathed at the base and bearing geminate reddish spikes $1\frac{1}{2}$-2″ long with long awns. Joints of spike and pedicel of ped. spkt. clothed with long hairs below, expanded above into a funnel-shaped 2-toothed limb.

A very common and abundant grass in poorly stocked forest. Fls. *Nov.* *Culms* yellow. Cauline *leaves* 10-20″ by $\frac{1}{4}$″ thinly hairy on the ribs above, often pubescent beneath, ligule short scarious truncate. *Sessile spikelet*, Gl. I $\frac{3}{8}$″ linear-oblong truncate 3-nerved on each side of the infolded centre, margins strongly inflexed; II hyaline 1-nerved with fine awn $\frac{1}{3}$″; IV hyaline 2-cleft with an awn 1″ long or more. *Ped. spikelet* Gl. I flat 9-nerved 2-cuspidate usually with a scabrid awn $\frac{1}{4}$-$\frac{1}{3}$″; IV finely awned, with 3 st. and a 3-fid quadrate scale.

6. A. intermedius, *R. Br.* Sudugan, *M.*

A very variable grass 3-7 ft. erect or with decumbent base, and rootstock usually densely clothed with buds. Nodes (especially above) nearly always with a dense ring of hairs, and leaves with long hairs near the base or hairy. Panicle usually small $2\frac{1}{2}$-4″ but attaining 10″ in some varieties, branches slender usually opposite and decussate with a bulbous base, spikes usually simple towards the end of the branches, $\frac{1}{2}$-$\frac{3}{4}$″ long, joints fragile. Sessile spkt., callus shortly hairy, Gl. I $\frac{1}{10}$-$\frac{1}{8}$″ flat oblong 5-7-nerved often pitted, margins involute with smooth or scabrous keels; II faintly 3-nerved keeled; III hyaline; IV an awn $\frac{1}{2}$-$\frac{5}{8}$″.

A very common forest grass, sometimes only 9″ to 2 ft. on dry open ground and up to 7 ft. in valleys. Fls. *Nov.-Feby.*

The smaller varieties are apparently annual.

L. 1-2 ft. by $\frac{1}{3}$-$\frac{1}{2}$″ broad usually keeled below, tips filiform, sheaths hairy above, in one variety very loose and hairy throughout. *Ligule* very short with long hairs. *Panicle* often red, rachis and branches glabrous but usually with long villi in the axils, tips of joints and pedicels truncate, margins hairy. Gl. I of ped.-spikelet, 5-9-nerved often with a small circular pit.

8. **A. assimilis,** *Steud.*

A very distinct grass with creeping rootstock well marked by its hard almost *woody* slender polished stems, short leaves and diffuse short pyramidal panicles 2-3″ broad and long with few-fld. spikes $\frac{1}{4}$-$\frac{1}{3}$″ long on filiform peduncles.

Valleys. Fls. *Oct.-Nov.*

Often sarmentose and proliferously branched, nodes bearded. Lower *leaves* broad, upper linear 3-4″. Nodes of *panicle* and rachis of spike and pedicels of spikelets hairy. *Spikelets* 2-3 prs, with usually terminal ternate. Joints and pedicels slender villous ending in a minute cup. Sessile spkt., Gl. I 2-5- usually 4-nerved, margins incurved, keels ciliate; IV a slender awn under $\frac{1}{2}$″. Ped. spkt., Gl. I $\frac{1}{8}$″ 5-7-nerved lanceolate acute.

10. **A. squarrosus** *L.f.* Syn. A. muricatus, *Retz.* Sirom, *S.*; Kus-Kus, *Eng.*

The sub-genus Vetiveria, Hack, is raised to generic rank by Stapf and the name becomes V. zizanioides, *Stapf.*

A tufted perennial grass 3-5 ft. high with stout spongy aromatic roots and rather rigid sub-erect glabrous leaves 1-2 ft. with scabrous margins. Panicle 6-12″ with many whorled spreading or ascending branches terminated by a long many jointed spike. Joints and pedicels filiform (not channelled) with truncate tip not bearded. Callus of sessile spikelet slightly bearded. Gl. I coriaceous with muricate keels; II coriaceous 1-nerved, keel muricate; III lanceolate acuminate 2-nerved; IV linear-oblong mucronate or shortly awned.

Chiefly in low open ground, not very common in Singbhum. Common in Manbhum, *Camp.*, frequent in other districts.

The dried roots are well known, being the material of which Khus-Khus tatties are made.

19. Heteropogon, Pers.

Sessile and pedicelled spikets very dissimilar, in terminal solitary many-jointed spikes, the lowest two or more pairs of sessile spikelets differing from all the upper ones, closely imbricate, male or neuter. Sessile spikelets sub-terete or Gl. I dorsally flat; II obtusely keeled; III hyaline; IV reduced to a long stout awn.

1. **H. contortus,** *Roem.* Syn. Andropogon contortus, *L.* Sauri *M.*; Saiyu, *Ho.*; Sauri ghas, *S.*; Chorant, *Kharw.* Spear grass.

A well-known grass 1-3 ft. or in fertile ground 5 ft. high, with leaves scabrid above, ligule membranous truncate ciliolate and spikelets in dense imbricate spikes terminating in the long twisted awns of the sessile spikelets which are furnished with a pungent callus bearing a barb of stiff hairs.

Gregarious. Throughout Chota Nagpur esp. on the hills, but also in open ground in the valleys. Fls. *Sept.-Dec.* Fr. *Oct.-Jany.* but all the fruits may not become detached until *March.*

Used much for thatching. The young grass is a fair fodder, the old grass is also used for fodder but only because there is often nothing better, it causes a reddish colour in the dung of horses, and sometimes severe ulceration (from the spears) in the gums of cattle and horses. It is a pest to forest officers from the barbed callus penetrating the clothes and flesh. The awns, as in other awned grasses are very hygroscopic and by their contortions and the barbed callus the fruits readily penetrate to a position favourable for germination.

20. Cymbopogon, Stapf.

Usually tall perennial often scented grasses. Spikelets paired sessile and pedicelled, in short spikes which are geminate and usually divaricate on a slender often very short peduncle which is sheathed by a spathe. One or more of the sessile spikelets at the base of the spike different from all the others. Spathes with their geminate spikes variously arranged in racemes and panicles, each order of branching being in its turn sheathed by a leaf or bract. Spikelets several pairs. Sessile spikelets above the lowest fem. or 2-sexual, dorsally compressed, Gl. I. flat, with inflexed margins and often winged keels, sometimes grooved or pitted, awnless; II cymbiform, keeled; III oblong hyaline; IV narrow hyaline 2-cleft and awned, *pale* minute or 0. Pedicelled spikelet male or neuter.

1. **C. Martini**, *Stapf*. Syn. Andropogon Schœnanthus, *L.* (F.B.I). Sail tati, *K.*; Nanha dudhi ghas, *S.*; Rusa oil grass.

A tall sweet-scented grass 6-8 ft. high with glabrous, straw-coloured leafy stems with flat leaves 6-12″ by $\frac{1}{2}$-1″ with a rounded or sub-cordate base. Geminate spikes divaricate or deflexed on a short peduncle from a spathe $\frac{3}{4}$-1″ long, forming a copious narrow leafy panicle. Gl. I of sessile spikelet (except the lowest) channeled below the middle and with a rib on the inner side opp. to the channel.

Fairly common from Singbhum to the Santal Parganahs. Chiefly in the valleys near watercourses and on the northern or shady sides of hills in the forest. Fls. *Nov.-Jany.*

L. smooth below, with scabrid margins above. *Spikes* $\frac{1}{2}$-$\frac{3}{4}$″ joints $\frac{1}{8}$″ 3-toothed villous, terminal spikelets 3-nate. *Sessile-spikelet* $\frac{1}{8}$″, keels of Gl. I winged above; keel of Gl. II also slightly winged above; IV an awn $\frac{3}{4}$-1″ long, its very narrow base with 2 filiform lobes. Gl. I of *ped. spikelet* 8-10-nerved.

The source of the oil known variously as Rusa, Palmarosa or East Indian Geranium, "the yield from the fresh grass is about ·3 to ·4 per cent." *Stapf.*

21. Apluda, L.

Spikes of only 1 joint in copious leafy and bracteate panicles, rachis or joint (sometimes considered as the thickened pedicel of the upper spikelet) stout, easily recognized by its curious shelf-like base on which the lower (or sessile) 2-sexual spikelet is seated and bearing a terminal male or neuter spikelet. In addition to these is a third basal and sessile spikelet reduced to an empty glume (usually hard-coriaceous) faintly 2-nerved and lateral to the plane of the other two. These three spikelets are subtended by an awned bract separated from them by a very short internode, the whole cluster is on a slender pedicel. Pedicelled clusters several in a fascicle with often small bract-like scales at the base and some of the clusters reduced to single glumes, the whole fascicle in a spathe, and the spathes on branches of a lower order. The perfect spikelets consist of Gl. I coriaceous many-nerved; II boat-shaped, keeled, gibbous; III M. hyaline, St. 3; IV small hyaline 2-sexual.

1. A. varia, *Hack.* Sub.-sp. aristata, *Hack.* Tati, *K.*; Dhudhia sauri, *S.*

A tall grass often 6-8 ft. with a rather stout perennial rootstock, flat leaves 12-18″ often 1″ broad and glume IV of the perfect sessile spikelets with a geniculate awn $\frac{1}{4}$-$\frac{1}{3}$″ long.

A very common forest grass. Fls. *Nov.*

In sub.-sp. mutica Gl. IV is very rarely awned. I am not sure whether this occurs in our area, but there are two varieties which look very distinct in the field, *viz.*, one in which the small few-fld. spathes, which are often purple, are closely arranged on a spike, and another in which the spathes with dense clusters of spikelets are widely separated on the usually flexuous rachis.

22. Anthistiria, L.

Tall grasses. Spikelets in capitate spikes, the four lowest bract-like, male or neuter, in a whorl or decussate pairs and forming an involucre to one or few sessile 2-sexual spikelets and two or more pedicelled spikelets. Spikes subtended by a bract or spathe, fascicled, the fascicles panicled or sub-solitary on the branches of the copious panicle. Sessile spkt. linear-oblong, Gl. I coriaceous not keeled; II coriaceous 3-nerved, keeled; III hyaline 1-nerved; IV usually reduced to a very long and stout awn, or awn O. Ped.-spkt. male or neuter awnless.

A. Spikes in globose or fan-shaped fascicles.
  - Perennial. Involucral bracts or spikelets $\frac{1}{3}$-$\frac{1}{2}$″ 1. *imberbis.*
  - Annual. Involucral bracts or spikelets $\frac{1}{8}$-$\frac{1}{4}$″ 2. *ciliata.*

B. Spikes on slender peduncles, one or few together from a spathe, in large slender panicles 3. *gigantea.*

1. A. imberbis, *Retz.*

A leafy grass 5-6 ft. high with leaves about $\frac{3}{16}$″ broad and with the spikes in spathaceous fascicles on short capillary stalks in the axils of leafy bracts, the globose or fan-shaped fascicles panicled. Spikes inside the involucre reduced to one sessile and two barren slender pedicelled spikelets. Sessile fertile spikelet brown with an awn 2″ long.

Nalas and depressions, chiefly on the shady sides of hills. Fls. *Nov.*

Bristles on spikelets and spathe, if present, few.

2. **A. ciliata,** *L.*

Somewhat resembling the last or weak and somewhat scrambling. Spikelets and spathes under the spikes usually clothed with numerous tubercle-based bristles and spikelets much smaller than in last. Awn 1-1½″.

Moist grassy places. Fls. *Nov.*

3. **A. gigantea,** *Cav.* Kus ghas, *S.*

A very large cæspitose grass 10-20 ft. high with stout rootstock, flattened stems, and markedly equitant leaves 2-5 ft. by $\frac{1}{3}$-$\frac{3}{4}$″ with scabrous margins. Panicles very long slender with nodding branches. Involucral spikelets $\frac{1}{3}$-$\frac{2}{3}$″. Fertile spikelets 2-3 densely rufously hirsute.

Along nalas and ravines, not very common. Fls. *Nov.-Dec.*

L. glabrous. Callus of sessile spikelet pungent barbed with rufous hairs, so that the ripe fruits become a pest in places where it is frequent. *Awn* usually absent.

Cynodon dactylon, *Pers.* The Dub grass although of little forest value deserves notice as being probably the best fodder grass, at least for horses, in India.

It is a prostrate and ascending somewhat glaucous grass with short stems and markedly distichous short leaves with a hairy ligule. The *spikelets* are minute $\frac{1}{12}$-$\frac{1}{10}$″ secund in 2-5 digitate spikes 1-2″ long on a slender erect peduncle and with very slender rachis. *Glumes* 3 only, I and II empty ovate with scabrid keels, III larger cymbiform awnless with scabrid keel and margin.

Comparatively scarce in Chota Nagpur, usually in damp sandy places.

Eleusine Coracana, *Gærtn.* Iri, *Ho*; Kode, *K.S.*, is a grass very commonly cultivated for its grain. It is 1½-3 ft. high with compressed stems and 4-6 digitate stout usually incurved spikes. It is rather stringy as a fodder. A wild species E. ægyptiaca, *Desf.*, with more slender spikes

$\frac{1}{2}$-1″ long and spikelets at right angles to the rachis, is said to be a good fodder by Campbell. It is a common grass flowering in the rains.

Triticum vulgare, *Vill.*, the wheat. is only very sparingly cultivated, and **Hordeum vulgare**, *L.*, the Barley, more frequently, both more especially in the plain at the foot of the Palamau hills. Barley may be distinguished from the bearded wheat (which is the only variety I have seen cultivated) by the spikelets being 2-3-nate in the hollows of the rachis and by there being only 3 glumes (of which 2 are empty). In Triticum the spikelets are solitary and 3-more-flowered above the empty glumes. The lateral spikelets in Hordeum may be imperfect. There is no special Kol name for either.

27. Phragmites, Trin.

1. P. Karka, *Trin.* Jankai *K.* The Reed.

A very large grass 10-20 ft. high with rather close jointed hollow leafy stems, often widely spreading by means of stolons and its creeping roots. L. stiff erect distichous 16″ by 1″. Panicles very large and compound, grey or brown with innumerable slender rather large spikelets terminating the very slender branches. Rachilla jointed between the glumes and with long silky hairs above glume III.

Watery places, sandy beds of nalas and rivers, frequent. Fls. *Nov.-Dec.*

L. with scaberulous margins. *Panicle* 12-18″ by 9-12″ *Spikelets* with several glumes, I and II empty persistent, unequal, 3-nerved ; III largest $\frac{1}{3}$-$\frac{1}{2}$″ long lanceolate, 3-nerved acute, others aristulate, all widely spreading in fruit.

The stems are made into shepherd's pipes, and are used for preparing fish traps (Kumbat, *K.*) The tender shoots are greatly appreciated by horses but produce diarrhœa in excess.

28. Bambusa, Schreb.

Large bamboos, cæspitose or not, stem sheaths very broad. Transverse veins of leaves reduced to a pellucid dash or dot. Spikelets capitate in panicled spikes, 1-many-fld. Lowest 1-4 glumes empty. Fl.-glumes ovate lanceolate with 2-keeled palea, uppermost imperfect. St. 6. Ovary oblong or obovate with hairy tip, stigmas 2-3. Pericarp thin adherent.

A. Branches below unarmed.

Spikelets terete.

Stems cæspitose. Palea cymbiform. Anthers obtuse . . . . 1. *Tulda*.

Stems scattered. Palea ovate. Anth. tips long apiculate or penicillate . . . . 2. *nutans*.

Spikelets compressed. Culms often yellow . 3. *vulgaris*.

B. Stems with armed often leafless branches at least below . . . . 4. *arundinacea*.

1. B. Tulda, *Roxb.* Pepe siman, *K.* (*f. Gamble*), Makor, *Mal Pah.*

A large cæspitose bamboo 2-4″ diam., internodes 1-2 ft., white-ringed below the nodes, with walls $\frac{1}{3}$-$\frac{1}{2}$″ thick. Stem sheaths 6-9″ by 6-10″, narrowed upwards, tip rounded or sub-triangular; blade hairy within with long-fringed auricles. L. 6-10″ by $\frac{3}{4}$-$1\frac{1}{2}$″, base rounded.

Cultivated, and perhaps wild in the Santal Parganahs (but see remark under B. nutans.) Fls. sporadically and gregariously.

L. glabrous or hairy beneath, glaucescent. *L. sheaths* with an oblong often long-fringed auricle. *Spikelets* 1-2 bracteate polished, sessile, 1-3″ long, in distant loose heads or half whorls on the glabrous branches of the panicle. Empty *glumes* 2-4, *Fl.-glumes* 4-6, $\frac{1}{2}$-1″ long with many distinct nerves. Keels ciliate, tip penicillate, 3-5-nerved between the keels.

Used for building and basket making.

2. B. nutans, *Wall.*

This bamboo is scarcely distinguishable without flowers from the last, it is said however to be recognized by the scattered culms and to be less hairy and bristly than B. Tulda. A bamboo common on trap rocks in the Rajmehal hills and cultivated by the Paharias agrees in these particulars with B. nutans better than with B. Tulda, but it is evidently the species from the S. P. which in the Cal. Herb is called B. Tulda by Gamble. B. nutans is ordinarily considered to be confined to the Himalayas and Assam. My field notes are as follows :—

Culms about 3-4″ diam. with internodes 18″ *not caespitose.* Stem sheaths 8-12″ densely covered with black deciduous bristles at back. *Blade* triangular acuminate with rather small fimbriate auricles. *L.* softly downy (white when dry) beneath, with scaberulous margins, ending in a twisted scabrid point. Base generally obtuse or sub-acute, not cordate, rarely rounded but attenuate into the distinct $\frac{1}{8}$″ petiole ; nerves 8-9 each side of mid-rib.

3. B. vulgaris, *Schrad.* Bansini. *Beng.*

A commonly cultivated bamboo in gardens, sometimes with the stems a bright golden yellow. *Nodes* with a hairy ring. *L.* tesselate with the pellucid cross nervules hairy beneath when young, leaf-sheath appressed white hairy. *Culm-sheaths* clothed with brown hairs, blade 2-6" by 4", base with rounded falcate fimbriate auricles.

4. B arundinacea, *Willd.* Katanga, Katam madh, *K.* Ketua, *Beng.*

A very large bamboo densely cæspitose and with numerous horizontal branches below, which, as well as many of the other branches, are armed with recurved thorns. Internodes usually short usually about 1 ft., sheath about as long much over-lapping at the base and open above, young densely yellow-hairy, blade short 2" up to 4". L. rather short $2\frac{1}{2}$-7" long nearly or quite glabrous, their sheaths pubescent.

Wild along ravines in Singbhum. Brandis says that it apparently flowers gregariously every 30 years or so. A large number of clumps came into flower in Dehra Dun in 1907 in April, and fruited July, the panicle occupying the whole culm.

L. with 5-6 prs. nerves* each side of the mid-rib, ending in a short stiff filiform point. *Clusters* very large and dense about 1-$1\frac{1}{4}$" by 1-$1\frac{1}{2}$" close. *Spkts.* $\frac{1}{2}$-$\frac{3}{8}$" long. Lodicules and keels of the pale bearded.

29. Dendrocalamus, Nees.

1. D. strictus, *Nees.* Buru Madh, or Mat', *K.*, *S.*

A more or less cæspitose bamboo 2-3" diam. Young stems glaucous with a waxy bloom, old yellowish green. Lower stem-sheaths 3-12" narrow, blade not very distinctly differentiated triangular, not or scarcely auricled. Leaf-sheaths rough-hairy or glabrous, blade $\frac{3}{4}$-1" broad glaucous and softly hairy beneath. Fls. in prickly heads, hairy. Empty glumes 2 muticous (Gamble says spinescent), upper two flowering spinescent.

Hill forests, very common. Fls. sporadically every year in *Nov.* Deciduous.

Culms sometimes nearly solid. Internodes 12-18". *Stem-sheaths* glabrous or covered with harsh hairs, striate, top rounded ciliate. *L.* with rounded base and a fine twisted tip ; nerves* 3-6 each side of mid-rib, transverse nervules reduced to pellucid dashes.

A very strong useful bamboo; but the Singbhum culms were not favourably reported on for lance shafts by Messrs. Manton & Co. to whom some specimens were sent by Mr. E. R. Stevens. The new shoots are eaten.

Var. sericeus, *Munro* (Sp.) only grows on Parasnath. It is distinguished by having softly silky spikelets and obtuse anthers, the anthers of the type being apiculate.

30. Cephalostachyum, Munro.

1. C. pergracile, *Munro*.

A handsome cæspitose bamboo with culms about 2″ diam. Stem sheaths light brown deciduous 5-6″, young with felted deciduous shining black hairs without, blade triangular acuminate only 2″, felted within towards the base, with densely fimbriate setose sometimes reflexed auricles, ligule hardly any. L. 8-10″ by 1-1½″ with twisted tip and scabrid margins.

Sides of valleys in Singbhum but rare (Luia in the Kolhan, Kiringka Lor in Porahat).

Wall of culms very thin. *L.-sheaths* with closely ciliate margins and with long setæ or bristles above when young. Pellucid nervules usually joining two tertiary nerves. *Inflorescence* (*fide* Gamble) a large panicle with verticels of long drooping filiform spikes, bearing distant broad heads of spikelets supported by small chaffy sheathing bracts; the rachis very slender, wiry, thickened above, and 1½-2″ between the clusters. *Pale* long, apex deeply bifidly-mucronate.

The green culms split and crack in drying in Chota Nagpur, but Gamble says they are used for building in Burma.

---

* NOTE.—The "nerves" refer to the stronger nerves each side of the mid-rib.

APPENDIX I.

THE BLAZES OF TREES.

In marking trees for felling among the tall stems and numerous valuable species of the Eastern Himalayas, the writer found the blaze a most useful subsidiary character for determining species, where the foliage of the trees could not be clearly distinguished from that of their neighbours in the tangle of verdure overhead.

By the blaze is meant the mark made by removing a piece of the bark off the trunk by a downward stroke of a cutting instrument. It is not however easy to put into writing all that may be learnt in the act of cutting, and the following is an incomplete and merely preliminary account of the blazes of a few of the Chota Nagpur species. Incidentally it may be remarked that the blaze is often a useful way of determining the species of trees which compose a freshly cut stack of fuel.

The characters chiefly employed are :—

(*a*) Colour and surface of the outer dead bark, and its thickness.

(*b*) Thickness of the bark as a whole.

The thickness of the bark, both (*a*) and (*b*), varies with the age of the tree as well as with the species, so that no absolute measurements can be given.

(*c*) The *feel* of the cut, or its *texture*. Some barks, for instance, are stringy like the Sal, others give a distinctly *gritty* cut, as in Litsæa semecarpifolia (not a tree of our area), others a *cheesy* cut, others are very *hard*.

(*d*) The colour of the blaze. This may be uniform, or more frequently, the successive layers of the bark which, owing to the cylindrical form of the trunk, can all be exposed in one cut, are somewhat differently coloured. The colours are always enumerated from the outside inwards, ending with the colour of the freshly exposed wood if characteristic. If the colours of successive layers alternate, the word *banded*, is employed. Thus the alternation of successive layers of bast fibres and phlœm parenchyma may produce a banded red and white. Owing, presumably, to oxidation of cell contents, the colour of the blaze darkens after a time, but in some cases this is so rapid that the change is visible immediately, and the colour may turn from light to deep brown in about a minute. The Cordiæ are a good example.

ANONACEÆ.

Alphonsea ventricosa. Bark smooth, thin. Blaze thin brown layer, then white.

Milinsa velutina. Bark grey, rather cracked, moderately thick to thick. Blaze dark-brown, then thick light-brown or dirty brown with lighter streaks. Wood white.

Polyalthia cerasioides. Bark not thick, rough, grey. Blaze deep brown then yellow, only the yellow noticeable in young trees.

Saccopetalum tomentosum. Bark brown, nearly smooth or, in old trees, fluted. Blaze, thin outer brown layer, then narrowly banded yellowish or light brown and white. Wood white.

LAURACEÆ.

Litsæa polyantha. Bark smooth. Blaze somewhat *grating*, a mixture of brown and white.

BIXACEÆ.

Cochlospermum Gossypium. Bark thick, fluted. Blaze deep brown and rather hard outside in old trees, light brown streaked with white in young trees, a thin layer near the cambium with orange-coloured juice. Wood very porous.

Flacourtia Ramontchi. Bark nearly smooth. Blaze rather hard, pale brown.

SAMYDACEÆ.

Casearia graveolans. Blaze streaked yellowish and white. Wood pale.

Casearia tomentosa. Bark cinereous, rather rough, thick. Blaze hard, pink or in old trees, crimson, with thin bands of pale brown, inside pale yellowish, wood yellow.

DILLENIACEÆ.

Dillenia aurea. Blaze dark-crimson, usually with a light crimson border inside and out. Wood brownish.

Dillenia pentagyna. Blaze light crimson, then white or streaked light crimson and white.

MALVACEÆ.

Bombax malabaricum. Bark very thick, young spinous, old flaky. Blaze soft, dark pink, streaked with pale pink and white.

Kydia calycina. Blaze white, faintly pink at the margins.

TILIACEÆ.

Grewia asiatica. Bark smooth thick. Blaze thin brown outer layer, then light pink streaked white, the harder and softer bast tissues distinctly zoned.

G. elastica. Bark as in type. Blaze pink (or in old trees reddish-brown), thinly banded with white, with well-marked pores, rather fibrous, scarcely distinguishable from the last.

G. elastica can usually be distinguished by the red bark on the twigs.

G. lævigata. Bark grey smooth, with slight horizontal stipular ridges. Blaze soft thick white with streaks of light brown.

STERCULIACEÆ.

Sterculia colorata. Bark smooth light-grey. Blaze white with thin yellow margins, somewhat streaked cream or yellow.

EUPHORBIACEÆ.

Bischofia javanica. Bark smooth. Blaze pink streaked with darker pink.

Bridelia montana. Blaze similar to B. retusa.

B. retusa. Bark nearly smooth in young, flaky in old trees, moderately thick. Blaze dark crimson or red.

Glochidion Gamblei? (*vide* p.) Blaze deep crimson, white inside.

G. lanceolarium. Bark grey striate smooth. Blaze thin, brown or grey outside then a delicate pink, then white or yellowish-white in centre.

Phyllanthus Emblica. Outer bark very thin papery. Blaze deep crimson, hard.

Trewia nudiflora. Bark light grey, old flaking in thin patches. Thin raised stipular lines on the branches and young stems. Blaze pale yellow or nearly white, hard with a thin outer chlorophyll layer.

(This tree has often a remarkable resemblance to Gmelina in bark, blaze and leaves. The latter tree has no stipular lines and the cut is much softer.)

OCHNACEÆ.

Ochna squarrosa. Bark smooth, light. Blaze hard dark pink finely streaked with white, then white.

BURSERACEÆ.

Boswellia serrata. Very thin grey flaky outer bark with a chlorophyll layer beneath. Blaze flushed with light and darker pink, from it exudes small drops of resin.

Garuga pinnata. Bark pale grey, slightly flaky on old trees. Blaze with a thin or thick (according to age) deep brown outermost layer (dead bark), then pink or deep crimson often white streaked, rather hard. (According as to whether the particular portion of the tree blazed has recently shed its outer layer of bark or not, a chlorophyll layer or the deep brown outer layer is present.)

RUTACEÆ.

Ægle Marmelos, var. (*vide* p. 217). Bark light grey. Blaze harsh, light brown.

MELIACEÆ.

Amoora Rohituka. Bark smooth. Blaze thick crimson with bold white streaks.

Cedrela Toona. Bark brown-grey flaky. Blaze first dark brown (onter dead layer) then bright crimson, streaked with white which rapidly turns yellow, then soft whitish, then (on the wood) yellowish.

Soymida febrifuga. Bark dark brown, splitting int oblong flakes.

ANACARDIACEÆ.

Odina Wodier. Bark cinereous, flaky on old trees below. Blaze rather hard, margin dark brown, then bright crimson streaked pale pink or white.

Semecarpus Anacardium. Blaze deep red, rather thick, then (wood) white.

Spondias mangifera. Bark smooth very thick. Cut rather tough but not hard. Blaze pink or light red alternating with narrow zones of lighter pink.

SAPINDACEÆ.

Sapindus detergens. Bark grey slightly fluted, thick. Blaze crimson, delicately zoned with few white streaks. Wood brownish.

Schleichera trijuga. Bark thin. Blaze very pale pink slightly mottled yellow darkening to brown.

CELASTRACEÆ.

Elæodendron glaucum. Bark grey nearly smooth thin (but see note). Blaze rather hard, dark red, then (wood) white. The cut is followed almost immediately by a *flow of water* from the lower edge of the cut.

Note.—A tree of $4\frac{1}{2}$ ft. girth had hard somewhat thick red brown outer layer, then whitish, and wood reddish.

Siphonodon celastrineus. Bark grey slightly rough. Blaze thin grey layer, then yellow, then (wood) white.

RHAMNACEÆ.

Zizyphus Jujuba. Bark grey rough. Blaze thin, brown, then thick dark pink.

Z. xylopyra. Bark thin. Blaze crimson streaked with white. Wood white.

APPENDIX I.

MIMOSACEÆ.

Acacia arabica. Bark cinereous, rather cracked. Blaze very hard similar to A. Catechu but lighter pink. Wood white.

A. Catechu. Bark black or cinereous thick cracked. Blaze very hard, outer dead bark (thickness very variable) vandyke brown, inner deep pink.

Albizzia Lebbek. Bark cinereous not very thick. Blaze red.

A. odoratissima. Bark smoothish. Blaze thick, very deep crimson, then (wood) white.

A. procera. Bark pale green or white, or in old trees grey. Blaze with a green chlorophyll layer, then red in old trees.

CÆSALPINIACEÆ.

Bauhinia malabarica. Blaze thin, light brown (outer dead bark), then light bright pink.

B. purpurea. Blaze brown, then with or without a pink band, then pale yellow rapidly darkening slightly zoned with white parenchyma, then paler and nearly white, then in center (wood) yellowish.

B. racemosa. Blaze dark pink.

B. retusa. Blaze thick, dark grey brown (outer layer), then very pale pink.

B. variegata. Blaze pale pink or flesh-coloured, turning darker pink on exposure.

Cassia Fistula. Bark smooth, pale or white. Blaze rather hard, red brown slightly streaked.

PAPILIONACEÆ.

Dalbergia lanceolaria. Blaze with a thin chlorophyll layer, then cream rapidly turning bright yellow-brown, then (wood) white.

D. latifolia. Bark grey flaking. Blaze cream-coloured or white streaked with a cream or yellowish tint, rapidly turning yellow-brown.

Erythrina suberosa. Bark hard, brown fluted, very thick. Blaze light yellow, then dark yellow.

Ougeinia dalbergioides. Blaze finely closely streaked with crimson or blood-red on a white ground. A red juice soon exuding from the cut.

MYRTACEÆ.

Barringtonia acutangula. Bark thick dark grey distinctly furrowed on old trees. Cut cheesy. Blaze pink.

RHIZOPHORACEÆ.

Carallia integerrima. Bark rugose thick. Blaze red-brown, outside with cheesy cut, then harder, pinkish-brown, inside (wood) hard dirty white.

COMBRETACEÆ.

Anogeissus latifolia. Bark white. Cut rather soft. Blaze, a thin chlorophyll layer; then brown-pink, than pale yellow or white, center (on wood) pale brown.

Terminalia Arjuna. Bark pale. Blaze with thin outermost layer, then crimson distinctly zoned, then an inner white border surrounding the yellow-brown center.

T. Chebula. Bark flaky. Blaze hard deep grey-brown outside, then reddish-brown or red, then yellowish.

T. tomentosa. Bark cinereous, thick. Blaze as in T. Arjuna.

CORNACEÆ.

Alangium Lamarckii. Bark very pale brown or grey, slightly longitudinally cracked. Blaze thin, narrow dark brown outer layer, then pale yellow.

ARALIACEÆ.

Heteropanax fragrans. Blaze thick cheesy, yellowish.

ULMACEÆ.

Celtis tetrandra. Bark smooth pale with faint stipular lines. Cut hard. Blaze white copiously sprinkled with brown dots and transverse lines. Center white.

A chlorophyll layer is present where the bark has been recently shed.

Holoptelea integrifolia. Bark pale or cinereous smooth or somewhat flaky, thick when old. Blaze cream-coloured streaked with light brown. (The white and cinereous barked trees may be different species or varieties, *vide* p. 389.)

MORACEÆ.

Most species exude a milky juice on being blazed.

Artocarpus Lakoocha. Bark grey flaky in small scales. Blaze red, immediately followed by drops of white milk.

Ficus nervosa. Bark smooth grey. Blaze hard, brownish. Cut followed by a flow of water and latex.

F. retusa. Bark smooth, thick. Blaze reddish, streaked. Cut followed by a flow of latex.

Streblus asper. Bark light grey. Blaze, outside a thin chlorophyll layer, then white, followed by a gradual darkening and a slight exudation of small drops of latex

APPENDIX I.

SALICACEÆ.

Salix tetrasperma. Bark (in old trees) fluted. Blaze thin pink band, then white.

SAPOTACEÆ.

Trees of this family yield a milky latex on being blazed.

Bassia latifolia. Bark nearly smooth brown. Blaze thin brown, then rather thick or thick red. From this latex oozes out from tubes visible to the naked eye.

EBENACEÆ.

Diospyros cordifolia. Bark dark very rugose.

D. montana. Bark light-coloured, smooth grey or reddish. Blaze rather thick, -yellow, gradually deepening on exposure to brown, wood cream coloured.

D. sylvatica. Bark smooth black or black and white (latter perhaps due to a parasite or epiphyte). Blaze light brown then white.

D. tomentosa. Bark black rough. Blaze chrome-yellow. The bark and blaze of D. melanonylon is similar.

D. variegata (p. 411). Bark smooth. Blaze pink.

OLEACEÆ.

Linociera intermedia. Bark brown, slightly flaky. Blaze, mottled brown, yellow and white, then white.

Schrebera swietenioides. Cut cheesy. Blaze pale yellow and white.

APOCYNACEÆ.

Most species exude a milky juice on being blazed.

Holarrhena antidysenterica. Bark thick smooth. Blaze brownish exuding latex from the layer next to the wood.

Wrightia tomentosa. Bark rough with lenticels only. Blaze soft, thin chlorophyll layer, then nearly white or a pale greenish-brown with copious latex. Wood white.

BIGNONIACEÆ.

Stereospermum chelonoides. Bark grey nearly smooth. Blaze with thin grey outer layer, then thick pale yellow or cream-coloured layer distinctly zoned with thin hard and soft layers.

BORAGINACEÆ (Cordiaceæ).

Blaze at first nearly white, quickly turning brown in all the species examined.

Ehretia lævis. Bark smooth pale grey or white. Blaze white with small brown streaks on the inner side. The whole quickly darkens and the inner bark turns deep brown.

VERBENACEÆ.

Gmelina arborea. Bark light grey, sometimes lightly transversely furrowed, flaky in isolated light coloured patches when old, thick. Blaze with a thin chlorophyll layer, then thick pale yellow with rough cut, then white with soft cut. Inside (on wood) yellowish.

Premna flavescens. Blaze white slightly streaked with yellow.

Premna latifolia. Blaze white.

Vitex glabrata. Bark pale. Blaze nearly white.

V. pedunculata. Blaze light yellow or cream turning darker on exposure, inside light brown.

RUBIACEÆ.

Adina cordifolia. Bark light-coloured, patchy. Blaze, outermost layer brown or absent (from exfoliation). then pink with an inner white border. Center (on wood) yellowish.

Anthocephalus Cadamba. Bark brown. Blaze, outer dead layer brown with patches of red, then thick yellow-brown, then white.

Gardenia turgida. Bark white. Blaze with a chlorophyll layer, then white with yellow specks. Wood cream-coloured.

Hymenodictyon excelsum. Bark dark grey, rugged, thick. Blaze deep brown, then soft pale pink streaked white, inside yellowish. Sometimes the blaze is nearly white, streaked brownish-red or yellow.

Ixora undulata. Blaze pink, then white.

Morinda tinctoria. Bark grey, fluted. Blaze grey brown, then whitish, center (on wood).

Nauclea purpurea. Bark smooth. Blaze light yellow, turning brown.

Randia dumeterum. Bark nearly smooth, thick., Blaze cheesy pink.

Stephegyne parvifolia. As in Adina.

Wendlandia tinctoria. Blaze light rose-coloured, then white (on wood).

APPENDIX II.

GLOSSARY OF BOTANICAL TERMS USED IN THE FLORA.

Abruptly acuminate, passing suddenly into a tapering point at the apex.

Accrescent, continuing to grow ; enlarged.

Achene, a dry 1-seeded carpel of an apocarpous fruit, *e.g.*, the pips of a strawberry.

Achlamydeous, without covering, a term applied to a flower devoid of any perianth.

Acicular, needle-like, long slender and rigid.

Acropetal, with the youngest organs nearest to the apex.

Aculeate, prickly, usually applied to somewhat curved prickles like those of a rose and which are not morphologically branches.

Acuminate, ending in a tapering apex.

Acyclic, not arranged in whorls. A term applied to the parts of a flower when these are arranged spirally on the axis.

-adelphous, combined in groups.

Adherent, when the members of a flower become united in the course of growth to the members in a different whorl and of a different character, *e.g.*, when the stamens become united to the corolla. Cp. coherent.

Adhesion, the state of being adherent.

Adnate, see adherent. Adnate anthers, see Anthers.

Adventitious, not arising in the regular order from the growing apices but subsequently and irregularly.

Albumen, a general name for the nutritive tissue stored up in a seed outside the embryo, whether endosperm or perisperm. Albuminous, containing albumen.

Alternate, the position of lateral members on an axis when neither opposite nor whorled.

Amphitropous, said of an ovule which is curved round so that one end approximates to the other. Funicle dorsally attached.

Anatropous, an atropous ovule is an ovule inverted on the funicle or stalk in such a way that though the nucellus remains straight the micropyle is directed towards the point of origin of the funicle which is adherent to the side of the ovule. *Vide* also Ovule.

Androecium, a collective word for all the stamens in a flower.

Annulus, a row or group of specially thickened cells on the sporangia of many ferns.

Anterior, the side remote from the parent axis, the ventral side. The antithesis to posterior. Unless twisting of the pedicel has taken place the anterior sepal or sepals of a flower in an inflorescence will be the lower sepal or sepals, the upper one or ones will be called posterior and the side ones lateral.

Anther, that part of the stamen which contains the pollen. In Angiosperms (*vide* Introduction, p. 49) it usually consists of 4 cells, loculi or pollen sacs (microsporangia), one pair on each side of the anther constituting the "anther-lobes." The cells or loculi often coalesce so that only 2 or even one cell is present in the ripe anther. When the loculi lie their whole length on the relatively broad connective, which then appears as a continuation of the filament, the anther is called *adnate.* When the filament appears to end at the base of the anther, the latter is called *innate.* If the anther swings freely on the top of the filament, it is called *versatile.*

Apetalous, without petals or corolla.

Apocarpous, see ovary.

Areola, a space marked off from the rest by some line, nerve, colouration.

Aril, an envelope which grows up from the base of the seed and more or less completely covers it. It is usually fleshy, *e.g.*, the flesh on the Litchi seed, the red covering on the Kujri (Celastrus paniculatus) seed.

Aristate, awned.

APPENDIX II.

Ascending, becoming erect from a prostrate or sub-prostrate base.

Asperous, rough with small papillæ.

Atrophy, the partial or complete suppression of a member.

Auricle, an ear-like appendage.

Awn, a rigid very fine or almost hair-like terminal appendage, *e.g.*, the appendage on the ears of barley or the terminal twisted appendages of the Spear-grass.

Axil, the upper angle formed by an axis and a lateral member, such as the angle formed by a leaf-stalk with the stem from which it springs.

Axillary, situated in an axil.

Axile, situated round an axis. Axile ovules are those situated on the column passing vertically through the center of an ovary, which column may be either a free axis, or formed by the meeting of the internal walls of the ovary.

Axis, any member which bears lateral subsidiary members may be called the axis of such subsidiary members.

Baccate, berry-like.

Balsam, a resin dissolved in an ethereal oil.

Bark, all the tissues alive or dead situated outside the cambium ring.

Basal-nerved, with several equally, or sub-equally strong main or primary nerves starting from the base, cp. penninerved. See also Nervation.

Basifixed, fixed by the base to the stalk. Cp. peltate, dorsifixed, etc.

Bast, a system of tissues distinct from the Xylem or wood and in Dicotyledons lying mostly outside it. The tissues of most economic importance in the Bast are the *fibres* which yield such materials as jute, hemp, and other textiles.

Beaked, provided with a firm excurrent solid or narrowly tubular prolongation which is often sharply marked off from the body of the organ. (The term is not applied to leaves.)

Berry, typically a fleshy indehiscent fruit with many seeds. The covering or *pericarp* consists of a thin skin or *epicarp*, a fleshy portion or *mesocarp*, and sometimes a firmer hard inner portion or *endocarp*. Where however the endocarp becomes stony or hard the fruit becomes a drupe. Examples of a berry are the Jamun (Eugenia), Mehrli (Flacourtia), Brinjal (Solanum). The term is sometimes extended to include fruits which are not typical berries but which resemble a berry in most characters.

Bifid, 2-fid, divided into two parts about half-way down.

Binate, 2-nate, two members arising together from the same point.

Bi-pinnate, pinnate with the pinnæ, or some of them, again pinnate.

Bi-pinnatifid, pinnatifid with the segments again pinnatifid.

Bisexual, 2-sexual, containing both fertile stamens and carpels with ovules.

Blade, the expanded part of a leaf, bract, etc., as distinct from the stalk.

Bostryx or Bostrychoid cyme, see Helicoid cyme

Bract, a reduced leaf. Bracts are usual on an inflorescence and often bear a flower in their axils.

Bracteole, small bracts occuring on the axis of a next higher order than that on which the bract is situated. If bracts and bracteoles appear to arise from the same axis, the bracteoles will usually be in a different position, thus in dicotyledons if the bract is ventral the two bracteoles if present are usually lateral.

Bullate, raised between the nerves.

Caducous, quickly falling off.

Calycine, resembling a calyx in texure rather than petals.

Calyptrate, falling off as a cap without expanding, *e.g.*, the petals of many vines.

Calyculus, (1) a calyx-like assemblage of minute leaves subsidiary to the true calyx and outside of it or (2) a calyx-like organ, *e.g.*, in some Loranthaceæ of which the morphology is doubtful, and may be a part of the torus (as in Escholtzia).

Calyx, the outer of the floral envelopes where these are differentiated into calyx and corolla. The term is also used where the inner floral envelope or corolla is considered as suppressed. See Flower.

Calyx-tube, the tube or cup formed by the cohesion of the leaves of the calyx. Also applied to an annular zone of the torus which grows up and bears the calyx or sepals, and frequently other members such as petals, etc., on its edge, see however, *Hypanthium.*

Campylotropous, see Ovule.

Capitate, clustered together into a head or ball. (2) Knoblike.

Capitellate, in the form of a very small knob.

Capitulum, a head of flowers.

Capsule, a form of fruit which becomes dry when ripe and opens by two or more valves.

Carpel, the modified leaves which bear the ovules. The carpels occupy the center of the flower when present (*e.g.*, in female or hermaphrodite flowers) and together form the ovary. q. v. See also Intro., p. 49.

Carpophore, the axis of the ripe ovary from which the separate ripe carpels are sometimes pendant.

Caruncle, a peculiar growth at the apical or micropylar end of the seed.

Catkin, a peculiar form of inflorescence consisting of an elongated axis clothed with bracts in the axils of which are

1- rarely 2- sexual flowers usually without, or with very inconspicuous, perianth. The whole inflorescence is deciduous in one piece.

Caudate, furnished with a long slender tail-like tip.

Chartaceous, paper-like in texture.

Cladode, a leaf-like branch of only one internode, *e.g.*, the so-called " leaves " of Asparagus.

Clavate, club-shaped.

Claw, the narrow or stalk-like base found in some petals.

Coccus, one of the lobes of a fruit, each of which is usually derived from a single carpel of the ovary, and when ripe, becomes more or less detached from the other cocci and often from the floral axis. Cocci may be dehiscent or indehiscent.

-coccous, in composition, *e.g.*, 5-coccous means composed of 5 cocci.

Columella, a term applied to the persistent axis of the fruit from which the rest of the fruit falls away in some cases when ripe.

Commissure, the plane of division between two carpels in Umbelliferous fruits.

Complicate, folded together lengthwise upon itself.

Compound, composed of two or more similar parts, thus a compound leaf is composed of two or more separate leaflets, a compound inflorescence of smaller inflorescences.

Connate, united one to another. The term is used of similar parts only, such as sepal to sepal or petal to petal, etc., *e.g.*, the petals of the Cotton plant; but the union of dissimilar parts, as, *e.g.*, petal to sepal would be termed " *adnate.*"

Connivent, weakly cohering or adhering.

Contorted, applied to a bud in which the parts have their margins overlapping and are at the same time rolled up.

Convolute, rolled up.

Cordate, shaped like the conventional heart (as on playing cards), or with the base heart-shaped.

Corolla, one of the envelopes of the flower and a collective name for the petals. The corolla if present is usually situated within the calyx, but rarely the calyx is absent. It may usually be distinguished from the calyx not only by its position but by its peculiar texture and colour, *e.g.*, the red petals of a rose.

Corona, a ligular outgrowth from the corolla or petals on the inside which sometimes appears like a second corolla, *e.g.*, in Pancratium and Daffodil.

Corymb, a form of inflorescence in which the several branches or flower-stalks arising at different levels reach more or less the same level at the top.

Costa, see Nervation.

Cotyledon, a leaf present on the embryonic plant while yet in the seed. The cotyledon (in Monocotyledons) or cotyledons (in Dicotyledons and Gymnosperms) in some species never expand but are absorbed by the germinating plant, in other species they appear above ground as the first green leaves of the plant. *Vide* Intro., pp. 49 and 53.

Cusp, a short hard point or tip; sometimes also used in the sense of a short pointed tip from an otherwise obtuse leaf.

Cuspidate, furnished with a cusp; in the second sense sometimes used as a short expression for abruptly acuminate.

Cyclic, with the parts arranged in whorls, not spirally.

Cyme, a system of branching in which the main axis ceases to grow or terminates in a flower, the secondary or lateral axes from beneath the apex continue to grow beyond the parent axis and may be likewise superseded by branches or axes of a higher order. Cp. *raceme.*

Decandrous, 10-androus, with ten stamens.

Deciduous, falling off, cp. *caducous*.

Declinate, inclined to one side, and often ascending at the tip.

Decompound, very much and repeatedly branched.

Decumbent, having the lower parts prostrate.

Decurrent, prolonged downwards from the base.

Decussate, in planes at right angles to one another.

Definite, not varying in number.

Deflexed, bent downwards.

Dehisce, to open by the separation of the walls or valves.

Dehiscent, dehiscing when ripe.

Dentate, with teeth projecting more or less perpendicularly from the margin.

Denticulate, with little teeth, or points along the margin.

Depressed, sunk in.

Diadelphous, 2-adelphous, in two bundles. A term applied to stamens which are grouped into two lots; one lot may, however, contain only one stamen.

Dichasium, a cymose method of branching in which each axis ends in a point or flower from beneath which a pair only of opposite lateral branches arise.

Dicoccous, 2-coccous, consisting of two cocci.

Didymous, consisting of two equal or similar connected halves or lobes. In the case of anthers, the term is especially applied to those with two rounded lobes without separating connective.

Didynamous, in two unequal pairs.

Diffuse, lax and spreading.

Digitate, spreading like the fingers of the hand. In the case of digitate leaves, each leaflet is properly provided with a short stalk or petiolule, if this is absent the leaf is palmately compound or palmati-partite. (q. v.).

Dimerous, 2-merous, with the parts in pairs.

Dimidiate, half wanting or rudimentary, or appearing to be so.

Dimorphic, occurring in two different forms. Syn. Dimorphous.

Diœcious, where the sexes occur on different individuals, the male flower on distinct trees from the female, as, *e.g.*, usually in the Papaya (Carica).

Diplostemonous, with the stamens in two whorls, those of the outer whorl opposite to the sepals, those of the inner whorl alternate with them.

Disc, a swelling or swellings, sometimes glandular, of the torus inside the calyx and usually inside the andrœcium.

Disciform, disc-like in the popular sense of the word disc.

Distichous, disposed alternately in two opposite rows.

Divaricate, spreading in opposite directions from a common base.

Dorsal, situated at the back of; same as *posterior*, see anterior.

Dorsifixed, fixed by the back of, in contrast to the state of being attached by the end or margin.

Drupaceous, more or less resembling a drupe.

Drupe, a form of fruit consisting of a more or less succulent pericarp which encloses a single 1-many-celled stone, *e.g.*, a plum. The stone in a drupe is the inner portion, or endocarp, of the fruit, and is to be distinguished from a hard testa of a seed. The stone may contain one or more seeds.

Drupel, each of the small drupes which may be formed from an apocarpous ovary.

Ebracteate, without bracts.

Echinate, with long spreading spines.

Ecology, see œcology.

Edaphic, depending upon the nature and condition of the soil.

Effuse, a term applied to an inflorescence with loose widely spreading branches.

Emarginate, having a deep dent at the apex. If the dent is broader and shallower it becomes retuse.

Embryo, the new plant from the time of its inception in the fertilized ovule and until the germination of the seed.

Endosperm, the tissue formed within the embryo-sac or macrospore subsequent to fertilization (in the case of Angiosperms) and destined to feed the embryo. In Gymnosperms the prothallium (though a secondary endosperm may be also developed). Cp. perisperm.

Entire, with the margin or edges not toothed or cut but even and continuous.

Epicalyx, a whorl of bracts just beneath the calyx and in some respects resembling it, in other cases stipular appendages of the sepals which also resemble a secondary exterior calyx.

Epicarp, the outermost layer of the fruit.

Epigynous, an epigynous flower is one in which the torus or receptacle grows up at the circumference carrying with it the calyx, corolla and stamens and completely enclosing the ovary. An epigynous calyx, stamens, etc., refers to this superior position with regard to the ovary or pistil. Cp. perigynous, hypogynous.

Epipetalous, situated on the corolla or petals. The position of epipetalous stamens may be either due to the growth of a common zone of the torus carrying with it both petals and stamens, or to the growing up together of both corolla an stamens (*i.e.*, adhesion of corolla and stamens).

Epiphyte, a plant which grows upon another plant without, however, drawing its nutriment from the living parts of such other plant. Cp. parasite.

Episepalous, situated on the sepals, (2) situated opposite to the sepals.

Equitant, in two vertical rows with the bases of the outer sheathing the bases of the inner leaves, *e.g.*, in many of the Iris Family.

Erecto-patent, between erect and spreading.

Erose, appearing torn or frayed at the edges.

Evanescent, quickly disappearing.

Exalbuminous, without albumen.

Excurrent, running out beyond the margin.

Extra-axillary, situated away from the axil of the leaf to which it is nearest.

Extrorse, applied to anthers which open towards the circumference of the flower and not towards the pistil. Opposed to introrse.

Falcate, somewhat curved.

False septum or dissepiment, an inner wall of an ovary which is not formed from the incurved edges of the carpels and is usually of late development.

Fascicled, closely aggregated.

Fastigiate, with the branches all upright.

Female, a female flower is one which bears an ovary containing ovules capable of fertilization and becoming seed, and does not bear stamens. A flower which only bears an imperfect or functionless ovary (pistillode) is not considered a female flower. A *female plant* is one which only bears female flowers.

Fertile, a fertile flower is synonymous with a perfect female flower. A *fertile stamen* is one that developes functional pollen, in contradistinction to a staminode. A fertile frond in a fern is one that bears sporangia.

-fid, used in composition, divided about half-way down Cp. -partite, -lobed, -sect.

Filament, the stalk of an anther, *i.e.*, the lower part of a stamen. It may, however, be absent, in which case the anther is sessile.

Filiform, very slender, hair-like.

Fimbriate, clothed with filiform appendages.

Flabellate, fan-shaped.

Flower, the organs of reproduction (stamens or pistil) together with the usually more or less modified portion of the axis (torus, receptacle) on which they are inserted, and together with the specialized leaves (perianth, calyx, corolla), if any, which surround or envelope these organs.

A *typical* 2-sexual flower consists of (1) two circles (whorls) of perianth leaves, the outer of which is green and herbaceous (*calyx*), the inner (*corolla*) white or coloured and of different texture (petaloid), (2) one or more whorls of male organs (*stamens*), (3) one or more *carpels* which bear the ovules. All or some of the above parts may be arranged spirally in some flowers, and any or all may be absent with the exception of a single stamen or a single carpel. (*Vide* Intro., p. 65.).

-foliolate, in composition refers to the leaflets in a compound leaf, *e.g.*, 3-foliolate means with 3-leaflets.

Free, not united with other members.

Free central placentation, where the ovules are situated on the axis of a unilocular ovary.

Frond, a term applied to the leaf of a fern.

Fructification, a fruit or aggregation of fruits, including

such parts of the axis, bracts, etc., which are accrescent in fruit.

Fruit, the ovary (in the case of an apocarpous ovary, *all* the carpels) and its contents after the fertilization of the ovules, including in the case of inferior ovaries the accrescent or investing part of the floral axis, *e.g.*, apple.

(NOTE.—Some botanists term each carpel of an apocarpous fruit a fruit.)

Frutescent, becoming shrubby.

Fruticose, shrubby.

Fugacious, rapidly dying or falling off.

Funicle, the stalk by which the ovule is attached to the placenta of the ovary.

Furcate, forked.

Gamo-, in composition means united or in one piece, *i.e.*, not divided to the base into separate members, *e.g.*, gamophyllous, with the perianth leaves united at least below; gamopetalous, with the corolla more or less tubular below, etc. The term is used even where theoretically, perhaps, the lower or tubular portion is an annular zone of the floral axis of the same texture as the leaves, petals, etc., concerned.

Geminate, in pairs.

Gibbous, swollen on one side, humped.

Glabrate, nearly glabrous.

Glabrous, without any hairs.

Glabrescent, with deciduous hairs, becoming glabrous.

Glaucous, of a blue-green colour.

Glume, the bracts and bracteoles on the spikelets of the grasses and sedges.

Gonophore, an internode of the floral axis between the corolla and stamens, and hence bearing both the stamens and the pistil. Cp. Gynophore.

-gonal, in composition signifies -angled.

Gregarious, occurring associated in large quantities, *e.g.*, the Sal tree.

Gynœcium, the carpel, ovary or assembly of carpels in a flower, together with their appendages (style, stigma).

Gynandrous, with the stamens adnate to the pistil.

Gynandrophore, same as gonophore.

Gynobasic, arising from the base of the carpel or ovary.

Gynophore, an internode of the floral axis between the stamens and the pistil, so that the pistil is considerably separated from the stamens. Cp. gonophore.

Hairy, clothed with somewhat long, not very dense hairs. Cp. pubescent, villous, etc.

Haplochlamydeous, with only one whorl of perianth leaves.

Hastate, shaped like an arrow head in which the basal lobes or auricles spread more or less at right angles to the rest of the blade.

Helicoid (cyme), a form of sympodial cymose branching in which the newer axis always arises to the same side of the parent axis, so that the sympodium becomes more or less spiral, *e.g.*, each half of a pedate leaf. Syn. bostrychoid.

Hemicyclic, with some of the floral members whorled or cyclic, and others spiral, *e.g.*, with the calyx and corolla in whorls and the stamens and carpels spirally arranged as in Clematideæ.

Hermaphrodite (flower), a flower in which both stamens and ovary are present and functional

Heterochlamydeous, with the perianth distinctly differentiated into a calyx and a corolla.

Heterogamous (a term usually restricted to the flower-heads of the Compositæ and the spikelets of grasses) where the flowers are of two kinds differing in sex in the same head or spikelet, *e.g.*, male and female, male and hermaphrodite, etc.

Hilum, the scar on a seed indicating the point of separation from the funicle or stalk.

Hirsute, with a thick covering of somewhat firm moderately long hairs. Cp. hairy, pubescent, villous, etc.

Hispid, with short scattered very stiff hairs or bristles, sometimes the base of the hair only is stiff. A hispid surface feels harsh to the hand.

Hoary, grey or white.

Homogamous, a term usually restricted to the flower-heads of the Compositæ and the spikelets of grasses where the flowers are all similar to one another in sex in the same head or spikelet.

Homoichlamydeous, where the different whorls or members of the perianth or floral envelopes are all similar in texture, *i.e.*, not distinctly differentiated into calyx and corolla. Cp. Haplochlamydeous, Heterochlamydeous.

Homologous, of similar morphological significance.

Hygrophyte, a plant requiring a constant supply of moisture all the year round.

Hypanthium, a more or less tubular or flask-shaped zone of the floral axis which grows up above the level of the ovary and bears on its margin or at different levels the floral envelopes and andrœcium. It is sometimes constricted above the ovary and prolonged into a 'beak' above it It is either green or coloured, specially in fruit. The ovary may lie free within it or be closely invested by (adnate to) it, in which case it may be referred to as the ovary-wall. See also Calyx-tube.

Hypogynous, situated on the torus at the same level as, or below the level of, the base of the ovary. Cp. perigynous, epigynous.

Imbricate, overlapping, with one sepal, petal, etc., outside all the others (*i.e.*, its margins are free) and one inside all the others.

Incised, deeply cut.

Incurved, with the ends curved inwards or towards the axis.

Indefinite, of varying number and usually numerous.

Indehiscent, not opening by valves or pores. The liberation of the seeds of an indehiscent fruit takes place through the consumption of the fruit by animals, or through the rotting of the pericarp.

Indumentum, the clothing of hairs, scales, etc.

Induplicate, rolled inwards on both sides.

Inferior, an inferior calyx, stamens, etc., implies insertion at a level below, or near, the base of the ovary; an inferior ovary implies that the sepals, stamens, etc., are inserted on the torus at a level above, or near the top of the ovary. Cp. epigynous.

Inflorescence, an axis or assemblage of axes especially devoted to the bearing of flowers and including the flowers and their bracts and bracteoles.

Infructescence, an assemblage of fruits including in many cases the more less modified axes which bear them.

Infundibular, funnel-shaped, having the lower part tubular and gradually widening upwards, as in a chemical funnel.

Innate, said of stamens in which there is a distinct transition from, or articulation between, the anther and the filament in contradistinction to one in which the connective appears merely as a continuation of the filament. Cp. *adnate.*

Integument, one of the coats or envelopes of the nucellus of the ovule. There may be one or two integuments which grow up from the base of the ovule completely investing the nucellus with the exception of a minute channel at the tip termed the *micropyle,* through which in many plants the pollen-tube finds its way to the embryo-sac.

Internode, the space between two leaves or metamorphosed leaves.

Interpetiolar, said of stipules situated between the bases of opposite leaves, and which are frequently more or less connate so that each pair, made up of one from each leaf, may resemble single stipules.

Intrapetiolar, said of stipules when each pair of a single leaf unite together within the axil of the leaf.

Introrse, said of anthers which open towards the pistil. Cp. *extrose.*

Involucre, an assemblage or whorl of bracts or leaves situated close beneath a flower or inflorescence.

Irregular, unsymmetrical, *i.e.,* not being capable of division into two similar halves by any plane parallel to the axis. Sometimes also used for flowers in which some of the members in the same whorl differ from others but in which the flower can be divided medianally into two similar halves, see zygomorphic.

Isomerous, with the number of members in each whorl the same.

Isostemonous, with the stamens equal in number to the normal number of its sepals or petals or (in haplochlamydeous flowers) to the tepals.

-jugate, in composition in + + pairs *e.g.,* multi-jugate= in many pairs.

Keel, the anterior petals in the Papilionaceæ; a ridge shaped like the keel of a boat as in the adjective *keeled.*

Laciniate, irregularly cut into very narrow lobes.

Lanceolate, shaped like a lance head. A lanceolate leaf may or may not taper as much at the base as at the other end, but if it is much wider near the base the leaf will become ovate-lanceolate.

Lateral, situated to the right and left of the median plane, see *anterior*.

Latex, milky juice.

Leaf, leaves in the broad morphological sense are lateral exogenous outgrowths of an axis originating below the growing apex in acropetal succession from the undifferentiated tissue of the growing point, and differing in form from the axis which produces them.

In its typical form a leaf consists of a flat expanded green blade, or in a compound leaf several blades (*leaflets*), a stalk or *petiole*, and two lateral appendages at or near the base of the petiole (*stipules*). Any of these parts may be absent or the leaf variously metamorphosed into foliar tendrils, bracts, scales, petals, etc., etc.

The growth and life of a leaf is usually strictly limited, it never bears flowers, but it often bears sporangia (as in ferns, carpels, stamens). It usually bears a bud or shoot in its axil except in the case of many metamorphosed leaves. In descriptions of shape, etc., the word *leaf* merely denotes the *blade* of the ordinary foliage leaves.

Leaflet one of the blades of a compound leaf (see above). A leaflet may usually be distinguished from a simple leaf from its position (one very frequently terminating the foliar axis) and from its bearing no bud in its axil.

Leguminous, resembling the peas and beans in the nature of the fruit.

Lenticel, cortical pores. Usually lens-shaped or elongate small dots or excrescences on the bark, they are filled with loose tissue, the intercellular spaces of which serve as a passage for oxygen into the inner tissues.

Lepidote, covered with small flat scales.

Ligule, a membranous outgrowth from the surface of an

organ. In grasses, the membranous appendage at the mouth of the sheath.

Ligulate, strap-shaped.

Limb, the expanded part of a corolla, petal, etc., in contra-distinction to the tube or claw.

Lobed, cut less than half-way down into more or less rounded segments.

-locellate, used in composition to indicate the number of locelli or cells in an anther, especially before the fusion which often takes place on dehiscence.

-locular, used in composition to indicate the number, etc., of cells or compartments in an ovary or fruit, or in a ripe anther just before dehiscence.

Loculicidal, a mode of dehiscence in which rupture takes place through the middle of the outer wall of each loculus. Cp. septicidal.

Loculus, a compartment of an ovary or of an anther.

Lodicule, small scales, usually much swollen at the time of flowering, occurring in the flowers of many grasses and by some supposed to represent the inner whorl of a rudimentary perianth.

Lyrate, with a very large terminal lobe compared with the smaller and narrower lateral lobes.

Macrosporangium, a sporangium which contains one or more macrospores. In the Gymnosperms and Angiosperms the macrosporangium is represented by the nucellus of the ovule.

Macrospore, a relatively large asexually produced female spore, represented in the Angiosperms and Gymnosperms by the embryo-sac.

Male flower, a flower which bears fertile stamens but not fertile carpels. An abortive pistil may be present in a male flower or not.

Marcescent, remaining attached in a withered state.

Marginate, with a margin of a different character from the rest of the member.

Median, lying in the plane drawn through the center of the member and the longitudinal center of the axis bearing the member.

Mericarp, one-half of a schizocarpous fruit.

-merous, in composition, indicates the number of members in each whorl, *e.g.*, 5-merous.

Microsporangium, a sporangium which contains microspores. In the Gymnosperms and Angiosperms each loculus of an anther is a microsporangium.

Microspore, relatively small asexually produced male spores. In the Gymnosperms and Angiosperms the pollen grains are the microspores.

Micropyle, the canal through the integuments of an ovule at the apex of the nucellus.

Mixed Forest, forest composed of a large number of different species rather than of one or two gregarious species.

Monadelphous, more or less united into one bundle by the filaments.

Monochlamydeous, the same as haplochlamydeous.

Monœcious, bearing both male and female flowers on the same individual.

Mucronate, tipped with a short hard usually blunt point.

Muricate, covered with scattered short firm thick or conical spines.

Muticous, without appendages.

-nate, used in composition, arising from the same point or whorled, *e.g.*, ternate leaf, with 3 leaflets digitately arranged.

APPENDIX II.

Nervation, the arrangement of the fibre-vascular bundles in the leaves. The method of describing the nervation differs somewhat in the Flowering Plants and Ferns.

I. Flowering Plants. The nerves or ribs which spring directly from the petiole (or stem in sessile leaves) are termed *Primary Nerves.* The center one or if there is only one is the *Mid-rib.* If there are several primary nerves spreading from the base the leaf is *palmi-nerved* or palmately nerved, 3-nerved, 5-nerved, etc., refer to the number of primary nerves. If all the primary nerves are parallel or nearly so, the leaf is *parallel-nerved.* The larger nerves which spring laterally from the primary nerves are the *Secondary Nerves,* and those that arise from these the *Tertiary Nerves,* which may, as well as the nervation of a higher order, be also called the nervules. If the nervules are very numerous and anastomose with one another the nervation is *reticulate,* but this expression is sometimes also used merely as the antitheseis of parallel-nerved.

II. Ferns. The continuation of the stipes or stalk of the frond into the blade is called the rachis, or primary rachis, in a compound or deeply divided frond, rachis or mid-rib, in a less divided or simple frond. The branches from the primary rachis in a bi-many-pinnate or deeply 2-many-pinnatifid frond are the *secondary rachides,* and the branches from these again the tertiary rachides according to the state of division of the frond. The nerves which spring from the mid-rib or rachis of a simple frond or from the secondary or tertiary etc. rachis, as the case may be (depending on the degree of branching in the frond) in a more compound frond are the *costæ.* Those that spring from the costæ are the *veins.* and those of a higher order the venules. A costa is hence the mid-rib of a lobe.

Node, the plane of insertion of a leaf on the axis.

Nut, a hard, dry 1-seeded indehiscent fruit.

Nutlet, the dry 1-seeded lobes of some fruits each of which becomes detached like a separate fruit. See also coccus.

Ob-, in composition means inversely, thus an ovate leaf has the wider part towards the base, an *obovate* leaf is inversely ovate and has the wider part towards the apex.

Obdiplostemonous, diplostemonous in which the members of the outer whorl of stamens are opposite to the petals, and those of the inner whorl opposite to the sepals.

Oblique, when referring to shape means with one half more largely developed than the other.

Oblong, longer than broad and with the sides more or less parallel.

Obsolete, not developed.

Obtuse, blunt or rounded.

Ocreate, said of stipules which are united into a tube round the stem.

Oecology, the science of the relations of an organism to its environment.

Opposite, on different sides of the axis with the bases on the same level.

Orthotropous, an orthotropous ovule is straight with the micropyle opposite to the chalaza or base from which arise the integuments. Cp. anatropous. *Vide* also Ovule.

Oval, broadly elliptical.

Ovary, the part of a flower which contains the ovules and consisting of one or more carpels which cohere by their edges to form one or more closed cells or chambers, the *cells* of the ovary. An ovary is *apocarpous* if the carpels composing it are free from one another, in which case each carpel forms a separate chamber by the incurving and meeting of its edges (see suture). An ovary is *syncarpous* if the carpels composing it are united to one another. A syncarpous ovary is 1-celled where the component carpels only cohere by their edges or where the coherent edges are incurved without reaching the axis, it is 2- or more-celled where the coherent edges of the carpels are sufficiently incurved to meet one another in the axis of the ovary, so as to form walls, or *septa.* Septa sometimes arise also by vertical walls between the axis of the ovary and the mid-ribs of the carpels. (See also Pistil, and Introduction, p. 49).

Ovate, egg-shaped with the broader end towards the base.

Ovate-lanceolate, ovate-oblong, etc., between ovate and lanceolate, between ovate and oblong, etc.

Ovule, usually small or minute bodies attached to the carpellary leaves (carpels) in the Gymnosperms, and usually to the carpellary leaves, but sometimes on the base or on the free axis of the ovary in the Angiosperms, always in the Angiosperms inside the closed ovary. The ovule consists of a central portion (*macrosporangium, nucellus*) and nearly always of one or two integuments which envelop the nucellus by growing up from its base, it is attached by a stalk, *funicle,* to the placenta or is more rarely sessile. If the ovule and nucellus are straight with the micropyle opposite to the base (chalaza) the ovule is *orthotropous,* if it is inverted so that the funicle is adnate to the side (forming the *raphe*) and the micropyle is directed towards the placenta it is *anatropous,* in this case the nucellus remains straight between the chalaza and the micropyle, but if the whole ovule including the nucellus is itself curved the ovule is *campylotropous.* In this case, the embryo also becomes curved. On fertilization and consequent development of the embryo, the ovule becomes the *seed.*

-partite, in composition means cleft nearly to the base. Cp. -fid, lobed.

Pedicel, a stalk. Usually the stalk of a single flower of an inflorescence, or the stalk of a fruit, etc., above the calyx.

Peduncle, the stalk of an inflorescence or of a single flower when this forms the inflorescence.

Petiole, the stalk of a leaf.

Pale, palea, (adj. paleaceous), a chaffy scale; specifically the upper of the two bracts which subtend a flower in the Gramineæ. The palea of the gramineæ is most frequently 2-nerved and may possibly represent two connate tepals of the outer perianth whorl.

Palmate, radiating like the spread fingers of the hand. A palmate leaf may have the segments cut nearly to the base but if the leaf actually becomes compound from the sinuses reaching the petiole it becomes *digitate*.

Palmatifid, palmate with the sinuses reaching about half-way down.

Palmatipartite, palmate with the sinuses reaching beyond the middle.

Palmatisect, much cut in a palmate manner.

Palmi-nerved, with the primary nerves radiating from the apex of the petiole.

Panduriform, fiddle-shaped, with the base and end broader than above the base.

Panicle, a repeatedly branched inflorescence.

Papilionaceous, shaped somewhat like the flowers of a pea or bean. A typical papilionaceous flower has a corolla with a large posterior petal (*standard*), two lateral petals (alae, *wings*), and two anterior petals more or less combined into a *keel*.

Papillæ, small multicellular outgrowths from the epidermis.

Pappus, the scaly, hairy or feathery modified calyx of the fruit of some plants especially of the Compositæ.

Parallel-nerved, with numerous nerves from the base running more or less parallel and close to one another, as *e.g.*, in the leaves of Bamboos, etc.

Parasitic, drawing sustenance from the living tissues of other plants.

Pari-pinnate, pinnate with the leaflets in pairs and no terminal leaflet.

-partite, in composition means cleft considerably beyond the middle. Cp. -fid, -lobed.

Pectinate, with narrow segments spreading like the teeth of a comb.

Pedate, a form of branching in which the segments of each half of the leaf forms a helicoid cyme.

Pedicel, a small stalk. Especially the stalk of a single flower of an inflorescence to distinguish it from the peduncle.

Peduncle, the stalk of an inflorescence, or of a single flower when the inflorescence is 1-flowered.

Pellucid, translucent.

Peltate, shield-shaped, round, like the indusium of some ferns ; (2) of leaves, attached to the petiole in the center of the blade, or at least not by the margin.

Penni-nerved, with one mid-rib and secondary nerves from it. Cp. Nervation, basal-nerved.

Pentadelphous, applied to stamens aggregated into 5 groups.

Pentamerous, with five members in each whorl.

Perianth, a general term for the floral envelopes including both calyx and corolla, but more especially when there is no such differentiation into calyx and corolla.

Pericarp, the whole outside of the fruit including the epicarp, mesocarp and endocarp.

Perigynous, a term applied to the flower or to the sepals, petals, or stamens when these are raised on a zone of the torus above the level of the base of the ovary when the ovary is free in the tube so formed or only adnate by means of the intercalated disc. Cp. hypogynous, epigynous.

Perisperm, nutritive tissue of the nucellus which remains in the seed until absorbed by the *germinating* embryo.

Persistent, not falling off.

Perulate, wrapped in scales.

Petal, one of the divisions of the corolla.

Petaloid, of a more or less delicate texture and white or coloured. Cp. sepaloid.

Petiole, the stalk of a leaf.

Petiolule, the stalk of a leaflet in a compound leaf.

Phylloclade, a branch compressed so as to resemble a leaf and performing the functions of a leaf. Cp. cladode.

Phylogeny (adj. phylogenetic), ancestry from forms or groups which differ specifically, or generically, or in more important characters, from the existing species or group.

Pilose, with rather long, not dense nor very silky hairs.

Pinna, the branches of a bi-pinnate leaf. See pinnate.

Pinnate, a compound leaf with two or more leaflets springing from each side of the axis or *rachis*. If the leaflets are odd so that the rachis terminates in a leaflet, the leaf is *imparipinnate*, if the leaflets are even with no terminal leaflet, the leaf is *paripinnate*. If the rachis of the leaf bears one or more pairs of secondary rachides which latter bear the leaflets, the leaf is *bi-pinnate*. If the secondary rachides bear again rachides the leaf is *tripinnate* and so on.

Pinnately, in a pinnate manner, *i.e.*, with the branches springing from either side of the central axis, cp. palmate (adv. palmately).

Pinnatifid, deeply lobed to about half way down or more, with the lobes pinnately arranged.

Pinnatisect, pinnatifid down to the mid-rib.

Pinnule, the ultimate free divisions or leaflets of the frond in ferns.

Pistil, a collective word for the ovary, style and stigma.

Pistillode, a rudimentary pistil.

Placenta, the surface to which are attached the ovules.

Placentation, position of the placenta.

Plicate, plaited.

Plumose, feathered.

Pod, typically a dry fruit derived from a mono-carpellary ovary, elongated in shape and dehiscing along one or both sutures, such for instance as a pea-pod. In a more extended sense any fruit of the Leguminous order or other fruit resembling a typical Leguminous fruit.

Pollen, the male spores which are developed in the pollen-sacs or loculi of anthers.

Polyadelphous, in many bundles.

Polygamous, bearing male, female, and hermaphrodite flowers on the same plant.

Polypetalous, with the petals not combined into a tube (p. 50).

Posterior, see under anterior. Postichous, hinder, at the back, posterior.

Prickle, a pointed spine-like process originating from the epidermal. or epidermal and subjacent, tissue only. Cp. thorn.

Primary nerves, see Nervation.

Protandrous, the anthers ripening before the pistil is ready to fertilization.

Pseudocarp, a fruit or cluster of fruits together with the accrescent axis, peduncle or other parts not usually considered to belong to the fruit proper, but which become fleshy in fruit.

Puberulous, slightly pubescent.

Pubescent, covered with close short fine hair. Pubescence is a denser shorter state of hairiness than hairy.

Punctate, marked with small dots.

Pungent, with a pin-like point capable of penetrating the flesh.

Putamen, the hard endocarp, especially a many-celled endocarp, of fruits.

Pyrene, when a putamen breaks up on ripening into several parts each enclosing a seed, each such part is called a pyrene. Cp. coccus.

Quinate, with five segments or leaflets.

Raceme, an inflorescence in which the main axis continues to grow and the lowest flowers are the oldest and open first. *Racemose*, a form of branching in which the main axis continues to grow and always remain stronger than the lateral axes which successively spring from it. Cp. cyme.

Rachis, that part of a pinnate leaf which bears the leaflets; in a bi-pinnate leaf the primary rachis bears the pinnæ the secondary rachides the leaflets. (2) The axis of an inflorescence.

Rachilla, the axis of the spikelet of grasses.

Radical, direct from the root.

Raphe, the ridge or course of the funicle along the side of the ovule to which it is adnate in anatropous ovules.

Raphides, acicular crystals sometimes found embedded in tissues (and in some cases visible as small raised lines on the surface).

Ray florets or ray flowers, the more or less zygomorphous flowers found at the circumference of many umbels, flower-heads, etc.

Receptacle, the portion of the axis on which is situated the florets in a capitate inflorescence, or on which is situated the parts of the flower in a flower.

Regular, with all the members symmetrically disposed around the geometric center of the flower, and with either all the members in a single whorl equal and similar or if dissimilar then with one half of the whorl similar to the other half.

Reniform, kidney-shaped.

Repand, with a wavy margin. The sinuses being more shallow than in *sinuate*.

Replum, a partition of the ovary which is not a part of the carpels.

Retinaculum, an upcurved acute subsequently hardened process from the placenta (possibly a modification of the funicle) on which the ovules and seeds are borne in most Acanthaceæ.

Retrorse, directed backwards.

Retuse, with the apex depressed so that there is a sinus at the tip, which is less deep than in emarginate.

Rhacis, rhacilla, see rachis, rachilla.

Rhizome, an elongated underground stem with apical growth.

Rotate, a corolla with a very short tube and a horizontally spreading limb.

Rotund, roundish, not angular.

Rugose, with numerous minute elevations and depressions.

Ruminate, with the testa of the seed projecting as points and plates into the albumen.

Runcinate, incised with the lobes directed backwards.

Saccate, bulged into a small sac or cavity.

Sagittate, arrow-shaped with the basal lobes directed

backwards. Cp. hastate.

Salver-shaped, with a long tube and comparatively short horizontally spreading limb.

Samara, a fruit with the pericarp compressed and expanded into a wing, or each part of a schizocarpous fruit in which the pericarp is thus modified.

Saprophyte, a plant which feeds upon decayed organic matter.

Sarmentose, with long arching slender branches which are often sub-scandent.

Scabrid, covered with small hard hairs or points so as to feel rough to the touch.

Scabrous, very scabrid.

Scape, a peduncle which rises direct from the root.

Scarious, dry and membranous.

Schizocarp, a fruit which splits up into two or more distinct portions (mericarps, cocci, etc.) each resembling a separate fruit.

Sclerenchymatous, applied to tissue, consisting usually of more or less isodiametric cells, in which the cell walls are very greatly thickened and hardened.

Scorpioid, with the (apparently) lateral axes forming a double row on one side of the usually curved (apparent) main axis or sympodium.

-sect, in composition means deeply cut, especially cut nearly to the axis.

Secund, all inclined in one direction.

Seed, the ovule after fertilization and development of the embryo. The seed consists of the more or less modified integuments of the ovule which become the *testa* or seed coat (see also aril, arillus), sometimes a part of the tissue of the nucellus which becomes filled with food material (perisperm), frequently a tissue which has become developed inside the embryo-sac (endosperm), and finally the more or less completely developed and differentiated embryo.

Sepal, one of the divisions of the calyx.

Sepaloid, green and resembling a sepal in texture rather than a petal. Cp. petaloid.

Septicidal, a mode of opening of a fruit by means of a split through the median plane of the interior walls or dissepiments so that the fruit becomes more or less separated into its component carpels. The separation usually begins by an opening at the top of the fruit. Cp. loculicidal.

Septifragal, a mode of dehiscence in which a central column bearing the septa or part of the septa remains while the exterior walls of the fruit separate from it. Cp. loculicidal, septicidal.

Septum, an interior wall.

Serrate, toothed like a saw with the teeth inclined forwards.

Serrulate, serrate but with the teeth minute.

Sessile, without a stalk.

Seta, a long stiff hair. Setaceous, needle-like; very slender and tapering and of no appreciable width; more slender than in linear.

Setose, beset with setæ.

Silky, sericeous, covered with very fine adpressed silky hairs.

Simple, not composed of a number of similar parts, opposed to compound. A leaf is simple even if segmented provided that the divisions are not separated by portions of the axis destitute of blade.

Sinuate, somewhat deeply waved. Cp. repanu.

Sorus, a group of sporangia.

Spathe, a large bract which sheaths an inflorescence or

part of an inflorescence, at least, in its young state.

Spathaceous, sheathing and not divided up into distinct sepals, petals, etc.

Spicate, spiked, with the flowers in a spike q.v.

Spiciform, resembling a spike in appearance.

Spike, a form of racemose inflorescence in which the flowers are sessile on the axis.

Spadix, a spike with an enlarged fleshy axis and usually enclosed when young in a spathe.

Spikelet, the ultimate parts of the inflorescence of grasses (rarely an inflorescence consists of only one spikelet) and Cyperaceæ are called spikelets. A spikelet in the grasses consists of an axis (rachilla) with usually three or more distichously arranged bracts (glumes), of which the lowest two (one or more) are usually empty and the others contain an opposing bracteole (pale) and a male or female or 2-sexual naked flower. See also glume, pale, lodicule.

Squarrose, with numerous close-set spreading leaves, bracts, or tips or processes of leaves, bracts, etc.

Stamen, a modified leaf which bears the microsporangia or pollen-sacs. A typical stamen consists of a stalk (filament) and the specially modified part (anther) which bears the pollen-sacs. See also anther.

Staminodes, imperfect or reduced or rudimentary satmens which do not bear fertile pollen.

Stellate, spreading in a star-shaped manner.

Stigma, the part of a carpel especially adapted by means of papillæ, viscosity, etc., to receive the pollen grains. The stigmas of the several carpels forming an ovary may be separate or united, stalked or sessile.

Stipes, a stalk, especially the stalk of a fern leaf.

Stipella, the stipule of a leaflet.

Stipitate, stalked.

Stipule (adj. stipular), stipules are a pair ot processes

(often absent) one of which springs from either side of the leaf base (*i.e.*, where the stalk of the leaf or the base of a sessile leaf leaves the stem) and either membranous or foliaceous in texture, usually small but sometimes exceeding the leaf-blade (which they often protect) in bud.

Stolon, a slender stem usually furnished at first with scale-leaves only, springing from the root or base of the stem and extending some distance under or on the ground, ultimately rooting and giving rise to a new plant.

Strophiole, a thickening about the hilum or base of a seed, perhaps of the nature of an incomplete aril.

Style, a slender outgrowth or appendage of a carpel bearing the stigma. The style may be absent. In an ovary of more than one carpel the separate styles may be distinct or more or less connate into one; in the latter cases the stigmas may be distinct or fused.

Subulate, awl-shaped, *i.e.*, slender and tapering to a point.

Suffrutescent, somewhat shrubby.

Sulcate, grooved.

Superior, situated above another member. A superior ovary has its base above the insertion of the calyx, a superior calyx is inserted at a level above the top of the ovary.

Suture, a seam, the line marking the connate edges of a carpel and sometimes also the line marking the mid-rib of the carpel.

Sympodium, an apparent main axis made up of the lower parts of successive axes each of which has completed its growth after giving off the strong lateral shoot which in its turn forms part of the sympodium.

Syncarpous, see ovary.

Synandrous, with the stamens united throughout.

Syngenesious, with the anthers cohering

Tendril, a filiform sensitive organ which winds round supports to enable weak stems to reach the light. Tendrils are of various morphological origin in different groups. Some may be modified branches, other leaves, another the end of a leaf rachis, etc.

Tepal, a division of a perianth, a word applicable to either a sepal or a petal.

Terete, cylindrical.

Ternary, with 3 members in a whorl.

Ternate, 3 members digitately arranged, or starting from the same node.

Testa, the outer covering of a seed.

Tetradynamous, with 4 long and 2 short stamens.

Thorn, a modified shoot or branch in the form of a hard spine.

Thorn Woodland, forest composed principally of thorny species.

Thyrse, a close panicle more or less spindle-shaped.

Tomentose, with exceedingly close matted short pubescence.

Torulose, alternately swollen and constricted.

Torus, the portion of the floral axis from which spring the perianth, stamens, carpels or any portion of the flower. The torus may therefore be convex, cylindrical, concave, etc. Same as receptacle in some senses.

Trichotomous, with the axis successively dividing into three branches.

Tricoccous, ultimately splitting into 3 cocci.

Tri-pinnate, with the primary axis of the leaf pinnate with one or more pairs of the pinnæ again pinnate and with one or more pairs of the secondary pinnæ pinnate.

Triple-nerved, 3-nerved, with 3 nerves from base, with 3 primary nerves.

Tri-quetrous, with 3 sharp corners.

Tropophilous, plants adapted for a physiologically wet climate at one season of the year and a dry climate at another season are termed tropophilous.

Truncate, as though cut off at the end.

Turbinate, top-shaped.

Turgid, tense as though with pressure from within, swollen.

Umbel, an inflorescence in which the branches all radiate from the top of the peduncle. If these branches each terminate in a flower th umbel is simple, if they are again umbellately branched, the umbel is compound.

Unilocular, applied to an ovary not divided up by partitions into separate compartments.

Urceolate, flask-shaped and broadest below the middle.

Valvate, said of sepals, etc., when they are only connate in bud by their edges which do not overlap.

Ventral, the lower side.

Ventricose, suddenly bulged.

Venulose, with vein-like raised markings.

Verrucose, covered with wart-like small bosses.

Versatile, said of an another which is attached above its base to the attenuated tip of the filament on which it swings.

Verticillate, whorled

Villose, villous, covered with long fine soft hairs.

Virgate, with slender erect rod-like stems or branches.

Viscid, with a sticky secretion.

Xerophilous, adapted by structure to conditions of drought.

Xerophytes, plants which inhabit localities where they are subject to conditions of physiological drought.

APPENDIX III.

Table for Conversion of Metric and English Lengths.

Inches.		Millimetres.	Inches.		Millimetres.
$\frac{1}{32}$	·03	0·79	$\frac{17}{32}$	·53	13·5
$\frac{1}{30}$	·03	0·8	$\frac{9}{16}$	·56	14·3
$\frac{1}{25}$	·04	1·0	$\frac{19}{32}$	·59	15·1
$\frac{1}{20}$	·05	1·3	$\frac{5}{8}$	·62	15·9
$\frac{1}{16}$	·06	1·6	$\frac{21}{32}$	·66	16·7
$\frac{1}{15}$	·07	1·7	$\frac{2}{3}$	·67	16·9
$\frac{1}{12}$	·08	2·1	$\frac{11}{16}$	·68	17·5
$\frac{3}{32}$	·09	2·4	$\frac{23}{32}$	·72	18·2
$\frac{1}{10}$	·10	2·5	$\frac{3}{4}$	·75	19·0
$\frac{1}{9}$	·11	2·8	$\frac{25}{32}$	·78	19·8
$\frac{1}{8}$	·12	3·2	$\frac{13}{16}$	·81	20·6
$\frac{1}{7}$	·14	3·5	$\frac{27}{32}$	·84	21·4
$\frac{5}{32}$	·16	4·0	$\frac{7}{8}$	·87	22·2
$\frac{1}{6}$	·17	4·2	$\frac{29}{32}$	·91	23·0
$\frac{3}{16}$	·19	4·8	$\frac{15}{16}$	·94	23·8
$\frac{1}{5}$	·20	5·1		1	25·4
$\frac{7}{32}$	·22	5·5		2	50·8
$\frac{1}{4}$	·25	6·3		3	76·2
$\frac{9}{32}$	·28	7·1		4	101·6
$\frac{5}{16}$	·31	7·9		5	127·0
$\frac{1}{3}$	·33	8·5		6	152·4
$\frac{11}{32}$	·34	8·7		7	177·8
$\frac{3}{8}$	·37	9·5		8	203 2
$\frac{13}{32}$	·41	10·3		9	228·6
$\frac{7}{16}$	·44	11·1		10	254·0
$\frac{15}{32}$	·47	11·9		11	279·4
	·5	12·7		12	304·8

INDEX.

I.—GENERAL AND ENGLISH.

M

N

II.—VERNACULAR.

E

F

G